I Remem

BALANCHINE

By George Balanchine and Francis Mason

Balanchine's Complete Stories of the Great Ballets

101 Stories of the Great Ballets

I Remember
BALANCHINE

*Recollections
of the
Ballet Master
by Those
Who Knew Him*

FRANCIS MASON

ANCHOR BOOKS

DOUBLEDAY

New York London Toronto Sydney Auckland

AN ANCHOR BOOK
PUBLISHED BY DOUBLEDAY
a division of Bantam Doubleday Dell Publishing Group, Inc.
666 Fifth Avenue, New York, New York 10103

ANCHOR BOOKS, DOUBLEDAY, and the portrayal of an anchor
are trademarks of Doubleday, a division of Bantam Doubleday
Dell Publishing Group, Inc.

I Remember Balanchine *was originally published in hardcover by
Doubleday in 1991. The Anchor Books edition is
published by arrangement with Doubleday.*

*Grateful acknowledgment is made to the following:
Lincoln Kirstein, for permission to reprint his letter of July 16, 1933, about Balanchine.
The manuscript of this letter is in the collection of the Wadsworth Atheneum, Hartford, Connecticut.
Camille Hardy, for permission to combine her interview with Maria Tallchief with the author's in
the narrative that appears here.*

BOOK DESIGN BY BONNI LEON

Library of Congress Cataloging-in-Publication Data
Mason, Francis.
I remember Balanchine : recollections of the ballet master by those who knew him /
Francis Mason. — 1st ed. in the U.S. of America.
p.   cm.
Includes index.
1. Balanchine, George.   2. Choreographers—United States—
Biography.   I. Title.
GV1785.B32M36   1991
792.8'2'092—dc20
[B]   90-3732
CIP

ISBN 0-385-26611-1
Copyright © 1991 by Francis Mason

FIRST ANCHOR BOOKS EDITION: APRIL 1992
10 9 8 7 6 5 4 3 2 1

To
Natalie Bodanya and
William Gorman (1910–82),
who introduced me to
Balanchine's ballets,
and
Lawrence Sherman,
Balanchine's first editor, and mine

INTRODUCTION

At Balanchine's funeral services in New York in 1983, I was reminded that ballet has a family tradition: what individual dancers learn from a ballet master is the essence of what is passed on. As hundreds of grieving dancers and others who had been close to Balanchine moved to the open coffin to make their farewells, I knew that the future of his ballets, his teaching, and much of what ballet as an art means to the world today depended on them, the living vessels of what he had taught and showed. What would they have to say about him, his teaching, and his ballets? When immediate sadness had passed, I promised myself I would try to find out. The recollections gathered here are the result of that search.

I knew before I began that Balanchine recalled in mere words would not be enough. From the time I first met him in 1948 and wanted to hear what he had to say about his ballets, he always said that seeing them was enough: words about them, how he came to make them, or about his life were of little use. If these recollections bring readers to any closer understanding, it is because of the eloquence with which his dancers and colleagues remember Balanchine. I have never known so many people so eager to talk about a man. To all of them Balanchine was clearly a dominant figure: in talking about him they explained themselves, relived their careers, made sense of their lives, assimilated the past for the future. To each and every one the longevity of his ballets mattered. Balanchine may have made some of them unhappy periodically, but he left most with joyous memories. One who says he made her miserable (she never got the roles she wanted) asserts that dancing his ballets—the act of performing as he wished—was so physically exhilarating that she thrived on it. Another claims that this giant of a teacher–choreographer–artistic director had feet of clay, but "nobody's perfect."

When the first biography of Balanchine was about to appear in 1963, he gave me the advance copy of the book that had been sent to him, saying, "Take it; maybe you will be interested. I'm not." We were in Hamburg, where I had come to see his production of Gluck's *Orfeo ed Euridice* for the Hamburg State Opera and the new ballet he had made for it. He talked to me about the pleasure he took in this opera, which had played such a big role in his life, and in the Hamburg dancers who had danced his ballet. He also spoke of Suzanne Farrell, whom I had seen at a rehearsal in New York the previous year, and a ballet he was making for her and Jacques d'Amboise. He would not talk about the book. For years the world has known of Balanchine's reticence to discuss his ballets. He preferred, even within the immediate ballet family, to speak cryptically when asked what a particular ballet was about. He might say, "About twenty-eight minutes." For the press, which he was wary of for many years (justifiably: it took John Martin of the *New York Times* fifteen years to respond with warmth to Balanchine's cause), Balanchine played the chef who was concerned only with cooking up entertaining menus.

Working with him in the early 1950s on the book *Balanchine's Complete Stories of the Great Ballets*, I found him completely generous and forthcoming. Convinced that the book would help ballet, he talked at length in a relaxed and candid manner with me and Lawrence Sherman, our editor, about his work. I shall certainly never forget the first time he described the Maryinsky Theater in old St. Petersburg and ballets by Petipa: real water, cascading fountains, huge shipwrecks, trying to convince an unbelieving American that these Cecil B. De Mille effects were everyday miracles at the Maryinsky in tsarist days. He came to love ballet when he found himself onstage performing in Tchaikovsky's masterpiece *The Sleeping Beauty* during his second year at the Imperial Ballet School. The theatrical power of dance began to run in his veins. I had a feeling he'd never been asked particular questions about *The Sleeping Beauty* and the other big productions. He told me that what I'd seen at the Metropolitan Opera House in the Sadler's Wells productions of these ballets was peanuts. We went through all the old ballets scene by scene, in my effort to get his impressions. His descriptions of the Garland Dance in *The Sleeping Beauty* which *he* had danced, told of a huge ensemble compared to the meager British version. Everything grand was possible because of the Imperial Treasury and the Tsar's commitment to the theater, because of the soldiers who labored below stage to make waves, the low cost of labor, and the vast corps de ballet of children available to the Imperial Theater.

New York City Ballet audiences were to learn many years later exactly what Balanchine meant by the choreographic intricacies of the Garland Dance in *The Sleeping Beauty* when he staged it during the Tchaikovsky Festival of 1981. It was, as he had told me in 1950, a much more intricate and complicated manifestation than Sergeyev had produced in London. Balanchine waited until his final years to stage the Garland Dance, the merest *fragment* of his favorite Tchaikovsky ballet. If he could not do the whole *Sleeping Beauty*, he would at least have the Garland Dance right. The idea of doing the complete Tchaikovsky ballet one day was an extravagance he could afford to postpone. After all, what would it be in the end but a retread, or his version of a retread? Balanchine's priority was now, the elusive moment, the making of new transitory butterflies, the giving of everything, by himself, by his dancers. "What are you waiting for?" was his perpetual question.

This book recollects the tremendous amount of time Balanchine gave to his dancers, friends, and associates. His presence in most of their lives was determining. Teaching the course "Working with Balanchine" at New York University's School of Continuing Education in 1984, I became freshly aware of how little the ballet master's art is generally understood. Many participants in the class did not realize that Balanchine actually showed his dancers their parts by dancing and demonstrating himself. They were astonished when Maria Tallchief, Patricia McBride, and others spoke of the power and eloquence of what Balanchine would show in the studio. "To be a choreographer," he said, "it is first of all necessary to be a dancer, a good one, better than others, so you can show new things." The choreographer has to be a good dancer in order to feel in his bones all the possibilities of expression. "Good" was always the ultimate adjective for Balanchine; "great" was excessive.

Ballet is a hands-on matter; choreographers show and touch and manipulate to get what they want. Balanchine had such a give-and-take relationship with his dancers that he had only to indicate what he wanted before they would be dancing it. He would show steps and sequences, watch the dancers copy him, and change things if they did not suit the particular performer. Following and responding to his suggestions, they felt that they were participants in a remarkable creative process; it was not just him, it was them.

Even rehearsing dancers in roles he had made for them years before, Balanchine was calm and collected. On occasion I would watch him late at night in one of the studios at the old School of American Ballet and wonder why he was not exasperated when the dancer he was working with never quite got what he was showing. *Why* couldn't the dancer copy the tension and relaxation Balanchine himself was so clearly demonstrating in a certain gesture? But Balanchine maintained his cool, repeating the gesture and acting as if all would be well. He conveyed trust. Invariably the next performance by the dancer was better, and eventually it got close to what Balanchine wanted. His long, drawn-out "Thaaaat's right" was always hoped for.

Documents in Balanchine's life are very few. Of his youth, he spoke of love for the church, music, and reading. Balanchine would not have known ballet except for his sister's interest in it. He attended her performances with his parents. Nowadays all children trying to get into the School of American Ballet in New York apply precisely because they wish to be in *The Nutcracker*, a ballet they've been taken to by their parents. Balanchine had no such ambition. He auditioned for the Imperial Ballet School in St. Petersburg because he was there at the time his sister auditioned and a friend suggested he try. His success in getting in clearly meant little to him. "My parents stuck me in ballet school when I was small," he told Solomon Volkov. The year was 1913 and Balanchine was nine years old. The only subjects he was good at, he said, were music and religion. He hated the ballet school so much he ran away, but he was brought back and worked in a state of bewilderment and despair before he got onstage in *The Sleeping Beauty* and found his raison d'être.

Before that, he had his faith. His uncle was a priest, later archbishop of Tbilisi, and as a child Balanchine participated in church ritual. He spoke later in his life of playing church on his own, of blessing objects, of making the sign of the cross in his own private church theatricals. He spoke of this in much the same way that Laurence Olivier spoke of the influence of the church on his youth. Olivier said that playing the altar boy was his first experience of the stage. You got up in front of people who watched you, you had obligations.

The only evidence we have that Balanchine's father believed in him was his wish to place his son in the Imperial Ballet School. The family's financial situation was such that his father, Meliton, was obliged to place all three of his children in state-supported schools. Meliton was a musician, a composer, the Glinka of Georgia. We know also that Balanchine's mother was young George's companion at the piano. He was also devoted to his German nurse-maid, Barbara.

When Balanchine was born, his father was forty-two. A generous man of volatile temperament, Meliton once won a state lottery and went so mad with joy that he gave away much of the 100,000 rubles, paid for the publication of Glinka's letters, opened a restaurant, went broke, started a factory, became bankrupt, and was put under house arrest. The young Balanchine who looks out at us in the early photographs is not a child wishing to be discovered. He is already performing, his chin and nose a little high in the air. Soon after Balanchine was placed in the Imperial Ballet School, his family retired to their country home in Finland, where he could seldom see them. Then his father was given a post as cultural minister in Georgia and left for Tbilisi. Balanchine's brother, Andrei, was sent to join his father, then his mother and sister moved to Tbilisi also. On weekends, when other children visited their families, Balanchine would occasionally visit his maternal aunt. He never saw his mother or his sister again. His father and brother came to Petersburg for his marriage to Tamara Geva. And he saw Andrei again only after forty years when Balanchine returned to the Soviet Union with the New York City Ballet and when his brother visited him later in New York.

In an early photograph of the two young brothers, five-year-old Andrei looks vulnerable alongside his lofty, experienced brother. Balanchine was called Rat at the ballet school because he sniffed and showed his teeth. But otherwise he was Georges, in the French fashion, not Georgi or Yura as one might expect. He was already a child apart. Felia Doubrovska, older than he, saw Balanchine in a studio at the school and told me that nothing escaped his attention. His contemporary Alexandra Danilova came to know him at nine and marveled at his self-possession and control. By the time Tamara Geva saw him, he was glamorous, handsome, and showing everyone what to do.

He pursued his music in tandem with his dancing for many years, an enormous burden for a young person who wished to excel at both arts. He entered the Conservatory of Music not at his father's urging but at the suggestion of one of the teachers at the ballet school who recognized his gifts. One day at the age of seven as he succeeded in playing a Beethoven sonata, he knew music was for him. "Music, according to Tchaikovsky, reconciles us to life forever," he later told Solomon Volkov.

The documents of Balanchine's career at the Conservatory show that he was seriously gifted. When he could no longer go on with his work there and had to give everything to his dancing, he was such an accomplished musician that he could play entire Wagner operas at sight for Tamara's father, and improvise at the piano to accompany silent films in movie theaters.

Deprived as he may have been in Russia during the revolutionary time, Balanchine was also enriched. Once when I told him about what seemed to me an experimental dance performance, he said, "Oh, we did that years ago; in Russia and afterward. Really, I have done everything." Happenings, plastic enveloping the stage, technical devices to enthrall and distract, words and chants in dancing, running amok: nothing surprised him. He had tried it all in the revolutionary period—in reaction to, or out of admiration for, Kasyan Goleizovsky and Nikolai Foregger—or in the Diaghilev period. He and his colleagues performed in music halls, workers' clubs, and for the army. When he left Russia, he knew the German nightlife of the 1920s. Vaudeville in England was the only place he and his little troupe of dancers could get a job in 1925. Later they were able to link up with Diaghilev and renew their Russian connection.

The Diaghilev opportunity—becoming ballet master at twenty-one to the world's most eminent impresario—was the job of a lifetime. Balanchine had begun to make ballets when he was fifteen in Petrograd, and trained young dancers until 1982, the year before his death—sixty-three years of close work with some of the most beautiful women in the world. He married four times. He enjoyed many alliances. The specter of a bluebeard of a ballet master bending glorious girls to his will excited a tabloid curiosity he always deftly bypassed: "I am a cloud in trousers," quoting Mayakovsky.

Yet the women in his life moved Balanchine to make ballets to the music that inspired him. His mother was no sooner gone from his life—leaving Petrograd to join her husband in Georgia—than Balanchine began making ballets for young goddesses. Early on in his work a persistent theme was established: the man seeks the absent beloved, pursues his ideal, but she always eludes him. That was his way of making ballet endlessly interesting. When asked why his work was so abstract, he would say, "What is abstract about a man and a woman together onstage? You already have a story watching what they do." They seldom find each other or stay together long in Balanchine's ballets. Only *Firebird* ends in a wedding. The young god Apollo who teaches the Muses to dance and blesses their feet must leave for Olympus; Orpheus the musician sees his wife die as he tries to lead her homeward; the boy in *Le Baiser de la Fée* is summoned by his muse; the composer Schumann goes mad; and Don Quixote, seeking a beloved Dulcinea who appears to him in many guises, servingmaid as well as Madonna—are all Balanchine heroes. Balanchine had music and the theme of seeking, finding, and losing within him. All he needed was beautiful women, dancing the way he wanted, to make the ballets.

Lacking a family, Balanchine found one in fellow dancers and musicians. Concurrently, he found refuge in the church of his childhood. Its rituals and liturgy provided lofty models to emulate and gave him a sense of duty and obligation toward music and ballet.

When Balanchine's friend W. McNeil Lowry asked him in his old age what God meant, Balanchine replied, "God is this wonderful dress you see. Even now, always, I have to say I couldn't just think of God in an abstract way, to connect with Him just by spirit, by mind. You have to be really mystic to sit down and meditate, to worm down in yourself. But I can't do that. As they say, my work is what I see, with moving, with making ballets. So too with God—He is real, before me. Through Christ I know how God looks, I know His face, I know His beard, I know how He'll talk, and I know that in the end we'll go to God. You see, that's how I believe, and I believe so fantastic . . ."

At Easter time in 1950, when I was walking with Balanchine near his apartment, we passed a Catholic church on Lexington Avenue as people were pouring out onto the sidewalk. We paused to wait. Balanchine turned to me and said, "Do you believe?"

"Yes, but I don't go to church," I said.

"But you believe," he said. "I go to church but nobody knows."

Balanchine had so many beautiful women around him most of his life that he seemed to require no other family. That was true everywhere—at the ballet school in Petrograd, at the Maryinsky Theater, with his own Young Ballet, with Diaghilev's Ballets Russes, with the Royal Danish Ballet, with the new Ballet Russe de Monte Carlo and his own Les Ballets 1933—before he accepted Lincoln Kirstein's invitation to America, where he found the women he admired most of all. From 1933 to 1948 he made ballets at the School of American Ballet, for the first ballet ensembles he and Kirstein formed, on Broadway, in Hollywood, and even at the circus and the Metropolitan Opera. It was a new repertory based on the rhythmic gifts he adored in American dancers. Itinerant and happy to be employed, he made ballets, too, for the Ballet Russe de Monte Carlo and Ballet Theatre. Only in 1948 did Balanchine and Kirstein succeed in establishing a home at the City Center in New York. From the New York City Ballet, Balanchine's family circle expanded throughout America. Through no insistence of his own, his influence began to prevail. He had no inflexible doctrine about teaching, about how to train fine dancers, no textbook of his own; he would not be glued down. What was right one year for the dancers in his company could be different the next; it all depended on the particulars of time and place. He could work with everybody—a circus girl like Constance Clausen, a Metropolitan Opera soprano like Natalie Bodanya, a hoofer like Ray Bolger, as well as a dancer of the magnitude of Mikhail Baryshnikov. When Baryshnikov left the New York City Ballet and became head of American Ballet Theatre, I visited Balanchine as he recovered from heart surgery. I asked him what he thought of the move. "That's what I wanted, my own company. Why shouldn't he try?"

While the gifts and proficiency of his dancers changed over the fifty years he was in America, they all had in Balanchine a common bond. In his final months many of them came to his hospital room in fear and trembling that he would not recognize them. But, catching sight of old familiar faces, bodies, and voices, he perked up and was warmly welcoming. The receptionist at the hospital told me one day that he had never seen so many beautiful women. Near death, Mr. B welcomed his family as they came to say goodbye.

Balanchine died early on Saturday morning, April 30, 1983. Russian Orthodox funeral services began on Sunday evening and continued to the burial on Tuesday. As I watched the dancers move toward the coffin, it was clear that their love and devotion were incalculable. I asked myself at the time, was it like this at Shakespeare's death? Did the actors from his Globe Theatre and all over England come to mourn at his bier and wonder, too, would there ever again be such a poet? Balanchine to me had Shakespeare's power: both recognized nobility and grandeur, the high and the mighty, romance, courtliness and passion; and both also had a common, comic touch. We do not know what Shakespeare's mourners had to say, what the members of his Globe Theatre could have told us about him and the world is poorer for it. Shouldn't we know what Balanchine's colleagues had to say?

This struck me all the more as time passed. "Ballets," Balanchine said, "are like butterflies." Here today and gone tomorrow. Could Balanchine be caught on the wing of remembrance? Based on the remembrances gathered here, I venture to say Balanchine was absolutely right that his professional rather than his personal life was of interest. He woke up early in the morning, did his washing and ironing while listening to the radio and thinking about what ballets he would like to make and the class he would teach in a few hours. He would talk on the telephone with his assistant Barbara Horgan about what the day promised, have breakfast at the Empire Hotel grille with a favorite dancer, teach class, work through lunch on company business, and during most of the year, when the NYCB was performing, rehearse or make ballets all afternoon, maybe change clothes, watch the performance onstage (coaching his dancers before and after), then go out to eat and drink with people he wanted to be with.

He had a piano in his apartment and his office where he could play and transcribe scores about which he cared. He was always reading and had a substantial library of Russian books in his office and a small room in his apartment filled with books—poetry, plays, novels, and volumes on science and religion. He read to learn. Two books that deeply engaged him in his later years were *Jesus of Nazareth* and *From Jesus to Paul* by the Hebrew scholar Joseph Klausner. I once asked Balanchine why he didn't watch television. He said, "I'm always doing the laundry." He reserved his time for his dancers and music—the inspiration of his ballets—and for reading and thinking.

He thought much about politics, and his views were conservative and right-wing. He and his close friend the composer Nicolas Nabokov, whom he knew from Paris in the Diaghilev days, were always engaged on this subject. After World War II, Nabokov became a key adviser to American authorities on Soviet cultural matters. He and Balanchine had no patience with Soviet cultural overtures to the West and always questioned the sincerity of Communist gestures of that kind. Freedom in the arts was what mattered first to Balanchine.

For this book, I interviewed a hundred and fifteen colleagues of Balanchine's over the years, men as well as women. While women to Balanchine meant ballet itself and were the essential part of his life, the men who partnered them onstage were important, too. They represented, at one remove, Balanchine himself; they made it possible for the beauty of his ballerinas to unfold. Playing that cavalier role as well as independent starring roles of their own, the men contributed much to the Balanchine legacy.

The only man who did not respond to my request for an interview was Mikhail Baryshnikov, who learned many roles when he danced for Balanchine. Other lost narratives are from Jerome Robbins and the late Antony Tudor. Jerome Robbins, whom I interviewed, is writing a book of his own and asked that I not include here the few words he could then give me about his close association with Balanchine. Watching Balanchine rehearse Robbins for his masterful performance in the American revival of *Prodigal Son* in 1950, I was aware of the mutual respect of these two artists. Robbins should have more to say about Balanchine's creative process than anyone else.

Antony Tudor died before I could talk with him at length about Balanchine. What did Tudor, the master of ballet drama, have to do with Balanchine, the classicist? In 1987 I was invited to the offices of the Swedish Consulate General in New York to see a superb Swedish film about Tudor and his ballets. Before the showing of the film, I talked with Tudor and mentioned Balanchine's admiration for his ballet *Romeo and Juliet.* He said, "*What* did you say?"

I repeated what Balanchine told me years ago as we assembled narratives of a number of *Romeo and Juliet* ballets for a new edition of *Balanchine's Complete Stories of the Great Ballets.* He liked Tudor's *Romeo and Juliet* most of all. "It's the only one," he said, "the only *Romeo and Juliet*, really, that is truly English, with true English music."

Tudor's eyes filled with tears. He asked, "Did he really say that?"

"Of course," I said. "Didn't he ever tell you?"

"No," Tudor said, "and I can't tell you how pleased I am to hear it. I owe my beginnings to Balanchine. I was just a boy in a butcher shop in London in the late 1920s, but I saw the last two seasons there of the Diaghilev Ballet. I saw in 1928 Balanchine's ballet *Apollo* and in 1929, *Prodigal Son*. When I saw *Apollo*, I said to myself, 'I want to be able to make people move like that.' The following year, with *Prodigal Son*, I felt the same way. The result was that I went to Marie Rambert to learn how to dance and began to make ballets."

"Did you ever tell Balanchine that?" I asked.

"No," he said.

Another missing link is Vera Zorina, who says she is writing other books and has asked that I not use here the long interview she gave me at New York University in 1984. I am sorry the reader is deprived of her eloquence about the extraordinary human being she found Balanchine to be.

I interviewed Suzanne Farrell, who was so important to Balanchine, twice —once at length for the "Working with Balanchine" course and again briefly

Introduction

in 1989. She, too, has asked me not to use here what she had to say. She has written her own book, *Holding On to the Air*.

I understand Tanaquil LeClercq's reluctance to speak of her life and work with Balanchine. The glory of her career, tragically cut short by polio, is often mentioned in this book.

She was Balanchine's last wife. While he may have wanted another and yet another, I believe he settled in the 1970s into a Don Quixote period of generosity and understanding. In this period he welcomed Suzanne Farrell back to the New York City Ballet after a long absence. Upon her return she again inspired new ballets, but there were others, too. Karin von Aroldingen, Balanchine's last muse, inspired the masterpieces, *Stravinsky Violin Concerto* and *Robert Schumann's "Davidsbündlertänze"* and other ballets. She included him in her family and made him happy in his final years. Her name resembles his mother's Von Almedingen, before she married. With her, he had come home.

For a man who would not be encumbered by heirs, he had a huge family, linking together thousands who taught thousands more. Gathering for dinner one night in Philadelphia with Barbara Weisberger and members of her young Pennsylvania Ballet, he said, "Let's all join hands, like elephants join their tails and trunks. What you are doing is following what we began."

One of his dancers, Marian Horosko, reminds us here that Balanchine "loved to twine and intertwine arms, legs, and bodies onstage. They were rest patterns for the eye and for the dancers." At Balanchine's funeral, her generation of dancers from the 1950s stood together. "When we left the church, there were so many people outside on the steps that we had to twine our way down. There we were, unconsciously holding hands as he had taught us and slowly winding down through people on the stairs as if in a ballet."

Francis Mason

ACKNOWLEDGMENTS

I am grateful to the many associates of Balanchine who so generously gave me the interviews on which this book is based. Beginning with interviews conducted in a symposium for the Dance Critics Association in June 1983 and for the course "Working with Balanchine" at New York University's School of Continuing Education in the autumn of 1984, I have spoken at length with more than a hundred dancers and colleagues of the ballet master.

Joel Lobenthal is responsible for the book's existence. This fine writer insisted that I fulfill my promise to talk with Balanchine's heirs. He said, "You are the only writer who knows all of them, and they know you. As Balanchine used to ask, 'What are you waiting for?' "

Almost all of the interviews, which I recorded on tape, were transcribed by Shields Remine, my colleague at *Ballet Review,* whose vast knowledge of ballet history made his texts exemplary.

Don Daniels, writer, critic, and associate editor of *Ballet Review* for many years, knew Balanchine from the 1970s, when he worked on the staff of the New York City Ballet. Lawrence Sherman knew Balanchine from the 1950s, when he became his first editor, and mine, for the book *Balanchine's Complete Stories of the Great Ballets.* Joel Lobenthal's first printed work was an essay on the career of Tanaquil LeClercq for *Ballet Review.* While these three worked closely with me in editing the transcripts to produce the personal narratives the reader will find here, I alone am responsible for these texts. I have made every effort to preserve not only the voice but the substance of what each person had to say.

Lincoln Kirstein kindly gave permission to print the letter about Balanchine which appears here for the first time. The manuscript of this letter is in the collection of Wadsworth Atheneum, Hartford, Connecticut.

I conducted all the interviews for this book with the following exceptions: Elizabeth Souritz interviewed Nina Stukolkina, Mary Fraker interviewed Ulla Poulsen and Dawn Lille Horwitz interviewed Ray Bolger. I am grateful to these eminent dance historians for this material. An interview with Maria Tallchief

Acknowledgments

by Camille Hardy has been combined with my own. I wish to express my thanks to Camille Hardy for that privilege. Joel Lobenthal joined me in talking with Alicia Markova on one occasion and Dawn Lille Horwitz joined me in talking with Katherine Dunham.

The Dance Collection of the New York Public Library, the world's greatest gathering of materials relating to ballet's past and present, I consulted regularly as I prepared for interviews and edited them for publication. For many kindnesses and the answers to my queries, I am indebted to Madeleine Nichols, curator of the Dance Collection, and to Susan Au, Francis Dougherty, Lesley Farlow, Dorothy Lourdou, Lacy H. McDearmon, Monica Moseley, Judy M. F. Moshonas, Karen Nickeson, and Else Peck.

The New York Public Library made it possible for me to work for six blessed months in the Frederick Lewis Allen Room at the main building on Fifth Avenue and Forty-second Street. To the library and especially to Wayne Furman, I am indebted for that privilege. I am deeply obliged to Sidney Offit for animating me to seek this ideal refuge for a writer in New York City.

Lydie Marshall, a remarkable teacher and writer of cookbooks, gave me the title for this book. Visiting her and Wayne Marshall in Paris in the summer of 1989 as I prepared to interview Boris Kochno, I told her about the book, which I then thought of as *Working with Balanchine.* She said, "That's all wrong for the personal book you're telling me about and the book I want badly to read. Call it *I Remember Balanchine.*"

The understanding of my editor, Jacqueline Onassis, made this book possible. Shaye Areheart's editorial patience and wonderful suggestions I shall never forget. Bruce Tracy smoothed many paths. To Deborah Artman, for daily concern and guidance over many months, I shall always be beholden. My agent, Joan Brookbank, held this whole project together from beginning to end with extreme fortitude and good humor.

Susan Edelman of New York University's School of Education proposed the idea of the *Working with Balanchine* course I led in 1984. Leslie Berlowitz, Vice President of New York University and director of the Humanities Council, invited me to lecture on Balanchine the following year. I am immensely grateful to both of them. The material I gathered for those projects contributed importantly to the foundation for this book. Throughout my work on the book I have been fortunate to talk with Marvin Hoshino, whose knowledge of Balanchine and love of his work is extraordinary.

For help in many aspects of the book's preparation, I am also indebted to Pamela R. Berdan, Shelley C. Berg, Warren Bodow, Richard Boehm, Merilee and Roy Bostock, Denis Donoghue, the late Parmenia Miguel Ekstrom, Maren Erskine, Paul Fasana, Rodger Friedman, Rachel Godfrey, Hubert Gold-

Acknowledgments

schmidt, Maryann and Allan Gottdenker, David Gray, Ann Hageman, Jay Hewlin, Dale Hoffer, Marvin Hoshino, Patricia Jarrell, Mary D. Kierstead, Abner Klipstein and Ronald Klipstein of Qwik/Cassette Corporation, Heike Kordish, William Lawson, Yvette and Daniel Lebourge, Don McDonagh, Maitland McDonagh, Brooks McNamara, Dominique Nabokov, the late Walter Neiman, Nancy Reynolds, Helene Sadovska, Barbara Schlain, Robert Sherman, Stephen Temmer, Alexandra Truitt, David Vaughan, and Anne Williams of Ballet Society.

CONTENTS

Contents

Contents

I Remember

BALANCHINE

ALEXANDRA

DANILOVA

Trained in St. Petersburg, Russia, at the Imperial Theater School, Danilova became a soloist of the State Theater of Opera and Ballet. She also danced with Balanchine's Young Ballet and left Russia with his touring group in 1924. Dancing leading roles for Diaghilev's Ballets Russes, de Basil's Ballets Russes, and the Ballet Russe de Monte Carlo for more than twenty-five years, she became in Europe and the United States a favorite ballerina. She has staged for many ensembles ballets in which she starred, danced on Broadway, appeared in the Herbert Ross film The Turning Point, *and written her autobiography,* Choura *(1988). She taught at the School of American Ballet from 1963 to 1989 and received in 1989 the Kennedy Center Award and New York City's Handel Medallion.*

I Remember Balanchine

BALANCHINE AND I AUDITIONED FOR THE IMPERIAL THEATER SCHOOL IN ST. PETERS-burg. First there was the medical exam, to see if the heart was strong enough so that you wouldn't drop dead in the middle of a dance, to see that you were not bowlegged or nearsighted. Then there was the artistic examination: they asked you to skip, to run, to do little movements. Out of two hundred and thirteen girls, they accepted seventeen, because the school was small. It was run on the private capital of the imperial family. After a year the original seventeen had been reduced to nine, then to seven. It was a hard competition. We were about forty-five girls and thirty-two boys altogether, small in comparison to our School of American Ballet. But then, before the Revolution, everything was *intime.* Now it's for everybody.

I entered the school one year before Balanchine. His sister Tamara was in my class. She was not talented for dance, no sylph, really a tomboy, and left after two years. Their mother was sweet. I remember Balanchine's father, but soon they both left Petrograd. George always had a picture of his father. He kept to himself. Most all the pupils would stay in school all week and then go home on Saturday afternoon and stay with their families until Sunday evening. George couldn't because his family moved to the Caucasus. Others would talk about their families, but he did not.

There were two female monitors who looked after the girls, and two men who attended the boys. They made sure that you had good manners and behavior. We would get up at eight. The governess would see that the maid rang the bell. They would open the covers on your bed, and you would go to the washroom. There they waited with a jug of cold water. They would pour it on the back of your neck and down your shoulders and body to toughen you. Five girls could be doused at a time around a circular washbowl. As a result, we didn't get colds. It was good for the circulation.

One of the men in charge of the boys was Grigori Grigorievich Grigoriev, who befriended Balanchine. He encouraged George to study music at the Conservatory and often invited him to his apartment, but George dwelt inside himself.

Boys and girls were separated except in certain classes, where we would do double work and ballroom dancing. We did the Viennese waltz and all the quadrilles. The first boy I liked was Balanchine. He was my pal. Another boyfriend among the students was Slava Slavianinov. I also admired Anatole Vilzak, a sort of puppy love. In our early years we didn't care about boys. The flirtations started at sixteen, in our last two years. You'd drop a book, hoping the right boy would pick it up. In our ballroom classes the boys and girls would be divided. The ballet master would say, "Now invite a partner to dance with you." Little by little, real flirtations started.

After the Bolshevik Revolution, when I was fourteen, the ballet school was closed. I went to visit in Cossack country with my family. A director of the school took George to Finland, I think. Then Lunacharsky, the new Communist Minister of Education, insisted that the school be reopened. Ballet, he said, was not decadent but a part of our culture. The old Bolsheviks had good ideas. They weren't just murderers.

We learned in the revolutionary time the value of life. In our teens we had experiences that others acquire after sixty years in this world, if then. Hunger, for instance. George told me in those days he was so hungry he wanted to steal. I think he did steal. At a time like that you learn the value of friendship. If you have to choose between lovers and friends, to me it is friendship, because it's forever. The other comes and it's marvelous, like the wind, but breezes come and go. Friendship stays. There is no life without friendship.

Balanchine was a good dancer. At the Maryinsky Theater he danced the pas de trois from *Paquita* in the annual performance of the school—two years before his graduation. Mr. B., as everyone called him later in America, danced very well. Later, he had an operation on his knee and had to quit dancing and only do choreography. In mime he was also marvelous. In Fokine's *Petrouchka* he did the old man on the balcony so well that nobody looked at the dancers!

I remember seeing one of Balanchine's first ballets, the pas de deux called *La Nuit.* He was sixteen, and the music was by Anton Rubinstein. It was presented in our own little theater in the school where we had annual school performances. The ballerina Olga Mungalova danced it with him. There he included for the first time an overhead lift of the ballerina in arabesque. The boy carries the girl away—he gets her. That dance gave me my first hint of romantic love between men and women. Madame Revoshevskova, the director of the school, said, "That was really terrible—indecent." She didn't like me either.

The repertory of the Maryinsky Theater was very Victorian. When Balanchine started to choreograph, he was considered so *moderne* that they wanted to fire him. I think they were simply jealous. When we finished school, George organized the Young Ballet. He had us dancing not only to music but to poetry as well. The poetry was recited, and we danced to it. We did everything. That's why I am so difficult to please nowadays with new choreographers: there wasn't anything we didn't do in the Young Ballet!

Because the management of the State Theatre of Opera and Ballet, which the Maryinsky became under the Bolsheviks, thought Balanchine's work was too advanced, after a couple of performances of the Young Ballet we received a notice that if we continued to dance with him we would be expelled. We didn't want to be expelled, and so we excused ourselves and

3

were very upset. I think that's when George began to think about leaving Russia and going abroad where he could express himself.

Even in those difficult days, I noticed that George seldom lost his temper. But if he did lose it, watch out! I never caught any of this, but once I saw him lose his temper and throw people across the room. Later, here in America, I only knew him to lose his cool when a girl in the company showed up one day in rubber pants. He screamed, "Get her out!"

Before we left Russia, Lopukhov choreographed a *Firebird* which I danced at the Maryinsky. In *Dance Symphony,* Lopukhov's theme was the creation of the universe, a theme that eventually became boring (everybody choreographed ballets about the creation!). But even a modern choreographer like Lopukhov would have been jealous of Balanchine—like Salieri of Mozart. Balanchine had to leave Russia and join Diaghilev's Ballets Russes to be given a free hand. The public in Paris was accustomed to innovation.

Balanchine was busy always with his music. He went to the Conservatory. He didn't have many friends. One was Slava Slavianinov. Balanchine, his new wife Tamara Geva, Slavianinov, and I were walking together and met a gypsy fortuneteller. Gypsies always know. Balanchine paid her to tell his fortune. She said, "He will fall in love with a friend of his youth, and I can tell you her name." She said the name of that friend would be Alexandra. I was embarrassed, but I did not forget the prophecy.

My decision to leave Russia with Balanchine was not difficult. I wanted to go abroad. It was such a gruesome existence. We had nothing to eat, no heat. I thought, "I have one life, I shall try to get away." When Vladimir Dimitriev planned to send a group of young Soviet dancers abroad and invited me to go with Geva, Balanchine, and Efimov, I was thrilled and left with pleasure. I thought I would maybe spend the summer in Europe and come back. The Maryinsky had promised me a big role, so I just packed a little suitcase. Later, when we had been in Europe for months, the Soviets sent telegrams and threatened to fire us, but we ignored them. I was young and just said, "No."

But before joining Diaghilev we toured the spas in Germany and performed. Somehow we went to Vienna to hear Rachmaninoff. With Balanchine we went backstage to congratulate him on the concert. Balanchine said to Rachmaninoff, "May I make a dance to your music?" Rachmaninoff said, *"My* music? *Dance?* Get out!" Here we were reminded that in Russia dancers were not acceptable in society. Balanchine never forgot the insult. Rachmaninoff was insufferable. Russians are strange, not like other people. Remember, Russians are half oriental: this may explain the strange things they do sometimes. And why they don't forget.

On the German tour, I did the pas de deux from *Coppélia,* Act III, with

Efimov, George composed a waltz he dedicated to me, and he choreographed a Scriabin solo for me as well. Geva and I did an oriental dance from *Khovanshchina* with a tambourine. And *Matelotte,* a sailor dance, with Balanchine and Efimov. We had a lovely time in Germany.

Beginning with Balanchine, I have spent all of my life with avant-garde people. Diaghilev, however, I was frightened of. I didn't know why. He was not severe or frightening in himself. But first of all, he was such an important genius. It is always difficult to deal with genius and authority, as with a professor at your university. In Russia we say that such a mind is twenty-five years ahead of the rest of us.

In Diaghilev's company, we all began to realize how versatile Mr. B. was as a choreographer. I worked in the opera in Monte Carlo as a member of the resident Diaghilev company. I did *L'Enfant et les Sortilèges,* a butterfly in Balanchine's choreography. In Mr. B.'s work in opera we could see tremendous variety.

Massine was terribly jealous of Balanchine. He once appealed for a new project to Diaghilev, who said Balanchine had already asked about something similar. Massine said, "Oh, Balanchine steals my ideas!" Diaghilev was amused. With Balanchine, Diaghilev would come and say, "George, I don't like that part, it's a little bit slow. Can you change it?" Balanchine would change it. If a dancer couldn't perform a step well, he would alter it. You came to rehearsal and he never stopped, creativity poured from him. I began to realize that this was an extraordinary man.

Balanchine confessed his love for me in 1926. Everyone noticed that he was moody and not talking. I said, "What is the matter?" He said, "Well, don't you know? I love you." Balanchine's attitude toward the women he fell in love with was that of a painter toward his model. I had noticed that he was very protective of me. Once he had criticized me for gaining weight, so I took too many diet pills and passed out. When I woke up, Balanchine was standing over me. He shook me, brought me to my senses, and lectured me on using such pills.

When Balanchine made *Apollo* in 1928 he had us flex our feet, shortening them in our toe shoes, and half the theater in Paris was stunned and liked it and the other half did not. And we used angular hands instead of rounded classical hands. Without any ceremony Apollo lifts Terpsichore onto his back! It was free movement. That is what Mr. B. gave us: a completely new vocabulary.

Stravinsky was a charming man, with a lot of punch. He was like Balanchine's father, who was a musician too. I was introduced to Stravinsky as George's wife. He respected me. I liked him, which is more than I can say for George's other Russian friends, Nabokov, Kopeikine, and Tchelitchew. Boris

Kochno was another strange one. He was responsible for the subjects of many of Diaghilev's ballets, including those by Balanchine. Diaghilev liked Boris. They were not lovers, but Boris was Diaghilev's secretary. Balanchine and Boris were close friends. They understood each other.

All of Diaghilev's ballets had a story or an idea or some kind of goal. It was never just dancing to music. I think that's why we danced each part so differently, interpreted it so differently.

The last time I saw Diaghilev was at Vichy in the summer of 1929. Diaghilev gathered us together the last night and congratulated us on the season. He said he had signed a contract for Covent Garden next season, then we would go on to Berlin. "I can't kiss everybody, but you, Choura, I will kiss good-bye." Within a few weeks he was dead. That was the end of Diaghilev's Ballets Russes.

Balanchine was in London then, working on a film. George was asked to do *The Creatures of Prometheus* at the Opéra in Paris for Spessivtseva, whom he adored. (She was a beautiful woman with a beautiful body and beautiful technique but an empty head.) But George got pneumonia which developed into tuberculosis. I took him to Switzerland to a sanatorium. That left the field free for Lifar. George was generous with Lifar. He told him, "You do the ballet. I will give you all my ideas, and you can do it." Lifar did do it, and the ballet was a success. When George recovered and returned to Paris, he and I went to the Opéra, saw the ballet, and wanted to go backstage. The man at the stage door told us, "You can't come in." We were astonished. "Those are Monsieur Lifar's orders." I never forgave Lifar for that. George made Lifar's career as a dancer by giving him unparalleled roles in *La Chatte, Apollo,* and *Prodigal Son,* psyched him into being a choreographer (his first ballet for Diaghilev, *Renard,* had been a disaster), and he did this!

Soon George went to Denmark, and I went to Monte Carlo for the opera season. We went where there was work; we were always separated. He started to have friends I didn't know. I had friends he didn't know. I said, "Let's call it off." I wrote him a letter asking for the break. Balanchine wrote me a letter. It was *triste.* He was hurt that I had left him, sad because we had had a very good life. We never quarreled. It was perfect. One season Balanchine had used Vladimiroff's and Doubrovska's apartment in Monte Carlo to invite Diaghilev to dinner and entertain. We were so young. I think from the beginning George loved me, but he didn't know how to show the love. He always spoiled me. He always brought me something back from his travels. When I asked for something, he went out and bought it. Once he bought me three dresses. But when he came back from Denmark, he brought a new American automobile!

After the separation, I was in London doing *Waltzes from Vienna* for a year.

He was with the De Basil company in Monte Carlo. One day we met on the street in Paris. I told him we were going to work together again. He said, "What do you mean?" I said, "Well, I signed a contract with De Basil." George said, "But I didn't invite you." I said, "Massine invited me." He said, "Massine?" George had done one season for De Basil, but De Basil did not tell him he had hired Massine as ballet master for the next. When I first appeared in America with the De Basil Ballet Russe at the St. James Theater in 1933, Balanchine did not come to see me. We were finished as husband and wife.

But I did see him at the School of American Ballet later, where I always went for class. At one lesson there at the barre were all the wives and ex-wives: Geva, Zorina, Tallchief, Tanaquil LeClercq, and myself. Balanchine was mad for Zorina. She was beautiful, with blond hair and blue enamel eyes. She had a boyish figure, with wide shoulders, thin waist, and thin hips. She dropped Balanchine eventually, but afterward she did not do much on Broadway. Balanchine was very noble about it. He was a romantic man. All of his fantasy is romance, isn't it? He was romantic with each of his wives and between wives as well. He knew how to behave with nobility when one of his romances left him.

I worked with George again at the Ballet Russe de Monte Carlo. I danced in *Serenade.* At that time *Serenade* had only one heroine. The girl in the ballet who leads the boy to the girl who lies on the floor is his wife. I asked Balanchine who she was, and he told me that. She is his wife and together, he said, they pass down the road of life. I, the girl on the floor, was pitied by the man, but I was a frivolous girl who had one affair after another. Then I was left alone.

I think Balanchine asked me to teach at the School of American Ballet because he believed that I would do what he asked for. I did not meddle in his affairs, and he seemed to be comfortable with me. We kept a certain distance from one another except for our professional work. We collaborated on the 1974 production of *Coppélia* for the New York City Ballet.

I saw George during his last illness. He was asleep when I came into the room, then he woke up and saw me. It was difficult because he couldn't follow the conversation. But he was tender and happy toward me. In his final years he said to me one day that, when people asked when he was going to marry again, he would reply, "Thank you very much. No more!" I believe that was the time a dancer in the company wanted him to marry her. He told me, "I am interested in art now." I said, "Yes, I understand." Each age brings us something. After sixty you don't think about romance, you think about philosophy.

I think all those girls, the beautiful ones, did not understand George. A

European woman takes care of a man. We are brought up that way. American women, with a different history, joined their men in conquering the land and their living. Men appreciate that and get down on their knees and offer everything. That is why American women are spoiled.

When Balanchine fell in love, maybe the girl would fall in love, too, but not one hundred percent. He actually never found, I believe, his one hundred percent beloved. Maybe that is why he was so creative. His life was creating, having satisfaction in searching.

Now the Soviet companies want to dance the Balanchine repertory. I once asked him if he would do a ballet for them. He said, "If they said, 'Oh, you must do a ballet,' then I would say all right." But the Russian choreographers at that time would have been jealous if Balanchine had had a success. I saw the Kirov's productions of *Scotch Symphony* and *Theme and Variations* in 1989. I think Balanchine would have been pleased. It will take years for the Russians to catch up. Perhaps when the Russians have experienced his ballets there will be a choreographer born in Russia who will be inspired by them. In politics, Gorbachev is a very capable man, but he can't do it alone. The Russian people have been so beaten down by Communism, they don't believe in the possibility of change for the better. They are afraid that if they show something new they will be punished like the Chinese students. Let us hope things will change.

Now people worship Balanchine, but for maybe forty years many, including critics, thought he was crazy. The same with Stravinsky. I am often asked, "What would have happened to Balanchine if Lincoln Kirstein had not asked him to come to America?" Balanchine used to say, quoting an old nurse, *"If* mushrooms grew in your mouth, it wouldn't be a mouth, it would be a kitchen garden." These ifs are silly. But one thing is sure. Balanchine's friendship with Lincoln was fantastic. Kirstein was the Rock of Gibraltar. Whatever George wanted, Lincoln was a hundred percent behind him. Maybe Lincoln did not agree, but he was behind him. Always. Sometimes you'd think Lincoln would say, "Now, really, George, that's crazy." But Lincoln never did. George was very lucky to find Lincoln Kirstein. Friendship is what means most.

TAMARA

GEVA

Dancer, actress, and Broadway star, Geva was born in St. Petersburg in 1907, daughter of the art collector Levki Gevergeyev (later curator-director of what became the Leningrad State Museum for Theater and Music) and a music hall singer; she trained at the Russian Imperial Ballet School and danced for Balanchine in his Young Ballet. She and Balanchine were married in 1922. He choreographed a Rubinstein Romance and Valse Triste for her and she sang in night clubs, accompanied on the piano by Balanchine. Balanchine and Geva left Russia with the troupe organized by Vladimir Dimitriev (1924) and joined the Diaghilev Ballets Russes. After she and Balanchine separated, she toured America with the Balieff Chauve-Souris, appearing in dances made for her by Balanchine. She starred on Broadway in Whoopee, Three's a Crowd, Flying Colors, A Divine Drudge, The Red Cat, and in On Your Toes, choreographed by

Balanchine. Appeared in Idiot's Delight, The Play's the Thing, The Trojan Women, Dark Eyes, Peepshow, Twentieth Century, No Exit, *and in the motion pictures* Their Big Moment *and* Manhattan Merry-Go-Round. *The author of* Split Seconds, a Remembrance *(1972), she was choreographer for the film* Le Spectre de la Rose *and directed the BBC television documentary* Diaghilev: A Portrait *(1979).*

Tamara Geva

IN MY BOOK *Split Seconds,* I CHARACTERIZED GEORGE AS A MIXTURE OF POET AND general. I met this creature of extremes in Petrograd in 1920, when I was admitted to the Theater School. Although I was not yet thirteen, I was not a child—I was already a woman. Childhood is short-lived in convulsive times of hardship, fear, and famine. That experience sends one ahead of one's years, a bit confused but eager to face a better future.

The school was segregated; boys and girls were kept apart except for such occasions as adagio and ballroom classes, and it was at one of these that I met George. We were in the middle of a ballroom class, being instructed in a minuet, when the door opened and the director of the school walked in, bringing with him a young man. They both stood to the side watching us work. The young man was of medium height, thin, with a handsome Roman-like face and long hair which instantly labeled him a rebel. Long hair was not exactly the order of the day at that time. But since my father, a brilliant man, also wore his hair a bit long, I considered it a sign of asserting oneself and found it rather attractive.

In a little while the two visitors approached the teacher and, after a short conference, the young man took over the class. He led us through new and intriguing combinations, taking part in it all himself, and the whole class came to life in a burst of new excitement.

I was told that his name was George Balanchivadze, a young dancer and an aspiring choreographer. He was always called Georges, in the French way, seldom Georgi Melitonovich. To my surprise, after the lesson, he picked me out and asked me if I would like to work with him. That was how George Balanchivadze, later Balanchine, entered my life in a relationship that lasted a lifetime.

George was beginning to be known as a choreographer of promise. He tried out his imagination on me. In the olden days, anyone connected with the Maryinsky Theater or the Theater School was forbidden to appear on any other stage, but in the revolutionary time, when people were struggling for survival, the authorities overlooked the rule. George began making dances for the two of us. We would appear in little theaters that sprang up all over the city, for a prosaic recompense of a few pounds of flour, salt, coffee, and other staples. Coffee was marvelous because after it was brewed you could take the grounds and mix them with a little flour and, if you were lucky, you added a little sugar and baked it all into cakes. They were nothing like our cookies, but they filled the stomach.

George's family was cut off in the Caucasus. He lived in a room on the top floor of the Theater School. Then came a disastrous period when pipes froze, heat was cut off, and food rationing was lowered to a minimum. The school closed and George lost his living quarters. Immediately my father brought

George to live with us in our huge, twenty-three-room apartment. Dressed in several layers of clothing, he and I worked in a nearby private studio.

My father and George respected each other. Father liked Wagner, and George used to play Wagner for him at the piano. George became ill when he was living with us, but with the help of the famous Professor Pavlov we nursed him back to health.

In the course of the next two years George's dedicated work gained him a reputation. In 1923 the Mikhailovsky Theater gave Balanchine a chance to do the entrance scene in the opera *Coq d'Or*. (The Mikhailovsky staged lighter operas for short runs.) His dances departed from the usual expression of the oriental mood; they changed his staging later on because they were not quite ready for such liberties.

When Balanchine organized the Young Ballet, he startled the audience by choreographing the *Funeral March* of Chopin, a distinct departure from the lighthearted choreography of the time. It was easy to get an idea of Balanchine's dances in those days because to a recurrent question, "Why are you doing this?" he would always reply, "Why not?" George always wanted to bring in the unexpected. Sometimes he would plunge into extremes. For instance, the duet, *Enigma* (1923), we danced barefoot, but it required real technique. It was a terrific success and was done before Isadora Duncan came back to Russia. I shall never forget her performance: Wagnerian music, with a symphony orchestra down below in the pit, and up on the stage of the Maryinsky this lady stretched out on the floor. She lay there for a long time while we were all waiting for something to happen.

Balanchine was a good dancer, light and wiry. He was given solos at the Maryinsky Theater. He performed the hoop dance in *The Nutcracker* as I've never seen it done before or since. He never touched the ground, flashing in and out of the hoop. At one performance at the Maryinsky, he did the *lezghinka,* a warrior's dance. He had two knives and accidentally hit himself in the knee. As a result, he had a broken cartilage that moved in his knee, and every now and then it would get locked completely. After that he always had trouble with that knee (the cartilage had to be removed eventually).

There was a pas de deux to Rubinstein's *Romance.* It had an arabesque supported by a kiss. Balanchine was on his knees, and I had to hold myself in an arabesque just on my mouth or lose my balance. I didn't hold it long, believe me. That's an example of erotic dance that Balanchine could produce —he always had a little bit of eroticism everywhere in his work.

As time rolled on, our friendship gave way to a more intimate relationship. My father, in his wisdom, gently suggested that perhaps we should marry. "Times are hard," he said. "You never know where life will throw you. If you don't like being married you can get divorced later."

It was prophetic. The marriage came just in time because, soon after, a smart and sly man, Vladimir Dimitriev, succeeded in getting permission from the government to take a small group of "young Soviet talent" on a three-month tour of recitals in Germany. He also arranged to be the manager of the group. On a rainy morning George, Danilova, myself, and a young dancer named Efimov left on a German boat, never to return.

For the tour Balanchine included *Valse Triste* (1922), in which I was a somnambulist, dressed in a tuniclike dress down to the knees. That dance frightened the audience because I moved forward toward the very edge of the proscenium as though I were blind and were about to go right off into the pit. The solo prefigured his ballet *La Sonnambula.* In Germany, George and I would do the modern dances, Danilova and Efimov the classical variations. We were a flop in Germany, absolute disaster. We danced in all sorts of places—beer gardens, open theaters, vaudeville. We followed dog acts, apes, and elephants. We even appeared in an insane asylum.

Anton Dolin, the star Diaghilev dancer, saw our troupe at the Empire Theater in London. There we played on the same bill with American singers and vaudeville. Our program was essentially the same one we had done in Germany: George and I in a pas de deux; a solo for me; Danilova with Efimov; Danilova in a variation, etc. We did *Orientalia,* in which George played a blind beggar in the street, an old man with a bear, and I was either his daughter or his dancing girl. He rolled out a little carpet, sat down, and mimed playing a string instrument, and I danced on the rug. When we finished the dance, we packed everything up and went away. It was a very strange little dance to music by Cui. We were at the Empire Theater for only ten days or so. We were fired because we had costumes with old-fashioned hooks and snaps, and it took us too much time to change from one costume to another while the orchestra played the same piece over and over. The audience got tired and protested. Meanwhile, Anton Dolin was enthusiastic about us. He alerted Diaghilev, who asked us to come to Paris and snatched us up for the Ballets Russes.

As a wife, I lived with George only three years, but as we remained friends for life, I grew to know him pretty well. He had a good sense of humor, leaning toward the ridiculous; some of his expressions were hilarious. Outwardly he was calm—nobody had ever heard him raise his voice— but inside there were often emotional eruptions, and many a time, knowing that I would never betray him, he would come to me and let that misery spill out. We had many secrets, one of them never to be discovered until his lawyers dug it up after his death.

He was very religious, his faith so deep that normal troubles of existence never touched him. He was absolutely sure that God was on his side. Politically, he was of the almost extinct species—a monarchist. He loved pomp and crowns and never forgot that as a young boy he was presented to the Tsar after one of the performances at the Maryinsky Theater. His hatred of the Soviet Union was maniacal. I never understood it since he did not suffer any more than the rest of us in the revolutionary years. In fact, he started his work with the encouragement of the government.

I remember when the Soviet poet Yevtuchenko came to New York and read his poems at the State Theater. George and I sat in George's seats in the front row of the first ring. Whatever one's opinion of the Soviet Union, Yevtuchenko is a very talented poet, but George fidgeted throughout the reading. At the end I said I wanted to meet Yevtuchenko because my friend, the great writer John Steinbeck, had met him in Russia and told me a lot about him. But as we approached the poet's dressing room George firmly refused to go in.

"Shame on you," I said. "This is your theater. Where is your hospitality?" and without any further ado I threw the door open and pushed him in. For a while he was furious but later we laughed about it.

There was a streak of the dictator in George, a benevolent dictator, but a dictator nevertheless. In his world of dance he was king. He treated his dancers and associates with a strong but affectionate hand. He was also a mystic in touch with forces unknown to us and he depended on them. I remember one morning at Diaghilev's when he was about to begin choreographing a new ballet and the company was called to rehearsal. We found him sitting down, staring into nowhere, eyes blank. We waited but he remained motionless. Finally the stage director came up to him and asked what was the reason for the delay. Without a direct answer George said, "Intermission. Let them go for half an hour."

"But you have not started yet," the bewildered man gasped.

"My rehearsal," George said, "I can call intermission whenever I want."

And so we were let go. When we returned we found him still sitting there, but when we were all in he rose and began to work, one movement after another pouring out of him, like a broken dam, imagination soaring.

I was in *Le Chant du Rossignol* (1925), which was first done by Massine, but Diaghilev didn't like it and asked George to redo it. They wanted to find a thin, small girl who could be put in a cage and be a nightingale. They found her in the person of a fourteen-year-old called Alicia Markova. She was marvelous. I don't know how she had such a technique at that age. Danilova and I were two ladies-in-waiting. One day Markova became sick, and nobody could take her place. A princess was coming to the performance, and

Diaghilev would not tolerate a cancellation. So George put on white tights and got in the cage. When he emerged, he burst into some light fantastic dance, trying to remember his own choreography. Of course, he couldn't dance on pointe, so it was quite different. He didn't imitate a bird when he danced, but he laughed himself sick. So did the audience. George loved playing tricks. At Christmas in *Boutique Fantasque,* he came out on stage as St. Nicholas in a beautiful Renaissance costume. He adored makeup; the less he looked like himself, the more he loved it. In *Firebird,* as the monster Kastchei, he had his mustache coming out of his nostrils. He loved putting the dancers off and breaking people up onstage. That is strange because his character in life, the way I knew him, was quite different. There was a contradiction in his character. He was a mystic. He believed totally in his destiny. He never doubted it, even in the most difficult moments. When I would say, "What do we do now?" he would reply, "We wait. Something will happen." If anybody worried in those early days, you couldn't make him worry. He knew. It was going to be. "Don't worry." And at the same time he would do all these silly things onstage.

With Diaghilev we were used to dancing to a certain tempo in Stravinsky's *Firebird.* Once Stravinsky himself conducted. He raised his baton, and everything was suddenly three times as fast. To keep up with Stravinsky's tempo, everybody was tripping and falling over each other. George said, "That was the right way to do it. We are always slowing everything down in life."

When George and I would move into a new place, he never did anything to the rooms as far as furnishing them or decorating them were concerned. He only cared about the piano and the kitchen. He played and composed beautifully. He had two or three musical compositions. I would suggest to him, "Show them to somebody." He never would. He thought that his musical compositions were below his other talents. But he was a good musician. He would sit at the piano with Rieti and not only try to learn a score; sometimes they changed it together. He did the same thing with Stravinsky.

When Balanchine did *Prodigal Son,* he had severe disagreements with Prokofiev, who was old-fashioned. George told me that Prokofiev wanted to do the ballet much more traditionally, with a real banqueting table and wine and fruit and everyone at the feast behaving like in court. The debate nearly wrecked the production. Finally Diaghilev took George's side. As a result, thank God, there is hardly anything in the ballet that is old-fashioned.

When we separated and I had an offer to go to New York, George choreographed three numbers for me, each distinctly different. The first was to music by Glazunov, a classical, romantic powder puff that I danced between two wooden borzoi dogs. The second was called *Grotesque Espagnol* to the music of Albéniz, a composite of a bullfight scene in which I was at once a matador, a bull, and a priest and in which at the end I killed the bull but fell dead myself. That created a sensation. The dance critic of the *New York Times,* John Martin, wrote two articles about it. The third number was to Prokofiev's *Sarcasm,* an abstraction to a changing rhythm, a challenge to the audience. I was half harlequin, half pilot. The audience responded to it with chuckles of amusement and at the end applauded wildly. Thus I introduced George's work to America and set out on my own independent career here.

Four years later, when I was in my first Broadway show, George knocked on my door. He came straight from the boat, having deposited his suitcases at the hotel. We picked up where we left off. I learned about the big project of a school and ballet company and, since George knew hardly anyone in New York and spoke no English, he spent a lot of time with me.

The building of that now great establishment was rocky, but they succeeded—that great trio of Balanchine, Lincoln Kirstein, and Eddie Warburg. On March 1, 1935, at the Adelphi Theater, I danced George's ballet *Errante* at the first performance of the American Ballet.

On Broadway, George and I were united in *On Your Toes* in 1936, when I was coupled with Ray Bolger. (The revival on Broadway in 1983 claimed choreography by Balanchine, but it was far from the truth since George was already confined to the hospital.)

Following *On Your Toes,* I went to Hollywood. George came soon afterward, signed by Samuel Goldwyn. The story goes that at the first meeting with the big boss George was asked how many dancers he needed. He mentioned a certain number of boys and girls and then added, "And thirty midgets." Stunned, Goldwyn asked him, "Why thirty midgets?" George replied, "Little midgets won't cost too much." Later I asked George if that was true, and he replied, "Sure. Why not?"

There were years when working territory separated us, but the close relationship remained. However, when my book came out he suddenly and with no explanation stopped talking to me for a year. Eventually I learned the reason. In my book I described him as a man possessing all the frailties of human nature, whereas he wanted to be remembered only through his work. With time that rift healed and the relationship returned to normal.

At the end, when he was ill, I spent a lot of time with him at the hospital. I would cook Russian food, bring it there, and spoon-feed him. I just sat next to him, watching. His memory grew dimmer and time lost its meaning for him, yet one day he astounded me. He motioned me to get closer and whispered in my ear, "Remember, we leave Wednesday . . . don't forget." And I answered, "No, I won't forget." It was eerie to see him fall into the past.

One day Kramarevsky, the dancer and teacher at the School of American

Ballet, came to visit, and we both sat with George. Kramarevsky, the good friend, decided to amuse George. "Do you remember Vertinsky?" he asked gently. Vertinsky was a composer-lyricist, a sort of Cole Porter of Russia, who was greatly admired. George nodded and Kramarevsky burst into reciting one of Vertinsky's poems. Then he stopped. "That's all I remember," he said apologetically.

A glint of light came into George's veiled eyes. He opened his mouth and recited the poem verbatim to the end.

One day I found him clutching a small icon in the palm of his hand. He brought it to my face and repeated several times, "Must believe . . . must believe . . ." and closed his eyes. With every hour he seemed to grow farther away into the distance, like a shrinking shadow.

I think I was the last visitor. I left him at four in the afternoon on April 29, 1983. Early the next morning he died. Farewell, George. May the angels you loved so much keep you in peace.

YURI

SLONIMSKY[*]

A friend of Balanchine's youth, the eminent Russian ballet historian and critic Yuri Slonimsky (1902–78) wrote biographies of the French ballet masters who dominated the Russian repertory in the nineteenth century and of the Russian choreographer Lev Ivanov. He was a founder of Balanchine's Young Ballet in 1921.

* Yuri Slonimsky's account of Balanchine's youth originally appeared in *Ballet Review*, Volume 5, Number 3.

I Remember Balanchine

BALANCHINE and the New York City Ballet visited the Soviet Union for the second time in 1972. Soon after their return, Balanchine told me of his friendship and respect for Yuri Slonimsky. I began a correspondence with the Soviet critic. Knowing of Slonimsky's long acquaintance with Balanchine and his unique knowledge of the choreographer's youth, I proposed that he undertake recollections of Balanchine's early years and the choreographer's first ballets. Balanchine concurred in this idea; the following essay, translated by John Andrews, and compressed for this volume, first appeared in Ballet Review, Vol. 5, No. 3. *To read a recapitulation of such a time from the point of view of a Soviet critic and historian must be of special interest to those, who wish to have a contemporary's account of the background of Balanchine's early work. While Balanchine left Russia in 1924, when he was twenty-one, Yuri Slonimsky remained there.*

Several of Yuri Slonimsky's books are well known in English through the enterprise of the late Anatole Chujoy, who translated them for special issues of Dance Index *and* Dance Perspectives. *A number of crucial texts have yet to appear in English. Born in St. Petersburg in 1902, Yuri Slonimsky was educated in the law and in the arts. He began to review ballet performances when he was seventeen and at twenty translated certain of Noverre's* Letters on Dancing and Ballet *into Russian for the first time. Monographs on* Giselle *(1927, since revised and much amplified) and* La Sylphide *began his career as a major ballet historian. Biographies and extensive essays on the choreographers Charles Didelot, Jules Perrot, Arthur Saint-Léon, Marius Petipa, and Lev Ivanov have been important sources to ballet scholars for many years. His book,* The Bolshoi Ballet, *appeared in English in 1971.*

F.M.

April 1976

ON AUGUST 13, 1913, THE COMPOSER MELITON BALANCHIVADZE PRESENTED AN APPLI-cation to the inspector of the Theater School in St. Petersburg. He wrote: "I most humbly request Your Excellency to accept my son Georgii among the daytime students of the school for special education in the art of dance." The following year Georgii was admitted "at the treasury's expense" into the boarding school. And thus Georgii Balanchivadze began his life in ballet. Under his pseudonym, George Balanchine, devised later by Diaghilev, he has acquired fame throughout the world.

Balanchine spent just over ten years in the Russian ballet, seven as a student in the Theater School and three as a dancer of the Maryinsky Theater.

What advantages did this promising dancer and natural ballet master have at his disposal? What did he receive from his family, his school, and, later, from the theater? In what conditions did his creative individuality take form? How did the October Revolution affect him? He spent seven of those ten years, after all, in the most complex circumstances of the revolutionary period. What determined his artistic direction? . . .

In a small room, in St. Petersburg in 1889, there lived two young men— the Balanchivadze brothers. The younger, Vassily Antonovich (1870–1952), was a student at the Academy of Fine Arts in the classes of Repin and Makovsky. He later became a prominent artist, a professor of painting, and an actor in the theater and cinema. He was awarded the honorary title of Meritorious Artist of the Georgian Republic. The elder, Meliton Antonovich (1862–1936), studied in the Conservatory of Music in the composition class of Nikolai Rimsky-Korsakov. Meliton Balanchivadze became one of the founders of classical Georgian music, the composer of the opera *Darejan Tsbieri (Guileful Tamara).*

In those earlier years, however, after struggling for three years with little money or support, the two brothers were forced to end their studies. Vassily left for Georgia. Meliton occupied himself with teaching and musical composition. He wrote articles for the *Russian Musical Gazette.* He organized concerts ("Georgian Evenings") in St. Petersburg and Tiflis, with performances of the Russian classics, his own adaptations of Georgian folk songs for chorus and orchestra, and his own romances, arias, and dances from the opera which he had begun to sketch.

In 1898 Meliton Balanchivadze married Maria Nikolaevna Vasilyeva, who worked in a bank. The young couple had difficulty making ends meet when suddenly in 1901 an enormous fortune fell upon them; they won two hundred thousand rubles with a lottery ticket. At last it was possible to breathe freely and to devote oneself to a single passion—music! Good-natured, sociable, fascinated by all conceivable enterprises (George would inherit these characteristics from his father), Meliton succumbed to the persuasion of friends and decided to become an entrepreneur. He built a crucible factory in Luga, launched it triumphantly, but soon went bankrupt. The musician Balanchivadze was too far removed from commercial affairs and financial manipulations to succeed.

He was obliged to return to teaching. The family had grown in the meantime. Tamara was born in 1902, George in 1904 (January 9), and Andrei in 1906. They were all to take positions of eminence in the world of the arts. Tamara finished the Academy of Fine Arts in Tbilisi and achieved renown as a painter. Andrei wrote the music for the first Georgian ballet, *The Heart of the Hills* (1938). A professor of the Georgian Conservatory of Music and a National Artist of the Georgian Republic, he has been chairman of the Georgian Composers' Union.

Meliton Balanchivadze was not long dismayed by the failure of his business. In the evenings in his home there were readings and performances by

his guests, many of them leading cultural figures; and the host would recip-
rocate by performing his own musical works. Discussions and arguments
were loud and passionate. The children often demonstrated their talents
also. Andrei and George played nocturnes and marches which they had
composed themselves, preferring these genres above all others. They performed the four-hand piano pieces of Haydn, Mozart, and Schubert.

The Balanchivadze children were nurtured on music as a source of incom-
parable beauty and inspiration. Their parents sometimes took them to the
theater, mostly to opera and ballet, where the performances of celebrated
singers and dancers developed in them a love for the art of the theater, for
the combination of music, choreography, and painting.

The impressions he had absorbed induced George to put on performances
of his own. His "troupe" consisted at first of two "staff" performers—himself and his sister, who also painted the scenery. His brother served single-
handed as an entire orchestra. Occasionally in these performances and cos-
tumed concerts the neighboring children would participate. The family
album has preserved for us several photographs of these "performers" with
their "manager." Was this not the origin of George's need to compose
dances, a need which would fill his entire life?

In 1913 Tamara was admitted to the ballet section of the Imperial Theater
School in St. Petersburg. According to Balanchine his parents did not agree
about his future. His mother wanted him, like Tamara, to go to the Theater
School. But his father preferred a military career. Apparently for financial
reasons it was necessary to place the children in some kind of school where
they would receive room and board. Balanchine says that his fate was resolved accidentally. One of his father's acquaintances in the ballet discerned
in the boy an aptitude for the dance and helped him enter the Theater
School. This was not at all a simple matter—significant patronage was required. And so the school accepted him as a daytime student along with his
sister and took him into the boarding school a year later.

The separation from his family was difficult. He suffered, protested, and
even ran away, which nearly caused his expulsion. But he had to reconcile
himself to the situation. And gradually George began to find solace in his
lessons of music and dance. He had an excellent music teacher, E. F. Klop-
stok, who gave special attention to this gifted child. He also studied violin.
With his dance teachers Balanchine was equally fortunate. His first instructor was S. K. Andrianov, a classical dancer who loved his students and
scrupulously supervised their studies. The second teacher to whom Balanchine considers himself indebted was P. A. Gerdt, a veteran of the Russian
ballet and an outstanding classical dancer of the second half of the nineteenth century. Gerdt had a striking ability, rarely found in ballet, to com-

bine techniques of dance and gesture into a choreographic form. Serge Diaghilev held Gerdt in high esteem and had sought his participation in the "Russian Seasons" he organized in Paris. In the ballets of Tchaikovsky and Glazunov, Gerdt's performances were related to the music as to a source of vital rhythm which controlled the movements and plasticity of the dancer. Boris Asafiev, the writer and composer, asserts that Gerdt was one of the few people who grasped intuitively the meaning of Tchaikovsky's reforms in the ballet, expressing them perfectly in his artistic performances. Gerdt was a student of Christian Johansson, who had inherited from his teacher, Bournonville, the pedagogic methods of Vestris. He conducted a class from which there emerged many brilliant dancers; the most brilliant was Anna Pavlova. Balanchine is mistaken, I believe, in calling Gerdt his teacher; in those years Gerdt had stopped teaching and only led exercises or reviewed classes—and classes not of classical dance but of mime and support. Nevertheless, until 1916 he appeared on the stage demonstrating his astonishingly expressive movement and gesture.

"These two men," Balanchine said many years later, "instilled in me a respect for the movements of the human body. They taught me to utilize to the maximum the expressiveness of the arms, the legs and the body. They provided me with experience of exceptional importance for the future." L. S. Leontiev, his teacher in the later years at the Theater School, was another important influence.

Of prime importance to the students of the ballet school is their participation in actual performances with the great dancers of the day at the Maryinsky, the imperial theater. This experience reveals the beauty of the art of dance to an inquisitive eye and can captivate young students for their entire lives. The repertory of the seasons from 1915 to 1917 permits us to name several productions which gave this essential practice to the school's pupils.

Balanchine appeared in the third act of the famous ballet *Paquita,* in which Petipa, drawing from images of his youth, composed unequaled children's dances—a polonaise and a mazurka. Sometimes performed today, these short masterpieces of choreography deserve to become more widely known. In those years, they were almost always danced in the school's concerts and graduation performances. Balanchine also took part in the dance of the Arab boys arranged by Petipa with astonishing simplicity and rhythmical inventiveness in the second act of *Raymonda.* In the first act of *Don Quixote* he was one of the Spanish boys running about the stage in the crowd, and he performed classical Spanish dances which can still be recognized, in Gorsky's production of the ballet, as a model of Petipa's art. *The Nutcracker* in those years was seldom performed except for its second and third scenes. And in them, among the pupils of the younger classes, Balanchine danced in the divertissement. He also participated in the march of the toy soldiers in the ballet *The Fairy Doll,* arranged by the Legat brothers, and distinguished himself among the young boys in Fokine's *Polovetsian Dances.*

His ability to understand and perform any theatrical task, his excellent memory and stage presence made him stand out among his contemporaries. Balanchine also performed at the Alexandrinsky, the drama theater, in plays that required boys. There, from behind the scenes, he could watch entire plays and could memorize with exceptional ease the monologues he liked most of that theater's many great actors. The closing monologue of Chatsky in Griboyedov's *Wit Works Woe,* as performed by Y. M. Yuriev, left such a strong imprint on his mind that even now he can recite it expressively and distinctively from beginning to end. He played the role of the boy-servant Famusov in Griboyedov's comedy. Actually, Balanchine often appeared more frequently at the Alexandrinka (as the theater was familiarly called) than at the Maryinsky. He acted in plays by Ostrovsky, Molière, Leonid Andreyev, and others.

The source of Balanchine's most vivid impressions as a child, and later as a young man—the ballet which directed his thoughts toward the future and made him fall in love with the art of dance—was *The Sleeping Beauty.* Not without consequence have many children—Pavlova, Fokine, and Ulanova—seen this production in what is now Leningrad and acquired a burning passion for ballet.

Balanchine's debut on stage in *The Sleeping Beauty* among the children in the Peasant Waltz with garlands (first act), his participation in the suite of the fairy Carabosse (prologue) and in the dance Hop o' My Thumb and the Seven Brothers (final act), opened before him an enchanted world of sound, color, and movement. Despite the existence of such masterpieces as *Giselle* and *Swan Lake,* the classical heritage has no production which can seduce audiences in so many ways as *The Sleeping Beauty.* Throughout the production in those days, there were marvels of special effects: in the large fountains with multicolored lighting, in the growth on stage of lilac bushes, and in the great scene of people and horses posing majestically on a moving floor. . . .

The leitmotif of *The Sleeping Beauty,* expressed in its music with unprecedented strength and reflected in its choreography, corresponded to Balanchine's view of ballet and gradually became the leading theme of his work. "Long live the sun, away with darkness!"—the words of Pushkin come to mind more than once when we see and hear *The Sleeping Beauty.* The affirmation of the beauty and radiance of existence, the triumph of day over night —this is what music in union with dance must celebrate. Tchaikovsky, in *The Sleeping Beauty* more than in his other ballets, "makes us happy," as Balanchine has said. The dance, in full harmony with the music, fills us with bright joy. This is why, ever since those early years, Tchaikovsky is for Balanchine one of the few composers who can provide an inspirational base for choreography.

The size of the ballet companies of the imperial theaters at that time, the training of the corps de ballet within a single system, and the unusual richness of expressive forms—character dance as well as classical dance, pantomime as well as dance, a highly developed technique of group dances and pas de deux as well as the art of the solo or individual variation—all this made the Russian ballet unique. Its abundance of talented performers was without parallel. These dancers demonstrated a new level of classical and character dancing that had been developed in the Russian school.

But the state of political-moral reaction that dominated Russia after 1905 cast a shadow on the imperial theaters: it somehow suddenly became apparent that the art of ballet was marking time, that it was losing its creative potential. What could be done to overcome this problem was simply not known. Several attempts to create monumental choreographic works similar to earlier triumphs met with failure. The one exception was *Salammbô*. Choreographic miniatures, brief attempts at the art, predominated. They were produced, usually, for benefit or charity performances. New productions of any size were created more and more rarely. They lasted but briefly and their quality provoked criticism for unoriginality. Even such innovators as Fokine and Gorsky could not display their full range on the Russian imperial stage. Most of the ballets beginning about 1910 were created abroad in the "Russian Seasons" of Diaghilev. He was the one who attracted the most gifted artists—artists concerned for the future of their native culture. While Paris and the world saw that Russian drama, opera, music, and painting could demonstrate the greatness of Russia's achievements, the ballet in the imperial theaters at home was obliged to subsist in an atmosphere of spiritual poverty. This situation was viewed with alarm by leaders in the Russian theater—Stanislavsky and Nemirovich-Danchenko, Lunacharsky, Benois, and Meyerhold. Even the great Pavlova abandoned Russia, feeling the sterility of creative art in the oppressive, stagnant atmosphere of the imperial theaters. The dismissal of Vaslav Nijinsky was a typical act of thoughtlessness by the court theaters. This dancer required ballets where his individuality could be shown with full force, where the voice of his time would find expression. But there were no such ballets on the imperial stage at that time.

No one could make ballet in the imperial theaters thrive and move forward. Moreover, if a man existed who could foresee the future, no one would have listened to him. Even the director of the theater in Petrograd,

Telyakovsky, spoke bitterly about this. His superiors, he said, simply wanted an amusement, a toy—as they regarded ballet in general—and above all, they wanted it unchanged, in its old form. In order to break through this impasse, fundamental transformations were necessary in Russia. They were heralded by the salvo of the ship *Aurora* in 1917. Balanchine at that time was thirteen years old.

Let us shift now to the years 1918 to 1920. The civil war, the blockade . . . Petrograd, it seemed, was dying. The streets were empty, the windows of inactive shops were boarded up or broken. Transport (trams, motor vehicles) often came to a halt for lack of electricity and gasoline. Light often went out, throwing the streets and apartments into darkness. Hunger and cold tormented everyone. In homes and offices small iron stoves were set up with smokestacks extending through ventilation windows toward the street; furniture was burned for fuel, even valuable antiques—it didn't matter. There were days when workers received an *osmushka* of bread—that is, one eighth of a pound. One was fortunate in institutional canteens to get soup made from frozen potatoes or millet with vobla. All ablebodied men were mobilized for the country's defense. There were enterprises, institutions, and organizations from which all the employees went to the front. Old clothes and shoes wore out, new ones were not produced. People showed unusual inventiveness recutting, darning, and patching secondhand materials not even meant to be clothes and shoes. Curtains, draperies, coverings, and nightshirts were transformed into dresses and suits, leather upholstery was used for homemade shoes or their repair—if these materials were not exchanged for potatoes and flour.

"People belonging to the refined elite," a journalist has written about those times, "thought that the end of Russia, science, and culture had come, that they were the last bearers of a sacred flame and that with their own departure all would perish." The theme of the "demise" of the Russian ballet never left the pages of the hostile press of the White Guards. Moreover, in an open letter to A. V. Lunacharsky in 1920, the ballet critic Volynsky predicted: "The ballet is approaching a fall into oblivion. . . . In two or three years it will be completely destroyed." Four years later he wrote of the "slow dying of the entire organism of ballet . . . the school is dying before everyone's eyes." In a number of articles he repeated this refrain. The ballet in those years was surrounded by shortsighted, skeptical, whimpering, panicky, and fault-finding observers. And there was indeed reason for their lamentation. One need only remember that all of the prerevolutionary ballerinas except Olga Spessivtseva, all of the leading male dancers except Semyonov, the most important teachers (Nicholas Legat, Olga Preobrajenska, and others), the leading ballet master, Michel Fokine, and the principal director, Nicholas Sergeyev, in varied circumstances found themselves outside of Russia. . . .

There is a Latin proverb: "Among weapons the muses are silent." But despite the experience of centuries confirming its truth, the muses this time did not remain silent. On the contrary, under the thunder of cannon the voices of the muses sounded forth more strongly than ever. Their power extended widely over people who just before did not even know of the theater's existence. . . .

At the ballet performances in those years one could see many poets, painters, actors, composers, and critics. The list of balletomanes of those years—artists, writers, architects, scholars, military men, doctors—is enormous. Their impassioned influence on the young ballet contributed in no small measure to an infusion of intellectual oxygen, to an enrichment of the spiritual climate of the ballet theater.

Among the younger ballet dancers there were the famous names of the future. Leading performers graduated from the school—Shavrov, Dudko, Lavrovsky, and Gusev. And already the character of the first great Soviet male dancer, Alexei Yermolayev, who graduated in 1926, was becoming distinct. Finishing the school together with Balanchine in 1921 was Lydia Ivanova, his friend and partner in concerts and a participant in all of his first ventures, who three years later died before her talent was fulfilled. The first performances of many student dancers at this time—Vaganova, Jordan, Ulanova, and Vecheslova, who graduated from 1926 to 1928—had already attracted attention. There were the promising debuts in the school theater of the first star of Soviet ballet, Marina Semyonova (who graduated in 1925), and the exceptionally distinctive classical ballerinas Mungalova and Mlodzinskaya, who graduated in 1922, and Tangieva, who graduated in 1923 and soon became the first star of Lithuanian ballet, one of the founders of choreographic education in that republic and a prominent ballet master and teacher. We should not forget the appearance in those years of two more performers—Vassily Vainonen (1919) and Leonid Jacobson (1926)—who would later become major ballet masters.

When in history as we know it, in such a short period, not to mention such very difficult material circumstances, had so many talents emerged? The calm, self-satisfied, carefree existence in which the imperial theater had prided itself disappeared in the civil war. Good food, clothing, transport, heating, well-ordered living—all that had vanished. A great many fine young people every day searched for and prepared fuel for the kitchen where, of course, there was insufficient food all too frequently. More often, they boiled water-and-carrot tea. Central heating was unthinkable. One would walk about the school in an overcoat.

The manager of the troupe, the dance artist and teacher L. S. Leontiev, called his young pupils little heroes and defended them from the attacks of slanderers and complainers. In his words, they "endured resolutely the burdens and deprivations of the winter of 1919–20," when "the situation reached a critical point and in the middle of the winter even classes had to cease for a time." The children appeared in ballet, opera, and drama performances, changing clothes in dressing rooms where the floor and walls were frozen with ice. They often walked great distances to the Maryinsky Theater, sometimes even twice a day, making their way through dark streets covered with deep snow along paths as in a field. Sometimes they could find work as loaders. This enabled them to arrange "sumptuous feasts" with menus of rusty herring, dried vobla, frozen potatoes or their peelings, oil-cakes, and pies made from coffee grounds. Saccharine was used for sweetening; sugar was an unavailable delicacy. At first the storerooms of the imperial school helped to provide clothing. Then the students might turn to the grandmothers' and grandfathers' sturdy old fabrics of rather curious style from which they would cut, sew, and patch up clothing and shoes.

Look at a 1921 photograph of Balanchine surrounded by his classmates and colleagues; among them are the rising "stars," Ivanova and Danilova. One cannot fail to notice the oddity of the young people's costumes borrowed from their relatives' wardrobes. Balanchine's white summer trousers were a rarity. One of the girl graduates made a blouse for herself from her grandmother's colored umbrella. But this exotic improvisation surprised no one. In 1922 Fokine's Petrograd relatives wrote that the men could not attend the planned celebration for his birthday at the Maryinsky Theater because among them they had only one pair of pants! All of this, however, was of no importance compared to the unlimited creative possibilities that now existed. The mood of optimism characteristic of youth also had an effect.

Of no small importance was the awareness that everyone was living in the same way and that everyone considered their burdens insignificant in the broader perspective. People were fighting, working, serving—laboring self-lessly. The students of the school—about to become performers—lived like everyone else and shared the hardships of the people. Without their knowing it, this had an enormous importance.

The revolutionary situation itself brought substantial changes in the school's character, in the teaching staff, and in the social consciousness of the students. Ethnic, religious, and other restrictions for admission which had existed before the October Revolution were abolished. Admission became possible for gifted overage children who surpassed the students already in the school in their level of development. The students had to equal the level of these newcomers. In 1921 the school numbered around two hundred students compared to eighty or one hundred on the eve of the Revolution.

In March 1919, Andrei Oblakov was selected and confirmed as director of the ballet school in Petrograd. He played a big role in the education of future dance artists and gave special attention to Balanchine. A former dancer of the Maryinsky Theater, a witness to the Parisian triumphs of the Russian ballet, and an impassioned admirer of music in general and of Stravinsky in particular, Oblakov helped to open the windows and doors of the "ice house," where room for thought and creativity was clearly lacking. To facilitate the flow of new ideas from the Revolution and to respond to the desire of the students for social relevance—were these not the most important tasks before the emerging Soviet school of dance?

On October 16, 1919, a historic event took place. A general meeting of students was held, creating a student committee. A veritable explosion occurred in this previously voiceless, submissive environment. As demanded by the students, a second general meeting was held on October 24 at which passions raged. The students remembered the humiliations and insults received from some of their teachers, the ignorance and stupidity of others, and the despotism of still others. They demanded their dismissal. At the same time they drew up a "Program of Activity and Objectives of the Student Committee." This "Program" contained demands to organize lectures in dance history, to expand the music library in which many classical and most modern composers were completely absent, to introduce a course in aesthetics, to teach the fundamentals of staging and set design, and to permit the study of set design for those who were interested. It included the innocent request—though very important for an understanding of their growing needs—that the students of the older classes be provided with a box in all the former imperial theaters at all performances. The "Program" was signed by all students at the meeting, including Balanchine.

In the demands of these young persons one cannot fail to perceive the changes taking place—a desire to know the world far beyond the limits of ballet, to achieve a sense of the art of dance which had been viewed from time immemorial merely as a craft, to master thoroughly the entire profession, and to read its "literature"—that is, its performances, which were previously inaccessible. The student committee made itself the vanguard of social and artistic life. Its functions, *ex officio*, were not great, but they expanded with the silent approval (if not the private advice) of Oblakov.

Starting with the distribution of rations, with duties in the dining hall and other jobs, and also with participation in arranging holiday conferences, concerts, and so on, the committee gradually achieved a determining voice in many areas. From month to month the committee acquired new active members who adopted the experience of the "veterans."

From the moment of the committee's organization in 1918, the students of the School of Russian Drama began to have secret and then open contacts with the pupils of the ballet school. I say "secret" because, at first, attempts were still made to seal off the girl pupils from the "pernicious influence" of outsiders. Into the breach between the two schools, once again in secret at first, there came students from other educational institutions in the arts. Going to theaters (including ballet theaters), studios, concerts, and literary evenings—previously forbidden—became first a normal pastime and then an integral part of one's self-education. The school gradually grew in active members. As a friend of Balanchine's since 1918, and of the other pupils as well, I was on good terms with Isaenko and Oblakov. I became a habitué of the school concerts and evenings; I even took part in certain projects of the students and the direction. With my help Vladimir Dimitriev and B. Erbstein, then students of the former Academy of Fine Arts in the class of K. S. Petrov-Vodkin, entered the school. Both had already distinguished themselves as pupils of Meyerhold, as painters in the theater, and as teachers in art courses of the Baltic naval fleet. Moreover, they had frequently come forward in the press and at meetings, calling for a renewal of the ballet. They became frequent guests of Oblakov and were sought after for rehearsals and performances at the school theater. Erbstein drew sketches of costumes for students and helped in selections from the old wardrobe.

In the school's history lessons the previously unrecognized Communards, Decembrists, the members of "Narodnaya Volya" took on real flesh and blood to become true heroes. For the first time one could hear the freedom-loving poems of Ryleyev, Pushkin, Lermontov, and Nekrasov, which the curriculum had "delicately" avoided before the Revolution. The children had access to the works of Russian poets of the end of the nineteenth century and the prerevolutionary period. The doors to the director's apartment were open in the evenings to all who wished to come. Widely diverse young people from the school and outside world would come there. Oblakov's sister played quite well on the piano and acquainted those gathered with contemporary music. He himself would tell about the "Russian Seasons" of Diaghilev. According to Kostrovitskaya, Oblakov introduced the pupils to the poetry of Mayakovsky, which captivated the boys in particular. The girls preferred Akhmatova and Esenin.

The healthy spiritual climate of the school could not have been better for

Balanchine. A number of people encouraged and guided him, watched his growth and inspired him with confidence in his abilities. Above all I will mention the school's inspector, G. G. Isaenko—an old man who had worked in the school for thirty years. In the words of the leading dancer, Pyotr Gusev, a contemporary of ours, Isaenko "produced the strongest impression by his extravagance, his force of will, and his sharp wit." He was even almost dismissed in 1919 at the demand of students who were offended by his sharpness, overbearing manner, and severity toward the young boys. Among these students, of course, were Balanchine and Gusev. But Isaenko did not harbor any ill will; he was close to his students, shared everything that he had, and let them make use of his wardrobe. "We were afraid of Isaenko," Gusev has recalled, "but he was an interesting man and in the last analysis we loved him. He told endless stories from his long experience as organizer of the touring performers of the Alexandrinsky Theater. He had an incredible knowledge of dramatic performances, of plays, and of theater life. He told short stories, more like anecdotes, but with brilliance and always with a moral. Every day, every hour Isaenko thought up some unusual remarks, conversations, stories, and tricks, unlike any others. In this respect, Balanchine loved to imitate him. Among students everything original and clever was valued and would flourish. Isaenko, in this regard, had a direct influence on Balanchine."

Oblakov did even more for him. "On first impression," Gusev recalled, "he seemed inactive, he didn't involve himself in our affairs, he didn't stop by or make remarks, he didn't analyze stage performances. But on occasion, unobtrusively, he would have individual discussions—though not with everyone. He gave particular attention to Balanchine, Lydia Ivanova, and Mlodzinskaya. He also showed some interest in Mungalova and me. The subject of these discussions, as a rule, remained a secret. Judging by the advice Oblakov gave, he thought about everyone's future in terms of their actual interests and artistic tendencies. He supported Soviet power with sincerity and with conviction. He knew how to ridicule philistine dissatisfaction and whimpering. Discussions with him made an impression. His advice and predictions were more than intelligent; they showed great insight at times. Balanchine often talked with Oblakov. He never told us about what exactly, but he spoke of him with respect and he didn't like the students to make fun of him. And Oblakov, speaking of Balanchine, told us that a great talent was developing."

We should not forget Shiryaev (1867–1941). A grandson of the composer Pugni and a student of Gerdt and Petipa, he was a character-dance soloist in the Maryinsky Theater from 1885. At the end of the 1890s he helped Petipa revive old ballets and rehearse new ones. . . . Gusev recalls: "Everyone worshiped Shiryaev. He was an idol of the students. He didn't like the compositions of Balanchine; that was no secret. He openly made fun of Balanchine's classical dances. He could hardly have influenced Balanchine except in his deep respect for Petipa." But this influence alone could not have been more important at a time when the name of Petipa was almost an insult for many so-called reformers of the arts. And there is nothing to conceal. We were all at first unable to see beyond certain flaws into the priceless value of the old.

Gusev's recollections of the school's popular informal concerts are interesting: "We dramatized the song, 'What are you dancing, Katenka? The polka, the polka, Mama.' There was a hussar, unsuccessful matchmaking, and lively dances. Balanchine played the piano, I was the director, but who portrayed Katenka, the hussar, and others—I don't remember. In the finale of the overture for *Carmen,* when the music sounds the theme of fate, a part of the orchestra fell down as if dead on the first chord, another part on the second chord. All of the direction, the composition of texts, and the musical arrangements for all dramatizations were done by Balanchine. There were many amateur evenings. Balanchine participated without fail either on stage or at the piano. None of the teachers interfered. Oblakov and Shiryaev in particular gave their support to these ventures. A new instructor, Pavel Akorchev, often played with Balanchine in pieces for four hands. A large audience would gather by itself. The interpretations of Akorchev were always professional. Balanchine went to concerts all the time, obtained music, and acquainted us above all with Rachmaninoff, Medtner, Scriabin, and Chopin.

Unexpectedly, another instructor appeared at the school—Iosif Vaks—either a student or a graduate of the university. He was intelligent and modern with a sense of humor. I personally first heard about Mayakovsky from him. He brought into our particular little world news of what people were doing beyond the limits of Rossi Street. Oblakov supported Vaks. His ironic attitude toward our activities offended us. But still, he was able to show us that, unconsciously, we were not in step with the times. There was one student whom Vaks singled out and always followed with interest—and that was Balanchine.

However great the burden of study and, especially, practice at the theater, the students were restless and eager to know everything and do everything. They wanted to try everything themselves and test their abilities. Some took up singing lessons, some drawing, and some worked at the art of drama. In the summer of 1919, Balanchine submitted an application to the director of the Conservatory, Glazunov, to audition for entry into a piano class. He was accepted into the class of Professor Sofia Frantsevna Zurmullen. A student of Leschetizky, she was invited to teach at the Conservatory by Rubinstein himself, at that time in his older years. She valued Balanchine's gift for the piano very highly. There follows an interesting appraisal of Balanchine by Zurmullen in 1922, given in the form of answers to an administrative questionnaire:

7. . . . a good ear, rhythm, good arm, good fingers.
8. Talented and very musical. He worked under the most difficult conditions. For the first year and a half he was a pupil of the State Ballet School, did not have his own instrument, and could only play in the large theater hall, which involved great inconveniences. Finishing the school, he continued to live there under the same conditions and only in March of this year did he acquire an instrument for himself. His ballet activity left him exhausted.
9. I hope that he will be able to finish the Conservatory successfully.
10. Until March of this year he played in the winter in the unheated theater hall, sometimes even with gloves.
11. He did not play at the [Conservatory] evenings.
12. [He performed] the Rondo in E flat major of Weber, the Sonata in E flat major of Beethoven, Prelude and Fugue in E major of Bach, "At the Fountain" of Arensky, the Waltz in A flat major of Chopin, the Etudes in C sharp minor and C minor of Chopin, Noveletta in E major of Schumann, and the "Chanson Triste" of Tchaikovsky.

Balanchine did not succeed in finishing the Conservatory. But nevertheless Zurmullen turned out to be correct: Balanchine became an accomplished musician—and not only a pianist. He attended classes of harmony, studied counterpoint and composition, wrote music, and most often improvised easily and quickly, as if drawing from innumerable prepared ideas. He wrote compositions for piano and dance, for recitation to music, and for voice. To this day the conductor Mravinsky remembers Balanchine's music composed for poetry he had written himself. The beginning ballet artist emerged in the role of composer and the student composer in the role of poet. Balanchine even played his works before L. V. Nikolaev, a stern professor who listened to the gifted young man with some indulgence. Working in the theater, Balanchine frequently tried his hand at the violin, the French horn, the drums, and the trumpet. And always he mastered the music despite the difficulties of quickly learning any new instrument. Judging from the recollections of ballet artists of the older generation, the compositions of Balanchine were somewhat lacking in originality. They were more like reminiscences in the manner of Chopin, or of Liszt, Tchaikovsky, Rachmaninoff, Scriabin, and Arensky. It is worth noting that he rarely composed dances to his own music, but most often used the works of composers of the nineteenth century and the beginning of this one.

In any case, Balanchine in those years made himself into a professional musician within the ballet theater; this to a large extent determined the character and direction of his creative work in the future.

Speaking directly to the students of the Theater School in Petrograd in October 1918, Lunacharsky, the Minister of Education, said: "You are young, and youth after all is revolutionary in its essence. Inclined by nature toward risk, it loves the excitement of novelty. A time such as the present, therefore, for you winged young people is the most appropriate and the most happy. . . . It is for you that we are building and to you that we are giving the best we have."

One of the idols of the young was the poet Mayakovsky. Balanchine nourished a particular admiration for him. He made himself a walking almanac on Mayakovsky, recited his verse, met with the poet himself, and was highly proud of his acquaintance with him.

The young people loved the lines from *Mystery-Bouffe,* full of challenge to the old theater:

> We are tired of heavenly sweets,
> We are tired of paper passions.

Lines from the same source became widely familiar to us:

> We want space!
> Today
> Over the dust of the theaters
> Our slogan will catch fire:
> All is new!
> Stop and marvel!

. . . It was at this time that fate led me to the ballet school where I would largely remake my own life. I will explain briefly how this happened.

Early in the fall of 1918 the doors on Theater Street were first opened to "outsiders"—as all were called except servants living at home, students, and relatives who came to see their children on holidays. Even now I remember the piercing glare the imposing doorkeeper directed toward me. But he was powerless to prevent an intrusion. At the insistence of Lunacharsky, the ballet school shared its premises with the newly organized School of Russian

Drama. The auditions for admission which began on a certain day brought me, along with other hopefuls, to Theater Street. And the first person I saw was a youngster in uniform—black trousers and a navy-blue jacket with a stand-up collar, on the tabs of which were large silver lyres with laurels. A thin and very pale boy with hair parted in the middle, with large eyes— rather sunken and sad, it seemed to me—and with a kind mouth (this impressed me most), he walked toward me quickly with a light gliding step like a dancer in a *lezghinka.** He explained very courteously how to get to the school theater, and later, meeting me after the audition, gave me the name of a man who invited me for a visit—the ubiquitous G. G. Isaenko. This first messenger of the ballet world was Georgii (everyone called him Georges) Balanchivadze. And so, in the early fall of that distant 1918, several events occurred in one hour which are inseparable for me. I penetrated into the "cradle of dance," crossing through the school's entrance; I made, without suspecting it myself, a first step toward ballet which had been foreign to me before; I met a certain pupil who began every day to show me the basics of classical dance; I acquired a guide in the labyrinth of ballet—and a friend.

The young dance student appealed to me. He soon visited our home and instantly won over my family—my father, who viewed my interest in ballet with some skepticism, my mother, younger brother, and two sisters. Balanchine possessed an astonishing ability to win people's favor, to inspire sympathy—just like the heroes of old ballets, in fact, with whom everyone fell in love at first sight. This was due to his sincerity, his modesty, and above all to his kindness. I single out this final trait; it was one of the primary determinants of his behavior. He responded eagerly to any need and offered help without ostentation. According to an Indonesian proverb, it is not the person who gives assistance who merits nobility but the person who allows himself to be given assistance. It seemed as if Balanchine was happy for the opportunity to render any service and be grateful for it. Those years instilled in people a deep sense of fraternity, mutual help, and an organic need to share all one had.

Balanchine apparently liked the atmosphere of my family and came to visit us often. My sisters both studied piano at the Conservatory—the older one in the class of the very same Zurmullen. My brother, the same age as Balanchine and a gifted musician by nature, spent hours improvising at the piano and became friends with George. They often played together, dreaming up dance compositions.

Gradually, Balanchine came to know all of my close acquaintances as easily as he had come into our home. My great friends, the artists Dimitriev

* A folk dance of the Lezghis, tribes in Daghestan on the Caspian Sea.

and Erbstein, valued at once his outstanding qualities—beginning with his striking appearance and attractive personality. Balanchine, like many of our companions, was "desperate"—as Mravinsky called those of our age with impassioned yearnings for cherished goals.

The intelligent and perceptive Isaenko replaced my first dance teacher, Sakselin, with Balanchine and explained the reason for the change to me some years later: "There exist different flowers. Some blossom in the early spring, live for a day or two and vanish. Others are summer flowers; you won't find them in the spring or fall. And then there are flowers which stay in bloom from spring to late fall. Balanchine belongs to this group. And you, too, will stay ripe for a long time. Therefore, you need him and he needs you."

And I really did need him. I will depart from the main line of the story and tell what Balanchine did for me. It was he who first brought me to that enchanted world which lay behind one of the entrances to the former Mary-insky Theater. The children by tradition called it the "Interdict"—a distortion of the foreign words on the sign which hung over the backstage doors of the performers' entrance: *"L'entrée sur scène est interdite."* Woe to him who dared ignore this injunction and penetrate into this "holy of holies" of the theater! The gates of this realm had their own Cerberus in the person of the doorkeeper, who knew the performers and would allow the school's students inside only on the word of an accompanying instructor. The small vestibule before the entrance was always crowded with the ecstatic admirers of the performers. Their great happiness would be to see in the flesh their "object of worship"—and, if successful, to present flowers or a letter with a declaration of love—and to hear one or two words from the "divine" lips.

No one would dream of going backstage and, speaking truthfully, I had not shown any interest in doing so. My dance lessons had, at first, seemed only a prerequisite for entering the School of Russian Drama. (That is how Isaenko explained it.) When Balanchine and I became friends, this necessity developed into daily contact with him, but it still did not by itself turn me into a lover of ballet. The turning point in my consciousness occurred when Balanchine took me into the "Interdict." He did this very simply. He made an agreement with the students, who all knew me by then. They surrounded me in a dense mass so that to distinguish a stranger among them would be almost impossible. And intentionally clustering together before the entrance, they crossed the Rubicon. The backstage smell, the scurrying of people busy with their work, the adjustment on stage of decor with illegible words painted on the back, the performers behind the curtain repeating various steps or simply warming up—this private side of the theater, bereft of the illusions which can so entrance an audience, made a tremendous impression on me. Uncontrollably, and inexplicably to me at that time, I trembled with happy excitement before an unfolding new world, a miracle. Balzac has written that only one feeling in the years of youth can rival the feeling of love—the strongest in a person's life—and that is love for art. And Belinsky declared it a love "with all the forces of the soul, with all enthusiasm, with all frenzy of which only ardent youth thirsting for elegance is capable." It came to life in me then, on that day and at that hour when I saw before me the ordinary and far from attractive everyday life of the theater and, moreover, at an ominous time for the theater.

While I was straining my eyes at the stage from the wings, a ballerina walked up. Dressed in a sweater and woolen socks over her tights, she wore, too, a large shawl. She said timidly, "May I lean on your arm?" And receiving the answer yes from an unsteady, enraptured voice, she did lean on it, as on the barre, and began to do all kinds of *battements* and *développés*—the very same ones which I had been repeating mechanically every day with a teacher, never imagining that they could mean more than a routine boring exercise. It was as if I had been transformed; a new way of seeing and hearing came to me. A miracle had happened.

In the film script for *Cinderella* by the remarkable Soviet dramatist and storyteller, Shvarts, Cinderella asks a page whether or not he is a magician. He answers, "I'm not a magician, I'm still only studying . . . but love helps us to make miracles."

Balanchine then was still only a sorcerer's apprentice. But still, he could well have repeated the words of Shvarts's page. His sympathy toward me, a part of his natural kindness toward people, allowed him to make a genuine miracle. I found in one instant the enchanted world which would possess me for the rest of my long life.

One can study the arts of drama and opera in a library and at home by reading the texts of plays and musical scores. To master the art of choreography in that way is not possible. One can read a ballet text only by watching performances in a theater, by participating in them, and by going over parts with those who retain these "texts" in their memory. There are no printed means for fixing a choreographic text. Dance notations and films for everyday work in the school or theater are of little benefit. This is why the fate of a ballet artist depends entirely on the repertory which he masters in the process of specific "reading."

In the season of 1918–19 the repertory in Petrograd included *The Sleeping Beauty, Swan Lake, Raymonda, Giselle, Le Corsaire, The Little Humpbacked Horse, Paquita, The Daughter of Pharaoh,* and *Esmeralda.* There were the one-act ballets of Petipa—*Cavalry Halt, Caprices of a Butterfly, The Trial of Damis;* also *The Magic Flute* of Lev Ivanov, *The Fairy Doll* of the Legat brothers, *Eros* (to the Serenade for Strings by Tchaikovsky), and *Jota Aragonesa* of Fokine. Petipa's *Talisman* and *Bluebeard* appeared sporadically in the repertory. In all, there were eighteen ballets.

The following season, 1919–20, was in many respects critical. But nevertheless the theater retained in the repertory the same number of titles. It only replaced some ballets with new ones. *La Bayadère* appeared, and *Vain Precautions (La Fille Mal Gardée), Harlequinade, Don Quixote, The Nutcracker, Le Pavillon d'Armide, Chopiniana,* and *Carnaval.*

The wealth of the repertory and its regeneration gave the school's pupils a great deal. It meant, in essence, that they received and assimilated new and important impressions constantly. It is sufficient to point out that *La Bayadère, Don Quixote, Harlequinade, Chopiniana,* and *Carnaval,* after all has been said, are priceless jewels in the ballet heritage. All of the pupils, including Balanchine, took part in these ballets. Balanchine, moreover, danced in a number of opera productions—in the brilliant *Polovetsian Dances (Prince Igor),* the grotto of Venus (*Tannhäuser*), and the scenes in hell (*Orpheus and Eurydice*). The *Polovetsian Dances,* as well as *Chopiniana* and *Jota Aragonesa* (in which he may have participated and which he definitely saw), could not but have an enormous importance in the biography of a ballet master. With these productions, immediately recognized as classics in the new Russian repertory, Fokine became a twentieth-century master. In them he achieved an astonishingly complex simplicity and an ideal interdependence of music and dance. In full harmony with Glinka's score, Fokine's *Jota* makes a clarion call, a hymn of light, as it were, a triumph of national spirit. The best works of Balanchine seem to grow out of his experience of Fokine.

Gusev says that "Balanchine called *Chopiniana* his favorite ballet and often by himself performed various dances from it." The perfection of its Romantic dance forms and the unprecedented intricacy of its symphonic composition unquestionably deserved the boy's close attention.

Before the Revolution, the practical experience of the students was limited to the performance of children's dances in productions of the Maryinsky Theater, to rare performances in the small school theater, seating little more than one hundred, and to participation in the graduation production. Periodically, there were other appearances of particular students in dramatic productions. But now appearances acquired diversity and depth and demanded hard work. There was talk about how the school theater had come alive and active, producing ballets or fragments from them and concerts of mixed genres, at times composed and organized by the students themselves. We might describe it today as undergraduate training.

From the first years of the Revolution the ballet school established a new form of contact with the public, perhaps the most important form of contact for a Soviet performer's education. Concerts were held in workers' clubs, in army units, in literary and scientific institutions. In 1919 the school obtained use of the palace in the former Tsarskoye Selo for the summer vacation of the pupils. Not inappropriately, this town took on the name Detskoye Selo (Children's Village). Pioneer camps and kindergartens gathered there. Scientists and writers went on vacation in the health centers. The school presented several concerts in the town hall for the regular inhabitants and their summer guests. The performing pupils could now examine the repertory. They could feel out, interpret, and assimilate its wealth of styles, distinguishing what they found most attractive and rejecting what was not to their taste. They had the opportunity to generalize their impressions and form guidelines for the future.

It is no more possible here to review every ballet and its influence on Balanchine and his comrades than to give one's impressions in one brief essay about the treasures of the Louvre, the Hermitage, and the British Museum. But certain moments must be mentioned.

In the theater Balanchine found a veritable "library" of ballet unlike any other in the world. It contained works created by European ballet masters for the past hundred and fifty years. These men, the great choreographers, had sought artistic truth, each perceiving it in his own way. They had used the widest variety of themes, images, genres, and styles, and had approached from different angles the most important problems of choreographic creation. They differed from each other in their conception of the nature and purpose of ballet and their own mission in it.

In addition to his striking ability to assimilate what he "read," Balanchine had an even more precious capacity to retain any impressions in the depths of his memory and reproduce them according to need in an original form. Of course, at the time of which we are speaking, Balanchine was still only a young student trying to make the best of his situation. But already he was preparing to make the first attempts at giving an account of what he had learned. The ability to absorb what he saw and to preserve it in the recesses of his memory was of great benefit for his choreographic self-education. The established repertory of the theaters did not exhaust his interest. He derived no less from the contradictory, occasionally absurd and fantastic avant-garde which had arisen then in the tempestuous sea of experimentation around the former imperial theaters. A mastery of the old in combination with the often bitter early experience of Soviet ballet saved Balanchine from a need to reinvent the wheel. The talented ballet masters of the West have sometimes arrived at the truth and then reached the heights of their creative powers in the middle or later years of life. For Balanchine the seeds of his long future career were already sown at the beginning of the 1920s, at the dawn of youth.

Ballet belongs to those arts which acquire the right to that name only in the finest productions performed by the finest artists. One can read a mediocre novel, watch a mediocre play, and even listen to mediocre music. Not with ballet! Looking at outwardly attractive, technically trained dancers, with the privileges and corresponding rewards of leading performers, one can still remain completely unmoved or even lose one's interest in a performance altogether. The most critical and valuable element is missing. Conversely, for the sake of a brilliant artistic personality on the stage an audience is prepared to be very tolerant, readily sacrificing stunts and acrobatics. The sole presence of this precious quality turns an ordinary master into an artist. It evokes and intensifies in the audience a feeling of spiritual identity; the person on the stage embodies an ideal and inspires a belief among those watching that they can also attain this ideal. Furthermore, only the finest performances of true masters of the dance, capable of expressing the life of the human spirit in plastic images, will reveal the beauty and poetic truth of the ballet theater.

In this respect Balanchine was fortunate. On the stage of the Maryinsky Theater there were artists—men and women—who possessed the secret for penetrating to the essence of particular dance forms. As a boy he most admired Karsavina and Vladimiroff. It is not difficult to guess why. They used a palette of the most brilliant dance colors, appeared on the stage in a wide variety of styles, and believed in dance as a manifestation of human passions. But in recalling those years, Balanchine fails to mention adequately the name of the ballerina who was the favorite of the young people, including the author of these lines. This was the great Russian actress Spessivtseva. It is as if she did not exist for him, although she had no equal in talent, depth, and spiritual force and although she was the idol of the Dimitriev group with which Balanchine was associated. How can we explain this? Is it perhaps in the distance between their manners of self-expression and in the divergence of their interests and approaches to ballet?

In his first steps as a performer and ballet master, Balanchine showed a rather clear desire to make dance a celebration of happiness, gaiety, and joy without introspection or dramatic contradictions. This was the natural reaction of all our young people to the long period of domination in the theater by the prerevolutionary frame of mind—and even of Fokine and Gorsky, not to mention the lower gods of the ballet Olympus. With rare exceptions, Balanchine preferred ballets that were harmoniously clear, well balanced, and peaceful, expressing all possible shades of optimism. *The Sleeping Beauty,* therefore (rather than *Swan Lake*), was for him the ideal of beauty of the old ballet, although as a ballet master he did present *Swan Lake,* too, and valued *Giselle* very highly as an exception—the second act more than the first. Like Fokine, he considered dramatic dances easier than joyful ones.

His sympathies for performers were determined in the same manner. Above all others stood Elizabetha Pavlovna Gerdt. She was in truth an inimitable example of dance art, inheriting her talent from her father. All of her steps blended by themselves with the dance music. The lines of her body in movement drew a clear, harmonious, resonant form with absolute purity and completeness. Gerdt remained unsurpassed in *The Nutcracker* and especially in *Raymonda.* (We considered the variation of the last act to be perfection.) Thanks to her, the gigantic edifice of *The Sleeping Beauty* was accepted as an unequaled masterpiece of plastic form.

In my mature years, on rereading my essay on Gerdt, which was one of my first appearances in print, I recognized that it was unsuccessful. How could I have made such a mistake? The correct answer came from Lisovskaya, a ballerina of the 1920s and 1930s. "One should not look for a storm of passions in Gerdt and consider its absence a deficiency. From this there arises the false impression that she is cold and empty. This is a delusion. One must simply apply different standards. She is warm and alive like a Greek statue. Can one judge sculpture according to the laws of drama?" This is true. The plasticity of Gerdt's dancing was related in harmony and tranquillity to the statues of antiquity. One can achieve such form only on the highest levels of dance art. That it is not the goal of everyone in ballet is another matter. Balanchine, I think, understood the essence of Gerdt's art and valued her for precisely what I could not see at that time.

Spessivtseva was in this sense the antithesis of Gerdt. The beauty of her dance was always illuminated from within by a restless and excited brilliance. Spessivtseva did not joke with dance or amuse herself or flirt. She did not show the fluctuations of love and disappointment as Lukom did so well. Only rarely did her dancing evoke smiles, even where this would have been appropriate, as in the first acts of *Esmeralda* and *Le Corsaire* or *Giselle,* for example. She rose to the summits of great art as a fragile, lovely flower being destroyed by mounting misfortune. Her longing for happiness was doomed from the very beginning. The voice of unrelenting fate, the cry of a wounded bird, pierced the hearts of those in the audience with a presentiment of tragedy.

However, as often occurs in art, indifference or even opposition to a particular artist in no way precludes the possibility of influence. On the contrary, in arguing with an author, we often absorb against our will certain of his ideas, images, and themes which we reexpress in our own way. And so it was with Balanchine. Tchaikovsky's apprehension and anguish, the melancholy that dominates certain of his works, found their best interpreter of my time in Spessivtseva, yet once again found similar expression in such productions of Balanchine's as Tchaikovsky's *Serenade* or the Elegy of the *Suite No. 3.* At the time of our early youth, of which I am writing, the unconscious influence of Spessivtseva was even greater than in the following decades when the Apollonian concept of dance, supported by the neoclassical music of Stravinsky, became dominant.

There are books which capture one's interest from the first page. And there are works of literature or music which do not produce such an impression. One reads or listens through them with indifference, sometimes with a certain boredom or disagreement. But when the years or decades pass and one again comes across that book or piece of music, it can suddenly become a great discovery and can captivate one for a long time or even forever. I remembered this not only and not so much in connection with Spessivtseva as in connection with Petipa; his name alone in those years embraced for us the entire ballet horizon of the nineteenth century. More than anything else, we wanted to overcome the power of the past, which we identified to a certain extent with blinders preventing us from seeing the future. With the passing of time, Petipa—a synonym for "old relics belonging in archives"—became our contemporary and friend in contemplating new paths for the ballet theater. This metamorphosis is indeed astonishing, but also historically logical.

The year 1921 heralded victory over the enemies of the Soviet Republic. Theaters on the verge of closing regained their spirit and became active; an inflow of fresh forces made it possible to begin staging new ballets.

This year was unforgettable for Balanchine as well. His graduation examination for dance took place on April 4. Vaganova, Romanova, Vecheslova (Smetkova), E. Gerdt, Leontiev, Ponomarev, Chekrygin, Shiryaev, and other teachers signed the document of approval. The committee decided "to present all of the pupils in separate pieces in an exhibition performance for the press and public." Chekrygin arranged a ballet by P. Gerdt, *Gavotte,* to the music of Saint-Saëns. Balanchine and Lydia Ivanova were assigned the major roles. Before the premiere Ivanova became ill. The performance would have been postponed had not another graduate, Vdovina, taken her place. Not only the director but Balanchine as well helped to prepare her; this reflected the practices of rehearsals and staging which Shiryaev had cultivated in the school. The press reacted to the new performers positively but without great enthusiasm: it saw an unoriginal performance similar in nature to *La Fille Mal Gardée* but of lesser quality in all respects; improvised participation of the principal female performer and especially of the female character dancer; insufficiency of classical style in the female group and its almost total absence among the men. But with good reason the newspapers wrote about Balanchine as an "especially reliable partner" and noted that he stood out in the divertissement with a "technically difficult *lezghinka.*"

Those who wish to study the biography of Balanchine as a performer will have some difficulties. The reviews in Russia are limited to the mention of his name among other performers. In the programs we find his name rather infrequently and in very modest places—in the Peasant Waltz in *Swan Lake,* the beggars' dances in *Esmeralda,* the Minuet in *The Sleeping Beauty,* the dance suite in the *Grotto of Venus* from *Tannhäuser* and so on. The programs then often listed a few well-known names in the group dances and concealed the rest with the words "and others" or "artists of the corps de ballet." The lists of participants posted by the direction and management have generally not survived. In brief, the documents do not allow an enumeration of Balanchine's roles or a precise characterization of his position in the company. One thing is certain: in 1923 he was an artist of the thirteenth rank and received 2745 rubles—a small sum, although nominally significant.

Does this mean, then, that Balanchine was only an average member of the corps de ballet incapable of anything greater? Not at all. His brilliant talent as a dancer was noticed while he was still in the school. It was for Ivanova and Balanchine that Shiryaev mounted the unpretentious old ballet, *The Magic Flute,* with music by Drigo. Balanchine performed in divertissements many times in the school theater.

His friend from those years, Tatyana Bruni (later a famous theater artist), remembers: "I first saw George at a school concert in the charming Chinese theater of Tsarskoye Selo. It was in a pas de trois from *The Fairy Doll*—Lydia Ivanova, Efimov, and Balanchine. Lydia completely eclipsed her partners, it seemed to me. The boys simply were very funny; one was happy, the other (George) was sad. They emphasized their roles very strongly. Perhaps Balanchine demonstrated there his instincts as a ballet master. I know that they had danced this piece before with Barysheva, when, I believe, they were still just children." Balanchine also performed the role of the hero in *The Magic Flute,* which required both classical dancing and acting. In the pas de trois, composed by the Legat brothers for themselves, the two male dancers competed with each other in a variety of very complicated classical dance steps or opposed each other in a somewhat grotesque style. This required considerable dance artistry and a dramatic presence. "The polka-folichon resembled a cancan; Balanchine performed it energetically with the pupil, Mungalova. He wore a dress coat *incroyable,* she wore a tutu embroided with pink ribbons. They both kicked up their legs as high as possible in an obvious parody of operetta performers." Balanchine was a reliable partner for any female dancer and sometimes substituted for leading performers in large ballets. He danced with Gerdt, for example, in *Swan Lake* and *Chopiniana.* But he was not a real classical dancer. Who knows? Perhaps a lack of natural gifts as a classical dancer helped him as a ballet master to become an expert on classical dance. Vaganova, after all, was most effective as a teacher in developing precisely those movements for which she had the least natural aptitude as a performer.

After the Revolution the system of ranking all public employees, including the artists of the imperial theaters, was abolished everywhere. Dancers were required to perform without regard to their rank and salary. And Balanchine observed this rule. He did all that he was assigned without protest, and with exuberance and individuality. His creative interest centered on fiery, complex, emotional dances. The traditional treatment of lyric themes (the timid male dancer pining away for his embarrassed and frightened female partner) did not suit his temperament. He sought dances with bright or even loud colors and vigorous, stormy emotion and energy. Such roles were few in number and older dancers did not readily relinquish them. In any case Balanchine did attract attention, as in an article summarizing dance for 1921: "Among the gratifying developments of the year it is necessary to include as well . . . the highly successful graduating class of the school, which has immediately become active. A part of this class, to do an unprecedented thing, has begun to appear in solos." There was praise for him in an enumeration of the new dancers' successes.

On April 4, 1922, in *The Nutcracker* at an anniversary performance in honor of the dancer Vill, Balanchine achieved perhaps his greatest triumph before an audience up to that time. I. B. Rodersen wrote in *Zhizn Iskusstvo:* "Second only to the ballet's heroine, one must single out G. M. Balanchivadze, who performed in the *Danse des Bouffons.* With his technical virtuosity and beautiful performance the young artist raised a storm of applause from the audience." But even earlier, on February 5, the critic Edmund Stark gave special mention again to Balanchivadze for the divertissement from *The Nutcracker:* "the dance of the jesters produced a furor . . . Balanchivadze performed this difficult acrobatic piece with striking agility, lightness, flawlessness, and grace." The praise for his performance in this dance gradually grew into a large chorus. N. I. Nosilov proclaimed him "a superb jester, striking for the boldness of his movements with a hoop." In a word, the dance caused a sensation. It conquered the audience from the front rows to the upper balcony. After Balanchine I saw many splendid dancers skillfully manipulating a hoop while leaping in the air, and many masters of artistic gymnastics who could execute such maneuvers with brilliance, but no one has ever erased him from my memory.

Everyone who saw him said the same thing. The highly respected ballet critic and theorist Volynsky, noting the "great success of the young and exceptionally musical dancer," wrote: "Balanchivadze dances a jester with a hoop—essentially a trepak with the lively rhythm of a folk dance. He stands obliquely in the hoop with his profile toward the public wearing a sparkling silver costume. His face is deathly pale from excitement. A tall youth [slightly exaggerated—Y. S.], he is full of wild tension. He waves the hoop and throws it under his legs. Then he sweeps it around himself and moves underneath like a hurricane. [Boris] Romanov won fame in his day in this piece. But Balanchivadze today has outdone Romanov with his young, energetic, and superbly disciplined talent. Certain details of the trepak come as a total surprise. But they are carefully thought out in harmony with the dance's general character. They lead one to assume the inspiration of an experienced teacher. Is it Shiryaev? I could imagine no one else."

Balanchine was in fact very excited. This was his first responsible solo in the theater. He had had it in mind for himself even in his years as a student when, along with other boys, he imitated the excellent performers of this piece. The chance to "compete" with reputed masters made it all the more important to him. Shiryaev actually did help the young dancer: he had performed as a soloist in the Dance of the Jesters and, with his exceptional memory, he demonstrated for Balanchine many nuances and details with which the piece had been enriched. Balanchine, though, did not simply select what he liked from the experience of the past. Being by nature a creative artist, he introduced his own ideas into the technique and content of assigned pieces. I will not try to say now what he derived from his predecessors through Shiryaev and what he invented himself. He won the favor of the audiences with both.

Tatyana Bruni recalls: "Swiftly and sharply he leaped into the air through the hoop, rolled himself into a ball and made still another zigzag with his knees squeezed up to his chin. He created the illusion of an unbelievable, impossible jump. This was a revelation, like the best dances of Vasiliev and Baryshnikov today. He was helped by a long, dark red wig which suited him very well. And he wore black and yellow tights with stripes and sparkles almost like those worn today." Bruni asks, "Was this an accident? Or was this dance especially well suited to his talent?" I will allow myself to offer a suggestion. Lev Ivanov's choreography for this dance and the individuality of Balanchine's talent presented him with the opportunity, for almost the only time in his career as a performer, to express his innermost feelings and the voice of the time. His dancing reflected the triumph of a man who had made the air his element. This produced a tremendous response from audiences. Balanchine's performance in some way corresponded to their own sentiments about the world. For good reason the committee for the celebration of the sixth anniversary of the October Revolution included his dance in a concert at the Maryinsky Theater. Those in the audience gave their full approval to this dancer who was driven by the same impulses they felt themselves. The dance also expressed personal qualities which have already been mentioned: desperation, passion, audacity, conviction in the overcoming of all obstacles. Balanchine's best role became his trademark.

It was a fine and auspicious beginning. Balanchine might have continued in other roles that seemed almost specially created for him: Polovchanin, the jester of *Pavillon d'Armide,* the hero of *Egyptian Nights,* and others. But he did not continue, although he did well among the leading performers of the *Polovetsian Dances* and in the role of jester in *Armide.* This created the impression that Balanchine had spent himself in one part, that he was a performer of one role! The real story was more complicated. He could not cope with certain roles and solo parts, to others he remained indifferent, and for others still he had no offers. Besides, he had a way of shining so brightly, like "a bald spot," that people would involuntarily follow him with their eyes until he left the stage. Here is how Kostrovitskaya describes him in the first scene of *Esmeralda:* "And suddenly a cripple appeared on the stage, moving about almost on all fours with one eye, protruding ears, and an enormous, swollen, potatolike nose. He moved and used pantomime in such a way that the audience burst out laughing and everyone onstage laughed hilariously to the point of tears." Two years before, a similar incident had occurred in the opera *Enemy Force.* Among the crowd onstage a tall, sullen fellow appeared, twisting his arms and legs like a circus contortionist. The audience's attention was involuntarily distracted from the great Chaliapin. The mime in the opera, Cherkasov, and the dancer in the ballet, Balanchine, showed a longing to create their own unique images.

Mostly, however, Balanchine's limited development as a performer must be attributed to unbelievable overwork. He was torn between daily work in the theater (rehearsals in the morning, performances in the evening), studies at the Conservatory, earning money for subsistence by playing the piano in Vecheslova's class (from 1921 he played three hours a day) and for dances at concerts and the movies. He had no time to spend on training! And without training the development of even the greatest talents is impossible. It is necessary, moreover, to spend hours working before a practice-room mirror to begin transforming technique into art. Where would these hours come from? Indefatigably, he went to premieres of the Petrograd theaters and to visiting performances of the Moscow theaters, to philharmonic concerts and stage productions, to art exhibitions and museums. He could not deny himself contacts with new developments in the arts, of which there were so many at that time. He participated in the innumerable controversies concerning literature, music, and dance. Very sociable, readily making friends and engaging in intense discussions on the most diverse subjects, he was easily accepted into every circle. He undeniably did spread himself thin from the viewpoint of colleagues in the theater who had only one goal—to dance more and better, to climb up the ladder to leading roles. He did appear disorderly, unpunctual, because of his incessant desire to succeed in everything, to fulfill all of his responsibilities, and to satisfy all of his desires. Such a lifestyle could not fail to have an effect on the young Balanchine, already somewhat weakened by years of undernourishment. It exhausted him physically and interfered with his purely technical development. It prevented him from concentrating all of his soul and talent on something specific, important, and decisive. But then, it also stimulated his spiritual growth and his general creative development. He was at an age, furthermore, when other interests and matters attract young people.

Balanchine was not alone in living this way. The entire generation—some more than others—possessed an insatiable appetite for knowledge of the surrounding world. Balanchine and Lydia Ivanova, more than others in the ballet, were capable of neglecting their artistic interests for something which they considered immeasurably more important and urgent.

The Revolution brought a sharp, unavoidable need for change in the theater. We felt this more with our hearts than with our minds. Somehow the joys and misfortunes of many ballet heroes of the classical heritage had faded. The color of many previously popular ballets had dimmed; their clichés and styles seemed inappropriate and obtrusive. All that had been taken for granted now required a thorough reevaluation. One thing was clear—the old could no longer provide the entire content of creative life in the face of the gigantic historical changes that were taking place.

As always, in an epoch before or during the rebuilding of a country's social-political life, there arose the "eternal questions" of art—of ballet in particular. What does the ballet represent? The Minister of Education, Lunacharsky, gave an answer in a general way in his essays, public speeches, and conversations in the theaters and in the school. The revolutionary masses, he said, had little cultural entertainment; they deserved spiritual nourishment to help in understanding the world and in determining their own place in it. One of the primary "tasks" of the theater, therefore, is "to preserve for the people and for future generations the best of what was created in the past and to present it in the best classical forms as perfectly as possible." And, Lunacharsky added, it is necessary at the same time "to instill in our cultural climate a desire for new art, a great love for every aspect of this new art." Of course, Lunacharsky said more than once that "a new culture will ask the opera and ballet that they not relate to real life by imitating the dramatic theater." The practical meaning of this with respect to the ballet has been understood by different people in diametrically opposed ways.

It is not surprising that heated debates developed. Is everything in the old repertory good? Are the old fairy-tale plots acceptable? What are the criteria for making decisions, for determining new directions? Subjects which go beyond standard love themes into the great issues of society and humanity? Forms of expressive movement which differ radically from the traditional forms of classical dance? Music which reflects the nature of the new century either in content or in novel forms of expression?

In the school and in the theater, backstage and in the audience, in and between classes, at concerts, youth gatherings, and art exhibitions—everywhere there were impassioned discussions on these themes, leading at times to sharp disagreements. Balanchine was swept along in the search for truth and began to speak out. He improvised his speeches, not overly concerned with whether he reproduced exactly what he had said before. As his creative thought became mature in these arguments, he grew determined to prove his correctness in practice and to define his attitude toward the ideas of others.

There was no shortage of people then who claimed to have made "discoveries." The radicals denounced from the start all that was old in ballet. Ballet, some said, had grown illogically from a supporting branch of the theater into an independent one. Not using words, it attempts in vain to express the content of an action. The only way to preserve its right to exist is to incorporate a written text for dramatic actors or opera singers. These proposals, however, despite their theoretical elaboration, held little interest for Balanchine, although he did apparently arrange some dances to vocal music and poetry. This is not ballet but a synthesis of drama, opera, and choreography. As an exception, something of this nature might be used in a particular production. But it cannot possibly constitute the basis of a new ballet theater, for it lowers the dance to the secondary function of a divertissement.

The adherents of such proposals completely repudiated the experience of the ballet of tsarist Russia. They thought it appropriate only for the archives. They wanted the former imperial theaters scrapped as incapable of creating anything new. A revolutionary people needs a revolutionary art. And revolution, they said, means the total annihilation of the old machine of government, national economy, and culture and the building of a new machine. It is easy today to ridicule people who could identify the process of social, governmental, economic transformations with the process of cultural and artistic regeneration. Our poor heads back then were spinning with such slogans. They were spinning not only from exhilaration but also from frustration. What could replace the indisputable wealth of the past which, incidentally, was having an obvious success with new audiences, with the representatives of the future?

The talented producer-director of the so-called "machine dances," Nikolai Foregger, supported such views to some extent. Emphasizing the widespread urbanization of social life in the twentieth century, he called for the composition of dances which would create a dynamic image of complex mechanisms and would glorify the technological revolution. Foregger had a novel idea: people imitating particular mechanical components, coming together to form a machine. This at first brought applause. It was certainly new, different, and interesting. But the questions which disturbed us remained unanswered as before.

Isadora Duncan and her disciples proposed to replace ballet with free movements to classical music. They saw the purpose of twentieth-century dance in the individual freedom of semi-improvised emotional and physical expression to music. The barefoot admirers of Dalcroze tried to popularize this kind of movement, never suspecting that they were changing dance and music equally. Duncan, thanks to her great talent, did not simply reject the conventions of classical dance. She had a stubborn determination to affirm the pathos and heroism, the sorrow and joy, which broad masses of people felt and which ballet lacked. However, she had an extremely limited range of movements and at times discredited her very best intentions. Balanchine, like all of us, went to Duncan's concerts, applauded her performance of the Sixth Symphony of Tchaikovsky and of the "Internationale," agreed that the liberation of the body was to the music's advantage, and recognized her talent as an artist. But he remained indifferent to her practical proposals as well as to the proposals of other advocates of rhythmic movement. Many of Duncan's adherents were, of course, organized in studios at that time. We shared the feelings of the well-known literary critic Shklovsky: "Classical art is infinitely more advanced than Duncanism. . . . We welcome . . . the arrival of this missionary, Isadora Duncan, but we welcome her from a high vantage point!" Time has proved him correct.

The press, the folklorists, and many people active in the theater—some very prominent—fought to replace classical ballet with folk dances, with ethnographic presentations of Russian and foreign celebrations and ceremonies. The "Russian Wedding" presentation, for example, fascinated and delighted many people with its diversity of folk dances and songs. We at-

tended productions of the Ethnographic Theater and respected its creator—
the theater critic, Professor V. N. Vsevolodsky. We were amazed at the
novelty of its methods. Even now one of the little folk tunes illustrated by a
dance comes to mind: "Make way, everyone, it is our turn now. My partner
and I, there are two, two, two, two, two, two of us!" "This dramatized
dance," says Gusev, "was intricately constructed and polyphonic." Experiments of this kind clearly influenced the use of Russian dance folklore in
ballet (especially for the choreographer Lopukhov), but we did not consider
them a substitute for the earlier ballet theater.

Wishing to make ballet performances more meaningful for audiences of
workers and peasants, the management of the academic theaters tried to
make new ballets on subjects from everyday life that made use of pantomime and character dance. This was a tempting idea. Hadn't Fokine secured
considerable success with *Jota Aragonesa* and *Petrouchka?* With the full approval
of my ballet friends, I referred then to *Petrouchka* in the press as a brilliant
pantomime and contrasted it to the traditional *Giselle.*

The system of acting in Italian improvisational comedy, worked out in a
modern form in performances by Radlov, Miklashevsky, and Soloviev, attracted great interest. Gymnastics, acrobatic partnering, circus clowning
prompted many fresh, clever, and striking ideas for ballet masters and performers. In particular, they could enrich the technique of male support in
duets, complicate the movement of the female dancer, make the dance more
varied, intense, and dynamic, and arouse the interest of the mass audience
attracted by gymnastics, sport, and physical culture.

In this direction, the choreographer Kasyan Goleizovsky succeeded more
than anyone else during the first years after the October Revolution. His
compositions demonstrated a traditional range of body movements enriched
by acrobatics and artistic gymnastics. Uniting these new movements to the
traditional ones that had been freed from the canons and conventions of
ballet, he was so talented that we at first thought he had answered the
question, "How should we proceed?" The resources of the human body, the
wider range of colors and movements, could not leave an audience unmoved. All the more so since Goleizovsky used music of the twentieth century—Rachmaninoff, Scriabin, and others—interpreted by the talented
dancer Zinaida Tarkhovskaya. "Goleizovsky seemed miraculous to us," recalled Gusev. "Balanchine raved about him. We never missed one concert of
his Chamber Ballet and spoke about it endlessly." The themes of some of
Balanchine's first works show the imprint of these concerts. But time
quickly scattered our illusions. The words of the French encyclopedist
Diderot come to mind: "Man displays himself on an endless stage. But why
does he do this?" Is it really just to demonstrate agility and grace alone?

Those who opposed the destruction and radical transformation of the old ballet did not form a monolithic camp. Some demanded the preservation of "everything as it is" and the "patterning" of new productions on the earlier ones. Others believed that the new should differ from the old, but precisely how they could not say. The attempts of Chekrygin, Leontiev, Petrov, and other by no means untalented ballet masters to work along traditional lines did not meet with success. A number of the older ballets without great content and of inferior musical quality were dropped from the repertory *(The Daughter of Pharaoh, Le Roi Candaule).*

Attempts to "perfect" and "correct" old ballets by giving them new "modern" scenarios or by reorchestrating their antiquated music also met with failure. Pouring old wine into new bottles is useless. And practice has shown that it is unnatural. Something completely different was necessary.

The young Balanchine was fortunate. For four or five years he saw with his own eyes many well-trodden paths and crossroads of ballet experimentation. Some of what was tried then in Petrograd and Moscow would seem much later in the West almost like the discovery of the twentieth century; decades of bitter practical experience would be necessary before coming to the conclusions that we reached at the end of the 1920s.

Balanchine—the youngest person in our group—was torn by incompatible desires. He might try to make a career as a ballet master. He was studying in the Conservatory with great intensity—not only the piano, but also the fundamentals of musical composition. Both the Conservatory and the theater demanded full-time work. A desire possessed him, however, to create dances. Of course, he could not be expected at the age of seventeen to be able to decide between the professions of musician, performer, and ballet master. Usually such a problem arises much later—not before the age of twenty-three to twenty-five on the average, if one considers those famous dancers who have decided to become ballet masters. Balanchine represented an exception to the rule. Dissatisfaction with the affairs of the theater had been softened by time. His friends and fellow dancers were pestering him, "George! Tell me what to dance! Help adapt this old piece! Arrange a dance for me to this music!" Balanchine, who always found it extremely difficult to say no, would try to satisfy these requests on the spot. In 1923 he ended his studies at the Conservatory. Euterpe, the muse of music, did not suffer, however. Both she and Terpsichore, the muse of dance, had much to gain, for both would collaborate in his creative work. Most outstanding ballet masters of the past approached musicians as friends, colleagues, and musical amateurs. This was not necessary for Balanchine, who could approach them as a fellow musician. At the same time, the composition and performance of

51

music was not an end for him but a means—a means of achieving physical expression for intangible, deeply felt emotions. Balanchine was filled with many embryonic ideas for dance. To bring them to life he sat behind a piano, attended concerts, and read music.

I am not mistaken in using the word "read"; I am using it in its literal sense. Balanchine differs from the great majority of ballet masters who must depend on live performances or on recordings in that he *reads* music. That is, looking at a score, he can hear the music with his mind. Of course, he was then just setting out in what would eventually become his constant occupation. Playing or improvising music, he was searching for sounds in the same way that a poet seeks the music of verse. From the plasticity of music Balanchine derived a plasticity of body movement. This is the essence of the contribution, begun by Fokine, to the choreography of the twentieth century. The outstanding musical theorist Boris Asafiev (he was highly respected by us and had a sympathetic attitude to Balanchine's first experiments) has said: "Music is energy. More than that, it is energetic; there are wonderful possibilities for making visible that which is heard. The history of great choreography is the successful embodiment onstage of musical form." This notion pertains directly to Balanchine's creativity as a ballet master.

Of Tchaikovsky it has been written: "Fundamental to his nature was a need and an ability to compose dances." This need was so irrepressible that melodies came to the composer at the most inappropriate times instead of at work or by request. As a result, Tchaikovsky would write down new themes wherever he could—on magazine covers, on scraps of paper, in notebooks, on postal forms and envelopes. Dances arose in Balanchine's imagination just as forcefully and haphazardly. Appearing suddenly, of course, without forethought and proper development, his "melodies" sometimes remained isolated in a composition or even lacked stylistic compatibility. But the ease with which they came into existence astonished and fascinated us. Especially if his dance forms arose in direct response to music which he loved, they then acquired greater unity and clarity. They belonged to the music. In short, they were more than mere improvisations. We did not yet know the dictum of Bournonville in this regard—a ballet master perceives the world through a prism of dance and refracts its images into the images of dance. This was Balanchine's distinctive trait, marking the difference between him and other neophyte ballet masters. While their ideas (of a subject, a situation, or a theme) preceded a composition and made it contrived, those of Balanchine flowed directly from music or from a choreographic image flashing in his imagination.

Hemingway once said of one of his heroes, perhaps having himself in mind: "He could not keep from writing." And he explained this not by a feeling of duty. "It is simply peristalsis, simply an enormous enjoyment." The young Balanchine could have said the same thing about himself. He was literally bursting with an abundance of dance themes. They sprang forth automatically when he heard music. And music surrounded him day and night, whether he performed in the theater, served as an accompanist at dance lessons or at silent films, studied with Zurmullen at the Conservatory, listened to philharmonic concerts, attended theater rehearsals or, finally, simply relaxed behind a piano. Themes came to his mind in dances which he saw or performed himself. Either in sympathy or disagreement with their authors, he wanted to "play them through again." Themes arose in the ensuing discussions in which he preferred to respond with dance compositions rather than with words. Little by little his soul flew further away from actual performing. He began to compose dances in which he excluded his own participation or kept it to a minimum.

I will never forget the impression made on me by *Orientalia,* with music by Cui, which he choreographed at a time when he had already become well known. A female oriental dancer came out on the stage (Mlodzinskaya performed this part, and later Gevergeyeva—Tamara Geva) accompanied by an old man with a tambourine. The old man sat on the floor with his legs crossed in oriental fashion and "spoke" to the dancer with sounds from the tambourine as if prompting her movements. This work always had enormous success. The dancer always took bows for a long time as the "old man" stood modestly behind her. One might have imagined that this was only an accompanist if one did not know that this role was performed by the nineteen- or twenty-year-old Balanchine.

Here I must express an assumption of mine. Balanchine has often said that his intention to create dances first arose involuntarily and inadvertently. This is true. But still, he had sources of encouragement; one of them perhaps is worth philosophizing about.

With the beginning of the 1920s he had reached the age of love. His first passions go back to that time. It is noteworthy that they generally led him to compose dances for the girls to whom he was paying attention. And it is still more noteworthy that the girls soon distinguished themselves in these dances, even if their talent was not otherwise apparent. In this way, I believe, one aspect of Balanchine as a man and artist took form. He searched tirelessly for a girl with talent who would inspire him in turn to affirm the beauty of a dance created in honor of his love and in admiration of her gifts. Is this not the source of Balanchine's satisfaction in those works which minimized his own abilities as a performer in order to "paint" a captivating portrait of the ballerina?

Balanchine's first ballet was presented in the season 1919–20. He arranged *Night,* a romance by Anton Rubinstein, for two students at the school, Olga Mungalova and Pyotr Gusev. The work had a great success. It survived for years, even decades, although losing, it is true, the first "touch" of originality. People began to speak of Balanchine as a prospective ballet master.

Next he began to choreograph works for his most talented girl friends—especially for Lydia Ivanova, his partner in school productions and concerts. Restless, inventive, intelligent, eagerly absorbing impressions of life and in love with music, she was a talent like Balanchine himself. And later he did the same with Alexandra Danilova, a brilliant, beautiful dancer, though slightly reserved. In 1922 he lived and worked with the gifted young artists who were his former classmates. They appeared at concerts with him, organized performances together, and supported each other in numerous ventures. They formed a group which the press soon called the Young Ballet—an important name in the history of Soviet choreography and in Balanchine's biography.

Fedor Lopukhov, then just starting his career as a ballet master, devoted himself to these gifted, tireless, unselfish, and promising young people. Lopukhov's importance in Balanchine's destiny and that of his friends is so great that a few words must be said about him.

Stravinsky's first ballets, *Firebird* and *Petrouchka,* appeared on the stage of the former Maryinsky Theater in 1920–21 [ten years after their Paris premieres—Ed.]. A little later, Balanchine obtained the music for *Pulcinella,* Stravinsky's ballet based on Pergolesi. In those days, Balanchine, Dimitriev, and Erbstein, a real trio, discussed everything new that was happening in the arts; although very close, they did not demand agreement of each other. Stravinsky's scores were joyous discoveries for them and for us all, opening up new worlds of music and choreography. *Petrouchka* delighted us with its elements of E. T. A. Hoffmann, Alexander Blok *(Balaganchik),* and Russian farces and folklore. We were enraptured by Leonid Leontiev (the understudy of Nijinsky in the Paris "Saisons Russes") as Petrouchka, Alexander Orlov (another leading performer in Paris) as the Moor, and Lukom as the Ballerina. Nevertheless, as has already been said, Fokine's images and poetry left us in some doubt. Was this the correct path for ballet? *Firebird,* choreographed for Petrograd by Lopukhov, showed him to be an inventive ballet master capable of bringing dance into an organic unity with exceptionally complex music. The Dance of the Monsters, completely unlike Fokine's, won us over with its polyphonic correspondence between choreography and music. We at once singled out Lopukhov among the other directors of the time. As a matter of fact, he was the first and only ballet master at that time in Russia who could analyze dance forms from the past and who sought and often found an explanation of their poetic strength and logic. (He wrote about this subject in his book *Paths of a Ballet Master,* 1925.) It is true that our trio did not always share his opinions on projects for reviving certain works; still under the influence of certain talented schemers, we strayed in our search for truth. But this did not strain our relations with Lopukhov; it even helped. The paradoxes and self-assurance of his pronouncements, where discoveries alternated with clear mistakes, suited us perfectly. We were just as "possessed" as he was, were "kindred souls," and had certain common opinions. Members of the group, trained by Lopukhov, facilitated contacts. His belief could be summed up: it is necessary to experiment as much as possible in various directions; it is necessary to rely, however, on the experience of classical dance in old ballets; it is necessary to make dance the central force of a performance. This coincided exactly with what Dimitriev, Balanchine, and others of our group thought and said.

In the spring of 1922, Lopukhov proceded from words to action. He proposed to Balanchine's group that it join in his undertaking with a ballet to the music of Beethoven's Fourth Symphony. This production was experimental, unfunded, and had to be rehearsed in the summer, during vacation. Balanchine and his friends accepted without reservation. I will give the names of the other participants (most of them came to Lopukhov from the Young Ballet, which was then forming): Danilova, Ivanova, Koukal, Lisovskaya, Raupenas, Tiuntina, Frangopulo, Gusev, Lavrovsky, Mikhailov, Kirsanov, Balashov, and Tomson. Only two of the participants had graduated before the Revolution—Andrei Lopukhov and Ivanovsky. They were soloists and "choir leaders," so to speak. The director, Alexander Gauk, took care of all musical matters.

I will not relate the history of this production's creation or analyze its choreography. The initial ideas and methods of Lopukhov are what is important. They left a permanent imprint on Balanchine's creative consciousness—even perhaps when he no longer remembered where they came from! Lopukhov popularized his ideas in a pamphlet devoted to the performance. He believed that, in addition to program ballets with plots, ballets without plots must be created—something analogous to symphonies or instrumental ensembles. He called his own production *Dance Symphony.* It needed a new form of choreography, he wrote, "with dance that is free and self-contained." He sought "themes of universal significance, not embedded in any story, which can be transposed directly into choreography," without the application onstage of other arts. The art of dance is great because it creates all accessories itself; they are absent in reality, but emotionally felt. Dance, arising from music and merging with it—this is the dance symphony; dance and music alone form the content and purpose of the production. The dance symphony is realized through classical dance and, if necessary, through character dance—either separately or alternately or combined. So he believed.

For all who participated in this production, who witnessed it, *Dance Symphony* (subtitled *The Majesty of the Universe)* became one of the most memorable and important events of their creative lives and a springboard for further development. No one could ignore it—even if his interests centered exclusively in dramatic ballet. As for Balanchine personally, one could consider *Dance Symphony* his beginning in the sense that he had found in Lopukhov's production the force of a positive example. Balanchine respected Isadora Duncan for the boldness of her interpretation of great music in dance, but he saw a deficiency in the choreographic embodiment of her ideas. Lopukhov inspired faith not only in the possibility of interpreting music in a worthy manner but also in the need to create such a genre in ballet.

Balanchine valued the discoveries of the great choreographers of the past but was often indignant, too. He blamed them at times for a lack of consistency, for turning away from the unity of dance and music, for not fully revealing the self-sufficient power of classical dance. Lopukhov was not entirely free from this last sin in *Dance Symphony*. But on the whole this work was a triumph of classical dance, creating a magnificent world of its own poetic forms far surpassing the limits of the conventional ballet love triangle. *Dance Symphony* was inspired by Beethoven—by his lyricism, humor, sadness, meditation, his tenderness and humanity. Fokine's *Les Sylphides* perhaps surpasses Lopukhov's work in its perfection and completeness. It contains many valuable discoveries in dance symphonism. Our opinion then, however, was that *Les Sylphides* should be considered the pinnacle of the past century's great choreographic achievement and did not belong to this one. In the drawings of poses and groups from Lopukhov's production by the artist Pavel Goncharov, a new plasticity and a new emotion become obvious in the lines of movement. Even now when this genre has become universal and has provided many fine examples, we can value all the more easily the bold, innovative idea of Lopukhov. It gave rise to a new field of dance expression, where dance and music find their greatest affinity. Balanchine's work as a choreographer and his subsequent achievements owe much to Lopukhov's *Dance Symphony*. It is only a pity that many ballet masters have forgotten Lopukhov's important warning. The new form of dance production does not replace the previous form, he believed. It should exist alongside the synthetic program ballet as, in music, the dramatic forms (opera, ballet, oratorio, etc.) coexist with purely symphonic and instrumental ones. I will make one more point myself. *Dance Symphony* represents the "concert" pole of musical-choreographic art, while program ballet represents its opposite theatrical pole. But the center of the *Dance Symphony* is onstage, in the theater.

In the fall of 1922 Lopukhov presented *Dance Symphony* to the Theater Council in Petrograd and to other artistic representatives. The reaction was strong and contradictory. Supporters and critics did agree on one point: they had seen something qualitatively new, expressively performed by gifted enthusiasts. The public, which saw Lopukhov's production on March 7, 1923, was somewhat reserved. The work was just too different from the traditional concept of ballet. Presented after *Swan Lake, Dance Symphony* could only tire audiences. Lopukhov's pretentious program and fantastic commentaries on *The Majesty of the Universe* did not contribute to success. A scandal developed in the press. For a long time the senior ballet critic and theorist, Akim Volynsky, had disliked Lopukhov, considering him untalented and even harmful, with pretensions to the role of leader of the Petrograd ballet. In the eyes of Volynsky, Lopukhov was undermining the classical heritage, although he had successfully revived many old ballets that had faded with time. Volynsky believed that his friend Nicholas Legat, who had replaced Petipa as ballet director of the Maryinsky Theater, was the only man capable of protecting the classical heritage. He demanded that Legat be summoned to "save the ballet." In a number of essays (one of which, on Lopukhov, was entitled "A Worthless House Painter"), Volynsky insultingly disparaged everything Lopukhov had ever done. He attacked *Dance Symphony* in particular and condemned his choreography for the Waltz of the Snowflakes in *Nutcracker*. He urged that the famous members of the Maryinsky Theater be called together from around the world before it was too late. Only this, he proclaimed, could save the Petrograd ballet from an imminent and inevitable extinction. Salvation, he asserted, could not come from the Theater Street school or from the academic theater. It could come only from his own school, which respected and developed those traditions which Lopukhov and others had trampled upon.

To tell the truth, the young people had an ambivalent attitude toward Volynsky. They valued his intelligence and his talent, which were evident in his analyses of dance forms. But at the same time they were indignant at his claim to the right of sole "prophet of Terpsichore." They were revolted by his arrogant attitude toward young people who were inspired by the Revolution and by his vicious attacks on the leaders of academic ballet. It would not have been so bad if Volynsky had directed his criticism only at the directors of the theater and ballet school. He had an essentially negative attitude toward Fokine and Alexander Gorsky. He found fault with much of the creative heritage of Petipa, combining justified criticisms with absolutely unobjective accusations. But even this we could endure. When, however,

Volynsky began to promote his own school and Legat as the sole legitimate and irreproachable sources of knowledge, this was too much for many people—both "the old" and "the young." The presentation of a concert by a group of Volynsky's in the winter of 1923 exhausted their patience. Many people unexpectedly spoke out against him. Balanchine, who normally did not express himself in print, wrote an article for the magazine *Theater*. In it he defended Lopukhov, exposed the flimsiness of Volynsky's claims, and thoroughly analyzed his school.

"It lacks the basic rules of classicism," wrote Balanchine. "It has no 'backbone,' no development, no plasticity; the movements are crude; the technique is simplistic; the contortions are gratuitous; the mime is impossibly bland. There is nothing to say about the men: they are sickly-sweet shopkeepers who pretend to be leading dancers. . . . All of this taken together creates an oppressive feeling which one cannot easily shake off. The press led us to expect from this school a solution to the problems of Russian ballet. [This was the title of Volynsky's pamphlet, raising vital problems and offering utopian solutions.—Y.S.] We see, however, that our hopes have been completely dashed.

"For reforms we need reformers and in the 'Technical School' they do not exist. To the proliferation of ballet studios we must add yet another . . . and we are no better off than before."

This salvo of Balanchine's was devastatingly on target. He received support from Alexei Gvozdev, who declared in *Petrogradskaya Pravda* that "Volynsky had no grounds for creating a school," much less "a poor shadow of the former Maryinsky Theater. This is a far cry," he concluded, "from the renewal of the ballet." The founders of the so-called "eccentric actor factory," Kozintsev and Trauberg, wrote an anonymous, scathing satire against Volynsky. It began: "A nightmarish tragedy unfolded yesterday within the walls of the former Maryinsky Theater. The celebrated critic, A. Volynsky, was offered the post of ballet director." The satire went on to describe Volynsky's first production: "The flower of society was in attendance. The foreigners firmly believed that the spectacle would bring back memories of the good old ballet. Volynsky was greeted in Greek by the girl pupils of the ballet schools. His admirers offered to start a collection for the maker of his statue. At the insistence of Volynsky, the director of the ballet, the critic Volynsky delivered a lecture before the performance and read a review afterward." Listening to Volynsky, "someone died while whispering, 'Too much water under the bridge.' A few dozen people managed to stay alive for the next hour. These survivors fell sick with dancing; their bodies were covered with spots. Doctors have called this illness the Volynka. A quarantine was imposed on the Young Ballet and the evening courses of the Theater Street ballet school. A ten-year abstinence from tutus, pirouettes, and pliés was prescribed." The satire completed the rout of our "enemies" and left us in indescribable childish ecstasy.

Volynsky responded with an article, "Woe is Me!," in which he directed all of his fire at Balanchine. He recalled that he had praised his performance in *Nutcracker*, but that Balanchine had begun to fade, to become anemic, and to burn out almost completely on the boards of the former Maryinsky Theater. Volynsky expressed regret for this in a jeering tone: "I feel sorry for this once promising minor talent. . . . The young artist has pursued the peculiar genre of quaintly licentious dance on the Petrograd stage." He "could not even finish reading [Balanchine's] critical remarks. They are wordy, confused, semiliterate, and nervously strident." He then added the insulting lamentation, "These poor children! These poor analyzers!"

This was already the voice of a man wailing in the desert. The "poor children" emerged from the discussion with greater strength. The accuracy of their posture was confirmed by events and by an increased respect from critics and the public.

I wrote many articles in the press in 1923. One of them, "The Paths of Ballet Regeneration," was a direct response to Volynsky's criticism of Lopukhov and the young people. It was precisely they, I said, who must resolve the fate of ballet. The return of the so-called "eagles" could change nothing significantly, for we had to overcome the stagnation and crisis which arose before the Revolution, at the beginning of the new century. "The first step toward regeneration is to make youth the rational successor of a past that is correctly understood and appreciated." The little-known ballet master Lopukhov would mean much more in this task than many of the eagles who had long since dissipated their abilities. I also wrote in the same article, "A ballet master must create a sonata and symphonic form of dance. . . . Ballet must finally become a self-sufficient dance art, an end in itself. . . . Lopukhov has correctly foreseen this in his attempted *Dance Symphony.*" Another of my articles, "The Language of the Female Dancer," was intended to affirm the immutability of classical dance as an eternally vital foundation of the ballet theater of all ages. Applying this thesis to practical examples, I published several essays on Spessivtseva, on the ballets *Giselle, Esmeralda,* and *Swan Lake,* and on the specific nature of expressive art in ballet —a mastery of movement embodying the themes of both the production and the performer himself.

These essays were not the results of my personal reflections alone. Their content at times originated and received analysis in my conversations with friends in the Young Ballet. Gradually we all began to occupy definite creative positions. Our ability to make judgments developed, either alone or with others. We could express our thoughts better in practice—some of us in painting, some in the performance of dance, and Balanchine in choreography. We acquired then a feeling of fellowship; like fighters for a common cause, we identified our like-minded allies as well as our implacable adversaries; we sharpened any weapons that were inadequate for the struggle being waged.

All of this was to Balanchine's advantage. There was seldom a new enterprise without his participation. At the beginning of 1923, for example, it was announced that the Chamber Ballet, directed by Goleizovsky and about to settle down in Petrograd, would introduce a class in choreographic improvisation in addition to the classes in drama. It was entrusted to Balanchine.

The Young Ballet was Balanchine's accidental brainchild. This was not a company of dancers in the generally accepted meaning of the word—a continually active artistic organization with a definite concert program. Some abandoned the group for a time or for good while others came into it; and still others only joined for one or two performances. But the core remained unchanged.

Vera Kostrovitskaya has recently recalled her confrontation with the "leaders" of the school's graduates for 1922 and 1923: "The first meeting was conducted by Gusev. He asked us sternly what our credo was. Not fully understanding what that meant, we answered in a chorus trying to be brave: 'We want very much to dance; we will do everything that George finds necessary.' In the depths of our hearts we believed that with dance one could do everything—conquer evil, make people happy and better. Dance should embrace large spaces—not only in the figurative but in the literal sense of the word. We dreamed of traversing in a few leaps the entire Field of Mars (an open area today, the Square of Those Who Died for the Revolution). Furthermore, we considered revolution and new dance to be synonymous but were embarrassed to say so. Gusev seemed to us so grown up and wise. And we expected new dance from Balanchine."

Of course, this aesthetic credo was childishly naive and obscure. One would not have expected it to be anything else. The important thing was the undivided absorption in one's calling, faith in it, and a desire to devote all one's time to the fulfillment of one's cherished dream. After beginning work in the Young Ballet, listening to Dimitriev, Balanchine, and Erbstein, and their conversations with supporters of their new projects, Kostrovitskaya formed a clear idea of the group's essential beliefs. "The art of dance must not be a diversion. It must exalt human souls, purge them of their darker impulses, and encourage noble actions in daily life as well as genuinely great heroism. Content, dictating form, determined the direction of the group's work."

Many of the group's members came directly from the list of performers of Lopukhov's *Dance Symphony*. To Ivanova, Danilova, Lisovskaya, Tiuntina, and Raupenas, newcomers were added: Mlodzinskaya, Mungalova, Kostrovitskaya, Stukolkina, Mazikova, Bazarova, Faber, Arkhipova, Eliseyeva, and the gifted student Tamara Gevergeyeva, now Geva. It was no longer necessary to fight for group performances somewhere on the fringe of the city or in a club. Representatives of the Young Ballet and the group as a whole were now sought after as guest artists. The press began to report on the group's activity, its successes and plans; the dancers' names became prominent on posters and playbills. Balanchine was treated with respect conferred on only a few celebrities. His photograph appeared on the cover of the magazine *Theater.* This indicated public recognition of his personality and of his enterprise.

The Young Ballet could now indulge in fond recollections of the way it had begun. The gatherings at Dimitriev's home, in Tarkhovskaya's room, where everyone had to bring a log to keep the fire in the small stove burning. How the dancers begged relatives for fabrics, selling or exchanging them sometimes at the market, to obtain the necessary material for costumes, and how they worked in common, sewing and dyeing. Concerts when no one knew who could get away from the theater to participate and who would do what. All this was recalled with laughter.

Balanchine had now become a master. But in his behavior he was still everyone's friend, extremely unpretentious and easygoing, readily joining any company. Someone remembered an acrostic written by Balanchine as a child in school, and it became a kind of calling card for him in our circle:

> Fate smiles on me.
> I am Ba.
> My destiny in life is fixed.
> I am Lan.
> I see the keys to success.
> I am Chi.
> I will not turn back now,
> I am Vad.
> In spite of storm or tempest.
> I am Ze.

(The last syllables of the Russian words corresponded to the separate elements of his name.)

I Remember Balanchine

Everyone loved Balanchine for his way of doing things and, in particular, for how he disposed of the first earnings of the Young Ballet. He named those members who were most in need and proposed that before everyone else they be provided with what they urgently required. This noble gesture was characteristic. He cared little for himself but was always considerate of his comrades.

It is very difficult to make a list of the Young Ballet's repertory and to evaluate it. Much has been forgotten, much is perceived differently today, and much was not even properly evaluated at that time. I will leave this task in part to Vera Kostrovitskaya, who wrote down, at my request, her recollections.

She tells of a conversation of Balanchine with the group's members, which apparently took place in the spring of 1923: "He outlined the first concert in three sections. For the first section he proposed that each of us choose freely what we most liked from the old ballets and prepare the pieces as we ourselves felt them and as we wanted to convey them to the audience—to do our own interpretation. (This was very appealing, for in the theater we did not get solo parts. They were given only to Ivanova and Danilova.)

"He proposed that we form the second section from his concert pieces and from our own dances, which we had performed while still at the school on the initiative of Oblakov. Andrei Alexandrovich had selected music for some of us in accordance with our individual natures and had given us confidence that we could interpret this music in dance. These experiences had given us many joyful, happy days then.

"He rehearsed everything himself and made gentle, always good-natured remarks, mostly in regard to the musical side of the performance.

"I will enumerate what was prepared. Not everything has remained in my memory. The first and second sections of the program consisted of the following: 1. Mungalova and Gusev: adagio from the ballet *The Little Grace*. 2. Mlodzinskaya and Efimov: adagio from the ballet *Les Sylphides*. 3. Stukolkina, Kostrovitskaya, and Mikhailov: pas de trois from the ballet *Paquita*. 4. Danilova: dance of Berenika (with a snake) from the ballet *Egyptian Nights*. 5. Mazikova: *Flight* (Schumann)—her own choreography. 6. Faber: *Flight of the Bumblebee* (I don't recall whose music)—her own choreography. 7. Kostrovitskaya: *Ecstase* (Gan)—her own choreography. 8. Ivanova: *Valse Triste* (Sibelius) —her own choreography done together with Balanchine. 9. Mungalova and Gusev: *Night* (Rubinstein)—choreography by Balanchine. 10. Mlodzinskaya: *Dying Swan*—her own choreography. 11. Kostrovitskaya and Mikhailov: *Elegy* (I don't recall whose music)—choreography by Mikhailov. 12. Danilova and Balanchine: *Poème* (Fibich)—choreography by Balanchine. 13. Geva and Balanchine: adagio with high lifts (I don't recall whose music). 14. Stukolkina and Mikhailov: Spanish dance (I don't recall whose music)—choreography by Balanchine. 15. Ivanova: *Spring* (Grieg). 16. Lisovskaya: idyll to music of Davidov—his own choreography.

"For the third section, Balanchine decided to choreograph the *Funeral March* of Chopin."

All of the preceding works were choreographed, rehearsed, and successfully performed at various times. But of course, at the first concert of the Young Ballet in the building of the former city Duma on Nevsky Prospect, only some of them were presented.

Of three pieces of Balanchine, Kostrovitskaya says: "In 1920, a sensational rumor spread through the school. A student of the graduating class, Balanchine, had composed a dance to a romance of Rubinstein, *Night,* and behind closed doors guarded by Oblakov and Isaenko was rehearsing it with two students, Gusev and Mungalova. The new work was performed to piano and violin at the next school concert. (Oblakov invited a young violinist.) After leaving the school, Mungalova and Gusev continued to dance this piece for a long time on various stages in Petrograd.

"We were accustomed to seeing in the former Maryinsky Theater and in the school the usual adagio développés, traditional turns from fourth position which the ballerina performed with support from her partner. Before the turns, there would be fear on her face, and a relieved smile at the conclusion. There was none of that here. Rubinstein's *Night,* in Balanchine's dance, was a lyrical duet of restrained passion—half poses, half arabesques . . . tender passages of adagio without the conventional movements of legs raised on the principle 'the higher, the better.' Of course, later on in various concert pieces, artists performed love duets, called adagios, with disregard for the traditions of Petipa. But then, and especially in the school, this was completely new.

"And in 1921 there were still few who appeared onstage in tunics. Dancing on pointe was done only in tutus. The head was adorned with diadems, artificial flowers, and various tinsel. Mungalova wore a light, bright tunic, and instead of the headdress a narrow ribbon was tied freely around her blond curls.

"After *Night,* I saw another new work of Balanchine's, *Poème,* with music by Fibich. He danced in it together with Danilova. If one can call the romance of Rubinstein a poem of passionate love, then the dance to the music of Fibich was a poem to perfect beauty. The irreproachably formed Danilova with her finely molded, severe features framed in golden hair, wearing a transparent bright blue tunic, was the embodiment of pure, cold beauty. Balanchine, also very handsome, lifted Danilova in the classic arabesque and lowered her softly on pointe. The adagio began, but again without the usual turns and technical tricks (although Danilova had many opportunities to do them). Sometimes these performances were accompanied without violin, only by a piano, but the lines of the dance were so melodious that one could always imagine the violin's presence anyway. At the end of *Poème,* Balanchine carried Danilova off, lifting her high in an arabesque with his arms extended. One had the impression that she herself, without a partner's support, was gliding through the air away from the audience to finish 'singing' her dance somewhere far, far away. The *Poème* gave rise to many imitations.

"One of our concerts took place in the building of the Institute of the Living Word on the square of the former Alexandrinsky Theater. Seats for the audience were arranged in an amphitheater, as in the circus; the stage was a semicircle. With this in mind, Balanchine choreographed the Chopin *Funeral March* for a circular stage, but in such a way that it could be performed, if necessary, on an ordinary stage with little modification.

"In the first tragic section of the march, six female dancers stepped out slowly on pointe, one after another, bowing their heads with sorrow and crossing their arms downward. Reaching the center of the stage, all of them separated with the same steps into a large circle. Raising their crossed arms into the air for a second, they dropped to one knee, facing the outer part of the stage. They bent forward, arms and head toward the floor.

"Then, to a new musical phrase from the same passage, three young men carried away a girl lying on her back, whom they had lifted high on extended arms." (Mungalova and Geva performed this role alternately without any fear during the high lifts, which everyone was still afraid of then and didn't know how to do properly. The young men were Gusev, Balashov, and Efimov.) "They proceeded slowly across the entire stage, slowing down even more at moments of *forte,* and lowering the girl to the floor at the opposite exit. At the same time, they dropped to their knees in the same pose as the others.

"The middle, lyric section of the *March* began. With a radiant face Danilova appeared; with light, flying steps she went around each kneeling figure as if to waken the pure, human soul from an eternal sleep. Scarcely touching them, she gave them life and, making them rise slowly one by one, she executed slow turns in attitude. Everything somber disappeared; the folded arms became straight; the expression of the faces changed; their eyes became bright, focused on something beautiful far away. (This is how Balanchine explained it to us.) There were arabesques on the floor with the body bent forward followed by deep backbends. . . .

"In the third section of the *March,* musically analogous to the first, all of the dancers—Danilova first, followed by the young men with the girl on their arms and the other six girls—went slowly from the stage one after another, as in the beginning, stretching their arms forward in a gesture of hope.

"Dimitriev drew sketches for costumes for the *March*. We sewed and dyed them ourselves from old calico which we found at home. The short, gray, close-fitting, sleeveless dresses had a black and silver pattern. The plain gray caps with small discs on the sides over the ears were also embroidered in black and silver. The usual ballet tights and slippers completed the costume."*

Did this theatrical representation of Chopin's funeral music, so important for concert pianists, have any particular meaning? The music alone was commonly used for tragic processions and demonstrations, so great was its emotional impact. Certainly, an important message did exist in this new and unusual choreography: one recalled the events in Western Europe and in Russia, ravaged by wars and destruction.

Bruni writes about Balanchine's *Funeral March:* "With this work one can begin to speak seriously about Balanchine as a ballet master. I believe this was his first work with Dimitriev, marking the beginning of their unfortunately brief creative friendship. The work made a great impression on me then, an impression of something really new. As best I recall, the cortege came onto the stage through the audience under a spotlight in the dark. The groupings were composed in a very interesting, individual manner. The tragic feeling was vividly expressed. It seems to me that one could look at this work even now."

I do not know if Bruni is correct on this last point, but in those days this dance never left any audience unmoved. It was too evocative of what they had lived through themselves. And not only visually! Chopin's march accompanied those who had fought for the Revolution on their final journey. It alternated at funeral ceremonies with the famous revolutionary song, "You Fell Victim in the Fateful Struggle." For the ballet of those years this work was a direct reflection of modern times. And the devices of composition were prompted by modern dramatic methods. The slightest opportunity was taken to lay a bridge between the audience and the stage, emphasizing the unity of what was being performed and what had been experienced, the unity of spirit between the audience and the stage heroes. This explains the passage of the dancers followed by light through the audience and the mod-

* Kostrovitskaya adds: "We also made the costumes for the first section ourselves. We sewed tunics and did over bodices from old theatrical costumes, since those in the wardrobe were inappropriate. There was no money for anything new. Our earnings in the theater were hardly sufficient to buy the most modest food."

eling of sculptural groups as if to generalize individual experience. In this respect, Meyerhold was the teacher of everyone—including Balanchine.

Quite another matter was the success of Sibelius's *Valse Triste*, performed by Ivanova and choreographed by her together with Balanchine or under his direction. A kind of Duncanesque rhythmic plasticity found vivid expression in this work. This was the opinion of the reviewer Cherepnin, who was far from well disposed toward the Young Ballet and who preferred the supposedly more modern Moscow ballet to that of Petrograd. In February 1924 the Young Ballet dared to make an excursion, unprecedented for that time, to Moscow. It performed in the former Zimin Theater there.

Cherepnin (under the pseudonym LI) reacted to the concert negatively—"astonishingly crude, in poor taste, quite vulgar." But approving certain details of the performance, he later wrote: "Nevertheless, the performance reveals some touches of a positive nature, which might be instructive for our Moscow professionals. In one small composition . . . there appear two devices of great expressiveness. . . . The female dancer, developing her feelings of horror and moving in a kind of emotional crescendo in a straight line from the rear of the stage to the footlights, unexpectedly, at the last instant of highest intensity, turns her back to the audience in a quick motion and becomes frozen for a moment. This fermata makes an enormous impression. . . . In the same piece the final emotional intensity is conveyed superbly with a completely new device—the silent scream of a widely opened mouth. The author, as I discovered, is a young character dancer of the academic theater, Balanchine."

The successful work of the designer, Dimitriev or Erbstein—I do not remember which one—did not go unnoticed. LI also praised the costuming enthusiastically: "The simple, loose, white tunic of the female dancers with two frills bordered with white satin braid, supplemented by something like a shawl stretched over the shoulders to the hands and falling freely on the back . . . as described here with perhaps a black Spanish chignon—what an excellent costume for the four soloists in the last act of *Don Quixote!*"

The effects described by the reviewer really did make a big impression. Balanchine was not alone in seeking an intensely dramatic plastic expressiveness for dance and in achieving his goal. In Ivanova he found a champion of dance, equal to himself, with whom he could capture the audience. One can see from Cherepnin's account that they succeeded. This is confirmed by those who remember this work. (And there are many who do. It has lasted to the present day in the performances of various female dancers.)

Pyotr Gusev at that time was Balanchine's closest friend, his principal collaborator and the leading male dancer of the Young Ballet. He later became a partner of Ulanova, Lepeshinskaya, and other famous ballerinas. Today he is an Honored Artist of the U.S.S.R. and a professor at the Leningrad Conservatory. He succeeded Lopukhov in supervising the training of young choreographers. Gusev speaks of his memories of Balanchine with great affection. "What attracted me most? Everything. The initiative, the invention, playing the piano, uninterrupted composition. Through Balanchine I learned much music and I learned much about music. He generated a contagious excitement for everything new. And it was fun to be a kind of guinea pig to him. He always used Mungalova and me like this; and then later he would give the particular work in question to others. We didn't mind in the least. We knew that the next day he would drag us back onstage and torment us until night with more experiments. What a joyous torment this was! *Night* was a direct imitation of the early Goleizovsky. The animal passions, so to speak, sex—though of course, not with the present connotations! It would seem more than modest today, even 'chaste.' We were reproached then for indecency."

A few words must be said about the performers. They decided the fate of the production. Gusev became known in the Soviet ballet as the "king of support." In his agility, strength, and boldness, he was a partner without equal, an intelligent, expressive artist with a broad range of dramatic resources, from the still unsurpassed Girei to the comic Franz in *Coppélia,* to the young dandy in a duet with Lepeshinskaya. Here he danced with her to a humorous Russian song in the astonishingly exact manner of a Strauss waltz. As for Mungalova, she was the only female dancer of her kind whose line was perfect no matter how whimsical. Lopukhov, in fact, used this quality in 1927 when he created for her the original role of the Ice Maiden in the ballet of the same name. It was in this piece that certain acrobatics par terre, first tried by Balanchine, became an integral part of the classic dance. Balanchine used the natural expressiveness of Mungalova in the same way. But he knew how to make the line of her movement quivering, fragile, agitated by youth, and overflowing with feeling.

"The adagio of Arensky," Gusev continues, "if I am not mistaken, was performed by Balanchine and Geva. I remember that in this piece for the first time a woman arched into a 'bridge.' This shocked people then but was accepted. But when her partner leaped across the 'bridge,' making a grand jeté with his bent leg, this produced general indignation and protest. Even Lopukhov told us that such a stunt was coarse and served no purpose. We told Balanchine to listen to the criticism and remove the jump. But he stubbornly continued to jump all he wanted. And later on Mungalova and I did the same thing in a duet of acrobats, in the opera *Judith,* which Lopukhov choreographed. We noticed that many revue or vaudeville dancers did it as well. While with Balanchine it expressed an emotional climax, with the imitators its meaning was lost. Only the bare stunt remained. Actually, I think Balanchine also got the idea for this work from Goleizovsky, although it contained no direct borrowing.

"Mungalova and I for a fairly long time danced a waltz and adagio to Balanchine's music, which he choreographed. I remember the theme of his adagio, but the waltz I have forgotten. There were exercise movements—full *plié, tendu, battement, grand battement, ronde de jambe par terre,* and *frappé.* I remember that sequence. The piece was choreographed on a strictly classical base, in which I see the influence of Lopukhov. There were, however, some unusual lifts. In particular, the finale: the female dancer is carried off in first arabesque on extended arms. This was new, though two or three years later it had become a cliché. Balanchine apparently liked the piece—perhaps because its classicism was not violated and the music corresponded to the dance. Lopukhov gave lavish praise to him and us for this work. Balanchine's choreography for Bizet's *Symphony in C* and his compositions to music of Tchaikovsky evoke in me certain associations with these earliest choreographic works of his."

Gusev continues: "I will say a few words about the relationship between Balanchine and Lopukhov. When we were preparing *Dance Symphony,* Lopukhov did not fully explain to us the structure and composition of his work. He showed us what to do and we did it. We would not have understood all of the finer points of the choreography (two, three, and four parallel 'voices' in choreographic counterpoint, the leading 'voice,' the accompaniment, and so on), if Balanchine had not given it deep thought and had not interpreted it for us with admiration and amazement. In his treatment of Chopin's *Funeral March,* I see the influence of Lopukhov's *Dance Symphony.*"

Whatever reservations one might have about the work of Balanchine and the Young Ballet, this was a very significant and necessary enterprise. It is not surprising that many authorities spoke out in its favor. A survey of the press in 1923, when the group's members had already been determined, when a repertory had been formed and concerts had become frequent, shows that the Young Ballet had acquired a real reputation in the theatrical world. . . .

On June 24, Erbstein devoted a large article to the Young Ballet. Despite his favorable disposition toward the ballet master and the group, the article is not without criticism: "In the works of Balanchine, in general, there is much that is accidental, sentimental, or naturalistic and externally showy. But specific superb details (the development of movements over the entire stage and even beyond it) permit one to expect significant achievements in the future." And further on: "This evening has demonstrated that slowly and painfully, as with all living things, ballet is being reborn; its new and much-needed modern, monumental style is beginning."

On July 21 in the pages of *Petrogradskaya Pravda,* the composer and music critic Anatol Kankarovich wrote that an absence of outstanding innovators in Petrograd like those in Moscow (the theaters of Meyerhold, Vakhtangov, Tairov, and others) "made one search inquisitively for any attempts to renew drama, opera, and ballet in Petrograd." The search led Kankarovich to the Young Ballet, which he commended for "desiring new forms and new content, seeking new music for the embodiment of its new ideas." However, he added, "it lacks knowledge and experience, and most important, a sure leader." The writer was certain that all this would come, that theorists would be found "if with only the clear awareness of the need for change, of the decay of the old theatrical forms." He noted that the group consisted of the theater's most talented youth. As one of its initiators he named Balanchine, "who has shown himself to be an interesting choreographer." He listed the leading female dancers: Danilova, Ivanova, Geva. He wished for the group "enough tenacity and energy for the full realization of their ideas on art."

In these observations of a thoughtful professional there was much truth. A sense of conscious and confident progress was what the Young Ballet's leadership lacked most at first. With the entry of Dimitriev into the group sometime during the season of 1922, its direction became somewhat more distinct. If Balanchine was the group's soul, as it were, Erbstein its heart, and Gusev both the right arm and ambassador of Balanchine onstage, then Dimitriev became the artistic organism's head. Their strengths complemented each other and brought effusive praise from the newspapers.

Gvozdev wrote in *Krasnaya Gazeta* on May 20, 1924: "From the time of Michel Fokine, not one ballet master, not one pioneer in choreography, has succeeded in firmly establishing himself and in creating not only something new but something really interesting. In just the last few years, G. Balanchine, while still inconsistent and not yet in possession of his artistic identity, has attracted general attention as an unquestionably talented, if uneven, choreographer and as the leader of the group, the Young Ballet. I heartily welcome his attempts. . . . I appreciate his ability to rejuvenate classical dance with new lines, brilliant poses, and bold, unexpected passages."

A university professor, a leader of the theater of the Institute of Art History, a major theater critic and philologist, Gvozdev had shown sympathy for Balanchine from the start. He had noticed the young artist at the institute's evening performances, had asked me about him, and learning that this was Balanchine, was very pleased that he frequented the institute—one of the city's leading centers of creative thought. Gvozdev took to heart everything that the Young Ballet created. He was especially sensitive to the indifference and skepticism which were then widespread in certain theatrical circles. Many people felt that innovative intentions and experiments led inevitably to sparse results. Gvozdev had written bitterly in *Zhizn Iskusstvo* on May 10, 1924: "There is no lack of sincere enthusiasm and devotion to work among the young performers. On the contrary, when you look at these young people filled with the desire to find something new coming into contact with the artistic exploration of our days, when you see the inspiration which permeates all their efforts, you cannot but be excited at the prospect of building a great artistic enterprise combining their energy and talent with the studio's systematic cultural organization. It is too painful to see the apathetic and indifferent attitude toward this fresh and tempestuous current which rushes toward new art only to crash along shallow and false channels."

Life itself required a change of attitude among the leadership of the academic theaters. The new creative tendencies in the field of choreography, particularly in the work of the Young Ballet, were becoming provocative. Lopukhov followed the young Ballet intently and jealously. (Jealousy is an ineradicable and fruitful trait in the arts; it produces creative tension and self-criticism and stimulates an enrichment of one's skills.) He promoted young dancers who had distinguished themselves at the group's concerts. He formed close ties with its leaders, attended performances where Dimitriev and Erbstein participated as designers, argued with them until hoarse, and examined closely the creative work of Balanchine.

It was Balanchine's good fortune to have the sympathy of many "old people" active and knowledgeable in the performing arts. The talented theater director V. A. Dranishnikov, aware from their first meeting of the young man's promise, singled him out from the mass of ballet performers. As Kozintsev said of such people, "They could see beyond the wild talk and recklessness of the young, maturing individuals whom they respected. They understood that a new day had come; what this would mean for art it was difficult to determine, but the important thing was not to lose what would grow and develop." One such person, forgotten today, was the ballet director A. N. Maslov. "He instilled in me," Lopukhov has said, "a taste for reading, for reflecting on art, for visiting museums." The "exceedingly modest, erudite, honest, and goodhearted" Maslov had been a member of the ballet performers' strike in 1905, was expelled because of that activity from the imperial theaters, and returned to the stage only after the Revolution. His experiences had left a mark on him, making him taciturn and reserved. But they had not destroyed his love for everything progressive and talented.

"I often saw Maslov," writes Gusev, "talking with Balanchine." This man knew how to influence and was highly educated. Maslov was the only outsider who attended rehearsals of the Young Ballet. Sitting somewhere to the side without speaking, he would watch for hours these young people brimming with life.

At the beginning of the 1923–24 season, Balanchine was named a ballet master of the Maly Opera Theater. There was a small troupe of eighteen ballet dancers who could serve in various genres. Balanchine choreographed three works there.

On September 22 the season opened with a new production of Rimsky-Korsakov's opera, *Le Coq d'Or*. As stated in the playbills and programs, the "choreographic part" belonged to Balanchine. This meant that he composed not only specific dances but directed the movement of entire scenes. A document has been preserved in which Balanchine summarized his work as consisting of "two apparitions in the first act, of the choral group, of the Tsaritsa of Shemakhan, of Dodon and the pupils in the second act, general march in the third act." Asafiev wrote: "The cinematographic posing of the female dancer [the Tsaritsa of Shemakhan] is unnecessary ballast." However, "the procession in the finale of the second act is enchanting." He noted in particular an "eroticized orientation" and stated that the opera production was "stylized in the spirit of very old Russian miniatures." Asafiev's review was generally favorable, but Strelnikov, the composer, wrote an attack criticizing the opera performance and singling out the choreography. "Apart from the diffuse quality of the dances in the second act, it is simply incomprehensible to me how such a capable and musically gifted 'choreographer' as G. Balanchine can overlook the distinct alternation of groups in the procession—all of these separately characterized warriors, the retinue, the reindeer, the giants—and how he could so entangle the design of the music's plastic reproduction. Even worse, how he ever got the idea of choreographing the Russian G-major theme in its final somber return using four frail bayadères—all this escapes me."

I remember that we took this criticism much to heart. Especially since its author, a fine musician, was well disposed toward Balanchine and believed in him. But the fact is undeniable that Balanchine worked on the choreography in a rush, breaking away for a few hours from his duties as a performer and his work with the Young Ballet and not bothering himself with a thorough study of the music. Strelnikov was apparently correct in concluding that there had not been enough orchestra rehearsals, "as a result of which the dances were thought out over a piano."

On September 30 on the same stage, there was the premiere of Shaw's

Caesar and Cleopatra in a production by the Academic Theater of Drama. The poet-humorist Alexandr Flit wrote the following comment:

> To show the queen in a bar
> They struggled with all their might
> Egyptian vignettes and foxtrots
> Academically to unite.

He was ridiculing the efforts to "modernize" the performance, which began with a prologue in a bar. The critics denounced this vulgar attempt to unite "grotesque historical method with modern reality." Nevertheless, the bar drew wide comment in the press as an interesting place for a performance— without, of course, any connection to Shaw's play. Balanchine is not named in the reviews, but his contribution is mentioned. It concerned, as Balanchine himself has stated, "the pantomime and dances of the first act and all the plastic movements of Wolf-Israel, who played Cleopatra. We practiced them at her home." A reviewer suggests this was useful: the actress "demonstrated an excellent culture of body movement. It is a highly instructive example for the other members of the troupe."

On December 15, 1923, also in the same place, there was the premiere of *Eugen the Unfortunate* by the German dramatist Ernst Toller. A gloomy expressionist play, stark and pessimistic, it dealt with postwar Germany in the grip of inflation and the terrible misfortune of many families whose breadwinners had never returned or had become invalids. Balanchine was again assigned the "choreographic part." He collaborated this time with one of the persons closest to him creatively, the artist Dimitriev, who worked as designer.

The well-known literary critic, Professor B. Eikhenbaum, sharply criticized the performance, devoting some attention to the choreographic episodes: "shadowy dances in the latest fashion . . . cripples on crutches stretching their arms out to the audience." In his opinion, all this was an "amusing stunt for today's theatergoers—nothing more." I. Rabinovich saw the performance differently in his review. He praised "the splendid clothes, the adaptation of Kuzmin's music, the interestingly conceived and performed choreography of Balanchine, and the pleasing, diverse styles of Dimitriev's scenery. All of this, taken by itself, was not at all bad—especially the scenery of the third act, which received long applause, the silhouetted dances in the windows of the second-floor café and the street itself. In the composition of the separate scenes, one sees the great culture and inventiveness of contemporary direction. The invalids' supplication for charity against the background of the mechanical steps of ballerinas creates a strong impression." I fully endorse this judgment. The particular scene which he described was worked out collectively by Dimitriev, Balanchine, and the director. Balanchine choreographed the dance expressively. As for the stylish, popular dances behind the café windows, this device, I believe, was inspired by an enthralling episode that had occurred in a mass dramatization on November 7, 1920, *The Taking of the Winter Palace*. Just as the Red Guards had broken their way into the palace, lights came on behind hundreds of windows on all floors, showing them in silhouette fighting hand to hand with the defenders of the fallen regime, and showing the high officials, clerks, and servants fleeing the palace. This pantomime had been splendidly directed by Levitsky, an actor of the Alexandrinka and a former military officer.

In March 1924, according to a review in the evening edition of *Krasnaya Gazeta* (March 19), the principal ballet master of the Maly Opera Theater, Chekrygin, "rearranged the choreography of *Le Coq d'Or* without Balanchine's knowledge." "Wouldn't it be better to create something new?" the reviewer asks, in discussing other aspects of such changes. I have not found a reply in the press nor do I recall the circumstances of this rearrangement. In fact, no one does. I imagine that it was in response to criticism in the press. This is a trifle, however, compared to the unprecedented fact that at the age of twenty Balanchine had been made a ballet master and entrusted with considerable responsibility. But this appointment did not diminish his astonishing ability to do a great many things simultaneously. Information taken from the press shows how intense his activity was.

On December 11, 1923, *Le Coq d'Or* was presented at the Maly Opera Theater; on December 12, *Caesar and Cleopatra;* on the same evening Balanchine performed in the opera *Tannhäuser;* on December 15 came the premiere of *Eugen the Unfortunate;* he danced on the same day as one of the Polovetsians in *Prince Igor;* on December 19, Balanchine performed in *Swan Lake,* on December 20 in *Tannhäuser,* on December 21 in *Prince Igor,* and on December 23 in *Le Corsaire.* At the same time he choreographed new dances for the Young Ballet and helped prepare a program for the opening of an artistic cabaret, the Carousel, collaborating with the directors Evreinov, Petrov, Tversky, and Miklashevsky, and the artists Akimov and Benois (the son). His name figures in the list of sponsors alongside those of A. Tolstoy, Zoschenko, and other writers, and outstanding dramatic actors, such as Nikolai Simonov. This again testifies to his popularity and creative reputation.

The Young Ballet, meanwhile, was going at full steam. Balanchine received numerous requests to choreograph dances, which he could barely satisfy. Elizabetha Gerdt asked him to arrange a dance for her benefit performance in May of 1924. *Krasnaya Gazeta* wrote: ". . . without departing from the basic principles of the classics, Balanchine strives to imbue the dance with something new and personal. He uses particular dance positions very successfully."

Even accidents were reported by certain sarcastic journalists. *Krasnaya Gazeta* noted on January 19: "The young ballet master continues to search for ways of reviving classical ballet forms. Under his direction are many recent young graduates. The courageous ballet master-innovator used Mungalova and Bazarova simultaneously in one supported dance. The experiment ended with the fall of one of the female dancers, who suffered an injured back and bruised shoulders." It was not serious and she recovered, but the magazine *Zhizn Iskusstvo* chimed in with the following verse:

> Thirty years I've lived, O gods,
> And did not know till recent days
> That to break one's back and legs—
> This is searching for new ways.

The magazine also printed a caricature of Balanchine by the ballet artist Khrapis, in which he used Mayakovsky's famous line to convey what was most characteristic of the young ballet master—"All is new! Stop and marvel!"

On May 20 *Krasnaya Gazeta,* in a review of a demonstration concert by the Young Ballet, tried to summarize its two-year experience. "Yesterday's demonstration performance is a faithful barometer of the young ballet master's creative fluctuations. From the old classic adagio to modernism (a foxtrot), his style for the moment involves a skillful combination of extremes. It is difficult to say at which stage of his creative work he established himself definitively, but through his efforts a fresh stream has flowed into choreography which no one can now stop. Balanchine is bold and insolent, but in his insolence one can see genuine creativity and beauty. Balanchine's character dances are much less successful than the classical and abstract ones. They lack vividness and color, strong temperamental movements. Although in the classical work he does misuse poses, he combines them in such an interesting way and creates such beautiful if unexpected transitions that one can grudgingly excuse this defect." The reviewer then contradicts himself somewhat, stating that for "everything hackneyed and conventional Balanchine managed to find new, liberating forms." The review concludes with the words: "from the stage has come a burst of fresh air—the Young Ballet has proven its viability."

Balanchine, as we know, took a great interest in the activity of FEKS (the "eccentric actor factory"). In 1923, while its members were preparing their program for publication, they invited Balanchine to work with them and to help in its elaboration. He devoted himself to this task with full enthusiasm. Unquestionably, he was drawn to them by their audacious, defiant rejection of the "theatrical gods" of the past and their yearning to embrace and master everything which might be of use in the future when, it was hoped, art would join with revolutionary reality and win over the broad masses.

"It wasn't easy to understand the aspirations of the young people of those years," Kozintsev has written. "It seemed impossible to them to combine the feeling of novel happenings in life with the old forms of art. Everyone tried to find some new unknown form. This was a period of stormy searching, of astonishing honesty, and remarkable confusion." He mentions further "the foolishness of the young," their "unwise steps" and "irrational fantasies," and "the wild diversity of their crazy ideas and inventions." All of this can be related to Balanchine and to the entire Young Ballet—but with one substantial qualification. The experience of the times, discussion with sympathetic "older people," the sober intelligence and foresight of Dimitriev, who tempered Balanchine's most improbable fantasies, and their own practical work up to 1924 obliged them to draw certain conclusions forming the basis of further activity. It was futile to regard the conservatism of classical dance as a synonym for reaction. Classical dance, in fact, proved to be most viable in its assimilation of new forms, devices, and nuances.

But, in Kozintsev's words, "impetuous youth, without thinking, tears the old material into shreds and then tries to adopt everything which was formerly forbidden and alien to art." This is how Balanchine began. Reflecting innumerable influences, he tried to do everything at once. He made studies of rhythmic movement, seeking a new choreographic fabric for the cantilena. He introduced, sometimes successfully, brilliant acrobatic elements into the pas de deux; high lifts and the upward flight of the female dancer expressed joy and exhilaration. He made frequent use of splits, the "bridge," and other devices from clown or acrobatic acts. He paid tribute to "Duncanism" in movement which attempted to transcend the traditional range of ballet steps in order to convey through dance the fleeting nature and immediacy of deeply felt emotions. In brief, he did indeed introduce into the structure of ballet everything which had previously been considered alien.

The resistance of the "fabric" of classical dance, both pliant and unyielding in its poetics, gradually tempered his wild nature. Envying the ease (which time has shown to be illusory) with which his contemporaries in other fields of art repudiated their forebears, admiring those in FEKS for whom "all is possible," the ballet master Balanchine became convinced more and more of the invincibility of the old academic dance whose doom had been predicted along with the theater of the past.

The initial, sharply critical attitude toward the classical heritage gradually changed into admiration for its finest examples. The activity of Lopukhov, whom we at first considered a mere restorer of antiques, played a positive role in this regard. The older people whom we respected found like-minded thinkers among us—Dimitriev more than anyone else. The great masters of classical choreography, whom we had virtually consigned to the debris of ballet history, turned out, upon examination, to have been innovators for their time. Noverre and Dauberval, Didelot and Perrot, Saint-Léon and Petipa, Lev Ivanov and Fokine gradually became, in their best works, not our adversaries but our friends, allies, and contemporaries. It turned out that the right to innovation is acquired only by the most faithful inheritor of the great traditions of the past. The choreographers of the past influenced Balanchine through their productions and helped him to look toward the future. From Ivanov through Fokine and Lopukhov to Balanchine there is a thread of continuity of perception—like a line of music acquiring visible form in the plasticity of dance. Imperceptibly in those years the foundations of his future activity were being set.

Other aspects of Balanchine's outlook became firmly established with the years. Among them, in his attitude toward the ballet dancer. The dancer is both the servant and ruler of the ballet master, the performer of a "text" written for him by the choreographer, but also the person who decides the fate of the author's treasured ideas and who alone can win the audience's heart. Another conclusion which Balanchine came to adopt is that melody with rich harmony must always predominate in the dance. And his conviction became stronger that the leading theme of choreographic creativity was the theme of joy, ecstasy, rapture, and happiness.

A new project of the Young Ballet was begun in January 1924—*Pulcinella* with music by Stravinsky and based on Pergolesi. Balanchine confronted for the first time a work of relatively large dimensions, and for him it represented a leap from the classical music of the nineteenth century to the music of the twentieth century. He had not always approved of Stravinsky. In 1918 he had taken part in the premiere of *The Nightingale* but regarded the music almost as cacophony, as we all did. Two or three years later *Firebird* and *Petrouchka* radically changed Balanchine's attitude toward the composer. He became interested in other works by Stravinsky performed in philharmonic concerts, and obtained a piano score of *Pulcinella* from Dranishnikov, if my memory serves me right. It was discussed at length in our group, I remember, and pleased everyone. *Pulcinella* attracted Balanchine with its embodiment in dance of the masked-comedy system of stage characterization.

Meyerhold had long been drawn to acting of this kind, reminiscent of popular street shows. The Theater of National Comedy, organized by Radlov, had argued in its behalf. Balanchine was impressed by the score's organic combination of Pergolesi's simple melodies with the extremely modern rhythmic orchestration of Stravinsky.

For the first time he had to give thought to conveying external dramatization in dance, to creating distinctive dance characteristics for various roles. This was a test of his art as a ballet master. To combine the wealth of musical-dance forms with the dramatization of a story is a highly demanding task. Balanchine's accumulated experience allowed one to anticipate an interesting choreography for this music of greater complexity than he had ever known before. Circumstances, however, were not favorable. Gvozdev writes about this in an article dated May 20, 1924. The independent activity of the Young Ballet had not led to the development of full-time work. Because of their responsibilities to the theater, many of the group's leading members could no longer rehearse on the side. Dimitriev became less active and more absorbed by productions in dramatic theaters. Erbstein also. Slonimsky was preparing his work for a diploma at the university, as well as a monograph on *Swan Lake* and a ballet scenario for Shostakovich. In order to present *Pulcinella* and to display his capacities to the fullest, Balanchine needed material and creative support from the theater, scheduled rehearsals on the academic stage, a permanent manager, a director, and the participation of the leading performers. This he did not have. The Young Ballet was threatened with inevitable disintegration.

At the opening of the summer season in Pavlovsk on June 15, a concert of the Young Ballet directed by Balanchine was held, as it later became clear, for the last time. He danced an adagio of Saint-Saëns with Danilova, an adagio of Arensky (the exit of Cleopatra) from *Egyptian Nights* with Geva, and the *Elegy* of Rachmaninoff with Geva and Efimov. In addition, Ivanova danced a waltz by Drigo from the ballet *The Lovely Pearl*, and performed her best piece, the *Polka* of Rachmaninoff. Danilova performed the *Waltz* and Geva the *Polka* of Vilbushevich.

On the following day a terrible accident occurred; it shook the entire theatrical community in Petrograd: while on an outing in a boat, Lydia Ivanova drowned.

This news reached me in an army barracks where I found myself at the end of May, having been called into the service following my graduation from the university. For me, with the death of Lydia and the dispersal of the Young Ballet, the spring of youth had come to an end. And perhaps not only for me. Perhaps for Balanchine, too, and for many of our contemporaries. Could this be why Balanchine, talking in 1972 with a correspondent of *Komsomolskaya Pravda* about his youth and about his meetings with Mayakovsky, referred to those distant times as "the best years of my life"?

NINA

STUKOLKINA*

Nina Mikhailovna Stukolkina danced with the Petrograd Theater of

Opera and Ballet (now the Kirov) from 1922 to 1958. As a teacher

of character dance, she has worked in Minsk, Tashkent, and other

Soviet cities.

* Nina Stukolkina was interviewed by Elizabeth Souritz.

I Remember Balanchine

IN 1922 I JOINED BALANCHIVADZE'S YOUNG BALLET. WE ALL BELIEVED IN HIS TALENT and were ready to do whatever he asked us. He was very independent. I disagree with those who, while writing about him in those days, try to make us believe he was directed by someone, influenced, told what to do. Of course Balanchine was interested in everything that happened at that time in the theaters; many works of art made an impression, but he already knew his way. I remember how impressed we all were when the Goleizovsky company came to Petrograd in 1922. We saw his dances (I remember in particular *Salome)* and late one night went to his hotel to tell him how interested we were. He was very kind to us, but still I don't believe George was imitating him. I personally became very interested in Foregger's "machine dances." I even went for a while to work with Foregger but soon got disappointed. I don't think Balanchivadze cared for Foregger as much as I did.

Some of Balanchivadze's dances were versions of old, well-known works —for instance, his *Dying Swan.* The movements were different from Fokine's version, more angular, and the costume was different. As I remember it, it had something oriental in it, maybe even trousers, though I may be wrong.

I recall a solo called *Valse Triste:* a girl rushing about pursued by something dreadful, maybe Death. Lydia Ivanova danced it. Later, when she died in a boat accident, we all felt it was a premonition. I also remember two group works I took part in, *Marche Funèbre* to Chopin and *The Twelve.* We were asymmetrically moving groups with no real soloists; at times one dancer detached from the group and performed a combination of movements, as if pronouncing a "sentence," then disappeared into the group. The choreography was fluid and strictly subordinated to the music, one pattern running into the other with strict musical and choreographical logic.

Our dance group performed while a group of students chanted Alexander Blok's poem, "The Twelve." What we did was not pantomime, illustrating the text, but a dance. The dance had movements very much like Russian folk dances. The rhythm was difficult to grasp. Before performing it to Blok's text, we had many rehearsals with Balanchivadze counting for us.

BORIS

KOCHNO

Librettist and writer, born in Moscow in 1904, Kochno met Serge

Diaghilev in 1921 and served as his secretary and artistic collabora-

tor until 1929. He continued to work with Balanchine on ballets and

musical comedy and founded with him Les Ballets 1933. In 1946,

Kochno founded Les Ballets des Champs-Elysées with Roland Petit.

He is the author of Diaghilev and the Ballets Russes *(1970)*

and Christian Bérard *(1987).*

I Remember Balanchine

IT WAS FORTUNATE FOR BOTH BALANCHINE AND ME THAT HE JOINED DIAGHILEV. WE hit it off together right away. He was exactly the same age as I was. We were like brothers. To Alexandra Danilova, as well, I was close—we were very young kids. I was there when Diaghilev auditioned Balanchine and his little group. I remember Balanchine danced a pas de deux with Danilova. I have a photograph of the dance somewhere, Balanchine lifting up Danilova, who covered him with her skirt.

Balanchine wasn't interested at all in money. But he had a cashier in Vladimir Dimitriev. Dimitriev tried to make people believe that he was the inspiration behind Balanchine's work, but he was a cashier. Thanks to him, Balanchine, Geva, Danilova, and Efimov were able to leave Russia. George was always grateful to Dimitriev for this. After a certain time George did not have a need for Dimitriev. But Dimitriev could never let George alone.

From the beginning, I thought it was exceptional that Balanchine, such a great person, could be so colorless. Perhaps he changed later in life, but when I knew him, from his arrival at the Ballets Russes until 1933 when he went to the United States, he had an absolutely colorless personality. Some people, when you see them on the street, are so magnified that they fill up the street by their presence. Others may be great, but they do not correspond to our vision of a great person. George was like that.

Balanchine had no intimacy with Diaghilev, no closeness. There was a kind of mutual understanding, but Balanchine was not a member of Diaghilev's family. He was more of a *naïf,* surprisingly blessed, but a guest. Diaghilev was more intimate with Nijinsky and Massine, but not with Balanchine, Nijinska, and Fokine.

Nijinska was not pleased that Balanchine had joined the company as a choreographer. But George was absolutely indifferent toward her and Massine. Massine was perhaps a little more important, but Balanchine was Balanchine with Dimitriev in his corner. As long as he could do his own work, he was indifferent. This was unusual: to have such a colorless personality and to be exactly what you want to be! From time to time George was very humble. You could never tell what he would say. When somebody called him a creator, he would answer, "But the only creator is God." If someone asked him what he thought of such-and-such a choreographer, he would say, "And who *are* the other choreographers?"

Diaghilev wanted to have another Russian choreographer at the time George came to us. Kasyan Goleizovsky was well known at the time, but Diaghilev couldn't get him. I think Diaghilev expected to engage George more as a dancer than a choreographer, at the beginning. He did not know Balanchine's capacities and thought, "We will see what kind of choreographer this is." In the few ballets he danced, Balanchine was wonderful. He liked to be comical, and sometimes he overdid it.

So it was a wonderful surprise when Diaghilev, in order to try out this young man as a choreographer, asked him to do *Le Chant du Rossignol.* Massine had done a complicated version of this Stravinsky score which was never understood by the public. And so Balanchine did his first work, which was an excellent job. You cannot imagine the appearance of Markova in *Rossignol.* Matisse did a new costume for her as the Nightingale, white and covered with diamonds. The first appearance of Markova was in an enormous cage carried by four boys; inside, in a frenzy, she made all of her diamonds shine. It was an unforgettable performance. And that was the revelation of Balanchine—and Markova too.

Diaghilev realized that with Balanchine he would not have to make a new choreographer. He had made Nijinsky and Massine choreographers but now he *had* one in Balanchine. Diaghilev felt that he would not have to explain the music to Balanchine and what could be done with it; this was part of Balanchine's knowledge. Diaghilev trusted him entirely. Balanchine knew what he was doing from the beginning.

After *Rossignol,* Balanchine did *La Pastorale* to my scenario; it was a sensation too. George trusted me enormously. I would give him my ideas of what a ballet should be, and he would try to understand. He knew that I admired his work and he trusted my intelligence. We had two very different temperaments.

Prodigal Son began as a musical score by Prokofiev, but Prokofiev's scenario was absolutely stupid. I thought at the time that Diaghilev wanted a ballet with an idea that would be simple and as well known as *Romeo and Juliet;* and it came to me to suggest *Prodigal Son.*

Balanchine and I did a number of ballets in which parties occur. One was *Cotillon,* another, the same year, was *Le Bourgeois Gentilhomme.* It is difficult to revive ballets such as these, which were so typical of their time. How can you revive a dead horse (and a ballet *is* a kind of horse)? When Balanchine and I did *Cotillon,* it was done with a certain ease, in joy and friendship and the enthusiasm of Bérard, Balanchine, and myself. It was not necessary to "interpret" this ballet—it was not in any rigid sense a dream narrative. Most important, I think, is the way fate presents itself in Balanchine's ballets. The ethic of a Balanchine ballet—the rich possibilities, the suggestions, in the midst of nothing much happening—is more important than explaining the ballet as a "dream." The ballet provides another floor for us to live on for a moment, a higher floor on which we briefly live. This has nothing to do with mysticism. At the time that I knew him, Balanchine never exposed his religious beliefs. He was simply religious.

After the first performance of *Cotillon* in Monte Carlo, Balanchine, Bérard, and I went to the bar of the Chatham Hotel. It was time for the fireworks, which they perform on the beach on the national day, to begin. Balanchine, for the first time, suddenly became serious, became grand, and said to me, "I feel tonight we have really accomplished something."

Balanchine always wanted to be free to do what he wanted. That's why we did not stay longer with Blum and De Basil. We were comfortable with their company, but after the success of *Cotillon* and *Le Bourgeois Gentilhomme*, they began to impose their ideas and we didn't like it. That's why we left the Ballets Russes de Monte Carlo and started Les Ballets 1933. Balanchine wanted to do his own things. He knew perfectly well that nobody can be free at the Opéra, not even Serge Lifar. In the 1920s, Balanchine did not like Serge Lifar at all. But he knew that Lifar was the best interpreter for certain roles. It had nothing to do with liking people. In the Diaghilev days, Balanchine knew very well that Lifar's only hope was to rephrase Balanchine and to be a choreographer.

There was an element of inspiration about Balanchine's work. One can never tell where inspiration comes from. Balanchine would arrive at rehearsals as though he were just walking past the open door. He happened to see that the dancers were doing something, and he wanted to see what it was—when actually everyone was waiting for his arrival. But the appearance he gave was of someone just passing by. Balanchine was a passerby. Since he had to do some choreography, he would say, *"Bon jour."* He would take a chair. He never arrived with preparation for every note of music. He started doing this movement and that, showing the dancers what they had to do. Then at a certain moment it became something much more than just himself and his ideas. He started to work as a somnambulist, without knowing what he was doing. And all this was quickly done, with the greatest assurance. When he finished, he would sit and ask the dancers to show him what he had done, and he would seem to be very astonished. That is what I call inspiration. I think the inspiration went beyond individual interpreters—it could have been anyone. True, he liked some of his dancers personally. He would dine with them, or sleep with some. But the inspiration was not a question of who danced. George was quite an ordinary person except for his spirit. He was absolutely modest about his great gifts. He looked like a very ordinary person, but at times he was inspired. And afterward he returned to his own ordinary life. He did his best work unconsciously. He was astonished when he looked at people dancing what he showed them. Everything depended on the degree of inspiration, and his was the highest.

NINETTE

DE VALOIS

Born in 1898, studied with Field, Espinosa, Nicholas Legat, and Cecchetti. De Valois danced in 1922 for Massine and Lopokova before she joined Diaghilev's Ballets Russes as a soloist (1923–25 and again in 1926). Opening her own ballet school in London in 1926, she founded the Vic-Wells Ballet, later the Sadler's Wells Ballet, and finally the Royal Ballet (1956), of which she was the founding director. Author of Invitation to the Ballet *(1937),* Come Dance with Me *(1957), and* Step by Step *(1977), De Valois was made a Dame of the British Empire in 1951 and Companion of Honor in 1983.*

I WAS IN THE DIAGHILEV COMPANY AT THE TIME BALANCHINE, DANILOVA, GEVA, AND Efimov joined us. We still had Nijinska with us as choreographer. It was suggested that Diaghilev felt the young Balanchine would be a future choreographer. Which made an interesting moment. When we were in London, I and four or five other girls got a summons to go to Madame Serafima Astafieva's studio on a Sunday morning, because the young man joining the company was to arrange a piece of choreography on us for Diaghilev to see. So there we all went, angry about having our Sunday morning lost. Except we did like Balanchine, he was very sweet, only twenty. Of all things, he arranged a little number for the five or six of us to the *Funeral March* of Chopin. I only think of that music for royal family funerals. It seemed so strange that he used that. Diaghilev came in about two hours later and looked at it with Kochno and Grigoriev. That was the start.

Diaghilev had to have someone to follow Nijinska as choreographer. She had announced she was leaving. And here was this young man. When he arrived with the company in the South of France, they gave him a lot of ballets to do in the operas. He arranged a lovely pas de trois for me, Danilova, and Doubrovska. I've forgotten the opera, but it was a beautiful dance, I've always remembered it. It was just a straight pas de trois in a little *opéra-ballet.* Choreographers usually don't take any trouble with jobs like that. Balanchine didn't have to! It was quite a joke to him, the whole thing. He just did it. It was all there. (Later, when he went to the Metropolitan Opera in New York, it was disastrous. He couldn't live with them, they wouldn't let him do anything.)

The Russian producer of the operas was very struck with Balanchine. We had to listen to an oration of praise for Balanchine in Russian the day after the premiere of the Ravel *L'Enfant et les Sortilèges.* We were all overawed. But I happened to look around, and Balanchine was in hysterics. It didn't mean anything to him. He thought the man was terribly funny.

Diaghilev of course saw everything Balanchine did. He was a new little sprig of a choreographer for Diaghilev. Remember, Diaghilev had had four choreographers: Fokine, Nijinsky, Massine, and Nijinska. None of them stayed very long; Massine had the longest reign. But Balanchine stayed until Diaghilev's death. Balanchine was an independent person, we didn't know his views—he just took the job of choreographer and did it. We loved him for it because he was such a relaxed person. Quite beyond his being so brilliant, he was so easy, you were never nervous when you were working with him. He didn't get you into a state of nerves as perhaps even Nijinska could. There was none of that at all. He was a friend, you were working for a friend. That was very nice for us all and, young as he was, it was charming.

Danilova was lovely; Geva was a beautiful dancer too. It was new blood in the place. And then Balanchine with all his talent. We were all very good friends.

Balanchine made a big change in the Diaghilev company. He brought back far more classicism. We had had a *demi-caractère* period with Massine. Nijinska started to move out of that, but Balanchine brought back a lot of pure classicism. When he arrived, he was horrified with the dancing of the company. He didn't think any of the dancers were any good. He was looking for classical dancers, and such a lot of them were character dancers.

Nijinska was taking the classes when he joined us. He took the class but Balanchine had his own views. Pedagogically, he was most knowledgeable, particularly for a choreographer, because most choreographers are not so interested in teaching. He was excellent at that. He was good at mime, too. We used to rush in and watch because he was so funny in *Petrouchka.* He was the old man on the balcony. It was marvelous what he put into improvisation in that role.

I don't think there was great rapport between Diaghilev and Balanchine. Massine did much more what he was told. Balanchine knew what he wanted to do, where he wanted to go, all the time. I may be quite wrong. During the most important period, when Balanchine really took over, I was not there. Balanchine was just a boy who had come into the company and whom Diaghilev had his eye on. But I saw everything they did in all their seasons in London. It was a Balanchine era. Balanchine managed to dominate the Diaghilev company just as Nijinska and Fokine and Massine had done. He was the last of the great ones who gave the Diaghilev ballet its particular aura. It was marvelous, too, the way Balanchine could move on later to something like a Cochran review. He was very adaptable, with a great sense of theater.

The Balanchine ballet I admire most is *Orpheus.* If you see a good performance of *Orpheus,* it's lovely. I have always loved it.

ALICIA

MARKOVA*

A student of Astafieva and dancer with Diaghilev's Ballets Russes, Markova was the heroine of Balanchine's Le Chant du Rossignol (1925). Danced with Ballet Rambert, the Camargo Society, and the Vic-Wells Ballet (1931), becoming its ballerina in 1933. Frederick Ashton created Les Rendezvous for her, and she was first British Giselle and Odette-Odile. With Anton Dolin founded Markova-Dolin Ballet in 1935. Danced with American Ballet Theatre (1941–44; 1945–46), where Antony Tudor created Romeo and Juliet for her. Guest with many ensembles internationally; with Dolin founded Festival Ballet (1949). Retired in 1963, and directed the Metropolitan Opera Ballet until 1969. Her eightieth birthday was celebrated at a gala performance in London in December 1990.

* Alicia Markova was interviewed by Joel Lobenthal and Francis Mason.

THE FIRST TIME I MET GEORGE WAS WHEN HE CAME TO AUDITION ME WITH DIAGHILEV and Kochno. I was fourteen. I had seen George dance at the old Empire Theater when he and his small company, the Russian State Dancers, performed there. I was very involved in classical training at the time, and remember a pas de deux danced barefoot. There were fabulous lifts. I was most intrigued. Never did I think that I'd ever meet those dancers. Then Diaghilev brought Balanchine to audition me. I didn't realize why. I didn't realize that Diaghilev, Balanchine, and Kochno had already discussed the Stravinsky ballet *Le Chant du Rossignol.* Balanchine saw my capabilities; I did everything I ever knew, including acrobatic things, anything that came into Balanchine's head. When Diaghilev said, "Do you think it'll be all right?" it was for George to say yes or no, and George said, "Yes." I was his first baby ballerina.

George tried to help me, show me, but he was a *very* quiet person. At that time he didn't speak any English. I didn't speak anything *but* English, but somehow we got along. George always showed respect for the dancers. If he was rarely critical, it would be in the form of sarcasm that would cut like a knife.

I joined the ballet in January, leaving London for Monte Carlo with Ninette de Valois, and when we gave the performances in the Salle Ganne in 1925, Diaghilev gave me variations to dance in the divertissement: the *Pizzicato Polka* from *Sylvia* and the Rubinstein *Valse Caprice,* which George rearranged for me. George and Tamara Geva did a fabulous pas de deux, and I was so excited! It was the one I had seen at the Empire.

When I arrived in Monte Carlo, Diaghilev decided I should do the White Act of *Swan Lake* for the divertissement. We had to find a partner short enough for me. Efimov was chosen and George rehearsed me. About that there was quite a contretemps between Grigoriev, the regisseur, and George. George had just come from Russia and was trying to give me a more recent version. I'd never seen *Swan Lake* (the West hadn't seen it then). When Diaghilev came in he said, "Oh, don't worry," because I was getting tired and near tears. "We'll have a rehearsal tomorrow." He said he would bring in somebody to decide which version we would use and to help me. The following evening he arrived with Kschessinska, the retired ballerina who had been the Tsar's favorite and was teaching in Paris. She coached me. Balanchine's version was different only in musical details, accents. His accent was always up. I've used that version to this day.

George did all the opera ballets at Monte Carlo. The very first opera ballet I was in was the world premiere of the Ravel *L'Enfant et les Sortilèges.* He gave me the smoke/fire role and had me pirouetting like mad out of the fireplace; and in the second scene I was the little squirrel. I used to turn like a top, which George adored. I could do double turns in the air, like the boys; he used them as Ashton did later in *Façade*.

Balanchine never got excited. During parties for the company he always used to sit alone or look immediately for the piano and just sit and play. For George, it was music always. Since I was the baby and didn't dance at parties, I often used to sit on the piano bench next to him. I loved the music, and I'd sit and just listen while he played. I didn't talk a lot, and it didn't matter. George never said much. One knew what he felt when one's name went up for a new ballet. I took it that one had passed muster. His corrections took the form of, "Why do you do so-and-so?" That's all. Then you would suddenly think: *"Am* I doing so-and-so?" "Yes, you did." "All right, if it isn't good, next time I'll try and remember."

Rossignol was an isolated role, a little bird, and it didn't involve partnering. Balanchine would demonstrate what he wanted me to do. Stravinsky used to come to rehearsals. At the beginning the music was *very* difficult. Stravinsky played the score for us, and then they got a pianola and we had it on a roll. Stravinsky conducted the ballet at one point. Imagine, at fourteen, I was dressed by Matisse and Stravinsky was my conductor! I should be terribly spoiled after that! We always had fine conductors. I was always *very* fussy. The composer and the musicality were important. We were brought up that way. None of this business of the conductor waiting for the dancer. I think that was why I always enjoyed working with George.

A choreographer or a painter must clean the slate, forget his old works, if he is to start anything new. That's what George and Massine used to ask me to remember. I have a good memory. I think I could recall the choreography for the first variation in *Rossignol*. The action of the ballet wasn't divertisse-ment style. It went straight through. But there was the marvelous pas de deux between Death and the Nightingale.

Rossignol was filled with inventions that have become commonplace today, because subsequent choreographers have stolen them from George. George even stole from himself. For example, when you see two boys take the girl, slide her along the floor, and then lift her into a big *jeté*, that's taken from George. The first time he used it was in *L'Enfant et les Sortilèges*. Choura was the Butterfly, and she would come running in and the men would catch her and slide and lift, like a butterfly suddenly darting and landing. George always had ideas. He wanted to see whether something would work.

La Chatte I danced with Lifar. When I followed Nikitina in the role, George redid the variation. He made it a very difficult one for me, with syncopations and corkscrew pirouettes. The other dancers said such things would ruin their legs, but I was young and willing to try. It didn't hurt me.

George's ballets in the operas were always interesting. At one big gala it was decided that the Schubert *Marche Militaire* would be danced by thirty-two girls, like the chorus girls on Broadway. George adored chorus girls, even though he'd never been to the States. I remember we were all sizes and we were all in it: myself, Tchernicheva, Choura, and Doubrovska. But the way George arranged it, it looked as though we were all the same height. He had us all on pointe, with chiffon skirts, pale pink shoes and tights, and with shields over the chiffon and swords and helmets. He had us marching on pointe. We started out and he gave us a little pat, and we entered like chorus girls one after the other and bent our swords down. That was an effort! There was one performance only.

George was a wonderful dancer and a fine partner, too, until his knee operation. After that he did character roles—for example, the old man in *Three-Cornered Hat.* He used to play the old showman who stands all the way through *Petrouchka* until he's called to get the Magician and the body. In *Boutique Fantasque* Balanchine was the King of Spades in the mazurka. He did his own makeup and used to draw spades on his cheeks. Once, when Sir Thomas Beecham was conducting, Balanchine came on in *Tricorne* with a little goatee. And earlier, to see him dance the *lezghinka,* the Georgian dance, that was out-of-this-world excitement.

George wanted me to learn Terpsichore in *Apollo* when he came back to Ballet Theatre in the 1940s, but I couldn't because I was doing Tudor's *Romeo and Juliet.* Hurok decided that the least important ballet for me at the box office was the Balanchine, so he put someone else into it.

The last time I saw George was at a big dinner the Royal Society gave in London, when Lincoln Kirstein received the medal of the society from Prince Philip. We were having champagne, and George arrived. Ninette de Valois and I had not been sure he would attend. I was *so* happy to see him. He used to tease me. Because of *La Chatte* he used to say, "Where's little pussycat?" (Also, I loved cats.) The first thing he said to me that evening, as always, was, "Are you married?" Every time he met me he used to quiz me, "No marriage?" That last time I laughed and said, "You don't realize. I'm still waiting for you to ask!" We had the most wonderful roars of laughter together. When they announced dinner, he turned to me and gave me his arm.

ULLA

POULSEN*

*Born in Copenhagen in 1905, Ulla Poulsen studied at the Royal
Danish Ballet School and joined the Royal Danish Ballet in 1921.
She became a soloist in 1923. As guest ballerina she performed with a
number of European companies and returned to the Royal Danish
Ballet to dance from 1934 to 1939. She taught ballet in Denmark
until 1947.*

* Ulla Poulsen was interviewed by Mary Fraker.

I MET BALANCHINE IN LONDON IN 1929. I WAS TAKING LESSONS FROM KARSAVINA, the Russian ballerina, who had been with Diaghilev for many years. My brother-in-law, who was going to be head of the Royal Theater in Copenhagen, called me on the telephone: "We need somebody to make something new for the Danish ballet. Do you know anybody or can you get suggestions from Madame Karsavina?" Karsavina told me, "I know a young dancer and ballet master who has been with the Diaghilev company, George Balanchine."

I don't think Balanchine appreciated the Bournonville style then but he agreed to come to Copenhagen, and I was glad because our ballet was boring at the time. We only had some old Bournonville ballets; I wanted to see and learn something new. Balanchine said he would bring some of the best-known of the Diaghilev ballets—*Schéhérazade, The Three-Cornered Hat, La Boutique Fantasque*—and two of his own, *Barabau,* a very grotesque little ballet, and also *Apollon Musagète.*

He came to the Royal Theater at the start of the 1930 season. Our ballet was not on the level of the Russian ballet in technique, although we had our own Bournonville technique, which is not easy. But it was so different from what Balanchine had been used to!

Before the first ballet evening there was a special performance, and Balanchine choreographed a trio for Elna Lassen, himself, and me. His own role was not very big. He had stopped dancing because of his health, but I know it was something that he loved. *Liebestraum* was about a man who loves two women, but one he loves more. I was the woman he was leaving behind. It was a very emotional piece. First, we were together, then he didn't know which one he wanted. The dance was more mime, not so much a pas de deux. He had come to the Danish ballet and found that we had much expression. So he managed to make ballets with mime and emotion, instead of the Russian style with the brilliant dancing, turns, lifts, and technical solos.

At Christmastime, Balanchine and I danced *Le Spectre de la Rose,* which I had learned from Karsavina in London. Every year at that time there was a charity evening for the poor of Copenhagen at Concert Pamail near the Gallery Theater. They asked us to contribute something. Balanchine said, "We can do *Le Spectre* together for the charity concert." He made the male variation a little easier. There was no window for the big leap, but Balanchine did it very well.

He was clever to teach us emotional dances. The only one that was technical was *Apollon Musagète. Schéhérazade* was not too difficult but it was beautifully made and had a big success because it was oriental, something the Danish audience had never seen.

La Boutique Fantasque was amusing with its different dolls, and the Spanish ballet, *The Three-Cornered Hat,* was also new. I had just been in Spain taking lessons in Spanish dancing, so it was not so difficult for me. Spanish dancing in Bournonville was almost on pointe, but Balanchine used real Spanish dancing.

At the special performance following the untimely death of Elna Lassen, Balanchine danced the male role in *Chopiniana.* It was the only time that he danced it. He knew the ballet from his years with Diaghilev, and I don't think he changed anything. It was performed only the one evening. He danced very beautifully. At all the points where Elna Lassen should have danced, the spotlight was empty. Elna Lassen was a beautiful dancer and a really fine person. She was very light, and she jumped very well. Balanchine was especially moved when she died, a suicide, to all our sorrow.

Balanchine was only in Copenhagen for a season and could not really take over. The company needed someone who knew the Bournonville style, who had grown up with Bournonville. That was Harald Lander, who was just returning from America.

Balanchine also staged Richard Strauss's *Josephslegende* (1931). It had movement that we were not used to, but there was a great deal of mime. I was in an Egyptian garment. Unlike some of the other dancers, I could move in my costumes. I remember that Balanchine wanted me to sit on Børge Ralov's shoulder. Ralov was small and very thin. I said, "Oh, I've never done that, not in Bournonville. What would Bournonville think?" It was a sexy ballet. When Joseph would not go to bed with Potiphar's Wife, she was very angry. This was quite new for me and for the critics. They said it was new for the Sylphide! They didn't think I could do it. As Potiphar's Wife, I had to whip Joseph to get some excitement. It was rather terrible, because Joseph didn't want to have an affair with Potiphar's Wife, so she had to get it another way. I could act. The only thing I couldn't do was a real Balanchine ballet, because I had weak feet.

Balanchine's *Barabau* was not liked by the Danish audience. It was an amusing, grotesque little ballet. We liked it because it reminded us of *La Sylphide* and some of Bournonville, but the audience wanted to see another kind of ballet. The critics wrote terrible things, and it was taken off. But the other Balanchine ballets continued to be danced for some time. Then Harald Lander put all of his own ballets into the repertory.

Balanchine and I were very good friends for many years after he left. When his wife, Tanaquil LeClercq, was ill with polio, we went to Copenhagen to be with him.

TAMARA

TOUMANOVA

Danced as child with Anna Pavlova's company and at Paris Opéra.

Trained with Preobrajenska and danced Balanchine's ballets in De

Basil's Ballets Russes de Monte Carlo (1931–32): Le Bourgeois

Gentilhomme, La Concurrence, *and* Cotillon. *She was one of*

his "baby ballerinas." For Balanchine's Les Ballets 1933, he created

roles for her in the first Mozartiana, *in* Les Songes, *and in*

Fastes. *In 1941 he created* Balustrade *for her (Original Ballet*

Russe). At the Paris Opéra in 1947 she created the adagio in Balan-

chine's Le Palais de Cristal *(later called* Symphony in C) *and*

in his revival of Le Baiser de la Fée. *Appeared in motion pictures,*

including Tonight We Sing, Invitation to the Dance, *and*

Torn Curtain.

BALANCHINE WAS CLOSE NOT ONLY TO ME BUT TO MY FAMILY. TO UNDERSTAND, you must know a little about them. My mother was not a dancer: her family would not permit it even though they loved ballet. She and her parents used to go to the ballet at the Maryinsky Theatre in St. Petersburg, where they were all great admirers of Olga Preobrajenska. As a young girl Mama made up her mind that one day her daughter would be taught by Preobrajenska and become a great ballerina. Soon after she married my father, an engineer and colonel in the Tsar's army, they were separated by war and revolution. I was christened on a train as my mother tried to reach Vladivostok, which was still White Russian. Reunited there with my father, we moved to Shanghai, but Mama wanted to go to Paris. My father had been a brilliant success as an engineer in Shanghai and won prizes; he wanted to go to Cairo, which had need of engineers. We went to Cairo but Mama couldn't stand it. "Our child must grow up in Paris." So Papa left everything, and we came to Paris. There Mama found that Preobrajenska was teaching in Paris. Mama took me to her and wanted me to start studying. Preobrajenska said, "She is too small. In Russia we start training at seven, eight, nine years. How can I start her at five?" Mama said, "Please, Madame Preobrajenska, try." After the second lesson she told my mother, "All right, leave her. I will take care of her." Soon I was dancing for Pavlova and appeared at the Opéra. In 1929, Tatiana Chamié and Nathalie Branitskaya, who were in the Diaghilev ballet, invited Mama and me to see the Diaghilev company at the Sarah Bernhardt Theater. We saw Nicolas Nabokov's *Ode* with Danilova and Doubrovska and the Tchelitchew costumes. I was so excited because *Apollon* was on the bill. Between the *Ode* and *Apollon Musagète,* I went backstage. There I saw Diaghilev, Balanchine, Lifar, and Tchelitchew. Tchelitchew said, "This is the little girl I saw at Paris Opéra. She's incredible." Balanchine sort of looked at me and said to the group, "That's too young, too young. In Russia we didn't do that." Two years later Balanchine came to Preobrajenska's studio. She had known him from his childhood, when she auditioned him for the Imperial Ballet School. Balanchine was a shy man, but they kissed. She said to him, "Let us show you what my students can do: Here is Tamara Toumanova, Baronova, and Stepanova." When I danced, Balanchine was very enthusiastic. Preobrajenska said, "Ask her to do anything. She will do." Balanchine asked me what kind of music I liked and my interests. I said, "For me, music is very important." He said, "Do you know music well?" I said, "I can play for you." I sat at the piano and played Mozart. Then Preobrajenska said, "Would you like her to do an improvisation?" Balanchine turned his head a little bit on the side and said, "All right. I would like it." Balanchine was taken by me and said to Preobrajenska, "May I talk to the young lady?" Preobrajenska said, "Yes, but she has a mother who is an absolutely wonderful woman. May I call her?" So Mama was summoned. Balanchine said, "I will take her into *Orphée*. I am doing at Théâtre Mogador *Orphée aux Enfers*, the Offenbach, and I think your daughter is extraordinary, and I will take her and give her a very important part. Doubrovska will be the star, and your daughter will be the second star."

The next day when I went to class Balanchine arrived again, this time with Colonel de Basil. Again I danced for him. Balanchine said to Mama, "After seeing Tamara, it is difficult for me to think that she should start at the Mogador. I think she is a potential true ballerina. And I am going to take her in the Ballets Russes de Monte Carlo that we are putting together now. This is Colonel de Basil, the director of the company. Irina Baronova I will take for *Orphée*."

Balanchine was an extraordinary creature. How he took care of me: he used to tell Mama what to do, what food to give me, not to overdo! He presented me to the greatest individuals; this was the beginning of my true artistic career. I really think that Balanchine looked upon me as his own child. He would play with me. After a rehearsal of *Cotillon,* if I had done a very good rehearsal or performance, he would go to Pasquet, a wonderful patisserie in Monte Carlo, and buy me a magnificent chocolate that I could never afford and give it to me and say, "You must eat that. That's good for you." On my twelfth birthday he gave me a little gold watch from Cartier. Boris Kochno gave me an ivory elephant. Balanchine always had great respect for me as an artist, and he made great demands on me as a worker. He treated me on the same professional level. But so kind. He never raised his voice. He was always, to the end of his days, so quiet, with so much tenderness. To me he became the emblem, the ideal.

Don't think that I didn't notice how all the ladies were in love with him. Not long ago I found a diary that I wrote at the time, and I say in it, "Oh, oh, oh, Tamaritchka, careful, careful!" Because I understood that this was an appealing gentleman to all those ladies. They were flirting with him and he would take one or another out to dinner. One day Mama and I were going back home after the performance, and we had to pass the Café de Paree. I said to Mama, "Someday I will be sitting as well in that Café de Paree." Mama said, "Yes, yes, yes, when you are grown." And Balanchine was sitting there with one of the dancers and with Dimitriev. As I was passing, Balanchine said, "Good night, have a good sleep because tomorrow we have a lot of work to do." I said to Mama, "This is disgusting. Here I am the ballerina of the company, and I can't even sit in the café." Mama said, "Young girls of your position do not sit in the café." But Balanchine knew that I was sensitive about such things. I remember a performance of *Tannhäuser* with the great French tenor Georges Thill. Thill saw me on the stage and Balanchine called to me. He introduced me to Thill, saying, "This is Miss Tamara Toumanova, the ballerina of the company." Thill looked at me and said to Balanchine, "George, this is impossible, this is a child." Balanchine said, "And what a child!" My feeling for Balanchine is not only for a great master but for the way he treated me as a human being.

Right after *Cotillon,* Balanchine did *La Concurrence* (1932) for me, with Derain and Auric. During rehearsals Balanchine would not only demonstrate the steps, he would explain the idea. For example, every time he did a choreography for me, even a brio choreography, there was always a nostalgia, a sort of *tristesse.*

I first appeared in *Concurrence* as a vision in a long blue dress with a large bow on the left shoulder. Then later I changed costumes and became the young girl. There was a competition of *fouettés,* and on each side of me there was a dancer competing to see who could do the most turns. When the competition was over, the girl was alone, the lights dimmed, and I walked about on pointe, then went down to my knees and was very sad. You really didn't know if the girl was real or not. I have a feeling that she was an illusion; she didn't belong to the crowd of the *concurrence.* There was always a tremendous fantasy in everything Balanchine did. I think that's why he touched the audience.

In Balanchine's *Le Bourgeois Gentilhomme,* I danced Lucille, who does not want to marry her intended. David Lichine was extraordinary as the Moor; he had such a personality, and Balanchine caught his quality. Lucille is terrified and a little wild, like in the Strauss score. But by the end she accepts the betrothal. Balanchine made a pas de deux in which Cléonte put his arms about me and I would shiver: it was in the music. My whole body was shivering. No one had choreographed such a moment before.

In the summer of 1932, Balanchine started new ballets for his Les Ballets 1933, ballets like *Mozartiana,* and even *Errante,* which I did not dance. *Errante* was actually done in a style for me, with long hair, very dramatic. The woman tried to find her fate, she went through much suffering, and she could not find peace. She could not find what she was looking for. I adored that ballet, but Balanchine called me and said, "Tamaritchka, I have to talk to you about something very important. We have a very hard time with money." I said, "Yes, I know." And he said, "There is a lady by the name of Tilly Losch, and her husband is very, very rich. And he is now going to be the supporting power of the company." That was like a knife in my heart. Tears started to fall. And Balanchine said, "Tamaritchka, don't cry. I cried so many times before I could think how to tell you. But we have no alternative." But Balanchine spared me having to show the role to Madame Losch. He himself taught her the role.

When I joined Balanchine in Paris for his Les Ballets 1933, he played the piano for practice rehearsals. He was so charming and full of life. Each movement of *Mozartiana* was beautifully dovetailed, like lace. Bérard dressed me in a black tutu, not at all short. It was between a Degas length and a short tutu, up to the top of the knee. There were ostrich feathers in the hat. I represented a magnificent racehorse, proud, without putting the nose up, but with that look of nobility, pride with technique. This is what Balanchine gave me. There was no chichi. It was elegant, strong, magnificent, without any smiles. Balanchine did the most difficult footwork in that ballet. Everything was with dignity, but fast, exciting, alive.

Tchelitchew did fourteen portraits of me during that season. I have one with a magnificent inscription. The other thirteen were bought by Edward James. Tchelitchew had great admiration and friendship with Balanchine. He would say to me, "You listen to him. You listen to Balanchine and you listen to Mama."

Balanchine always thought he was a good comedian. He thought he was very funny. But I never thought of him that way. He had his own tremendous sense of humor, but he was better in serious or sad roles. One day Jasinsky, who was dancing *L'Errante* with Tilly Losch, got sick. Balanchine took over the role. He had not done one classroom exercise for months, but he performed this difficult role with wonderful innovations. The Tchelitchew costume was tights up to the waistline and nothing above. Balanchine was in such good form that he danced the role as if he had just finished another ballet and now was doing *L'Errante.* But this was not a comedy, it was more a mystical ballet. I think Balanchine was very mystical.

He was religious. This feeling that he had for a higher power made a strong link with Mama. Still, he was down to earth. He liked to cook, he liked to buy beautiful things, but I think basically with Balanchine there was a deep religious feeling. From the beginning he showed a capacity to remove himself from all of us. Was it in his work? Was it during dinner? Was it during a walk or discussions? He could remove himself. I think the quietness with which he worked, choreographed, inspired everyone, had a great deal to do with his religion.

Balanchine had two things: he had a tremendous zest for life, and he also had a gift to retire within his own world, to just go away and not hear anything. I think that's why the music helped him tremendously, by allowing him to sit down at the piano and really get away from the world with that music. I understand that. Since my very young days, music has been a part of me. Without music, it's impossible.

I think Balanchine lived in his own world. I don't think many people really realized his sensitivity. And I am afraid that some people took advantage of it. Balanchine was a solitary person, very much apart. When he played the piano, he would not even know who existed. I heard him once at his apartment in Monte Carlo play Tchaikovsky. Mama and I were invited to dinner that evening, and we came early. Dimitriev was there. But Balanchine never even realized we were present. He played, little insects buzzing around him, and he didn't even notice. When he finished he turned and said, "Ah, hello." We didn't breathe, none of us breathed. And after dinner he said that he had a gift for me. We all got very excited. He gave me a recording of the "Symphonie Pathétique." I have the old records still, they are not broken. Perhaps he was preparing to do a ballet for me to the music. I think that Balanchine saw in himself and in me the same qualities.

He was a brilliant man who knew what other people thought. He loved to see them think differently than himself. He liked the idea of having a game of thoughts. That's what he liked in me and Mama and Papa, because we stood our ground. When Papa said something in his military way, Balanchine enjoyed it because it brought him to a world he admired. He loved the military. Balanchine loved strength, the ability to keep yourself going. He thought like that himself. And he found in Papa an extraordinary knowledge of literature that he liked to discuss with him: Pushkin, Lermontov, Gontcharov, and Ivanov. I have books that he gave my father as presents: *Pique Dame* and *Eugen Onegin* in beautiful editions. Papa was very close to Balanchine, especially in 1939 in New York. Balanchine was then in a sentimental, difficult mood, very sad. Being the romantic that Balanchine was, he fell in love many times—perhaps not love but infatuation. He was open with Papa, knowing it would go no further.

He loved Mama very much. He was alone when he left Russia and before, he had no family. He loved Mama and Papa because he found a family. That is why he gave his love to us, because we had a very strong family tie. When I was married, even then Balanchine loved to be surrounded by us. It was his family.

I knew Balanchine when I was such a little girl, and I knew him when I became a grown-up, and I knew him when I married. I think that Balanchine had so much, he was like an ocean. I think the waves kept coming to him, waves of extraordinary creativity, always alive like an ocean. He would not rest, he was always interested in a new phase, new ways to express. Balanchine was Georgian and had a fullness of soul that was so abundant that he wanted to give more and more of the things of his life so that they would not disappear after him. That must be why he had so much enthusiasm, ideas and love of talk, why he created so many things for young dancers. Even when he was eating he had enthusiasm. Balanchine, unlike other choreographers, did not settle down with the coming of age. He wanted to have more waves, more electricity out of himself. I think he saw kinship with me, with my *tristesse*, with my being part Georgian. Because his sister Tamara died, I have a feeling that he looked upon me like his sister.

When Balanchine came to America in 1933 and I did not, he was very hurt. Actually, Colonel de Basil tricked me into joining his company—I thought that Balanchine would be there too. Colonel de Basil wanted revenge against Vladimir Dimitriev, Balanchine's manager. Balanchine was so grateful to Dimitriev, who had helped him get out of Russia. But actually Dimitriev was himself possessive and vengeful. As a result of the misunderstanding caused by De Basil and Dimitriev, Balanchine would not speak to me when I did come to America. Lucia Davidova was the one who brought us back together again as friends.

Balanchine didn't like to see me taking unnecessary medicines. For example, if I took an aspirin in front of him, he would make such a face. I remember that at one time he was smoking quite a lot, but later he looked upon cigarettes almost as a vice. I worked with Balanchine, studied with him, took his lessons—and never in my life was I hurt by his instruction. Every time I came to New York, I would run to the School of American Ballet and look forward to his classes. I've never had any tendonitis from taking classes with him. I improved immensely, I had more speed, I had more authority, and—more important—I had a freedom of the body from the speed. Usually, when you do precise things, speedy things, your body gets cramped. But with Balanchine it was absolute harmony of arms and body while your feet were doing those extraordinary little Scarlatti-like details. After three weeks of study with him, in the fourth week you realized that you had made a step forward, you could do more than you could before.

Balanchine loved teaching. He brought a great deal of enthusiasm to his teaching, and he was proud when the teaching was successful. He did not like to teach people who did not understand him. Let's face it—not everybody understands. He loved teaching people who understood what he was after.

Balanchine was proud of his work on Broadway. He took me to see *On Your Toes, I Married an Angel, Cabin in the Sky,* and *Where's Charley?* As I have said, he liked to have fun. Neither on Broadway nor in the movies did he work only to make money. He adored to do movies and shows. In 1936 I was too young and inexperienced for *On Your Toes,* so I was a bit shocked. Ray Bolger was extraordinary and Tamara Geva was marvelous in it. No one before or since has presented a star as he did Zorina. What Balanchine gave Vera Zorina and myself was the likeness of the sun and the moon. Both.

Balanchine had so many ideas that his collaborators gratefully took his suggestions for costuming and lighting. Larry Hart, a fantastic gentleman with ideas and a sharp intelligence, worshiped Balanchine.

I remember New York in 1941 and the excitement of a new Balanchine ballet. I had come back from Australia with the De Basil Original Ballet Russe and Balanchine did *Balustrade* for me with Stravinsky and Tchelitchew. I was dancing at the Fifty-first Street Theater. Balanchine and Stravinsky and Tchelitchew came to every one of my performances. I danced also *Swan Lake, Choreartium,* and *Symphonie Fantastique.* We were in the third week of the season when they came to my dressing room and said, "Tamaritchka, we decided that we want to give you a gift, a diamond necklace. The diamond necklace will be a ballet of the violin concerto of Stravinsky, and Tchelitchew will do the costumes and scenery, and you will be the one for whom it will be created." I said, "This is beyond anything I could ever dream." We began to rehearse the ballet. Balanchine brought the recording of the Samuel Dushkin performance. He played my part for me, and he said, "Tamaritchka, don't be alarmed by the sound because this is a very special sound, very clear, very pure sound, and you will understand it more when you start rehearsing it."

He said one day, "Stravinsky is dying to come to rehearsals. He wants to put his nose in, but I will not let him until it's done." When the piece was done, we went into the big rehearsal room, and Stravinsky came along with many other people, including Tchelitchew. Stravinsky was absolutely enchanted. He said, "George, I think this is the epitome of what I thought." He went into ecstasy.

When Balanchine and Stravinsky were together, they were like two incredible teachers. Balanchine would stand next to little Stravinsky, and they would walk together, Balanchine always saying, *"Da, da, da."* He never said, "No." I think that he became like a little boy in Stravinsky's presence.

Easter was early in 1941. Balanchine arranged for us to celebrate Easter in our suite at our hotel in New York. He ran out and bought all the food. I went to church with Papa. I remember we came home, and Balanchine said, "We've got to buy some little fish and a little bit of sour cream." Mama arranged everything with him on the table, I think Balanchine was grateful to religion for his own gifts. I remember when he came back from the 1962 tour to the Soviet Union with the New York City Ballet, he came to visit us in California, and he was so excited. I think he missed Russia very much; Russia for him was of tremendous importance.

He and Mama discussed Russia a great deal, and he and Papa talked of it too. Papa was much older than Balanchine. The relationship gave Balanchine a chance to feel that there was that old Russia. He always talked with

Papa like he was his son. After all, Balanchine loved his own father very much. And it was important for him to open his heart.

When I got married in 1944, I didn't tell Balanchine because he was in New York. Flying was not like it is today, especially in the middle of the war. My husband, Casey Robinson, liked Balanchine immensely, and Balanchine liked Casey. But I did not send him an invitation to the wedding because I planned to call him and say that I had been married. I was married in our church in California, the Russian Greek Orthodox church, the Virgin Mary Cathedral. The wedding was very *intime.* When I was standing at the altar after we were pronounced man and wife and receiving congratulations, suddenly I saw Balanchine. He came up to me and kissed me and congratulated Casey, even kissed him. And I said, "Georgi Melitonovich, how incredible. You are here." He said, "How can I miss the marriage of my daughter?"

Balanchine was invited back to the Paris Opéra by Roger Desormière, who had been one of Diaghilev's conductors. When Balanchine was in California in 1946, he said to me, "You know, I am going to Paris in 1947. Would you be interested to go?" At that time I was married and making films. Balanchine said, "Desormière didn't want to write you straightforwardly first, before asking me if he could write you and invite you." I said, "That would be magnificent." Five days later I got a letter from Desormière saying that they would be more than delighted if I would accept the contract to come to dance at the Paris Opéra for six months. I answered immediately that I would be delighted.

Balanchine loved Paris. He loved the Paris Opéra theater. He loved the grandeur of the *foyer de la danse.* He loved the surroundings. And I don't blame him. I think it's one of the most beautiful settings. And then he wanted to do ballets with me. He did *Serenade* first, cast with all Paris Opéra people. Then Balanchine said to me, "You know, Tamaritchka, I am going to do *Baiser de la Fée* and I want you to be the Bride." He augmented it for me and dressed me beautifully. At the end of the ballet he brought down a net curtain, and you could see the boy climbing up the staircase. I was looking for him, and the lights were made to look like ocean waves. I was taken by a wave, and I looked for the boy and tried to find him and could not. I would think that I had found him, but actually I would be looking into the audience. I would stand in arabesque and then cry. And again I couldn't find him, and at the end all the waves of the ocean took me. It was one of the most touching choreographies I have ever danced.

One day I got a call from the regisseur of the Opéra, who said, "Miss Toumanova, Balanchine is waiting for you at the rehearsal." I said, "What are we rehearsing?" And he said, *"Le Palais de Cristal,"* "the ballet of Balanchine to Bizet's Symphony in C." Balanchine had never said a word about it, not one word. So I dressed quickly, took a taxi, got to the Paris Opéra, dressed, went upstairs, and Balanchine was standing with his hand on his hip and looking at me with a half smile. I said to him in French, "Please excuse me, *maître,* I am late." And in Russian I said, "You didn't say anything to me about *Palais de Cristal.* I don't know what it is." He said, "You don't have to know. You just start rehearsing." So we rehearsed the pas de deux of the second movement, which he called "the black diamond." On opening night when I finished, lying back on my partner's knee, bending back to the audience, I was met with a dead silence. I said to myself, "My God, did they like it or not?" Suddenly the whole audience just screamed.

When Balanchine would bring his New York City Ballet to the Greek Theater in Los Angeles, he always called me and invited me to the ballet. He would wait for us outside the stage door so that we could come backstage and tell him what we thought. He was always so childlike and so adorable. Once at intermission he introduced us to Karin von Aroldingen. He said, "You know, this is Mama Toumanova. When Tamara and Mama were in Paris with me at the Paris Opéra in '47, Mama Toumanova used to break in Tamara's ballet shoes, soften them, so that Tamara would not suffer."

I would say to him after a performance in Los Angeles, "Oh, it was a wonderful performance," or "She was wonderful." He would look at me and sniff. He did not like to take compliments on anything he did not want to. I always called him after a performance on television, and he was so humble. He would say, "Did you really like it?" When he received the Kennedy Center Award, I called him up to congratulate him. "Georgi Melitonovich, you looked so magnificent." He said, "Really?" I said, "Yes, Georgi Melitonovich." He was a little puffed up. And I said, "Georgi Melitonovich, you were proud and magnificent, like always." He was so happy.

Today there is no great master. There was Diaghilev and there was Balanchine. There were Fokine and Massine. They're all gone. Now everyone does his own version of the classics. The dancers dance beautifully. The new choreography is fantastic. But there is no guidance. You have to have a tremendous strength over yourself. You have to learn—you cannot just go and dance. You have to think what you are doing: how you are dressed, how the role absorbs you. When you do the ballet classics, you can polish them, you can do them a little stronger, but you cannot take away the design, the beauty of what was created by Petipa and other geniuses. You cannot take the Beethoven Seventh Symphony and rewrite it. The Seventh Symphony of Beethoven is the Seventh Symphony. It stays forever. Dancing itself is fantastic today, but the something extra is not there. It is missing.

When my father died, I was at home in Bel Air, and Balanchine came out to see me. I had lost weight at that time and could not listen to music or anything. Balanchine came, and we were sitting in our breakfast room overlooking the garden. It was beautiful there, looking out on the garden through the French windows. We were sitting having coffee. Balanchine said, "You see, Tamaritchka, Papa is not gone. The sun shines. He is here with you." That is Balanchine, the fineness of his heart, of his spirit.

DIANA

MENUHIN

Diana Gould was trained by Marie Rambert and Mathilda Ksches-sinskaya. Chosen both by Diaghilev at fourteen and by Pavlova at sixteen, the deaths of both soon after prevented her joining their companies. She danced for Massine in Max Reinhardt's The Miracle, *and was engaged as soloist in Balanchine's Ballets 1933 at its inception. She also worked with Woizikowsky, Lifar, and Nijinska during her seasons with the Markova-Dolin Ballet in England. She also acted in plays in London's West End. She gave up her career on marrying Yehudi Menuhin in 1947. The first part of her autobiography,* Fiddler's Moll, *appeared in 1984.*

FROM THE BALLETS RUSSES FOR HIS NEW BALLETS 1933 BALANCHINE BROUGHT WITH
him the lovely Tamara Toumanova, all of thirteen—or was it fifteen? Anyway, I do remember celebrating her fifteenth birthday repeatedly over the
years, which makes it difficult to be exact. What one can easily be exact
about was that she was young, beautiful, and had that marvelous rock-hard
technique that Preobrajenska gave her and Baronova.

With Roman Jasinsky as principal male dancer and a little padding from
the vast pool of dancers to be found in the various Paris studios, Balanchine
had a small but strong company which suited his needs, for he had no use
for the old-style corps de ballet, which to him represented a dreary frieze
that filled in blank spaces, dressed the stage, and permitted the soloists to
catch their wind in the wings.

For Edward James, with all his taste, his vision for painting, it was an ideal
moment to try to make a company in the image of Diaghilev. I had known
him when I understudied Tilly Losch in the part of the Nun in *The Miracle,*
and Tilly of course I knew well: naughty, mischievous Tilly with her huge
ice-blue eyes and her beautiful, erotic arms and hands; Tilly who ran circles
round the fresh-faced, eternally boyish Edward; Tilly who was the despair
of Balanchine, who found his inspiration totally blocked when it came to
devising a ballet for her; Tilly who finally triumphed in *L'Errante* and *Anna-
Anna.*

Anna-Anna was a typically thirties-Berlin production concocted by Kurt
Weill and Bertolt Brecht on the subject of the seven deadly sins. Some of us
loathed it because any leftover dancers (like yesterday's cold meat) had to
pull on huge cloaks which covered the head as well and rush on brandishing
poles vaguely and exuding either sin or the punishment of same—Tamara
Sidorenko and I never did find out what we were doing. And in *L'Errante,*
Pavel Tchelitchew and Balanchine, having draped the stage with four kilo-
meters of white silk and flooded it with very ingenious lighting, put Tilly
into a marvelous dress of emerald-green satin with a great wide train, which
we would gather up in the wings and let fly as Tilly ran on looking suitably
bewildered.

To be working at last in Paris, in the very theater, the Champs-Elysées,
that had seen the premiere of *Sacre,* was thrilling. The rehearsals were
strangely spasmodic, sometimes in the afternoon, sometimes at night. As
one was never sure what was going to be rehearsed, one simply turned up—
and anyway, to watch Balanchine at work was no time wasted. I remember
one rehearsal in the upstairs room to which Josephine Baker came, almost
unrecognizable with clothes on and no bananas.

Gradually the ballets took shape: *Mozartiana, Les Songes, Les Sept Péchés
Capitaux, Fastes,* and *L'Errante,* to which George suddenly added a sixth: *Les*

Valses de Beethoven. Based on the Greek myth about Daphne's spurning of Apollo, it was choreographed mainly for Tilly and Jasinsky. A rich and not very gifted South American called Emilio Terry designed a dotty decor and hideous costumes. There were the four elements: Earth, Air, Fire, and Water. I was Earth, in a deplorable sort of chiton in Bovril-colored chiffon (Old Mother Manure, I called myself).

On the opening night, trembling with nerves, we were still awaiting the headdresses backstage, the audience clapping with impatience, and panic all around. At last Karinska arrived in a flurry and a taxi. She handed me a monstrous sort of cairn at least two feet high and made of plaster and mud. I put it on my head, tears pouring down my face, and appealed to George. Mine was the first solo, and I was to be found reclining on something or other (a plaster couch, I think) extremely uncomfortable as the curtain lifted, from which I had to spring into fourth position on pointe, flinging the top half of my body back as far as it would go (Balanchine had discovered that I had a double-jointed back). What was to happen to this monument on my head is anybody's guess and very obviously *my* funeral. Fortunately, George lifted the thing off, wiped my tears, gave me a kiss and a gentle push—"Go on—go on, Dianotchka"—and I ran, knees knocking, to take up my lonely position onstage and try not to listen to the mounting anger of the derisive applause. Despite lovely solos for Prudence Hyman as Air, Sidorenko as Fire, and Ouchkova as Water, the ballet did not set the theater alight and was dropped. No one really minded, for the difficulty of turning Daphne into a laurel bush proved insurmountable. I remember a whole lot of messing about with green branches made of paper leaves, Tilly trying to hold them in such a way that it would appear that the metamorphosis from nymph to shrub had really taken place; not all the wistful wonder and rolling of those ice-blue eyes by Tilly did much to convince the very chic audience that it was not a rather sorry affair. Farewell, Mother Manure!

The real excitement began much earlier, though, when we got out of the rehearsal studio and onto the stage and into our dressing rooms. At last one saw the various collaborators Boris Kochno, Balanchine, and Edward James had brought together: André Derain, with his enormous, casklike belly and his jolly bulging eyes; "Bébé" Bérard, all mince and wince (he was perpetually having toy rages and being offended); "Pavlik" Tchelitchew, with his beautiful, haggard, romantic face; "Nika" Nabokov, a marvelous Russian with a mane of dark blond hair and witty blue eyes. These latter two would take me all over Paris on various purposeless and very Russian outings to see friends who were usually absent or to chatter with American expatriates and have tea. (Tchelitchew would read my hand: "Dianotchka, you have the palm of a very old lady!") And there were Henri Sauguet, always smiling and pleasant, and Darius Milhaud, a big, lemon-colored face and dreamy black eyes. All of them would be walking up and down the stalls or watching their ballets, discussing changes and adjustments with Balanchine; and I realized how privileged I was to belong to this moment of creation: not one stale, taken-out-of-the-cupboard-and-dusted-over ballet; all fresh or rarely heard music, fresh designs, fresh ideas. It is an earnest of Kochno's grip as well as Balanchine's genius that any of it came to fruition. There were moments when one felt a certain lack of roots, of the security that the well-tried ballets gave, a sensation of giddiness at the almost blinding vision, the newness of it all—so many conceptions, so many precarious births, so much peril taken quite calmly. For I cannot recall one angry word from George as he took us through the steps, the *enchaînements,* the solos, the pas de deux, adjusting, readjusting here and there. One day, while we were walking together in London, he said, "You know, to my mind, ballets should be only topical—disposable. Once they have lasted a season, they should be thrown away."

He worked with a loose hand—no shouting, no commands, simply showing the steps, correcting, adjusting with a precision and a musical perception that were the joy of any dancer who has had to struggle with intractable arrangements ill fitting the measure and the rhythm, cutting across phrases and melodies, twisting instincts and one's mind in the process.

Near the end of the London season Balanchine took me for a walk in the warm July night. "Dianotchka," he said, "today a man came to see me, an American, and said he could offer me a school and company if I go to America—would you please come?" Longing to say yes but young and frightened at such a long leap into what might be the dark, this idiotic English virgin said no. Even though we must have circled that square a dozen times and Balanchine pleaded and I was torn in two, my fear and my cowardice won, and sadly we returned to the hotel and said good-bye.

History knows the rest: the American was Lincoln Kirstein, and Balanchine never looked back.

LINCOLN

KIRSTEIN

Man of letters and the arts, born in Rochester, May 4, 1907, attended Exeter and Harvard, published his first book, a novel, **Flesh Is Heir,** *in 1932. Poet, historian and art critic, he has written many books. Among them:* Dance: A Short History of Theatrical Dancing *(1935); with Muriel Stuart,* The Classic Dance *(1950);* Movement and Metaphor: Four Centuries of Ballet *(1970); and* The New York City Ballet *(1973). His* Collected Poems *appeared in 1988. Founded in 1934 with Balanchine and Edward M. M. Warburg the School of American Ballet and the American Ballet which became resident at the Metropolitan Opera in 1935. Established Ballet Caravan, 1936, to present new work by American choreographers and, with Balanchine, American Ballet Caravan, which toured Latin America in 1941. Pfc, U. S.*

Army, 1942–45. Founded Ballet Society with Balanchine 1946.

When that became the New York City Ballet in 1948, Kirstein

became general director, which he remained until 1989. From 1934

to 1989 he was president of the School of American Ballet.

Lincoln Kirstein

WHEN Lincoln Kirstein visited Venice in August 1929 at the age of 22, he accidentally found himself a part of the funeral of Serge Diaghilev. His coming upon the funeral service at the Greek church of St. George was prophetic. Kirstein knew all about Diaghilev and had attended performances in Paris and London of his Ballets Russes. Kirstein thought even then that ballet should flourish in America too. His favorite choreographer was George Balanchine, whose work he had seen in the Diaghilev repertory. In 1933, visiting Paris, Virgil Thomson arranged for him to attend rehearsals of Balanchine's Les Ballets 1933, which he followed to London. Through Romola Nijinska, Kirstein met Balanchine backstage at the Savoy Theater. They arranged to meet at the home of Kirk Askew.

Kirstein asked Balanchine what he was going to do next. Europe appeared to be closed to the choreographer, where all the big jobs were taken by the natives of each country. The English would not give him a labor permit to stay. Kirstein asked him to come to America. Balanchine said, "Yes, but first a school." After that meeting, Kirstein came back to his hotel and sat down to write the following letter to his close friend A. Everett Austin, Jr., director of the Wadsworth Atheneum, the museum at Hartford, Connecticut, where the manuscript is part of the collection. *

F.M.

Batt's Hotel
Dover Street, W.1
[London]

July 16: 1933.

Dear Chick:

This will be the most important letter I will ever write you as you will see. My pen burns my hand as I write: words will not flow into the ink fast enough. We have a real chance to have an American ballet within 3 years time. When I say ballet, I mean a trained company of young dancers —not Russians—but Americans with Russian stars to start with—a company superior to the dregs of the old Diaghilev company which will come to N.Y. this winter and create an enormous success purely because though they aren't much they are better than anything New York will have seen since Nijinsky.

Do you know Georges Balanchine? If not he is a Georgian called Georgei Balanchivadze. He is, personally, enchanting—dark, very slight, a superb dancer and the most ingenious technician in ballet I have ever

* Printed with the permission of Lincoln Kirstein.

seen. For Diaghilev he composed *The Cat, The Prodigal Son, Apollon Musagète, Le Bal* of Chirico, *Barabau* of Utrillo, *Neptune* of the Sitwells, and many others. This year he did Tchelitchew's *Errante,* Bérard's *Mozartiana,* Derain's *Competition* and Bérard's *Cotillon.* He is 28 yrs. old, a product of the Imperial schools. He has split from the Prince de Monaco as he wants to proceed, with new ideas and young dancers instead of going on with the decadence of the Diaghilev troupe, which I assure you, although it possesses many good, if frightfully overworked dancers, is completely worn-out, inartistic, commercial. Now Balanchine has with him Tamara Toumanova, the daughter of a general Toumanov, and a Circassian princess. She is 14 yrs. old. I enclose what the best ballet critic in England says about her. Her technique is phenomenal. Preobrajenska, her teacher and Pavlova's great rival says she is unbelievable, in 3 yrs. a real phenomenon. Balanchine adores her, has really created her: made her blossom out. Toumanova is so *photogenique* she has refused 2 movie contracts: She wants to dance above all. *"Il faut danser."* The Monte Carlo Ballet wanted her on a *10* yrs. contract. Balanchine refused to tie her up for so long: they dismissed her. Enclosed are her photos. Balanchine also has her partner Roman Jasinsky. He is a Pole from the Warsaw School. He is extremely beautiful, a superb body and by way of becoming a most remarkable dancer. He promises far more than Lifar who is absolutely spoiled and is artistically through, a terrible snob and cabotin. Jasinsky works all the time, is a fine mime, modest, a bit dumb, but marvelous in an expert's hand like Balanchine. I wish you could have seen him in the marvelous pas de deux in *Mozartiana.* Toumanova is a sombre little girl, a tragic face and a rather firm heavy build, a dancer in whom the masculine strength and feminine art is superbly intertwined. Jasinsky is older, about twenty: but less mature. But his pirouettes, his entrechats are fine and he will be a superb artist. These 3 have *nothing* to do now. I prepared the following and they are willing and eager to do it.

To have a school of dancing, preferably in Hartford: it is distant from New York—plenty of chance to work in an easy atmosphere. Balanchine is socially adorable, but he hates the atmosphere both of society, as such (Lifar loves it) and the professional Broadway Theatre. For the first he would take 4 white girls and 4 white boys, about sixteen yrs. old and 8 of the same, *negros.* They would be firmly taught in the classical idiom, not only from *exercises* but he would start company ballets at once so they could actually *learn* by doing. As time went on he would get younger children from 8 yrs. on. He thinks the negro part of it would be amazingly supple, the combination of suppleness and sense of time superb. Imagine them, masked, for example. They have so much abandon—and disciplined they would be *nonpareil.* He could start producing within 3 months. Now, if you could work it he could use your small theatre: [in] a department of the museum a school of dancing could be started—entirely from the professional point of view. But since *no* tuition fee will be charged, the dancers will be picked for their *perfect* possibilities and they will have to sign contracts to prevent them from appearing anywhere else, except in the troupe for 5 years. This will obviate the danger of movies or Broadway snatching them up after they have been trained—better than anybody else in the country. In the meantime Balanchine and Jasinsky and Toumanova will serve as demonstrators and models. Thus, you can already see in a girl not yet 15 and a boy of 20, finished dancers, artists of *conviction.* Now, Madame Nijinsky, her name is very important, has given me the rights to *Sacre du Printemps, Jeux, Faun, Tyl Eulenspiegel* and 4 unproduced ballets, the benefit of his *untried* system of training of dancers. She also volunteers to lecture with me, at these demonstrations where one could also see the dancing of Toumanova and Jasinsky. I intend to get engagements charging $100 a lecture from Harvard, Boston, *Worcester,* Springfield, Northampton, Bennington, New Haven, New London, Poughkeepsie, Bryn Mawr, Wesleyan, Philadelphia and 3 or 4 times in N.Y. This will prepare the way for the company, which will give performances *not* at the theater, but always kept on an educational level, with museums. This takes us out of the competition class, obviates us from theatres—managers etc. In the meantime Balanchine, Jasinsky, Toumanova and her mother must live. Toumanova can't go anywhere without her *ma.* She is a nice woman, has starved for years and could keep house and cook for them which she has always done. It would be necessary to have $6000 to *start* it. That guarantees them for one year with passage back and forth. I count this sum as dead loss. Though it won't be at all because by February you can have four performances of wholly new ballets in Hartford. Balanchine is willing to devote all his time to this for 5 yrs. He believes the future of ballet lies in America as do I. I see a great chance for you to do a hell of a lot here. The expense can be under*written,* say I glibly, but you must realize how much this means. So I have to be arrogant, by Phil *Johnson* who is willing, myself, *Jim Sobey,* Jere [Abbot],* the Lewisohns, the *Cotters* etc. in N.Y. who are willing and I feel sure there are others. This school can be the basis of a national culture as intense as the great Russian Renaissance of Diaghilev. We must start small. But imagine it. We are exactly as if we were in 1910, offered a dancer only less good than an unformed Nijinsky, an incipient Karsavina, a maître de ballet as good as Fokine, who would also be delighted to

* Shared director's authority with Alfred Barr at the Museum of Modern Art in New York.

117

cooperate. It will not be easy. It will be hard to get good young dancers willing to stand or fall by the *company*. *No* first dancers. No STARS. A perfect ESPRIT DE CORPS. The ballets I have discussed with Balanchine out of American life are these—

Pocahontas: classical ballet with décor from American primitives: music from 17th century English suite de danses.

Doomsday: décor by John Benson after New England gravestones. Libretto on Salem themes by Katherine Anne Porter, the superb biographer of Cotton Mather. She is working on it now.

Uncle Tom's Cabin: ballet au grand serieux avec apotheose: by E. E. *Cummings*. He is doing it now on my suggestion. Music by Stephen Foster. Décor by WHOEVER.

Defeure of Richmond: Débacle dansé on a libretto of John Peale Bishop, I've spoken a lot about this to him. Virgil Thomson is excited about the music. All about Southern *swords* and roses.

Flying Cloud: a ballet of the days of clipper ships: a dock in New Bedford or

Moby Dick by Jere Abbot.

Custer's Last Stand: After Currier and Ives, the circling Indians: corps de ballet shooting at the chief dancers in the center. Ponies: Ritual of scouts going out, Indian dances *stylisé*.

Then there are Balanchine's own ideas: a great erotic ballet which is to die. Nijinsky undone ballet to an organ and Bach's preludes and fugues— abstract in the baroque manner, and so much else.

I know Stokowski will cooperate musically. It is absolutely necessary to keep Balanchine to ourselves. Not let either Stokowski, the *League* of Composers, the *Juilliard* or the Curtis Institute get ahold of him. He is an honest man, a serious artist and I'd stake my life on his talent. In two years, unhindered by petty intrigue, by rows between Tchelitchew and Bérard, between the Monte Carlo ballet, Lifar and the Paris Opéra, unworried about how he could both live and call his soul his own which he has not done since Diaghilev died, he could achieve a miracle, and right under our eyes: I feel this chance is too serious to be denied. It will mean a life work to all of us, incredible power in a few years. We can command whom we want. We will be developing new talent. It will not be a losing proposition. Conceived as an educational institution under the title of The American Ballet, or the School of Classical Dancing of America or something, it could travel, on small tours, at first, simply *as* a school and get a considerable return. We would have to do a little theatrical camouflage at first. A few leaps by Jasinsky or a few *fouettés* by the adorable Toumanova will lift a roomful off their feet, cheering. I wish to God you were here: that you could know what I am writing is true, that I am not either over-enthusiastic or visionary. Please, please, Chick, if you have any love for anything we do both adore, rack your brains and try to make this all come true. If not as I outline, then some other way must be feasible. WE have both done harder things than to raise $6000. Hartford is a perfect place for it, I think. You will adore Balanchine. He is no trouble, i.e. not personally difficult in any way. He could come over in October or even sooner. When you have thought of this, considered it, talked it over with Russell, Jere, Joe Marvell, even Winslow Ames and Francis Taylor—talk to Muriel Draper too. She knows a lot about such things. But please wire me, give me some inkling as to how you will receive this letter. If not I can't sleep. I won't be able to hear from you for a week, but I won't sleep till I do. Just say *Proceed* or *Impossible.* If *Impossible,* I will try to think of something else, but as I see it, Hartford is perfect. It will involve no personal loss. The $6000 is just a guarantee, for poor Balanchine, who is responsible for Toumanova and Jasinsky: he has been tricked so often.

We have the future in our hands. For Christ's sweet sake let us honor it.

Yours devotedly,
Lincoln

Wire me here:

Renowned for being at least twenty-five years ahead of everybody else, Lincoln Kirstein promised Balanchine in London in 1933 that before Kirstein was forty Balanchine would have a ballet company and a theater of his own. In 1948, when the New York City Ballet came to be, Kirstein was off by only a year. Lincoln Kirstein's invitation to Balanchine to come to America, his selfless, single-minded, and tireless commitment to Balanchine and his work for fifty years is the most inspiring story of patronage and collaboration in the history of the arts in the United States. The artist's work survives; patronage is often forgotten. Kirstein's continuous patronage of the man who made possible the growth of the classical dance in America, who made possible an unfolding of national talent Kirstein knew to be there, should never be forgotten. What Pope Julius II did for Michelangelo is nothing compared to Kirstein's commitment to Balanchine.

F.M.

EDWARD M. M.

WARBURG

Founder of the School of American Ballet with Balanchine and Lincoln Kirstein and of the American Ballet, Edward Warburg was born in New York in 1908. At Harvard as undergraduates, he, Lincoln Kirstein, and John Walker, later director of the National Gallery of Art, established in Cambridge the Society for Contemporary Art, a precursor of the Museum of Modern Art. He taught art history at Bryn Mawr College, was on the staff of the Museum of Modern Art, and vice director for public affairs of the Metropolitan Museum of Art.

I Remember Balanchine

I WAS AT THE DOCK WITH LINCOLN KIRSTEIN TO WELCOME BALANCHINE TO AMERICA when his boat came in. My involvement with Balanchine started because Lincoln's family and my family were great friends and business associates. My brother-in-law was the head of Abraham & Straus in Brooklyn, and Lincoln's father, Louis Kirstein, who looked just like Balieff, the impresario, was head of Filene's department store in Boston. Lincoln grew up surrounded by first-class writers and first-class everything else. Lou Kirstein himself couldn't have been less interested in the arts. Lincoln's mother, Rose, was interested simply because she wanted to keep up with her children. Their house on Commonwealth Avenue in Boston was a most wonderful mix of antimacassars and old-fashioned furniture with Negro sculpture (all genitalia clearly on view) and schmaltzy Jewish cooking, hors d'oeuvres and everything else coming around all the time as the young people brought in all their way-out artistic friends. Lincoln took a year out between school and college to work in a stained-glass factory. He was a friend of most of the artists by that time and was years ahead of all the rest of us in intellectual maturity. When we entered the class of 1930 at Harvard, John Walker and Lincoln and I used to have bull sessions. My interest was, How does art support itself? How does an artist—musician, dancer, composer—make enough money to last until the next successful work? Lincoln, who had spent summers in Europe following the ballet and other things, said there was only one art form that would give the artists that opportunity. And that was ballet. Diaghilev had shown, he felt, that you can have the painter do the decor and the maquettes for the costumes, you can have the score written by the composer, and you can have some outlet for the dancers other than Radio City Music Hall. The Music Hall and vaudeville were at that time about the only dance we had, except for what was called modern dance (Martha Graham at its best, but more liable to be Denishawn).

Lincoln, John, and I were trying to find a way by which, through a percentage take of the box office, artists could continue to work in a cooperative way toward making art. No one at that time was bright enough to think about the fact that there was a thing called labor unions, which of course absolutely blocked this. Lincoln was our authority—we didn't know whether he was right or wrong—but he said that of all the people in the ballet the only one who had any view of the future and wasn't just rehashing and redoing old stuff was George Balanchine. Lincoln said Massine had had his day, and there wasn't anybody else. The question with Balanchine at that point was betwixt and between the petite James, Mr. Edward James, Marshall Field's strange brother-in-law, and an uncertain future. The petite James had married Tilly Losch and they put on Balanchine's *Errante* and other Balanchine ballets in a brand-new dance company called Les Ballets 1933, with performances in Paris and London. Balanchine's *Errante,* which he later did with Tamara Geva and Vera Zorina, is one of the good ballets I'd like to see revived.

And so we thought, if we could only get Balanchine. Lincoln called me up one day out in the country and asked, "Can I come out and see you?" I said, "Sure, Lincoln, always." So he came out by train to White Plains. I know the exact spot in the woods where we walked. He said, "Eddie, I know you've never seen a ballet, I know you don't know the first damn thing about it, but on the basis of what we were discussing at college in terms of patronage of the arts, let me tell you that our one chance seems to be possible. I've talked to Balanchine in London, and he is ready to come over and find out if there is a place and whether there is a possibility to start a school of ballet. He asks that we pay a round-trip for himself and for his business manager, Vladimir Dimitriev. Now, I'm perfectly ready to pay for one of the tickets, round trip, but I'm coming to you to ask you, will you pay for the other?" He added, "I've got Chick Austin ready to welcome them to the Wadsworth Atheneum in Hartford and its new auditorium and new wing. He'd love to have a ballet school there. It all looks ready made."

I said yes. I didn't follow it up and then suddenly I got a call. I was told, "They are arriving, Balanchine and Dimitriev." "All right, Lincoln," I said, and we came down to meet them. Balanchine and Dimitriev spoke very little English. My French isn't that good, but we could make ourselves understood. But you didn't need any language to know what Mr. Dimitriev was interested in, and that was money. As far as Balanchine was concerned, you realized that was the *last* thing he was interested in. He was fascinated by all kinds of things, but you never quite knew what. The Rockefeller Center buildings had just been built, so we took him up to the top so he could look over the Manhattan skyline. He looked over east to the General Electric building with its Gothic tower and said, *"Ah, vous avez aussi votre ruines."*

It was hard to lead Balanchine into what you might call "Americanizing experiences." We took him to Broadway shows. We showed him the sights. He wasn't much interested in the sights. I don't recall his caring for the museums at all even though Lincoln and I made it clear that we did. I didn't recall Balanchine's being interested in looking at pictures except Tchelitchew's paintings. They knew each other from Paris. And Antheil, the musician he knew from Paris. Lincoln tried to bring in various people *he* was interested in, Americans, but it wasn't easy. First of all, very few of them had language bridges to walk on. Tchelitchew was the most articulate man of all. I don't know anybody who spoke as well about art as he did. He would take a pencil and while he was talking be drawing on the tablecloth the most extraordinary illustration of what he was talking about. You wanted to grab hold of the tablecloth and take it with you, but there was always some monkey wrench in every one of his paintings and drawings, something that just loused it up a little bit. He had a terribly hard time. Tchelitchew would not be recognized even to the extent that he is today if it hadn't been for Lincoln. The same thing is true of Nadelman and Lachaise. There's no question about it. *And* George. Lincoln *fought* their way in.

In the ballet school the major elements did not include George, funnily enough, although he was of course the important artistic presence. But we weren't dealing with artists. We were dealing with organization. Plus trying to get the thing into the black. Eugenie Ouroussow, the secretary, a beautiful girl and a charming woman, was marvelous. And there was Vladimiroff, the great ballet teacher, who was the ham par excellence, absolutely kosher ham, but a wonderful, wonderful guy. Plus Dimitriev, the sinister *éminence grise*, who was trying to figure out when he had us safely enough hooked to put the bite on. Which he did about four times. Threatening strikes, threatening return to Europe, threatening everything, leaving us high and dry unless we did what he said. More money! He paralleled himself to George all the time in terms of salary, and George wouldn't even know about it.

The initial idea was to place the school in Hartford, where Lincoln said Chick Austin wanted us at the Wadsworth Atheneum. Balanchine and all went up there and tried it out. But to them and the Russian Tea Room crowd, it was the provinces, amateur night, and they wanted to be in the *center* of things. So the studios at Fifty-ninth Street and Madison had to be rented. We had to redo the whole place, and then we had to sign up anybody, depending upon their talent and also their financial status. Agnes Meyer's daughter, Kay Graham's sister, was one of the elite, she had no ballet talent whatsoever, but she did have money, and she did have private lessons with Vladimiroff. Then came the push. We started off with a bunch of field hockey kids from Philadelphia, the Littlefield Ballet crowd, who all were healthy and brassy, plus a few shaggy-looking male dancers, who had been lifting weights and maybe had done some dancing. William Dollar was by far the outstanding one. Before we knew it, there were many students at the school, the training was good, Balanchine began to make a ballet (what we know today as *Serenade)* and to rehearse *Errante* and *Mozartiana*. We were a ballet company in the making. At one o'clock in the morning, after hours of rehearsal, we would adjourn to the Russian Tea Room, which was sort of a club, and Balanchine and Dimitriev and friends would discuss the Bolshevik Revolution. "You remember the Revolution? You remember when we had nothing to eat but herring heads?" They'd sit there and wallow in the misery of that memory. All except Nicholas Kopeikine, the pianist. He would be sitting smirking in the corner with the pleasantest memories obviously going through his head. I said, "Kopeikine, you don't seem to have the same reaction. What were your feelings about the Revolution?" "It was *whann-derful.*" *"What* do you mean, it was *'whann-*derful'?" "Every night the whole Russian Navy used to break down my door." So there was that kind of a world as well.

Suddenly it was decided that what *I* wanted more than anything else for *my* upcoming birthday was a performance by this company of ballet dancers at the family place in White Plains, New York. We put up a platform on the lawn which to this day has never recovered; there is still a brown spot in the grass. We hung spotlights from the roof. My poor mother put on a buffet for two hundred guests before the event. We had a piano hidden in the bushes which Nicholas Kopeikine played. The show started. It was the first performance of *Serenade.* The dancers stood with their arms raised to the moon and the heavens, and the heavens responded with heavy rain. No moon. We were wiped out. We never got beyond the opening theme. Lincoln jumped up onstage and announced the performance would be held the next night. Mother had to repeat the meal; it was Sunday, and where do you get the food? "Do you expect me to have . . . ?" Yes, please, Mother. In the midst of all this chaos of screaming kids changing in the dressing rooms by the swimming pool and the garage, Vladimiroff was saying, "Say, *bébé,* this is just like the old days in Russia. By chance, do you happen to have a cigar?" This I didn't need. The next night, June 10, 1934, *Serenade* went on as scheduled with a miraculous girl, Marie-Jeanne. She had long legs and long feet and did the child who gets lost in the forest, plus *Mozartiana* and *Songes.* Vladimiroff said that Marie-Jeanne in the "Ave, Verum Corpus" of *Mozartiana* reminded him of the debut of Pavlova. (That was about 1899, when Pavlova joined the Maryinsky Theater in St. Petersburg, when Vladimiroff was a six-year-old kid.) But he partnered Pavlova in her final years and knew what he was talking about. The audience was mostly Lincoln's friends —Askew, Muriel Draper, Julian Levy, and that kind of world. My poor parents had no idea what hit them.

The School of American Ballet really got into its stride after the summer break, and we thought we'd take Chick Austin up on his offer of a performance in the Avery Memorial Theater of the Wadsworth Atheneum at Hartford. We called ourselves the American Ballet and put on *Serenade, Alma Mater,* Balanchine's first bit of Americana, and *Transcendence,* for which Franklin Watkins designed the costumes (*"Merde,"* said Tchelitchew). I stood at the back of the house and got the applause going at the right minute.

Then the cry came in unison from Dimitriev and Balanchine and the crowd at the Russian Tea Room: "We've got the most whann-derful man who is going to manage us and will take us on a transcontinental tour." His name was Merovitch, who had toured the Don Cossacks and Chaliapin. Well, Merovitch didn't take much persuading. It was all a question of "I'm *sure* Mr. Warburg and I will understand." Ha-ha. Well, I didn't understand what the hell he was talking about.

We played New York, the Adelphi Theater, with Tamara Geva, Balanchine's ex-wife, as heroine ballerina. She was great, but "disaster" is too small a word for the season. Lincoln and I sat in the empty house with our hands cupped, covering our eyes. By the third performance, there were about five members of the ballet company's families in the audience. Nobody in the place at all. An usher tried to move Lincoln and me off the stairs as we sat in the back of the house in our despair. We had to explain to him that we owned the bloody company and to let us stay. A popular success it was not. John Martin of the *New York Times* felt that anybody except Martha Graham moving when music was being played was committing a sacrilege.

Then Merovitch toured us. It turned out, of course, that he and Dimitriev had Kirstein and me, two dumb Americans, rich kids, in a corner. I was the guarantor of everything: dancers, orchestra, and God knows how many rehearsals, etc. Plus equipment, buses, everything. Plus mothers! Lincoln then curiously formed a fifth column with George and left me with Dimitriev to be eaten alive. We get to Scranton, Pennsylvania, I am summoned, and we go bust. No more money! The musicians said I had to pay for them. "But, Mr. Warburg, you can't leave us in Scranton!" That had to be settled amicably. It was settled amicably all right, in a costly manner. Right across the country, everybody who had ever put an ad in the paper about forthcoming appearances by the American Ballet wanted money. Lincoln kept saying, "Eddie, you've got to settle with them because otherwise we'll never be able to go on and have a tour. These are the same people we'll always have to use. So if you want this thing ever to succeed . . ." So I died ten thousand deaths.

So then we got mixed up with Edward Johnson, who managed the Metropolitan Opera. It was front-page news when he took the American Ballet to the Met. But when we said after we got there, "Why can't we have a ballet evening?" it was "Nix." Balanchine staged the ballets for the operas, but how in that primitive theatrical place could they have been really great? But his ballets became the only lively things in the operas. They showed up the Met and were therefore resented.

One time they gave a girl who was to dance in *Aïda* a costume she couldn't move in. Balanchine said, "Eddie, go up to Fifty-ninth Street and get any costume she can move in." So I got it and came back with this thing, and the man at the stage entrance says, "Whatta you got there, Mr. Warburg?" And I said, "The costume for the kid who's gotta dance in about twenty minutes."

He said, "For God's sake, put that under your coat. You gotta have a union truck bring that in here or they'll stop the whole damn performance." The Met always promised Sunday night ballet evenings. It never happened.

The equipment of the old opera house was primitive. The boys blackened their bodies to dance in *Aïda,* but there was no running water or showers to wash it off. They had to fill up tubs and gather round them in a circle, so that each guy could scrub the back of the kid in front.

The Stravinsky Festival of 1937 we had to do ourselves, pay out every cent for every aspect. I commissioned Stravinsky to do a new score for Balanchine, *Jeu de Cartes,* and we put on the first performance in America of the Stravinsky-Balanchine *Apollon Musagète,* plus the premiere of the Stravinsky-Balanchine *Le Baiser de la Fée.* In those days we could not pay for music and lighting rehearsals, and we were on tenterhooks. Opening night, the New York Philharmonic was in the orchestra pit. Stravinsky was to conduct. When the audience was all expectant at curtain time, it was my job to tell the maestro we were ready. I went to Stravinsky and said, "Maestro, please." Stravinsky said, "I cannot." My stomach fell seventy feet. He asked me, "Have you seen the program for this evening's performance?" "Of course," I said. "What's the problem?" He said, "It says in the program *'Apollon,* music by Igor Stravinsky.' I will not conduct." I could not understand; the ballet did have music by Stravinsky. The maestro elucidated: "Program should read *'Apollon* by Igor Stravinsky.'" As if it were new Apollo Belvedere, *sans* Balanchine. He was offended that anyone else should be acknowledged! The choreographer and the designer meant nothing to him. The assistant conductor was standing by. I turned to him as calmly as I could and said, "Will you please take the podium?" The words were not out of my mouth before Igor rushed past him into the orchestra pit. The rest was Stravinsky-Balanchine history.

Some years later, when my wife and I were having a drink at the St. Regis, I saw Igor and his wife across the room. I thought it proper to pay my respects. I went over and identified myself, but Stravinsky looked at me blankly. He had no idea who I was. Since I'd paid for the first Stravinsky Festival, I was somewhat amused and mentioned the incident to Balanchine the next time we met. He said, "Eddie, you don't understand. Stravinsky took a long time to die, he forgot so much. It was all there in his head, but he could not get it out of his mouth."

Audiences everywhere are always looking for things they recognize or remember from a previous time. Balanchine's *Orpheus and Eurydice* at the Met was nothing that they had ever seen before. New things are very upsetting. This was all mime and dance, with the singers in the pit, and onstage everyone walking through wonderful, beautifully lit, diaphanous sets by Tchelitchew. It was stylized dancing, stylized mime, glorious, but it went on forever and no action.

There was one thing at the opera which was heaven. For Wagner's *Rhinegold,* there was a man by the name of Zachsa who was a stage director from Hamburg, I believe. He said, "Mr. Balanchine, you know Wagner's opera *Rhinegold?"* Balanchine said, *"Da."* He said, "At the Metropolitan the Rhine maidens hang on a trapeze forty feet above the stage and they swim. I want they should be ballet girls. At least one should be black-haired, another brown, and another blond. They must be musical so they know *how* to swim. They must understand German so they know *when* to swim. Above all, Mr. Balanchine, they must not vomit!"

Balanchine seemed perfectly happy and quiet and amused by all this, and he was pleased to see some of his favorite singers. But he had no use for the organization of the place and was unhappy on that score. No wonder he turned to Broadway. He'd somehow got mixed up with Larry Hart's manager, "Doc" Bender, who was a dentist. How he got to be a manager, I don't know. He also was a pimp.* But, through Larry, he also got Balanchine the opportunity to do *On Your Toes.* Dick and Dorothy Rodgers were terribly straitlaced. They hated Larry's entourage. It was a very odd kind of world. There was always some little tap-dancer boy and Larry in a turkish towel, having just had a "massage." Into this world came this vague, dreamy character with such good manners and such kindliness: Balanchine. He was told by the dentist, "I'll take care of everything, don't you worry," and the big push for the show was on. The show had Ray Bolger, and Balanchine was fascinated by Bolger. And Tamara Geva was in it: she and Bolger stopped the show every night with *Slaughter on Tenth Avenue.*

Balanchine could fantasize and execute anything. Remember Zorina in *Goldwyn Follies* coming out of the water and dancing on the mirrored surface? It was *Swan Lake* in the New World. He liked to show Hollywood and Broadway how to do their own trade. He liked to show them up a bit. He was competitive. He respected Ray Bolger as he certainly respected Fred Astaire, although he never worked with him. And he rather liked being with Sam Goldwyn in Hollywood and working on ideas that Sam would never dream of having. Incorporating ballet into a musical on Broadway, remember, had

---

* A contemporary of Lorenz Hart's has recalled to me an alternative lyric written by Hart for his and Richard Rodgers's song "There's a Small Hotel" from *On Your Toes:*

> Looking through the window
> You can see three boys and Bender.
> Bender's the ender.
> Who wants Bender?

—F.M.

its snob appeal. Dick Rodgers was terribly pleased to have something more than A-B-A music to write for. He had Robert Russell Bennett stretch out something into *Slaughter on Tenth Avenue.* One of the stories at the time was that Rodgers didn't know what Balanchine wanted for the ballet's music. He said to Balanchine, "I will write anything. What do you want? Do you want something special?" And Balanchine said, "No, you write. I do." So Rodgers went and made this long thing, which he'd never made before, and Balanchine didn't change a thing. He just did it.

With the ballet *Alma Mater,* which we did in the early days, it was the same kind of thing. He said to Kay Swift, "Write me a waltz." She gave him a whole sequence of things, and he played with them. The sets and costumes were by John Held, Jr., but Balanchine was no good for that kind of Americana then. He couldn't do for football in *Alma Mater* what Loring did for horseback riding in *Billy the Kid.* I think he was equally awkward with *Stars and Stripes* and with *Union Jack.* You can laugh at them, not with them. They're *charming,* an awful thing to say about an incredibly talented guy.

One time Lincoln said to me, "Eddie, will you do me a favor? Will you go with me to my father? I've got to put the bee on him for some money. He likes you." I said, "Oh, sure. I'd love to see Uncle Lou." When we got there, Lou said, "What's on your mind, Lincoln?" Lincoln splutters through a presentation. Lou says, "Eddie, you heard what he said?" "Yeah." "Understand a word he said?" I said, "One or two. But I know what he's trying to say." And he said, "Do you think it's a good thing?" I said, "Yes, I do." "Do you think I should put money in it?" I said, "Lou, why do you fight immortality so? You might become famous from this. You're never going to become famous otherwise. Here you may become the great patron of the arts." He laughed and said, "All right, I'll go along." Thank God for American ballet and Balanchine—he did!

LUCIA

DAVIDOVA

A close friend of Balanchine's for many years, Lucia Davidova translated the selected letters and diaries of Vera and Igor Stravinsky, Dearest Bubushkin, *edited by Robert Craft (1985).*

OUTSIDE THE DANCE WORLD, I WAS BALANCHINE'S BEST PLATONIC WOMAN FRIEND. George treated women as females, not as great friends, and certainly not as intellectual companions. I told him I would teach him friendship. I knew that every woman he had an affair with was discarded sooner or later. They discarded him, or more often he left them. I told him, "If we have any kind of relationship, I'll be one of the discarded ones. But this way I might be your friend for life," which I was. I said, "You are so great, you could teach us everything in art, but I might be able to teach you how to be a bigger and better human being."

I met him almost the moment he arrived in New York, when he was brought to my house by a mutual friend. We didn't take to each other at once, but he felt very at home with me. He didn't speak English too well and it was nice for him to have a Russian person close to him. Little by little it turned into a real friendship. I became close to him in times of real stress, for instance when he became desperate about Diana Adams. He was really in love with her, but his wife was an invalid and he didn't know what to do about it. He tried for three years or so. Then finally he said to his wife, as he told me, "Tanny, if I go on with my marriage, I think I'll stop creating. I know the stimulus. In order to continue working I have to follow my love." But then when Diana left him he was disconsolate. He said, "Somebody just put their hand on my head and is holding me under the water, and I don't know when I'll come up."

When Balanchine came to America, Geva was already here, and he thought that he might catch up with her again. Then she married my ex-husband—Balanchine was absolutely outraged. How could she prefer someone else? She outwilled him, in her way. She was the first one in the New World and he followed.

During the thirties I had my own house, but I lived only on two floors and rented the other three. One time during those years, George didn't have a place, because he'd lost his last apartment. I invited him to come and take a floor above me and just pay what he could. "I'm going to Europe," I told him, "and I would be delighted if you'd stay." When I returned, he said, "You don't mind, I'm not only here but Zorina moved in too." It was a great surprise to me, because to have him was one thing, but to have a ménage was another. Zorina had a big open car and a big dog: she was a star and she was putting on a little bit. Of course I couldn't expel him, but he knew that it wasn't a good thing to do. He soon moved out and found somewhere else.

When their marriage broke up, it was shattering to him. I wouldn't plan for an evening without saying to myself, "I have first to check if George is alone." Then, one time later, I think it was after Diana, he begged me to go to Paris with him. We lived in a third-rate hotel around the Étoile, because that's all he could afford. I tried to remind him that after every breakup he'd say, "I can't see how I could have been in love with a woman who has a heart of a hausfrau"—or things like that. Each time when a new loss came, I'd say, "You remember how you couldn't get over that last hausfrau? Well, you will get over it, once more." And then each time there was a new one. For his creativity he needed a real emotional, sexual attachment. And the periods of depression afterward were not bad for his creativity because, when a man suffers, even that is useful for his work.

He really took Maria Tallchief, I believe, because he was upset about the previous one. I said, "Now tell me, truthfully, if she wasn't an American Indian, if she wasn't a virgin, not a Russian or an American girl, would you have been interested?" He was interested in trying a female of the species he had never had before, including one of our black entertainers who was famous in Paris. He did that purely to see, "I wonder how a Negro woman is?"

He liked elusiveness in a woman. About one of the wives he said, "I don't need a housewife. I need a nymph who fills the bedroom and floats out. This one always washes her leotard, she is a housewife and doesn't know that I don't need that in a woman." He always wanted romantic elusiveness. In his ballets the man always seeks and the woman flees. That is the typical picture of his life. He really can't catch her and in a way, the minute he does, she is less important. *Ivesiana* is an example of this in his work. He is down on the ground in "The Unanswered Question" and can't touch the girl. That is the beautiful part and descriptive of the man.

Suzanne Farrell was always elusive and not interested. He said, "I introduce her to Stravinsky and Tchelitchew and other people, yet I'm fully aware that she'd rather chat with her girlfriends from the ballet school about nothing." She was quite bored and told him so and he was very upset about that. I think Suzanne, through her association with George, developed as a human being. When he originally met her she was not really a companion for him, culturally.

When Stravinsky came to live in America, George had an apartment on East Fifty-seventh Street. To my knowledge, there was no particular woman in his life then. He had been quite strapped financially, but he was going to give a dinner for Stravinsky. George said to me, "When Stravinsky comes, it'll be easier for me if you are here." Socially Balanchine was quite gauche, and of course in this case he was worshipful. Besides having cooked all day and bought the most expensive things, he found two bottles of wine he couldn't possibly afford. When Stravinsky appeared George said, "Now, we have lovely wine." "What for?" Stravinsky replied. "I always bring my own, because nobody at the moment can offer me what I drink." George was crestfallen; he had spent practically a month's salary on those two bottles.

Twenty years later George said to me, "You know, Lucia, I'm going ahead and doing the choreography for *Agon* and maybe it's entirely different from what Stravinsky would like. Here I have conceived something and am going ahead with it and I don't even know whether I'm on the right path or not. Would you do me a favor? Bring him to a rehearsal so that I can know his reaction." So I asked, "Mr. Stravinsky, George begs me to bring you to rehearsal." "Oh, I don't like to go," he told me. "Please," I implored, "you know how much it matters to him." At that time the Stravinskys lived in the Ambassador Hotel. I had a nice car of my own. He said, "Well, all right. If you'll lunch with me and drive me over yourself to the rehearsal, and take me back, then I'll come." Stravinsky watched the rehearsal and said, "That's fine, that's fine, I like it very much." He suggested that when the four men begin the ballet they should turn their backs to the audience, but beyond that it was "just fine." George was in seventh heaven.

I loved George, I worshiped his work. I always wanted to do things for the good of his ballet company. I knew he should take Baryshnikov, but George didn't want another star in his company. At that time he was ill in the hospital. I tried to push Baryshnikov little by little, but it wasn't a go. Finally I went to see George in the hospital. I said, "Now you must promise me: take Baryshnikov. He is Russian, he understands the way you want. He never will go against your orders or directions, but you must take him. Just promise me." I practically made him do that. Soon after, he called Baryshnikov and said, "Do you want to come tomorrow and start rehearsing?" It was very unexpected.

George held Fokine in great respect. When George was very young Fokine was an innovator. That's why he respected him so and, unlike many people, George didn't change his mind afterward. George said, "He has his place."

Someone said to me, I think quite rightly, "It wasn't just Lincoln helping George; George helped Lincoln." Lincoln used to call up and say, "This or this is a disaster and it's all going to tumble." George used to cool him off and say, "Now wait, just wait." Yet, in spite of their wonderful association, they were never close to each other. Let's say they didn't speak the same language. Once or twice when Lincoln was inviting George for dinner, he'd say to me, "Come along, it'll be easier for me." They needed each other, but they never felt on the same ground, somehow.

I had a great friend who owned a tremendous estate in Connecticut. George was married to Tanny at that time and he was dying to have a little place in the country. I arranged that my friend would sell George a beautiful piece of land on top of a hill, at a ridiculously low price. He could take twenty years to pay. It was exactly across the road from Lincoln.

George had a little streak of cruelty, conscious or unconscious. I ascribe it to his being Caucasian. He had men who were useful to him, like Volodine, who was in the corps de ballet and shared an apartment with him. He did everything for George in the household, because George didn't want to go shopping and wash his underwear or clean the bathroom. But when George married Zorina, he said to Volodine, "You have to go find your own apartment now." Volodine was upset. He was Balanchine's cook and valet and friend, always fetching and carrying for him. He even went out on the George Washington Bridge and considered throwing himself off. So after George moved away with Zorina, I gave Volodine a little bedroom on the fifth floor and almost saved his life.

When the Bolshoi Ballet came here the first time, George gave a small supper for them and invited me. The then head of their company said to George, "Why do you make ballet like baking a pie and cutting it in small pieces? Here you give an evening and it always is subdivided into three or four ballets. One day you will come back and do what we do, give one great big evening." "No," George said. "I think one day you will come and do as I do." And now the Russians give one evening of several ballets. If George were alive I think he would be ambivalent about the Russians doing his things. On the one hand he would have said—publicly—"I don't want them to; they don't dance well enough." On the other, he would tell himself, "But in the end they *are* doing my things!"

ERICK

HAWKINS

Studied with Harald Kreutzberg and at the School of American Ballet. A member of the American Ballet, 1935–37, he danced in the Balanchine repertory and in the opera ballets of Balanchine at the Metropolitan Opera. As a charter member of Ballet Caravan, he danced in Harlequin for President, Pocahontas, *and* Filling Station. *He choreographed his own* Show Piece *for Ballet Caravan in 1937. He danced with Martha Graham from 1938 to 1951, when he established the Erick Hawkins Dance Company.*

I Remember Balanchine

I STOOD RIGHT BESIDE BALANCHINE WHEN HE ARRANGED THE FIRST GIRLS FOR *Serenade* in 1934. I was one of the first four men in that ballet. I was full of beans. Balanchine used other men for his other ballets. I was crushed. I'm sure they could do more than I could, but I could tell in my heart that they didn't understand what the idea of his dancing was all about. So I said, "I want to see Mr. Balanchine." I remember going into the office. Balanchine, Lincoln Kirstein, and Eddie Warburg were there. I said, "Mr. Balanchine, do you think I can be a dancer?" He said, "Well, you're supple." Balanchine was very wise. He went on, "I can't tell what you can do until you do it." That put it right back onto my talent and my desire. Afterward I thought frequently of what he had said. It was right after that that Balanchine let me teach. I must have been the first teacher who came out of the School. There was a little hole in the studio door, and Balanchine and Vladimiroff could watch me. I taught there for over a year. Today I sometimes let people start their teaching at my studio early like that, even when I know that they haven't assimilated very much. Teaching is a way of learning. That was probably the most important insight that I had from Balanchine.

In my heart I know that Balanchine was more excited about me than anybody. He was reviving *Mozartiana* in 1935. When George Chaffee was out of the first trio one day, I said, "Mr. Balanchine, can I do that?" The trio had double air turns. I remember I couldn't do them well. But sometimes a dancer doesn't know everything technically, but his spirit gets him through it. Mine did. Also I was in *Dreams* in 1935. I was the Knave with a sword. Balanchine came up to me after we got back from the performance at Warburg's estate. I was sitting next to Gisella Caccialanza and Leda Anchutina, and Balanchine said something about my spirit.

When Balanchine did something that was poetic, even in class, I reacted. In his Gluck *Orpheus* at the old Met in 1936, Balanchine had just Amor, Eurydice, and Orpheus—the three of them—onstage for the last act. I remember going in and sneaking around and just sitting there and watching. It made me burst into tears. Another moving Balanchine work was *Cotillon.* I've often wondered why people didn't see what Balanchine was doing. It was poetry in the sense of really making something. I don't know where his poetic gift came from. Somewhere you develop it in your inner life, and you go out and honor it and trust it.

When I got out of Harvard, by sheer accident an Italian friend had to go to London. He called me and we went. We saw the De Basil company's repertory for a week. In Balanchine's ballet *Concurrence,* a competition between two tailors, there was a tailor shop on the right side of the stage. Tamara Toumanova made her entrance around the corner, and I don't remember anything but the beauty of her looking around that corner. Everyone's tried to evoke it. Such moments are very deep, and that's what art is. I have always struggled to do what I want to do in that kind of way. Audiences and everybody are always after me to do the razzmatazz, the double air turns. Balanchine did that at times. I suppose he had to. I went to every rehearsal of the American Ballet because I just knew that I was going to be a choreographer.

When I did *Show Piece* for Ballet Caravan, Lincoln brought in Balanchine to look at it. Shortly after, Balanchine said that, of all the works produced by the Caravan, "That's the piece of choreography that's been *done.*" Perhaps I picked up something from him. His lesson was a guide.

ANNABELLE

LYON

Studied with Michel Fokine and Alexandra Fedorova. Annabelle
Lyon was a charter student at the School of American Ballet and a
dancer in Balanchine's American Ballet and in Ballet Caravan. She
created roles in Balanchine's The Card Party, Reminiscence,
and The Bat. *In 1940, she became a charter member of Ballet*
Theatre.

I Remember Balanchine

I WAS A STUDENT OF MICHEL FOKINE IN MANHATTAN, BUT THE ARRIVAL OF THE BAL-
lets Russes de Monte Carlo in New York in 1933 provided my first opportunity to see ballet. I was taken with the humor of Balanchine's *La Concurrence,*
and the humanity of it. It was something we could relate to, in our present
world, as opposed to all the fairy tales and abstract works. I remember
vividly Léon Woizikowsky's tramp, scratching all over, and then going into
one of the shops and coming out dressed up as a dandy. And Balanchine's
Cotillon was so beautiful—it would spark all kinds of feelings.

After seeing Balanchine's ballets at the Ballets Russes, I read about the
School of American Ballet opening. Fokine had gone to Europe to stage
ballets, so I was free to audition. I was accepted and began. It was a totally
different experience from Fokine, who had everything set, choreographed in
advance: you had to do exactly what *he* wanted, while Balanchine choreographed for *you,* for the dancer he was working with. It was tailor made.
Also, Fokine was very formal. You looked up to him as you would to a god.
He was remote, not to be touched, whereas Balanchine was approachable.
Fokine had so much to offer that no other teacher I've ever been to had, but
the School was more fun. We had Pierre Vladimiroff as our principal teacher;
he was wonderful.

I was involved in Balanchine's ballets right away, because with the School
he began rehearsals. The first one was *Serenade,* and it was quite a fantastic
experience. When he originally did *Serenade* in 1934, the first movement concluded with the entire corps de ballet doing a sequence of *fouettés.* (Later he
changed it to *piqué* turns.) I couldn't do *fouettés,* so he had me run offstage just
before that. Then, before the waltz began, he brought me back. I was the one
who comes in late, looking for her place. Now when people try to put a
meaning to that, it always tickles me. I didn't have strength in technique,
but I had a sense of all things I had learned with Fokine. So Balanchine used
a lot of lyric movement whenever he did a piece on me. It showed me to my
best advantage, but it became tiresome. I longed to do something different,
and later, when the Metropolitan Opera did *The Bartered Bride,* I asked him if I
could be in the polka, and he let me. That was a great relief.

At that time, Balanchine was not recognized by the critics or the public; he
was very vulnerable. I remember when we took the American Ballet to the
Adelphi Theater on Broadway he was nervous, and rather showed it. In
Reminiscence, the entrance for my variation was from a back wing; I was to
bourrée out with my back to the audience. I didn't have a strong technique
and had trouble with my ankles. Balanchine ran around from the front wing
to the back after I was already onstage and called out, "If you feel like you're
going to fall, just come off." I was so shocked! He was that nervous.

When we went to the Met, Balanchine seemed to take most things in stride, except once, when John Martin, the dance critic of the *New York Times,* was invited to a rehearsal. Martin arrived early and was sitting in the auditorium. An usher questioned his presence there, and Martin left. Balanchine was very upset about that.

One of the first dances he choreographed in *Jeu de Cartes* for the first Stravinsky Festival was my variation, which was totally different from the usual lyrical *bourrées* that I constantly did. I was the Queen of Hearts. I also did a Broadway show with Balanchine, *Great Lady.* That's where I first met Jerry Robbins. Nora Kaye was in the corps de ballet, and Alicia Alonso and her husband Fernando, and Paul Godkin. Bill Dollar helped choreograph. Leda Anchutina and I made more money than we ever had in our lives. We thought we'd end up being wealthy, but the show only ran two weeks.

After the Stravinsky Festival by the American Ballet at the Met, there was a reception. We were all invited to come, but I didn't. Balanchine asked my roommate, Gisella Caccialanza, where I was. "Oh, Annabelle didn't have a dress to wear," she told him. One day in Los Angeles he told me to wait for him after rehearsal. In the ballet company he had a very close friend, a Russian by the name of Volodine. So I waited and Balanchine and Volodine took me to the Bullocks Wilshire department store. Balanchine told the salesperson to bring out evening clothes that would be suitable for me. He was very, very particular. He said "Now, bring out something with a jacket, because she'll need one." They brought out this beautiful dress. It was white with a gold metallic thread in it, very simple with a flared skirt. The jacket was fitted, with a tie at the waist and one at the neck. It was simple and classic. Then he said, "Well, she'll need shoes and a bag." They outfitted me, and it cost a small fortune. I felt like Cinderella.

BARBARA

WEISBERGER

Studied with Marian Harwick in Brooklyn, the School of American Ballet in New York, and with Dorothie Littlefield in Philadelphia, she taught in Wilkes-Barre, Pennsylvania, and in Philadelphia, where she founded the Pennsylvania Ballet. She is now the Artistic Director of the Carlisle Project in Carlisle, Pennsylvania.

I Remember Balanchine

I STARTED DANCING IN A LITTLE NEIGHBORHOOD IN BROOKLYN WHEN I WAS FIVE AND A half. It was Midwood, Avenue J, in Flatbush. I had a great teacher, Marian Harwick, who was also a fantastic woman. She was a beautiful, natural dancer and had performed at the Met during the time of Gatti-Casazza and Rosina Galli. By the time I was eight, she didn't know what else to do with me. She heard about the opening of the School of American Ballet. She called Eugenie Ouroussow and said, "I have this child." Eugenie said, "Well, don't bother, we don't have children's classes, we expect to have them later and we'll be in touch." My teacher said, "No, you have to see her now." She was so pushy, Eugenie relented, and I auditioned at eight with Balanchine, Lincoln Kirstein, and Vladimiroff.

I was a little frightened because nobody spoke English. Kirstein didn't ask me anything. He just stood there like a big lion. My teacher didn't use French ballet terms, so when they asked me to do something, Ouroussow would translate. I don't know why in the world they took me. There weren't any children in the School. I had to take class with what was then the company. I was S.A.B.'s first child student. It was Balanchine's first company and beautiful: Heidi Vosseler, Holly Howard, Helen Leitch, William Dollar, Charles Laskey, Erick Hawkins. Daphne Vane might have joined a little later.

The only teachers in the School at the beginning were Vladimiroff and Balanchine. Several months later, I remember waiting to take class and a girl came who was five or six years older than I. She had a boyish bob and was skinny. It was Marie-Jeanne. She might have been twelve or thirteen. She was the only other child. Later they started the first children's classes, taught by Dorothie Littlefield.

I never took her classes because her students were beginners. I was already much too advanced. I was at the School from 1934 through 1936. I remember sitting in the corner while Balanchine was creating *Serenade*. I remember the wonder of that and the moment when Heidi Vosseler was lifted by the men and carried off at the end and saying to myself, "That's what I will do when I'm grown up. That's where I will be."

As a teacher, Balanchine was an authority figure but not frightening. I always seemed to be in a class with mountains around me, the dancers were all so much bigger. There were very big men, especially Charles Laskey and Erick Hawkins. I remember that they were always very sweet to me. I was very shy. In the dressing room I was very modest, and the women were walking around without clothes, and I used to have my mother take me to a corner and say, "Hide me, Mommy." It was a little bit awesome. It took me a little while to understand class work, but I followed, and I always did it. One time I remember feeling both frightened and elated because Balanchine had to demonstrate something, indicating me, and he said, "Do it like she does."

Balanchine's class was a regular ballet class with nothing idiosyncratic. He made me part of the class. I had to be absorbed into it. And in Vladimiroff's, too. In fifth position *port de bras,* Vladimiroff always folded his arms over, draped very close to his head, very much like the picture of Nijinsky in *Spectre.* His hands were open and beautiful, and he would drape them very close. His shoulders were always high, too.

In between the three or four classes at the School each week, I continued to study with Marian Harwick at her studio in our neighborhood. And in addition I was going to school. It was terribly tiring, and Marian and my mother reached a decision that I'd better take class instead with Margaret Curtis at the Metropolitan Opera at Thirty-ninth Street. The Met was a little closer. Miss Curtis was Nora Kaye's teacher, among many other dancers'. Nora Kaye and Ruthanna Boris had just left to dance. And so I was waiting at the Met for Balanchine when he came with the American Ballet in 1935.

My mother had received a note from Lincoln Kirstein when I left S.A.B. "Please bring her back. I'm so sorry that she isn't there," he wrote. For a long time my mother kept that note. When he came to the Met, Balanchine remembered me. Through every stage of my life, no matter how many years were in between, Balanchine remembered. I was in his ballets at the Met. I was in *Aïda, Le Coq d'Or*—anything that could use children. I did things like the Prince in *Lohengrin,* where I didn't dance but was carried across in a little boat. I was in operas with Ezio Pinza, Lily Pons, Lawrence Tibbett and Kirsten Flagstad. We did the Moorish dance in *Aïda.* Daphne Vane was in the center, and I remember Balanchine teaching it to us. *Aïda* was done very often, and I was there when Giovanni Martinelli had a heart attack onstage.

Balanchine always seemed a little bored by the opera ballets, but he was never bored when he was with his own people. I think he didn't relish the atmosphere at the Metropolitan Opera. I saw the ballets he did for the company there: *The Bat* and *Card Game.* He called them by their American names, all the time. He looked forward to his 1937 Stravinsky evening. I remember when I was late once for a rehearsal of one of the opera ballets, and I was so worried. The subway was held up, and I came running and practically in tears into the middle of the rehearsal. Balanchine was so sweet to me. "Where *were* you?" He never scolded. I don't remember him ever scolding. He never lost his cool.

I stayed with Miss Curtis at the Met until 1940, when my father got a position in Wilmington, Delaware. There was a local teacher who was very happy to have me, but I could teach her. Someone told my mother about

Dorothie Littlefield in Philadelphia. I had never taken from her when I was at S.A.B., so it was like a brand-new experience. Not only did Dorothie teach for Balanchine, but he had come to her when he couldn't find dancers that pleased him. Both Catherine and Dorothie Littlefield had worked with Balanchine at Preobrajenska's studio in Paris years before.

When I graduated from high school at sixteen, I was determined to dance. Catherine Littlefield invited me and two other dancers in the class to join her for Barrie's *A Kiss for Cinderella* on Broadway. But my mother and I didn't think I should, perhaps because there were some very frightening ladies saying things like, "Well, if you want to do this you're going to have to sleep with a few men!" It scared the heck out of me, so I went to college, to the University of Delaware. I married when I graduated, and that took me again to Philadelphia. When my marriage broke up, I returned to where my parents lived then, Wilkes-Barre, Pennsylvania, and I began teaching ballet in a little dancing school there. In the early fifties my school had grown so that I had about two hundred students. I had become a driven teacher in my late twenties and a choreographer for my recitals. I took my students in the summer and on holidays to S.A.B. They were always put in the top classes. I was in an elevator and there was Mr. B. I looked at him, and he looked at me, and he said, "Hello, Barbara." I said, "How do you remember me?" He said, "I never forget." He remembered without question. He wasn't pretending to. He had the facility of remembering people no matter how they had changed or how many years had passed. Through my pupils, he was aware of me.

In 1960 the first Northeast regional ballet festival was held in Wilkes-Barre. A year and a half later there was a regional festival in Dayton, Ohio. Diana Adams was the adjudicator, and Balanchine came with her to the festival. He was wonderful. He made me feel so good because I was teaching so well, and he watched my ballet, *Symphonic Variations.* Lincoln Kirstein was there too, along with Balanchine and W. McNeil Lowry. Lincoln came to me and said in a very gruff manner, "Your ballet was the best thing on the program, and you know it." Lowry was already doing research, and I met with him and talked about the regional ballet movement. He listened quietly.

Then in the summer of 1960, out of all that, the School of American Ballet invited teachers from around the country to come to New York to have seminars with Balanchine. I was one of the teachers. During the seminars, Kirstein had a gathering. It was crowded, and Balanchine talked to us: "In this vast country it is unbelievable that there are so few outlets. I can't even absorb the talented dancers in my own School. I will help if you want my help. I don't have money, but I have costumes, and I have music, and I have some ballets, and I will help you."

At the same time I was approached by people in Philadelphia to come and teach there. I innocently went to Mr. B. and I said, "You know, Mr. B., if you're very serious about doing this, the place to start is Philadelphia." Balanchine put his hand on my head, and he said, "Well, Barbara, you must do it." And that's how it started.

From the very beginning, Balanchine was there to help. It was Balanchine who said that it might be helpful to start with an institution that already existed, so we associated ourselves with the Philadelphia Lyric Opera. Balanchine said he would be the artistic adviser of such a group. He let me take any dancers I wanted. I took some from the School of American Ballet, some from New York City Ballet. I said that if I could keep the company that I pulled together to do the operas I would have one of the major companies in the country at that time.

The first opera we did was *Faust* in the 1961–62 season, and the impresario was Fabiani, a fight promoter who adored opera. He was so excited about having Balanchine advise us that they put back the Walpurgisnacht ballet and Frank Moncion came and did the choreography. We did two seasons with the Lyric Opera. I said, "We're going to start a school, and then we're starting a company." I had about seven hundred and fifty dollars of my own money, and I had a lovely woman who lent me about fifteen hundred dollars. We found a studio on Walnut Street and opened in October 1962. It was five hundred dollars a month for rent. I had about three thousand dollars. We ran out of money immediately and were locked out. Freddie Franklin gave auditions for scholarships, and dancers came from all over. I had maybe fifty students to start. None of our teachers got paid.

Balanchine came to Philadelphia constantly. We were a group of dancers struggling, really struggling, locked out of our studio for lack of rent money. Balanchine's visits bolstered our morale. I would let him know I had a group of people who might give us some money, and he would not hesitate to come, never questioning. He never stood on ceremony. It was always down to basics: this is what you do, it is important. Balanchine's utter simplicity and absolute sense of values about what is right came through.

On one particularly happy visit we all decided to take him out to dinner at a fancy restaurant off Rittenhouse Square. There were eight or ten of us altogether and we were seated at a round table and were just loving our togetherness. The two gentlemen who owned the restaurant recognized Mr. B. and sent over a magnum of champagne. He didn't drink it. He had his schnapps, but we had our champagne, ordered a feast, and soon reached a state of blessed euphoria. Suddenly we realized that we might not have enough cash to pay for the dinner. This was the pre-credit-card era. The bill hadn't been presented, but very smoothly we began passing whatever money we did have under the table. He couldn't see us doing it, but of course he knew. He had sensed the situation, and he interrupted himself to remark casually, "Oh, this is on me. Don't worry about it." And then he put out his arms and said, "Let us hold hands." You may know the wonderful analogy he made about dancers and elephants, comparing us because we need each other and herd together. He talked about that while we held hands, and then he said, "This is the way it used to be with my company when I started it."

Balanchine did not change. He was always warm and giving. To me he was a sort of demigod, despite his unpretentiousness. I would say, "Why do you do this? Why are you doing so much to help?" At one point the company was dying. We had no money, and I was spending my own money. I met with Mr. Lowry and he said, "Try to hold on. Maybe there'll be a possibility of helping in the future. Don't give up." Balanchine came and he knew how desperate it was. I was at the hairdresser's and was called to the phone. Eugenie Ouroussow spoke to me and said, "Balanchine has something to say to you." He got on the phone and said, "Barbara, I spoke to my friend Mr. Lowry and said he must help Barbara and her pussycats, and so we have some money for you. And here's Eugenie, and she'll tell you about it." Eugenie got on the phone and said, "We have forty-five thousand dollars from the Ford Foundation." With that money I was able to bring dancers in for rehearsals at forty-five dollars a week and to pay back all the people we owed. Pat Wilde came, and we had our very first performance in July 1963. We did a jazz ballet, my *Symphonic Variations,* Virginia Williams's setting of *Pas de Dix* (1955) and a Williams ballet to American folk songs. We performed on an estate in Paoli with a natural amphitheater. There were nine hundred people in the audience, hanging on trees, sitting in the knolls of the hill. Balanchine and Mac Lowry were there. We had our first performance in Philadelphia in April 1964 at Irvine Auditorium at the University of Pennsylvania. We did *Concerto Barocco.*

Balanchine was our artistic adviser for a number of years. I liked what he liked. I tried to get close to what I felt he would want things to be. We always had some dancers joining from S.A.B. or New York City Ballet, and we worked well for what we were. But I knew, and this was quite clear to him, that the performance was not going to be as it would with his own company.

We talk of Balanchine's genius and the extraordinary "assemblage" that constitutes his style, if you will. What is greater, actually, than the choreography is the symbiotic relationship between his School and the New York

City Ballet. It wasn't enough that he created the work on the company; it had to involve a transference from those he trained. I once thought it was the School that fed into the company—but how he liked to see the movement and the dancers in his choreography is the basis for the training in the School. The development goes both ways, and that is what makes a great company—and a great style—possible.

RAY

BOLGER[*]

Born January 10, 1904, Ray Bolger performed in vaudeville, on Broadway in The Merry World *(1926) and* George White's Scandals *(1931) and starred in* On Your Toes *(1936), choreographed by Balanchine. He worked with Balanchine again in* Keep Off the Grass *(1940) and* Where's Charley? *(1948). His motion pictures:* The Great Ziegfeld *(1936),* The Harvey Girls *(1946), and his definitive Scarecrow in* The Wizard of Oz *(1939). He died January 15, 1987.*

* This interview was conducted by Dawn Lille Horwitz.

I WAS THE GUY AT THE SENIOR PROM IN HIGH SCHOOL WHO WAS DISGRACED BECAUSE HE couldn't dance. The girl walked off the floor and left me standing there. This changed my whole life. After school I was working at the First National Bank of Boston. I decided the only way I would be a social success in life was to learn to dance. So I went down to O'Brien's School of Social and Formal Dancing. I could not afford to take a lesson, but O'Brien was a very gracious man. This is how I got my first and beginning dance instruction.

I ran into a fellow who was anxious to become a professional dancer. He was a shoe salesman—Thom McAn Shoes in Boston. I wasn't anxious to become a dancer. I really had no desire other than to learn the social aspect of dancing. But he showed me a tap step, and suddenly I became enamored of being able to make my feet sound like a percussion complement to the music. From these humble beginnings, one day I was doing some steps, and I ran into Sania Russokov, of the Russokov School of Russian Dancing. He had danced with Pavlova and Nijinsky. He said, "I have this Russian School of Dancing here," and I said, "Oh, I noticed the sign." We became acquainted, and he invited me to come in and do what I'd like to do in the studio, and what I liked to do was to learn whatever I could. And that's how I got into ballet. During the day and evenings I would go to Russokov's ballet school, fix up his books, and then go into any class I could, go to the barre, do the barre exercise and create a dance form of my own. I did the school's recital. I was the star. I had a vivid imagination. I did a Chinese dope fiend dance. I did some tap dancing, which I really knew nothing about at all, nothing technical. The only technique I ever had in my life was what I picked up at the school by going to the barre and learning about turning out and hand positions and things of that sort. And I worked very hard at what I was doing.

I went from the school to the Bob Ott Musical Comedy and Repertory Company. (You had to have the "and" in there because that showed that they had one dramatic show a week.) A man came looking for girls for this show, and I talked him into hiring me. After the Bob Ott Musical Comedy and Repertory Company, I played the Rialto Theater for about six weeks in 1923. And that was the start of a whole new era. Dr. Hugo Reisenfeld created stage shows for motion picture theaters between the silent pictures. They were like pageants. At the Rialto Theater we had Ben Bernie and his Orchestra in the pit and Ray Bolger and a lot of names that nobody ever heard of on the stage. And then the picture would come on, and we would lie down on a cot and rest and then go back and do another show. We did four or five shows a day.

When I was in *George White's Scandals* and *Life Begins at 8:40,* I always choreographed my own material. Then I did *On Your Toes* with George Balanchine in

1936. Balanchine was without a doubt one of the divine characters on this earth, a heavenly person. He didn't speak much English then, so we didn't have a language that we all understood. He was a fantastic musician. We got around to understanding each other very well, in whatever language he spoke. If he spoke Russian or French or German or his version of English, it was easily understood, because any movement Balanchine made was a whole choreographed picture, a whole ballet in itself. This man I adored. He took a fancy to me because I had some kind of musical background, loved music and had heard a symphony orchestra and seen Pavlova and Nijinsky. So, for example, I was very aware of the satire in *On Your Toes'* Princess Zenobia and *Slaughter on Tenth Avenue* ballets. Very few of the rest of the cast were aware of it. *On Your Toes* was really the first show ever to integrate dance and action, even before Agnes De Mille. I don't think Aggie would have done any show if it hadn't been for *On Your Toes.* The audience would not have accepted it, as original as she was.

I was instrumental in arguing for what I thought was right for the book. You don't write, you don't tell somebody to do something. But you say, "I think that if you were to do something like this," and then finally you fight with them. Balanchine was aware of the integration of the show and aware of the type of humor. Between Balanchine, my wife, and me, we had more understanding as to what that show was about than anybody else. Richard Rodgers wrote the *Zenobia* ballet, but that was actually a job of arranging, more than anything else. But *Slaughter on Tenth Avenue* was Richard Rodgers.

Balanchine and I went up to the great ballet studio way at the top of the Metropolitan Opera House to work with a marvelous girl pianist on the piece. Balanchine was not only a musician but also a quick study. He was a brilliant brain, quick and humorous and happy when he discovered something. Rodgers's music became to him rather a challenge. He could see the beauty in the theme. He could see a great deal of romance, and he could also see the innocence of my character. So he made a sexy ballet without ever touching. "No touch. Oh, no, no, no touch." I would reach for her breasts, and her hand would come up. Her hand would raise, my hand would reach, and she'd jump. I'd get behind her and I'd climb over her, using balletic form, turned out. When I got away from the original turnout, I'd get into another kind of move, so that we were creating moves and creating drama and humor all the time. "No touch! No touch!" It was really sheer delight. And so when I got around to the tap-dancing effect, I said to George, in French, *"Les percussion."* He stopped and listened and said, "Yes, that's right." When it came to the end of the ballet, where I had to do my own thing, I did a lot of eccentric jumping up steps, anything that I liked, a hodgepodge. Nothing really had any form to it. I was trying to avoid any form, to make it look like it was pure desperation. You've got to do a step. You've got to jump up. You've got to keep dancing. You've been on for fifteen minutes. You've been doing this thing and you've had a fight and you've leaped over the bar. You've done all of the acrobatic kinds of things that you do in this sort of ballet. And I still had to live. "I want to live. And if I stop dancing they're gonna shoot!" That was the end, and Balanchine just let me go.

Tamara Geva had been married to Balanchine. He put on the most elegant thing, the *Zenobia* ballet, for Geva and Demetrios Vilan, a pas de deux in the "classique" form. It was satire, but some people didn't get it. They didn't know what was so funny. Dwight Wiman said, "George, look at the way he is grabbing her!" Balanchine would have Vilan start to do a classic lift, but his hand would slip. Opening night in Boston, Tamara was mad; she was so upset that the audience laughed. It was a funny audience, a funny opening, because half the audience laughed and the other half said, "Shhhhhhhh!"

The Boston critic Elliot Norton was in on the satire. When he saw it, he adored the show and thought it was great, marvelous, the greatest thing that had ever happened to show business, a brand-new idea. And he gave Tamara Geva a great, great kudo for being a great satirist. At rehearsal the next day, she walked on the stage and said, "George! Where are my laffs? I want my laffs!"

Four years later I worked with Balanchine on *Keep Off the Grass*. We wanted to do a ballet. We got Dukelsky—Vernon Duke. We got the Russian contingent together, and we did a *Raffles* ballet. *Raffles* was the only ballet Balanchine choreographed for the show. *Raffles* was a real ballet, and the other things were only junk. That show was a revue, just entertainment stuff. Balanchine choreographed that ballet for me as a kind of favor. We were very, very fond of George. George Balanchine's idea, his love, was to form the kind of ballet company he eventually did bring about in his New York City Ballet. Where is he going to get the money to do it? If he gets one percent of the show, it's going to let him survive. If the show does thirty thousand dollars, he'll get three hundred dollars a week, and in those days he's going to be able to survive and do his work. That was the main reason he choreographed the *Raffles* ballet. Who would ask him otherwise? I wouldn't ask George Balanchine to do a lousy revue like *Keep Off the Grass*.

In the *Raffles* ballet Raffles was a thief. In an apartment he breaks in through the window to steal a pearl necklace, and he has to get the pearls from around the woman's neck. He's a very famous, very elegant thief. The ballet had me, a girl, and some props. It was a pantomimic ballet, whereas *Slaughter on Tenth Avenue* was a dramatic ballet.

Betty Bruce was in *Keep Off the Grass*. She was a good tap dancer. Balanchine made a dance for her. What he did was to take the tap dancing out of just steps and to give it a form. I never used tap dancing just as tap dancing *per se.* Doing eight bars and then sixteen bars of one step after another bores me. I try to tell a story in the course of the dance. For instance, *The Old Soft Shoe* is about a man who thinks he is the most elegant dancer in the world. It's in his whole form: he wears a homburg hat and he puts it on his head and tilts it. He's even got ballet movements with his hands. He's so elegant. And the satire of it is that he uses the same step that anybody else would use, the simplest of all tap-dancing steps. It's his attitude of thinking of himself as too elegant that gives the dance its humor. The audience senses what you're doing. I like to kid myself. I like the fact that when I think I'm a great dancer I must almost trip or slip or fall. Balanchine loved this. He thought it was marvelous. I notice that he used certain things of that sort in his ballets. He used mistakes in his ballets a good deal. He was a quiet humorist.

Balanchine was the greatest influence in the dance world on my life. He made me want to go back and study. I started to work with him prior to *On Your Toes.* And when I didn't have work with Balanchine, I went to a dancing school, went to the barre and did nothing but exercises, for my balance. Balanchine impressed me so much as the ultimate in dance, as the ultimate in the drama and joy that dance can give, that I wanted to work. After that I even took tap-dancing lessons so that I would know what I was doing. I took tap from whatever teacher I could get, and finally I found a young fellow by the name of Kelly who was a very good teacher, and I went back to the fundamentals. He was in New York, and then he became my assistant choreographer on my television show. Russokov gave me the opportunity to stand at the barre, and Balanchine made me understand what good the barre would do you in a dancing life.

My wife and I produced *Where's Charley?* along with two partners, Feuer and Martin. In that show, Balanchine choreographed the numbers *Pernambuco* and *Red Rose Cotillion,* a lovely duet. I'm a good waltzer on the ballroom floor, and I also know the Viennese style of waltzing. The *Ashmolean Marching Society and Students' Conservatory Band* was Balanchine's, too.

As you've probably noticed, in all of Mr. Balanchine's works, his hands are terribly important. He uses the whole body. This is what I learned from him: the humor, from the top of my head to the tip of my toes to the soles of my feet, to the turnout, to the turn-in, the strength of the turnout. And he paid attention to the music.

He had a fantastic sense of humor. Like all great intellects, his humor was deep. To dance his material is a rewarding thing. The timing is impeccable. Balanchine not only absorbed American culture, American humor, American rhythms, American music, he went further than that: that further is Balanchine. Balanchine just doesn't go around the corner to see what's happening. He wants to walk around all the blocks. We have different kinds of music. Balanchine understood Schoenberg and Honegger and Bartók. He has to be the greatest choreographer ever. He allowed all the other choreographers to do what they wanted to do and they had never been able to do. He also taught them a little something: that in the American musical you don't have to do kick, stomp, thump, turn, jump, turn, kick. You can *dance.* He opened up a whole new world for the American musical comedy stage.

The Broadway work did nothing particularly for Balanchine. He was above that sort of thing. He didn't have the kind of ego that has to flaunt innovations or influence. Of course, anything that you do teaches you something. What Broadway taught Balanchine I don't know. Perhaps it taught him something that was important in his life, that there are other things besides Bach, Beethoven, and Brahms. Some of these things come from America. When you look at his modern ballets, you can see that Balanchine loved, adored, and worshiped such things. Hoedowns would be wonderful things to Balanchine. There was no jealousy in his body. His Americana works have been magnificent. You can see great study and thought behind them. The man is a lesson, a lesson on how to work, how to study, how to never let yourself down. Whenever I am in New York, I look at his repertory at City Ballet. It's a privilege. I saw him in New York when I was worried about his heart condition. Balanchine and I were the same age.

RUTHANNA

BORIS

Trained at the Metropolitan Opera School of Ballet with Giuseppe Bonfiglio, Margaret Curtis, and Rosina Galli, at the studios of Graham, Humphrey-Weidman, and Holm, and at the School of American Ballet; danced with the American Ballet and Ballet Caravan; she performed on Broadway and joined the Metropolitan Opera, where she was prima ballerina. *As a member of the Ballet Russe de Monte Carlo she choreographed* Cirque de Deux *and* Quelques Fleurs. *Joined New York City Ballet as a guest artist and choreographed* Cakewalk, Kaleidoscope, *and* Will o' the Wisp. *She has made ballets for the Royal Winnipeg Ballet, the Eglevsky Ballet, and the Houston Ballet. She is professor of dance and professor of psychiatry (emeritus) at the University of Washington in Seattle and is president and executive director of the Center for Dance Development and Research in Albany, California.*

I Remember Balanchine

I WAS IN THE ORIGINAL *Serenade* IN 1934; YEARS LATER, FOR THE DE CUEVAS BALLET and Toumanova, Balanchine made one big role out of all the smaller parts. Toumanova did the first and second entrance. There was only another person when the adagio began, when the Angel came in. Ballet Russe got that version, too, and Danilova danced it that way. When I joined Ballet Russe I wanted to dance that role because I identified with *Serenade.* And when I did finally dance it, I felt more and more strongly that it showed a pattern in Balanchine's life: a figure comes in and all the configurations change. That figure initiates the change but does not participate in it. Then, finally, she does the finale looking for her place, and the whole group turns away. In the end she's the one that goes to heaven. I knew by then that Balanchine had had tuberculosis. He said to me once, "You know, I am really a dead man. I was supposed to die and I didn't, and so now everything I do is second chance. That is why I enjoy every day. I don't look back. I don't look forward. Only now."

He started *Serenade* on a nice sunny day. There were seventeen girls in class. "Today I think I'll make a little something," he announced. He excused the gentlemen and started putting girls in place and standing back to see what it looked like. Annabelle Lyon and I were the two smallest, and we already knew that he liked tall ballerinas. He took forever to arrange everyone; he wanted all his girls to show. He placed Kathryn Mullowny, Heidi Vosseler, Holly Howard, until finally Annabelle and I were the only two left, standing across from each other. Her face told me what I felt: "Oh, God, we're too small; we're going to be the understudies." But then he jumped up on the bench and summoned us: "Ruthanna, Bella." We came running and he put her in front on stage left and me on stage right. "Like hungry birds in the nest," he told me later. We were starving for steps.

He was looking for a way to begin. He started talking about Germany. "I was there with Diaghilev. There is an awful man there [Hitler]. He looks like me but he has mustache. The people know him, they love him. When they see him, all people do like that for him." I still didn't know who Mr. Hitler was. "I am not such an awful man," Balanchine continued, "and I don't have mustache. So maybe for me you put together this. Your hand is high, and then falls down and thrusts forward."

I adored Balanchine. I waltzed up to him when I was fifteen and said, "Mr. Balanchine, I want to be a choreographer like you. How do you do it?" He replied, "I can't tell you how you will do it because I am not you and I don't know how I do it. I don't think I am even yet choreographer. I make some steps for my friends. They are nice. Sometimes it's all right. But I will tell you what you have to do. You have to be very good dancer yourself. I didn't say famous, I said good. You have to know how dancers feel. You will never know unless you have done it. Then you have to know music very well." He went on and on about that. "Then you have to look everywhere, everything, all the time. Look at the grass in the concrete when it's broken, children and little dogs, and the ceiling and the roof. Your eyes is camera and your brain is a file cabinet."

When he was choreographing one ballet, he put us all on our knees a long time. "Well, you know, when I began I was dry," he explained. "I didn't have idea. And I had twelve pages of awful music. I didn't know what to do. I go in studio and I sit. I watch dancers. They put leg on barre and I get idea. But I look and I think of that awful music, what will I do, and I have to put them off. And mind open and picture come suddenly of that man on Broadway, with wheels, with pencils." He was referring to a World War I veteran who had no legs, who used to sit on a skateboard on Broadway. "He was one of the first people I meet in America," Balanchine told us. "When I saw this man without legs, I put all on your knees and I can begin."

I never knew anybody who trusted his unconscious and was able to follow it through as much as he. I had millions of little examples of how that happened, one when he made *Le Bourgeois Gentilhomme.* It was done in a great hurry. Balanchine kept saying, "I have a nice little pas de trois for you and Danielian and Nikita Talin." Berman designed a Columbine costume, with curls and a hat, but Balanchine hadn't yet made any choreography. I kept saying, "But Mr. B!" He reassured me. "You learn very fast. I will do for you." About a day and a half before the premiere, he finally got around to it after a performance one night. Nikita was Pierrot and Leon was Harlequin. We came in with three little screens and put them down and danced. The idea was they both wanted me and he made a big promenade where Leon had my hand and Nikita was pulling my foot. Balanchine put it together very fast; finally he came to the end. It was about two o'clock in the morning by then. "I have to make finale. But I am so tired I could kill myself." And so he had us set up our little screens. I was in the middle and Leon came up from behind his screen and approached me. I said, "No," and he killed himself and disappeared. Nikita came up and I told him, "No," too. He went down behind his screen. I ran around, they were both dead, so I killed myself too, and that's the way it ended.

After class one day Balanchine said, "I want to talk to you. I think you have to start to teach." "Oh, no," I protested. "I will never be a dancing teacher. I'm going to do *Swan Lake* and then I'm going to die." "You have gift," he said. "You will be good teacher. I will give you the most easy class." He gave me the advanced professional class, which was comprised of all my friends. For a week I came wearing a different chiffon every day and carried on like an idiot. Balanchine sat on the bench and wiggled his nose and batted his eyebrows and eyelashes. He didn't say a word, however, until after class on Friday. "You don't get salary this week because you didn't teach one class. You performed for them. You make nice choreography. I will steal your steps, a little bit. But you didn't teach." He pointed to the bench. "Until you can sit there and let them find, you are not teaching. You have to look, not do yourself, or they will only copy you. They are good dancers. They know everything. What would you like to see them do different than they do?" "Number one," I said, "I cannot stand the way they look in the mirror. They spend the whole class there." "What else?" he prompted me. "They don't run very well, particularly the women in their toe shoes. They make too much noise and they don't move." "Well, then you have something to teach. Do."

The next lesson I turned everyone away from the mirror and started them running, everywhere and every possible way and configuration. While I was doing that Mr. Vladimiroff arrived on the balcony to watch. Eugenie Ouroussow came in next. Then Mr. Oboukhoff. When I came out, Miss Ouroussow said, "Come into the office. I need to talk to you. Mr. Vladimiroff has complained that you are breaking tradition. The class is only running. They are not doing *enchaînement.*" She told me Mr. Balanchine was waiting for me. He asked how it went and I told him, "We're beginning to break some ground. I'd like to do it again tomorrow." "Good," he said and walked out. As I walked out Mr. Oboukhoff hit me on the back and congratulated me. It was only Vladimiroff who made the scandal, but to keep him happy they called me into the office with Balanchine congratulating me in private. Balanchine told me, "You know, when I am dry I go to Oboukhoff's class and take it with my eyes. And I am full. He is such a choreographer." Balanchine used to ask him to do a ballet, but he never would. "No, too sad, too sad."

After I retired from dancing, I was sitting on the bench with Balanchine at the School of American Ballet while he rehearsed. As they were working, he said to me, "You know, those men in Tibet up in the mountains. They sit nude in the cave and they drink only water through straw and they think very pure thoughts." I said, "Yes, the Tibetan monks. The lamas." He said, "Yes. You know, that is what I should become. I would be with them." And then he looked around and said, "But unfortunately, I like butterflies."

ELLIOTT

CARTER

Educated at the Horace Mann School, at Harvard, at the École Normale de Musique in Paris, and in private studies with Nadia Boulanger. Musical director of Ballet Caravan 1936–40. Among his many compositions are the scores for the ballets Pocahontas *(Ballet Caravan, 1938) and* The Minotaur *(Ballet Society, 1947). Taught music, history, and mathematics at St. John's College and music theory and composition at the Peabody Conservatory, Yale University, and the Juilliard School. Elliott Carter received the Pulitzer Prize for Music, 1960 and 1973; the New York Music Critics Circle Award, 1962; the Creative Arts Award of Brandeis University, 1965; the Gold Medal for Music of the National Institute of Arts and Letters, 1971; the Handel Medallion of the City of New York, 1978; and the National Medal of the Arts, 1985.*

I Remember Balanchine

Carter, I believe, has a grasp of Balanchine's gifts no one else can match. We all know that Balanchine was a graduate of the Conservatory of Music in Leningrad, that he was a gifted pianist and could transcribe for piano the scores he envisioned for ballets. But dancers and musicians as well as critics have difficulty describing the process by which he used music to arrive at his choreography.

When I came to know Balanchine in 1948 through the composer Nicolas Nabokov and Patricia Blake, the choreographer knew that I had been a student of Nabokov's and Carter's at St. John's College in Annapolis. As I tried to draw Balanchine out about how he made his ballets, he always deflected the conversation to the mysteries of space and time. Did I think it was possible to know things as they are or did I interpret them as phenomena in the eternal space/time situation? Music was Balanchine's time, yet the stage space he filled with dancing seemed mysteriously occupied with movement that unfolded almost independently of the music; his imagination was not enslaved by music's time-keeping but seemed freed by it. How he filled space with dancing, aside from the music, the here and now of the situation, the needs of the moment and the particular dancers available to him, seemed indescribable. I felt that he did not wish to explore a gift from God. He would simply shrug as I tried to decipher the process of the unfolding of his ballets, saying, "You will see." If Balanchine were alive today, the conversation I should most like to hear would be between him and Elliott Carter, our finest composer.

F.M.

I SAW ALL THE 1933 BALANCHINE BALLETS THAT WERE DONE AT THE THÉÂTRE DES Champs-Elysées when I was a student in Paris. It was a most remarkable occasion: in my opinion, I never saw anything quite as interesting as that again from Balanchine. It seemed to me that was one of his highest moments. He said to me once that one of the problems later, when he came here, was that he felt obliged to do ballets that would be successful. He felt responsible to Lincoln and to the whole company. As time went on, from my point of view, he began to lose some of that very novel character that was striking at the beginning of his career. It occasionally showed up again, as in the case of the Webern ballet, *Episodes* (1959), and in some of the Stravinsky ballets, but mostly his whole point of view began to change, I think quite rightly from the point of view of running a ballet company. It was unfortunate that he was the person involved so closely with running the company. It was a shame there wasn't a ballet company to hire him to do just Balanchine things. Instead he was the leader who felt the whole ballet company rested on his back. But in 1933, with Edward James's money, in Paris and London he could for the first time in his life do what he wanted to do. Occasionally he had that opportunity again. Gluck's *Orpheus* (1936) at the

Metropolitan with Tchelitchew's sets was an extraordinary production, I thought. I don't know how they got the money together for *Orpheus,* but it was a failure from the point of view of the Metropolitan Opera season. It was never done again, which was unfortunate, because it was a very unusual, moving spectacle. I went to the rehearsals with Tchelitchew, whom I knew pretty well also at that time.

In that production I remember one scene with what looked like actual trees with roots hanging down. The underworld was a whole forest of roots and trees. You could see the trunks of the trees halfway up the stage. It was extraordinary. I remember going to a rehearsal and hearing Lucrezia Bori, one of the directors of the opera at that time and very important, be absolutely scandalized, wondering why they ever allowed anything like this to be shown at the Met.

Also done at the Metropolitan, the Stravinsky-Balanchine *Jeu de Cartes* (1937), or *Card Game* as it was called later, wasn't such a good idea as a ballet in itself, but the music was wonderful. I thought Balanchine was stuck with just the cards. It would have been better if he'd made the Joker more devilish. The music is full of parody, suggesting *The Barber of Seville;* Figaro there, like the Joker, is a character who breaks everything and causes problems. *Le Baiser de la Fée,* which he also staged first at the Met, was another matter, a very good production, but it disappeared all too quickly. It must have been too elaborate to put on. The ending of the ballet was like the ending of *Errante,* with the main character climbing on a rope ladder up to the top of the stage.

The reason Balanchine interested me so much began on the Riviera in 1932, when I saw *Cotillon.* The ballet was mysterious; things happened that you couldn't explain. The Hand of Fate, I remember, was the important figure in the entire work. Toumanova was the heroine. She was ravishing at that time.

Concurrence was different, much more straightforward. The story was clear although I don't remember what it was. It had much less atmosphere, a humorous piece in the common world of people but as seen through the eyes of modern painters.

I came to know Balanchine through the composer Nicolas Nabokov, a great friend of mine for many years, and through Tchelitchew.

I wrote the music for the ballet *The Minotaur* with the idea that Balanchine would do it, but then in 1947 he went to Paris and John Taras choreographed it. I don't think Balanchine ever liked the music very much. I'm surprised he didn't like it because it sounds, in a recording by Gerard Schwarz and the YMHA Orchestra that's just been made, so much like the kind of music I would have thought he'd like! We had talked about the libretto and worked it out together.

He suggested many things; it was a collaborative libretto. It was my idea, an idea that was somewhat in the air, because of everyone's awareness in the post-World War II period of the concentration camps; we were discovering then all the horrors that had happened. This was a kind of ballet picture of those horrors: the Minotaur eating up its victims in a cave, in a labyrinth, was symbolic of it all. I think Lincoln wanted Balanchine to do this ballet. I have the feeling that Balanchine was doing what he thought Lincoln wanted him to do. He seemed to be interested. There was one big moment in the ballet which he invented and which was a very good idea, at least it seemed so then, to me. When Pasiphaë is raped by the bull, she falls over panting. Her heartbeats become the hammering and building of the labyrinth. That transition from one scene to the other I put into the score. That was very striking, making the analogy between the heartbeats of the woman who became the mother of the Minotaur, and the labyrinthine imprisonment of the Minotaur—that was a touching and moving idea.

Another Balanchine ballet I remember was Stravinsky's *Danses Concertantes* (1944). That was a beautiful ballet that got lost, with wonderful scenery and costumes by Eugene Berman. That was a great shame. In Ballets 1933, there was *Mozartiana,* with an extraordinary set by Bérard. The front drop was an enormous red curtain painted in a very rough style with the little child Mozart playing a grand piano.

I used to go often to Balanchine's rehearsals in the old studios at the School of American Ballet at Fifty-ninth and Madison. I remember meeting Céline, the novelist, there one time. When you saw Balanchine indicating the dance, showing the choreography to his dancers, it seemed as though he was just inventing things moment by moment, as if there was no plan for anything, as if he was improvising, rather than having one general big picture. But then when it actually happened onstage the ballet didn't seem like that at all, you saw the whole thing he had in his mind.

Some years ago, in a conversation with Allen Edwards, I spoke about my interest and thinking about musical time. They were very much stimulated, I said, "by the kinds of 'cutting' and continuity you find in the movies of Eisenstein, particularly *Ten Days That Shook the World* and *Potemkin,* and such as are described in his books, *Film Sense* and *Film Form.* I was similarly interested by the onward-moving continuity in the ballets of George Balanchine—every individual momentary tableau in the best of his ballets is something that the viewer has seen interestingly evolved, yet it is also only a stage of a process that is going on to another point; and while every moment is a fascinating and beautiful thing in itself, still what's much more fascinating is the continuity, the way each moment is being led up to and led away from—something you are not aware of in the ballets of most other choreographers as being anything of interest or which has even been thought about much. Indeed, the Balanchine ballets have been very stimulating to me in this way ever since 1933, when I saw many of them in Paris. They have been important as an example, in another art, of what one might do with music: one wanted to have very vivid moments, but what was more interesting was the process by which these moments came into being and by which they disappeared and turned into other moments."*

I don't think I could say it that well again! Balanchine doesn't follow the music exactly. What's interesting is the fact that he's making a choreography that is basically a comment on the music and not a specific Mickey-Mousing from one measure to another. Take *Serenade,* for instance; there are different movements in the score, but in the ballet when one movement ends the people who are to dance the next one are already onstage: he's linked up the movements, and the choreography is in some ways made more continuous and different from the music. This remains fascinating for a musician to see, how he's constantly developing a choreography that's tangential, somehow connected to the music.

One of the things you didn't know about Balanchine's ballets was whether there was an element of fun in it all. That you could never tell. The humor of that period was very concealed, I think. People did things very seriously when they were meant to be funny, like some of Cocteau's work. You can't really tell whether you want to laugh at it or not. I think there's some element of that in Balanchine. That's one of the things that's interesting about it, the ambiguity of character at times. I think that's fascinating. As I knew Balanchine, I don't ever remember him laughing, even with Nabokov or Tchelitchew. But I remember him smiling a great deal. Like Stravinsky, he told those funny kinds of jokes based on twisted words. Of course, that's inevitable in a person who is foreign, who's always thinking about language. And there were little comic turns. Stravinsky was broadly comic, even to the point of being extravagantly too funny, clownlike. Balanchine never was like that. He was muted in some curious way, as a person—controlled, somehow.

The reason why I don't like to go to the ballet now is that I just see work that very pedestrianly follows the music. On the other hand, it's not something that is so divorced from the music that we find that there are two different things going on at the same time, like with Merce Cunningham and others. That bothers me somewhat because it just seems so random and

* From *Flawed Words and Stubborn Sounds, a Conversation with Elliott Carter* by Allen Edwards. W. W. Norton & Co., 1971.

rather arbitrary. The mind can't focus on the fact, as one can with Balanchine, that here's somebody thinking about music and treating it as if it were something ballet is a comment on. With Balanchine one constantly wonders what it is he's seeing in this music. That constantly keeps you awake, is constantly provocative.

Some of the Massine ballets on big symphonies were very striking: the *Symphonie Fantastique* of Berlioz, one of the Tchaikovsky symphonies, and the Fourth Symphony of Brahms. Massine was much more literal than Balanchine. He had a good sense of the big spectacle and made a big show out of the whole thing. But his ballets had none of the intensity and fascination that Balanchine was able to achieve without any scenery and without much show.

Balanchine's Bizet *Symphony in C* is extraordinary, I think. You have there the sense of all sorts of patterns with the dancers rushing across and around the stage. It's a series of visual impressions that all lead from one to the other. I recently attended a festival of music in Turin, in Italy, where the leading architect was Juvarra, who designed so much of St. Petersburg. St. Petersburg, Balanchine's home, is really more Italian than anything else. And it's that fancy, that element of elaborate, extravagant baroque, that you find in Balanchine and in Tchelitchew. There is in their work a Russianized version of late Italian baroque architecture which Juvarra and the other artists in Turin excelled in. You see a great deal of that in Turin, in the churches, in the hunting lodge. Perhaps Balanchine's whole sense of sumptuous extravagant design came from St. Petersburg, which was built largely by Rastrelli and other Italian architects.

Balanchine had Stravinsky always, until almost the end of his life. And Stravinsky himself, instead of Russianizing things, as he started out by doing, got more interested in Tchaikovsky and less in Mussorgsky and Borodin and the rest of them, and changed entirely into a neoclassic composer. It was a good deal like Balanchine, using classical material in his own personal way. Both of them were refugees, so to speak.

Balanchine's ballet *Robert Schumann's "Davidsbündlertänze"* (1980) is most compelling. It is obvious that the vision of what the entire suite of Schumann's piano pieces is about is the dominating thing in the ballet. And it conditions every part of the ballet in some way or other. Even the life of Schumann and the madness of his later years—all of this somehow is focused on, is all expressed in the choreography. And the whole idea of constant flow, a very romantic idea, is always present. It's all about the wind blowing and people coming in and flying around, all a part of the German Romantic movement. The dance doesn't do it note by note or beat by beat, but it conceives the whole as having some sort of a larger meaning than the

small details of music. That's part of what's interesting about it, Balanchine's presenting his notion of what Robert Schumann's vision of music
was. That's very moving, I think. He was genuinely interested in who Schumann was, the whole world of which he was a part, and then suddenly
having this constant growth of madness in his life. That was always implicit,
of course, in the German Romantic movement. Many people were afflicted
by madness and were interested in madness. For instance, even Edgar Allan
Poe.

Errante, to come back to Les Ballets 1933, was certainly partly connected
with the German Romantic period, as was *La Valse* (1951)—the sense of fleeting moments, which I think is obviously something Balanchine was moved
by. He was always finding ways of expressing it, from *Cotillon* to the Robert
Schumann.

MARIE-JEANNE

Born in 1920, Marie-Jeanne (born Marie-Jeanne Pelus) studied at the School of American Ballet as one of its first pupils. Balanchine made star roles for her in Concerto Barocco and Ballet Imperial. She led the 1941 tour of South America by American Ballet Caravan and was a member of the Ballet Russe de Monte Carlo and the New York City Ballet during its first year. She rejoined the company in 1953 and retired in 1954.

I Remember Balanchine

I'M A REAL NEW YORKER, A LATIN FROM MANHATTAN. BEFORE WORLD WAR II, Manhattan was wonderful. My mother knew the ballet because she had been a Parisienne. When I was thirteen and a half, on New Year's Eve of 1933, my mother wanted to show me what ballet was. And I didn't want to go. I wanted to see some Disney movie. She dragged me, literally, to the St. James Theater, to the De Basil Ballet Russe de Monte Carlo. I sat there enthralled. I remember *Cotillon,* Riabouchinska in *Les Sylphides,* and Danilova, Baronova, and Toumanova. I knew that that was it. And on the second of January 1934, I was enrolled in the School of American Ballet, which had just opened.

My first class at the School was with Dorothie Littlefield. And then Pierre Vladimiroff and Muriel Stuart. I had very little class work with Balanchine in the early years. They were all good teachers, but the atmosphere of the School was not very disciplined. I don't think that I myself ever had real discipline. It was too easy for me. So I never developed self-discipline. I don't think that I remained in the beginners' classes with Dorothie Littlefield for very long. She was really quite the perfectionist in barre work—very clean, very precise, very fluent. Balanchine started with the Littlefield students from Philadelphia, and they were very well trained.

When I was sixteen, I was already rehearsing for Ballet Caravan, and taking classes with Vladimiroff. I adored Vladimiroff—his classic Maryinsky Theater style, his combinations, his finesse. No wonder Pavlova wanted him to partner her! Musically, he was very careful about what he wanted. Vladimiroff knew what he wanted and used it. He was very calm, and in the beginning he was still able to do ten pirouettes and he had a lovely soft use of the arms. His jumps didn't have to be high. His combinations were fantastic. When I teach, I use his combinations still. And I heard that he was a great poker player.

After Vladimiroff left, we had Anatole Vilzak and Ludmilla Schollar and Anatole Oboukhoff. I adored Vilzak's adagio class. He used me as his partner, and he was wonderful as a partner. But later on I realized that I never really learned anything from Vilzak, except he was a stickler about turning from tight fifth. I learned more from his wife, Schollar.

Tamara Toumanova took classes for quite a while with Vladimiroff, and I loved watching her. I was thrilled to have someone like that in class. Annabelle Lyon had real ballerina quality. I remember Annabelle at the Met during the American Ballet period. Balanchine made a lovely role for her, a menuetto to Bizet. And there was Gisella Caccialanza, a great Cecchetti dancer, and Leda Anchutina, a brilliant technician. Among the men, Lew Christensen, Paul Haakon, and Paul Godkin were in class. And William Dollar. Balanchine did beautiful things for Bill, really lovely things for his body. He was unique. He moved in his own way. He had a very rubbery body. He had started quite late in ballet, and he had an extraordinary technique. He could throw himself into extraordinary doubles and make it. He had beautiful line.

I tried to dance full out in my classes. After all, that's where you test your technique. I was too young to dance in the Metropolitan Opera productions by Balanchine's American Ballet, but I saw them all being rehearsed. I saw *Errante.* Tamara Geva was divine in it. She didn't do anything but run in that long train. And that was one of the first things that I was ever in by Balanchine. I was the Child in *Errante.* Charles Laskey was my "father" in the ballet, and I held on to his hand. He walks, and I'm following him, and then I see a flower, and I run to the flower and pick it, and I believe I gave it to Geva. And then I ran off. It was just a walk-on, but I remember it vividly. I remember Lincoln Kirstein being so impressed that he ran to my mother and said, "Did she ever have acting lessons?" My first recollection of working with Balanchine is rehearsing *Errante* with him. I had met him before, but that was very early when we did all that at the Warburg estate in White Plains. Balanchine started the rehearsals several months before the performances.

Balanchine used Erick Hawkins brilliantly in the beginning. He made *Alma Mater* (1935) for us. We went up to Hartford, Connecticut, to give performances. I was in *Mozartiana* (1935). Our version was very close to the Ballets 1933 version. The "Ave, Verum" was with four strings attached, and when he redid it later he did not use the strings.

Today, when *Serenade* is danced, it is very Fokiney. But it was not at all like that. It was very sharp, very precise. Balanchine redid *Serenade* for me. He reset it so that I did all the little solos at the same time that he added the Russian dance. This was in 1940 for the Denham Ballet Russe. (Later on, I danced *Serenade* with the New York City Ballet.) Of course, if Balanchine deliberately wanted to change a ballet, he'd change it. *Concerto Barocco* especially. He changed *Barocco* musically, making it fit the beat. Today's dancers do it slower; they do to two beats what we did on one beat. So it's much easier today. It doesn't have the sharpness, and it doesn't have the flow of the adagio. It's not the fault of the dancers—today's dancers are far superior to what we had in our day. *Barocco* killed me. I never got off that stage for seventeen minutes. I had just a tiny breather right at the end. Originally in *Barocco* I was to have been with Brigitte [Zorina], but at the last minute she did not join the company. She was to have been one of the violins, I never knew which. It would have been a different ballet, I am sure.

Ballet Imperial was no masterpiece, and it didn't kill me except for the opening cadenza. It was extremely uncomfortable. Usually George never did anything that was uncomfortable, perhaps because musically his choreography was perfection. But the cadenza in *Ballet Imperial* was difficult in an uncomfortable way. George just threw it in, and I don't know if I did what he wanted—those crazy things that he would invent. I don't think he knew either. It was difficult, and it made me terribly nervous. I was never sure I was going to be able to do it. And it wasn't technically difficult, really. It was just a crazy thing. Of course, there were some passages that were hard: there were a lot of double *sauts de basque* on the way. But I enjoyed doing those things. So do all five-year-old ballerinas! It was the same in the Bizet *Symphony in C*, where I did *entrechat dix*, which nobody does today.

In South America, Balanchine made a Rossini ballet, *Divertimento*, in which I had a pas de deux with Fred Danieli and a Tyrolean solo that would bring down the house. (He used the beautiful costumes from *Les Songes*.) Dancing to Rossini was so exciting. I had to do encores of the Tyrolean dance and repeating it nearly killed me. It was one of Balanchine's flashy, very piquant solos. He made that solo for me in ten minutes before curtain time. He threw the ballet together because we had no closing ballet.

When I danced Terpsichore in *Apollo* I had to do doubles on the diagonal. Nobody ever did them. Eventually, Balanchine would change details for whatever dancer he had. Perhaps that's why he didn't like to redo things. He liked to keep doing new ballets. He always said that he had no interest in his past ballets. His only interest was what he was doing now.

As a ballet master, Balanchine was not a torturer. Quite the contrary. He was strict when he wanted something, but he never worked to harm his dancers. The only time I saw Balanchine ever get mad was at the Fifty-ninth Street School, and he never raised his voice. If he got mad, he'd just walk out. And that made us feel much worse than if he had screamed and gone on. As a teacher, he could get a bee in his bonnet about something. He would work an hour and a half on one thing. Back in 1952–53 he decided that you can't put your heels down in landing. What he was trying to avoid was landing heavily—boom! He told me he was trying to teach his dancers to land like Eglevsky, who had a fantastic, slow, catlike takeoff and landing. So all of a sudden no one could put his heels down. It was a teaching fad. But Balanchine wanted you fit. The girls worked to be fit, dieted, even to the point of anorexia. I don't think I was ever as thin as George wanted me. My frame was not built that way.

Creating roles for dancers was an instinct with Balanchine, just as choreography was just an instinct. He could put it together without thinking. It was all music. He was such a musician. I knew George only when he was choreographing for me. What he gave me I just did. I did it the way he wanted, of course, and he didn't have to tell me how or why. He was working with what I had. Of course, the ballet had to be Balanchine's. That was the most important thing. The choreography was the important thing, not the dancers. After the South American tour he swore that he never would have top stars again. He tried very hard not to have any stars. He didn't want any stars. Balanchine was the star. He was not interested in personality. (Except, of course, if he was madly in love with somebody.)

Nobody escaped George. He had so many girls in the beginning. I think he went through all of them. It was just something you had to accept, that he was that fickle. But my love for him was as my master. He was *my* master. And that's what I loved. Unfortunately, I told him one day on the South American tour that I loved him as a master, rather than as a man. It was a very wrong thing to do.

I had been with George off and on throughout the year. He was breaking up with Brigitte (Zorina), and I was with him. He knew I wanted children and he didn't want children. He used to say, "I can't have children. They'd look like me." And he'd make the most terrible face, and he'd say, "Brigitte said that if I had children they'd all look like me." He was always sarcastic about my wanting children: "You should go and teach little children since you want to have such little children." But I was an only child and I am very seriously family-oriented. My big desire and dream was always to have a large, tight-knit family, which I never had. I never married the right man to have a tight-knit family. George couldn't see that, of course. Balanchine had loved his mother in his youth, but as an adult he always searched. He was incapable of really giving in depth. He probably couldn't have given affection to a child because he was the one that had to be on top. I think he probably would have been afraid to have children. A child would have required something that he couldn't give. At least, that's what I felt. There was some sort of insecurity there. Balanchine was charming and egotistical —with his charm alone, he would not have had to be good-looking.

Balanchine was furious with me when I married. I went back to Argentina with my husband, Alfonso de Queseda, and lived there awhile, and I wanted a child very badly. Balanchine came to the Teatro Colón to set *Mozart Violin Concerto* (1942). He came to me and asked me to be in it, and I said no. I don't think he ever really forgave me. But after I had my child at the end of 1943, I came back and we were friends again.

Twelve of us from the School went to Mexico and had an opera season there. In 1945, Balanchine did an *Aïda,* a *Faust,* and a *Samson et Dalila.* We did *Concerto Barocco* there. And we did *Apollo* with Lew Christensen, Nicholas Magallanes, and myself. Also, in 1944, there was a Salvador Dali ballet, *Sentimental Colloquy,* for the Marquis de Cuevas's Ballet International in New York to the music of Paul Bowles. Dali was at rehearsals with his wife. It was choreographed by Balanchine and credited to André Eglevsky. André and I were veiled in yards of fabric. André was the only good male dancer around at the time. He had a lovely technique, a lovely jump, a lovely *plié*. He could do wonderful turns. He was not a very exciting dancer, however.

In Mexico City in 1945, Balanchine made a dance to music from *Faust* for me and Fred Danieli. He did a beautiful adagio and a solo that was very lovely. And I did *Le Bourgeois Gentilhomme* (1944; original production 1932) with Leon Danielian at the Ballet Russe de Monte Carlo. I enjoyed it so much, I had a ball doing it. It was not a matter of showing off our technique, it was just so much fun. Freddie Franklin gave it to me, and he loved me doing it. I did not perform it for long; Nathalie Krassovska took over the role. But whenever I did it, it was wonderful.

I felt lost when Balanchine ran off to Hollywood. He put me in the Ballet Russe de Monte Carlo because he had no company. I was always very unhappy without George being there. I had been trained by him. I had had him from the beginning. And that was his period with Maria Tallchief. Balanchine started Ballet Society, and he didn't ask me to join. I was never in Ballet Society. I finally went back to dance for Balanchine in the New York City Ballet in 1948, but that was short-lived.

TODD

BOLENDER

Studied with Hanya Holm and at the School of American Ballet; member of Ballet Caravan and founded American Concert Ballet with William Dollar, where he choreographed Mother Goose Suite. Principal dancer and choreographer for Ballet Russe de Monte Carlo. Joined Ballet Society in 1946 and for Balanchine created roles in The Four Temperaments and Agon. Choreographed The Miraculous Mandarin, The Still Point, and Souvenirs for New York City Ballet and has choreographed for numerous Broadway shows. Ballet director of Cologne, Frankfurt, and Ankara operas. In 1980 became artistic director of the State Ballet of Missouri in Kansas City, for which he has made many new ballets.

I Remember Balanchine

I FIRST ENCOUNTERED BALANCHINE AT THE SCHOOL OF AMERICAN BALLET. I HAD BEEN A modern dancer; modern seemed to be in vogue then. I had come from a small Ohio town to search for knowledge about dance movement. At that time there were incredibly talented people in the field of modern dance— Wigman, Graham, Humphrey, Weidman—but I chose a man named Edwin Strawbridge briefly before becoming completely overwhelmed by Wigman, so I switched to begin studies with Hanya Holm, Wigman's American counterpart. After a year with Hanya, I got a job with the W.P.A., and Arthur Mahoney, a choreographer for W.P.A., became my first ballet teacher. He was a taskmaster, insisting I take two classes a day. One of these classes was with a charming old Russian teacher who insisted I learn double *tours en l'air* and *brisés volés.* I heard of Balanchine and the School of American Ballet, such good reports that one day I ventured to Madison Avenue and Fifty-ninth Street—the old Tuxedo Building that housed School of American Ballet on the top floor. It was a four-story walk-up. I watched classes. I liked them and the big open studios. I took some classes. It was clearly a structured training, it seemed right. But I needed a job. I got into a Broadway operetta, choreographed by Chester Hale, famous on Broadway at that time as choreographer for the big ballet he produced weekly at the Capitol Theater for his "Chester Hale Girls." He said, "I'll take you on one condition, that you will be in class every morning for two and a half hours, so that I can keep an eye on your development." Hale was a Cecchetti teacher. Balanchine was not. I studied with Hale every morning for two and a half hours and at School of American Ballet every afternoon, rehearsed all afternoon, then took two more classes at S.A.B. I did that for a long time, then danced in the operetta at night.

One day at S.A.B., a tall, thin, bullet-headed young man came in to watch Muriel Stuart's class. They talked a lot and at the finish of class Kirstein called me to his office and said, "Where did you come from?" and then immediately, "Would you like to join a small ballet group?" The operetta was about to close. It was a most timely invitation. So, in the autumn of 1937, I joined Ballet Caravan. The repertory was small, but what there was I liked: Loring's *Yankee Clipper* and *Harlequin for President,* William Dollar's *Promenade,* Lew Christensen's *Encounter,* and Douglas Cloudy's character ballet about gypsies. Erick Hawkins's ballet called *Show Piece* was perhaps my favorite. The following year, 1938, Gene Loring created his masterpiece based on a Kirstein libretto and an Aaron Copland score, *Billy the Kid,* in which I was cast as the ubiquitous Alias.

During those last years of the 1930s, I liked to watch Balanchine's classes —so much different from Mr. Hale, or other teachers in New York. What seemed unique to me was that apparently each class he taught had a theme, in which Balanchine would concentrate on only a few movement ideas. When I first watched, his class was about *port de bras,* subsequent ones were about jumping and turning, and one I admired greatly was teaching dancers how to run. In those years only modern dance used running movement as dance. Balanchine had only begun to shake the nineteenth century out of twentieth-century dance. I began to realize he had a much wider awareness of movement possibilities than I had imagined, but then that was a period of immense importance to all dancers, choreographers, and artists.

Because I was friends with Bill Dollar and Lew Christensen, Balanchine would arrive from his very busy schedule and invite us to have coffee downstairs at Sammy's Delicatessen, and there we would eat, drink coffee, and talk for hours. These after-rehearsal snacks happened with enough frequency that I began to look forward to them. Balanchine was a great talker, loved to tell stories and jokes, nor did he mind when we didn't think the jokes were all that funny. I got used to his heavy accent and indeed he would often have his Russian pals along. I even learned some Russian words, but then Russian dancers were everywhere at that time. The two Ballet Russe companies were regular visitors to New York, never at the same time, and many of the dancers lived and taught ballet in or near the city. Besides Sammy's, another place to gather for a snack was the Russian Tea Room. That was long before it became a famous, expensive after-theater spot. So I got to know Balanchine as a friend before I ever worked for him, which was not to happen until Nelson Rockefeller arranged with the United States State Department to send Ballet Caravan, in a much inflated size and repertory and with Balanchine as artistic director, to South America in 1941. So, in the blistering spring days before setting sail for Rio, rehearsals were going on around the clock. There were no unions, and we worked from early morning until late at night. I was a member of Balanchine's *Ballet Imperial,* a ballet created to be the "grand" ballet for our repertory and finely choreographed for the unbelievable talent of a French-American eighteen-year-old product of the School of American Ballet named Marie-Jeanne. At the same time and for the same dancer and for the same tour, he created one of his truly great works, *Concerto Barocco.*

Upon returning to the United States, Balanchine arranged for some of us to appear in a Broadway production of *Die Fledermaus* called *Rosalinda.* An instant success, it ran for one year and a half. His dances for this production were elegant and charming.

Balanchine and I would meet occasionally in passing at the School of American Ballet. One day he asked me if I would like to work with him on a program to be given at Carnegie Hall with the National Orchestral Society with Leon Barzin conducting. He began with Tanaquil LeClercq and me and any girl student who could stand up and created a superb choreography for the Mozart *Symphonie Concertante*. One day he handed me a music score and said, "Why don't you do this little piece?" He pointed out the waltz from the second orchestra suite of Tchaikovsky. It was very reminiscent of Balanchine's *Serenade,* the one ballet by which I measured every ballet I saw. And so I did my own little *Serenade,* using the S.A.B. students. When John Colman, the incredibly gifted pianist, who was there playing for classes or rehearsals, failed to appear, Balanchine would play for my rehearsals. We did several programs together with Leon Barzin and the National Orchestral Society. On the second program Balanchine gave me a Bach piece to choreograph. I again used all the girl students and one boy student eleven years old who, I was convinced, would become a good dancer. His name was Edward Villella. It was apparent he could be a dancer simply from his excellently proportioned body and fine intelligent face and head and the beginnings of a strong, clean technique.

The following summer I prepared a small choreography for Jacob's Pillow, which Muriel Stuart had asked me to do, using Stravinsky's *Pulcinella Suite.* One day Balanchine walked into the studio and asked what we were doing; could he watch it? We gave him a very energetic performance. He asked if Sergei Denham of Ballet Russe had seen it. Did I mind if he invited Denham to see it? I did not. Denham arrived the next day, liked the ballet, called it *Commedia Balletica* and opened it at City Center in New York in September 1945. Mr. Denham had asked me to dance in my own ballet, and when Ballet Russe went on tour, he asked me to join the company in Chicago. After every performance in Chicago, Balanchine would want to have dinner and would gather up Maria Tallchief, Choura Danilova, sometimes Freddie Franklin and me, and we would have wonderfully hilarious times together. Balanchine loved telling bawdy jokes, occasionally embarrassing Maria; however, not Danilova, who would often be doubled over in laughter.

Shortly after this Kirstein and Balanchine began Ballet Society. The first role I danced in Ballet Society was in the variation of Phlegmatic in *The Four Temperaments.* When Balanchine began rehearsals on this work, he had asked me one day after class if I would come back to school about 7 P.M. because he wanted to work a little on an idea. He also asked John Colman to play at that time. That first evening of rehearsal he did the entire opening of that particular variation. It wasn't long but wonderfully innovative and rather complex. Balanchine didn't tell me that variation was called Phlegmatic. In showing the movements, he would say, "I want you to be very soft, like a cat, then very big and very long movements." He would indicate movement that would flow from one thing to the next with a beautiful continuous line. It seemed dramatic to me, wonderfully pliable, oddly mysterious, as through many layers of movement. Then suddenly Balanchine said, "Well, that's it, that's finished." John Colman looked up from the piano and said, "You mean that's the end of the introduction." Balanchine said, "Well, maybe. Maybe we can't do any more." Then John said, "But that's only the introduction— now begins the development." Balanchine said, "Well, we'll think about it." Nor did he touch that section for a while.

Then one day he called me into rehearsal to continue working on the Hindemith with the four tallest girls he could find—each six feet tall. And then he worked very fast. It seemed to almost fall into place. At first it seemed not at all difficult, but as I worked on it, I realized it wasn't easy at all but immensely difficult. It took me years to learn how to dance it. The Seligmann costumes were an uncomfortable-looking and -feeling arrangement of materials. My costumes were made of the most expensive suede. At times I used to feel I was dancing the costume, and only later when Balanchine discarded all the costumes and put us in black tights and T-shirts did I begin to understand the enormous power contained in the choreography.

The last ballet in which Balanchine choreographed a part for me was *Agon*, a beautiful pas de trois and a solo called Sarabande. He seemed never to tire of rehearsing the pas de trois and often up to curtain time would have us repeat it many times. Nor did I ever get weary of dancing it. But then, once I learned to dance a role in one of Balanchine's ballets, it was forever a pleasure. Learning this required a long time.

When Balanchine said that he would be remembered as a teacher as well as a choreographer, he was indicating the vital importance of training in preparation for performance. It is rare a dancer ever has, as Balanchine was, as fine a teacher as choreographer. He was an invaluable teacher. Certainly he created an approach and understanding of technique that is entirely new and in some instances still controversial—and has been since I began training with him. I was appointed director of the Kansas City Ballet in 1980, which has since become State Ballet of Missouri through affiliations with St. Louis. I wanted to begin a school at the same time I started the company, so that in a relatively short period of time I could begin to accept students in programs and then as apprentices before finally making them full-fledged company members. I remembered very well how important the School of American Ballet had been in helping Balanchine establish any of the various ensembles he created—American Ballet Company (1932), Ballet Caravan (1935), American Ballet Caravan (1941), Ballet Society (1946), and New York City Ballet (1948). Una Kai became our ballet mistress and Diana Adams was director of our school. We are direct descendants of Balanchine, the teacher and the choreographer.

NATALIE

MOLOSTWOFF

Director emeritus of the School of American Ballet, with which she has been associated since 1938, Natalie Molostwoff was born in Baku, Azerbaijan.

I CAME TO THE SCHOOL OF AMERICAN BALLET BECAUSE I WAS FRIENDLY WITH EUGENIE Ouroussow, who was there from its inception. The School was small and intimate then, completely different from what it is now. We never had anything like a staff meeting. We had the fifth floor of the Tuxedo Building on Madison Avenue and Fifty-ninth Street. All around were studios for other artists. They were not supposed to live there, but they did. Balanchine was in and out because he did a lot of work with musicals and in Hollywood. That was not what he really wanted to do. Broadway is so different from ballet. There are constant changes and cuts and it's never ready, and you work at the end before you work at the beginning. I remember when the tryouts for *House of Flowers* were playing in Philadelphia in 1954, we all went down to see the performance and keep him company. It was not his milieu at all. He was so alone until we came. He didn't mix with the rest of the cast.

But during the thirties, ballet didn't pay, it was not popular, and George needed money. He would go to the Russian Tea Room with a friend and before he got up to pay the bill there would be six or seven people sitting with him, and he paid for them all. At that time he didn't have a personal secretary, so I used to write his checks for him and take care of his bills. I was shocked at the way he spent money. He didn't save. He didn't know the value of it.

Vladimir Dimitriev, who left Russia with Balanchine and came to America with him, was a tyrant, a difficult person to work with. He was supposed to be running the School administratively. He was very intelligent, loved power, and he exploited Balanchine. Without Balanchine he couldn't have earned a penny. He also chiseled Lincoln out of a lot of money. Dimietriev retired after I'd been at the School about a year, and Eugenie would work out with Balanchine who was to teach: Vladimiroff, Oboukhoff, Miss Stuart, Kyra Blanc.

Distant Balanchine was not, but knowable, I'm not sure. He would lose interest in a particular group of friends and move completely to another. He needed change. At one time he was friendly with Valodin, who had a ballet school in Westport. He knew him very early on, from his first days here. Then at one time there was Arshansky. Balanchine and I were never intimate, but we were very close friends. He used to spend a lot of time at my place on Fire Island. We used to have dinners together here in New York, always with a group of friends. And then suddenly it ceased. I never understood why. He would spend a lot of time in my office at the School, but there was no more closeness. In the last few years of his life I was always extremely happy to be invited to his Easter suppers, late at night after church. He'd spend the entire day preparing all kinds of food. At one time Natasha Nabokov was also a close friend of his. They even traveled the country by car to California and back. He was interested in her son Ivan, who was then a young kid. That friendship also disappeared completely. And then there was Dr. Bender, Balanchine's friend and adviser on the American way of living. He would call the School and demand, "Balanchine!" I tried to teach him to ask, "May I speak to Mr. Balanchine?"

In the summer of 1945, Balanchine and I took a small company of about fourteen dancers to Mexico to appear in various operas and ballets: Nicky Magallanes, Marie-Jeanne, Yvonne Patterson, and Bill Dollar were the principals. Patricia Wilde and Georgia Hiden were with us too. Mr. Balanchine was not very happy then because Vera Zorina had suggested a divorce. He liked having the chance to go away. Traveling by train was not easy during the war. I had to keep an eye on twelve young girls, to stop them flirting with the Mexicans, who were very impressed with their blond good looks. I had to bring them back alive. Everything would have been very difficult on that trip if it had not been for Balanchine. He could handle any situation. I remember one time when the dancers were to appear in *Aïda.* He looked at the costumes and said, "Absolutely not: dirty, filthy, no good." He decided to go create new ones. I was about to pack my suitcase and go back to New York. I just couldn't cope, I can't sew at all. But he made it so simple, saying all we needed to do was take measurements, buy so many bras, and then buy some orange material and cover each bra with something orange. The girls were delighted. Balanchine had this wonderful gift of making everything appear simple.

You could tell him "No, I don't care for your new ballet. It doesn't appeal to me." He'd take that better than if you told him that you didn't like the way he fixed food. One time when he was married to Tanny, he hosted a dinner and served mayonnaise that he'd made himself. Edith LeClercq, Tanny's mother, said that it wasn't good, the consistency was wrong. I told Balanchine, "One of your guests thought that the consistency of the mayonnaise was not up to par." And he said, "I know who it is. Brooks Jackson. He is never going to be my guest again!" I couldn't possibly tell him that it was his mother-in-law.

Every day there was a reason for him to come to the School. He would arrive and be silly, or tell us lots of extremely dirty jokes. He also talked a lot about what ballet he was going to do next. Once on Fire Island, when Tanny and Edith LeClercq were there, he described *Tyl Ulenspiegel,* giving us the whole thing, how it was going to be.

I think he liked the "unattainable." Once he attained, he lost interest. But he also told me that he never left any of his wives. He said they all left him. Tamara Toumanova left him, definitely. I think she was in love with someone. He told me that Danilova once said to him in Paris: "I'm going out to a cocktail party. George, you stay here, you're such a bore that people don't enjoy drinking with you." He really was miserable during Zorina's day. She was very close to her mother: together they sort of had no use for him. She married him on the rebound. Balanchine was at the School one day during a difficult period with Zorina. We were suddenly ordered to leave the building because of a fire. We rounded up the dancers. Balanchine and I stayed until the last student left. He was cool, calm, and collected. "I don't care," he said. "I just don't care now whether I live or not."

He told me that for Christmas at home they would have a feast. Mother and daughter Zorina would share presents. From Balanchine there were all kinds of gifts for Zorina, and then she would say, "And this is for you, George." It was something that he could live without. Once when he came back from a tryout of a musical, he found that Zorina had moved with her mother into an apartment in the Ritz Tower. When he got to the apartment, they said, "This is going to be your room." It was the maid's room, near the kitchen. So he picked up his suitcase and left. That's how they separated.

With Maria, I think Balanchine was on the rebound. He was very unhappy when they met in California. With Tanny, I heard that the marriage was breaking up and they would have separated if she had not become ill. Two months after she was stricken with polio, the School sent me to Copenhagen, where she was in the hospital, as a Christmas present. Tanny was just out of the iron lung, but she was in despair, in tears. She was white and slack as a piece of paper and scared to death. Edith LeClercq and Balanchine had adjoining rooms at the Hotel d'Angleterre. He was staging one of his ballets for the Royal Danish company in gratitude for Tanny's hospital care, which was paid for by the government. That was the only time he left the hospital. The rest of the time he would sit with Tanny. At Christmas he used Vera Volkova's kitchen to prepare dinner for her. I was instructed to bring from New York a bottle of bourbon, marshmallows, and sweet potatoes. He purchased the turkey there, cooked it, and with great difficulty moved it all from Volkova's house to the hospital.

Tanny couldn't even lift her fingers. It was horrid. Balanchine really saved her from insanity. He made what he called a five-year plan for her. He said, "This is our first five-year plan, this is our second," and got her to accept the situation. Then he couldn't continue, and it was very tough on him. Balanchine would go to the theater to give class, rehearse, then come home to feed her, and go back to the theater. I think somebody else should have taken care of her physically.

Finally, Tanny gave him an ultimatum. There was to be a gala with a big supper party on the promenade of the State Theater. Before that night's performance, as Balanchine was leaving, Tanny told him, "If I'm not there at your table when you come back I'm not going to be here." During that evening she moved to a hotel.

Balanchine and Suzanne Farrell sat as guests of honor at Mayor Lindsay's table. I was at the next table, with John Taras and Edith LeClercq, Tanny's mother. At one point Edith said, "I'm going to go over and ask him, 'Where is your wife, Mr. Balanchine? Why isn't she here with you?' " I said, "Edith, listen to me. If you do that, your daughter will never forgive you. I'm your friend." "You're no friend," she insisted. John took her by the arm, escorted her to O'Neal's across the street, and took her home.

I think Tanny and Balanchine's separation was a bigger blow to Edith than to Tanny. Balanchine moved into a studio apartment on West End Avenue, and gradually he and Tanny became friends again. He never forgot to send her something beautiful for Christmas or her birthday. He provided for her. There was no bitterness.

Our trip to Russia in 1962 was hard on Balanchine. He left us to come back to America in the middle of it. He stayed with Tanny awhile and then returned to join us. He didn't like the Soviet regime, of course. The moment we arrived in Leningrad, before we unpacked our suitcases, he grabbed me by the arm and said, "Let's go and I'll show you where I lived." It was not far from the hotel, and we ran there. It was a very nice little square. He was very excited, and then Leningrad became very disturbing for him. He met people with whom he'd grown up, he found them in their misery: they had no rights, they had no money. They couldn't get into the theater to see the performance, so he arranged a special performance in Leningrad and invited all of them to come for free.

The company was a great success in Russia. In Tiflis, all the tickets were given away to the higher-ups. The crowd who couldn't get tickets broke down the door and rushed in like a river. During the Cuban crisis, we were performing in Moscow at the Palace of Congresses in the Kremlin. Nancy Lassalle cabled us from London that war might break out. "Situation is serious. Take care." We were warned by the American Embassy, "If war is declared don't come near us, you're on your own, don't expect us to do anything." We were instructed in the event of any difficulty to pull the curtain down and stay put. We were not to leave the theater. But the performance that night in Moscow was wonderful; there were many curtain calls, one after another. They would not stop applauding. Finally Balanchine appeared before the curtain and told the audience: "If you want us to perform tomorrow, we will have to go home and rest. We thank you for this reception."

KATHERINE

DUNHAM*

Trained at the University of Chicago and founded school and dance company, Ballet Nègre, in Chicago (1931). Studied with Ludmila Speranza and Mark Turbyfill and researched native dance and culture in Caribbean (1937–38). Her company appeared in **Cabin in the Sky,** *staged by Balanchine (1940), and it toured United States and Europe for over twenty years and appeared on film:* **Carnival of Rhythm** *(1942) and* **Stormy Weather** *(1943). Opened school in New York in 1945. Author of* **Katherine Dunham's Journey to Accompong** *(1946),* **A Touch of Innocence** *(1959), and* **Island Possessed** *(1969). Director of the Performing Arts Training Center at Southern Illinois University, East St. Louis branch.*

* Katherine Dunham was interviewed by Dawn Lille Horwitz and Francis Mason.

I Remember Balanchine

BALANCHINE was no stranger to musical comedy in 1940 when he collaborated with Katherine Dunham on the dances in the musical play Cabin in the Sky. *In England, after Diaghilev's death, he had created dances in* Wake Up and Dream *(1929) and* Cochran's 1930 Revue. *On Broadway he had made dances for the* Ziegfeld Follies *(1936) and choreographed the Rodgers and Hart musical* On Your Toes *(1936), which included Tamara Geva and Ray Bolger in the ballet sequence* Slaughter on Tenth Avenue. *In this show, for the first time in American theater history, the phrase "choreography by" was used in the program.*

Balanchine made dances for Babes in Arms *(1937),* I Married an Angel *(1938),* The Boys from Syracuse *(1938), and in 1940 two musicals,* Keep Off the Grass *and* Louisiana Purchase. *In that same year came* Cabin in the Sky *with the program credit "Entire Production Staged by George Balanchine."* Cabin in the Sky *had two black heroines played by Ethel Waters and Katherine Dunham, an angel and a devil, who competed for the body and soul of Little Joe.*

F.M.

I KNEW BALANCHINE FROM THE TIME HE CAME TO CHICAGO TO SEE MY COMPANY. WE were appearing in the Sherman Hotel in a sort of nightclub act. He immediately wanted us for *Cabin in the Sky,* the whole company, and he wanted me for the role of Georgia Brown. He had seen us in *Le Jazz Hot* in New York and then he came to Chicago to see us with Vernon Dukelsky—Vernon Duke. What amazed me was that Balanchine wanted me to sing, too. I did sing a little in *Le Jazz Hot* and I'd done one song in the nightclub show. But the idea of the whole thing, with me in a show with Ethel Waters, who was holier-than-thou in those days, was really a great risk on his part. At the beginning, when I understood that he was to be the choreographer, it did not go down so well with me. But watching us in our own classes and training and the company's use of their bodies, he finally felt that we should work together, which we did. In the hell scene, where the Devil comes and shows his power, we worked together. I'd go to Balanchine and say, "Let's try this . . . let's do that," and so forth. And being a Georgian Russian, he felt the rhythms, you know, and the strangeness, for this was a little bit avant-garde then, the way that I approached choreography. We worked together with no problem. I would make a suggestion and he would keep it or else he'd make a suggestion and I'd say fine. We just worked together. He knew Vera Mirova and Ludmila Speranza, with whom I had worked. Speranza was my major teacher. She had been at the Kamerny Theater, Moscow, the big theater at the time. Speranza came to this country in the Chauve-Souris. "Black Ballet and Variety" is a way to describe our shows. But our work needs drama. It needs people who are actors as well as dancers, who can do indigenous material from a number of countries and still do the cakewalk.

Balanchine seemed to like this. He really seemed to love our style. I lost touch with him after *Cabin in the Sky*. But in those days he and Vernon Duke used to come after the show. We'd all meet at my house. And once I think Stravinsky was there. Balanchine wanted Stravinsky to do something for me, but at the time I guess I was a little disorganized, and Stravinsky was involved in something else for Balanchine. But he did persuade Stravinsky to give me a tango. Somewhere it's in our music, and I've never done it. I keep thinking I must find it. I don't think anyone has done it. It's autographed to me by Stravinsky. He saw *Cabin in the Sky* because he and Balanchine and Vernon Duke were very close. Balanchine was interested in seeing me develop, and I suppose he knew the problem that I would have in developing myself alone. I kept the company with me.

Later I saw a movie he made with Zorina, *Star Spangled Rhythm* (1942), with the *Old Black Magic* number. It made me mad because I wanted to do it. Zorina was floating around being balletic. I don't think I saw much of Balanchine or his work until 1947. But I did see him once around 1947. Tedesco wrote the music for *Octoroon Ball,* a ballet I wanted to do. But it required more ballet technique than our company had. And I couldn't concentrate on anything but touring my company and putting on the shows. So I asked Balanchine about doing it with me. He knew Tedesco and was vaguely interested in the idea, but it meant his company learning our technique as well as our company learning his. He said to me at that time, "You invest too much in the individual dancer. A dancer should be an object for a choreographer. The dancer should not think." Well, we had it out about that. I never ask anyone to do something they don't want to do, and I insist that they know the total complex of the role they're playing. That's my problem now with the Ailey dancers. I haven't had time enough to get to them, really. I said to Balanchine, "No, as a choreographer I don't want simply to use the dancer as a pawn." I want to instill in the dancer a person, and a person that has to know how to do whatever he's assigned. That's the anthropology coming out, of course. Balanchine didn't do *Octoroon Ball,* but he did urge Arthur Mitchell to do it. Two or three times Arthur Mitchell said how much Balanchine wished I would show him the script and do this particular ballet. But I didn't, and we haven't done it. I was a little annoyed with Balanchine at the time, but I didn't realize that mixing the techniques would have been disastrous for what he was doing. Ballet Society was just getting off the ground. But he had some experience in Latin America. I remember when he and Vernon Duke were planning their first vacation, they were going to go to Cuba.

In *Cabin in the Sky* we had fantastic drummers, two Cubans and one Haitian. The music together with the dance and what they contributed to the libretto—Balanchine really appreciated all of that. We would talk things out first. We'd have a pretty clear understanding. At one point he wanted me to come in on the Egyptian ballet wrapped up like a mummy and be unwound like Cleopatra on the floor. I didn't like that. I think I had seen Ruth Page brought in as a mummy in one of her ballets. Karinska, the costume designer, and Balanchine were of course very close friends. And I liked Karinska very much. So I got on the phone and explained to her how I didn't mind coming as the Seductress but being a mummy was out. My husband, John Pratt, did the costume and Karinska understood. It really was Nefertiti, with a headdress. The costume was covered with pebbled gold material. It was split in the middle, from the waist down, and my navel was open. That's what they objected to in Boston! It was beautiful, flimsy, filmy, and so forth. Balanchine admired my husband very much as a designer. And Karinska also felt that I'd feel more comfortable in his clothes. I don't think I wore a Karinska costume at all in *Cabin in the Sky*. The company did. Karinska made me a street suit, an afternoon suit, that was just beautiful. And my husband admired her very much. He admired the fact that she went around in tennis shoes and didn't try to compete with her models.

Cabin in the Sky was a big success on Broadway. The only problem was the musicians' union's strike. That's what did the show in. You couldn't play the music on any radio station. In those days the popularity of the music from a show as you heard it on the radio could make or break it. Because of the strike, they never did a real record of the show. I think Ethel Waters recorded something and Johnny Latouche, who was the lyricist, did some sort of trial record, where he sang all of the songs, but a commercial record was never released. I don't think they got the music published in time to have it make any difference. *Cabin in the Sky* played nine months at the Martin Beck Theater and then we toured. Before we opened on Broadway we tried out in Boston, where I was censored for the bare navel in the Egyptian ballet. We had a desperate time determining what to do. My husband thought up a large yellow diamond, fake of course, so from then on I had a diamond in my navel. That made it even naughtier, but the censor didn't pick it up. Balanchine loved all that.

In "Dry Bones," my kids, very slightly clad, would pat "them bones from the finger bones to the" this and this and this. They had a kind of swaying movement with it, sort of wiggling their bottoms. Ethel Waters was standing right behind them while the whole chorus sang "Dem bones." One night she went past my dressing room and stopped to say, "I may not know nothin' about no anthropology"—there had been an article in the paper about my going to Yale for a lecture demonstration—"but I sure know when I see a lot of asses swingin' around."

Balanchine and Vernon Duke wanted to open the show with the black choir singing a Russian dirge. I think it would have been wonderful. Ethel Waters hit the ceiling. "My people aren't going to sing none of that." So they took that out, and it was just spirituals. Little Joe is dead. She raised him alive. Todd Duncan is the angel who brings him back to life, Ethel prayed so hard. Well, I think Balanchine and Dukelsky were both disappointed that it did not have that sort of avant-garde air.

Balanchine liked the rhythm and percussion of our dances. I think most Georgians have a good sense of rhythm from what I've seen. And I think that he probably had been so deep into classical ballet that working with us brought out some of that naturalness that is native to Georgians. I don't think before he'd ever worked with black people, but he certainly wanted to work with us. Maybe he learned that we were just people. He had no prejudices that I know of. That was good for me too. He picked us out, remember. It was an ideal collaboration. As I look back on it, we were really great friends as choreographers together.

JOHN

TARAS

Trained with Fokine and at the School of American Ballet; danced
with Catherine Littlefield's Philadelphia Ballet in 1941 and joined
the American Ballet Caravan tour of South America; danced with
Ballet Theatre 1940–45 and joined De Basil's Ballet Russe as dancer
and regisseur·in 1947. Choreographed ballets for Ballet Theatre, the
Markova-Dolin company, and The Minotaur *for Ballet Society*
and Design With Strings *for the Metropolitan Ballet. Ballet mas-*
ter, New York City Ballet 1960–84; ballet master of Paris Opéra
Ballet 1969–70; associate director, American Ballet Theatre, 1984–
90, Taras has choreographed many other ballets and staged Balan-
chine ballets for numerous ensembles.

I Remember Balanchine

I WENT TO STUDY WITH FOKINE TO LEARN HOW TO MAKE DANCES FOR PLAYS I WANTED to be in. That's how I got started in ballet. Fokine classes dealt with his own ballets. I watched at first. I had never been trained. He didn't train. I never was told how to turn out. Barre was given by his son upstairs. And then we came down to the salon, and sometimes Fokine would play the piano and sometimes he would sing. Once he sang a phrase from *Schéhérazade.* And all of this went into my head. I couldn't do it, but of course I loved every step. I was sixteen. I was like a sponge.

At that time I was fortunate enough to have a friend who was a publicity agent for Broadway. So I got to see all of Mr. B.'s musicals. I saw *On Your Toes* (1936), *Babes in Arms* (1937). I also managed to see the Stravinsky program at the Met (1937): *Apollo, Baiser de la Fée,* and *Card Party (Jeu de Cartes).* And I saw the Gluck *Orpheus and Eurydice* (1936) at the Met. Balanchine had dancers flying through the air in the hell scene, which was like a concentration camp. Bill Dollar came flying in as Amor, and he had enormous wings. Lew Christensen was wonderful as Orpheus.

I began attending Balanchine's and Kirstein's School in 1940. And I managed to get into *A Thousand Times Neigh,* which they were doing at the Ford Pavilion at the 1939 World's Fair. I went to Anatole Vilzak. I studied with Madame Nijinska. I studied with a woman called Madame Anderson-Ivantzova. Balanchine was not around in 1940. Nicky Magallanes, Todd Bolender, and I joined Catherine Littlefield's Philadelphia Ballet because she was doing a short tour. When we came back, we got the news that Lincoln and Nelson Rockefeller were organizing a tour to be sent to South America to try to develop inter-American cultural relations. That's when I first came into contact with Mr. Balanchine. There I found Bill Dollar, Lew Christensen, Gisella Caccialanza, and Marie-Jeanne.

There was one ballet for the Latin American tour called *Divertimento* (1941) which Balanchine whipped up when we needed a closing ballet at the last minute. We hadn't had time to do it in the rehearsal period in New York. We rehearsed it when we finally got there. Balanchine had planned to rehearse it on the boat. It took two weeks to get to Rio at that time.

Balanchine worked closely with Marie-Jeanne in choreographing both *Concerto Barocco* and *Ballet Imperial.* She was an extraordinary girl. She was very energetic, strong. Oddly enough, she was not tall. A great many people think of Balanchine ballerinas as being Amazons or giantesses, but she was quite small. She had very long legs and very long feet, so when she was on pointe, which was quite often, she looked tall. She did not have much neck, but she had a strong upper body. I've never seen anyone who had her drive. If you had seen her in *Ballet Imperial,* and then saw the people who came after —and there were many great dancers who came after her—I feel you never

196

saw *Ballet Imperial,* unless you had seen Marie-Jeanne. It was done for her, that's what the ballet is about. When you change casts, the ballet is divine but it's not the same ballet. I find that happens so often with Mr. Balanchine's work.

I think that's also true of *Barocco,* which was also done for her. *Barocco* has become rather a tepid, bland classical work now. And it was a jazzy work when we first did it. Full of odd hips, odd turned-in things that you don't see anymore. All the dances have syncopation that lies under the Bach music. And now it's rather romantic and lyrical. It became diluted. I think the same thing is true of *Ballet Imperial,* that the characterization came—I'm totally convinced—entirely from Marie-Jeanne's body and from her personality, and from the way he used her. She was terrific. I remember a variation she did in the ballet *Divertimento* to a Rossini score *(Matinées Musicales; Soirées Musicales;* overture to *La Cenerentola),* orchestrated by Benjamin Britten. We used the overture for *Cinderella* as the finale. Marie-Jeanne did a variation, a Tyrolean dance, that brought the house down. It was the only time on that tour in South America that we ever had to repeat a dance. And she was the original Harlequin in *La Sonnambula.* She was extraordinary.

Balanchine would adjust his ballets for later casts. For example, *Concerto Barocco* has lost some entrance steps because of Suzanne Farrell's bad knee. And the later dancers said, "Oh, we don't have to do the *jeté* because she could not." He took Terpsichore's *jetés* out of *Apollo* because of Suzanne's knee. He just gave her *développés.* There was a reason. And, also, Balanchine did get bored from seeing things over and over again.

The wonderful thing about Balanchine ballets is that they survive cast changes. Sometimes there is even an improvement. I'm thinking of Peter Martins in certain roles that he inherited. We had never seen a *danseur noble* like that. Being a ballet master, one sees these ballets year after year in different productions, and if you are not there all the time, if you are not insistent on maintaining details, a lot of things disappear. Special characteristics of the work disappear. I used to dread it if I didn't go to a rehearsal that Mr. Balanchine himself took. I knew that if I wasn't there he'd change something, and so I would try to go as often as possible. He would suddenly see a step that we had been doing for a long time but that he would not like because the dancer was not doing it properly. And he would change the step. It wasn't because the step wasn't right. It simply was not being done well. So he would change the step.

Eventually I became a ballet master and worked with European companies. I would make ballets for repertory needs or because the poor ballerina was sitting in the corner and didn't have a ballet. When I returned to the United States, Balanchine suggested that I stage *Sonnambula.* He didn't remember it. He came and watched my rehearsal and then he asked me if I would like to stay. Of course I was delighted.

Now I am ballet master at American Ballet Theatre, which asked me to join. If Mr. Balanchine were still alive, I could not have left his company. I felt that my one usefulness was to help him when he was getting older and doing things he shouldn't have—things I could do for him. I could help with his load of work. Now that he's gone, it's another world.

FRANCISCO
MONCION

Studied at the School of American Ballet; appeared on Broadway in Balanchine's choreography for The Merry Widow, Song of Norway, and The Chocolate Soldier. Charter member of Ballet Society and New York City Ballet. Created roles in Balanchine's Divertimento, Orpheus, The Firebird, and many other ballets.

I Remember Balanchine

PEOPLE DIDN'T USE THE EXPRESSION THEN, BUT I WAS "BLOWN AWAY" WHEN I SAW Balanchine's dances in the movie *Goldwyn Follies.* I wrote requesting a catalogue from his School of American Ballet. They sent a brochure designed by Tchelitchew, stating requirements for admission. They were too formidable for me to think of applying. I used to work out at the Sixty-Third Street Y, however, and there I met a man who turned out to be a friend of Eugenie Ouroussow, who ran the School. "Did you ever think of dancing?" he asked, and sent me to the School to audition. I was already sixteen or seventeen, but I was pliant and acrobatic. In 1939, I started out on a partial scholarship. Then I saw Marie-Jeanne in *Ballet Imperial,* and that sealed my doom. This dancer, Balanchine's favorite at that time, had an extraordinary body. Her legs seemed to start up in her chest. She had long feet, too, which you'd think would be an advantage, but it wasn't because going from flat to pointe —she had long toes—was a great effort, you saw, as she so effortlessly got on pointe and did *relevés* the distance she rose through. Here was a dancer who could never fake anything; it was all there and controlled. When that lady took an arabesque, you saw the whole sculpture, strong, from the feet up. In addition, she was an intelligent individual with temperament and feeling, with a great sense of movement.

One day at the School, Natasha Molostwoff came to me and said, "You see this? This is what you owe. It's astronomical! We will tear it up. We'll start all over again under a different basis. You can pay when you can. Just dance." Balanchine in those days was a shadowy figure: a lean, darkish man with a hawklike face, bony, who kept coming in and going out. Then came the New Opera Company and Balanchine's *Ballet Imperial* with Mary Ellen Moylan and Bill Dollar. When the curtain went up about fifty percent of the cast was shivering with fright, all onstage for the first time. He'd just drawn us out of the School, but he rehearsed us himself and made it work. Then I had to leave and go into the army. When I developed pneumonia and had spots on my lungs, I was discharged. I came back to the School and took a job at Radio City Music Hall, doing performances of *Bolero.* Then I joined the cast of Balanchine's *Merry Widow,* and next came the De Cuevas Ballet International, in '44. There I danced Edward Caton's ballet *Sebastian.* The story was elaborate—a prince is having an affair with a courtesan, much to the distress of his two jealous sisters, who in turn own a slave. After the De Cuevas season was over I came back to the School. Balanchine had a seminar and spoke about how superfluous a complicated libretto was. He gave his spiel about ballet not being able to show who's a sister-in-law, etc., while I sat, fresh from my laurels as *Sebastian.* Winking at me, he added, "Oh, of course, there may be some times when you can show slave!" He always knew everything that was going on.

At Ballet Society, Balanchine put me in *The Triumph of Bacchus and Ariadne* as King Midas, where I performed angular kind of modern dance movements. I came out with the courtiers, who rolled coins back and forth. The minute I touched the coins they flipped to the gold side, and the same thing with the people whom I touched. Obvious, but it worked. Balanchine's Midas was so desperate for gold that he scratched the earth with his fingernails to try to find more. George wanted the audience to hear the scratching but the orchestra covered it. Bacchus and Ariadne were Nicky and Tanny, dancing a typically enwrapped Balanchine pas de deux. The ballet was inspired by a poem of Lorenzo de' Medici about the beauty of youth which flees away so fast.

These were the days in Ballet Society when we had several performances a year and in between nothing. You went to class and kept in shape but you gained weight. Once the rehearsals began, so did the crash diets. Everyone would get desiccated. In *Bacchus and Ariadne,* Marie-Jeanne was a nymph like wood-tempered steel. She'd bend back and forth in total abandon. I remember one performance she came across in a diagonal, with Herby Bliss marvelous as a satyr, flying. Her body twisted into back bends and forward and every which way. In the wings, she just collapsed, she was so weak.

We did *Concerto Barocco* together, and I remember the *piqué* walk-around, then the pull-away, and then arabesque *piqué* around and then facing and that pull-away. Marie-Jeanne said, "This pull-away is almost like an orgasm. It's a sensual, physical thing." I'd never thought about it in those terms, but it's terrific in good performances. It's the quintessence of a physical, muscular reaction to ecstasy.

Balanchine worked out all the variations in Haieff's *Divertimento* on me. I was the only one around and he grabbed me one day and said, "Come." The same with *Orpheus.* Nicky was somewhere else and Balanchine wanted to get started on the pas de deux of Orpheus and the Dark Angel. He said, "Now you come here and you do this and then do that." George and I were wrapped up in each other's arms struggling when Maria Tallchief came in. "Get your hands off my husband!" she laughed. "What's going on here! What do you want to eat tonight, George? Chicken again?" She'd finished class and was on her way to shop.

We dubbed Balanchine father, but I don't think it was returned that way; that would have entailed a tremendous amount of responsibility on his part! He was concerned primarily with the company, with the dancing. He used people as they came and went, the ebb and flow. I had low self-esteem because I came into the profession late and was never a classical dancer, although I studied the whole bit. I was never really considered a product of the School of American Ballet, although that was the only place I studied.

My relationship with Balanchine developed that way. I never felt easy about slapping him on the back the way some others did. I felt intimidated in asking him about new roles. If you pushed him into a corner, he would lash out. He could really get angry, but always in a cold, freezing manner. It was almost like he encapsulated himself in a defensive cocoon. I could never find a way to address him.

Divertimento was a great success when I staged it for Todd Bolender and the State Ballet of Missouri in 1987. Tanaquil LeClercq, who inherited the rights to the ballet, did not like it, however. "It doesn't have what you and Maria used to," she complained. "That's gone," I told her. "You can't expect things to look that way." Tanny and I both remembered *Divertimento* from when we had done it together. But translating it to other dancers is another thing entirely. What works in 1947 works in 1987 differently. One of the things you have to learn about recreating old ballets is that they're never the same. They always have to be reinterpreted. Critics want what used to be but it isn't available. Balanchine knew that better than anyone. He never wanted to look back. You'd say, "Didn't that used to be like this?" He'd reply, "It used to be rotten. Much better now." In *Vienna Waltzes,* he used the same Gold and Silver Waltz that he had choreographed in *The Merry Widow.* When I showed him what he'd done thirty years earlier, he wasn't too much taken with it. "Interesting," he said.

When we came back from our long tour to Australia, I heard he was going to do a new version of *Prodigal Son.* I was told by someone, "I heard that you are not going to be in it." Balanchine wanted someone else to tell me this, since I had danced the role for many years. He went to Vida Brown and Janet Reed. They said, "It's your decision, Mr. B., you must do it." It would have been as painful for them, since I was so established in the part. One day after class he sat down next to me tentatively. "You know, I'm thinking of doing a new version of *Prodigal."* "Oh, nice," I said. "Are you going to do new choreography, sets, costumes?" He said, "No, we'll keep this, we'll keep that." He hemmed and hawed, trying to tell me that I was no longer to be in it. "Do you mean to tell me that the response I've gotten from the audience over eight or nine years doesn't mean I'm more than just adequate in the part?" I asked. He said, "The audience doesn't know anything." "What about the critics?" "Oh, never listen to critics. You see, the ballet never looked right. Jerry Robbins wasn't good. He's small, but not enough; he's too big, not strong enough. I always thought maybe it should be small Italian boy, you see."

Out of the blue, he asked me one day at the Broadway school, "What do you want to do? Be a poet, a painter? Go out and work? Do you want to go to South America?" "Mr. B., I'm perfectly satisfied," I told him. "I have commitments and responsibilities. I don't want to go anywhere." I felt he wanted to get rid of me, and I wasn't ready to go. He took me out of *Midsummer Night's Dream,* then he thought if Cornell Crabtree worked out in my part in *Midsummer,* he would work out in *La Valse,* too. He rehearsed with Cornell for weeks, and there went another role, lost. Then it was Karin von Aroldingen's debut in *La Valse.* The night of the premiere, the telephone went buzz. Dripping wet, I answered it. It was Sara Leland. "Hang on to your hat. Mr. B. wants you to come in and do *La Valse.*" I rehearsed and got through the performance. Later Peter Martins told me, "I've never seen that man so disturbed in my life." As he lit the ballet, Balanchine was pounding on the lighting booth, saying, "Where is Frank? I must have him." During the curtain calls Balanchine said, "I'm so glad you could come. You know, we just didn't have enough time to rehearse." They'd been rehearsing it for ages, but he wouldn't admit that he wanted me, needed me, for Karin. For forty years I'd lived with the man, worked for him, revered him, suffered with him, hated him, loved him. The man was a genius and he had clay feet. No one's perfect.

NANCY

LASSALLE

Nancy Norman Lassalle, Chairman of Education at the New York City Ballet, has been on its Board of Directors for many years. She is also a member of the Lincoln Center Council on Educational Programs.

I Remember Balanchine

ONE OF THE REMARKABLE THINGS ABOUT BALANCHINE I OBSERVED OVER THE YEARS WAS his strong sense of outreach to ballet schools and teachers throughout the country but most especially to children.

As a child myself I began to feel really intensely about ballet when I was a young student at the School of American Ballet in the early 1940s. I was able then to watch him work on *Concerto Barocco* with Marie-Jeanne. I would watch rehearsals and turn pages. I was hooked for good. After I graduated from high school and it became clear that dancing was not going to be it for me, I stayed close to my ballet family, Ballet Society by that time and the New York City Ballet, where eventually I was to make my contribution in the areas of educational programs and fund raising.

In the early days of the company, before we really got our feet on the ground, Balanchine was trying to reach out to a larger audience. Around 1956 or '57 we did an upstate tour financed by the New York State Council on the Arts. The company was broken up into small units, and different ballets were done in four different cities upstate. The tour also included lecture demonstrations.

When we came back to New York City we thought, "Why not go out and do this in the public schools?" Our little dance group, headed up by Melissa Hayden, included Suki Schorer and Pat Neary. We traveled around in my station wagon to all the boroughs. We had a little funding from NYSCA, but mainly we did it for free. That provided the base for the immense educational program we now do regularly. I think we were the first company to do that kind of thing.

Then Balanchine wanted public school children to come to the theater. He put me in charge of the special matinees for children which started in 1962. He felt so strongly that *all* children in the city should have a theatrical experience and come to know this beautiful thing, pure beauty. He was very clear about that and very determined that it should happen.

Balanchine felt the same way about using children in ballets. His earliest use of children was probably in *The Nutcracker,* but then in 1962 we had our first true benefit for the company with *A Midsummer Night's Dream,* where he used children again. We still do the children's matinees every year. It took away a whole day of rehearsing, but Balanchine was absolutely adamant about children coming to the ballet. His personal interest in it was tremendous.

My own feeling is that Balanchine never lost that sense of magic about the theater that he acquired when he was very young himself. From what we know, he wasn't terribly interested in getting into the ballet school. I'm sure that what finally committed him was being in performances. I think he suddenly woke up. All I saw of him during a long period of more than forty years confirms that he wanted the ordinary child to experience the magic of the theater.

When Balanchine worked with children he was very courteous, very peer. He worked *with* them. He knew they could do the things he gave them to do. He never gave them material he felt would be awkward. When you watched him working with children, you realized something wonderful must have happened to him during his own childhood. He probably would never have said so, but he clearly wanted them to have something of what he had. He did say when he put them in *The Nutcracker*, "I was a child in *The Nutcracker* and this is the way it has to be." He felt all of them must have that feeling.

Just as he had this special feeling for children, Balanchine cared deeply about the ballet teachers across the country. Back in the days of Ballet Society we were trying to get backing from the Ford Foundation for a study of the quality of the ballet schools in the United States. Balanchine was incredibly interested. He had obviously gone around to schools. In fact, I went with him to Philadelphia, later on, and saw what he wanted and how he talked to Barbara Weisberger at the Pennsylvania Ballet. He cared tremendously what they did. Eugenie Oroussow at the School of American Ballet finally ended up with the study, and I assisted a great deal for many years. Until the State Theater schedule became too demanding, he held seminars for ballet teachers from many different schools. When small companies would ask permission to do one of his ballets, he would say, "Oh, yes, give it to them. They should do it." His feeling was to help them, teach them.

The thing Balanchine gave me and so many other persons was a spiritual center. That's why I was there at the beginning and why I'm still here.

FRED

DANIELI

Fred Danieli was born in New York City on July 17, 1917. He was trained at the School of American Ballet and made his debut with Ballet Caravan. He also danced in William Dollar's A Thousand Times Neigh *at the 1939 New York World's Fair. Danieli joined the 1941 American Ballet Caravan tour of South America, danced in the Ethel Merman musical comedy,* Call Me Madam, *joined Ballet Society and created roles in Balanchine's* The Four Temperaments, *the Haieff* Divertimento *and in* Renard. *He choreographed* Punch and the Child *for the 1947 Ballet Society season. Danieli retired as a performer in 1949 and founded the Garden State Ballet. As artistic director of that company he choreographed a number of works, including* Divertimento, Peter and the Wolf, The Enchanted Piano, *and* The Nutcracker.

I WAS A SICKLY CHILD IN THE BRONX. SOMEONE SUGGESTED BALLET TRAINING. I STARTED ballet, liked it, and stayed with it. My first teacher was Dimanz, who had a small studio between Lexington and Park on Fifty-ninth Street. At one time he had had a very large school, but that's the way schools go: some years you are packed, the next you're not. The School of American Ballet was just up the street a couple of blocks. I began to go there. At seventeen I got out of high school and stayed with dancing. I took classes and got into a Broadway musical comedy, *On Your Toes.*

I auditioned for the show in the usual way. I think Balanchine recognized me from around the School. There were eight male dancers, and I was grateful to be one of them. There were also eight tap dancers in the show; they worked with Balanchine and a black hoofer, Herby Harper. Balanchine would arrange the sequences, but Harper would do the steps. Ray Bolger was a vaudevillian; his style was gawky but graceful. In *The Wizard of Oz* he made a perfect Scarecrow. At the time of *On Your Toes,* when he was younger, he could thank his wife for pushing him and making him work hard. She was the driver. Tamara Geva was a marvelous dancer, a very beautiful woman, and nice. Usually, stars would go in their dressing room and nobody could get to them. But Geva was not that way. You could talk to her and joke with her. Basically, she was a ballet dancer, and we were all in the same boat as dancers.

Balanchine was not snobbish or egotistical in any way. He was a very down-to-earth man, unlike Fokine or Tudor. I think that's why dancers liked him. Fokine had a studio-home on Riverside Drive, and I would take class with him once in a while. There was no comparison between his classes and those at the School of American Ballet. Fokine's studio was a home, a mansion. He had a big foyer, and the classes were held in a living room. Fokine was a nice guy. He never felt he got the acclaim that he should have gotten, but he didn't do any real ballets after the first ones for Monte Carlo; whereas Balanchine was so prolific, he just kept turning them out. Fokine couldn't understand why this young guy was getting all the attention and "I'm not."

I continued to take classes at S.A.B. during *On Your Toes.* I studied with Vladimiroff. Erick Hawkins studied at the School at the time and, being a dancer and being broke, he started teaching beginners' classes there. Erick was a Harvard man, so he and Lincoln Kirstein knew each other. Kirstein would take classes so that he could understand a bit more about ballet technically. Balanchine was not teaching classes at that time, but his presence was felt.

Balanchine's manager Dimitriev was also at the School. Not very many people liked him because he was so money-hungry. At that time there were no male students. I was the only boy around the School at that time. There were no scholarships. Dimitriev was making a nice salary, I believe.

Balanchine loved America, he loved Americans. Although he never thought we were great dancers, he always used us in intelligent ways. He was very good at giving the dancers what they could do best. In that sense I think he liked us. He was never impatient. He would never throw anything out because we couldn't do it the first time around, or the second or the third. He lived with certain things technically if they were too difficult. If it was still impossible after a week or two, he would change it. I can't remember in all the years I knew him that he ever lost his temper.

Kirstein would keep the dancers together by giving us work. He booked a tour in New England, and we played summer theaters on tiny stages in old movie houses. In Keene, New Hampshire, we played a movie house, and the only time they'd give us was 10 A.M., because they didn't want to lose money on the movies. We danced our repertoire, whatever it was at the time. The Adelphi Theater season in New York in 1935 had no audience. There was no audience for dance at that time. Ballet—and being a dancer—at that time were not really acceptable. Ballet Caravan did a performance in Milwaukee, and the next day the paper's headline was "The Airy Fairy Dancers Were in Town Last Night."

The American Ballet Caravan tour to South America happened because of Kirstein's knowledge and his acquaintance with Nelson Rockefeller. Rockefeller was head of inter-American affairs in the government in Washington and mapped out the whole tour.

I liked Balanchine's approach to ballet. If you worked with Fokine or wanted to be in other ballet companies, they would ask you to dance the variation from *Les Sylphides*. Balanchine never asked you to live up to that technical variation if you were a lead dancer; he would make something for you. Fokine and the others just had certain set patterns, and you fit into that or you didn't. Either you were that kind of dancer or you weren't.

I remember Marie-Jeanne after a performance of *Concerto Barocco,* tears streaming down from her eyes from exhaustion. *Barocco* was a hard ballet. The adagio was always the hardest. Marie-Jeanne never "marked" her rehearsals. In her attack and her approach, she always worked very hard. She was very strong and had big feet. We used to call her "Paddlefoot Pelus." She was a fantastic allegro dancer, but also good in adagio. That's what made her great. She had a good extension, but she could also move fast. Nobody could touch her when she felt like it.

I always remember Balanchine's use of his hands to indicate how the feet are to be shown. When a new work finally got along where you could perform it at tempo, he might bring in a recording and try to do it full out.

But normally he used a pianist, and he would have us work very slowly on certain sections if we had to. There is a strut in *Concerto Barocco* that Balanchine called a "Harlem strut." It's in the adagio when a group of the corps dancers have to move from one side of the stage to the center. They strutted, using the right arm. There was an awful lot of kidding around in rehearsals. We did that strut as a joke, and Balanchine liked it and kept it in.

When I got back to New York after World War II, I returned to the S.A.B. Even if you had other jobs, you went there to take class and see friends, Kirstein, and Balanchine. Lincoln had also been in the war. He was in Germany, and he wasn't too happy with war service. He didn't fight, but if you're in the army there's no one you can really talk to. He was noting collections of paintings the Germans had stolen and trying to set things straight.

I was in the Sanguinic movement of *The Four Temperaments* (1946). Long before the premiere, Balanchine was always working with scraps of the music, trying out movement, whenever he had studio time. Studio time was at a premium. We didn't have rehearsal space. We used the School of American Ballet after their classes were finished at six o'clock at night. Whenever he could get a dancer or two together, he would try things out. Balanchine never started a ballet at the beginning. He could start any ballet in the middle or the end, and later put it together. We knew that *The Four Temperaments* was not an ordinary ballet.

The Russian Kopeikine was the rehearsal pianist; he was fantastic. I don't think Balanchine was understood by his Russian friends better than Americans. He just felt at home with them. They all liked to eat and drink. How Balanchine could drink—usually vodka! He never got drunk. Later, when he came out to watch a class at our school in Newark, he would order a plate of spaghetti and some Jack Daniels.

I collaborated with Balanchine on the musical comedy *Where's Charley?* (1948). He took the job, and asked me to be his assistant. He said, "When it goes on the road, I'm not going to go with it because I have other things to do." When we went into it, the show's dance director had been Al White. It was a Ray Bolger show, and White had been assigned. He was a good choreographer, but not imaginative. He was very businesslike and matter-of-fact. *Where's Charley?* had been in rehearsal for a couple of weeks when we came in, and Balanchine and I sat in and saw what White had done. Then we rolled up our sleeves and went to work. We did the whole show all over again. It had a good run. Bolger was the whole show. He used to be exhausted because he had to make quick switches from one costume to another, and some of the costumes were wigs and dresses.

After I retired as a dancer, Balanchine and I remained friendly. I wanted to get married, start teaching, and open a school. I explained it to him, and he said, "Fine." We helped the Ford Foundation search for children for scholarships. At one time there were six of our students in the New York City Ballet: Gloria Govrin, Teena McConnell, Victor Castelli, Lynda Yourth, Christine Redpath, and Marjorie Spohn. I try to give my students Balanchine's attack and speed, as well as his theory of ballet—beautiful, technically correct movement without affectation. Balanchine didn't like prima ballerina mannerisms. That's why he liked Americans, especially women dancers. He gave us *Concerto Barocco* and any of his ballets that would fit on a company our size, and he came to see the company. He was very generous with his ballets.

My wife Evelyn remembers Balanchine visiting regional ballet conferences of the National Association of Regional Ballet before the Ford Foundation grants. Once in the early sixties at the Northeast conference in Pennsylvania, he saw how large the organization of civic ballet companies had become, and he was asked to speak at a dinner attended by all of the heads of the civic ballet companies. Balanchine wanted to say something about the power of the organization to bring ballet to the public, to educate the public. He stood up, addressed the group, and compared their strength to the power of Jimmy Hoffa, the head of the teamsters union. Up to then, he really hadn't realized what was happening. He was overwhelmed by it. "I see what you are doing here with this organization—civic ballet in the Northeast. Look, you now have the power that Jimmy Hoffa has." He may not have known who Jimmy Hoffa was and what he was involved in, but he knew he was a very powerful man and chartered a powerful organization. It wasn't a long speech, but it was impressive. Jimmy Hoffa at a ballet conference, out of the mouth of Balanchine!

MARY ELLEN

MOYLAN

Studied with Alice Young and the School of American Ballet; danced in Balanchine's New Opera production of Rosalinda *and in* Ballet Imperial *(1942). Danced with Ballet Russe de Monte Carlo (1943–44; 1947–49). Balanchine made roles for her in* Pas de Trois for Piano and Two Dancers, Danses Concertantes, Le Bourgeois Gentilhomme, Divertimento, *and Sanguinic in* The Four Temperaments. *Danced with Ballet Theatre, where she performed the ballerina role in Balanchine's* Theme and Variations, *and with the Ballet Russe de Monte Carlo, where she was ballerina for many years.*

WHEN I CAME TO THE SCHOOL OF AMERICAN BALLET, I WAS FOURTEEN. I HAD LIVED IN Florida from the age of six, although I was born in Cincinnati. My mother was very knowledgeable about the theater. Her father, Tom Stall, was a big theater star in his day. He studied grand opera in Milan, where my mother and her brother were born, returned to the States early in the 1900s with his family, and went into the theater. He went into musicals. Remember the famous Florodora Sextette? Mother was an avid theatergoer. She loved the dancing and wanted to dance herself, but in her day it was frowned upon for young girls. So she contented herself with the thought that she would give her daughter ballet lessons one day.

I started studying in Florida at the age of six and was immediately doing some pretty awful things on pointe. But then a very good Russian dancer named Solomonoff and his wife appeared. I still had never seen a ballet. I didn't know what a dancer did onstage, I only knew what my mother told me. She liked Marilyn Miller, the Ziegfeld musical comedy star, and I think perhaps that's what she envisioned for me. So from the time I was six I was always going to be a dancer. My mother was very convincing!

Mother saw an article in a magazine about Balanchine's School of American Ballet. So when I was about eleven she took me there in the summer. She wanted to see what a little dancer in a St. Petersburg ballet school would look like in a New York school. S.A.B. was very encouraging during the month-long summer program. I returned for a second summer, and then when I was fourteen my aunt, who lived in Manhattan, said she would have me come and stay with her if I wanted to go to S.A.B. full time. Mother figured it would be very tight financially, but she could swing it for me to take one class a day. I was in B, the intermediate class. I left the tenth grade and came to New York in midyear. That was the end of my formal education; I'm self-taught, so to speak. The next year the School gave me a full scholarship, which was a lifesaver. My mother was a teacher, my father had died, and this was right after the Depression. The School has been wonderful to me all through the years.

The School opened up new vistas. Ludmilla Schollar, Anatole Vilzak, Kyra Blank, Vladimiroff, and Muriel Stuart were the main faculty members then. Later Vilzak and Schollar left and Oboukhoff came. When I think of how terrified of Oboukhoff I used to be! He would come and stand exactly in front of my nose while I was doing a *développé à la seconde* in the center of the floor. I was concentrating on my balance, and his face was right in front of me, not saying anything. I thought I would collapse. But one day I peeked in and saw him teaching the children. This roaring lion was like a gentle lamb. And I figured it was all a bluff; the next time he stood right in front of my nose, I just looked right back at him.

Mary Ellen Moylan

It was always a very special event when Balanchine taught, for he was working mostly in Hollywood and Broadway. I remember the first time, the students were abuzz in the dressing room. They seemed to come suddenly from nowhere to class. I found that I was corrected very much in that first class, which of course was a great honor, I was told afterward. I can remember standing at the barre in that mobbed classroom and his coming up and speaking in his very quiet voice. He was always very gentle, very quiet, never bombastic. Never pushing his weight around, which with us was, of course, considerable.

Balanchine didn't teach the way the others did. He didn't give a general type class. He'd give a barre and then center work, but it wasn't a division of, say, adagio steps, turns, little jumps, big jumps. He would often focus on a particular step. It might be a *tendu,* it might be a *glissade,* whatever it was that he wished to stress. I think he felt that the other teachers could do the general, well-rounded class, but he would rather impart some specific point to us. I'll never forget one *glissade* class, doing this very difficult connecting step over and over again.

He was very particular that the feet should be as expressive as the hands, that you should point, that it should have a snaky movement and a presentation. "Present the feet as you would the hand to someone with whom you're shaking hands."

My first appearance onstage in New York was in Balanchine's *Pas de Trois for Piano and Two Dancers* (1942). Nicky Magallanes and I did it for Russian War Relief. Theodore Chanler was the composer, and he played the piano onstage. His presence was an integral part of the ballet, he made the pas de trois.

We came in very casually. The pianist entered with us. Nicky had his towel, I carried an extra pair of toe shoes, and there was a barre set up onstage. The pianist sat down to play, and we started to do warm-up exercises which were very much the real thing. It was utter realism and simplicity and just "that's the way it is"—it was delightful. Then we came center stage and hovered around the pianist, involving him in our activity. I even played a few notes and leaned on the piano in an arabesque—he and the piano were incorporated into the choreography. Then we went into a pas de deux, a sort of blues, meditative, quite moody dance. Then a quick finale.

There wasn't a ballet company then, but in 1942 Balanchine was providing work for his dancers. The New Opera Company had him doing the ballets for several operas at the Broadway Theater, and he was also the choreographer of *Rosalinda* at the Forty-fourth Street Theater. He most marvelously put me in the *première danseuse* role in that production. José Limón was my partner. Can you imagine? I guess José needed work at the time. He was a lovely man. Here he had this little, young, inexperienced dancer as his partner, but he was a gentleman, looked wonderful in the uniform, and danced in the waltz sequence divinely.

At this time at the Broadway Theater, Walter Damrosch's opera *The Opera Cloak* was due to be given its premiere. But the producers felt that it would not be successful and planned to withdraw it after one or two performances. They must have known this well in advance because *Ballet Imperial* (1941) was being prepared to take that spot on the same bill with *Fair at Sorochinsk*. This was the first time that *Ballet Imperial* was seen by the general public in New York. I had seen the preview performance at Hunter College, and I had also seen *Concerto Barocco* (1941) with the original costumes before Balanchine took these ballets off on tour to Latin America. (I was still a student at the School.) It was fabulous. Marie-Jeanne did the leads in both, and she was spectacular. I thought she was just it—perfect. I adored her. Talk about role models—to me she was the perfect ideal of Balanchine.

Balanchine would call rehearsals for *Ballet Imperial* every day at the old School of American Ballet on Fifty-ninth Street and Madison Avenue. I would sit there as steps were choreographed here and there. I thought, "I wonder what am I going to do?" One day Nicky Magallanes came to me and said, "Come with me in the back of the room. I want to teach you the pas de deux." That was the first I knew I was going to do the leading part. Nobody had ever said a word to me. Nicky taught me and the next thing you know we were asked to do the pas de deux and on we went.

It was quite a thrill to make my debut in New York under Balanchine's aegis in two productions concurrently. I felt a great responsibility to do a good job for him and not let anyone down. When a person so young and inexperienced is onstage in a situation like that, I don't think they know enough to be as terrified as they should be. The big to-do at the last minute was how to fix my hair. I think it was Gisella Caccialanza who was helping me make these little curlicues. After the performance of *Ballet Imperial* I put on my cloak, left all my makeup on, and tore down in a taxi to the Forty-fourth Street Theater to appear in the second act of *Rosalinda.* It worked out perfectly. After a week or ten days, *Imperial* was finished, and I continued in *Rosalinda* for a year.

I don't think I have ever danced a more difficult ballet in my entire career than *Ballet Imperial.* One of the reasons was because the very first entrance onstage is to the piano solo. It requires turns on a dime and stop, and great control and speed. There is no preparatory warm-up with the audience. You come bursting in, and you don't have a way to ease in to meet your public. I don't remember what Balanchine said at the opening. I remember Zorina coming back that first night. She was wonderful.

Nick was a superb partner. I had worked with Nicky for all of my student years. He was generally my partner in adagio class, so we were already used to working together. At other times Eglevsky would come to the adagio class. I can remember his partnering me—and William Dollar.

As *Rosalinda* went on, I began to get a little bit antsy, since there was never any direct conversation with Balanchine about what might be. The School always told me: "Don't do anything. Balanchine is going to arrange, so stay put." There were discussions that perhaps he would find a niche for me at Ballet Theatre, but Sergei Denham, who was the director of Ballet Russe de Monte Carlo, had seen me in class and wanted me to come with his company. The idea appealed to me enormously. Here was Danilova, the great Russian ballerina, heading the company. To me, this would be part of my education. You learn the steps at school, but one also needs to learn how to comport oneself properly onstage, how to do a vast repertoire of various works in different styles, working with many choreographers. I felt strongly that the Russian tradition from which we all sprang was still in Denham's company. Many of my friends were joining: Nicky Magallanes, Herbert Bliss, Yvonne Chouteau, Pauline Goddard, Julia Horvath, Ann Barlow, all the people with whom I'd grown up at the School. So I went to Mr. Balanchine and presented him with the possibility. Would it be okay if I went in with that company at this time? He gave me his blessing, but he said, "Do not sign a two-year contract. Only sign for one year. No option." Denham didn't like that at all, but he accepted it, and the next year I was able to double my salary. I'm not very good at business. That's the only thing I was ever able to do that I thought was a coup.

It was wartime and traveling was very difficult. We were all in every ballet in one capacity or another. We were quite exhausted at night, but it was tremendously exciting. The Ballet Russe at that time was very poor in finances, though rich in talent, but they were trying to do some new productions for that year. They had Nijinska in to do *Etude,* as one of the new ballets. This was set to the Bach Brandenburg suites and some of the concerti, with the men and women dancers in unisex costumes without tights.

I enjoyed working with Nijinska. She was absolutely different from Balanchine. Her movement was earthy and heavy. She was an interesting character. There was no rapport as far as language went because everything had to be interpreted through her husband, but she was very sweet with me. She seemed to like me and put me in the girls' pas de quatre. It was all jumps, and it was hell. And then I rotated a solo to a polonaise, which was really lovely. I did that every third time. There was a definite breath incorporated into the dance; you actually breathed on cue. At least that's what she did, and I felt this aspiration as part of the dance, so that's what I did. And I went to the museum and studied the Byzantine eyes that she wanted—you know, you can learn a lot in the ballet.

The following year Balanchine came to the Ballet Russe. He gave us *Ballet Imperial, Concerto Barocco, Le Bourgeois Gentilhomme,* as well as a brand-new ballet, *Danses Concertantes.* It came into the repertoire during the summer of 1944, when the company was engaged as a group to be in the production of *Song of Norway,* which was making its debut in Los Angeles. Danilova and Freddie Franklin did the leads in the *Concerto,* and Krassovska and Danielian did some solo parts in the *Peer Gynt Suite.* Maria Tallchief and I did the next parts after that, and we also each understudied Danilova's role. When she became ill in San Francisco, Maria and I each appeared for about a week in her roles. The plan was that, while the company was in California, once the show was on and performing, our days would be taken up with rehearsing a new ballet for our own season. So while we were performing *Norway* at night, we rehearsed *Concertantes* during the day. I don't know what the union would say about that kind of activity today, but we did it then. It worked, and, my dear, no one complained. I mean, for the opportunity to work with Balanchine we would have danced all night and all day, too.

I think that *Danses Concertantes* was a particularly felicitous marriage of three components: choreography, music, and stage design and costumes. The Stravinsky score was perfect for Balanchine's choreography. The costumes by Eugene Berman were perfect as well. They showed the body, the legs, they were flattering and chic. Balanchine used four groups of three—a boy and two girls—and a lead couple. There were black accents on all the costumes, and the other colors were very vibrant: turquoise, chartreuse, a beautiful purple. Maria, Nicky, and I were shocking pink. Choura and Freddie, the leads, were a topaz color.

The whole company pulled out of *Norway* after two weeks, and *Danses Concertantes* was ready to open. But we were still rehearsing *Ballet Imperial* during our Chicago season, which was rather early in the tour. We'd rehearse after other performances; we'd stay on the stage and do *Ballet Imperial.* We were very close, pinched for time. One night I remember going with Choura, Freddie, and Balanchine to some cafeteria and eating cornflakes. You think of people in the ballet in some exotic restaurant, but there we were.

Balanchine left after the Chicago season, once *Ballet Imperial* was launched. I was very happy to have the opportunity to do the ballet again, after having performed onstage in a multiplicity of roles, with Choura and Freddie and Leon around me. Maria did the pas de trois, and she was stunning. I feel we were very good for each other, Maria and I. She's a very precious part of my theater experience. *Imperial* had marvelous reviews in Chicago. *Serenade* had been in the repertoire the year before and was no longer a new ballet for

Chicago. But we had *Imperial, Barocco,* and *Danses Concertantes* right in the opening weeks of my second-year season: three Balanchine works newly done with Balanchine dancers. These ballets were done a lot on tour; they were the new works of the year, and they became the "ham and eggs" program. I feel that we were pioneers. We had five works of his that were presented the entire length and breadth of the United States, performed by dancers whom he had trained.

I remember *Le Bourgeois Gentilhomme* being quite delightful. Maria Ruanova had danced my part originally, in 1932. The pas de sept moved in a flying wedge, led by me, sideways onto the stage, as part of a big divertissement. In addition to the pas de sept, there was the Indian dance which Maria and Herby Bliss did, and a Blackamoor dance which Ruthanna Boris danced.

I left the Ballet Russe in 1946 to go back to Broadway, to work with Tudor on *The Day Before Spring,* with Hugh Laing as my partner. It was Antony's first show and probably his last. I don't think it was his cup of tea. I worked again with Balanchine in Ballet Society. Fred Danieli and I did Sanguinic in *The Four Temperaments*—an extraordinary pas de deux that was gravity-defying. It had a lugubrious quality of movement in the air without any preparation, elastic movement from place to place in another atmosphere. That's what I felt when I danced it—not jump, not an arc, but moving in another plane.

Tanny LeClercq was magnificent as Choleric. We'd been students at the School together. I remember when she first won a scholarship when she was about eleven. Her costume in *Four Temperaments* had a lot of ribbonlike things flying off it, so not only were her legs and arms going in many directions, but the ribbons were also sailing. Have you ever seen the great blue crane in flight? They are magnificent birds with long necks and long legs. The bars of their rear feathers are long and loose, and they flutter in the wind as the bird is landing. Tanny's movement reminded me of that crane, with the weight of the body and these delicate feathers trailing along. I can see it in my mind very clearly: certain things just stand out.

Before the opening, Balanchine was complaining about Seligmann's costumes being so voluminous that they covered the dancers' movements. I remember my costume was red, with matching tights and shoes, and it had white bandagelike gauze around the torso and a great big gauzy bow on one shoulder, gauze skirts, and big sleevy things. Balanchine was justly complaining to Seligmann: "Look! Mary Ellen! Where is Mary Ellen? We can't see her. We should take this off and this and this." And Seligmann was standing there, and he said: "Hah! Where is Seligmann?" They were destroying him. Not too long ago, in one of my art classes I met a fellow who studied with Seligmann. Small world, hey?

I only did two performances of Balanchine's *Divertimento* (1947), and I never saw it again. It was tantalizing to do roles like this only a couple of times. It's like having a banquet and just as you are about to eat the food goes back to the kitchen.

I was still in New York, studying singing and drama, and I was able to do another Broadway show. So I got into *The Chocolate Soldier* (1947), and Balanchine did three beautiful ballets for Frank Moncion and me.

Around this time Balanchine and Oliver Smith asked me to lunch at the Stork Club. They told me they wanted me to come to Ballet Theatre where Balanchine would make a new ballet, *Theme and Variations,* for me and Igor Youskevitch. The music was Tchaikovsky. I thought for a minute and said no. I had an opportunity to go back to Ballet Russe and dance all the big old roles and I preferred that. Balanchine was astonished, I think.

Some years later I did dance *Theme and Variations* with American Ballet Theatre. I made my debut in Paris with Igor Youskevitch in it. It was the company's first appearance there. Some years before, one of the French companies had appeared in New York. One of the dancers had political leanings that were not popular, and the company was booed. So we were not sure if there might not be a retaliation. We were performing in the Palais de Chaillot, not at all certain what our reception would be. But the curtain rose and the audience broke into applause. It was just overwhelming. They took us to their hearts immediately. What a sigh of relief! Later in that tour I did *Apollo* with Igor. In London George came and gave rehearsals. To have the touch of the master—there's nothing like it.

Years later I came back to New York after having lived in California. I went down to the School and thought I would drop in to say hello to George. I had never seen his new studios. George greeted me and turned to the dancers in company class and said: "This is Mary Ellen. She was the first."

CONSTANCE

CLAUSEN

*"Starlet" with Ringling Brothers and Barnum & Bailey Circus,
Constance Clausen performed in the elephant ballet by Balanchine to
Circus Polka by Stravinsky. Author of a memoir of the circus,* I
Love You, Honey, but the Season's Over *(1961), she is a
literary agent in New York City.*

I Remember Balanchine

THE BALANCHINE I KNEW ISN'T THE ONE THE BALLERINAS WRITE ABOUT. WE WEREN'T dancers. We were in the circus. He was never going to make us dancers, and he knew that. We were hopeless, particularly me. Most of the girls were acrobats or New York dancers. I was hired by accident to play Alice in *Alice in Wonderland.* I had long blond hair. John Ringling North saw me on the street in Sarasota, Florida, and said, "What beautiful long hair you have. You're Alice. You've got to be in the show." I told my father. He had always wanted to run away and join the circus. What else was there for him to do in Oshkosh, Wisconsin? He said, "You must go." I said, "I can't go off to the circus. It smells. I can't do anything. I'm the least athletic person in the world." I was always reading and going to movies. I couldn't even touch my toes. I went out to the circus and saw girls hanging by their teeth, their hair, their ankles, their wrists. I was terrified. I was nineteen. They took me.

They decided not to do *Alice.* They were going to do the League of Nations, and I ended up beating a drum in a Martha Washington wig. I said, "But I can't drum!" They said, "Fake it." So I was hired for my hair, yet through the entire show I wore a wig until finally I was cast as Cleopatra in the opening parade.

Finally Balanchine walks in. I can't tell you how beautiful he was, physically beautiful. I think he had a suede coat, and he was so kind. He called all the girls together and said, "Who has had experience with animals?" I said I had—I had come off a farm. So they brought up the elephants, and I nearly died. They were huge, and they were making all these trumpeting sounds. I was so humiliated, because I couldn't do anything. I couldn't do a somersault. So I said, "I've got to conquer this." I had been in parades and floats and the Spanish dance, but I never could tell left from right without finding my vaccination mark.

Balanchine explained that we would all be in the elephant ballet. Three of us were selected in each ring to actually work on top of the elephants. Balanchine was a pragmatist, he worked very hard. The girls all pranced out to Stravinsky's music with pink garlands—hoops covered with pink flowers. The garlands would sometimes snap up if you let go of one end, and they'd hit the girl next to you. We all came out in tutus and net hoods, so again my hair was under a hood. We wore ballet shoes with ribbons that tied. Then we danced madly to the Stravinsky score. (None of us had ever heard of Stravinsky.)

While the girls were still dancing, the elephant man would say, "Down," and the three elephant girls (I was one) would put one foot on the trunk, ride it up, put the other foot on the head, and go into an arabesque on top of the elephant, balanced on the head and the trunk. We were in the winter quarters rehearsal tent in Sarasota, and I would fall and fall and fall as I rehearsed this. The elephant men would be roaring with laughter because I would crash so terribly. This was my famous encounter with Balanchine. It went on for weeks. I was in agony. It was then that Balanchine walked over to the ring curve and looked at me with such sorrow in his face. He was a kind man; he knew we were hopeless. Balanchine said to me, "You must learn to land on the balls of your feet, my dear." I said, "But where are they?" I was falling twenty feet onto the ground, and if you don't know where the balls of your feet are, you land full force. I had a stone bruise that lasted twenty years.

Balanchine worked with a microphone, but he was always sweet and calm. John Murray Anderson, the famous New York theater director, staged our show; he would be yelling and giving us all nicknames. There were girls and clowns and people milling around; the horses hated the elephants, so there was drama constantly. Vera Zorina, Balanchine's current wife, danced in the middle ring with Modoc, the dancing elephant. Balanchine also did a fiesta number for the horses. We had to swirl Spanish toreador capes to music from *Carmen*.

The Ballet of the Elephants lasted only one season. The band went on strike, so the music was played on a recording. The man who played the records was dubbed "Stravinsky" until the day of his death. I called him "Igor." The costumes were kept clean, but at the end of a season you're a little tired. Strangely enough, Balanchine stayed with us all year.

Where can you go after Ringling Brothers? I went to MGM. Anything else would be an anticlimax. One day when I was rehearsing, an elephant man said to me, "You must go to California and go to MGM." He wrote the name of Frank Whitbeck on a slip of paper. Whitbeck had an unforgettable voice, he did all the MGM previews and trailers—"Gable's back and Garson's got him!" He had been an ex-circus billposter, and I was sent to him. He started me as a messenger. Every day he brought in a book for me to read, and every night I would report to him on the book. Then he'd bring me another one.

In the meantime Balanchine came out to Hollywood. It may have been to talk about making a film musical of *Jumbo*. I had to go by train to Sarasota, where my parents still lived. Two Pullman compartments down was Balanchine. We sat together on that train to Sarasota for two and a half days and nights. That's when I really got to know him. I said to him, "Why did you ever choose me? I was terrible!" He said, "Well, it was the hair."

I was reading Thomas Wolfe, then, and I was in love with Esther Jack in *The Web and the Rock*. We got to talking, and Balanchine said, "Oh, that's a real person, she's Aline Bernstein, the famous stage designer, we're really good friends." He knew at once all about the book and about their love affair. I had literally fallen in love with this woman. Balanchine said, "She has written two books, and if you ever go to New York, you must call her and tell her you're my friend. She will see you."

He was such a gentleman. I was still a kid, and he must have been bored out of his mind, but he was always, invariably, kind. He couldn't have been nicer. He would initiate a lot of the conversation, because I never liked to intrude on anyone. But he was so warm. He told me about his life, the cold winters in Russia, and how he practiced and practiced as a student. Mainly he talked about his childhood, about his sister Tamara. He talked about Dostoevski also, about Raskolnikov in *Crime and Punishment.* He missed Russia, although he wanted to be here in the United States. Balanchine and I were so hungry on that train and so sick of the food. Our train had to stop for every troop train. This was the war. We would sit on sidings for hours. Balanchine and I drank a lot of coffee. They had those great silver tureens of coffee on the train.

Eventually we stopped somewhere in Texas, and we said, "Do we dare run to a diner?" We got off the train and found this little coffee shop. And we almost missed the train! It was receding, going down the track in the moonlight. We yelled, but they didn't hear us. I've never run like that in my life. We were screaming, and Balanchine was yelling, "Come on! Come on!" We just made it.

I went back to MGM and stayed there until I became head of special promotion. Then I met my future husband and moved to New York. After I was here for about a year I suddenly remembered, "Balanchine. Aline Bernstein!" I called her up, and she immediately invited me to tea at her home on Park Avenue. My husband, coincidentally, had been signed by Selznick to play Thomas Wolfe. He was six feet three, very handsome in that glowering Wolfe way. Aline went crazy when she saw him. Aline and I became good friends. Esther Jack was so real, and Aline was so real. She made New York come completely to life. She wrote a brilliant book, *An Actor's Daughter,* about growing up where Macy's is located now; another one called *Three Blue Suits;* and one in which she told her side of the affair with Wolfe.

Since I lived on the West Side, I would run into Balanchine on the street for years, and he would always talk with me. He would say, "Now, have you read the Russians?" He would give me lists—Dostoevski, Tolstoy, Gogol.

I sent my book about the circus to Balanchine. I ran into him on the street and he said, "That was a wonderful book."

ROBERT

LINDGREN

Performed with Ballet Theatre, the Ballet Russe de Monte Carlo, and in Broadway musicals. Joined New York City Ballet in late 1950s. Established ballet school in Phoenix, Arizona, with his wife, Sonya Tyven. Formerly dean of North Carolina School of the Arts, he is president of the School of American Ballet in New York.

BALANCHINE ALWAYS USED A SENSE OF MOVEMENT, A SPATIAL DESIGN, RATHER THAN just giving steps. When he restaged *Errante* for Ballet Theatre in 1943, we wandered through waves of chiffon, as though walking underwater or through clouds. It was a little bit like the feeling in *Orpheus,* when he used the silk curtain. There was not much technical choreography. There were some lifts, mainly in the adagio.

At Ballet Theatre, Balanchine also did a restaging of *Helen of Troy,* the last work Fokine choreographed. After Fokine's death, Lichine tried to take it over. It didn't work, so Balanchine added his little bit. He staged a marvelous variation for Eglevsky, who was dancing the role of Paris. His costumes were wonderful: when he came out with a bunch of sheep at the beginning, he wore a green Tarzan outfit and ballet slippers. Later on, his body was bronze and he wore gold shoes. When he was given the key to Troy, he did double *cabrioles,* an entire circle of double *sauts de basque.* It was really a virtuoso variation. Eglevsky was famous for slow pirouettes; he would wind up with the key to Troy and do about twelve pirouettes, double, to the knee. They would lower the curtain while he was doing them, so that the double tour and the end would occur simultaneously. It was incredible. At the old Met, people would scream and holler.

When Balanchine joined the Ballet Russe de Monte Carlo the following year, the company had already lost Eglevsky, Markova, Zoritch. Slavenska was about to leave. Massine was gone and we didn't have any new ballets. Balanchine's repertory rejuvenated the company. He created a whole new look for us when he brought in about ten dancers from the School of American Ballet.

The *Mozartiana* he staged for the Ballet Russe was totally different than the one he did later for Farrell at the City Ballet. I danced a completely different gigue; none of it was in the classical movement it has now. It was all done with toes and heels and was percussive, like a Spanish dancer, with all sorts of stamps. The preghiera was so beautiful. Two boys came on in black, like in an Italian funeral, with plumes on their heads, and the boy in back kept his arms on the shoulders of the one in front. Marie-Jeanne hung suspended on the arms of those two. They lowered her to the floor and she did a dance. She had a white tutu and a black veil over her face. Dorothy Etheridge's number was also beautiful: fast work, *piqués* forward and back, a little bit like the Butterfly in Fokine's *Carnaval.*

Le Bourgeois Gentilhomme was a witty, charming piece, with some beautiful dancing. Dressed in yellow, Mary Ellen Moylan led a classical pas de sept, the girls wearing white. George Verdak and I were two fencing masters, wearing sumptuous costumes. We did a demonstration pas de deux. It was comedic: I finally killed George at the end and went over and carried on. The

Indian dance that Maria Tallchief and Lazowski did was terrific. Then there was a commedia dell'arte pantomime piece for Nikita Talin as Pierrot, Leon Danielian as Harlequin, and Ruthanna Boris. There was a little screen and they'd rise above it, each one stabbing the other.

Sonya Tyven and I met in Balanchine's *Baiser de la Fée*. We were partners in the circle dance, in the second scene. Sonya was so shy, and I guess I thought I was rather a smart-ass young thing; that's where our romance began.

Mr. Balanchine was notoriously unkind to retired dancers. He'd always say things like, "He was lousy. Heavy." The only vintage dancer I ever heard Mr. Balanchine hold up as a model was Spessivtseva. In the days of the Ballet Russe, he never even came and watched classes at the School very much. When I was first in the New York City Ballet, he said the teachers were "lousy . . . no understanding . . . old-fashioned." We'd ask ourselves, "Gee, how can he say the School's terrible?" But Mr. Balanchine kept on saying to us, "Faster, faster, faster. We can do a barre in twelve minutes." All those Russians at the School, though, they would do a barre in twenty-five minutes, then take half an hour on adagio for feet and leg work, and another half hour on allegro leg work.

Balanchine really became interested in teaching after the New York City Ballet came back from Japan in 1958. He had come to terms with Tanaquil's paralysis and he was returning to the company. He taught us every day and started to build up the tight fifths, the crossed positions, the accents, the velocity. In the beginning, the tempi were not what they became. I'd say that *Concerto Barocco,* and *Ballet Imperial* were much more leisurely in the early days.

Mr. Balanchine said, "Just do it." He said, "Everybody wants something different. For my ballets I like to see legs high. You can't tell if their hip is up or not but anyway it doesn't matter. I want to see the leg go up quickly." "But, Mr. Balanchine, what about their placement?" teachers asked at the Ford Foundation seminars. "Well, when I say 'placement,' if you fall over you have no placement."

MARIA

TALLCHIEF*

Studied in California with Ernest Belcher, Bronislava Nijinska, Mia Slavenska, and David Lichine. Joined Denham's Ballet Russe de Monte Carlo, where she began her studies with Balanchine. Danced in his Danses Concertantes *and* Night Shadow. *Married Balanchine in 1946. Danced* Serenade, Apollo, *and* Le Baiser de la Fée *at Paris Opéra (1947). For Ballet Society danced roles in* Symphonie Concertante, Orpheus, *and* Symphony in C. *For New York City Ballet created roles in his* Firebird, Bourrée Fantasque, *and many other ballets. Founded Chicago City Ballet and directed it for thirteen years.*

* This interview was conducted by Camille Hardy and Francis Mason.

I Remember Balanchine

WE *are so accustomed to thinking of Balanchine as the established ballet master that we forget that this was not always so. There were many hard years for him and Lincoln Kirstein and their ambition for a permanent ballet company that would establish the classic dance as they envisioned it in America. Balanchine, during times when making ballets onstage was not possible, took refuge on Broadway and in Hollywood to do what he could on other stages. From the time of his arrival in New York in 1933 to the founding of the New York City Ballet, fifteen years had passed.*

Balanchine never was to compromise what he wanted to do. Alexandra Danilova says in her remembrance that Balanchine always wanted to do it his way. I believe that the dancer who helped him most to do it his way, the dancer who with him established the reputation of the young New York City Ballet and led the public to appreciate his ballets, is Maria Tallchief. She it was who took the New York City Ballet over the top.

Today it is difficult to conceive the New York City Ballet pulling less than full houses, but look back to an earlier time during its first season at the City Center in New York in 1948, and you see that the New York City Ballet danced on Monday and Tuesday evenings only and that, while the house was occupied by all who knew and loved Balanchine's work, they could then be numbered in hundreds: maybe fifty percent capacity, as Lincoln Kirstein has recalled. The balcony was always full with students from the School of American Ballet and their families, and the public sitting nearby learned early to profit from their response. But the small group of Balanchine fans continually wondered, as we watched Serenade *(1934) and* Concerto Barocco *(1941) and* Orpheus *(1948) and the Bizet (1948)—where was the rest of the world? Where were the persons who, if they only gave themselves the chance to see Balanchine's work, would come also to love it? They were looking at ballet elsewhere. Why not at the City Ballet? They were flocking to Ballet Theatre at the Metropolitan Opera House, to the Ballet Russe when it came to town, to the international companies Hurok brought to the Met. That audience had not yet learned to see the ballet Balanchine's way.*

In 1949 things took a dramatic new turn. The movie The Red Shoes *with Moira Shearer had its premiere in New York, the Sadler's Wells Ballet from England came to the Metropolitan Opera House with Fonteyn and Shearer in a repertory dominated by evening-length ballets, and ballet boomed in an unprecedented fashion. Fonteyn in* The Sleeping Beauty *and* Swan Lake *gave us a splendid vision of what ballet had been in the past and how it could be recaptured through the reconstructions of Nicholas Sergeyev, who had worked with the Russian Imperial Ballet under Marius Petipa. Frederick Ashton in his ballets showed us that England, too, had a choreographer of consequence, a maker of ballets of wit and lyricism and drama. To many balletgoers in those days, Balanchine's company at the City Center seemed very small potatoes.*

That was in October 1949. Although I myself loved much that I saw at the Sadler's Wells Ballet, I remember expressing to Balanchine my anxiety about the overwhelming response to the English season. He sniffed and said, "The more good ballet we have in New York the better the public will know how to see us. You will see." And so I did and so did we all.

Less than a month after the Sadler's Wells Ballet finished its first season at the Met, the

Maria Tallchief

New York City Ballet began its second fall season at the City Center. On November 27, 1949, soon after the orchestra started to play the deep, ominous notes of the beginning of Stravinsky's Firebird, *the curtain went up on Marc Chagall's painting of the Firebird. It was greeted with applause. Attention, expectation was immense. When the front curtain rose and Prince Ivan entered to search the shadows of the Chagall forest, an amber spotlight whizzed in flight above his head. Before we could focus on what the spotlight was aiming at, the Prince had fled and the Firebird leaped onstage. Her dance and the pas de deux that followed were greeted by astonishing applause. As the story went on through the dance of the Princess and her friends and Ivan, the entry of the diabolical Kastchei and the Monsters, and the rescue of the lovers and their friends that the Firebird must inevitably make, the audience grew eager for new magic. Balanchine's choreography gave it. The Firebird's final, flashing entrance, sword above her head, her turning so rapidly around the stage that all the monsters fell before her, was a triumph. She then calmly put them all to sleep, the Prince and Princess were reunited, and the stage was set for the wedding finale.*

When the curtain fell on that mighty processional of Stravinsky's, the audience rose to its feet and began the ovation every Balanchine advocate in America had been waiting fifteen years to hear. The cheering was so loud, it was as if we were in a football stadium instead of a theater. A man standing behind me in the mezzanine yelled at the top of his lungs over and over, "Tallchief! Tallchief! Tallchief!" When Maria Tallchief took her first solo bow, I thought the roof would cave in. The applause went on and on, and there was no doubt that the New York City Ballet had scored an unprecedented success.

In the New York Times *the next day, the dance critic John Martin said that Tallchief danced like a million dollars. On second thought, he said, like two million dollars. The box office was deluged. The New York City Ballet from that point never looked back.*

F.M.

So many memories to recall! I well remember being with Lew Christensen at the opening of the Sadler's Wells Ballet at the Met in 1949. George had hurt his back making fun of me in rehearsals for *Firebird* (1949). He said, "You're striking like this and you mustn't." I was trying very hard as always to accomplish what he wanted, when he put his back out.

So Lew and I sat watching *The Sleeping Beauty*, and I remember Margot Fonteyn's first entrance as Aurora, Moira Shearer dancing the Bluebird pas de deux, and the huge, wonderful production by Oliver Messel and hearing for the first time the full Tchaikovsky score of this masterpiece. I thought, "My goodness, in a few weeks the public's going to see *us* in *Firebird.*" I was terrified.

The role of the Firebird *was* terrifying. George always said, "Don't choreograph in class," and I understand very well what he meant. But often in class that fall he was concentrating on certain steps, and finally I realized that my variation in *Firebird* was made up of every step I had done well in the last month in class, all put into one tiny variation just before the pas de deux with Prince Ivan. Balanchine had put all those steps together and I had to master *dancing* them all together. I had had my tonsils out at the time, and I really wasn't feeling very well. It has to be the most difficult variation on record. I would lie in bed before going to the theater, going over those steps and the breathing.

He choreographed the *pas de deux* for me and Francisco Moncion in, I think, one session. I remember many years later talking to Fonteyn about Balanchine's *Firebird* and how difficult it was to dance, because you went directly from that variation into the pas de deux, and you have to control your breathing because the movement never stops. For about two minutes, you're holding your breath. You're jumping constantly, and it's turned in, turned out, the way he wanted me to look. I thought it was practically impossible to dance. In the studio I worked alone with the old Stravinsky recording. At that time we had the old 78 rpm records, like breakable plates—long-playing records had just come onto the market. On my own I went over and over the variation while George choreographed the dances for the Princesses and the Monsters and Kastchei. My favorite part in the ballet was the berceuse, the lullaby, where the whole quality of the movement, the *port de bras* and the poetry, epitomized George's entire Russian background; it was all there, his schooling, even in how he asked me to place the feet.

Our opening night I'll never forget. My pas de deux with Francisco Moncion as Ivan was incredible. We started quietly, and when we got to the part where Frank took me to the corner, stage left, and I did what in simple terms would be called a back layout, the whole audience suddenly went "Aaah." It was astonishing the way Balanchine could produce a magical bird.

It's not true that before my first *Firebird* I baked an apple pie. Actually I lay in bed, shaking with terror. I was a nervous wreck because I thought, "Oh, Karsavina. I'm not Karsavina." We'd had our final dress rehearsal at seven o'clock that morning, which meant I'd arrived at City Center before dawn to start warming up. I'm a morning person, but Frank Moncion isn't. In the rehearsal, when I came flying across at Frank, I don't think he could see me yet and he was nearly staggered. And I did fly through the air. He seemed sort of stunned, and I remember we quarreled, even though I always made it a point never to quarrel with a partner. After all, you had to depend on him.

I still hadn't put on my complete costume, though we'd had many fittings. Madame Karinska would shine a spotlight on me, and she and George would discuss the costume, especially the feather for my headdress and how to make it glimmer. The headdress didn't arrive until just before I went onstage that first night.

We never expected such a big success. I don't think Frank was even planning to take a curtain call. He was still mad at me because of the way I flew, and I was furious with him. At the rehearsals, no one had "oohed" and "aahed" or said, "Oh, what a wonderful variation." So we didn't have any idea what was going to happen. And then it was as if we had triumphed in a football stadium. The next morning George and I were still in a state of awe. He couldn't believe we had made such a smash. He had done wonderful ballets always, but never anything like this. Years later he came out to Chicago to see the opening of my company, and he sat next to my daughter Elise as *Firebird* was being danced. He turned to her and whispered, "Your mother was wonderful in this ballet, and it was our first great success." But that morning after the premiere, he and I took a walk to calm my nerves, and in Mark Cross I bought a present for Frank because I felt so guilty. It was incredible what George did with not only my part but the whole of *Firebird*. I love his later changes in the Maidens' Dance. We did that version in the Chicago production, kept the old Monsters and the original Firebird solo and pas de deux. It was very difficult. Frank sprained his back and said to me, "You're doing too much." Although he did not conduct the first performance of George's *Firebird*, Stravinsky sent a telegram afterward congratulating both of us. I think he said, MY OLD FIREBIRD and CONGRATULATIONS ON GREAT SUCCESS.

Several years earlier, when I first saw Balanchine's *Ballet Imperial* being rehearsed with Mary Ellen Moylan at Ballet Russe, I wondered how could anyone move like that, at such speed and so precisely with those feet, those legs? I knew that was exactly the way I wanted to dance. Watching Moylan and Marie-Jeanne, I saw the swiftness and elegance of their legs and feet and knew that mine weren't like that, but that I wanted them to be. I was very determined. I was also very young. We all were. Four years later, after studying with Balanchine and the faculty at the School of American Ballet, my technique was radically improving. When I joined Ballet Russe in New York, I enrolled right away in the School of American Ballet. There I came to know the great teachers Pierre Vladimiroff, Anatole Oboukhoff, and Muriel Stuart. Working with these teachers, I knew how much I had to learn, and when I had Mary Ellen Moylan's example before me and Balanchine's ballets, I knew what direction to follow.

When he made *Symphonie Concertante* (1947), I was the only one who had danced professionally. Tanaquil LeClercq was a student, and everyone in the corps de ballet was a student. What he was doing was making the clarity of Mozart's music visible: he was teaching us how to dance. The style is very pure. There is no margin for error. You can't veer the tiniest bit. It's exact.

Even *Firebird* later on was danced by students, real students, very young students, in its first New York performances. Tanny and I even partnered each other in *Symphonie Concertante*. When I see *Symphonie Concertante* now, it's fascinating to realize that he made it on such young bodies. I was twenty and Tanny must have been sixteen. What a beautiful work! But what isn't a beautiful work of George's? I recently saw the American Ballet Theatre revival in Chicago. I said to George, "You know, I saw a ballet that you made for me, and I didn't recognize it." George would never have let us step on a bent knee, and I'm afraid I saw that on the A.B.T. stage.

Before I met Balanchine, I knew some of his ballets that had come to the Ballet Russe repertory—*Serenade* (1934), *Concerto Barocco* (1941), and *Ballet Imperial* (1941)—and dancers who had worked with him—Danilova, Frederic Franklin, Moylan, Ruthanna Boris, Magallanes, and others. This was the World War II period, when little was stable in the dance world. The only companies were Ballet Russe and Ballet Theatre, which toured the whole country, often in one-night stands, plus the early civic companies in San Francisco, Atlanta, and Philadelphia. Balanchine would join the Ballet Russe on tour to rehearse his ballets, but he was busy in Hollywood, working on *Star Spangled Rhythm* (1942) with Zorina, and in New York staging pieces for the New Opera Company. In 1944, in California, he choreographed the operetta *Song of Norway*, about the composer Edvard Grieg. The stars of the Ballet Russe, Danilova and Franklin, appeared in it, along with an ensemble from the company. I was an understudy for Danilova's Anitra's Dance in the *Peer Gynt* ballet sequence. I remember my first meeting with him. I was nineteen, and he had come to Ballet Russe to stage *Song of Norway*. I was absolutely astonished at his musicality. I remember standing next to Freddie Franklin, who was very musical himself, and doing the finale of Grieg's concerto. I was amazed. I realized that this was what I wanted to learn, how I wanted to dance. I had to start all over again. After the show opened in New York to much acclaim, new dancers had to be found to go into it so that the Ballet Russe could resume touring intact, and Balanchine was persuaded by Mr. Denham to become the company's resident choreographer. Soon he was beginning to prepare a new ballet, *Danses Concertantes* (1944), to Stravinsky's music.

By that time I had danced the second lead in *Ballet Imperial*. I remember Balanchine's joining us on tour at one point and rehearsing after the performance. Union rules now wouldn't permit such a thing, but because he was with us we got into our practice clothes and worked our heads off. When I see pictures of myself in *Ballet Imperial*, I can see why I needed intensive rehearsing!

I was fortunate to be cast by Balanchine in a pas de trois with Moylan and

236

Magallanes for the new *Danses Concertantes.* It may be hard to recapture the glamor of that premiere today, but it was memorable. Balanchine was working with a new Stravinsky score, and their friend Eugene Berman designed the costumes and scenery. Danilova, who had worked with Balanchine in his early years in Russia and then in Europe with him and Diaghilev, was to star once again. She and Franklin gave the Ballet Russe a new lease on life with their performances in *Danses Concertantes,* which was immensely popular, and we could look forward to working closely with Balanchine.

All this was of course providential for me. When he was with us on a daily basis and watching performances, Balanchine began to teach, and I would concentrate on the corrections. After the success of *Danses Concertantes,* Balanchine remade *Le Bourgeois Gentilhomme,* which he had created in 1932 to Richard Strauss's score and the Molière-Boris Kochno libretto. I was cast with Yurek Lazowski in the Danse Indienne.

Then Balanchine did *Night Shadow (La Sonnambula)* (1946), another triumph. The role of the Coquette that he made for me was in incredible contrast to the Sleepwalker's role, and I had a very difficult pas de deux with the Poet. It took a good partner because I was going from pointe and landing on pointe, and he was carrying me backward by my hand, but I don't have very strong arms. In order to sustain it, my legs had to do all the work. I'm told they've taken out that section in subsequent productions. It was hard to do. Of course, to my mind the great beauty of *Night Shadow* is the Sleepwalker, the role made for Danilova.

Balanchine remounted *Baiser de la Fée* (1940 production; original 1937) for Franklin as the Bridegroom and Danilova as the Bride. Both were extraordinary. Balanchine very much wanted me to dance the role of the Fairy, and of course I was anxious to do it. I remember we were on tour, and one of the dancers who had appeared in the piece when Balanchine first did it at the Met in 1937—I believe it was Annabelle Lyon—came backstage and George introduced me. "This is the lady who danced *Baiser de la Fée,*" he said, and then to her, "Maybe you remember some steps?" Of course she didn't.

Baiser always presented problems. In the first scene a baby is found. The Fairy arrives on a big carriage in a snowstorm. She finds the baby and, claiming him, kisses him. That's the Fairy's kiss: *baiser de la fée.*

As the ballet progresses, the baby, grown to manhood, is about to get married, when the Fairy, or ice maiden, comes to claim him from the Bride. In Andersen, I believe, he is dragged down under the ice. At the end of Balanchine's ballet, the Fairy is beckoning the Bridegroom up into a wintry sky. That vision scene has been hard to make work. At the Paris Opéra (1947) and the New York City Ballet (1950), we used a huge net as the final backdrop. I was at the top of it, looking upward and trying to move as if I were floating, while Nicky Magallanes (at City Ballet) tried to climb up the net toward me. The music is glorious, and the ballet would be a masterpiece if the libretto were clearer. It has other problems. You have first a baby, then a grown man. How do you show they're the same person? And then when the Fairy returns to claim the man, she comes disguised as a gypsy. Who she really is has to be made clear, too.

But the role of the Fairy/Gypsy is very dramatic and conveyed a great deal. Even the way you walked was important. When I entered as the gypsy, I walked on my heels, then took the Bridegroom's hand and began this wonderful dance, at the end of which I pointed and pushed him slowly toward his fate. Balanchine would demonstrate this eloquently. But he worried about whether the story action was clear. He constantly made changes but, as he said, you really can't make a certain kind of ballet work. As he would say generally about characters in a ballet's plot: "How do you know it's somebody's aunt? Do I have this sign saying 'Aunt'?"

But he expressed poetry and emotion and drama through the way he used the music. You saw the music as he used it. This was especially clear later in *Orpheus* (1948), in my pas de deux as Eurydice with Nicky as Orpheus. And frankly, I think, in the pas de deux of Orpheus and the Dark Angel, with the lyre as part of their duet. The lyre makes the dance almost a pas de trois, with the music.

Mia Slavenska also danced *Baiser*. I had studied with her when I was growing up in California. She was a very strict teacher. One of the reasons I joined Ballet Russe was because she invited Mr. Denham to come to class to see me. I was fifteen or sixteen then. Slavenska was a very strong technician, a beautiful woman, lovely face. I saw her dance *Giselle* and *The Nutcracker*.

As a young girl in Los Angeles, I studied ballet and the piano, too, and was already starting to give recitals. When I was fifteen, I played the Chopin Piano Concerto in E minor with an orchestra in Los Angeles. Meanwhile, I was studying with Bronislava Nijinska, who had choreographed the ballet *Chopin Concerto* to the same music, and by some incredible fate, I then danced it.

I'd been watching the Ballet Russe since I was a very young girl. Sitting in the peanut gallery at the old Philharmonic Auditorium in Los Angeles, I saw Toumanova and Riabouchinska and Danilova, Markova and Youskevitch, Freddie Franklin and George Zoritch, with whom I fell madly in love; and I saw my first Balanchine ballet, *Serenade*.

Nijinska had many ideas of her own about teaching, and also a way of presenting things. She taught us how to breathe so beautifully by incorporating the breathing into the steps. In fact, *Chopin Concerto* begins with such a movement, the way we held our hands on our bodies. I think one of the things that Balanchine found so interesting about me was that I had the kind of breathing he wanted. That's just about all I did have when I first met him —except for the piano. George and I used to play four-hand pieces, symphonies transcribed for four hands. After we were married, we actually had two grand pianos, and we would play two-piano transcriptions. Sometimes Nicholas Kopeikine would play too—the Beethoven symphonies. That was fun. George himself could transcribe music. I remember he transcribed the Bizet Symphony in C from the orchestral score to the piano.

Nijinska was a great inspiration to me. After I met her, there was no doubt that I wanted to devote my life to ballet. Her classes were very strict. As I tell my young dancers, we were not allowed to *hang* on the barre. We had to stand and wait for our turn, and we had to walk as if we were already onstage. Even today I find it infuriating when people walk casually into place to do their steps. With Nijinska, if you didn't feel well, you didn't come to class. And you didn't talk in class.

When I first watched Ballet Russe from my perch in the peanut gallery, I also was seeing the Fokine works that I would eventually dance: *Les Sylphides* and *Schéhérazade*. Balanchine was very interested in Fokine, I learned. Rather than talk about it, he'd show me what Fokine would do with movement.

When Danilova says Balanchine insisted that everything be done his way, I agree, but what's fascinating is that his way could suit so many dancers. I certainly didn't look like Tanny, my body wasn't like Diana's, but he brought out the best in each of us. And this is genius. His style allowed a performer's individualism to emerge. I'm sure all of his dancers feel the same way, at least those of us who were successful. But he really worked very hard with us at the time, because he had to build. At first Todd Bolender and I were the only professionals. Then along came Nicky, and later Melissa Hayden joined. Although Tanny was a beautiful talent, she was still a very young girl. And I actually had to learn all over again. I could do triple *fouettés,* I could do single turns, I could perform on a carpet and do double *fouettés—* but just pure classical dance? No. So what a wonderful challenge, and how lucky I was to be there, how lucky I was to know where I was, and that George was willing to work with me.

Phrasing and timing were the most important aspects of the technique as I learned it. In a demonstration with Walter Terry and Balanchine, I did an eight-count *développé,* straight up and out with the *port de bras* in the manner in which we most often see it done. Then George turned to me and demanded, "Now out in *one* count and hold the rest." That is an example of the simplicity of his style. The speed was not hard for me, because I always had more of a propensity for allegro dancing than anything else. Standing still was the tricky part.

George's insistence on the opening attack also gave his movement a sense of urgency and color. Instead of doing one *grand battement* on four equally stressed counts, we practiced beginning and ending in one count—and *right* on the count. You use more energy that way, investing the dance with a great deal of life and theatrical excitement. "Don't hold anything back," he chided us. The style is based on nearly perpetual motion as the body glides, darts, or spins from one classical position to another in his endless array of steps.

At the Paris Opéra in 1947 George was coaching Toumanova in *Giselle.* We were in the *foyer de la danse* back of the stage in the big house. I sat and watched, and it was absolutely beautiful. What is the Mies van der Rohe saying: "Less is more" ? Every movement was so spare. There were no extra gestures. Everything was simple, beautiful, poetic. I become annoyed when I hear famous people say, "Oh, Balanchine was not poetic." How can anyone say that when you have seen his poetry—in the pas de deux that he did for me in *Scotch Symphony* (1952), and in that wonderful adagio, the prélude movement, in *Bourrée Fantasque* (1949)? Certainly we learned how to move fast, and that's thrilling. But just think of the gestures in the adagios alone. Remember in *Scotch,* my partner and I are looking at each other in a certain way, but I'm not peeking at him or flirting with him. Something palpable is happening between us, though—what . . . and why? Nobody knows. Balanchine said, "It doesn't start with the face. What happens to the face? It must come from inside."

Balanchine had links with the Paris Opéra that never quite worked out. He'd been invited to head the ballet company there in 1929, after Diaghilev's death, but then he fell ill with tuberculosis and had to go to Switzerland instead. He suggested that the Opéra bring in Lifar, who was to dance a ballet George was staging. That was the beginning of Lifar's regime as director. Soon after George and I married in 1946, he was invited to stage three ballets at the Opéra and I was asked to appear as guest artist. I left Ballet Russe and joined George in Paris.

He staged *Serenade,* which looked beautiful on the Opéra's stage, but he did not win the popularity prize because he used not corps de ballet dancers but the *petits rats* from the Opéra's school, the very young dancers, such as Liane Daydé and Claude Bessy. George liked the school very much; now, Bessy's the head of it. And in the solo roles he used the company's youngest dancers, not any of the regular ones.

He also did *Baiser de la Fée,* with Toumanova as the Bride, and I danced my role of the Fairy/Gypsy. Balanchine taught *Apollo* to Michel Renault and Alexandre Kalioujny, and to me. Toumanova had rehearsed Terpsichore but became ill, so I ended up dancing the role with either man. I always felt I was bigger than Michel, so the moment when I was on top of his back was very difficult. That was my first experience with *Apollo*.

And then to Bizet's music we did *Le Palais de Cristal*, which became *Symphony in C*. Balanchine used each one of the *étoiles* for the leading roles. Lycette Darsonval did the first movement, Toumanova the second, Micheline Bardin —she had an incredible jump, like a man's—did the third, and Madeleine Lafon the fourth. The men were, respectively, Kalioujny, Roger Ritz, Renault, and Max Bozzoni. The dancers just out of the School moved really well, fast, which George liked, of course. You can see that in the choreography he made on the two demi-soloist girls in the first movement, originally Bourgeois and Jacqueline Moureau, at that time a brilliant dancer.

Leonor Fini designed the production, and each movement was a different color: short tutus, jewels all over. Toumanova wore dark blue. In the last movement, when all the dancers begin returning for the climax, the stage was a mass of movement and beautiful colors. The Parisians went wild.

This was the start of a new international situation. After the Sadler's Wells Ballet had its triumph in New York a couple of years later it toured the country, and Lincoln Kirstein invited its director, Ninette de Valois, to see the New York City Ballet. It was suggested that this young company and Balanchine should come to Covent Garden. Balanchine went first, in the spring of 1950, to stage *Ballet Imperial*. He very much admired Moira Shearer, to whom he taught the principal role. Then that summer the New York City Ballet danced more consecutive performances at Covent Garden and on tour in England than it ever had before. By the time we got back to New York, the company had acquired so much experience that our audiences were flabbergasted, especially over the dramatic improvement in every way of the corps de ballet.

George was teaching the company class; he was working very diligently with the whole company. He'd been teaching almost from the beginning, but I remember in one of his letters from London, when he was there staging *Ballet Imperial*, he wrote that, before our London season, he was going to come back and tell everybody what do to: "When I get back, I'm starting classes with a very few people, and we're really going to work. No more of those lousy *entrechats sixes*," he said. I think that's when he began to teach intensively.

I literally lived Balanchine style. I must confess, I was part of those lousy *entrechats sixes!* But he was a wonderful teacher, so patient. He once said to me, "Someday I'll be known more for my teaching than for my choreography." When explaining something he never said much. He didn't dissect. George wasn't scientific about the way he taught, although he was scientific in his thinking about it. He had a wonderful way of telling you how to do something without insisting upon it. He stated things in very simple terms so that we could understand. Once I was doing *battement tendu* backstage during the first year that I met him. I was executing them in my usual sloppy way, I suppose. As he came by he said, "You know, if you just do *battement tendu* well, you don't have to do anything else." This is why I do *battement tendu* with my Chicago dancers for at least twenty minutes during every barre. They probably get very bored with it, but we do it because George told me to. The position of the hips and abdomen is especially crucial.

Balanchine's way of teaching was classic, practical training. He taught us how to walk, how to run. I remember he would say, "The straight line is here," and we'd walk back and forth. He would take our hands and back and forth we'd go across the room, walking in fourth position. You have to extend your foot as if you're doing *battement tendu.* I see very few dancers walking or running like this now. If you were to perform a character, he didn't like to talk about it. He'd say, "Now you're going to be the Swan Queen," or "You're a sylph," and he would demonstrate. You'd learn from that—hopefully.

I never learned how to cook, though. George was a wonderful cook, and he'd talk about it for hours, almost to the point of boredom. On one occasion he invited the Stravinskys to dinner with Auden. I had come to know Stravinsky because he lived in California, and when George was courting me I lived in California. George would come out for the summer, and we would spend many hours with the Stravinskys, who lived not too far away from where I did. Madame Stravinsky had just learned from her doctor that she had a heart flutter, or something, so she couldn't have any salt. Russians, of course, salt everything, and use butter and cream everywhere. George figured out a menu but was rehearsing late and sent me home early to put the potatoes on—little bitty potatoes. The pot was boiling when the downstairs buzzer rang. Our guests. I was so nervous that George wasn't home yet. With the pot in hand I buzzed the Stravinskys and Auden up—we lived in a fifth-floor walk-up—but in my nervousness I spilled the potatoes on the floor. Our tiny kitchen was just opposite the entrance, but before I could clean up the floor there was a knock on the door. Stravinsky. He had climbed those five flights in about two seconds. My potatoes were all over the floor. "Oh, Maria," Stravinsky said, "they will taste much better like that."

I'm often asked about Balanchine's actual making of ballets. At home he never said, "Let's try this out." Dancing was for the studio, but his preparation of the music was often done at home. When we were preparing *Orpheus,* the music arrived piece by piece at the apartment. George played it over on the piano, literally every note. That's when I took up sewing! I couldn't keep listening to each note both at home and at the studio. He chose Nicky Magallanes as Orpheus and Frank Moncion as the Dark Angel. He and Stravinsky were very specific with each other about the length of each sequence in the action. The music for the pas de deux—in which Eurydice implores Orpheus to look at her, with dire results—was not completely written when Stravinsky came to the studio for the first time and saw George, Nicky, and me working on the steps for it.

Mr. Stravinsky was sitting there looking and I was sort of emoting when Stravinsky said, "Maria! How long it will take you to die?" Nicky was standing there, so I put my head on his shoulder and began to fall to the floor, as the choreography demanded, and hands reached out from where the silk curtain would be to drag me back to Hades. Stravinsky began snapping his fingers—snap, snap, snap, snap—I think it was four counts. "That is enough," he decided. "Now you are dead." And he put those counts into the score. No one was allowed to pad a part. Again, you see, it was exact.

I like to teach my dancers Eurydice's variation, because it is both short and intricate: so poignant—turned in, turned out—her intense longing. I remember how long I had to stand behind Eddie Bigelow and his big cape before we appeared. It was a very beautiful pas de deux in an extraordinary ballet. I loved seeing it later when Diana Adams danced the role.

What Stravinsky and Balanchine gave each other can never be overestimated. Whenever they worked together like this, or indeed whenever George took a composition of Stravinsky's and began to make dances, the world became a brighter place. When I was married to Balanchine, I must say there were times when his love of Stravinsky, his adulation for the man, seemed too much. He idolized him. As always, George was right.

LEON

BARZIN

Founded National Orchestral Association (1929) and became its ar-

tistic director. Musical director of Ballet Society from 1946 and the

New York City Ballet from its inception in 1948 until 1958.

I Remember Balanchine

M<small>Y ASSOCIATION WITH</small> B<small>ALANCHINE STARTED RATHER INFORMALLY BACK WHEN</small> I <small>WAS</small> head of the National Orchestral Association. I started that organization for the purpose of training young American musicians for symphony orchestras throughout the United States. In the early forties we were working out of the old Masonic Temple on Fifty-sixth Street, later to become the City Center. Balanchine's immediate interest was hearing new pieces of music read by the orchestra. When he heard the orchestra and saw me conduct he said, "You have a tremendous school of players here." Lincoln Kirstein said they had a school, too, the School of American Ballet, so why didn't we do things together? Finally we decided to start an organization called Ballet Society which was created only to do new works.

George and I were drawn to each other because I realized that he was an expert musician as well as a choreographer. Fridays we would gather at his apartment and play smaller works. Among those who attended were Nathan Milstein, the violinist. My instrument was the viola. I had played with the New York Philharmonic and was a member of its quartet. At these gatherings we played a lot of music that came out of the New York Public Library's collection. I came to realize that Balanchine had too much knowledge not to have studied music really seriously. I later learned he had attended the Conservatory in St. Petersburg at the same time he was going to dancing school. The Friday get-togethers were an amusement dating back to his youth in Russia. In Leningrad there was an organization called The Fridays made up of musicians and composers at the Conservatory who got together and played. One person would play a theme and others would put variations to it. When Balanchine said it would be fun to get together on Fridays but he couldn't find anybody to do it, I said, "Well, that's silly because I'll bring you four people any Friday you want."

These sessions grew and grew and Balanchine's own musicianship became more apparent. His friend Kopeikine always played the piano when we were redoing some score. Later Balanchine would go to the piano himself. He didn't have brilliant technique, but he had enough to be able to play modern scores. From these Friday night get-togethers, George became more and more interested in certain composers. We played a great deal the chamber music of Mozart, works which provided the background for such ballets as *Symphonie Concertante* (1947) and *Caracole* (1952). We played the chamber music of Tchaikovsky, where he found inspiration for other great works. The Bizet Symphony in C we learned about.

When the city of New York decided to make the Masonic Temple into a kind of cultural center and it was agreed to invite Ballet Society into the Center, the New York City Ballet was born. I was musical director for ten years.

Balanchine would not create a ballet without being inspired by music. I got to know him more deeply because I would suggest certain works. He'd say, "Well, well," and then about three weeks later he'd say, "I think you're right, Leon, I think we ought to do a ballet with that music." At a rehearsal of the National Orchestral Association we played a work of Schoenberg. George came in and said, "Oh, my God, this is a fantastic work." He was very impressed. It was opus 34 [*Accompaniment Music to a Cinema Scene*]. I said, "George, how would you like to do something very unusual?" And he said, "What do you mean, unusual?" I said, "If people come to the City Center to a ballet performance and hear that work, they're not going to be able to listen to the music, they're going to look on the stage. Let me play it once through"—it was only about eighteen minutes—"and then the stage lights will come on and there will be a dance interpretation of the same work." George took this suggestion and improved it. In 1954 he made first a dance ballet to opus 34 and then a narrative ballet. They were performed consecutively, and the audience began to hear Schoenberg.

At the City Center, the management would try to push us toward things they felt would be popular. We had done *Tyl Ulenspiegel* (1951) by Richard Strauss. That was a great success, and then they wanted to do *Don Juan*. I said, "What do you mean, *Don Juan?* That music doesn't fit a ballet. You take care of the management and money. Don't come and tell us what ballets to put on."

George and I, from the artistic side, were fighting against the economic situation. We did an American thing called *Western Symphony* (1954). Well, I didn't like that idea. And then we had one with a lot of regiments and the American Stars and Stripes. I got very annoyed with this direction because we had such a fantastic number of contemporary ballets that were really superior artistically, I didn't want to lower the standards. I didn't like the idea that people were coming and telling George, "We need money," so he'd have to do things that were more popular. George didn't like it either, but he was stuck. We had to be very careful how far we would go back on our standards. We wanted to go forward.

It was difficult to penetrate Balanchine's character. For a man who created such great ballets, in personal warmth he was a rather cold person. I got to him through music. In music he was sensitive. In life he was not. George was always interested in the bodies of his dancers and what they were capable of onstage. I think his marriages were all based on finding persons who could satisfy him as dancers. The best, of course, was Tanaquil LeClercq. When Tanny was about ten or eleven years old, her mother came to me, and I said, "For goodness' sake, get this girl to study music—and then dance." Which she did. She could dance to anything. She danced to music, not to counts. I remember when she caught polio in Denmark. She had just danced the last movement of *Western Symphony*. I came up and put my scarf around her, she was so wringing wet. The next morning she couldn't get up. That was the end. It was really a very tragic moment for the New York City Ballet.

Balanchine was only interested in people who could dance well. He didn't care if it was called the New York City Ballet or Prometheus Ballet. He had no great feeling about a name. If the company had failed economically he would have started the next day with some other group. And if the standards were not high, he didn't care if that went on the rocks. The standards applied not only to the choice of music but also to the performance. I'm the type of person who, after the fortieth performance, is still doing the first. I never gave in to the musical comedy mentality where you do it the thousandth time and you don't care what happens. George adored that. He said, "There is no second performance. They're *all* first performances."

EDWARD

VILLELLA

Studied at the School of American Ballet; joined New York City Ballet in 1957. Balanchine created a number of roles for Villella, including A Midsummer Night's Dream, Tarantella, Harlequinade, Brahms-Schoenberg Quartet, Rubies, *and* Pulcinella. *Danced many repertory works*—Prodigal Son, Theme and Variations, La Source, Donizetti Variations, *and* Night Shadow—*and famed for partnership with Patricia McBride and for appearances on American television and the musical stage. He is the artistic director of the Miami City Ballet.*

I Remember Balanchine

WHEN I BEGAN TRAINING AT THE SCHOOL OF AMERICAN BALLET, I WAS TEN YEARS OLD. I had come from a local school in Bayside, Queens, where I grew up. I got to the School of American Ballet because my mother really wanted to be a dancer. She took my sister so she could live vicariously through my sister. My mother was a forward-looking, progressive individual, and she decided that she was going to find a wave of the future for her daughter, and she discovered that there was a man called George Balanchine and that he indeed had a school of classical ballet. My sister auditioned and was accepted. Just as they were leaving, as an afterthought, my mother said, "You know, I have a son at home who also dances. He's really very upset about it." In those days, my heavens, a boy! They talked my mother into getting me into S.A.B. I was brought to the School, full of anxiety, but there was an inherent elegance about the place and about all the people there. Instead of being intimidated, I felt comfortable. It was a place to work, and it was a place without pretension. I guess I had supposed that there would be enormous pretensions. But there were none. And there was an incredible array of dancers. I found out that ballet was movement, a very wonderful and sophisticated form of movement. And what thrilled me about it was that it was so far beyond the sandlot athletics I was involved in. It had form. It had a structure. It was something to hang on to. It had something that would continuously develop you.

When I began my training, I had never seen a ballet in my life. I had no inkling what ballet was about. I saw my first ballet when I was probably eleven or twelve, and if I'm not mistaken it was the premiere of Balanchine's *Firebird* in 1949. The first actual dancing I ever did was with Balanchine and the company in a program at Carnegie Hall. I was about thirteen, and I remember Mr. John had made the hats. Tanny LeClercq was on the program and Nicky Magallanes.

I joined New York City Ballet in November 1957, just before *Nutcracker* began that year. I had spent the previous four years at the New York State Maritime College. I wasn't necessarily preparing myself for dance roles but soon I was deeply involved in the repertory.

I had a great deal of enthusiasm and very little experience. I hadn't danced in four years but I had a major passion for performance. So the moment I got on the stage, I didn't know about phrasing and shadings and artistry. I just went pow! Everything full out. I'd do a *plié* with the greatest passion in the world. In the first year or two I had absolutely no taste. I thought you just got out there and jumped as high as you could and you beat and turned. I was approaching it from the physical point of view, the athletic, rather than the artistic. I had no artistic framework.

New York City Ballet made its first tour to the Soviet Union in 1962. The second night of performances at the Bolshoi, we were doing *Donizetti Varia-tions.* I was very comfortable with the ballet, it was very easy for me to dance, and I felt like I was passing through the air with great comfort. I finished my variation, there was a breath, and then the house started to come down. There were twenty-two curtain calls, they were stamping their feet and chanting my name. They asked me to repeat my variation. They were yelling *"Bis"* and *"Encore,"* and I was thinking I wasn't much of an experienced dancer technically. It was unprecedented. We have never had a tradition for that kind of demonstration at the New York City Ballet. It's just not our style. I honestly didn't know how to behave, and I was going back and forth, and sweat was pouring down over the goose bumps on my arms. The conductor turned the music back, and everybody went crazy after the twenty-second curtain call. I was standing at the bottom of the stage, and when the conductor did that, I thought, "All right, I'll go back and do it." When I turned and started to walk upstage, I realized it was raked. And the variation starts with a diagonal down and across and a diagonal back up. Going down was fine. Coming back the second time is a major problem. It was a very exciting night for me. I was thrilled by it until I found out Mr. B. wasn't thrilled. He was not pleased at all. After all, his company was a no-star situation.

So I cornered Mr. B. It took about two weeks. I waited until it eased up in the fall in Moscow. I finally said, "You know, I understand you were not pleased." He got very nervous. And he never really told me why he wasn't pleased. I guess he didn't want that kind of demonstration for dancers in his company. But it was certainly nothing I had calculated or planned. He said, "Well, here in the Soviet Union, it's okay." But he clearly wasn't pleased. As the tour progressed and I danced the same role many more times, I got similar responses but, needless to say, I didn't do another encore.

By the tour to Russia, I had started to work with Stanley Williams, a brilliant teacher and coach at the School. He began to place me. Until then I had literally just danced instinctively. Stanley broke it all down for me. We used to sit in Carnegie Tavern until three or four o'clock in the morning over beers and talk about a *tendu battement* and how to do a double air *tour* and *entrechats six.* It was a very valuable moment for me and in a way valuable for Stanley because he was just becoming a teacher. He had just stopped danc-ing himself, and I was just becoming a dancer. I became the raw material for his energy and, later on, I think his genius. So, by the Russian tour, I danced with taste, with the right style.

We danced in five different cities in Russia, and each opening night we were met with thunderous silence at the end of every ballet and at the end of every variation. Then we found out that each opening night was attended

by the officials, the union people, the government. But from the second
night on it was just pandemonium. They would stay for half an hour at the
edge of the orchestra pit. There would be five or six hundred people chanting our names in unison. Balanchine would come in front of the curtain and
ask them politely if they would allow us to go back to our hotels and sleep.

Partnering Balanchine's ballerinas, the cavalier is aware of the remoteness
of the woman, but I also think there is a great deal of restraint and respect.
The middle movement of *Concerto Barocco* is almost Balanchine's pedestal to
women. That pas de deux is a wonderful example of his attitude toward
women, his respect for their influence on him and on ballet. All of his pas de
deux are similar. They are rarely overly romantic. There is always a sense of
detachment and respect. There's always a touch of story. He leaves you with
a theme and he allows you room to think. Often one idea in his pas de deux
is not being able to achieve an ideal or to be with the ideal. *Serenade* is like
that, and so is *Theme and Variations.* The theme is not always resolved. Perhaps
a lot of Mr. B.'s life was like that as well, not all of his relationships were
resolved.

One day Mr. B. came to me and said he would like me to learn *Apollo* to
see if I could dance it. He told me who to learn it from, and I did, and I
showed it to him, and he said, "You know, that's not Apollo." Somebody
else had showed the role to me, and I was very young.

I said, "Those are the steps and the counts." And he said, "Yes, but that's
not Apollo." He said, "What you don't understand really is that we're poets
of gesture. You see, we really speak with our bodies, but we also speak with
the insight of the gesture. You know, you really have to understand style.
You have to wear style." He was a man of sixty at that time, wearing a
double-breasted suit with loafers, and a cowboy shirt and string tie. He said,
"I'm going to dance Apollo for you." So he did, and it was a revelation. Then
I could understand what the man was talking about. It really was an understanding of the essence of the gesture. That was really what Apollo was
about. The relationship between Apollo and Terpsichore in the pas de deux
was also important—the essence of the gesture between the two. At the
beginning of the pas de deux, Apollo and Terpsichore touch their fingertips
together, and I said, "Jeez, that's really very beautiful." And he said, "Yes,
Michelangelo got that from me." That's the kind of conversation he would
prefer to have. He didn't want some kind of flamboyant intellectualism. He
didn't want you to be puffed up onstage. He wanted you to deal with essence. The most wonderful thing was that he was such a great dancer that he
would show you and you really didn't need words. He stood in front of you,
and you just tried to follow him. That was tough because his musicality was
so extraordinary, and stylistically the steps were so fascinating. To watch

him dance to jazz was out of this world. He was probably the single greatest dancer I have ever seen in my life. I do not mean technically, jumping high and doing nine pirouettes. I mean in dance terms, real dance. You had to imitate him. You knew that he was doing a step that would basically suit you. Otherwise, he wouldn't be doing it. So you knew that the step was within your grasp. You just had to focus. You had to be really fast to understand it.

When he taught *Bugaku* to Allegra Kent and me, he just showed us. He spoke to us with his body. He was just the most fantastic stylist. He wore style. If it was Harlequin or the gypsy boy in *Tarantella,* or Oberon in *A Midsummer Night's Dream,* he was the personification of what that role was about. So long as you looked, that was the conversation, that was the discussion. It was strictly visual. He would drop a word. He once said to me, "Everybody's dancing Apollo like a statue. Apollo is a devil. He's a rascal."

He was bored to death with *Prodigal Son.* He didn't want to bother with it, he just wanted me to dance it. He gave me the role because he thought it would be something that would be fine for my progress. I looked at it that way. He may have wanted the ballet back in the repertory, but he wasn't crazy about it. He showed me the opening in twenty minutes. He showed me the closing in twenty minutes. He showed me the pas de deux in half an hour. Then I never saw him again. That was it. Bang. He just left it like that. But he would come back after a performance from time to time and say simple things. As the pas de deux began he said, "Icons." That's all I needed. Why am I searching for feelings? Icons.

When *A Midsummer Night's Dream* was being done, I just assumed that I was going to be Puck. I just thought, "Well, I'm small and fast and wiry. I jump and beat." At that time, too, I was doing a lot of these short fast roles, and I was a little disappointed. But there I was, cast as Oberon. I had never mimed before. We had no mime roles whatsoever in New York City Ballet. The biggest mime role was Siegfried in *Swan Lake.* I had not even seen much mime because once you got into the New York City Ballet that's where you lived.

I didn't know how to even indicate "Come here." I said, "Well, how do you do that? Do we just wave?" I was terrified. I could dance all the steps, but the mime was foreign. I thought I was going to be a disaster. Balanchine didn't finish the mime sequences until three days before the performance. He said, "Oh, we'll do that later." All he did was work on the scherzo for me, a brilliant variation. I had all of that down, in the palm of my hand. But I had no connection with the rest of the ballet, and I couldn't get to the scherzo. I really wished there was another guy who would do all the rest.

Fortunately, there was Stanley Williams when Mr. B. didn't have time to work with me. Lincoln went to Stanley and said, "You know, Eddie's going to ruin the ballet." So Stanley came up to me, and he said, "Did you know you were going to ruin this ballet?" I said, "Well, not intentionally." He said, "Well, what is all this stuff, all this miming?" I said, "Well, I don't have any. He just didn't give me any." Stanley said, "Well, what did he tell you?" I said, "Well, he told me this and he told me that." Stanley Williams said, "All right, let's go in the studio and let's talk about this." And that's what Stanley and I did. We probably worked two hours a day for three days. I became a mime. And what was especially gratifying was that the morning after the premiere Balanchine walked in. I was standing and hanging on to a pipe at the old City Center, exhausted. He came in with his paper under his arm, in his trench coat, and walked by and nodded to me. He went about ten steps, and then he stopped, turned around, and came back to me. Here was a man who was not really comfortable being physical with another man. He put his arm around me, and he said, "You know, you dance excellently." He turned around and walked away. That was the most incredible compliment I ever got from Balanchine.

BARBARA

WALCZAK

Born in New York City in 1940, Barbara Walczak studied with Phyllis Marmein and at the School of American Ballet. She danced in Ballet Society and joined the New York City Ballet in the 1950s. Barbara Walczak created roles in Balanchine's Scotch Symphony, Bourrée Fantasque, Roma, Pas de Dix, *and* Western Symphony *and danced the Balanchine repertory for sixteen years. She now teaches in New York.*

I Remember Balanchine

BALANCHINE WAS SUCH A CHAMELEON: DEPENDING ON THE PERSON, YOU WOULD GET a different reaction. You'd probably get an intimate picture from some of his Russian friends, a different one from his dancers. I was never a part of the inner circle or of his social life. I was only a dancer on a professional level. He must have liked me to some extent because he did allow me to be a soloist. He gave me roles. On the other hand, he never displayed his liking very much. I feel that I was just not his cup of tea. Today, I can understand it. At that time, of course, I couldn't. Today, I can look back and actually feel that he was very good to me because after all I did not have his type of body, his looks. At that point, he liked the tall, svelte, very loose type of dancer. I had a good strong technique, but he made it clear to me, right from the start, that I was just not what he was looking for. Considering all that, he was really very good to me. When he did *The Spellbound Child,* I was one of the Numbers. I was in the corps of *Symphonie Concertante,* and when he did *Symphony in C* I was in the second movement corps.

Gisella Caccialanza was doing third movement *Symphony in C.* In one of those very difficult throw lifts, she tore her Achilles tendon, and Bea Tompkins had to step into her role. I was put into Bea Tompkins's role, one of the soloists in the fourth movement. I knew that it was because Balanchine could depend on me. I learned fast, I was strong, and I could get through it. But I remember talking to him once, when I must have been about sixteen, in his office at City Center. He said, "You know, dear, I know you someday want to dance *Swan Lake,* but you know if you ever do *Swan Lake* I will never come to see you, because you will be terrible." I was absolutely destroyed.

Throughout my career with him I had a whole series of encounters of that type. I even did Pat Wilde's role in *Scotch Symphony,* the Scotch girl. I think basically I got it because Lew Christensen, the ballet master at the time, felt that I would be good in it. Lew was a wonderful dancer and a splendid ballet master. He was fair, quiet. I did my first performance, and the next day we were warming up on the dark stage at City Center, with just the work light. Balanchine came up to me and said, "You know what Danilova said about you?" One of my teachers was Danilova, and I was very respectful and looked up to her very much. She taught us the variations classes. "She said you are terrible. I should take you out of the ballet immediately. You are no good." He never took me out of it, but this just ruined it for me. I was crestfallen.

Then again, strangely enough, during the Ballet Society and early New York City Ballet days, we had very long layoffs, and during those layoffs Balanchine would teach special classes to special dancers. It would be Nicky Magallanes, Maria Tallchief, Tanny LeClercq, and about seven others. He invited Barbara Milberg and me to join the class. It was a very elite little group. I was one of them.

It was a strange relationship. Maybe he felt that putting me down would make me work harder. At the Greek Theater in Los Angeles, Barbara Milberg and I were warming up, trying to do his *développé à la seconde* with the leg as high as possible. We were working so hard on it. He came up to me and said, "You know, dear, why don't you give up? You'll never do it right."

Finally he reached a point where there were many young dancers coming up, like Patty McBride, who had just joined the company, Suzanne Farrell at the School, and Mimi Paul. He really wanted to get rid of the older dancers. We could feel it. He made it very clear by simply taking all of my roles away, and he put me in that terrible South American ballet, *Panamerica,* in the back line of the corps with the newest apprentices. I was just sick. I was in tears constantly. My inner feelings that I could dance had been so undermined that, psychologically, I believed I couldn't dance. Those of us who were in the company from the very beginning danced eight performances a week and a minimum of two ballets a night. You would go from being a Monster in *Firebird* to first movement *Symphony in C.* You were used to dancing a great deal. As the company got larger, you performed less. And when you were made a soloist, you performed even less. It was difficult for my type of body to adjust to this transition.

One day I went up to Balanchine and asked him, "Mr. B., I've got so much extra time now, and obviously you're not happy with me. What should I work on? What should I do?" He said, "You know, dear, you're a very good dancer. But the young ones coming up are better." I knew it was time to leave. I knew that what he was planning to tell me was that he really wished I would go. At the end of that season I resigned. He left for Europe to do something, and then he called me back to help when he was resetting *Agon* the next season. He came up to me and said, "You never said good-bye." I think the reason I didn't say good-bye to him was that I had a nervous breakdown when I left. It was totally wrenching. I had danced for him from 1946 to about 1960. It had been my whole life.

When you are that vulnerable, when you're young and your ego's out there, you do feel that he was being cruel. But when you look back, from a later perspective, you realize that he would never compromise his creative concepts. If a dancer was not what he felt he needed for his creative juices, he would just eliminate the dancer. As soon as that dancer was no longer what he felt he could use, that dancer had to be eliminated. From a creative point of view, and from the point of view of a person running a ballet company, you can't be human. If you were, everybody would stay forever and everybody would be demanding roles, and where would you be? They can't all dance as long as they would like to, and they all can't do what they would like to. He couldn't be very human. I never cared for him as a human being, but I couldn't help but care for him very much as a creative human being—as an artist.

I think the reason so many of us did not opt to try for another ballet company where we might get better roles was because Balanchine was extraordinary: when he looked at you in class, you knew he wasn't looking at you, he was virtually looking through you. He could see everything that was wrong. He could see what he could make out of you or not make out of you. He saw things that no one else saw. You were naked in every respect—emotionally, physically. He saw the potential. He saw what he might make or what he wouldn't make. He saw the flaws. As a result, there was always the carrot: can I achieve something? Can I make this body do what he wants? Is it at all possible? At that time, he corrected far more than later. Diana Adams told me when she was running the School in the late 1960s or early 1970s, "He just doesn't teach the way he used to. He doesn't give the amount of corrections and the depth of corrections." I think one of the reasons was that, as the dancers began to have what he had always dreamed of—his line, his quality—he didn't feel a need to, whereas, with us, he had to make us look like something. We weren't what he wanted, but he had to do something with us. So in a way we were very lucky. We got so much from him that the other dancers never really got. Mr. B. changed over the years because the material he had also changed.

The second reason I think we all stayed was the feel of his choreography on your body. The feel of having him set the steps on you—of the music, of the counts, of the kind of kinesthetic movement and quality—was addictive. It felt so wonderful. No other choreographer felt that way.

He had Marie-Jeanne come in and teach *Concerto Barocco* to us. The experience of learning it from her and then from him was unforgettable. I would love to see a company today ask Marie-Jeanne to come in and clean it up. Would it look very old-fashioned? Would it look suddenly much more right? I would just like to see what it would look like. It's been lost over the years, and Balanchine let it be. It wasn't choreographed for a tall, long-legged, individualistic dancer. It was done for a woman with an incredible jump. My feeling with Mr. B.'s works is that most of the time the original version is the best. Over time he would change the ballet for different dancers, but the original had the emphasis: "This is the way this step has to be done and no other way." Then later it would get watered down. Now that Mr. B.'s gone, why not call these people back and say, "Reset it, let's see what it looks like."? What have they got to lose? Maybe it was better, maybe it was more interesting. What stubbornness that this can't be done while the original people are still alive! Tallchief is here, LeClercq is here. Not to use these people is a sacrilege. The difference between the original and today's *Barocco* is a timing difference, an energy difference. It was never meant to be lyrical. One difference was that many of the steps were very off-center. We were supposed to fall off. It was like waves on an ocean. The energy behind the steps was different. They were attacked more than they are now. They were not meant to be done with a soft attack.

Marie-Jeanne was phenomenal in *Barocco*. She was also in *Triumph of Bacchus and Ariadne;* she did a step on the diagonal, and it was electrifying. I was such an admirer of hers. I thought she was potentially a great dancer. There's something about her, a charisma. So many of Balanchine's ballerinas had it, each one in different ways, but very specific.

I've only staged a few of Balanchine's ballets for my school. Some of my students were ready, and I felt that they should experience what it's like. I did the third movement of *Concerto Barocco* as a lecture-demonstration in which I took it apart musically, to show what the counts are. We did it only to counts, no music. We did the counterpoint of dancer to dancer and the counterpoint of corps to soloists, and then we slowly added the music so that the audience began to see the complexity of the weave of the ballet. If you don't know anything about dance, you see the third movement of *Barocco* and you say, "That's very nice, very interesting." But you have no idea what's going on. The audience loved it.

My generation was blessed because Balanchine was so specific with us. The two solo girls in first movement *Symphony in C* are now totally different in the dynamics. There are few films from those years, alas. What I'm trying to do now is a book that would give three classes of Vladimiroff's, three of Oboukhoff's, three of Doubrovska's, and three of Balanchine's, all from the fifties. I feel I owe a debt to my teachers.

Balanchine mellowed over the years. When we were a small company, he was there for us and we were there for him constantly, from morning till night. He knew you. You knew him. As the company grew, there was not that familiarity. It became a big company. Also, when we were coming up, Markova, Danilova, and Baronova were dancers famous for their individual styles. As young people we thought, "Oh, you have to have an individual style." Balanchine hated that. He wanted pure movement with all the energy that your body could possibly put forth, done full out, but pure movement, with no stylistic mannerisms. He would tell us, "Don't listen to the music, just count." He was afraid that we would begin emoting. "Don't listen to the music. Just count. Don't look around. Look straight forward. Not too much *épaulement.*" I heard an interview a few years ago with Joe Duell, and he said that Balanchine had told his dancers, "Just listen to the music, don't count." I was flabbergasted. But the company had changed. This is why I feel that, were he alive today, Balanchine would be changing. He would not want a philosophy of "This is the only way." Some things remained absolutely the same. Certain fundamental concepts never changed. Other concepts changed totally—black to white.

One concept that never changed was always crossing the leg on a *tendu* forward and backward—that it should not be slightly open. Another was how the leg should move, not putting the heels down until you went up again. Certain matters of timing and of *épaulement* never changed. Also, his idea of arabesque was constant. He liked the arabesque with a slightly open hip. He did not like the heel showing. He wanted an elongated line in arabesque, not a square line, the old Cecchetti line.

The reason I was so interested in recording the old classes is that what we're losing quickly today is the old White Russian approach. The Russians who taught us were the White Russians, who left because of the Revolution and had the pre-Soviet style and technique. What we're losing is that background. The teachings of Vladimiroff and Oboukhoff came from Nijinsky, Pavlova, Karsavina, back through the Diaghilev company, back to the old French school. When we saw the Paris Opéra school demonstrate their technique here in New York in 1988, it was so similar to what we did in so many ways. This is what we're losing. I don't think we should lose it. I think it's important. If you want to do a good *Les Sylphides* or a good *Aurora's Wedding*, this is what you need.

When I watched Balanchine classes later, I saw that he was allowing his dancers far more freedom. When I recently saw *Serenade* at the School workshop performance, I could not understand what had happened. There was choreography missing. I think he just didn't have the energy anymore, he didn't have the strength anymore, to demand what he really wanted. The thing that bothers me is that there are tapes, films, that go back to the sixties. All the people who danced the ballets then are here: Sonya Tyven, Bobby Lindren, Maria Tallchief, Frank Moncion. I saw an *Orpheus* at City Ballet that appalled me. They did the steps, they were on the music, but they didn't have the foggiest notion of what he wanted. The part that I remember him coaching and working on for hours was the pas de deux between the two men with the lyre. He gave you the nuance, how that movement was supposed to be done. It was in the feeling of the movement and the way he would demonstrate how to throw the lyre and how to catch it, how the hand unfolded when the hand is put through the lyre. Moncion is here. It was done on him. He remembers every single moment. The throwing of the lyre has become very athletic. It's all gone: the unspoken menace of the Dark Angel, the way Orpheus is backed around as he goes down. The

Furies looked like dolls and the Bacchantes were mechanical. Balanchine would have the Bacchantes lunge and pull back with the look in the eyes and the hands and the body. But there was nothing. When Balanchine said, "When I go, it goes," he knew what he was talking about. The choreographer has to be there.

I remember Balanchine coaching Diana Adams in *Swan Lake*—the moment when the Swan Queen throws her arms open to stop Siegfried from shooting Von Rothbart and then runs to Siegfried and takes the arabesque on the arbalète just before she leaves. He showed her over and over exactly the way he wanted it, how he wanted the opening of the arms. Everyone said, "Oh, he really doesn't believe in stories." He didn't believe in schmaltz! But the movement had to have a quality that was very specific. He wanted his dancers to get it. He could go about conveying it in the most roundabout way. Walter Raines has a wonderful story. He was doing *Concerto Barocco* with the Stuttgart Ballet. Balanchine came to clean it up. Walter was trying to make something out of the man's role beyond the partnering. Balanchine said, "You know, dear, be avocado." Walter exclaimed, "Be an avocado?" Then Walter figured it out: an avocado is a bland part of the salad, but it's an important part. In other words, you are not prominent, but you're *there*. About a year later Balanchine came back to Stuttgart and went up to Walter and said, "Now you are avocado." He didn't forget. He was very specific about what he wanted.

Balanchine always said that he remembered the first impression of every single dancer. The first time he saw a dancer he had a specific concept about that person. He also used to kid around that dancers were different animals. He could be very wicked. I remember I was a porcupine. My friend Barbara Milberg, who was very beautiful, was a delicious mushroom. Tanny and Nicky and Maria were little monkeys—the best animal to be, the kind that can move and do anything. He had animals for everything.

Balanchine felt that Suzanne Farrell gave him what he wanted. She was the epitome of what he had been looking for all those years. She was pliable enough, young enough. Merrill Ashley said that when she was studying with Balanchine she was trying too hard to do exactly what he wanted, but that some dancers would do exactly the opposite, and he would love it. That was probably Suzanne. A lot of her *épaulement* is diametrically opposed to what Balanchine kept saying. Suzanne would fling her arms in whatever position, and he would be ecstatic. Then if you did it, too, he would come down on you like a ton of bricks. He changed, depending on the circumstances. Certain dancers, given that freedom, would look terrible. Other dancers should not be controlled because then they lose something. But you, as an instrument, could get very frustrated trying so hard to do what he wanted. Why can she do it and I can't?

I read the Gelsey Kirkland book, *Dancing on My Grave.* In ballet, you have to be capable of leaving the ego at the door and loving the act of dancing: that is the secret. If you go in there with preconceived notions, it won't work. Like Balanchine always said, "Didi, you're too intelligent. You think too much." You can't go in there with your ego hanging out. For Gelsey, nothing was right. In *Giselle,* the music was wrong. With Balanchine, she hated the Stravinsky music. In *Romeo and Juliet,* MacMillan didn't help her with her pinky, how it should be held. It's all wrong. Gelsey is a gifted technician, but she is not a dancer; by nature, she is not a dancer. You have to let a role happen to you onstage. That's what makes Makarova such a great dancer. She doesn't try and make any two performances alike. She allows her technique to be moldable, to be changeable. That's what makes her great. So does Farrell. Such dancers "let go" onstage. Gelsey's greatest moments were never letting go. It's never a flow. Take Makarova and Kirkland in the *Don Quixote* pas de deux. They're both technically magnificent. But from Makarova it's juicy, it's coming from the inside. It's not "Now I throw my head back, now I move my chin." Gelsey's technique was magnificent, but I wanted to shake her.

After I left New York City Ballet, I stopped dancing. I was married and I realized that everything was second best after working with Balanchine. Reluctantly, I began to teach. After years of teaching elsewhere, I'm now in Queens teaching for a small school run by Terry Cassese, one of my students from years ago. I have students—children and young teenagers—who like discipline and want to be good. You don't have to motivate them, they can't wait to get it. You're teaching, you're not being a psychiatrist. Some of my students are even talented.

JACQUES

D'AMBOISE

Jacques d'Amboise (born 1934) was trained by Maria Swoboda and at the School of American Ballet. He performed children's roles in Ballet Society from 1946 to 1949. In 1949 he joined the New York City Ballet, where he was active as a dancer and choreographer until 1986. Jacques d'Amboise danced almost every male role in the Balanchine repertory. Balanchine made twenty-four new roles for him. He appeared in motion pictures, including Seven Brides for Seven Brothers, Carousel, and often on television. As a choreographer, D'Amboise is known for many ballets, including Irish Fantasy, Tchaikovsky Suite No. 2, Saltarelli, an Alborado del Gracioso. In recent years his work for the National Dance Institute he founded has introduced hundreds of thousands of children to dance and performance. He is the author of Teaching the Magic of Dance, 1983.

I JOINED THE NEW YORK CITY BALLET IN THE FALL OF 1949, WHEN I WAS FIFTEEN. I danced in Balanchine's *Four Temperaments* with Yvonne Mounsey. Ashton came to watch me rehearse and perform it. He said, "I want him to do Tristan." That was for his ballet *Picnic at Tintagel,* my first major role. Ashton didn't tell us the story line for *Picnic,* but I had read *Tristan and Isolde, King Arthur, Sir Gawain and the Green Knight, The Song of Roland, Juan of Bordeaux,* and *Ariosto.* I read everything, from junk to the essays of Montaigne.

One of the first ballets I was in was Balanchine's *The Triumph of Bacchus and Ariadne.* Marie-Jeanne was unforgettable, like Suzanne Farrell in her variation at the end of *Don Quixote.* Marie-Jeanne was major, the essence of dance, a nymph. For Balanchine's dances Rieti used a countermelody from Lorenzo de' Medici. I'll never forget how exciting it was and how she danced.

Eglevsky and I handled the virtuoso male roles in Balanchine's company. There were so many for Eglevsky! What did Balanchine do for virtuoso male dancers later on? Nothing, compared to what he did for Eglevsky. Balanchine made his *Swan Lake* for Tallchief and Eglevsky. I was coming into my own at the time. Balanchine kept saying to me, "You, I want to do for you and Tanny, you and Diana. And I have special variation for you, boy should not do *entrechat.*" Balanchine was angry because André didn't do the steps he gave him. André did sixteen *entrechats* in place. Balanchine said, "It should be romantic. And it should be a sense of loss." He never did do that variation for me. Instead, he did another one, very difficult, that no one does anymore. Now the Prince just does pirouettes. Balanchine did fascinating, interesting steps. The opening night of *Swan Lake* shocked everybody—the black, white, and red costumes, and the swirling corps de ballet. Pat Wilde did a magnificent pas de trois, which my wife Caroline George danced later. Eventually, Balanchine took the pas de trois music and used it for the man's variation.

When I did the film *Seven Brides for Seven Brothers,* I missed being in Balanchine's *The Nutcracker.* I might have done the Cavalier, but when I came back Balanchine said, "You know, you weren't here. I don't have any role for you now, but the minute the season is over, next season, you will do it with Diana." He wanted me to partner Diana Adams and Tanaquil LeClercq because I was tall. But the roles had been done for Eglevsky and Tallchief. Eglevsky was injured, and Nicky Magallanes danced at the first performance. Eglevsky had a wonderful variation, skimming around the floor with lots of fast beats. I wanted to be in the ballet right away so I did the Spanish dance in place of Herbert Bliss.

In 1953, Leon Leonidoff of Radio City Music Hall talked Balanchine into staging a cotillion ballet up in Harlem in an armory. Everyone was sensationally dressed, and Balanchine staged all the marches and movements for the entrance of the debutantes. Tanny and I led the cotillion ball. *One, Yuletide*

Square was a television show that Balanchine staged in 1952, again under the influence of Leonidoff. It was a condensed version of *Coppélia,* with Robert Helpmann as Dr. Coppélius and Harpo Marx as one of the dolls. Tanny was so beautiful in it.

About a third of the *One, Yuletide Square* pas de deux is in the *Stars and Stripes* pas de deux. When Balanchine came to do *Stars,* he saved the pas de deux for last. The day before dress rehearsal, he still hadn't done it. Melissa Hayden and I were waiting for him to choreograph. Remembering *Coppélia,* I suggested something and asked, "What about this?" He said, "Ah, yes, we'll do that. Yes, that's fine." At the end I said, "Mr. B., do you remember that wonderful step where she does finger turns in an *arabesque penchée?* The turns should be way down and the boy has to run in and out." He said, "Good, put it in."

Balanchine gave me a wonderful role in *Ivesiana.* It was called Halloween, but Balanchine said it was George Washington's Barn Dance. Balanchine used Ives's Halloween music and another piece as well. I was a preacher, and the worshipers would all dance around me. I'd stop, close the Bible, throw it aside, and dance like mad, as though I got carried away. It was fun and zany, but Balanchine took the section out after a while because he felt the program was too long and the Halloween section created an imbalance.

Balanchine revived *Apollo* for me in 1957. This ballet turned around my whole idea about dance. Balanchine had worked for six months to teach Nicky Magallanes the role. The first two or three performances that he did were wonderful, but he wasn't able to sustain it. Nicholas Kopeikine said to me, "Jacques, you should go talk to Nicky to help you with Apollo." Nicky said, "Watch the way that Balanchine does it. Just copy the way he does it." He was right. It was so beautiful to watch Balanchine do it. Today, nobody can do Apollo. There isn't a dancer made today who can do Apollo right. I came the closest to it. No one is going to do it again because they don't have Balanchine as the model. They won't have been trained by Balanchine. You need here a modern dance basis with a classical ballet technique. You need to be musical, you need to be dramatic, you've got to be big, you've got to have looks, you've got to have partnering ability, you've got to be dramatic. And you've got to be *young.* You don't find a young man with all those other qualities. I was deficient in classical line. I never had the beautiful pointed feet and the long turnout. Those were my weaknesses in *Apollo,* and you need those things too. I had the other things, but I never was able to get out of *Apollo* everything that was in it. I worked on it steadily, and I understood it.

Up until *Apollo,* I just danced without much rehearsal. Everything was natural and a success; I didn't have to practice or worry about a role, and I thought that Balanchine was going to work with me anyhow and get me perfect. So I always waited for him. He was preparing the first performance of *Agon* and rehearsing that, but he showed me the steps for *Apollo.* Then he left me alone to practice. I would wait around for him to come and make me practice some more. Opening night was a preview benefit performance: the premiere of *Agon, Orpheus* and *Apollo.* I knew what I was capable of in *Apollo,* but I didn't even achieve fifty percent of it. People were saying, "Oh, you were so good," and I was embarrassed. So, before the official premiere some days later, I wrote on the bulletin board: "Wednesday rehearsal, Jacques, 3 hours in the morning; evening, 3 hours. Alone. Request." And then, "Thursday, 3 hours." And "Friday, 3 hours." When Friday came, I was fifty percent better. I discovered the right way to rehearse. I thought, "If I could improve this much in one role in three days, why don't I do this with *Swan Lake?"* Dancing became so much more interesting. It became not just fun but an odyssey toward perfection. Seeking excellence is the major concern of a professional artist. The minute you start giving up the search for excellence for money or because you're too proud to do that role—"Oh, I don't want to do matinees"—you are lost. If you lose one performance, you lose the opportunity to make yourself a little better. You're marking time, and you don't have that time.

When the company visited Monte Carlo one year, Balanchine worked with me on *Apollo* once more. "All over again," he said. He told me he had worked for almost a year with Serge Lifar. He said he hated it because Lifar had had a big success in *Apollo* and Balanchine did not. Balanchine got terrible reviews. "When does a god crawl?" one of the critics had asked. Balanchine was determined to do the ballet again in Monte Carlo with "you, Jacques, in it." He said, "This is where Lifar and I rehearsed, right there, on that stage, in this theater." We worked the whole week long, and Gjon Mili photographed us from the corners of the stage. The stagehands would come and try to sweep us off, but we wouldn't leave.

Gounod Symphony was done for Maria Tallchief and me. Balanchine hated it. It was stock work, thrown together. It was the only time I ever saw him in a fury at rehearsal. He had to do something for France with a French composer, and he had to do something for Maria. He hated "had to's."

Tchaikovsky Pas de Deux was done originally for Diana Adams and me. *Tchaikovsky* had one of the most fabulous male variations; the only dancers who ever tried to do it were Conrad Ludlow and I. Balanchine changed the variation for Villella. Actually, each dancer does his own variation. Now, nobody can do that original variation. It was so hard. First of all, there have been cuts in the music. The original was three times longer. I still remember it. It contained tremendous virtuoso leaps, bounding all over the stage.

At that time Balanchine was rehearsing morning, noon, and night to get Allegra Kent and me ready to do the pas de deux in *Figure in the Carpet.* Allegra got injured, so Melissa Hayden was thrown into the role. He did another pas de deux for Melissa, using some of Allegra's version.

Balanchine made the Act Two pas de deux in *A Midsummer Night's Dream* on me. It is not kept well in the repertory today because of its simplicity. You don't have to sell it, that's the problem. Everybody tries to sell it emotionally, but it does itself. The steps and the music do everything.

The Stravinsky *Movements for Piano and Orchestra* was done for Diana Adams and me. Diana wanted to have a baby. When she became pregnant, the ballet became Suzanne Farrell's. Balanchine was so angry at Diana: "She stabbed me in the back!" He walked out of the theater, and you couldn't reach him for two days. John Taras and I went to Betty Cage. We said we could put the ballet on. Taras would rehearse the corps, and I would take Suzanne and teach her everything I knew. For those few steps we couldn't do, we went to Diana, who was lying on a couch. She demonstrated the footwork I couldn't remember with her hands. After two days we brought in Balanchine. We said, "Come back, look at it." He looked at it, he liked it. "She's wonderful. She's wonderful. God has replaced my lost Diana with Suzanne." And Suzanne *was* wonderful.

The Chase was my first real choreographic work. Balanchine was always telling me, "Choreograph, Jacques, choreograph." It had a good role for Allegra Kent, and Balanchine loved the ballet. We'd sit and have coffee, and he would say, "Why don't you try this a little bit? Now maybe this." There were many flaws in *The Chase,* but there was some interesting choreography where I used fifth position turned in. Balanchine and Lincoln Kirstein encouraged me to make ballets all my time in the company. "Do works. Any time." After I did *The Chase* they said, "You're a choreographer." So I said, "Mr. B., I'm a dancer. I think I can choreograph. I'm going to test myself: in one year I will do three different ballets." And I did. I did *The Chase, Irish Fantasy,* and *Pas de Trois* to Stravinsky music, which was premiered in Florida by another company. Three ballets—a full program. I just wanted to see if I could do it. Afterward, I didn't worry about choreographing anymore. I also directed three musicals in the summers.

Balanchine revived *Ballet Imperial* for Suzanne and me. He had a big wig made for me. He said, "Your hair, you're always putting grease like an American boy. You've got to have lots of hair." He used all the original mime, and we had special lessons. He would say, "This would be the fourth finger. Heart is on the side, and then tuck and take a breath. Because love hurts, elbows have to come in." He eventually took out all the mime because nobody could do it. He didn't want to teach it, so he made some beautiful choreography to replace the mime section.

Davidsbündlertänze, what a ballet! Take just the four pas de deux. It's a whole love affair: a meeting, an argument, etc. They are a whole thing by themselves. Balanchine had it all in his head. He met me on the street six months before he did the ballet and told me all about it. He said that Suzanne and I would be the real lovers, and then there would be other couples who would represent different aspects of the relationship.

For the "Adagio Lamentoso" from the *Pathétique* for the 1981 Tchaikovsky Festival I found for Balanchine the little boy who appeared with the candle. He said, "Jacques, I want you to go find a little boy for me out of all the thousands that you are teaching. I want you to find one for me who will be like an angel." I found Adam Wagner.

When *Noah and the Flood* was being rehearsed for the Stravinsky Festival in 1982 Balanchine came to me during the rehearsal, clutched me, and whispered, "I have to see a doctor. I can't feel. I have to get out of here and see a doctor. Something's happened. Can you do something—take over rehearsal? You know what to do." I said, "Yes, Mr. B." He went out, and I started working. He came back: suddenly he was there, saying, "Now this, this, this." He was disoriented. We couldn't get anything from him. I put *Noah* together. At the end, he gave it to me too. He said, "I give it to you." One day I will take *Noah and the Flood* and rechoreograph it, keeping Balanchine and some things that I did.

On the Russia tours, the response of the audiences was unpredictable. Ballets like *Prodigal Son* that you thought would be a big success laid an egg in Tbilisi. Ballets that you didn't think would be a success were astonishing: *Episodes* in the Palace of Congresses before six thousand people. After my variation in the *Tchaikovsky Pas de Deux* in Leningrad, I got six curtain calls. Melissa had five or six after hers. Just before that, *Concerto Barocco* had barely gotten one call. Balanchine came backstage and it was hate, fury, and anger about the success of *Tchaikovsky Pas de Deux.* "Awful! They are circus. They don't recognize. *Barocco* they didn't appreciate." I said, "But, Mr. B., they loved it. Wasn't it a big success?" "No, no. This *Tchaikovsky Pas de Deux* ballet is not our company. This is not us. We are not circus." Then he started blaming Melissa, and he would have blamed me, too, except I was standing there. He said, "This ballet, I give it to you. You take this ballet. It is yours. It belongs for television. It belongs in concerts. It belongs in night clubs. A big success. You danced it beautifully. But it is yours. I give it to you. It is not a company thing." I was hurt because he really wasn't giving the ballet to me. He was furious in the same way he was when the audience screamed for Eglevsky and Maria Tallchief after *Sylvia Pas de Deux.* A day or two later he left Russia and came back to America for a while. He couldn't take it. Then he returned to us to complete the tour. We were in Russia for almost four months. He had to get away. The pressures were terrible. Later, he mentioned in a hangdog manner his giving *Tchaikovsky Pas de Deux* to me, and I said, "Now, Mr. B., you were just all distraught. You didn't mean it at the time."

RICHARD

THOMAS

Richard Thomas was born in Kentucky in 1926 and studied in Los Angeles with Bronislava Nijinska. He danced on Broadway, in Ballet Theatre, and in the Ballet Russe de Monte Carlo before joining the New York City Ballet. For many years he directed the New York School of Ballet and served as company teacher for U. S. Terpsichore, an associated troupe he founded with his wife, dancer Barbara Fallis.

I Remember Balanchine

WHEN I WAS SIXTEEN, I DROVE FROM MY HOME IN THE KENTUCKY HILLS TO SEE
Ringling Brothers and Barnum & Bailey Circus perform Balanchine's *Circus
Polka.* They didn't use the Stravinsky music because the touring orchestra
couldn't handle it; they played something classical. It was my first ballet.
You never think really of elephants moving with the speed and the agility
they're capable of, but George had them flying through entrances and exits,
picking their trunks up and bowing, pirouetting and running in circles. The
women came in on those elephants and danced on the ring curves and the
stages. I loved it.

I went into the Ballet Russe de Monte Carlo at the end of 1946. We did
Balanchine's *Night Shadow* and *Baiser de la Fée,* and the full-length *Raymonda* he
and Danilova staged together. Balanchine had left the company, but he was
in and out rehearsing, and was kind about our coming to the School of
American Ballet to take class. I was with them until 1949, in the Alonso
company for a couple of years, and then I joined the New York City Ballet. I
was one of the best corps de ballet boys ever. I did a lot of leading roles in
the company, too, and solo parts, not *premier danseur* roles, because I wasn't
even a very good dancer, but I could do what I was given to do fine.

George was a very classy man for a Russian. Russians can be one way or
the other. They spill soup on their front or they wear jabots and are very
French. He loved my son Richard, who was a child then; they had a grown-
up relationship. Balanchine would come and sit with him on the train on our
tours, and my son came along for all the rehearsals and classes. He had his
toys and played quietly. At the end of class Balanchine would say, "Now,
Richard, you come." George would give him little things to do with one of
the dancers, and then teach him to do a reverence. Jillana would take a
penchée arabesque and then my son would kneel and do promenade.

At one time there were a lot of people in the company who could cover
enormous spaces; Janet Reed could really move around—when you think of
the third movement in *Symphony in C,* and those wonderful double *chassé tours*
she did right and left. Janet was never considered a technician, but George
loved her sense of total abandon in the air. Vladimiroff was very much into
teaching people to move at the School.

I loved watching Balanchine wheel and deal, and do all his things with all
the dancers. Screw people he obviously did, right and left, in all kinds of
ways. I remember when Maria had been funny and wanted a ballet. Balanchine did *Gounod Symphony* for her, but this time he did not glorify his ballerina. He put her on pointe in *plié* all the time, which was not Maria's best
position. When Tanny or Diana did it, it was really quite lovely, but Maria
did not have that kind of physical look and it was perverse of Balanchine to

use her that way. André Eglevsky saw that Maria really didn't look good in this pretty awful ballet and he stepped out.

You couldn't best Balanchine, no matter what. One year I refused to be a Monster in *Firebird.* I had been there forever and I told the ballet mistress, Vida Brown, "You have three new boys in the dressing room. Put 'em in it. I won't jump up and down as a Monster one more time." The next day my name was on the board to do the *Head* Monster—it was the first time a male dancer had ever done the role. I was the Head Monster until the day I left.

Usually ballets would come up on the schedule and it didn't bother him at all: "Just rehearse with Vida," he'd tell us. But every time we got to Paris, George became very picky. One season at the Paris Opéra, we were in that big studio in the rotunda and he picked up our arms, feet, and legs: "We never do that! We never do this!" He nitpicked for hours until we were all mad, and then I realized: "It's Paris." He didn't care what they said about us in any other place. Perhaps because it was the scene of his early triumphs, he wanted us to be perfection in Paris.

Years later my wife, Barbara Fallis, who was also in the company, and I felt that it was time to go. I had been ill, I needed to leave and had been told by the doctors I couldn't make the tour to Australia. I was going to go anyway, but then there was an unfortunate incident. We really felt the company had taken advantage of us. Balanchine was upset about it and was doing this great number, until my wife told him, "George, I've worked with Fokine, I've worked with Massine. I've worked with many great dancers. You're not my God. You're another choreographer." She really hurt him to the heart, I think. I'm sorry it ended that way. But he had great respect for Barbara and me, in part because we never had the dependent relationship with him that so many did.

Several years later, when the School of American Ballet was moving to Lincoln Center, Lincoln Kirstein asked, "Dickie, do you want the old school?"—the space on upper Broadway occupied for many years by Balanchine's school. I had been there the day those premises opened in 1956, when the company moved from Fifty-ninth Street. Ballet Theatre, Bob Joffrey, everybody in the world wanted that space. I had a tiny little school on Fifty-sixth Street. I said, "I don't know how I'll do it, but yes, I want it." Don't ask me how I managed, but I knew I was going to go there. Balanchine said to me, "Why do you want a school if you have no company? What is the point?" I felt he was right, and so I started a company. After a certain point I wrote him: "Dear Mr. Balanchine, I would like to have something from the Balanchine repertory for my small company. I have a couple of very fine dancers, I have three or four very mediocre dancers, and then I have a whole lot of really terrible dancers. But I promise you that, if you will let me do something, I will never used canned music, even if it's a symphony." He replied, "Anything you want, you can have."

I think he was perfectly right in everything he did. I have no qualms in general about how he lived his life; he was walking on a higher plane than most of us. I don't want to put him on a pedestal as though he was the only great man in ballet. I never knew Fokine, but for my wife to talk about him was as exciting as anything, and being with Mr. Massine was one of the greatest thrills of my life. But when it came to intellect in ballet, I was very fortunate to work with George Balanchine. He gave me the key to the actual science, theory, and technique of ballet dancing. Each one of those steps has a meaning of physical energy, timing, and space. He taught me the value of the vocabulary, and that's what makes you an exceptional dancer. You don't even have to have a personality and still you can be wonderful. If you are touched by God *and* can learn what Balanchine had to teach, you become the most wonderful thing in the world.

Bronislava Nijinska, Balanchine, and probably Alexandra Danilova were the only people I've ever known who lived for dancing. They fed on other things only to support that. Nijinska had to choreograph; even when she wasn't involved, the orange trees in her grove were like a corps de ballet dressed in tutus. Balanchine had to choreograph. He didn't consider himself a teacher; he taught because he wanted the dancers to understand ballet so that he could use them to his and their own best advantage. There is no Balanchine technique; Balanchine taught classical ballet, what he learned back at the Imperial School. I learned it from him and Nijinska: they both said, "You don't come down, you go up."

Kinky *port de bras* was *choreography;* Balanchine's *port de bras* in class was pure Cecchetti. Everyone who came out of the Imperial School taught *port de bras* in circles. Balanchine worked from the hand to the rounded inside of the elbow, to the inside of the palm. "You do *port de bras* forward and back at the barre. You lean forward. You pick up the laundry. You lean back. You open your hands; the laundry drops. And then you pick up the clothes from the floor. . . ."

We very seldom had music in class; if we did, he wanted incidental pieces. He didn't like to ever work in 3/4. Now if I'm teaching a class of people that I have to see progressively, then I need to use 6/8, 3/4, 2/4. I have to use everything because they have to learn how to do it. But he didn't, and he didn't want 3/4 because he didn't want the extra beat because it was a waste of his time. He wanted everything pah-pah, pah-pah. If you want to get the actual accents, it's better to get rid of the other beat. Every now and then he could see, I suppose, that people would get bored and he let Kolya Kopeikine come in and play a little waltz.

He had his own preferences about people's looks. He told Michael Smuin he really couldn't hire him because he was too short. Michael said, "Well, I'm the same height as Eddie Villela." "Yes," Balanchine said, "but your legs are shorter." Michael replied, "But they touch the floor."

Danny Levans went to George when he left American Ballet Theatre. He wanted to work under Balanchine after hearing Barbara and me talk about him. Dan looked differently from the rest of the company and it bothered Balanchine, but he loved Dan in the classroom because Dan understood theoretically what was going on. He worked with Dan in some ballets. Then Dan went to him after about a year and a half. "You know, Mr. Balanchine, I really would like to know how you feel, now that I've been here this long." Balanchine said, "I will never do a great ballet for a male dancer again. You're a very nice boy, I'd like you to stay here as long as you want, but if I were you I wouldn't." Dan said, "Mr. Balanchine, I can't thank you enough." That was a great man giving good advice.

You cannot ask a painter to turn around and paint a work over again and, by the same token, choreographers should never rehearse their own ballets. They cannot put two and two together after the creation has been done. They start tinkering and changing, and they shouldn't. The New York City Ballet was there to allow Balanchine complete artistic freedom to create his ballets. That's what every artist wants, but I don't think it's the best deal. I am of the school that thinks a choreographer should never be the artistic director of a company. When that happens you wind up with a showcase for the choreographer. "Well, you don't want a museum," some people say. Of course you do; that's what a ballet company *is:* you must have *Swan Lake* to know *Agon*.

UNA

KAI

Una Kai (born 1928) received her early training from Vera Nemtchi-nova and the School of American Ballet. She danced with Ballet Society and was a charter member of the New York City Ballet in 1948. In 1956 she was appointed ballet master, and continued to perform until 1960. She has frequently staged Balanchine's works in the United States and abroad. She is ballet mistress at the State Ballet of Missouri.

IT'S SO PERSONAL, ONE'S RELATIONSHIP WITH BALANCHINE. IT'S ALL VERY INDIVIDUAL, each person's reaction to him. I think every person could write a book, as Gelsey Kirkland did, but they would all be totally different. Readers would say, "Can this be the same person they're writing about?" I was always so much in awe of him. We never had any conversations until I became his ambassador, putting on his ballets overseas.

When I came to work with him, I had seen some of his ballets. I thought they were weird, because my dream of ballet was like the first program that I saw when I was about five and living in New Jersey. My aunt took me into Manhattan to see the Ballet Russe. It must have been 1933 or '34. It's indelibly imprinted: *Les Sylphides, Petrouchka,* and *Prince Igor.* I thought it was just the most fantastic thing I'd ever seen. "That's for me," I decided. "I have to do that."

I grew up looking at that kind of ballet, so Balanchine's were a shock, but I quickly became enchanted with Balanchine and his work. It changed my entire approach to ballet, my way of thinking about it. Although it took me a long time to really come to agree with everything he said, the results were so visible that one had to agree with it. You finally had to accept it and say, "This works, not only on other people but on my body too."

I was lucky that I had very proper training from the beginning. After seeing De Basil's company in 1933, I had asked my mother to take me for ballet lessons. We went to a studio in East Orange, where Margaret Tarosova was teaching. The next teacher I had was Maria Swoboda in New York, from age seven until thirteen. At thirteen I started going to New York City to study with Nemtchinova at Carnegie Hall. I began taking private lessons from her on Saturdays, and that's where I met Oboukhoff. After graduating from high school, I decided that I wanted to go to the School of American Ballet, not because of Balanchine, but because I wanted to train with Oboukhoff.

The first ballet I danced with Ballet Society was Dollar's *Highland Fling.* That was the first time I saw Balanchine. I don't remember who was supposed to teach the pointe class but suddenly Balanchine was there instead. I remember that he corrected me the first day and then the next day he called me by name, which impressed me incredibly.

The first Balanchine ballet I did for Ballet Society was *Symphonie Concertante.* When he did it we were really students and the steps he gave us were those that students could look well in. I was surprised when Ballet Theatre revived it, because they have all those wonderful dancers who could certainly do a great deal more.

When Balanchine returned from the Paris Opéra in 1948, he came and taught the D class at the School every day; this consisted of the company and the School all mixed up together. He began giving us daily two-hour classes to speed up the process of technical expertise. He had all these young dancers whose style was not homogenized. He trained us to do the steps the way he wanted so that he could use them in his ballets. He started really digging in and choreographing ballet after ballet. It was intensive work. We had terribly difficult classes, long and concentrated, but the result was that in two years he whipped us into good enough shape to go to London and dance at Covent Garden.

The classes were hard on the body. We did twenty different versions of the same kind of step, without the chance to relax a bit by using other muscles. I think we suffered great pain during this period; in later years a lot of dancers refused to take his class because of this. They didn't realize that if you stuck with it you could overcome this. You had to live through the pain; a lot of dancers didn't want to do that. I never missed his class the entire time I was with the company. Balanchine always said that "dancers reach their prime at age thirty," and I think that at age thirty I could finally do whatever he required of me. It took a long time because my body was stiff. I really had to work just to achieve what I did, but he helped me to do it. I became what I considered a competent dancer.

We always danced *Swan Lake* and *Firebird* at matinees, forever. It really got boring for those of us who participated. Finally I decided that I couldn't face one more rehearsal of *Swan Lake* and asked for a leave of absence. I needed to refresh myself and decide what I wanted to do with my life. I thought that I probably didn't want to dance anymore, but I didn't know what else to do. Then one day Balanchine phoned and asked if I could go to London to stage *Bourrée Fantasque*. Vida Brown, who had been scheduled to go, was about to get married. I said, "Oh, dear, I know all the corps de ballet parts, but I have no clue as to what the soloists are doing." "Oh, you can learn that," he assured me. "Ask them and they'll tell you." So I went around and interviewed all the soloists, who were very helpful. The men showed me how they partnered the girls and so on. This was pre-video. I was so nervous that I lost eight pounds the week before I left for London, but I managed to put it all together.

After staging *Bourrée* in London, Balanchine sent me to Hamburg to do *Concerto Barocco*. I spent the Fourth of July with Melissa Hayden, who taught me both solo ladies as she was waxing her floor. Then Balanchine said, "Can you go to La Scala and do my version of *Swan Lake*, Act II?" I knew the corps parts, of course, and I knew the pas de deux because Oboukhoff had taught it in adagio class, but I didn't know what everyone did in the music Balanchine added from the fourth act. He said, "Come out in the hall and I'll teach it to you," and he partnered me as he sang. I raced home to my hotel and tried to write it down. I went off to La Scala and it was a struggle because I just couldn't make things fit together, somehow. The night I returned to New York, I went straight to the theater, and they were doing *Swan Lake.* The curtain went up and I was absolutely appalled: "Oh, my God, this isn't what I did in Italy at all." I raced backstage and said, "Mr. B., I don't know what to do; I've messed it all up." He said, "Oh, it's not that important. Doesn't matter."

When Tanny got sick and Balanchine was away, Lew Christensen and Todd Bolender were sort of running the company and Vida was doing recruiting and basic teaching. I started as ballet mistress because she needed somebody to help her.

The last time I watched Balanchine teach, I went back afterward to have a few words with him. He was still in the studio showing someone how to do *battement tendu.* I was really impressed, because he must have done that a million times in his life. He just persisted; I hope I can be like that. Every year we get people into our company and we have to start over, trying to integrate them so that we have a homogeneous style. It takes time. People resist because their early training is what they learn, and then that's it. I hope I can be as patient as Balanchine. He just started from the beginning every time.

PAT

McBRIDE

Patricia McBride, a pioneer member of Ballet Society and the New York City Ballet, retired from dancing early to marry Anthony Loussada and live in London.

I Remember Balanchine

WHEN I CAME INTO THE SCHOOL OF AMERICAN BALLET IN THE BEGINNERS' CLASS, my contemporary, Tanaquil LeClercq, a little wonder child, was in the top, professional class. When Ballet Society started, George just took the top classes, and that was the company. There was I among all these talented people. He was easygoing, absolutely charming. He obviously liked me enough because I could dance well and because I was probably quite a pretty girl. He was totally untemperamental.

He made *Élégie* in 1948 with Tanny and me. It was not a big piece. I think he liked the idea of the blonde and the dark-haired girl, almost the same height. It didn't matter that I wasn't as strong or anything like as able a dancer as Tanny. But he liked the kind of lyrical quality that I had, and I think he just liked the looks of us, frankly, two slim girls, about the same height, dark and blond. The ballet was all a tangle, on the floor, all intertwining, and just moving around. Tanny and I were inseparable in those days, he always saw us together. He did the *Élégie* again for Suzanne Farrell, but in a totally different way. I don't know that our version has been, in fact, revived. We did it in front of the curtain at the City Center. It would be nice to think that it was a major work but I don't think it was. He just came into the studio and showed us what to do. There was never any hesitation.

The other thing that was so wonderful was that Balanchine showed you what he wanted and almost marked it in a way. You weren't quite sure what he meant by the step or what the step really looked like. So when you did it, in a sense you could do it one of four ways and he might say, "Fine, fine, fine, yes, good." And in fact maybe if you did it the fifth way he would say, "Well . . ." and then he would do it again in his rough way. But you felt, in the end, that you were putting a stamp on it—and simply because you weren't sure what he was doing. It could be every time that you did it right. You felt that you were in some way, not collaborating with him, but playing a part in the process in an extraordinary way. So often he would show what he wanted in such a sort of enigmatic way that you could interpret it differently. You felt that you slightly played a hand in it, that he was in fact giving you a little rein. Maybe later he became more exact and specific about what he wanted. I felt that a lot of the steps, while they had a classical impetus or emphasis, were not totally classical positions. And so when he showed things to you, you really weren't sure where you were going and what the steps were. He could name a step, *"glissade, assemblé,"* you could do it, and there was no mistake about what he wanted. But if he showed a step that isn't classical in the vocabulary, there was a lot of scope to interpreting what he was doing. In the very beginning, we hadn't picked up his rhythm and what he was trying to do, and so maybe it felt more like we were

282

interpreting what he was showing. As you realized what he wanted, there might have been less and less interpreting.

Jerry Robbins, right from the beginning, wanted every finger in the right place. He obviously got his inspiration from the person and the way they moved. But with George it was more than that, a kind of collaboration where you had a little more freedom in interpreting what he wanted. Speaking of Jerry, Balanchine always gave everybody else the dancers they wanted. Jerry, Todd Bolender, the other choreographers, could choose. He took what was left. Of course, he got the lead he wanted, Tanny or whomever. And also he gave the other choreographers all the rehearsal time; he took whatever was left. And then it just poured out of him. He was amazing that way, incredible really. He never exploded, never yelled. And the activity in the company was total bedlam: people walking in and out. There was never any feeling that this was sort of sacred ground, and this is a genius working and tiptoe in.

As for dancing characters, dramatic roles like Eurydice, he always said that you mustn't analyze, just dance, that the steps will convey all the emotion. You don't have to think, just do the steps. You know, just straighten your knee, watch your feet, jump far, do the double *tour;* you don't have to worry about those things. Just worry about getting stronger, showing with your feet. On the other hand, we knew perfectly well that the dancers who had expressiveness were the ones that he was drawn to, those dancers who had this extra quality. He always acted as though that was of no importance, that you shouldn't think about "soul" or expressing. It wasn't what dancing was about. You didn't have to do any of that, just do the steps and it would all work out. Maybe it changed later as ballets became more concentrated and more difficult, but he needed to have technical whiz kids. On the other hand, when he found a dancer who had a certain quality, he didn't mind about that, did he? Suzanne Farrell could never do any of the really difficult roles. She couldn't dance like Merrill Ashley, technically. And there is no doubt which was his muse. But he never tried to get that. I mean, he never in class gave you an inch of the quality that Suzanne has. She was almost more like the Russians in the way she uses her back and her upper body. That's nothing he ever taught, wanted to teach, wanted to instill in the dancers. But when they had it, he was smitten by it.

I don't know how he'd feel about restoring his so-called "lost" ballets. When I see *Symphony in C,* there are so many things that are gone that I remember. I remember him saying that he didn't believe in the staticness of things. He'd probably loathe the idea of people coming back and trying to put in the original feeling for it. You know, the original things, the feeling of the works. It's terribly sad when you see it and all of those qualities that you remember aren't there anymore. It's gone. And all the emphasis isn't there. Sure, the dancers that were there—like Tanny, Maria, and all—could coach it and get that back.

The School is different, too, of course. We were taught by Vladimiroff and Doubrovska and Oboukhoff, and we had a lot of what we see in Russian kids today. But when Balanchine started to teach he wanted much faster footwork and the feet to be like hands, he wanted you to go faster and jump. He wanted to extend it all and he did. In a way, the early dancers of Ballet Society and the New York City Ballet almost had the best of both worlds. There was still a feeling of a complete body, of the arms being an integral part of it, and yet Balanchine was giving you these amazing feet. None of us could do what these School of American Ballet kids now can do, not by a million miles. But the whole side of things which we got from the old Russian input has disappeared. Young dancers now are infinitely more brilliant, but I think there's this other side that's gone. It makes the early ballets look very different. The lucky thing is that we still have Suzanne Farrell, we still have a lot of the authorities. She has just staged her first *Scotch Symphony* for the Kirov Ballet. That is wonderful.

Balanchine was a religious person. When I think of the people he was so taken with, who were his muses, all of them have this incredible other quality, this almost spiritual quality about their dancing. I think his pleasure was in that and his satisfaction with the form as he saw it, the way he felt that the form worked with the music, like another layer of the score. Obviously it all came to Balanchine with the music. The composer put the notes on the page like Balanchine put the steps on the stage. Neither the composer nor Balanchine thought, "What does this mean?" or "What is this going to contain?" It contains the composer's soul, feelings, everything, as the steps did Balanchine's. What did Mozart think about his music? Supposedly, he had shortcomings as a man, which no one wants to believe, but it doesn't matter. I mean, the output is the thing.

The spirituality in some of the muses—Suzanne certainly has it. Tanny had a different quality. She had a very stylish way of dancing and a very witty way of moving. She brought a kind of antic life to what she was dancing. And she was very musical, very intelligent, and a little distant. Later, she was technically more brilliant than I thought she would ever become. As the Dewdrop in *The Nutcracker*, he had really taught her. She had worked with him and she was like a little jewel. She was still Tanny, but she had her own kind of dance character. All of Balanchine's muses could illumine the choreography like an instrumentalist playing Schubert. Tanny illuminated in one way, and Suzanne illuminated in perhaps a larger way, a deeper way, or a way that was thought out. She brought out in George another dimension. Tanny gave, she determined what George gave her, and Suzanne drew out another side of him. That's why she, in a way, was a kind of major muse above all the others.

There are such parallels. If Mozart had a wonderful cello player around, he did a beautiful cello sonata and took off. It was the opportunity that started him. And the same way for Balanchine with Darci Kistler. The sad thing was that Baryshnikov came too late. Who knows what would have happened had he been there years earlier and George could have used his talents? And I think endlessly of George when I see Sylvie Guillem. He would have made something out of her. She's done a *Swan Lake* and an absolutely beautiful *Apollo* at Covent Garden, even with Jonathan Cope, whose innocence and dullness were all right because he looked wonderful. She sort of stirred him. I wish she could have worked with Balanchine—that would have been a delicious combination.

Balanchine, I think, would have been very amused by the joint appearances at the Holland Festival in June 1989 of students from the Vaganova Academy in Leningrad and the School of American Ballet. He would have had a very good time. He would have loved some of the Russian long-legged creatures. He'd have loved to have got his hands on them and given them a little lesson in how to get about. But the exchange is the important thing. I think the Russians will have benefited far more than the Americans. They've traveled around a lot. They're almost professional child performers. The Americans were all amazed at the instep the Russian girls have. We heard that the kids go back and talk and show each other steps, the Russian kids, the American kids. I wish there had been more exchange: perhaps the Russian kids could have done a Balanchine work and the American kids could have done *Paquita,* taught by the Russians. That would really have been an education. I rather love the fact that they are so different.

The Russians have gone bananas, and they now try to do these tricks: the leg up, the double *tour*—and nothing in between. And the kids are weak, they can't get on their pointes, they fall off their pointes totally. They have no strength in their feet. They have this gorgeous instep, gorgeous, thin, long line, and they can hit the poses, but they're zero in between. They don't dance anymore. That's what so amazing. The Russians are very astute in bringing the little kids who will seduce us until the end of time. That little boy with all that hair, when he was doing the polonaise—oh, I thought that was worth everything. But their *Paquita* is agony. Actually, a couple of the variations the girls do very, very well, but you know they can only do that step. It's all so set and dead and undancelike. But it was so wonderful watching all the classes, Russian and American. It was like finding out where Balanchine began as a child and how he made it into something new.

BETTY

CAGE

Associated with the New York City Ballet from 1947 to 1985, Betty

Cage was general administrator of the company for most of that period.

I Remember Balanchine

IN *the spring of 1985 Lincoln Kirstein gathered the members of the New York City Ballet together to tell them that Betty Cage, their general administrator, was resigning on April 30 after thirty-eight years of loyal service. He said: "No one can replace Betty Cage." Balanchine was the artist, Kirstein the animator of the New York City Ballet. Devoted to Balanchine's genius and to Kirstein's ambitions for him and the company, Betty Cage calmly set about doing what she could to fulfill their plans. They had had plans before that did not work out: their American Ballet, formed in 1935, vanished in 1938 as an independent performing entity. It became a part of the Metropolitan Opera to its disadvantage, went to Hollywood to dance for Samuel Goldwyn, re-formed in 1941 as American Ballet Caravan to tour Latin America but then dissolved. Balanchine worked on Broadway, for the circus, in Hollywood, and as ballet master for various ensembles. Upon Kirstein's return from World War II, he and Balanchine established, with Leon Barzin as musical director, Ballet Society, a private subscription enterprise devoted to new works in the lyric theater. Balanchine's* Four Temperaments, *the Ravel opera* L'Enfant et les Sortilèges *staged by Balanchine, the Menotti operas* The Medium *and* The Telephone, *and the Cage/Cunningham/Noguchi dance* The Seasons *were among their first presentations at the Central High School of Needle Trades on West Twenty-sixth Street in Manhattan. Ballet Society's business manager, Frances Hawkins, had rented office space at the new City Center of Music and Drama. This former Mecca Temple on West Fifty-fifth Street had become in the postwar years a people's theater, offering symphony concerts and opera at popular prices. The chairman of its executive committee, the distinguished attorney Morton Baum, was a gifted amateur musician who thought it would be good to offer ballet too. In 1947 he proposed the City Center as a home for Ballet Theatre, which had danced a month-long season in the house. Lucia Chase, happiest when her company danced at the Metropolitan Opera, refused.*

In 1948, anxious to broaden its audience, Ballet Society decided to rent the City Center for a season which would present the premiere of the Stravinsky ballet Orpheus, *which Kirstein had commissioned for Balanchine. The settings and costumes were by Isamu Noguchi. After the premiere, for Ballet Society's subscribers, the public was invited to buy tickets. Morton Baum happened by the City Center that evening, came into the theater, and saw* Orpheus. *He did not know Balanchine from Adam. He asked the box office, "Who are these people? I am in the presence of genius." He was told that Ballet Society was a private organization headed by Lincoln Kirstein. Baum said he wanted to see him. In his office several days later, after congratulating Kirstein on* Orpheus, *Baum asked him if Ballet Society would form a ballet company for the City Center similar to the New York City Opera. It could be called the New York City Ballet. Kirstein told him, "If you do that for us, we'll give you the best ballet company in America in three years." He walked across town to the School of American Ballet to tell Balanchine. Fifteen years after Balanchine's arrival in New York, it seemed possible that their dream of a ballet company with a permanent theater could come true.*

Baum's invitation to Kirstein has always seemed to me the most enlightened and generous gesture in American ballet history. With no knowledge beyond Orpheus, *Baum knew instinctively that Balanchine and Kirstein were the team to back. Fortunately, the three had*

Betty Cage

Betty Cage to mediate and guide them. At View magazine, working with Tchelitchew's friends, she had known the world of arts and letters and how to put out a magazine. How to run a ballet company headed by two of the most gifted persons in the world she learned in no time at all. The New York City Ballet, the first Balanchine-Kirstein partnership with a permanent home at the City Center, could not afford to fail. Betty Cage behind the scenes made it a success. Kirstein has spoken of her "protean task of being at once labor negotiator, certified public accountant, legal expert, mother superior, confessor, psychiatrist" and recalled that "she accepted strikes or threats of strikes with equanimity: they would pass. . . . She offered a patient ear, lively mind, dispassionate style and rational belief in powers superior to the fevers and complaints of lawyers, bankers, dancers."

Watching Betty Cage work, you would never have imagined that she was a person with a mission. She was just there to do what had to be done, a calm communicator. Not in the least officious in any superefficient fashion, seemingly casual and collected, she was nevertheless the efficient cause of all Balanchine and Kirstein desired. Because of her, their partnership flourished in their new theater as never before; it continued to do so when they moved to the New York State Theater at Lincoln Center. She continued as the company's general administrator until exactly two years after Balanchine's death.

In dance throughout history, there are crucial persons who make the impossible happen. It is my belief that Betty Cage was the essential colleague for Balanchine's resplendent creativity. She paved the way and made it possible for him to work with ease and confidence for thirty-eight years.

F.M.

MY INTRODUCTION TO THE WORLD OF BALLET CAME WHEN I WORKED FOR VIEW MAGA-zine. All four of us on the editorial staff were counted as charter members of Ballet Society because the Society had exchanged memberships for ads. I first met Balanchine very briefly when he came to the View office for an appointment with the editor. Lincoln Kirstein I knew better because he was a contributor. When the magazine folded, I called the Ballet Society office and asked if they needed anyone. They said no, so I took a job with Gotham Book Mart. One day Lincoln walked into the shop and said, "How would you like to work for the ballet?" I said I would love to but that I had called and they said they didn't need anyone. He said, well, they had fired the person who had talked to me. "So," he said, "come."

I didn't have a clear idea of what my duties were, but when I got there I found out that they just needed somebody to do everything that had to be done. This was 1947 when Ballet Society was a year old. No one had kept the books for several months, so I had to become a bookkeeper. I didn't know a thing about bookkeeping. Frances Hawkins, who was the general manager, didn't know much about bookkeeping either, but she said she had a friend who worked at the Museum of Modern Art and *she* would tell us about bookkeeping. So we called her, and she said, "Oh, well, just make up a trial balance." Frances thanked her and hung up. She relayed the message to me, and I had to ask, "Frances, what's a trial balance?" She said she didn't know, but we had an auditor and he would tell us. So I called the auditor and said, "We have to do something about these books, will you come?" That's what I mean by doing what had to be done. Somebody had to straighten out the books. I learned how to make a trial balance because I had to.

The programming for the year had all been laid out when I got there. The first performance they had after I arrived was *Far Harbour,* an opera by Archibald and Bergeson, performed at Hunter College Auditorium. The regular Ballet Society dance program was *The Triumph of Bacchus and Ariadne* on February 9, 1948.

April was to be a turning point for Ballet Society. Heretofore, all performances had been by subscription, but in April they rented the City Center Theater and gave four public performances. We had already commissioned *Orpheus* from Stravinsky for the spring. The program also included *Symphony in C,* which Balanchine had done for the Paris Opéra. It was after these public performances that Morton Baum, who was chairman of the executive committee of the New York City Center, got together with Lincoln and proposed that we become the resident company of the City Center. At that time Ballet Society's only continuing relationship with the Center was as a tenant renting office space. But in October 1948 we became the New York City Ballet.

In actual fact, I think Baum had offered the City Center to Ballet Theater before he offered it to us, but they turned it down, being content to stay at the Metropolitan Opera House. The City Center had very little space in the wings and wasn't really a suitable house for a ballet company, but it gave us a home, which was very important. We were new and considered a student company, but it was a way of establishing ourselves as a professional company.

Baum was good to work with. First of all, he was a very nice man, and he had certain feelings about music and art. He didn't know too much about ballet, but he loved music. He was a pianist, he loved performances and was completely committed to the idea of the City Center to have first-class performances at popular prices. He was helpful and easy to work with.

Balanchine, Lincoln, and Baum got along well. Sometimes Baum would suggest a ballet. Sometimes Balanchine would say no, sometimes he would say, "Well, maybe," sometimes he would even try and then say, "No, I really can't," and sometimes he would do it. *Liebeslieder Walzer* was one that Baum suggested. Another he suggested was Richard Strauss's *Don Juan.* Balanchine started it but finally said, "I can't use this music," and dropped it. Sometimes Baum would say something like, *"Four Temperaments* will never be accepted by the audience, George, you should drop it." But George said, "Well, they'll come around to it, we won't drop it." Baum never insisted on anything. He'd make suggestions, and if George accepted, fine, and if he didn't, fine.

Our first popular success as the New York City Ballet came a year later in 1949. It came about because the scenery and costumes for *Firebird* were available. Sol Hurok had them in a warehouse and offered them to Baum, and we bought them for five thousand dollars. Balanchine said, yes, okay, he would do it. The ballets we had done before were things that had been done as Ballet Society. They were not known to the public. People generally had never heard of *Orpheus.* They had never heard of *Symphony in C.* But *Firebird* they had heard of, they knew the music. *Firebird* was a great success with the audience, and it made Maria Tallchief's fame—started it, anyway.

My working relationship with George and Lincoln was not on an artistic level at all. I made financial judgments: "This is possible, this is not possible." Or, "If you want this very much, we'll try to make it possible." I didn't say, "You can't do it, it's going to cost too much," because in those days the City Center was not paying for new productions, only the company's operating costs. For new productions, we had to raise money outside. If we had money, fine; if we didn't have money, well, we didn't have money. The first year we did *Western Symphony* (1954) I told Balanchine we didn't have money for either scenery or costumes. He said, "That's all right, we'll do it in practice clothes and do it on bare stage. Later, when we have some money, we'll have costumes." Which is what happened. He was wonderful because he always understood the financial limitations.

In those early years neither George nor Lincoln was getting any salary. Everything we had went to the dancers. The only thing Balanchine got was royalties for his ballets, a modest twenty-five dollars per performance. He never got a fee for doing a ballet. Other choreographers represented in the repertoire would get a fee for doing the ballet plus a royalty per performance, but Balanchine would just do the ballet and receive only a royalty. To live, he did Broadway shows and worked at times with other companies. Because he wanted the company very badly, he sacrificed his personal needs to it. It wasn't until our first Ford Foundation grant in 1964 that George began to receive compensation. The grant not only stipulated that George was to receive a salary, but also that we commit a certain amount each year to new productions. That probably was the beginning of our stability.

Before that we had no fund-raising apparatus. The way money was raised was by Lincoln talking to a few friends and getting the specific contributions. When George needed money for a big production, he didn't come to me and ask whether we could afford it. I didn't have any veto power. He went to Lincoln, and Lincoln either raised the money and we did it, or he didn't raise the money and we didn't do it.

For a big production like *The Nutcracker* in February 1954, the expense was considerable and hard to figure. George wanted a huge Christmas tree such as he remembered from the old days at the Maryinsky, and he insisted on using children, which the Ballet Russe didn't do in their production. I think there were forty-two children in the first production we did, which was the same size ensemble as the adult company. The original production estimate provided by Lincoln to Baum was $40,000. It cost $80,000, in those days a lot of money, but when all the performances began selling out, it became a staple. By December of that same year we were doing a special *Nutcracker* season, and a tradition began.

I'm sure every ballet company is run differently. There's no formula. In our case it depended completely on the personalities of Lincoln and George. It ran according to the way they operated and the way they worked together. It doesn't happen very often that two major characters come together like that. When that happens, sparks fly. There was some sort of productive symbiosis between the two. I don't think Balanchine would have necessarily achieved what he did had there not been Lincoln. And certainly Lincoln would not have been able to develop the company had there not been Balanchine. Balanchine was the visible part of the theater, and Lincoln was behind the scenes, the catalyst.

There were many facets to Lincoln's character, and they all affected how he operated in the company. He was an art critic, he was an artist himself, a stained-glass maker, a poet. All sorts of things. I suppose you could say he was a Renaissance man, but not amateur or dillydallying. He certainly was an authority on art, on which he's written a number of books. He said he was the only person in the world he knew who had perfect taste. He said it not just once but often.

To the dancers, Balanchine was half father, half god, half choreographer; you would have to divide him into thirds or fourths, he was so many things to people. I never had that feeling of awe they had. I did have a feeling of how incredible he was. How could he keep doing one thing after another? You'd think he would run out of ideas, that he was finished, that there's nothing else left he can do. Then the next time he would do something completely different. He was an object of amazement.

Basically, it was Balanchine's company made possible for him by Lincoln. But Baum was a great support to both of them. They can give him credit for our being able to get started. A little story will show how Balanchine regarded him. Back in the days when Ballet Society was doing *The Triumph of Bacchus and Ariadne,* the Italian set designer Cagli gave Balanchine a Tarot reading. Balanchine asked him, "Am I ever going to have any money?" The cards said, "No, probably not, but that doesn't matter because there's a man who's going to be very helpful." Balanchine always swore that that man was Baum because it was around that time that Baum came into our lives.

Balanchine's gratitude to Baum was also evident when we had the big fight with Lincoln Center over the State Theater. Under the deal that was worked out by the Rockefellers—Nelson, who was then governor, and John, chairman of Lincoln Center—and other people for the city, the state was to pay for building the theater. But in order to justify the use of state money, the theater was to be the home of the City Center operating as a nonprofit enterprise devoted to presenting the best possible artistic performances for the people—not for the wealthy but for the people of New York. For the two years of the World's Fair, in the mid-sixties, the theater was to be run by Lincoln Center, but after the fair, the state was to hand the theater over to the city, and the city was to lease it to the City Center for the type of productions which they had been doing. Two years can be a long time. Before the two years were up, Lincoln Center had invented the Richard Rodgers Music Theater and promised that entity a home in the State Theater —which they really shouldn't have done because it was supposed to be handed over to the City Center. We at the City Center tried to compromise by offering the Music Theater a summer season, but it became clear that Lincoln Center didn't really want to hand the lease over to the City Center. They wanted to keep it and rent it a few weeks to the City Center. And they didn't want the opera there. They only wanted the ballet.

During these long and hard negotiations, we had a couple of meetings in my kitchen. One of these meetings was at the suggestion of Schuyler Chapin. He had just joined the staff of Lincoln Center as program director and was trying to make peace between the warring parties. He and Balanchine and I met in my kitchen. Schuyler was very nice and didn't hate us. At the end of our conversation, which was amicable, he suggested that we have another meeting and invite William Schuman. We agreed, and then I said, "Well, let's read *The Book of Changes* and see what the outlook is for this new thing." So we did, and it was funny because the reading was about being very careful because people were lying in ambush and indicating a situation you couldn't trust.

So we had our next meeting, and Schuman kept saying, "Oh, George, you and I are artists, we can talk to each other." He was trying to charm George. Everybody seemed to think that George didn't have a good sense of business. Just jolly him along, and he'll be all right. So Schuman finally came out and said: "George, we really want the New York City Ballet, but we really don't want the New York City Opera. Why do you feel so committed to the City Center?" And George said, "Of course I'm committed to the City Center, that's our home." And Schuman said: "But Lincoln Center could be your home. Lincoln Center could do for you what the City Center does." Balanchine then lost his temper and said: "Absolutely not. I trust Baum. We're not leaving the City Center. If the City Center doesn't get this theater, then we don't come." Then we went to *The Book of Changes* again, and it was very amusing.

Balanchine knew exactly what he was doing. He trusted Baum. Baum had saved us. Baum was the man in his Tarot reading. Which is not to say we conducted business in the way the Reagans ran the White House! We didn't consult astrologers. Our reading of *The Book of Changes* was a way of lightening up a rather tense meeting. But it was so apt, so good at describing this situation of mutual distrust.

So we won our fight and got the State Theater for the City Center. We worked wonders in the old City Center Theater, but it was hard. When the dancers made exits, they would run into the fly wall. As a matter of fact, Marie-Jeanne knocked herself out once making an exit; she went bang into the wall. It was not a proper theater. How we did *Nutcracker* there I'll never know, but we did it. Lincoln had always wanted Philip Johnson to design us a theater. He finally got it at Lincoln Center.

Over the years, Balanchine changed. In his professional career he went through periods and phases much as Picasso did. And as a person he was not stagnant. He was not the same man when he was seventy that he was when he was forty-five. His personal happiness was wrapped up in the well-being of the company and also in the careers of individual dancers. By turning dancers into more than they thought they could be and what he hoped they would be, he created them. That was his greatest pleasure, and that didn't change. He went through all his life being interested in and inspired by different dancers. Some provided inspiration longer than others, but there was always a succession. It was not just the marriages, but his interest in different dancers in the company and what they could do, and then working with their possibilities and choreographing for them.

But he was a most inconsistent person, even in his teaching. What he taught one day was not necessarily what he taught the following year. And the ballets changed, so there's no definitive version. Somebody will look at one company's version of, say, *The Four Temperaments* and say: "Oh, that's not right. They've changed the steps." They didn't change the steps, actually. They were doing a version that was done at a certain period. Balanchine changed the steps later, and the New York City Ballet is doing the latest version. The one that the other company does is closer to what we did in 1946.

And Balanchine respected a different approach. When Jerome Robbins joined the company, some tended to view it as a competition, but there was no way of comparing them. They were very different choreographers. They didn't work the same way, and they didn't produce the same sort of things. George was convinced that Jerry was the only choreographer besides himself who could be taken seriously. He didn't discount everybody else, but he thought Jerry was the principal person. Over the years he used Jerry as a dancer in his ballets, and he asked Jerry to help him choreograph the Monster sequence in *Firebird,* the battle in *The Nutcracker,* parts of *Jones Beach,* and, of course, *Pulcinella.* There was a close collaboration although they were very different. Jerry respected Balanchine, and Balanchine respected Jerry.

In an intuitive sort of way, Balanchine even understood the financial aspects of the company. When we were doing *The Figure in the Carpet,* an expensive production, we had a pool on who would come closest to what the final cost was going to be. Balanchine, myself, the staff members, and some of the dancers all paid a dollar into this pool. And who do you think won it? Balanchine. He didn't really know. He just had a feeling. He couldn't have said, "This much for costumes," or "The scenery is going to be this," or "The music costs are going to be that." He just had a sort of overall feeling.

I think few people have much understanding of what Balanchine was like. He wasn't somebody who was easy to know. He had different poses for different people and different groups. He had friends he talked politics to. He had musicians who shared his interest in music. And with dancers, that was a whole separate group of friendships. So any person who was only in one category can report only on one aspect.

For instance, his friendship with Nicolas Nabokov was completely different from his friendship with Stravinsky, even though both were musicians, both had composed for him, and both were Russian. His friendship with Nabokov was very deep, and he liked his music. He found in it exactly what he wanted for *Don Quixote.* But Balanchine kept changing things—he always fiddled with all of his ballets—and because Nicolas, as a close friend, was always there to write new music, the ballet was never really finished. They changed it every single year we did it. And the two agreed politically. All through the early years of the war, years when everybody was embracing the Soviet Union and helping the Russians, our dear friends and allies, Balanchine and Nabokov were staunchly anti-Communist. His friendship with Stravinsky, however, was completely outside politics.

Over the years, the way Balanchine looked at the company changed. In the beginning, it was a struggle, something to establish. In the end it was something that had reached a certain height, and he didn't envision it continuing beyond his participation. He didn't think of it as a permanent establishment, something that could go on year after year. It was something that happened in a certain period of time. It started, it grew, it developed, it reached the top, it's marvelous, there have never been better dancers, but it's not going to last forever.

At times, however, he acted as if *he* were going to last forever. And then toward the end he felt that he wasn't. When he began to feel there was a definite end in sight, his interest changed completely. He was not interested in preparing for the future of the company. He was not interested in naming a successor. Nor did he. Board members used to say, "Oh, George, have you ever thought of succession?" And he would say: "No, I don't think of succession. That has nothing to do with me. Besides, I enjoy life, and I'm going to live to be a hundred and forty-three, so why think about that now?" He didn't live to be a hundred and forty-three. But even if he had known that he would die before he was eighty, he still wouldn't have thought about succession.

People have observed that he was religious. I think he was always that way. I think it goes back to his early days in Russia, to his uncle who was a bishop or something. He loved the pageantry of the Church. He wasn't anybody who went to church every weekend, but he went on Easter.

Balanchine's worst time was at the beginning of his last illness, when his balance started to be affected. That really bothered him. He talked about it a lot. He said, "I put my foot here, and it ends there." I think it is so shocking that they never diagnosed his problem, not that they could have done anything, it turns out.

I don't think there is a definitive portrait of Balanchine. Everybody has a different view, a different perspective. Probably they are all true in certain ways and all lacking in certain ways. We have the ballets, of course, but I think it's true they may never be danced the way they were when he was doing them.

IGOR

YOUSKEVITCH

Born in Piryatin, Russia, in 1912, Igor Youskevitch was raised in
Belgrade and participated in the Olympic Games of 1932. Studying
dance with Xenia Grunt and Preobrajenska in Paris, Youskevitch
made his debut with Nijinska's company in 1934. He was a soloist
with the Ballet Russe de Monte Carlo from 1938 to 1943, dancing
in many ballets of Léonide Massine and Nijinska. He was in the
United States Navy during World War II. After the war Youskevitch
danced with Massine's Ballet Russe Highlights and joined Ballet
Theatre, where Balanchine made Theme and Variations for him
and Alicia Alonso. He also danced Balanchine's Apollo. Youskevitch appeared in the motion picture Invitation to the Dance
(1952). He retired from dancing in 1962. Youskevitch has taught

ballet in New York City, Massapequa, Long Island, and Austin,
Texas. He headed the dance department at the University of Texas for
many years and now heads the International Ballet Competition in
New York.

BALANCHINE TOLD ME ONCE THAT THE AUDIENCE WAS SUPPOSED TO LIKE MOVEMENT which is performed in inventive choreographic patterns. That's the goal of the Balanchine ballet, and one reason he shied away from depicting emotional involvements onstage. He felt these would distract the audience from enjoying the pure movement.

I asked him once about the second variation in *Apollo*. There was a movement with the hands, one in back, one in front. I tried to interpret it, and I asked him, "Is there any significance in this particular movement?" He said, "Oh, no. It's just the accent of the music." In *Serenade*'s ending I don't think he tried to create an emotional situation. In one of the productions of *Serenade* the men who pick up the girl and carry her away wore costumes resembling medieval uniforms, so you got the impression that something drastic was going to happen. He changed the costumes to get away from that.

When Balanchine choreographed *Theme and Variations* for me, we had arguments because he wanted me to do the part in a very abstract way. My idea leaned toward the romantic because the ballet was to convey a royal, imperial style, although with Balanchine's contemporary choreography. In order to convey that idea you have to indulge in something else besides performing steps. So I felt that I had to be much more romantic. We argued a little about it. I pointed out to him that if, during the dance, a girl falls into my arms, I cannot remain "abstract." I have to react somehow. Balanchine used to say very often that "Dance is woman." As a matter of fact, I agree with him in a way, because basically woman is born to dance, even if she is not a dancer. But art exists for both sexes; there must be equality.

After Balanchine worked for the Ballet Russe de Monte Carlo, we almost did a movie in Hollywood on Pavlova's life. He was engaged as the choreographer, and Tamara Toumanova was to play Pavlova. I was to play one of Pavlova's partners. We all met in Hollywood. The movie was never made, but we rehearsed for a good six weeks, having a very good time. I got well acquainted with Balanchine because we rehearsed a little and spent the rest of the time on the beach. Then we would go to his house and he would cook for us. We did not rehearse enough to have an idea of what the choreography would have been. Balanchine hung a rope in the studio, and Tamara did some pirouettes around it. Balanchine was trying different ideas.

Balanchine didn't like to argue. He had his idea. You had yours. There would be no real communication. He would say, "You have this idea, but why? Tell me." But Balanchine and I would argue because I felt that the ballet is one of the theatrical performing arts, and dance is only a method of interpretation. But, for Balanchine, dance was the thing in ballet. Even though we argued, and even though he was always asking me to be less romantic in *Theme and Variations,* later on I heard from other dancers who have danced the ballet that during rehearsals Balanchine would always say, "Oh, no, Igor did this, Igor did that." He used me as an example, even though he didn't like my interpretation!

If someone had asked Balanchine to describe his philosophy of dance, I don't think he would have been able to do it. He would have been handicapped to put into words his own philosophy. He was influenced by music, of course. That was his main source of inspiration. All mortals get inspired by the sound of the music, but Balanchine could be inspired by looking at the score, by the intricacy of the composition. That's what excited him, rather than the actual sound.

Because I was accustomed to dance classical roles and to modulate my dancing according to the subject and story, I had difficulty remembering the steps in *Apollo*. Balanchine never told me how to interpret the ballet. He never imposed in that way. He showed the steps. I fancy myself that I am sensitive to the choreographer. The second variation for *Apollo* is like a prayer to himself. It's "Oh, My Father" and so forth. But there is a middle part of the variation where the movement becomes quite abstract. That's where I had the trouble. To count and to have to remember which step followed where, with no emotional maturation to justify the steps—I always had trouble remembering them. If I didn't dance *Apollo* for some time I would go to Balanchine and say, "Please, remind me of this part of the variation. I have forgotten."

Balanchine changed a variation for me in *Theme and Variations*. Frankly, I did not like this variation for several reasons. It was not effective, it didn't do anything for me, and I don't think it would have done anything for the audience either. It was contemporary steps, small, nothing big. In addition to my not liking the variation, I felt it wasn't right for the ballet. So, in a diplomatic way, I talked to Balanchine and said, "You know, it feels not very comfortable. Would you consider rehearsing with me and changing?" So he said, "Well, all right, tonight we'll see what we can do." He came for the rehearsal. At that time John Kriza and I both rehearsed the ballet because Lucia Chase thought that Johnny would be able to dance it. So while Balanchine was standing at the mirror and thinking, we were fooling around in the back. One of us jumped around and did *rond de jambe*. Balanchine saw it in the mirror, turned around, and said, "I have a variation for you." He did it in five minutes, with the *rond de jambe*. I thought that he did well because most of the classical, old-style variations consist usually of three or four steps. To present an imperial ballet, it was stylistically proper to do so like that. And Balanchine's variation was quite successful. And I was comfortable with it.

Balanchine conducted a performance of *Theme and Variations* from the pit once. He conducted it very well. As a composer he did not do as well. When we were in Hollywood, Stravinsky lived there. Balanchine was a good friend of his, and I met him too. Russians celebrate their name day rather than their birthday, perhaps to avoid embarrassing questions. Balanchine, the pianist Kopeikine, and I decided that we should buy Stravinsky some Grand Marnier. Balanchine and Kopeikine sat at the piano and composed some music and then we put words in Russian to this music. We decided that, when we came to Stravinsky, Kopeikine would play it, and we would all sing it. We would present the bottle to him and he would be very pleased. It didn't happen that way. When we sang the song, Stravinsky got mad. He said, "Who in hell wrote this music?" For a few minutes he sat at the piano and tore this music to pieces. "This cannot be here, this must be *there*, this cannot be!" The whole composition was absolutely torn to pieces.

In his own works Balanchine was contemporary and forward-looking in his invention. In regard to classical ballet, he was just the opposite. He was at American Ballet Theatre when Lucia Chase decided to stage *Giselle.* Eugene Berman was supposed to do the new costumes and bring about the face lift. Balanchine advised us on certain scenes. One change he insisted on was to do the old Russian version of the ending of the second act. Instead of Giselle returning to her original grave, Albrecht would pick her up and bring her across the stage and deposit her in another grave. This grave was mechanical. When she was placed on it she would go down, grass would grow on top, and she would disappear. Dramatically, it didn't work at all. People laughed. I was looking for Giselle in the grass! It lasted, I think, one performance.

I also knew Balanchine's older version of the second act of *Swan Lake.* When I learned the second act, I did not know the full-length version. Only years later did I find out that the second act was done by Balanchine for Diaghilev. Balanchine shortened it at Diaghilev's request. I thought that Balanchine choreographed the version very well in the spirit of the ballet but without the old-fashioned pantomime.

Balanchine was the only choreographer I knew who was not interested in money. He didn't care about what he earned. He gave away his ballets for nothing. He would choreograph for nothing. He would give us a ballet to take to Argentina for nothing. This was very unusual among choreographers.

Balanchine was Georgian, exactly the same countryside Stalin came from. In a very mild way, he had that tendency of character. He liked to be in his own place and what he says goes. He would never lose his temper. He would not shout. He would not argue, but he liked everything to be done the way he wanted. In that sense I understood Felia Doubrovska's comment that you could not be chummy with Balanchine. He was a person you could not get too close to. He used to come to our apartment for Russian borscht and a little vodka, but we never got to feel "this is my friend."

JILLANA

Jillana (Jillana Zimmermann) was born in Hackensack, New Jersey, in 1934. She studied with Emily Hadley and then received a scholarship at the School of American Ballet. She joined Ballet Society in 1947 and became a charter member of the New York City Ballet in 1948. She became a principal dancer in 1955. Balanchine created ten roles for her. In 1957–58 she performed with American Ballet Theatre, then danced on Broadway in **Destry Rides Again** and returned to the New York City Ballet before retiring from the stage in 1967. She has been teaching for many years at the University of California at Irvine and at Dance Aspen. She conducts master classes and is writing a book on her years with Balanchine.

I Remember Balanchine

In 1947, when Mr. Balanchine asked me to join Ballet Society, I was twelve years old. When he taught at the School, everybody stood up a little bit straighter and pointed their toes a little bit harder. I was terrified of the staff at the front desk but never of Mr. Balanchine. He was always very kind, like a grandfather.

The first ballet I performed was the second movement of *Symphony in C.* I was the first little girl out in the *bourrées.* And I was so proud because I was out onstage all by myself, watching Leon Barzin, waiting for him to put up his baton and signal Go. After that I did *Serenade.* I considered myself very lucky to get into the company so young. There were older students who were not too pleased! I don't think there's ever been anyone taken in at that age.

I could pick up things quickly; that's why I got a lot of parts. Somebody would get sick, and Mr. Balanchine would look around and ask, "Anybody know it?" I would, and he would say, "Okay, do it." I would do it well enough so that he would let me continue. That's how I got to do the fourth movement of *Western Symphony.* For some reason, Tanaquil LeClercq wasn't able to do it. I was the first sister to run out and help the Prodigal Son over the fence. Mr. B. pinned on my costume.

Learning parts from Balanchine was always easy. I never had any problem figuring out what he wanted. It was so simple to follow what he did, even though he wasn't technically wonderful. He would just do it, and it was easy to pick it up. That was true the entire time I worked with him. He was so fast and knew exactly what you could do and what you couldn't do, what was right for your body, what was right for you. I never worked with anybody like that. I remember there were a couple of turns in *Swan Lake* I wasn't too comfortable doing. I've never been a turner. At one point I said, "Gee, Mr. B., I'm really uncomfortable with these turns." He said, "No, no, no, you can do them." He made me do them over and over, and I was finally able to do them right. But there was another part in which I felt uncomfortable, and I said, "You know, this feels really awkward." He said, "Yes, I'll change that for you." He knew the things you could accomplish if you worked on them, and he knew the things that might never feel comfortable. In *Liebeslieder Walzer* he would just do it, show it to us, and it would fit our bodies perfectly. I'm sure I would have had trouble doing some things he gave Melissa or Violette, but the things he gave Conrad Ludlow and me to do— well, it was us.

Other choreographers like Tudor were very particular about details, even with the *corps:* this finger has to be out here, you look this way, the head has to be that way, the eyes are looking this way. I also enjoyed working with Jerry Robbins. It just took him a little longer to choreograph anything. As far as I'm concerned there was nobody like Mr. Balanchine and probably never ever will be.

My fondest memories are of *Serenade.* I loved doing the Dark Angel. Even though there was no real story in it, I always had a story. I would make up different ones when I danced it, and I danced all the parts from top to bottom. I would make up stories about being in love with Nicky Magallanes and trying to get him away from whoever the other girl was, pulling and pushing. I made it into a love story for myself. I did that with a lot of ballets that didn't have stories. I could always feel something about them. They meant something to me. *Serenade* will always be my favorite. I think it is one ballet that never will be dated—never.

That goes for most of Mr. Balanchine's ballets. *Symphony in C,* for example —who can do anything like that now? And *The Four Temperaments*—can you believe how beautiful it is still? It was so different at the time they first did it. I was one of the Phlegmatic girls, and we all thought, "Gee, these are strange movements." But it is incredible to this day.

Balanchine not only understood each dancer's technical abilities but also which parts they would be good in. I think I was probably one of the ones who did a little bit more emoting than some of the others at the time. It's just in me to project. There's no way of stopping me from doing that. I loved *Nutcracker,* especially doing Dewdrop. I felt that was really dancing, even more than when I did the Sugar Plum Fairy. And I had a wonderful time as the Coquette in *La Sonnambula (Night Shadow).* There was a little bit of acting involved there, but since I was young, Mr. Balanchine explained that I was supposed to flirt like I wanted to have a boyfriend. But I sort of figured these roles out for myself! I don't think Balanchine ever gave roles to people he didn't feel could handle them.

In the early years New York City Ballet's ballerinas were all so varied. We didn't look like each other. Everybody had her own style. Maria Tallchief was so different from Tanny and from Patty Wilde. Today, the dancers are incredible technically, but I think they all look more or less alike. This would make it difficult to redo a ballet like *Don Quixote,* even if you could find a suitable successor to Suzanne Farrell.

For many reasons, I feel the time I was in the company was probably the best time to have been there. I get very upset these days when former dancers write, making Mr. Balanchine out to be some kind of villain. I have to read a little bit at a time, because I get so upset I can't go on. None of that sort of thing was true when I was there. I don't remember anything like that going on.

I recently got a letter from one of my students, a little girl, maybe twelve or thirteen years old. She's very talented. She probably has a chance to go on with her dancing, but her mother became so upset when she read a certain book that she won't let her child think about having dancing as a career. I tried to write back and tell her that the book doesn't describe how it really is or was. If the mother can't be straightened out, the little girl will probably just give it up and become a cheerleader. But I guess a good book won't sell as well as one that's got all this dirt and gossip in it.

When I write my book, nobody's going to buy it! I don't have anything bad to say.

I left New York City Ballet briefly in 1957 and 1958. I accepted an invitation from Lucia Chase to join American Ballet Theatre for a big European tour. After the tour I got into a Broadway show, "Destry Rides Again." I could only stand that for six months, and I wanted to rejoin the company. I went to Betty Cage and asked her, "Do you think Mr. Balanchine would let me come back?" She said, "Oh, I believe there is always that lighted candle in the window for you, Jill." Mr. B. always called me Jill, just Jill, never Jillana.

HUGO

FIORATO

Hugo Fiorato made his concert debut as a violinist at the age of six. He studied chamber music with Adolfo Betti. During the 1940s and 1950s he was concert master for Leopold Stokowski, Bruno Walter, George Szell, and Sir Thomas Beecham. He formed and for twenty-eight years played with the WQXR String Quartet. He has been guest conductor for the New York Philharmonic, the National Symphony Orchestra, and the Boston, Cleveland, Miami and Houston symphonies. With the New York City Ballet since its earliest days, he is principal conductor of New York City Ballet.

I Remember Balanchine

I FIND IT ALMOST IMPOSSIBLE TO DISCUSS BALANCHINE'S STYLE AS A CHOREOGRAPHER. If we take the works of Martha Graham or Fred Astaire from the beginning to the end, I think you're going to recognize them immediately. But Mr. B.'s career is more like that of Stravinsky, whose early scores—*The Firebird* and so on—are so completely different from those of his later period. I believe his genius stems from the fact that he was able to recognize the style of the composer he was working with, and then to make movement for that style that was so excitingly individual to watch. He always said, "The composer is my floor," and "Without the composer, what can I do?" When Balanchine did Ives he was a completely different person from the man who did *Agon.*

He had the faculty of not just interpreting the music or putting steps on top of the score. He added another dimension. It's as though he added contrapuntal rhythms, phrasing, lines, that made the score more attractive, interesting, and exciting, and clarified the intent of the composer. Balanchine added content that went with the music but was another part that became integral to that score. Who would listen to *Movements* of Stravinsky by itself? Not many people. But when you hear *Movements* and you *see Movements* through Balanchine's eyes and what he has added to the score, it becomes an exciting work. Or *Agon. Agon* is fabulous to hear when you watch his choreography.

Balanchine was something of a mystic. Often he would say, for instance, "I spoke to Tchaikovsky this morning, and he said he would help us." I remember when we first did *The Nutcracker,* at curtain time opening night none of the costumes for the second act had arrived from Karinska. It seemed as if we would have to end the performance at the intermission. But Balanchine said, "Don't worry. I spoke to Tchaikovsky and they'll be here." Sure enough, the costumes began drifting in. Dancers dressed in the hallways and rushed onstage.

From a conductor's point of view, Balanchine was a dream to work with. He didn't just insist on tempos, he knew what rubato was, and phrasing. He knew the character he wanted of the music. He never twisted the music to fit the dancing. He tried to the best of his ability, and his ability was superb, to keep the music as close as possible to what the composer intended in the way of tempo, feeling, and so on, and then he made the choreography fit the music. So I look upward always and say, "Thank you, Mr. B."

One time Balanchine conducted for us. We invited him to conduct *Symphony in C* at the City Center. The tempo went like fire. The dancers could hardly keep up with him. He knew, innately, what the tempo should be, probably better than anybody who ever lived. But when it came to doing it himself, he was so excited, so thrilled with having the orchestra, a whole new set of people to choreograph for! The dancers nearly went wild onstage. They began laughing. They couldn't help it. They just couldn't keep up with him. But it was marvelous. He conducted like an angel.

EDWARD

WILSON

Edward Wilson joined the School of American Ballet in 1949. He

was promoted to the professional Division at the School in 1951.

He has a Ph.D. from the University of California at Berkeley and

is curator of invertebrate paleontology at the Los Angeles County

Museum of Natural History.

I Remember Balanchine

BALANCHINE HAD TO HAVE ABSOLUTE CONTROL, COMPLETE CLOSURE. HE WANTED A very close relationship with women, a sort of Svengali relationship, so that he would run their lives and there would be no distractions. "Being a dancer is like being a nun," he said. Gelsey Kirkland said in her first book that he gave her amphetamines, and she either said or implied that he was occasionally snapping at her ass for sex. I don't believe either. The Balanchine I knew wouldn't do that kind of thing. He didn't chase men and he didn't chase women at that time, as far as anybody knew. Marie-Jeanne was exactly the physical type he wanted in the 1940s. She had long legs and beautiful feet, like two big phalluses. He wanted her badly and she was good in all of his ballets. She left him a couple of times, and he kept taking her back.

Balanchine was Russian. If Russians find life boring they do something to make it interesting, even something catastrophic—anything but boredom. Burn a house down, it doesn't matter what. Wonderful people—but. He was almost like a god. After he corrected you in class, I don't think you ever made that mistake again. Sometimes when the pianist wouldn't show up to play for class, Mr. B. himself would accompany us. For complicated combinations he would play simple tunes like "Three Blind Mice." He had a fine sense of humor; he didn't laugh out loud so much but he would smile; everybody understood what was going on. Many of his ballets were like that too. They were ballyhooed as being fancy, world-shaking premieres and then he would put on this simple little ballet. It amused him. He was always having fun with people and with audiences too.

There were a lot of people who worked much too hard for him. When I was in the company there was a very good technician named Joey Frank from Texas, who could do everything but was sort of a little butterball. He was dying to get into the company. Mr. Balanchine would keep telling him to try something, to accomplish something else. Then when he would manage to do it, Balanchine would say, "Well, if only you'll . . ." Finally it was *entrechats dix:* "If you can learn to do *entrechats dix,* I'll take you, Joey." And so Joey did learn to do *entrechats dix,* but he never got into the New York City Ballet. Balanchine never had any intention of taking him.

Mr. B. used to say to the girls, "I think you're getting a little fat." And they would tell him, "I'm on a diet." And he would say, "Don't do diet. Don't eat anything." So they didn't. Those poor girls, they missed menopause, they missed breasts. If they gained too much weight he took them out of the company, but on the other hand, audiences don't want to go and see a lot of fat women bouncing around on the stage. In order to see legs work, you can't have those big hammy thighs.

Maria Tallchief was a superb woman. She had bad feet and not particularly good legs, but she was an incredible technician. She was lots of fun. In

Firebird, she had to do a diagonal across the stage, turns in *attitude en dehors* backward—difficult. It was always stunning because she had a little cap on top of her head with sequins in it, and they spun out when she turned. She usually did two turns, but on the last sequence in an early performance she did three. You'd think normally that the audience doesn't distinguish between two and three, but one of the classic gasps went through the house. Balanchine asked her afterward what had happened and she told him, "I forgot whether I did one or two so I just did another one." She was such a worker and had such drive. Once, when I was at a dinner party with her, there was a lull in the conversation and she said, "Let's play Murder. I'll be the murderer." That's pretty much the way she ran her life.

Balanchine called me quietly into the office from a classroom one day and said, "We'd like to put you in the company." I was seventeen years old and in a daze. I left in a few weeks and went back to school. I had decided to give up dancing.

Ballet was a very interesting business, but I'm glad I'm out of it. I don't recommend it to anybody. Sometimes I think I would have been better off if I'd spent my time at the Harvard Business School. On the other hand, it certainly was a time in which I met marvelous people. I'm very grateful to Mr. B. for taking me in the company.

WILLIAM
WESLOW

A leading soloist at Ballet Theatre and the New York City Ballet, William Weslow danced for television and on Broadway. He was born in Seattle in 1925. His mother was a Ziegfeld dancer. He studied with Mary Ann Wells, Edward Caton, Anatole Vilzak, Vera Nemtchinova, and at the School of American Ballet with Balanchine, Oboukhoff, and others. He danced in Annie Get Your Gun, Call Me Madam, *and* Wonderful Town *before joining Ballet Theatre and subsequently Balanchine. Working first as a physical therapist with Alicia Alonso and Edward Villella, he has become famous as "masseur to the stars."*

I Remember Balanchine

MY FIRST REAL CONTACT WITH BALANCHINE WAS AT BALLET THEATRE IN 1950, IN Chicago, where his wife, the great Maria Tallchief, was dancing with the company for a time. I was in the corps de ballet. In the finale of Balanchine's *Theme and Variations,* the Polonaise, the boys had to cross the stage in big leaps to the sound of crashing cymbals. We cleared a path for Maria to come down to the footlights, or we were supposed to. Balanchine was watching a rehearsal. I had never danced the ballet before. Balanchine suddenly said, "Stop, stop. You—boy." Me, he meant. He was doing his nose mannerisms as he spoke to me, sniffing away. I was quick to pick up any sort of mannerism. "Boy—you. You must go up. And you go tremendously up. I know you have good elevation, but you have to go up and get *out of the way* fast, you see." Watching his nose, I began imitating him unconsciously. He said, "And don't do this nose. I do this nose. You *dance.*" He pushed me about eight feet, and I did what he wanted. Or so I thought. He said, "Come here. You, I want to tell you. You have to go up in jump and *out* and *away.* You can't be in the way, principal come in, and you're *in the way.*" There I was, going up in the air, and by the time I came down I was blocking Maria, who was coming down to the front. You don't block Maria's way. If you do, you've got a tomahawk in the middle of your forehead. I say that with admiration, because Maria was the greatest Balanchine dancer. I adored her.

That was my first part in a Balanchine ballet, but I knew his work. I saw Tallchief do *Firebird.* I loved the Balanchine ballets. I loved the way the company danced them. The feet were fantastic, and there wasn't all this posing and limpy arm movements. There were fast arm movements, crisp and peppy. The Balanchine arms were like a beautiful, machinelike mechanism. When I joined the company in 1958, Balanchine said, "Arms must be mechanical, must be perfect, must be across body, lots of movement, but movement must stop." The movement doesn't stop anymore. In many of his ballets today, the dancers keep moving their arms all the time. That is not Balanchine at all; he disliked that intensely. He would say, "You have to stop. You know, there is time to keep arms moving but then you must stop." That's the beautiful look of Balanchine. And that's what I don't see anymore.

I was taught by Balanchine to do *entrechat six* to *demi-pointe.* "And never the heels went down." Why can't you put the heels down? "Because you don't want to hear the noise of heel so you must strengthen the Achilles tendon. When you do *demi-pointe,* it get nice and strong. It will hurt for a few weeks. After that you will be much better." This also, he said, would help us walk the way he wanted, never flatfooted but on the ball of the foot. I found he was right. My Achilles tendon through the years with Balanchine did foreshorten, but I could do his work very well. I could move very quickly and quietly. On pointe it's a little more difficult, but the girls always tried to do what he wanted. With men it's easier because they're on half pointe. That is the look that he wanted. He didn't want any noise. He hated rosin, which caused a lot of squeaking.

Balanchine wasn't teaching much class in those days, probably because of Tanaquil LeClerq's illness. He was very devoted and wanted to be with her. When I joined the company, he didn't go on the big six-month tour of Japan and Australia because of Tanny. Later, when he began teaching, he didn't want to teach men. He only wanted to teach women, and he made it very plain to us by giving us *piqués* and *chainés,* all girls' steps and girls' arm movements. We all said, "Oh, my God, what is this?" He said, "We'll have men teach men, and I will only teach woman. Unless you want to suffer coming into my class, which I don't think you want to do. Only want woman, and you go with men classes. So I will do only what I want. Besides, men are no good. Awful bastards. Terrible. Woman is dance. Man is nothing. Only partner." He said that to me several times. Now, whether he was chiding me or not, I don't know, but I think he really meant it.

But he did wonderful roles for men! They were fabulous roles, but he really cared about the women. I asked him one time, "Who is your favorite male dancer?" Mr. B. said, "None, none. There has never been a male dancer that's ever been my favorite because I never think that men could dance well. It's only woman. Now man can take up space when woman is not onstage. But no, I don't have a favorite dancer. I've never liked the male dancer. Maybe one. Lifar—beautiful, almost like woman. And so I liked him because he was like woman. And maybe that's why I think he is at the time great dancer. He very pretty, very girly, you know, beautiful legs and feet and poses. Lots of poses. Like I do with girls. I used to pose him."

At that time we had a lot of conversations, arguments, and good talk. Many people said, "Oh, we are so afraid of him, we couldn't talk to him." I used to. He was wonderful and warm in those days. He used to coach us and touch us and it was absolutely fantastic with Balanchine. You felt he was like a father. He would touch you and say, "Now, you do this, do that, you have to do arabesque from here, not just cold arabesque, but from here." "From the heart?" I asked. "Not from heart," he said. "From soul. From soul comes—arabesque. You have to pose, you have to stretch. And arms. You have to go and you run. You run to her and you grab her and you pull her and you take her away." This was his favorite expression: "You've got to push her, take her away. You have to lift her and you have to go marvelous. You have to go way away and then come back. You let woman go because she is star. You just partner. You cavalier. But you have to let her do everything."

He used to partner me. I didn't have a great extension, and he used to hurt my legs, I would be trying so hard. He would take me around in arabesque because he said I wasn't doing it right with Patricia Neary. I said, "Well, it's easier to partner Pat because she is on pointe." He said, "No, it's easier to do Pat because she is a woman, and you're a man. It's very difficult to partner man. So you have to learn to partner woman, and when you partner woman, then you dance better." Of course, I never understood that at all. Occasionally, he would run and grab me. When we were doing *The Seven Deadly Sins,* he used me as a body to throw because I could hold myself well. Allegra Kent was supposed to do it, but when we threw Allegra she would crash onto the floor sixteen feet away. The boys couldn't catch her, so he thought, "Well, we'll throw Bill because he can stay together longer." Allegra's arms used to go, and she was very brave about it. She had bruises all over. So they threw me. I told the boys, "If you don't catch me, I'll slug you." Balanchine suggested, "Maybe closer than twenty feet—maybe ten to start." I said, "Thank you, Mr. B." So he would throw me: dum da dum da dum— "Throw!"—dum back—dum "Throw!"—bom bom bom. And then Allegra said, "Well, let me try it now. It's closer. I'm sure they won't drop me." So he said, "But go farther away for Allegra, because she's lighter, you see." So they went twenty feet away and, boom, she hit the floor again. She got up and said, "Let's try it again." And Balanchine would say, "No, we have to get closer now." They'd close in, so finally we caught her and threw her like twenty feet away. It was like a barrel roll sideways, quite amazing.

This was the period when Balanchine was so mad about Allegra, as well he should have been. He said she was a Brigitte Bardot, a great ballerina. He wanted to marry her, I believe. And of course Allegra fought it like mad. Every time he'd come near and grab her to show her a step, she'd go "Ooh!" and try to get away. Of course, she couldn't and didn't want to really, but she didn't want this marriage possibility to be interjected into all the wonderful steps he'd be doing for her. All the ballerinas who came later—Karin von Aroldingen and Suzanne Farrell—all picked up the mannerisms of Allegra, except that Farrell overdid them. But Allegra had just enough mannerisms to make her look very special. Lotte Lenya adored Allegra Kent in *Seven Deadly Sins.* Lenya said to me, "Oh, she is so beautiful. She will be the great ballerina if she only listens to Balanchine and doesn't get married and go off and have children."

Working with Balanchine on new choreography was a glorious thing. The only bad thing about it was that he sometimes put you down before you started. He would say, "You soloists up front, nothing special, no big part. You are going to be more or less like corps de ballet." Of course, we'd go "Ohhh." But then we would get so enamored of the steps he would give us that we'd forget. But he would put you down. That was his sadistic thing. He did that quite often as time went by, but not earlier so much. He would just take us by the hand and start to choreograph. He would always take the boy or the girl by the hand as he was thinking. He'd do a few nose twitches, lead you to the center, the music would start, and he would show you the steps. It would all come out and just flow.

In my view Tallchief was the greatest Balanchine ballerina, and I've seen them all since the 1950s. She was completely devoted to Balanchine at a time when her physical prowess was perfect. She was in the Ballet Russe de Monte Carlo, and when he found her there he just took her. She did everything he wanted her to do. Her arms were fantastic. She had musicality, one of the dancers with the greatest. Kopeikine, the Russian who played piano, a close friend of Balanchine, said that Maria could have been a great pianist had she not been a great dancer. Maria had a superb technique. She could *chaîné* and pirouette. She had great star quality. When she came onstage, it would light up. Anyone else would pale before her. She worked hard. After performances Balanchine would take her on the stage with the stage light and go over and over things. After *Pas de Dix* she would be soaking wet in her costume. One time he made her do *grand jeté en pointe.* He said, "No, make it triumphant." She did. Again and again. She said, "George, I'm awfully tired. *En pointe* is terribly hard on my feet and everything." He said, "Two more times." Which she did, for strength. She did whatever he said. This is why she was a great dancer. She never said no to him, like Gelsey Kirkland and others who said, "No, I don't want to do that." Tallchief was a complete Balanchine dancer.

In my early days at the New York City Ballet everyone sort of admired everyone else. We were all trying to do the roles the way Balanchine wanted —the same arms, the same footwork, conveying the same feeling. Balanchine said to me, "Everyone has to do the same arms. But each person has a different personality, so will not look the same. It's only the people who cannot do the steps I have to change for. So I change; I don't want to, but I do. There's nothing impossible. I will do other steps. I have millions of steps to give them. But I would like the same arms, the same steps because each dancer it will look different on. The same steps will look different on a different personality." He didn't want a lot of personality. He called it "ballerina mannerisms" later. He and I got into a big argument about that about Alonso and Alicia Markova. He never brought up Tallchief. One time I said, "You never say anything bad about Maria." He said, "I wouldn't dare. She'd kill me with a tomahawk. She is marvelous dancer."

I once showed Balanchine a picture of Alonso and me from *The Sleeping Beauty* in our Ballet Theatre days. I partnered her in the grand pas de deux. In the photograph I showed him she's in attitude with the leg up very high. Balanchine looked at it but didn't have his glasses on. He said, "Ah, is my dancer? Yes? Leg to arm. Yes. Who is that?" I said, "Alicia Alonso." "Oh, God, no, awful, never." I said, "What do you mean, never? You just told me how wonderful it was." "I didn't have glasses." I said, "Aha. See? You saw the line, she's perfect. Maybe she's a little heavy but that beautiful Balanchine line is there." He stormed off. He hated any ballerina he didn't have anything to do with. He loathed Margot Fonteyn. He said, "No arms, no legs, no feet, and hands like spatulas. She has no extension, nothing. Just creature with big smile come out on stage and everyone stands up and applauds. I don't know why. She doesn't do anything."

I said, "She doesn't have to do anything, Mr. B., she's so fabulous. She has a great personality onstage, a great warmth, she has great balance." Balanchine said, "Ah, but balance. Look at me. I can do balance." And he put his hand on my shoulder and balanced. "You see, I am Margot Fonteyn, but hands better." He showed me his hands. He hated her because he never had anything to do with her. He adored the other one, the redhead, Moira Shearer.

Balanchine loved the smell of women. He said, "When they get heated up, to put nose in certain places when they do exercise—*développé à la seconde* especially—odor wafts out and it's natural, it's natural. This I like. Men, they all smell the same. I don't know one from the next. But woman I like. I don't like perfume. Perfume masks everything. Masks dance, masks feeling, masks aroma, which is part of dance." He hated those rubber pants that some of the women used to wear at rehearsals or in class. He couldn't see if the legs were turned out, and it kept his nose away, too.

Balanchine was a wonderful person to work with. He used to touch a lot. He used to coach a lot. You felt that he wanted you, even the men, to do the best. He was upset with Edward Villella because Villella never took his class. This always was a thorn in his side, so he got back at Villella several times. One time was the opening night in London when Villella was supposed to dance the *Tchaikovsky Pas de Deux*. Balanchine changed it to what he called the "wop" number, *Tarantella*. Eddie didn't want to do *Tarantella*. It's a plaything, not a grand tour de force. Balanchine said, "We cannot—the orchestra cannot play that fast." So Villella did *Tarantella*. He would have been a sensation in *Tchaikovsky*, and Balanchine knew it. Balanchine used to harbor these grudges and then let them out at the most important times in a dancer's existence, at a crucial performance, like a London premiere. He did that to Villella, who only studied with Stanley Williams.

With Jacques d'Amboise, there was never any problem. Jacques worked with Balanchine and took his class. He was a fabulous dancer, a magnificent

Apollo. He had the beautiful body, and he had the Balanchine arms and the Balanchine look and the Balanchine mystique onstage. He had that marvelous presence. They really should bring back *Apollo* complete with Leto giving birth. The whole ballet should be brought back. Jacques was unforgettable when he turned and unwound the swaddling cloth and struggled to be born. Balanchine, I'm afraid, cut that out because he didn't want Baryshnikov to do the wild pirouettes at the beginning and create a sensation. Instinctively, I feel that, and a lot of other dancers feel the same. He wanted to cut it so that Baryshnikov wouldn't be the great star dancer at the New York City Ballet. Baryshnikov didn't get to show off at all with Balanchine, he wasn't the great dancer at all in the New York City Ballet. Every time Baryshnikov would do one of Villella's roles, Balanchine would say, "No, don't do great leap here, don't do that. We'll give you something simple, because you are a wonderful dancer. You don't have to do the bravura stuff. Just do something low, something simple." Baryshnikov would have to do it, and it would kill him. Balanchine kept saying, "Don't do this leap. Don't do that. Villella does this, we'll do something else." That's why *Prodigal Son* was such a disaster, I thought, on television. Baryshnikov had to wear that long cape that kept getting twisted in his legs. He was covered in the front. He has a beautiful body, but on television it didn't look like he had a body at all. He looked like a calf in a rainstorm. It just killed the whole thing. Balanchine knew that. He destroyed the whole thing.

I always wanted to see Jacques d'Amboise do *Prodigal Son.* I thought he would be magnificent and said so. But Balanchine said, "No, he's too big." Well, Balanchine had Gloria Govrin, who would make Jacques look like a pimple on an elephant's ass. But Balanchine always wanted a man to be small and subservient. "Man must be subservient. Is nothing. Is rotten. Woman is everything. Puts foot up. Shits on him. Pisses on him. Nothing. No. Get away. That's what he be with woman, who is domineering force," he used to say. "She has to be domineering. Has to be tall. Long legs, beautiful feet." Jillana was very good in the role of the Siren in *Prodigal Son.* Yvonne Mounsey was fabulous too.

Balanchine was almost never cantankerous and difficult, only when he had a bad day or something displeased him. But he could be mean. He got Erik Bruhn out of the company, having asked him in! Erik was a great star when he came. Balanchine hated his soul. He wanted to put him down like he did Baryshnikov. He did things to Erik like quickening the tempo. What made Erik leave the company was the tempo for his *entrechats six* in the Prince's variation in *Swan Lake.* Balanchine came with Robert Irving and said to Erik, "No, no, too slow. Must be fast. You may be star in Denmark, dear, but this is my company. We all must dance fast here, and we don't want applause here to ruin sound of music." Irving said, "Well, George, he wasn't doing it very slow." "No, must be fast." Before the performance Erik told Irving, "I can't do it his way; please do it my way." Balanchine was in the wings and told him: "I'll be here in the wings, and you can also be replaced, Irving. Remember, it's my company and my tempo, and I don't like this Danish dancer here being a big star; everyone's a star in my company. He's nothing special. He's in my company to dance, to learn my ballets." Erik was in tears. So the time came for the *entrechats six,* and of course Erik did them slow. He did a slow *entrechats six* against the tempi. The tempo for the male variation in *Swan Lake* should be elegant, I feel, and there should be time for the steps, but not slow like the Russians in the Bolshoi or the Kirov. Erik Bruhn always used to dance wonderfully and musically. He never ever slowed the tempo beyond what it should be. But Balanchine got at him, and he left the company. He could not take that buffeting of Balanchine's. Balanchine was clearly jealous of him for some reason. He could do that to dancers.

With Suzanne Farrell, however, he let her do anything she wanted. I asked him one day, "Mr. B., why is she not wearing any makeup?" He said, "Well, you know, she is very pale and very beautiful, and she wants to do that." I said, "She has all these mannerisms. You didn't give her these mannerisms. She's developed them from Allegra Kent." He said, "Well, yes, she's doing too much but, you see, if she does too much and does all these awful mannerisms, she'll never be able to leave me. No company will want her." Farrell did leave, of course, and she was wanted elsewhere very much. Years later, when she came back from Béjart, she danced better than I've ever seen her dance in her life. With Béjart, she had to wear makeup. She was very thin. When she came back, I said, "My God"—I saw her in the street and I said, "You look beautiful. But watch out, Balanchine is going to get back at you for marrying Paul Mejia. I'll tell you how he's going to do it—he's going to say you're too thin!" And exactly three or four weeks later she was heavier. I saw her on the street again, and she said, "Well, I have to do what he said, and I *was* too thin." I said, "Aha, you see, he's punishing you!"

Some people think Farrell was the greatest love of his life. That isn't true at all. He wanted to marry so many! Mary Ellen Moylan was a dancer who'd have put Farrell to shame in body, technique, and beauty onstage. Diana Adams had a gorgeous body for dance, beautiful feet and legs. She was tall and long. She was his idea of perfection, as Moylan was. Diana had more or less straight legs. She didn't have the tremendous hyperextension that Moylan had in the knee. Balanchine told Moylan not to put the legs together and not to put them apart in first position so the knees would bow. He said, "Bend your leg enough so that it looks straight." She used to practice for hours. She was a beautiful dancer. She should have married Balanchine. She'd have been one of the great dancers of the world if she had had his coaching, as Maria Tallchief had. Maria had his coaching for so long a time. That's why she was the best.

Balanchine was really miserable when these affairs would break up. He'd go into a real black funk, pout and walk up and down the corridors, go into his office, and you'd hear dark music from his piano. When he lost his finger, that was a terrible tragedy. He almost lost his mind when he lost that finger. It was an accident with the power lawn mower at his place in Connecticut. Ronnie Bates was up there that day and told me about it. He was mowing the lawn, and Balanchine said, "Oh, how does it work?" Ronnie said, "Now look—there's a big blade going around and there's a hole in there, but don't put your hand anywhere near this hole." Evidently Balanchine didn't know the machine was on. He said, "Oh, this hole?" And it went brrr. "Oh! Oh!" Ronnie grabbed his hand, and of course the finger was just a shambles. He tied the finger up and got Balanchine to the hospital. Ronnie said, "I don't know why he put his finger in there when I'd just told him not to." When I heard about this, I was deeply distressed. Balanchine was a great pianist and choreographer. He was very vain about his hands. He had beautiful hands. He went into a funk, and no one could get near him or talk to him. That was the terrible finger episode. Earlier, he had lost a lung. He couldn't marry Suzanne Farrell. He couldn't marry Allegra Kent. Several terrible things happened to him. That terrible death in the hospital, that lingering, with all those awful tubes, for weeks. He got punished severely for things in his life he didn't do well. I think we all get punished.

I've been punished. My terrible punishment was having to leave New York City Ballet, being thrown out when I loved it so much. I loved dancing. I had been there fourteen years. One day when I was watching rehearsal out front, Eddie Bigelow came to me and said, "Well, it's time you left the company, isn't it? Isn't there something else to do?" I was flabbergasted. And I said, "What do you mean?" He said, "It's time. Balanchine wants you out of the company. You're old, and you don't do too many roles, and it's time for you to go." I went to Betty Cage. She evidently hadn't heard about it. She said, "I'll arrange for you to talk to Balanchine." I talked to him a week later in his office. Barbara Horgan was there at another desk. I said, "You know, I'd like to stay at least six months longer to the end of the season." And he said, "Well, we don't want you to go to Russia." I told him I wanted to do character parts. He said, "You're too old. You have to leave company. We only want young, pretty dancers here. Old dancers—you see, when they get old they should just go away and die. This is what they should do, die. Because you're not pretty. No youth. We want youth in company. Besides, dear, you're not going to commit suicide, are you?" And I said, "To please you, no, I wouldn't, Mr. Balanchine." He said, "Well, is anything more to talk about? Six months, and then you go. Yes?" And that was that. He didn't say, "You have been a good dancer"—or anything. It was just, "Go away. Go away." I was close to tears. It was a terrible blow because I adored the company. But it wasn't as bad as for some of the other dancers —soloists—who were sent a pink slip through the mail. That is even worse. But of course I could not understand. I hadn't failed to do anything that he wanted me to do. There was no immediate cause, no scene, no screaming and yelling. I was just "too old."

I was so angry. My last evening's performance was in *Don Quixote.* Balanchine was doing the Don. There's a part where you hit him on the thigh with a sword. The Don didn't know where he was, and I was supposed to jump on him and make a big gesture of defiance on top of him. The Don is submissive to the armored men with swords. I was still so angry with the way Balanchine had thrown me out that when I saw his open thigh I hauled back with my big sword and hit him with all my might. "Unnnnn," Balanchine said. He staggered around and then everything was fine and the ballet continued. He had a mark on his thigh for three weeks to remember me by. He said after the performance, "My God, you hit me so hard, you almost broke my leg." I said, "I'm terribly sorry. You were in the wrong place."

PATRICIA
WILDE

Born in Ottawa in 1928, Patricia Wilde studied with Gwendolyn Osborne in Ottawa and with Dorothie Littlefield in Philadelphia before training at the School of American Ballet. She danced with De Cuevas's Ballet International (1944–45), Ballet Russe de Monte Carlo (1945–49,) the Metropolitan Ballet (1949–50), and the Ballet de Paris in 1950. She joined New York City Ballet in 1950. Wilde created nineteen Balanchine roles and danced the repertory for fifteen years. She left the company in 1965 and became principal of the Harkness School of Ballet from 1965 to 1967. She joined the faculty of the American Ballet Theatre School in 1969, was ballet mistress of American Ballet Theatre from 1970 to 1982 and director of its school, 1979–82. She is artistic director of Pittsburgh Ballet Theater.

I FIRST WORKED WITH MR. B. WHEN HE TOOK A GROUP TO MEXICO CITY IN THE summer of 1945. He had a commitment at the Palacio de Bellas Artes for us to do a couple of performances. The dancers he took included Marie-Jeanne, Nicholas Magallanes, Bill Dollar, and Yvonne Patterson, with a group from the School as well. We did *Apollo, Les Sylphides,* and William Dollar's *Constantia.* I remember getting sick—like everyone does in Mexico—and waking up and seeing Mr. B. sitting right beside me, holding my hand and saying, "You're going to be all right." We were all in apartments in one building. He really lived right with us, overseeing that we were getting the right food.

Marie-Jeanne was a terrific dancer. She was not very disciplined, but she was wonderful and a great help to me. She was always coaching me on the side—all through the Ballet Russe period, too. Nicky Magallanes was wonderful. How Mr. B. worked! It was like two months of every day working on *Apollo* with Nicky. I don't know what Mr. B. had to say about it, but I think he was really pleased with Nicky. Nicky worked hard; Mr. B. liked it when somebody had to really work at something that wasn't natural for him.

Before working with Balanchine, I had seen his *Danses Concertantes* with Danilova and Franklin. That ballet was absolutely charming. I remember Mr. B. making up a cute little song for Choura, so that she would get her rhythm right. It was to the tune of "Marietta" : "Marietta, da *di* di *di* di"—something like "If you do it right, you can't go wrong." Danilova could be really playful, very elegant, but also very French.

Mr. B. choreographed *Night Shadow* while we were on tour. He would take, for example, the four girls who were doing a Hoop Dance in the divertissement and rehearse after a performance. It was like real circus performers. We had funny pink bustled costumes and long yellow wigs that came right down to our rear ends. Another time he would take Nora, my sister, and Edwina Fontaine and Herby Bliss and Nikita Talin for the little Shepherds' Dance. And then, of course, he had to put them all together. I remember Balanchine in Houston at Christmastime. He loved get-togethers. Four or five of us would get together and take a suite so we'd have parties all the time, and of course he loved that. He'd entertain and tell stories and cook. It was a family time. Or he would come to us, to somebody's place right after the theater, and then we'd all go to somebody else's place the next night.

I stayed with the Ballet Russe for one year after Balanchine left. I was there four years—1945 to 1949. We did *Concerto Barocco* everywhere in those one-night stands all across America. Audiences loved it. On the road we also did *Ballet Imperial* and *Night Shadow.* They liked the Balanchine programs, including *Bourgeois Gentilhomme* (1944). There was a wonderful pas de sept in that ballet. Mary Ellen Moylan had done it first, and then Maria Tallchief. It was in the repertory for a long time. It went very well on the road. And there was *Serenade,* another Balanchine ballet we did constantly. That version was primarily for one ballerina, usually Ruthanna Boris or Marie-Jeanne, when she was there. I had a little solo part in Balanchine's *Baiser de la Fée,* a peasant dance. Choura was the Bride, and Tallchief was the Fairy. It was one of Tallchief's best parts. We didn't do a full Balanchine evening that often, but we did do them, in Houston and in some of the bigger cities. But practically any program that we did would have one or two Balanchine works on it.

Balanchine and Danilova did a three-act version of *Raymonda* in 1946. I had a solo in the big waltz in Act I, I did a big dance with Leon Danielian in the second act, and then in the third act, Leon, Gerty Tyven, and I had a fast *pas de trois.* Everybody was in *Raymonda*—Tallchief, Boris, everyone. I remember that it was quite successful, and of course it was a major production.

At that time I wanted to quit and study. I had been touring so constantly that I really wanted to work on my technique and improve in basic ways. So I went to Europe, where I wanted to just study for a year. I'd been saving up my money. My sister Nora was with Roland Petit's Ballets de Paris at that time. So I went over, and Roland asked me to guest with him. I did the Blue Girl in *Beau Danube.* His company was coming to the States, and he asked me to come with him, and I thought, "Oh, they're going to be a real flop, I'm not going to New York with them." But Broadway loved his company. I didn't go. I wanted to stay in Europe.

Then the Metropolitan Ballet asked me to join. I did *Swan Lake,* Act II, and ballets by Andrée Howard. When that company went down the drain I returned to Paris. Mr. B. saw Nora, my sister, in New York and said, "Where is Pat? Tell her I want to see her." He went to London to stage *Ballet Imperial* in March 1950 and I went over to see him. I was in the crush bar at Covent Garden with him. He said, "Well, Pat, you know I want you to come back and join my company." I said, "Oh, Mr. B., I love Europe, I'd really love to stay here." He said, "Well, yes, it's very nice in Europe, but we are coming to London, so come back and join my company. If you don't like it after we are in London, you stay here." So I came back, joined the company, and rehearsed. And my opening with the company was Covent Garden.

Madame Tamara Karsavina had a big reception at a hotel for the company, a party given by the Royal Academy of Dancing. Karsavina was absolutely charming. At this gathering some of the dancers said to me, "Oh, did Mr. B. find you?" I went looking for him. Finally I found him, and I said, "Mr. B., you were looking for me?" "Oh, yes. You know, Tanny had to go and have a corn removed from her foot, it's really infected so you do *Symphonie Concertante* tonight." I said, *"What?"* By this time it was about five o'clock, and the performances were at 7:30 P.M. I had never had a rehearsal, never done the piece. Balanchine said, "Lew Christensen will come to the theater, Todd Bolender will come."

I just grabbed my things and ran for a taxi, ran to the theater, slapped some makeup on, and never thought of saying, "I can't do it, Mr. B. It's impossible." So we get out there and go through the beginning and luckily it's Maria does one thing, and I was the second voice. So I just reversed what she did. We never got through the whole ballet in the rehearsal. During the performance, Todd would say, "Now, *piqué arabesque* on your left," and then they would turn me. "Okay, now change to attitude." They talked me through the whole performance. No fool would ever do it now. Mr. B. said, "I'm the only one who'll know if you make a mistake or not." This was not the first performance of the Mozart in London! Balanchine loved to do that to me.

Later at City Center I was cast for Sanguinic in *The Four Temperaments,* but I had never done it or had a rehearsal with Nicky Magallanes. Balanchine said that he would do a rehearsal with us. Nicky and Kolya Kopeikine and I were on the City Center stage waiting for Mr. B., and he never turned up. Nicky said, "Well, you'll just have to refuse to do it. This is impossible. He can't do that to you." Finally, a half hour before curtain, Mr. B. turns up. I said, "Mr. B., I can't do it." He said, "Yes, yes, you can do it. You'll be all right." I said, "But the music, I'm not sure that I'll be on the music." He said, "You know, you do it like it's a rehearsal tonight. It doesn't matter. You'll be fine. Nobody will know except me whether you're right or wrong. You'll be all right." He loved to send me out scared to death, see what you can do under fire. And then he would come back afterward: "You see? It went fine."

The London reviews were not that great in 1950 but the audience at Covent Garden was wonderful. Those fans in the gallery were informed. Balanchine seemed to be very happy in London. He was delighted to have his company there, and I don't think that he bothered really about the reviews. I think he was just interested in how we were dancing and that we were able to dance there a lot.

When we got back to City Center, we would do a season of only two weeks and then have so much time off. You'd rehearse forever. But Mr. B. was really working closely with us, teaching and doing new ballets all the time, and trying to find odds and ends for us to do, television for example.

Balanchine put on the *Minkus Pas de Trois* with Maria Tallchief and Nora Kaye originally, but I eventually did both of the women's parts. In *La Valse* I did the Third Waltz with Frank Hobi. I saw the ballet recently, and I really didn't think that Suzanne Farrell was right in it. She was playing it coyly. I liked Patty McBride. I thought she was the closest to Tanny. In *Western*

Patricia Wilde

Symphony, Tanny never played to the audience, was never cheap, she had that coltish chic fun.

I remember Jerry Robbins's performances in *Tyl Ulenspiegel* and *Prodigal Son*. In Paris the stagehands, who usually don't pay too much attention to what's going on onstage, all stood in the wings for Jerry. What an artist! He was right there in the company, taking class and working. He was a very good dancer.

When Balanchine did *Swan Lake*, Act II, in 1951, Yvonne Mounsey and I sat in the studio, looking at what he was doing, and saying to one another, *"How can he do this to Swan Lake?"* And then he created that really beautiful pas de trois for me. Yvonne and I could tell from the corps parts that we were cast demi-solo, but you just went to the rehearsal and he gave you the steps and you did it. He did it in one hour's rehearsal. In Paris I had a really big success with the pas de trois because it really allowed you to fly. The dance made the viewer think that I didn't touch the ground. I was in the air constantly, and really had to move. At the end there was a big series of *sissonnes* in one place, but from side to side, like a bird flying. My teachers in Paris, Madame Nora Kiss and Preobrajenska, were still there, and they and the audiences just loved it.

Balanchine's *Swan Lake* has a big finale, where we were really going fast in a flurry of movement, those big wonderful circles, running through each other. And he made that quick coda at the end of the pas de deux. Even the adagio and variation were faster. When I was the principal later, he changed the choreography. He took out the *ronds de jambe* for the ballerina and started with a *développé effacé* and then arabesque. He took out the slow start. And then at State Theater he changed the music, so there have been different versions.

When I came back from the European tour in 1953, my future husband, George Bardyguine, and I had acquired Brandy, a poodle, in Genoa. We had him with us on the entire tour. Everyone in the company adored this little ball of fuzz. We returned from the tour and were called for rehearsals for *Nutcracker*. George and I had got married that morning, December 14, 1953. Balanchine was just casting. He said I was going to do the Mirlitons. I was wearing a flower, but we hadn't told Mr. B. we were getting married. So I went to Vida Brown and I said, "You know, George and I got married this morning." She said, "Oh, does Mr. B. know?" I said no. So she went over and whispered to him, and he called me over and said, "Well, I'm so glad because I was wondering what was going to happen to Brandy." The dog! That was typical. George's family were having a dinner for us, just family and a few people. So Vida said to Mr. B., "You don't want Pat to rehearse

329

tonight, do you?" And he said, "Oh, yes, you know this is most difficult music, most difficult, and I want to do."

I had rehearsal supposedly from seven to nine. I got to the rehearsal at seven o'clock, and at nine o'clock we were still there. Nine-thirty, and the four girls behind me were saying, "He can't do this to you. He can't." I was doing *entrechats six* from pointe to pointe, *tour en l'air* landing on pointe. We finished the piece at ten o'clock. Then I went to the dinner. In the following weeks, I called in every day. I didn't have a rehearsal again for two weeks! He had made his point. Then I contracted mononucleosis, and I couldn't do the opening. Janet Reed did it, and the choreography was all changed. The version that I learned in rehearsal was never performed.

I went into *Sylvia: Pas de Deux* after Maria Tallchief. And also into *Pas de Dix*, which I learned from watching it. I remembered Choura in the old *Raymonda* because the variation was the same. I followed Maria in Balanchine's *Firebird*. The Firebird role was so marvelous. Maria was glitter, really a flame. The latest version at N.Y.C.B. has many of the same steps, but it's more like the Fokine interpretation than what Mr. B. made of it. *A Musical Joke* was done out in Stratford in 1956. All of us girls (Diana Adams and Tanny LeClercq and I) were staying with Mr. B. at his Weston house. We all stayed at the theater after the rehearsal, but Mr. B. went back home to cook. He was going to have this big dinner for us afterward. He made American, with ham, covered with brown sugar and maple syrup, and candied yams, all for after the performance.

I spent a lot of time with Balanchine and Tanny in the country in Connecticut in the mid-fifties. My husband and I would drive out from the city, and when we got nearby we would let Brandy out of the car. He would tear up the road and announce our arrival to Mr. B. And my husband and Mr. B. would spend the weekend cooking and working around outside. They built a little tool house and had various projects, and I would be busy baking bread. He was very informal in the country, always going around with his shirt off, working, getting the sun, digging around at the roses, cutting the grass. We'd start cooking in the afternoon and then sunbathe. Tamara Geva and her husband would come over. We'd all cook and sit around and talk. Mr. B. would bring something out of his wine cellar. We'd all have a great time. There was general conversation. Mr. B. loved to talk about science or the movies—anything but dancing.

He didn't tell me that he was going to do a ballet for me. When we started rehearsing *Square Dance*, Elisha Keeler, the square-dance caller, started coming to rehearsals. He also came out to Connecticut, too, and we talked over the calls. He used to drive me crazy. He wouldn't always call what I was doing. When I stage it now, I don't use the caller, I use the beautiful new man's variation that Balanchine made for Peter Schaufuss. The variation makes it much easier on the ballerina! When I first did *Square Dance,* I thought, "Oh, God"—I could hardly get through it. Then it was out of the repertory for a while, and we brought it back and I thought, "Oh, gosh, I'm older, I'll never get through this thing." I had a rehearsal in the afternoon, and then I had to go do the season's first performance of *Square Dance* in the evening. I found that it was easier, and this was long before the new man's variation was added. I thought, "What's going on? It *can't* be easier for me." But I had learned to pace myself. Even *Raymonda Variations,* with its very long adagio and two different variations, is not as hard as *Square Dance* without the man's variation—just from the point of view of stamina. *Raymonda Variations* had so much more breadth. With Mr. B., the statement is so complete that if you really just dance it, that is enough; but if you are then able to surmount any of the difficulties with real ease, you're able to bring that much more to it. He was always happy with that.

When Balanchine was in Europe with Tanny after her illness, everyone in the company felt that he would come back. I don't think that any of us thought that he would give up on the company, but we didn't know how long it would be and how he would feel when he came back to us. Tanny came back to America and was in the hospital in New York for a while. Balanchine was back and forth between the town and country. Then she was in Warm Springs, and he would go down there. But he was spending a lot of time in the country, preparing for Tanny's return, and planning on the works that he would do. My husband and I spent a lot of time with Mr. B. in those days. He was really going to do so many ballets, and he was preparing *Agon.*

Mr. B. was an awfully strong man and certainly very religious, too. I think he became more religious at that time. Balanchine was my son's—Yuri's—godfather. Yuri was born in Geneva when I was there setting up the school for Mr. B. At the baptism, the priest asked Mr. B. if he wanted a Russian Bible to read a long prayer for the godfather. Mr. B. said, "No, no, I know, I know." So he started off in Russian, and then suddenly he stopped. It seems that he said one word wrong. He realized his mistake, so he went back to the beginning and started all over again, and went right through to the end. Afterward the priest said, "What is this? Do you want my job?" As a young boy, Mr. B. had learned the prayer and he remembered. He said, "Well, I wouldn't have made a mistake at all if I hadn't . . ." The night before he had been out with Sophia Loren at a party, so he wasn't in the best of shape. In later years he did go often to church. We only went on Easter, but Mr. B. went often and was close to some of the priests. I think he needed that in later years.

When he came back to the company after Tanny's illness he was like a dynamo. It was as though he had been storing up all the things he wanted to do, and he had all these things he wanted to do for us all, and fantastic works were bubbling up inside. He needed to get them onstage, to give them to us all.

I think of Balanchine often. When you're rehearsing his ballets and somebody says, "Can I do this?" I'll say, "Absolutely not. That Mr. B. would hate." You know the things he wouldn't mind—a change in *port de bras* for example—and you don't want to incorporate something—more pirouettes, let's say—that he would not have wanted.

Mr. B. was very difficult sometimes because you never knew what he was thinking, and he could put you off. If you said, "Can I do something?" he'd say, "Hmmm, we see, we see." I remember when I first wanted to do *Swan Lake* he said, "Oh, you know, some people, you know, soprano, so she shouldn't do another role," and then later on he changed. "Everybody should do everything." He did whatever suited him at the time. One day it was the only way it could be, and the next it changed. Today, I find myself saying to a dancer, "Well, yes, you want to do it, go ahead and learn it and we'll see."

Balanchine will be remembered for his choreography but his teaching was fascinating. He changed our technique. His teaching will be remembered through his choreography. He changed the whole way that we think about dancing. I loved his classes. They were fascinating, and they changed so over the years. Early on he taught a ballerina class for Maria and Tanny and me in preparation for London, and Tanny had those legs flying all over the place. He would give us adagios where you had to hold your leg there for eight counts or something, and it was killing me. I felt that my leg was getting lower and lower. But then later on he would never do that. It was all the speed of the movement.

Balanchine changed. I remember a big argument that I had with him, I guess one of the only ones. Of course, I lost. I had been doing *Barocco* for four years constantly with Ballet Russe. Then I came to New York City Ballet, and he had changed a whole section of the steps in the first movement. I said, "Oh, Mr. B., how could you do that? It was so perfect. I couldn't make a mistake." He said, "No, no, too complicated. I want it more simple." I said, "No, it was perfect. Can't we do it?" "No, no. Must simplify, must simplify. Too busy, too busy." I think he really wanted to eliminate a little bit. Maybe in his mind it was clearer in the revision.

When we staged *Barocco* recently, there was an entrance in the third movement. In his last version of the ballet, Mr. B. has them repeating the sequence exactly the same. But earlier there was a wonderful entrance for the two ballerinas, where the corps de ballet is in the star formation at the beginning of the third movement, and the first violin ballerina comes in from one side and at that point the girls wrap up, and then when the other ballerina comes in from the other side they unwrap. He took that out. I don't know why. Probably Suzanne Farrell had a bad knee and couldn't jump. The entrance is *glissade, jeté, piqué arabesque, glissade, jeté, piqué arabesque.* So I put it back because it makes so much sense with what the corps is doing. I don't think that there was any need to make that repeat of exactly the same thing three times.

We have Vicky Simon to stage Mr. B.'s works for us. She knows exactly what the ballet is, and I say, "Well, Vicky, I remember this." And she says, "Oh, yes, well, you can do that. That version was done, so if you want to go back to that, that's within the style."

MOIRA

SHEARER

Born in Dunfermline, Scotland, 1926, Moira Shearer studied in Rhodesia and with Fairbairn, Legat, and at Sadler's Wells School in London. Made her professional debut with the International Ballet in 1941, joined the Sadler's Wells Ballet in 1942 where she became a principal dancer in 1944. In 1948 she appeared in The Red Shoes. *In 1986 she published* Balletmaster: A Dancer's View of George Balanchine.

I Remember Balanchine

THE ONLY TIME I WAS ABLE TO TALK TO BALANCHINE WAS IN THE REHEARSALS WE HAD for *Ballet Imperial* for the Sadler's Wells production in London in 1950. Up to that point I had just observed him and listened to him while he was working with everybody else. I got a clear impression of the kind of man he was, the type of mind, the type of attitudes, which I happened to like enormously. He was a man of such taste and cultivation, particularly for music and the ballet. I came to feel later that his visual sense, his sense of decor and costuming, were not so good. I think they took a secondary place. He could make errors in those areas. For many years he used no sets or costumes at all for his own company, and I wonder if it wasn't because he wasn't getting it right. For example, I would imagine that *Robert Schumann's "Davidsbündlertänze"* (which I've only seen on film) could look rather pretty-pretty and washed out onstage.

The ballerina role in *Ballet Imperial* was originally written for Marie-Jeanne, a fantastic virtuoso technician; he must have wanted to show every feat she could perform and put them all into one marvelous part. (Maria Tallchief told me that Mary Ellen Moylan was also wonderful in the role, perhaps the best.) It was wonderful to attempt. When I was working on it, what was lovely was feeling that he was pleased, that Balanchine knew that one was trying and there was a possibility that it might be good. All my relationship with Balanchine had to do with work. I never had a chance to sit down with him and just talk. He gave me the impression of a mind that was thoroughly taken up with his work and of a man with simple tastes. I cannot remember anyone else so immaculately turned out in dress. I think he was a private man, with a remarkable idea of his own, correct importance for ballet. I think he knew exactly where he stood in all of that and was glad of it. He wanted to improve his position over time and do even more, and I think he had a slight contempt for people who either wanted to exaggerate the importance of what he had done or who had not seen the point of what he was trying to do. His judgment of himself was quite good. In that, he was never conned.

I think he will always be, as he was in life, fairly enigmatic. There was something in that man's face that made you feel that, however well you knew him, you would never quite know him. It's a pale Georgian face, a real Mongolian face with a hint of a lot behind it which you'd never get at. There's something very interesting about that: in a way, it's wonderful that there is someone like Balanchine who is so endlessly fascinating. For example, he's the only choreographer who embraced change in his work, so that every ten years the fashion could alter and he would see the change exactly, with a true eye, unsentimentally, and with no nonsense about his "great achievement" because he knew he could do it better. I think he's unique in that.

Balanchine liked a certain type of shape in a dancer—long legs and not too much flesh. Actually, that's what a dancer wants, since to have a normal weight could be too much in order to dance. He liked strength very much—actual physical strength and stamina. You have to have line for his arrangement of steps. Everyone wants that, but he was looking for it especially. I think he liked speed and a good jump as well. Balanchine's choreography is never prissy, but you do have to be neat in order to fit the steps into the exact musical phrasing. I think musicality is the first thing he looked for. He wanted a lot, which is exactly as it should be.

I learned to play the piano early, and then, with serious ballet training at ten, I had to stop music. I admired Balanchine's tremendous ability as a pianist. It was also unique—I had never worked with so musical a choreographer. Balanchine had the ability to find his own music. Unlike a Frederick Ashton, he had strong ideas about music, he didn't need someone to suggest the music he might use. Balanchine and Ashton couldn't have been more different. One—Balanchine—so active, the ideas just pouring out; the other—Ashton—lazy, indolent, having to be goaded to work. And neither understood or particularly liked the other's work.

Obviously, Balanchine would have liked to stay in England and make his career here rather than in the United States. I adored *Union Jack,* especially that Scottish parade. The Brits were aghast, which I can only explain by jealousy, always jealousy. And *Agon,* which is such a funny, witty ballet, so smart and sophisticated, and which is always described here in London as merely an "abstract ballet"! Whenever I see Balanchine's company perform, I always feel so wonderfully happy when I come out. I find I'm smiling. You never get that at a performance in this country. To my mind, British ballet is rather leaden. Perhaps this is a quirk of mine, as a British person. Balanchine would change his work for the individual dancer. Over here, there's no change, and that's what we suffer from. Balanchine appeared genuinely interested in each dancer and in each dancer's very good qualities, as well as her less good ones. Look at the way he covered up for Serge Lifar, who never had a strong technique as a dancer, but Balanchine made him look fantastic. I wish that talent could be appreciated more in this country. No one over here seems to realize that there is room for everybody in a company. British typecasting is so boring in the end. Balanchine saw that you could have half a dozen radically different personalities all dancing the same leading roles. Adult English theater does not suffer from lack of variety!

JANET

REED

Janet Reed, born in Oregon, 1916, studied with Willam Christensen, Tudor, Celli, and at the School of American Ballet. She danced Odette/Odile in the first American production of the complete Swan Lake at the San Francisco Ballet. She joined Eugene Loring's Dance Players in 1942, moved to Ballet Theatre, appeared in the first casts of Fancy Free, Undertow, and other ballets, danced on Broadway in Look, Ma, I'm Dancin', and joined the New York City Ballet in 1949. From 1959 to 1964 she was ballet mistress of the company.

I Remember Balanchine

I MET BALANCHINE AT THE SCHOOL OF AMERICAN BALLET IN 1942, WHEN I CAME from San Francisco to join Dance Players in New York. He was teaching then, and I was just a newcomer in the back row. Marie-Jeanne and Zorina were there. Marie-Jeanne stood in the same spot all her career, right up front on the corner, where she could be seen. Everybody tried to get that front row; and I very seldom made it. Also in the front row were Bea Tompkins, Mary Jane Shea, Gisella Caccialanza, Zorina, Eugenia Delarova, Mary Ellen Moylan. Balanchine would concentrate on one step and work it. He would give a combination and then do it right, left, front, back, and he would twist it around—the same combination—many different ways, which I thought was really neat. He'd end up with lots of jumping. When it came to the jumps, that's where I could excel. I remember being extremely flattered when he stopped the class. We were doing one of those big leap things on the diagonal, and he stopped the class and had them watch me do it. That was really a high point in my life.

I had been hearing nothing but Balanchine for years, from the Christensens and Lew Christensen's wife, Gisella Caccialanza. Gisella always said, "Balanchine says . . ." Then I got to New York and everybody else was saying, "Balanchine says . . ." Anything he said they would take up and repeat. God has spoken. Balanchine had heard about me, although he didn't let on. At that time Balanchine didn't have a company. After Dance Players folded, Ballet Theatre asked me to come as a guest artist to do *Billy the Kid*. Then Tudor snapped me up, because Annabelle Lyon and Karen Conrad had just left, and he didn't have anybody to do the French ballerina in *Gala Performance*. He didn't have anybody for the young sister in *Pillar of Fire*. He put me in both right away. Before I signed any contract, however, Balanchine was very helpful. He said, "Don't sign a contract. Tell them that I want you first, and make them up the ante." At that time he was going to do a show with Rodgers and Hart. There was a part in it he thought that I would be good for. He took me to meet Larry Hart. It was at the old Delmonico Hotel. When we walked into this apartment, filled with smoke, Larry Hart was lying on a sofa. I guess he was ill at the time, and I didn't know that. The room was full of very tough-looking types, who were probably putting money into the show. When Balanchine came in, they said, "Where the hell have you been?" They sort of treated him like nobody. I was appalled that they would talk to Balanchine like that. He introduced me, and Larry Hart, very surly, just looked at me and said, "She's not the type." I wore my hair skinned back with a bun, you know, very ballerina, very serious, and I drew myself up and said, "I can be any type I want to be." I turned and left, but at the time I felt humiliated for Balanchine.

He tried to help me in all kinds of ways. In Ballet Theatre sometimes I had a hard time learning a role because there was no one to coach or teach me. They would just run through it very quickly, and I didn't get all the details and was left floundering. I would go find a space and try to work on it myself. If Balanchine happened to be passing by, he would stop and help me. He won my loyalty right from the beginning. He would help me on particular roles, like my variation in *Princess Aurora* or the ballerina in *Petrouchka*. I hadn't the foggiest about that part; it's hard to rehearse unless you have the support under the arms to do the steps. I didn't have that, and I would just hold on to two chairs. So I didn't know exactly how those steps were to be done, which were on pointe and which were off pointe. Balanchine had staged those ballets and worked in them himself in the Diaghilev company. I learned two or three variations for *Aurora's Wedding* and the *Bluebird*. Balanchine fixed steps and showed me how to make the most of them. He did that on his own. He was there in 1943 when Zorina came in to do *Helen of Troy, Apollo,* and *Errante.*

Then, in 1944, he choreographed *Waltz Academy.* I was in that (a pas de quatre with Albia Kavan, Fernando Alonso, and Harold Lang). That ballet has disappeared, but the costumes and the set were lovely, and the music, by Rieti. Balanchine gave me a variation that was difficult for me, sort of all on pointe, not coming off. I was not very strong on pointe to do these steps, but I finally managed them. I would say, "I can't do this." He'd just sit there and laugh. Then I finally did it. That particular step I often give when I teach a variations or a pointe class. Balanchine and Maria Tallchief invited Branson Erskine and me to dinner at "21" in 1948, when I was in *Look, Ma, I'm Dancin'* on Broadway. He asked me if I'd like to join the New York City Ballet. I said, yes, indeed. I didn't want to tour anymore. But I asked, "But what'll I do? I'm not a Balanchine dancer." He said, "Oh, we do something for you. We make something for you." So I joined. I had been excited about Balanchine's new company when I saw his *Divertimento* to Alexei Haieff's music and the Bizet *Symphony in C.* Mary Ellen Moylan was fantastic in *Divertimento.* And Maria danced it later. Bizet just blew one away. I thought that was the greatest. When I did get into the company, he let me do First Movement of *Symphony in C.* And then I changed to Third Movement. Of course both of them are very ingrained in my mind.

The first new Balanchine ballet I danced was *Bourrée Fantasque.* We were rehearsing, and in the third movement he couldn't figure out a way to finish. He was experimenting, he had the whole company running in circles, and I was standing in the center. There were about four circles—an inner, a second circle, a third, a fourth circle—all running, and then he would have them peel off and go into the wings. The stage was left bare. I was standing there in the middle. I put my hands over myself, covered myself as though I had been stripped naked, looked down and looked up and looked either way and went scuttling off. Balanchine roared with laughter. It was just spontaneous, as though everything had been ripped away and there I was, left exposed. It always made me feel good to make him laugh. That ending to *Bourrée* he didn't keep. But then of course later I saw it in *La Valse,* where he had them all circling around, with Tanny aloft.

Pas de Deux Romantique, which he made for me and Herbert Bliss, I try to forget. At that time I was not really at my top strength, and that was technically so hard, and I didn't really have the power to do it. Balanchine was thinking of me like a coloratura soprano and, as Richard Buckle later said, it was "A teacup *Tosca,"* a very sweet way of putting it. It was full of the most difficult and intricate technique, of tiny, tiny steps, and I worked very hard on it, but I was just not up to it. When I went to say good-bye to Balanchine at the end of the season, I said to him, "You made a mistake"—meaning he had made a mistake to use me in something that was technically beyond me. And he said, "I didn't make the mistake. You made the mistake." And with that we parted for the season. But I came back. He didn't hold it permanently against me.

Balanchine never admitted a mistake. Nothing was ever his fault. Sometimes he had some inner feelings of guilt, but he didn't let them out. When I was ballet mistress and we were in Hollywood, there was a boy there, fourteen or fifteen years old, who had been appearing in our productions out there. He wanted to audition for the company. I asked Balanchine if he would see this boy. Before a performance, we went downstairs underneath the stage where there was a platform that we rehearsed on. The boy was scared to death and had not warmed up. Balanchine came up to him and said, "Do a double air pirouette." And the boy just jumped up in the air to do a double pirouette and came down with such a severe sprain I can't tell you. And Balanchine muttered something like, "I shouldn't have had him do that. He should have warmed up." He walked away. But he didn't say it out loud. He just sort of muttered under his breath and walked away, leaving the boy in a heap, and I had to get ice and put him back together again. Balanchine just walked away. He had a streak of cruelty, but he also had some guilt under it. Think of the guilt he had about Tanny. Remember that he cast Tanny as a polio victim when she was a little girl in 1946. When Tanny got polio, he stayed in Denmark with her, and I think Kirstein for a while didn't think he was coming back. I'm sure Balanchine felt kind of responsible for this happening to Tanny. They had already split up. She was driving herself very hard to prove to him, to her mother, to whoever was expecting something of her. She was pushing herself very hard, and she was very run down when she contracted polio. I wasn't there, but I can well imagine.

Balanchine was a moral man and a hardworking man, but he was very superstitious. When somebody reminded him of someone he didn't like, he was tough on them. There was a girl in the company he didn't like. He said she reminded him of an older dancer. But this girl stayed on, she was a good dancer, she was lovely, she was very dependable, and then after a few years she left of her own accord. She went to Balanchine and thanked him for letting her be with the company and told him how much she enjoyed dancing in his ballets. Balanchine was so taken aback he couldn't get over it. He said, "Nobody has ever thanked me for being in the company." And this was the very girl he had clearly treated the worst. I just looked at him.

As a dancer, I never knew this side of him, but when I worked in association with him, as an assistant, as a ballet mistress, I saw it. I remember one Sunday morning rehearsing Edward Villella in *Orpheus,* in the Bacchantes scene. There was one section that was hard to figure out; we kept working and getting nowhere. Then Balanchine walked in. He had been to the sunrise Easter service at the top of a mountain in New Jersey. Alone. He stood at the top of the steps in the studio, and we all turned to him: "Thank God you're here." I said, "Please come help us. We can't figure this out." He just beamed. He was so happy, so pleased. He came down and rolled up his sleeves and went to work. I realized how much he needed to be needed. How much he wanted to have people need him. He said to me one time, "I can stand any amount of work. I can work endlessly. But I can't cope with human relationships, difficult relationships." He couldn't confront any emotional problems. And when he did, I realize now—looking back—that he actually got panic attacks. When he was taking care of Tanny during that period, he was having fainting spells. They were panic attacks. I didn't know anything about them in those days. I do now, having had a few myself. I know what he went through.

When he would come to me once in a while and say, "I really can't handle this. Can you do it?" I'd say, "Yes, I'll do it." But before I could even turn around, he was doing it himself. He would not let anybody take over. He would say to me, "Oh, I'm too tired. You rehearse it." I would start, and he'd be there like a shot. He wouldn't let not only me but anybody who wanted to replace him or do something that he thought was his job—he wouldn't permit it. He wanted to be The One. He wanted to be the only influence on his dancers. He didn't want anybody else. But there were times when he just wasn't there, and somebody had to make a decision. You'd go ahead and do it, but he didn't like it. It's only when he became ill that he really had to give over to Peter Martins and Jerry Robbins and Stanley Williams—but he didn't like it. He knew he needed them, but it must have been real hard.

When Balanchine staged the big ballet *Figure in the Carpet,* that was an obvious pitch to outgrow City Center. He always said, "We'll outgrow City Center. They'll have to build us a theater." He created the need by making the company bigger and bigger. We just exploded. That ballet was delightful. There were no videotapes or anything, but all of the principals are around, except for Magallanes—Verdy and Hayden and Jillana and Adams and Russell and McBride and Hinkson, D'Amboise, Villella, Francisco Moncion, and Mitchell—everyone's here, you see. Patty McBride had a dance with Nicky, her first big role. She was delightful in it. She came into the company the same year as Carol Sumner. I noticed in classes that Balanchine always picked out Carol Sumner as a dancer he was interested in. I kind of went the way of Patricia McBride. When she came into the company she made some mistakes in one of the first things she danced in the corps, and for the first time I saw Mr. Balanchine become irritated with her. She was scared to death, and he was irritated because she was slow or something. At my suggestion, she did some outside performing during the layoff and came back and then everything was fine. She could hold her own very nicely, but Balanchine never paid much attention to her. Up in the office, he'd lay out a bunch of pictures of dancers like Pat Neary or Pat McBride and then we would say, "Now which one do you think is going to make it?" I kept plugging for Pat McBride. I taught her Third Movement *Symphony in C* and my part in *Interplay.* Little by little, she began to get little things to dance. One time I found her in the wings very downcast. She seemed very discouraged because Balanchine didn't pay any attention to her and never spoke to her. I went upstairs and cornered him and said, "I think you need to talk to Patricia McBride." He said, "Oh, oh, yes, yes." He rushed down because he realized she was doing all right on her own and didn't seem to be needing him. She didn't go to him like some girls would and cry on his shoulder and try to get his attention. She never did that. He went and talked to her. She felt much better, and from then on he was aware of her needing him. As long as you could go it on your own, he didn't bother with you. You had to need him.

I didn't have the approach to him that other women had. I wasn't interested in him in a flirtatious way. I was not attracted to him, let us say. Not at all. But I liked him, I admired him, I was sympathetic, and I was loyal. When he was in Denmark with Tanny and people said, "Balanchine doesn't want to come back," I said, "What do you mean, he doesn't want to come back? He *has* to come back."

Eventually, with my family responsibilities, I couldn't carry on a double life, so I left. It was just one of those things. No good-bye, no nothing. Just, you're not there. But Kirstein thanked me. He said, "I'm surprised you stayed as long as you did."

Balanchine was always religious. He just didn't talk about it. He would always go to an Easter service and watch the sun rise. Religion was deeply ingrained from his youth, and when he got old he went back to it again. And of course superstition is so much a part of the whole Russian thing. At the time Balanchine died, around midnight, I saw a ball of fire go across the sky and said, "That means something, I don't know what." The next morning Francia Russell called and said Balanchine had died. I wrote to Lincoln Kirstein and said I was in the Port of Angels on the Olympic Peninsula, home of the gods, and saw this flash of fire cross the sky, and I could only think that it was Balanchine's soul.

Balanchine was sometimes taken in by people. There was a dentist he adored who acted as Balanchine's agent for a time. He also had a doctor at one time who had funny little ideas. Balanchine just thought it was great. He was very childlike, you know, about certain things. A curious combination of shrewdness and naivete and yet he had great command. Someplace I have a funny little photograph of Balanchine as a boy. As an older man he had the same expression he had as a little boy in that picture with his brother in uniform. Later a photograph was taken in Hollywood with John Clifford and his teacher Irina Kosmovska, and Balanchine has the same expression. Very looking down his nose: "I am much too good for this."

DIANA

ADAMS

Diana Adams, born in Virginia, 1926, danced in Broadway musicals before joining Ballet Theatre in 1943. She came to the New York City Ballet in 1950, creating ballerina roles in many Balanchine ballets, including Agon, Episodes, and Liebeslieder Walzer. In 1963 she retired from performing and taught at the School of American Ballet.

I Remember Balanchine

WHEN I WAS IN A COUPLE OF AGNES DE MILLE SHOWS, INCLUDING *Oklahoma*, THERE were always people around trying to sign up dancers. A sleazy agent—I don't remember his name—said, "I want you to come audition for Balanchine" for an upcoming show. So I went to this Broadway theater and did a couple of *tours jetés* in a basement studio. That was the first time I ever met Balanchine. He was terribly nice to me and said, "There isn't anything in this show for you." Of course I knew all about him because we went religiously to all the classes in New York. The young dancers went wherever he taught.

Our next encounter was at Ballet Theatre, which Tudor asked me to join. Lucia Chase was always trying to get Balanchine more interested in her company. She had him come in and rehearse the waltz in *Les Sylphides*, which was wonderful. She wanted Balanchine to restage everything in the classical repertoire, for example *Aurora's Wedding*. Balanchine rehearsed me in the first, fast Fairy variation: the "Finger" variation. I was terribly distressed because I had a vision of myself as being a dreamy, lyrical dancer, drifting about. He said, "Oh, no, you have to sort of flash around the stage." He kept saying to me, "Big girl, flashing around the stage, is wonderful." I thought he had misinterpreted my talent. But he always knew better. Very often he would see what people could do and look good in. He would see through what they thought they could do well. That was very hard on him because everybody was always arguing with him about casting. I think Balanchine had a kind of X-ray vision that allowed him to see what people's talents really were. I had been doing the Lilac Fairy variation. I think Balanchine thought I was quite boring as a lyrical dancer.

George cast me in his new ballet *Waltz Academy* for Ballet Theatre. Lucia said that Mr. B. had been in the office and that he wanted me to do everything. It was the first time I knew he thought I was good. I was the new girl in the company, and I think there were a lot of soloists and demi-soloists who were jealous. *Waltz Academy* was very pretty. It was a kind of ballet class. We did a little barre in the beginning and then a series of pas—a pas de quatre, a pas de trois, and then a pas de deux with Nana Gollner and Paul Petroff. The steps were so interesting for the pas de trois that I did with Miriam Golden and Johnny Kriza. Kriza, the signature of Ballet Theatre in those years, was so charming. I don't know if there was so much wonderful dancing coming out of Ballet Theatre at that time, but certainly there were lots of entertaining performances. Balanchine's *Theme and Variations*, which he made in 1947, has such a beautiful pas de deux. Maria Tallchief was always so terrific in the opening fast variations. She flashed, I thought, much better than I did.

Balanchine rehearsed me at length in Calliope's variation in *Apollo*. We went through every gesture. In the variation the Muse is making a speech, as in an oration. In his halting English, Balanchine was so eloquent. Balanchine must have rehearsed ballets like that thousands of times. I remember later he was almost wringing his hands over a *Prodigal Son* rehearsal—"I just can't rehearse this again." It was when Eddie Villella and I were going to do it. We were there for hours, going over how everything should look. Balanchine was so patient, but it was hard on him. He wanted to do new things. He wasn't living in the past. But nobody rehearsed like Balanchine.

Alicia Alonso left Ballet Theatre, and I was supposed to do lots of roles coming up. Then Alicia decided to come back. My husband, Hugh Laing, was furious. He said that would mean I would be doing less, and we should leave the company. We did indeed leave. Mr. Balanchine then came to our apartment and said he would like us to join New York City Ballet. He said he'd always wanted to work with me, and he wasn't a great admirer of the ballets at A.B.T. He liked Tudor's *Lilac Garden* and *Romeo and Juliet* and that was about it. Balanchine once said to me, "Tudor should have been a nuclear scientist or something." He felt Tudor's mind was too analytical for dancing, but there were things in his work Balanchine admired.

So the three of us—Hugh, Antony Tudor, and I—went to New York City Ballet. The move was very felicitous for me but did not go so well for Tudor and Hugh, although Balanchine was very generous with them. Lincoln Kirstein liked Tudor a lot and thought it was going to be wonderful to have him. Balanchine scraped together whatever he thought Hugh could do. And Hugh was so good on the stage.

Balanchine was teaching company class, and he also was teaching at the School of American Ballet, Tudor was still teaching at the Met, so it was an awkward situation. I, of course, wanted to take Mr. B.'s classes. There was a lot of pompous argument going on at that time about how Balanchine could dehumanize you, how you lost all your quality because you became a machine, so concentrated was he on technical prowess. That was a very shallow view of Mr. Balanchine's training. Everybody said that all he wanted was for you to jump and turn and get your leg up. I wasn't strong technically, and I thought, "Oh, this is going to be my demise because I can't do all those things the other dancers who trained with him can do." They were so strong. So I tended to be critical of him too. Then it became really difficult because Margaret Craske had worked, through Tudor, with Ballet Theatre a lot. She had an interpretation of Cecchetti technique that had her students leaning forward a little bit. I went from one teacher to the other, and Craske's influence used to drive Balanchine crazy. He used to say to me, "Stand up! Stand up!" The training got to be quite a controversy.

Serenade was the first ballet I did, and at the same time I was learning

Symphonie Concertante—Symphony Concentrate as we called it. I had to rent a studio and rehearse with a recording of the Mozart music because we just hadn't done ballets like that at Ballet Theatre. There weren't these concentrated ballets with so much dancing. It was an extraordinary challenge; I had to work on them myself in the studio to get them into my head. It was long, hard, and intimidating, but I loved doing *Symphonie Concertante.* I thought it was such a pretty ballet to dance. It was wonderful for schooling a dancer—I got schooled in it. Every time I made a move, Mr. Balanchine would suggest that I wasn't doing it correctly. That was unnerving, but it was the beginning of retraining myself. Tanny LeClercq worked with me. I hadn't known her before joining the company. Mr. Tudor liked her a lot. He thought she was very interesting, and when we went to performances at New York City Ballet he always said how Tanny was fascinating to him.

In the beginning I didn't have any attack. Everything changed for me when I was finally free to train with Balanchine, my husband was gone, and I was on my own. That's when I remember Balanchine's classes being so fantastic. He taught all the time. When we toured Europe, we had class every day no matter what. Balanchine loved to teach and everyone would be tired. Some dancers would not come to his class. But we were never without a class, and sometimes to our regret because Mr. B. wasn't terribly interested in sightseeing. No museums, just classes and restaurants. He had favorite restaurants in each city. He'd say, "Let's all go to the theater and have a class." We toured here in America. In Chicago we would have an enormously long, arduous, and fascinating class, and then we would go and eat. That was Balanchine's idea of the perfect schedule. He loved to teach dancers. He loved dancing, and he wanted it to be so wonderful; how you get it to be wonderful is to train people to do it.

Everyone at A.B.T. had seemed to be arguing about who was going to do what. But New York City Ballet was quiet and peaceful. Balanchine was so focused on dancing that temperament just didn't have anything to do with it. His interest was so totally focused. That's what he cared about, and he couldn't understand all the trappings. Arguing was just boring to him. He probably did have some casting problems, but he always wanted everybody to be happy.

I danced Terpsichore to André Eglevsky's *Apollo.* André was used to being treated like a star, which you were in Ballet Theatre if you got top billing. Nobody did that at New York City Ballet. So he always felt that he was being treated casually. He never understood that Balanchine respected all of his dancers. André wanted to have special treatment, he was always complaining. Balanchine admired Eglevsky's technique, he loved that soft, big jump, and he was always trying to enlarge Eglevsky's style, to get him to do different things. But André was always the same. Balanchine couldn't get him to change. I remember when André and Pat Wilde did the Third Movement of *Western Symphony,* and André just couldn't understand a ballet that had four movements and different principals in each movement. He was terribly insulted that he was doing this little Third Movement, despite the fact that it was so nice.

Mr. B. wasn't sympathetic to dancers who just wanted to go onstage and be impressive and safe in their dancing. Dancing was such a wonderful thing to Balanchine. It didn't matter what the critics said or what the audience thought. The thing was to dance something, not the impression that you made. His main interest in life was dancing, and so he would get over personal tragedies—even Tanaquil LeClercq's illness. That was a terribly hard time, that year. It must have been an experience that was excruciating. But he returned and made more ballets. That was what life meant to him. People came in and out, but dancing was the thing. I don't think this makes him an unfeeling man. It was just the way he was.

He returned to the company, after Tanny's illness, with *Agon.* We started with the pas de deux. It didn't seem to be anything bizarre. The thing that was fascinating was the music—it was difficult. That's what I remember mainly about the rehearsals, that the music was challenging. We had a great deal of fun, too, when we got to the finale. Stravinsky was at the rehearsals. Balanchine cared very much about his opinion. He's the only one I can think of whom Mr. B. would defer to.

Figure in the Carpet was fun to do, although I don't think Balanchine thought it was worth reviving. But it was certainly entertaining. You could never predict what Balanchine would think was memorable in his own work. It always surprised me to discover what he placed value on and what he didn't. *Barocco* was one of the ballets I loved to do. The other work that was a great deal of fun was the Five Pieces in *Episodes.* Balanchine was always looking forward to what was going to happen next. He wasn't one to dwell on his past glories. He looked for new talent because that made him want to choreograph.

Balanchine traveled with me on a couple of trips around the States for the Ford Foundation to look for scholarship students. It was really to help train me to see exactly through the superficial talent and to get my eye to see what might develop into an important dance ability. It was fascinating what Balanchine could see. It was never just the proportion or the physical gift. It was a whole quality. He could just see talent, which is not easy in dancing, because it often depends on how proficient you are. He could see in the beginning, before the students could do anything, what the possibilities were. That's really very tricky, to be able to do that.

At the beginning of the Ford Foundation program, I think Balanchine was worried about the training all over the United States. He said that it was not very good. He used to get so excited if we'd go to a school and he could see that the teacher was not training badly. To him that was so wonderful. But that didn't happen very often. That was the problem: if you gave all these young students scholarships and they had been trained badly, then when you brought them to New York he would have to untrain them. It was difficult to foresee that the training would ever get that much better, which it has, partly because of the Ford Foundation program. Balanchine wasn't a political creature in the sense of caring about the government, but he hated to see bad training and bad dancing.

On those visits, Balanchine would let me suggest who I thought was gifted and then we would talk about it. He helped me a lot. I had made mistakes. We had very different opinions, and he would explain to me why I hadn't seen something. I remember there was one little girl about whom I said, "Oh, she has such a nice instep." He said, "No, no, it's a bony foot. It's not going to develop." He could do a dancer's anatomy so clearly, almost like a doctor. He knew how it was going to develop. Balanchine saw things in Suzanne Farrell when she first came to the School that I hadn't seen—that one foot was better than the other, etc. Balanchine liked Suzanne right away.

Then there were lots of people Balanchine thought could have been wonderful dancers who didn't want to be. I remember so well his instructions in class to people who had good qualities on how those could become wonderful qualities. And the dancers themselves were not interested to hear what he was saying. I think that was sometimes very hurtful to him. Dancing was so important to him. I don't think it was as important to anybody else as it was to him. Everybody else wanted to have a little life on the side. Suzanne Farrell would listen to him. She heard every word.

A lot of people didn't even think he was right. Some dancers would say, "Oh, I hate his classes." That was heresy to me because I thought the classes were so extraordinary. The training was about how to dance well. He didn't concentrate so much on the men, but if he had a boy with an interesting quality, he would work with him. Edward Villella never took his classes, but Mr. B. still used him. Villella had that jump that was so lovely to see. Balanchine admired Stanley Williams. He said, "There are lots of people who can give class but Stanley can make people hear him." He liked Stanley despite the fact that there were a lot of things Stanley did differently. Balanchine watched Stanley teach things the way he wouldn't have taught them until they eventually found a middle ground.

If Balanchine saw a dancer who illuminated something in his creative mind—in other words, who inspired him—he just adored them. The inspiration was everything. What interested him in life was to see somebody move, or the way the body looked in movement, that produced in him an idea. It helped him to create. I don't fault him for that. I think that was what his life was about: creating.

When Balanchine spoke about his early life, it was never at any length. I think he cared a lot about his mother. When he spoke of her, it was with great reverence. It wasn't very often, but you got a feeling that she had been important to him, more than anybody else in his family. When he went to Russia, he wasn't even terribly interested in his brother. Everybody thought he should be, but he wasn't. Balanchine didn't fake, and that's why a lot of people disliked him. What he felt and what he thought: there it was. I don't think he was unkind, but he didn't flatter people.

I always thought of Balanchine as terribly Russian and romantic. Often he seemed to be very preoccupied. Tanny LeClercq and I had such a wonderful time together. Tanny used to make him laugh. She would bark like a dog and things like that. I think Balanchine is an enigma of a man. He was hard to understand, he had so many different qualities. I don't think in the end that I really did comprehend him: such a complex mind is not easy to define.

MELISSA

HAYDEN

Melissa Hayden was born in Toronto in 1923. She studied with Boris Volkov in Canada and with Anatole Vilzak and Ludmilla Schollar in New York. Hayden danced briefly at the Radio City Music Hall and joined [American] Ballet Theatre in 1945. She joined New York City Ballet in 1949 and retired in 1973. She danced many Balanchine roles, including twenty-three created for her. She appeared in Charles Chaplin's film Limelight *(1953) and is the author of* Melissa Hayden—Offstage and On *(1963) and* Dancer to Dancer, Advice for Today's Dancer, *1981. She directed a ballet school of her own in New York until 1983. She now teaches ballet at the North Carolina School of the Arts.*

I THINK OF BALANCHINE CONSTANTLY, IN THE PROCESS OF TEACHING YOUNG PEOPLE. I come from an experience of nearly twenty-five years with him, so in a sense I'm always aware of him. He wasn't really a teacher, more a magnificent coach, but in teaching I think of him because he had such high principles for the dance. Balanchine sometimes referred to himself as a teacher, but I think he entertained himself with some of those statements. He really didn't try to change you as a person. The wonderful thing about him was he didn't want to change you, he only wanted to give you more, for you to experience or discover more in yourself through what you could do. With him, you really got tuned in to possibilities within yourself. Balanchine had a grab bag of dancers at the beginning. He wanted diversity. He wanted everybody to dance with the same kind of technical impetus. That's why he taught the way he did. But he did not want to change you for uniformity's sake. That's a misconception. When someone says, "Well, he told me this," that concept was perhaps only for that person. When you hear one of those dicta, you must look at the individual artist he was speaking to, how they are involved with his choreography. It differs from case to case because he communicated and delved into each dancer differently. Basically, there were rules in what he was saying, and he could only relate his principles to a dancer who knew those rules.

Balanchine was not interested in checking to see if you knew the rules. He just used your possibilities. When he was choreographing, he would ask you to do something he had never done before in order to see if you understood and to see what came of it.

I began my dance training when I was about fifteen years old—I'm one of those surprise packages, a late starter. I used to swim all summer, starting when I was about six years old. Swimming is related to dancing in the looseness of the movement and the repetition. It keeps the muscles so malleable. If you've ever swum a mile at a time, you know there's a physicality in the whole body, in the respiratory system, the arms, the legs, you constantly have to kick and lift your arms and then breathe in a coordinated manner. I love the water. I swam all summer and winter, especially when I was in high school. I had coordination and a muscular sureness that went with movement. I did a bit of acrobatics at camp, where you did a little tap, modern, improvisation. I was just running all over the place.

When I came to Balanchine, I had had proper schooling because I trained with a Russian teacher in Canada, Boris Volkov. Dancers from the Ballet Russe and Ballet Theatre would stop off at his studio and take class in the late 1930s and early 1940s, dancers like Bobby Lindgren and Duncan Noble. I remember Volkov once entertained a group from the Denham Ballet Russe, he once hosted the Original Ballet Russe, and I met some wonderful people.

Eglevsky taught a master class that I will never forget in Toronto in 1939. He was a very good teacher. After I got to the United States in 1945, I was in Ballet Theatre and then with Alicia Alonso, so I did have a number of years of professional experience.

When I joined Balanchine, many of the dancers in the company had not had such experience. There was Tanaquil LeClercq, wonderful in the Second Movement of *Symphony in C.* But New York City Ballet had a wobbly beginning. I joined the company in 1949; we performed only on Thursdays through Sundays for three weeks. But there was a tremendous sense of excitement in those early days of City Ballet. There were more steps danced at N.Y.C.B. At Ballet Theatre there had been a more eclectic style, and having that initial experience at A.B.T. was a benefit. I have always felt that the drama of Balanchine's choreography is so subtle that you could even write a scenario dancing *Divertimento No. 15* relating to the music and the stage action. When I first joined the company, my attitude about dancing Balanchine was not based on technique. I didn't think that I should think about the technique. I danced all the movements in *Symphony in C,* and I thought each of the four movements had a distinct mood, another libretto. I really felt that was left to the imagination. I was very happy. I made up the libretto myself, in anticipation of doing it, while I was rehearsing or while I was onstage. Then later, as I continued in the ballet, I think I responded much more to the music and the choreography. I had studied music, and my response to music was a benefit in my response to Balanchine. I think Balanchine appreciated that. I studied piano at the Toronto Conservatory beginning at the age of seven.

At the beginning, the company danced ballets by a number of choreographers besides Balanchine. I think it was Lincoln's idea to make the company audience-worthy, to entertain the audience. You couldn't put on Balanchine ballets continuously. After all, he could only choreograph for the quality or the ability of the dancers. He grew as a choreographer as the dancers grew. If he changed *Symphony in C* or *Serenade* over the years, it was because the dancers could do more. He and the dancers developed together.

Working with Balanchine was never just a job. I believed in the growth of the company. I was really turned on by Balanchine's dances, beyond the physicality of them. His choreography was like a meshing and weaving to sound. To me, some of that choreography sang. You couldn't help but notice it if you were sensitive to such things. I wasn't an eighteen-year-old when I joined the company. I was nearer to twenty-six. I was a mature person and very much appreciative of what he was doing.

I looked forward always to doing *Serenade.* I used to look forward to doing *Western Symphony,* the second movement. That was such a tongue-in-cheek piece. When I did it in Paris, I said to him, "Well, how am I supposed to dance this?" He said, "Absolutely straight." I used to go to church dancing second movement in *Barocco*. In First Movement *Symphony in C*, I remember I was the Hostess with the Mostest. Second Movement *Symphony in C* is so very mysterious, the ballerina is untouchable, floating on clouds. Third Movement is like bubbles in a soda pop, you were bubbling all over the place. It always reminded me of the Third Movement of Tudor's *Gala Performance,* the French soubrette. You had to be as light as that. The Fourth Movement I didn't like, so I just danced it. I tried to do something with it. For me, it was always a shadow of the First Movement: can you dance better than the First Movement?

Jerry Robbins loved Balanchine like son to father. Balanchine was pleased that Jerry wanted to work with the dancers in the company. I think he respected Robbins's talent more than anyone, he respected Jerry's integrity, his ballets, his angst. Balanchine would give Jerry as much time as he needed. Also Balanchine put Jerry in *Prodigal Son* to dance the lead role. He was divine. Of the various people who did that ballet, I loved Jerry. He had a vulnerability. Jerry was an artist.

When Balanchine was making a new ballet on you, we'd go into a rehearsal room, and he'd start the music and say, "Now you do—try this." He always thought of me as a technical dancer because I always put something on top of it, it wasn't just technique. That meant that "technique" would be filling in more steps than somebody else could do and in a certain amount of time. I was precise. I didn't have any problems. The first version of *Valse Fantaisie* was done with Magallanes. We didn't have a pianist, so Balanchine started my little variation without music. We had an hour rehearsal without music, just counts. He taught it to me like that, and the choreography was set. It was so much fun. He said, "Now hop back like a skater. Now jump here." He just colored it for me, without the music. That's the way to learn choreography if it's so musically constructed. I also danced Tanaquil Le Clercq's variation in that ballet.

Tanaquil was magnificent, very unusual. She had legs that could do anything, and she had a temperament that had depth. In Jerry Robbins's ballets she had a sensitivity. I think she possessed artistry when she was born. She had a wonderful angular way of moving, she was magnificent in *Metamorphoses* and in *Bourrée Fantasque*. In *Western Symphony* she had a kind of chic. There's a marvelous film of it that shows her quality. And she had mystery in *La Valse*. That's not technically difficult, but she brought such a presence onstage for such a young person. That's the mystique of Balanchine knowing his dancer.

In *Jeux d'Enfants* (1955), I did the Steadfast Tin Soldier section as part of the whole ballet. It was charming. Later, in the seventies, Balanchine reconstructed that part for McBride and Schaufuss. The original was choreographed for Herby Bliss and me. But Roy Tobias did the premiere. I loved doing it. There were some marvelous steps in both the *pas de deux* and my variation that have been lost. Also, the end was much more difficult and much more interesting.

Agon is gone, alas. Now it's a watered-down version. It's become so changed that its purpose has been lost. Balanchine wanted it to be choreography to that marvelous, difficult music. Also, the first time you saw Diana Adams and Arthur Mitchell doing the pas de deux it was really awesome to see a black hand touch a white skin. That's where we were coming from in the fifties. It was marvelous what Balanchine did.

Because Mr. Balanchine loved his female dancers, a woman had to decide whether she could trust him in a relationship. I was not apprehensive, but personally I always questioned Mr. Balanchine's intentions. I suppose I was suspicious because I had seen the ploys and games he could exercise. Some people had been upset and hurt and even deprived. I had quite a thick skin about that. It was just water off my back when all the new young girls came in and became the apples of his eye, or when there would be only one apple that he could look at and other people left—sometimes very talented people —because they couldn't share his attention. They wanted his attention. It was very obvious when he did *Liebeslieder* (1960). He must have turned himself on with each of the dancers he worked with. He certainly did turn himself on with me, so I assumed he did that to everybody else, because they were all private rehearsals. Balanchine adored *Liebeslieder,* and he was in love with his girls in it. He couldn't take his hands off me. When the four couples got together for the finale, he would look at us and caress my neck, and I would look at him and think, "What's he going to do now? Everybody else is watching." Oh, he was just adorable. I loved it even though that man was making me nervous. I didn't want to have any liaison with him.

I really loved Mr. Balanchine. I will always love him. He was so much a part of my life. On the day he died, I realized I had spent half my life with this man. I adored his values and applied them to my own values. His tastes were sometimes very prejudicial, but for me he stood for so much class in his choreography. He could seem snobbish, but I don't know whether it was snobbism or shyness. Sometimes he appeared aloof because he didn't know what to say. He was shy and never comfortable in the American language. He always translated when he talked. He would turn to me and say something in Russian, and then he would say, "What am I saying to you? You don't know what I'm saying?" He spoke in Russian, and then he'd say, "You know, I could never write because I have to translate into English. I can't write." He envied anyone who could express himself in the English language. I couldn't understand his funny sense of humor. He spoke so fluently in French and, when his Russian friends were around, in Russian. But with people who spoke English, I had seen him give speeches and have a difficult time. He was constantly translating. Mr. Balanchine was a simple man but he had a mystery about him. For him, it was important to have something to believe in. He became proud of his position in the Church.

I told Mr. Balanchine that I was leaving the company, that 1973 would be my last year. I was having fun dancing a lot and doing so many ballets, and he said, "Would you like to do a ballet for a benefit? On May 16 we have a benefit, you don't mind doing this ballet?" I said, "No, I'd love it." He always liked Glazunov, so he made *Cortège Hongrois* for me. He made a beautiful pas de deux to lovely music. I loved the whole thing. I cried opening night. I didn't know my farewell would be that wonderful. It was a great honor he paid me. We did it in Saratoga, and on tour, and at the Greek Theater. People loved it, the whole ceremony of it. Whether he meant to do it or not, my farewell ballet was a gimmick that worked.

After my retirement from the stage, I would go over to the studio. I used to come up and watch him teach class. The whole company would be there. He would be rehearsing Baryshnikov with Patty McBride in *Rubies* and he would say, "Come sit with me." Then I would stay on to watch him rehearse *La Source*. He was very welcoming all the time. When I used to visit him in the hospital, that was very hard. I was able to be very open with him: we had no relationship except the working relationship.

VIDA

BROWN

Vida Brown, born in 1922 in Illinois, danced with the Chicago Opera Ballet before joining the Ballet Russe de Monte Carlo in 1939. In 1950 she became a member of the New York City Ballet, where she appeared in many Balanchine ballets and danced solo roles in the first casts of La Valse and Mazurka from A Life for the Tsar. In 1952 she became ballet mistress of the company, continuing on the staff until 1964.

I JOINED THE BALLET RUSSE WHEN I WAS SIXTEEN. TWO YEARS LATER, WHEN BALAN-chine staged *Serenade* for us, he picked me out for one of the four girls. Then another time we performed in Newark and he was there. We were all taking the train back to New York; it was very late on a winter's night. He was at the station, all by himself. I went up and said, "Mr. Balanchine, can I just say something? If you ever need a dancer, I'd love to work with you." Then I ran away, I was so nervous.

While we were in Ballet Russe, Helen Kramer, Maria Tallchief, and I had an apartment in New York. Maria came home one day and said, "What would you think if I marry George?" "George who?" I asked. That's how out of the whole thing I was. "George Balanchine?" I gasped. "It's up to you," I told her. "He'll do a lot for you."

I danced with Ballet Russe for ten years, then I worked for a year on Broadway so I could make enough money to go to Europe. I did some films with De Basil's company in Paris, and then, in 1950, I was dancing in Swe-den when I received a cable from Balanchine: AM DOING A COMPANY. WOULD LIKE YOU TO COME. Back in New York, I had four weeks to learn the repertory before we left for London.

In London the New York City Ballet worked very hard. We rehearsed, rehearsed, rehearsed, and the British loved our company. Even the stage-hands wanted to watch, because apparently it was so different from any-thing they'd ever seen. Lew Christensen was in London with us and did all the rehearsing. He was great, so nice, and people loved him. When he left unexpectedly Balanchine came to me and said, "Would you like to help me?" He realized he couldn't do too much for me as a dancer, because his favorite ballerinas were all very slender and tall, whereas I was shorter and solid.

These kids had been dancing these ballets for two years and here I was being asked to tell them what to do. I wasn't particularly popular! But Bal-anchine was very supportive of me. The patience he had was incredible. I'd rehearse the ballets and learn all the parts by dancing with the company. The best part was when he did a new ballet, I could be with him and learn it, and usually I was dancing in it, too. When he was choreographing *Metamor-phoses,* there were dancers three deep watching him demonstrate. Everybody crowded around, but from the back they couldn't see exactly. "They're not getting it back there," I told Mr. B., "so I'll go and show them." I used to watch him and then go to the rear and teach the rest of the company. I don't think those people back there liked that, but it worked. Tanny was gorgeous in that ballet. What a sad thing to lose her! She had such talent, she could do anything. Tanny's and Diana's movement was so beautiful because they always had line, even if they were executing an awkward movement. Balanchine was always trying something new. When he did *Ivesiana,* he said, "I don't do all these things for posterity. I know some of them aren't going to be any good. But I want to try them. I know I can do a classical ballet."

A lot of people felt Balanchine was very dictatorial. Well, it was his company! Mr. B. liked to make these little asides, but I really don't think he believed them. He'd do them as a dig, or to get a rise out of people. He loved teasing the young girls. But I don't think he realized that sometimes his quips upset them. I'd always tell them, "You know, forget it. He doesn't mean anything by that."

I loved dancing with him in the *Mazurka from "A Life for the Tsar."* But he was not a performer; he was so conscious of what was going on! Janet Reed and Yurek Lazowski were the stars, and most of the time we stood at the side and watched them. There he was, snapping his fingers. "Mr. B., you're onstage!" I reminded him. "But I'm so small," he said. One has to be a little bit of a narcissist to be on the stage, but I don't think he was.

I really don't feel that sex was a major part of Balanchine's makeup. He was married to the ballet, really, and he loved creating. That's where he got his stimulus. His idea of sensuousness was movement, I think. I don't think anybody was that turned on by him sexually. He wasn't what we used to call a wolf. He was not an aggressive lover.

I also feel there isn't that much emotional depth in his relationships onstage. It's a reaching out, but then going on to something else. His romances, for me, are a surface kind of thing. *Serenade* is Balanchine's most beautiful ballet. It's loving and the movement is beautiful to look at. But I didn't fall apart when he didn't get the girl.

MARIAN
HOROSKO

Born in Cleveland, Ohio, in 1927, Marian Horosko attended the Juilliard School of Music, Columbia University, and the Cleveland Institute of Music. She studied at the School of American Ballet and danced with the Ballet Russe de Monte Carlo and was a soloist with the Metropolitan Opera Ballet. She joined the New York City Ballet in 1954 and danced with the company until 1961. She has worked as an associate producer on television for WNET and CBS and broadcast on dance on WNCN and WBAI radio. A prolific writer on dance, she is also Associate Editor in Education at Dance Magazine *and author of* Ballet Technique for the Male Dancer *and* The Dancer's Survival Manual.

I Remember Balanchine

I CAME FROM A WIDE BACKGROUND—BROADWAY SHOWS, DANCING IN FILMS, THE BALlet Russe de Monte Carlo for a bit as an apprentice, and the Metropolitan Opera Ballet. Madame Doubrovska, who was so good to me in classes at the School of American Ballet, came to see me in *La Traviata;* she kept pointing me out to Mr. B. I stopped him on the street one day and said, "I can't stand the opera anymore. I want to dance in your company." He asked me to come audition. Roland Vazquez, my partner at the Met, and I auditioned and were both asked to join New York City Ballet.

I was told I would be expected to learn quickly, since there were one or two weeks to teach me parts of thirty-six ballets before going on tour. Mr. B. also said to me at that time, "You remind me of Zorina. I will never give you any solos." When I left because of a severe knee injury years later, and asked him why he never gave me anything but small parts, he said it was because I never asked for more!

Balanchine took a diverse group into his company in those days and coached them into his style. The coaching in his classes was first to get rid of all the little mannerisms and weaknesses we had picked up from other sources—the misunderstandings of good dancing. Then, in his rehearsals, his individual style was honed and perfected through his choreography. His schooling was good, but he wanted us to be even better. I would call his company class a *"classe de perfection,"* as they used to be called in earlier times. We had it almost every day after I joined in 1954. Coming from such an amalgam of jobs, one of the things I noticed immediately about Balanchine was the great economy of his choreography. With other choreographers, you had "catch" steps. If you wound up on the right foot after a step, and the next step also had to begin on the right foot, you somehow had to fudge your way between beats, to transfer quickly from right to left to right in order to be on the correct foot for the next step. It's an imperceptible moment, hopefully. In Balanchine's choreography, you never had something like that. When the Kirov recently performed *Theme and Variations,* there was a misinterpretation of what Mr. B. would insert as a quick *chassé,* but which the Russians performed as a "catch" step. If that movement is not performed elegantly and with speed, it makes the dancer look as if he has to adapt to the choreography. Such is not the case with Mr. B.'s work. When I saw the Kirov dancers, I thought, "Well, that's a normal error."

My comment is made with all due respect to the people who teach and rehearse his works. There was another moment in *Scotch Symphony* that required Balanchine's direction. Only he could make sense of this since it was one of his inventions. It's a kind of pile-up of people in that section of *Scotch,* the pose in an arabesque *à terre,* with the upstage hand raised overhead and the group sort of covers itself. Mr. B. used to call these poses a "muschel."

They were really a mess of legs, arms, bodies, and not a moment to lose to get into and out of one of these "muschels." He loved that term. What it should look like when it is properly done is a clam closing like a bud and then a sudden opening into a beautiful pattern. I guess he got that invention from the Paris Opéra's choreography where groups would come together and open up into a floor pattern. When the Kirov performed the "muschel" in *Scotch,* there seemed to be a moment of terror, all the bodies went tense, the faces lost their calm, and the shoulders went up. You could see them wondering if they were going to get their hands offered to the right person or make an obvious mistake. Panic set in. I know it used to happen to us too. With his beautiful hands and beautiful arm gestures, Mr. B. would direct that with a swing of his hand and say, "Indicate where you're going. Indicate your partner's hand." It was never to be a literal touching of your partner's hand. He wanted us to just know where our partner would be and where the hand was to go, as if in a dream. The Kirov began frantically waving hands. It's difficult to convey without demonstrating this movement, and it's so subtle that it sounds rather silly. But it's all just an illusion of a flower opening, a burst from a fountain, the unraveling of a ball of yarn. He loved to twine and intertwine arms, legs, and bodies onstage. They were rest patterns for the eye and for the dancers. Only he could really show a group how to pose as a movement, not as an inanimate cluster. Something inside has always to be moving, even in stillness.

At Balanchine's funeral, my generation of dancers from the 1950s stood together during the service. When we left the church there were so many people outside waiting for the casket to descend that we had to twine our way down the stairs of the church. There we were, unconsciously holding hands as he had taught us and slowly winding down through people on the stairs as if in a ballet. It was just an instinctive thing for us to do.

The other thing I noticed about Balanchine's style besides the comfort of the choreography was that there was never any waste. In movies you would very often find it necessary to do a certain amount of stalling in place until the cameras were on you. That was the kind of choreography I was used to, marking in place, then running to a spot or tactfully omitting steps in combinations that you could not perform neatly or with style. But in Mr. B.'s work there is never an unimportant moment, never a wasted movement, never a wasted count. The timing of his choreography, the musicality of it, reminded me of Massine. He was the only other choreographer I ever knew with the same sense of music, its inner rhythms and its big architectural curves.

Balanchine also had—and this is surprising in comparison to other, lesser talents—the capacity to self-edit. He would rehearse very quickly, knowing exactly what he wanted you to do at any moment, only hesitating a second or two to find out the mechanics of how to do it, and then sometimes edit it out. You could never understand why he would take something wonderful out. Sometimes it would be an entire passage, or a new ending. But he didn't fall in love with what he was doing—which is the downfall of so many choreographers—so that he could not remove it if it didn't work.

The piece that was thrown away was sometimes your solo, your little moment. But it was out. And he took it out for no personal reason other than that it didn't work in the whole. If it was your part he was working on, he made it work for you; but if it was out, it was because he wanted it out and it was not because he didn't like the way you did it. He would work on you until he was satisfied or he would change it for you.

Most choreographers will not self-edit so quickly. They start dickering with it. Finally, you might assume it was the dancer's fault because it wasn't working. It was never like that for Mr. B. Granted, he might store that passage away in his mind and use it somewhere else!

When I have spoken to Graham dancers during a recent seminar, I have found a similarity between Graham's company and the Balanchine company of the 1950s. There seems to have been a mutual time of family when all the members of both families, Balanchine and Graham, who had come from other disciplines and experiences, learned their new vocabularies and became so accustomed to working together that they practically wrote the choreography during its creation by the choreographer. The response was immediate understanding. The two groups think and act in the terms of the choreographer with such rapidity and understanding that they are participants in the creation. I experienced this with Balanchine, but, according to the Graham dancers, it is true for them as well.

Mr. B. worked very quickly, and during rehearsal he would do a combination on stage left, and those of us on stage right would immediately reverse the combination and do it exactly. Sometimes he would say, "That's what I want," when a dancer would perform it a bit differently in tempo or shape. And we would instantly do what we had just seen. There was no hesitation, no conversation about it, just the heat of mutual creation—director and executants, almost all equal.

Our audience then was a peculiar one that doesn't seem to exist anymore. We felt that the audience, small as it was, was with us every step of the way. We felt we were leading them, and they were willing to go, placing themselves into neutrality until they responded individually to what they saw. And that they would come back again and again to take another look. I feel that the company's audience today knows everyone by name, has favorites as in a baseball game, and is not there for status.

In the first or second *Nutcracker* season at City Center, during the change from the tiny Christmas tree to the big tree, the big tree always seemed to get caught in its own branches and struggled to disentangle itself and grow. It always seemed to need a little more music to move up grandly. Balanchine said to me, "Dear, we need more time for the tree. So we will have more music before the tree grows so the stagehands can disentangle the tree before it starts to rise. So you will hear the music and do something." Do something! Sure, I'd do anything for him. So, to my surprise, I heard the insert of the Tchaikovsky Violin Concerto cadenza in the place just before my exit, added some stage business, and slid softly offstage at the last note. In that company almost all the dancers would have known that violin work and would have done the same thing. I moved a chair, shook the draperies, looked out the window, checked the nutcracker in his bed under the tree, felt a chill, and wrapped my shawl tighter around me to fill in the time. I just did the things you'd normally do when you left a room for the night—a Christmas night. Balanchine just nodded when I reached the wings. It was all right. We were family.

There were fewer people in the company and more dancing for each member to do. Everyone did corps or solo parts as the need arose. Rank was not determined by how long you spent in the company but by what Mr. B. thought your rank should be. I remember seeing Maria Tallchief in the last line of *Symphony in C* when someone was missing. She knew the finales and just jumped in without thinking anything of it. We could enjoy all the roles. We just wanted to dance and be with him. Nothing else mattered. The income was terrible. I remember once we had to chip in because Mr. B. was robbed in a motel.

There was no ponderous development going on in Balanchine's creative process, no heavy thought about its meanings. You would see him stand there and stand there and seem to be thinking, listening to his inner music, anxious to move but unable to take a step that was not the evolvement of the last step. He'd have his arm around someone as a partner, his fingers moving, almost as if he were giving himself over to some kind of suggestion that was failing to tell him where to go. He wasn't eliminating a dozen ideas, he wanted to know what felt right to do. It was an instinct, and a beautiful instinct to watch. You were mesmerized. Sometimes he would watch two or three people do the indication he gave and then choose one over the other, not to make a personal choice of one person's ideas over another's, but to choose the better way to have us move to express his idea—what was comfortable for us. We were participants in the creation, entering into the atmosphere he created. It's heady stuff, as clear and exciting now, to me, as when I experienced it. You are on top of your capacities. He has taken you there.

And you dare not look to the past for any help. You are going into an unknown future.

Once you give yourself over to that state and follow your leader, you are in a spiritual state. These gifts are not learned, they are given. Some lead. Some follow. Some people say that the high a dancer feels is like that of a runner—endorphic. Sure, ten minutes after you start a class or rehearsal, the rest of the world melts away. But I'm talking about spiritual endorphins. Those only come to dancers who can place themselves outside of themselves.

Before he left the Metropolitan Opera, Balanchine gave an interview in which he said, "I will never tell the press what I think or be honest with them ever again. I will only tell them what I think they want to hear." I think he did that whenever he made a statement or gave an interview. Some critics think that what he said to them was thereafter written in stone. But he would contradict himself at the next interview. He was joking. With his mercurial mind, he tried to figure out what you wanted to hear and then he would say it perfectly seriously.

Balanchine could be quixotic and charming. He had little names for each of us. Mine was Ginger. He thought I was like Ginger Rogers. Part of Mr. B.'s glamor was that exotic glamor of the Russian Tatar, of a faraway difference that he had from us as Americans. When he was angry, he never raised his voice, but he would sit there and that face would become a mask. Those beautiful features would suddenly harden, and it would get very quiet, and you'd know that something was wrong. One hot summer night at the studios at Eighty-second and Broadway we were rehearsing *Swan Lake,* the earlier version, not the one N.Y.C.B. does now. *Swan* was not our favorite ballet to do. It wasn't his either. When you rehearse *Swan* everybody has to be at the rehearsal because there are so many crossings and so many patterns that have to be quickly assumed without hesitation. You have to know who is behind you, ahead of you, and when you're coming out for the pas de trois or the pas de quatre. So it was a boring rehearsal. Mr. B. sat there, and we were doing endless crossings. And then that hard face of his appeared, and everything got silent, and we knew that there was trouble somewhere. He said very quickly, "Are you bored?" Nobody would dare reply to that, except a new apprentice or somebody we had just picked up to add to the cast. One such girl said, "Yes," hoping to endear herself somehow. And he said, "Can you imagine how bored I am?" With that, he explained how, for every ten *Swan Lakes* we did, he could only do one *Agon.* It cost that much to be able to do one *Agon.* He said, "It better be good." Every *Swan Lake* had to be as good as *Agon.* One's energy had to be there one hundred percent all the time.

He said, "This is a moment of your life," and you were not to throw it away, even if it was a rehearsal.

As a teacher, Balanchine taught good dancing. When you think of how many generations of dancers participated in his ballets and teaching, only a few complain. One or two couldn't take it because of whatever previous experience they had had, whatever congenital reason or vindictiveness or purposeful misuse. Good dancing doesn't hurt the body. Beyond that, he created an aesthetic concept. It wasn't a matter of someone who invents a fall or deep knee bends. It was dancing that came to us over three hundred years of experience. What was different was that there was a rhythmic way that Balanchine was doing it that changed the look of it. This didn't change your bones; it didn't change your capacity to do it. I never had any injuries until a bad fall that was caused by fatigue.

Some people say that, without Mr. B. present, the ballets get too abstract and lose their effect. No. The loss is in the dancers. We have enough documentation to make Balanchine's work live. But there's great resistance for the performer who must make it live while performing it. There's a fear of making commitments, there's a fear of not driving oneself quickly enough, there's a fear of feelings. It is frightening to give yourself over, to forget everything you learned with such difficulty and to give yourself over to a director or choreographer and to trust him or her. I remember one *Serenade* that was so beautiful. One night something happened onstage that made us so together in spirit and movement that we breathed together and it was a perfect performance. We went into the dressing room in silence so as not to break the spell. It was a moment that we knew might not come again. That takes a group of people who are a family, who think the same way and come from the same source and are together for a long time and sacrifice in the same way to perform. I don't think that our dancers now want to dance badly enough to pay any price for it.

I remember not having more than five bucks when I danced for N.Y.C.B. But we had the security of knowing that Betty Cage and Lincoln Kirstein would take care of us. If we needed money, or if we had personal problems, Betty was always there to help. Lincoln was always there, looking worried. It wasn't just a job. Today, dancers get a good salary and have none of the long layoffs we had. There were times between seasons we would stand in unemployment lines. Sometimes Betty would ask us to go to Washington, D.C., for a three-day stint, and although that would interrupt our unemployment earnings and the waiting period, we would do so without hesitation. The real difference is that, for us, dance was a way of life. For dancers now, it is a career.

One night, while the company was traveling by train in Germany, I was wide awake sitting up in a compartment with the door open, and Mr. B. passed by. "Why are you up?" he asked me. "I can't sleep." He sat down and we talked of many things. He was relaxed and friendly—not the director. "What do you think your place is going to be in history?" I asked. "You have done so many great things." He said, "I can't outdo Petipa." "Why should you?" I responded. "You live in a different place and a different time." But that made no difference to him. I mentioned that he lived at a time of great competition: Robbins, Tudor, Graham, so many choreographers all over the globe, while Petipa had the one good company and reigned in a protected situation with the Tsar. He just nodded his head throughout. I mentioned Massine. "Oh, Massine, I know Massine," he said. I think there was some rivalry there.

So I asked again, "Where do you think your place is going to be?" And he said, "My place is with ghosts." He had this romantic, poetic turn that he used to explain himself. What he meant was that his place was in time, past and future, not in the present. "Do you compete with anyone now?" The question was not put so directly but over the course of a long conversation about many things. He would never answer a direct question if you pressed him. That's very Russian. He indicated that he was really competing only with ghosts of the past and the future. He didn't know where his place would eventually be. I sensed that he wanted a place in time and didn't know what the immortal place would be, and it seemed painful to him. He said he didn't care what happened after he was gone, but I think he did. He might not have cared about the company and the dancers, but he cared about his ballets and what his place would be among choreographers.

Doubrovska said to me once that Pavlova had come back from visiting a gypsy on the beach at Monte Carlo and evidently had been told something foreboding. She was very upset by it. She felt that she was not going to live much longer, that something was going to happen to her. Balanchine mentioned the story to me too. Evidently Doubrovska had told him, or they knew about it together. They felt that it was a symbol and a sign that the only response possible to life is fatalistic. The Revolution and the escape from Russia had been pure drama in their own backyards, and I think it made them very superstitious and fatalistic in general. They had an attitude toward life that they were going to play that game full out no matter what, and whatever happened to them was the hand of fate reaching down.

I had been sitting there on the train, writing letters. I had a certain talent for looking at people's handwriting and intuiting something about that person. I used it to begin a conversation. I certainly had never studied it. Mr. B.

wrote his name down for me. It was a little playful thing we did. I gave him a small slip of paper, and he could not contain himself, so he wrote all over the paper and onto the table. I said to him, "No one can contain you. You have too much energy." He said, "No, no, I'm Mercury."

BARBARA

HORGAN

Barbara Horgan began working at the New York City Ballet in 1953. Balanchine asked her to become his personal assistant in 1962, a position she held until his death. She is Trustee-Administrator of the George Balanchine Trust.

I Remember Balanchine

I DIDN'T GO TO RUSSIA WITH BALANCHINE WHEN HE WENT BACK THERE FOR THE FIRST time in 1962. He told me he felt as though he were being strangled when he was there. In the middle of the tour he left and came home. He was tired from his experience there, not by his brother or relatives, but the whole thing was overwhelming. Then he went back in 1972. It was a different Russia then, and he was confident. We had had a New York City Ballet triumph with the Stravinsky Festival of 1972, and that was Balanchine's pride. But the Soviet Union at that time had become more conservative, and there was not as much interest on the part of the audiences as there had been in 1962. There weren't as many accolades. But Balanchine seemed very secure, satisfied about what we in the New York City Ballet were doing in Russia and that the visit was justified and correct in the scheme of things.

At that time there was still a certain wall between the Balanchine the Russians wanted to recognize and the American Balanchine. Konstantin Sergeyev from the Kirov Ballet in Leningrad had come to Saratoga before we went on the 1972 Russian tour to tell us what ballets we should bring. I remember being told that Sergeyev should be allowed to tell Balanchine what to do! But, of course, being impatient and youthful and protective, I said to Balanchine, "You have to listen, you have to discuss things, and then you do what you want to do." But Balanchine had this incredible patience. I recognized that in many Russians I have met in my life. They are not unique, but they are different. Balanchine knew how to play the game: you are receptive, you are hospitable, you smile a great deal, and then you do what you want to do.

There was a certain repertory Balanchine wanted to take. He wanted to take *Stravinsky Violin Concerto,* which he had recreated from his older ballet *Balustrade* for the 1972 Festival. Sergeyev went to Saratoga to see it and, of course, didn't understand it, didn't want to understand it. What he could deal with was *Tchaikovsky Suite No. 3.* So there was a compromise. "I'll bring *Tchaikovsky Suite No. 3,* and I'm bringing my *Stravinsky Violin Concerto.*" Three dances from the Stravinsky Festival went, along with *Dances at a Gathering* and *Serenade.*

Balanchine was content with what he took. One of the problems with the tour was New York City Ballet's extraordinary, difficult musical repertory. We always have problems finding orchestras that can play our repertory well. The *Stravinsky Violin Concerto* was a real problem because we knew we would be getting different orchestras. We were doing four cities. We had four different orchestras and some repeat musicians. We started in Kiev, went to Leningrad, Tbilisi, and finally Moscow. We were grateful to have Sergeyev's help as an organizer for the tour. But it was not acceptable to have him inflict the taste of the Soviet Union on the choice of repertory.

Actually, it's not so unusual. When we started to go to Kennedy Center, Martin Feinstein, their director, would talk to Balanchine about the repertory he felt would sell, and he was absolutely right. He knew what to open with. He knew what to close with. If you wanted a two-week season, he said, "Something new here. Open with *Coppélia.*"

When Oleg Vinogradov of the Kirov came to the United States in 1986, his company was dancing on the West Coast. Several people sent me an interview he had given. It said he wished to acquire the Balanchine repertory but that since Balanchine's death it was very difficult to deal with the heirs. I decided there was a mixed message there. He wanted something, but he didn't know how to get it because the Balanchine estate was still in probate. It hadn't been distributed. Of course, everybody was doing Balanchine's ballets all over the world. Then a couple of more interviews like that one came to me through other people in cities the Kirov visited.

One night I was at a workshop performance of Madame Darvash where Judy Fugate was dancing. I ran into a colleague, Alex Dubet, who at that time was an agent. We happened to be sitting together, we started to talk, and the next thing you know we were talking about the Kirov. I said, "You know, the damnedest thing, I keep getting these articles where Vinogradov keeps saying he wants Balanchine ballets." Alex said, "Do you want to get in touch with him?" I said that I would like Vinogradov to know who I was and where I could be reached. Alex asked me to write a note to Vinogradov saying just what I had said to him. I did, gave it to Alex, and then got a phone call from a man representing Vinogradov who invited me to a performance of the Kirov in New Jersey. I remember having to get on a bus with all the New York critics on a Sunday afternoon. It was arranged for me to meet Oleg during the first intermission, and I literally had to fight my way backstage because there were many guards. Finally, there he was in a white suit, and he looked very handsome. He spoke to me in English, although he had an interpreter with him. He said that for many years he had wanted to acquire Balanchine. "It is my lifelong dream. I want *Scotch Symphony, Serenade,* and *Symphony in C.*" So I said, "Look, I think it can work, my only requirement is that you bring representatives of Mr. Balanchine's company—ballet masters from the New York City Ballet or ballet masters who worked for Mr. Balanchine during his lifetime—to mount the ballets. That is my only demand." He understood completely and said that would be fine. I asked how I could get in touch with him. He said to send a letter to him in care of the Soviet Embassy in Washington.

I prepared a letter, and my colleague and friend Eddie Bigelow helped me put some videotapes together. We decided, as long as we were going to do it, we would send videotapes of perhaps ten ballets including *Symphony in C* and

Serenade. We sent the letter and tapes, and between September of 1986 and November of 1987, I heard nothing. Finally I got a call from the Soviet attaché in Washington asking where my letter was. I said I had sent the letter and the tapes. He had never received them, so I had to start all over again.

I had a call from Dina Makarova, who had been with Natasha Makarova in Paris, and she said they had just been with Oleg in Paris, and he wanted a Balanchine evening as soon as possible. Then Rudolf Nureyev got in touch with Jane Hermann at the Metropolitan Opera and said, "What is Barbara doing? They want a Balanchine evening at the Kirov. Please help her." I said to Jane, "You know, it's just not that easy because I need to send people over. There are production values." Vinogradov didn't know what repertory he wanted, and I couldn't get hold of him. There was no telephone number to reach him, he was traveling all over the world.

In early 1988, when the Kirov went to Milan, I got in touch with Pat Neary, who was there. She found Vinogradov and talked to him and then called me and said, "Look, I don't think he has a clue as to what it entails to put on a whole evening. All he's thinking of is Balanchine, Balanchine."

In February or March of 1988, I called Jane Hermann. I knew she was bringing the Kirov to the Met in 1989, and at lunch I told her the whole history. I said, "I would like to engage you as a consultant to the George Balanchine Trust in order to negotiate with the Kirov for Balanchine ballets. You know who to talk to at Gosconcert in Moscow. You know who to talk to in Washington if necessary. I don't know anyone, but I'm prepared to deal, and indeed I have offered these ballets to Vinogradov for free." Jane Hermann immediately said, "Not on your life! If he wants to come into the twenty-first century, he has to deal with fees just like everyone else. Unless you really feel morally obligated." I said, "No, I don't feel morally obligated. But, on the other hand, money is not the object here. I feel very strongly that it is necessary to license the ballets in the same way everybody else acquires Mr. Balanchine's ballets."

Jane Hermann traveled to Moscow, and negotiations began. We made the decision that it shouldn't be an all-Balanchine evening. Three ballets were more than I could prepare and perhaps more than they could absorb. I talked to a great many people who had danced in Russia. Francia Russell had gone to Leningrad, and she suggested *Theme and Variations.* In the summer of 1988, Vinogradov came to New York, and all he wanted was *Scotch Symphony.* I made the cardinal mistake of thinking that the only reason he wanted it was that he thought it was Balanchine's Fokine ballet.

The Bolshoi dancers Andris Liepa and Nina Ananiashvili appeared as guest artists with New York City Ballet. Peter Martins had them dance Balanchine's *Raymonda Variations,* thinking that it would be easy for them since it is derived from Petipa. That's when I first saw what Balanchine had done with Petipa, how different the two styles were. George had arranged Petipa and had made the choreography more interesting, more modern. The experience was a nightmare for the two Bolshoi dancers. So I thought that Vinogradov was making the same type of mistake, thinking that *Scotch Symphony* was in a Fokine style. With an interpreter, I delicately broached the problem, and Vinogradov turned to me in perfect English and said, "You are absolutely right. There is an enormous difference between the school of Vaganova and the school of Balanchine. I know what you are saying because Mr. Balanchine told me this himself in 1972, which is when he recommended *Scotch Symphony* to me." "So," I thought, "okay, you've got it."

Vinogradov went to California. Francia Russell came down from Seattle and talked to him about *Theme and Variations,* and it was arranged for him to acquire *Scotch Symphony.* Francia was going to stage both, but she ran out of time and Pat Neary had to go into the hospital for a hip transplant. By fortunate coincidence, Suzanne Farrell had come to me and said that she was interested in staging Balanchine ballets. I asked her about *Scotch,* and she said that was the one Balanchine ballet she knew really well. So it was arranged for her to stage *Scotch* in Leningrad.

Francia went to Leningrad in September 1988 and spent three weeks mounting *Theme.* It was a difficult experience for her. Many of the dancers didn't know who Balanchine was. But, on the other hand, there was always a group of people who were interested, willing, and eventually converted. In the first three weeks she never had the same people twice. She never had a run-through. Vinogradov was away with the Scottish Ballet, so Francia had to fend for herself. When she came back, she was disheartened. I could see that she had struggled, and she hadn't felt that she had done well. She didn't feel satisfied. I asked her if there was ever a moment when she felt a dancer got it. She said, "Yes. When that happens it's an extraordinary moment." She said you could tell from their faces when they caught on. They would struggle and struggle with a combination, and when they finally got it, you could see that they had never felt their bodies move that way. That said it all.

Balanchine was always so patient. He never wanted Rome to be built in a day. Maria Tallchief told me a story about how he came to Chicago one day when she was auditioning dancers. Out of fifty, they only found one good one. She was upset and said, "This is awful. Isn't this a disgrace? Only one good dancer!" And George said, "Yes. Right."

In December, Suzanne went to Leningrad. She had a very good time because by then the dancers were a little more used to Balanchine, whoever he was, and *Scotch* was more in their style. It wasn't as fast, it wasn't as difficult technically. The problems are in the training. We all talk about the Kirov dancers' wonderful upper bodies, but they can't bend those upper bodies. They are held there by an invisible iron ramrod, so Suzanne had to work very hard on getting the girls and boys to move from the waist. But she found the experience to be most interesting, and she had the dancers to work with almost every day. She felt very satisfied when she returned to the United States.

We braced ourselves for the February premiere. Francia, Suzanne, and I flew over, and I was really very impressed with the work that they had done. I got there ten days before the premiere. Oleg was there, and I spent a great deal of time in the theater every day. These are the wonders of Communist art: "You want the orchestra tomorrow? Fine. How many hours do you want it? Six? Oh, okay, we'll have it." I was quite surprised when I saw the first rehearsal. I thought, "Goodness, this is kind of amazing." They worked every single day. It's not that the Russians don't work hard. They work very hard, but they work differently. Each day there was one more convert, and you could see so many of the dancers really trying to get the steps and the style. With *Theme,* of course, it's hard. It's hard for any company.

Vinogradov was very much there and supportive of Francia and Suzanne. His operation is like Balanchine's: it's a one-man show. Everything that goes on in that theater with regard to ballet is Vinogradov's policy. It really did remind me of how we work here with one artistic director literally in charge. Vinogradov did not play a role: the buck stops at his desk. I found him humorous, gentle, kind, and authoritative. He knows how to get what he wants. I admired him, and I enjoyed watching him work. He was gracious to all of us, he entertained us, and was friendly. He picked me up every day at the hotel and took me to the theater. I think he felt what we all felt: that this was a major step for them to take.

For the Balanchine repertory to be available to companies elsewhere is part of our tradition at the New York City Ballet. No matter how badly they are danced, Balanchine ballets look better on companies than other ballets, even ballets already in a company's own repertory. For me, Balanchine's ballets are many things. They are great teaching tools. They are tools to develop audiences and dancers. They are tools to develop taste and to develop your soul. That was the thing I suppose I felt most in Leningrad. There the arts are kindred spirits. There, too, they do a great deal more soul searching. We don't think of our souls here. We have too many things, I have far too many phonograph records, far too many stereos. If I could, I'd have four cars. In Russia, you have nothing.

I remember Oleg saying to me one night in the theater that they have many dress rehearsals open to the public before the actual premiere. I went to many performances and remarked how respectful the audiences were. He said, "Yes, but you know, in Leningrad, our audience comes as though they are going to church." I remembered Balanchine had said to me when he was upset that the theater should be like a cathedral. He was in the business of entertainment, and he was never going to cheat his audience, but on the other hand he wanted people to come into the theater with respect. But you know how we are: we come into the theater chatting, the first ballet is often missed because people are still settling down. Not in Russia. People wear the best clothes they can possibly put on. You can spot the tourists because they are the ones wearing T-shirts and sneakers. In Russia the arts are a solace.

I grew up in New York City. I graduated from high school in 1950 and decided not to go to college but to pursue an acting career. I enrolled in acting schools, had a coach, and enrolled in a dance class at Hanya Holm's school. One of her teachers was Alwin Nikolais, but I was dyslexic, so I had no coordination at all. My introduction to ballet came about through my friend the actress Wendy Drew, who had a half sister living in California who was studying ballet.

One day when the sister and Wendy's mother were to arrive in New York, Wendy called me and asked me if I could meet them. I had a car because my father was in the automobile business, so I drove out to Idlewild. I had said to Wendy, "How am I going to know these people?" She said she thought I would recognize her sister. Sure enough, this little girl came down the ramp holding a potted palm or avocado plant. I thought, "That's got to be the sister." It was. Her name was Iris Cohen, but she had changed her name to Allegra Kent.

Allegra auditioned for the School of American Ballet and was taken instantly. I started to see performances of the New York City Ballet with Allegra. The ballet made an enormous impression on me. About 1953, Allegra was made an apprentice in the company. One Saturday afternoon while I was selling records at Sam Goody a group of dancers from New York City Ballet came in. I recognized them as dancers, introduced myself, and took care of them. They were Barbara Walczak, Barbara Milberg, and Bobby Barnett. They invited me out for coffee, and the next week they came back again. They invited me to a party, and I went and had a wonderful time.

Then, in May, I ran into them on Fifty-sixth Street near the stage door of the City Center. They said, "Let's have lunch, but first we have to go upstairs to the office and get paid." In those days they were paid in cash. So I went upstairs with them. The City Ballet office had just been renovated. Lincoln Kirstein had put George Platt Lynes photographs on the walls, and they were really beautiful. I was looking at the photographs when a woman came out and said, "May I help you?" I turned around, and there was this beautiful dark woman, very young, I thought. I said, "Well, I'm waiting for the two Barbaras." At which point, they came out and introduced me to Betty Cage. She said, "What do you do?" I said, "I'm an unemployed actress. Do you ever use actresses?" She said, "No, but I could sure use a secretary." I said, "Well, I can type, as a matter of fact." I didn't tell her I couldn't spell. She said, "My secretary is in the hospital with a tonsillectomy, so I can't hire you permanently." I didn't want to be hired permanently. So she said, "If you want to work for a while, I can't pay you, but you can come and see performances for free." This was in the fifties when you were educating yourself. It was called "lifemanship." So the next day I started. I'll never forget walking in. I walked in, sat down, and thought, "I want to be here."

I met Mr. Balanchine. He came off the elevator, came in the office, and gave me a nod. He had just come back from La Scala, where he had done *Le Baiser de la Fée* and Tanny LeClercq had premiered Jerome Robbins's *Afternoon of a Faun*. At the end of the day they said that I had made an impression on Mr. Balanchine. He had wanted to know who I was. So there I was, and there I stayed.

I was trained by Betty, who is one of the most extraordinary people in the world. I came ill equipped; God knows, I was willing, but she had to deal with a dyslexic mind. She taught me how to do payrolls. She taught me how to do the typing for the casting. We did everything. There were three administrative people: Betty Cage, Eddie Bigelow, and myself. The really unglamorous administrative work was done by Betty and me. She had infinite patience. Why she put up with me I don't know, but she did. But I learned more than that from Betty. I had the privilege of watching her work with people. She had an extraordinarily magnanimous personality. She had loyalty, and she knew how to deal with people. It took a lot out of her, but she was very giving.

I can't speak for Betty, but we had, I think, the best of classicism in the art of ballet. The art we were privileged to work for is classic. It isn't around very much. Betty was a brilliant woman, a brilliant student. She had started life as a teacher. She came to New York and was hired by the editor of *View* and was very educated. I assume that the exposure to the gifts of Balanchine and Kirstein was solace for her soul. I can only say for myself that I never tired of the New York City Ballet. I was perhaps more visually oriented; Betty doesn't even have a television. I'm a voyeur like so many Americans. Betty is an intellectual. My voyeurism was saturated by Balanchine's work and the work of other choreographers.

The triumvirate—a sort of movable triangle—was George, Lincoln, and Betty. I was just lucky to be there. I was very much George's girl in the end. Ten years went by in which I didn't work for him personally. Then in 1962–

63 he asked me to be his personal assistant, although he never called me that. He said, "You are going to work, you will come and work for me now."

It was hard to have a routine working for Balanchine because he never did the same thing twice. He tended to have certain rituals, but rules were made to be broken, you know. We both woke up early. We tended to be morning people. More often than not, he would call me in the morning around seven or seven-thirty. He would ask, "What's happening?" and he was always funny. Sometimes he'd say, "Hello. This is George Balanchine." Or I'd hear water running and then I'd hear, "Where do you think I am?"

Balanchine made me laugh. People say, "What *is* she talking about?" I spent a lot of time with him, and he was amusing and pixie and fun. He had a lot of charm. He was really very "with it," and then sometimes he could be a real pain. Who isn't? If it was a day when there was a performance at State Theater, I would have his schedule for class and rehearsals. So the morning call would be a time to talk about other things that were to happen. "If you have time, would you stop by and see Betty, who is talking with so-and-so about such-and-such?" Then he'd say, "When do I start? Class is at eleven, fine, what do I have after?" But I wouldn't give him the entire day because he wouldn't want to remember everything. You couldn't always count on seeing him after class, so I had to program around that possibility. If there was something important, I had to say, "I really must see you," and often he would forget. I would have to remind him, but it worked very well. If something came up, I'd just go find and grab him. If he saw you standing at the door of the rehearsal room at the end of the rehearsal, he knew you wanted something, but if you did it every day he would walk right by you. You had to be smart. You had to make your own decisions. Meantime, I stayed at my desk. People always said, "You are so lucky, you can go and watch rehearsals." But I used to watch rehearsals on weekends because I couldn't leave my desk, what with phone calls and typing and people checking in. Many things had to be coordinated.

George had an incredible mind, and as I look back I think he had a game plan in the sense of development. Once he had his theater at City Center, he finally had his feet on the ground. It was really roots. Even though for the first few years we only had three or four performance weeks a year, it was the beginning. He had a place to show his art and the art of the company. Before I came in 1953, he had done *Firebird* and *Swan Lake.* I was under the impression that he created these works for box office. Morton Baum had wanted them. Probably there had been a discussion about *The Nutcracker* as well. When I arrived, the plans for *The Nutcracker* had actually long begun, and Betty was wringing her hands and defending George to Mr. Baum with regard to the kind of money it was going to cost. I remember the fights Betty would have with Mr. Baum and Mr. Falcone, our controller at City Center, about spending all that money.

I really didn't know Mr. Baum well. He was a music and opera man, but I think he realized that he had a genius on his hands in Mr. Balanchine, and ballet became interesting to him. He was one of those people who don't exist anymore. He was in total control of the scene. He didn't have to worry about the Ford Foundation. He was in control of the financial picture of both the opera and the ballet. He had his sources and his connection with the city. He was an intelligent and educated man.

Mr. Baum had graciously agreed to give us twenty thousand dollars for the production of *The Nutcracker.* George went out with Jean Rosenthal and spent it all on the Christmas tree. He knew what came first. Betty almost had a fit. She had killed herself to get the twenty thousand dollars. Suddenly it was gone. That was it. I wasn't present, but George must have defended himself. He knew that *Nutcracker* is ninety minutes, of which there is only twenty minutes of dance. The rest is scenic effects and pantomime. He had to find a way to get the scenic effects. In addition to his sense of tradition, he was a showman. He had worked with Goldwyn, Dick Rodgers, Larry Hart. He had been involved with Broadway for years. He also knew that this was going to be the company's meal ticket.

Mr. Baum enjoyed the success of *The Nutcracker.* He immediately announced that we would do four or five weeks of *The Nutcracker* the following November. This irritated Balanchine because, why November? The opera was in the house over Christmas, so it had to be November, take it or leave it. Slowly Mr. Baum began to trust us. He began to trust Balanchine and Betty. He saw that the company was being run by a woman who had credentials, loyalty, and who tried very hard to keep track of everything. This was not a frivolous woman. This was not Lucia Chase. This was a woman who was devoted to the cause and to the honor of the men she served.

I remember Balanchine's remark to me as we were standing waiting for the premiere of *PAMTGG*—which is always cited as George's great disaster. He turned to me just before the curtain went up and he said, "Next year, Stravinsky." The next year was 1972. He had to do one thing to get to another. Always there was a plan. Balanchine always seemed to have many ideas. In the beginning, one had to utilize those thoughts as conservatively as possible in order to save money and give the public something new.

In my opinion, George was not a universally recognized genius until 1972 and the Stravinsky Festival. Until then the fans may have recognized his genius, but the public finally had to acknowledge it. Back in 1952, I knew it, but I didn't know what to call it. It was just different from anybody else. I didn't know what genius was. Once he fought through the 1950s and toured and created works that could tour well, he began to bring more people into the company. He created works for individuals, so the menu was very large. "Now we will have a little pas de trois." "Now we'll do *Jewels.* " Who would have thought of *Jewels?* And how it worked! A whole evening of New York classic ballet under one title, a gimmick but a fascinating, genius gimmick.

Balanchine was superstitious, but I never paid much attention to it because I come from an Irish family (my mother is German), and they are filled with all that lore. I was told by my German mother to disregard that because it didn't mean anything in life. George would say things that were somewhat superstitious, but he was practical as well. I saw him on so many occasions being totally fearless with regard to decisions. He didn't have a nine-to-five job, and he took a lot of risks. He made people take risks in a business where risk will be the end of you. You knew that this was not a crazed genius making arbitrary decisions. He closed down the State Theater for one week in order to rehearse for the Stravinsky Festival. He knew that he couldn't do without it, and he knew that we had to have a Stravinsky Festival. We had been in the State Theater since 1964 and, at that point in his career and in the life of the company, it was time to make a statement. The Stravinsky Festival was the statement. It was a gamble that worked.

ARTHUR

MITCHELL

Born in 1934, Arthur Mitchell trained at the High School of Per-
forming Arts and the School of American Ballet, prior to dancing
with Donald McKayle's group. He joined the New York City Ballet
in 1955, where he danced until 1969, creating roles in **Agon, A**
Midsummer Night's Dream, *and many other Balanchine bal-*
lets. In 1968 he founded the Dance Theatre of Harlem where he is
artistic director. He has also danced on Broadway and choreographed
extensively.

I Remember Balanchine

WHEN I FIRST CAME TO THE HIGH SCHOOL OF PERFORMING ARTS, I STARTED GOING to City Center to see the New York City Ballet. At my graduation, Lincoln Kirstein offered me a scholarship to the School of American Ballet. That's when I became more and more aware of Mr. Balanchine. I went to all the performances, sitting in the second balcony. I'd say to myself, "Oh, God, I'd like to dance with this company. I'd love to dance *that* ballet, or that." I was very taken with the choreography, the musicality, and the wide range the company was given to dance.

I worked with Balanchine while I was still at the School, when I got into the Broadway show *House of Flowers.* He was the choreographer and I just marveled at seeing him so adept, going from one genre to the other. In a sense that prepared me for working with him at the New York City Ballet, but I never got the chance to know him until I received a telegram from Lincoln in the fall of 1955. He asked me to join the New York City Ballet and dance in the Fourth Movement of *Western Symphony* with Tanaquil LeClercq.

In talking with all the ballerinas at the time, I learned I should "always listen to Mr. B." Balanchine was mild in his manner; he would say what he had to, but with great quietude. Dance was my life, I would sit and watch everything whether I was in the rehearsal or not. I always put myself in his hands. He was a great teacher, once he knew you wanted to learn. But he was not going to seek you out.

You had to learn that many times he might be talking to you or about you, without talking specifically at you. Mr. B. said, "I want you to land like a cat, like André Eglevsky." Mr. B. had healthy competition impulses; he could do pirouettes and jumps and had that catlike feline quality. "Watch George," Maria Tallchief told me. When he did roles he became whomever or whatever he was talking about. You'd be talking to him and all of a sudden he'd transform into what he was describing. He particularly made a tremendous impact on all of us by his ability in partnering. Early on I learned that he had a wonderful ability to take both sides. He could waltz me around the room and do the girl's part or the boy's. I would say, "How do you do this?" and he would say, "This is the basics to start from and how to do it." And if you couldn't get it he'd say, "Well, watch So-and-so."

Balanchine took such care with each dancer. If you were having a costume made, he would come personally to Madame Karinska and say, "No, the wrong color, the wrong material," that sort of thing. Sometimes we would go shopping together and he'd say, "This color is very good for this ballerina," or "This person should make her hair lighter or darker." "Why?" I asked. "Because the color of her skin doesn't balance the color of her hair."

Once he knew that you really wanted to learn, he was willing to share his information with you.

Agon was a big step into really defining what we call neoclassical dance. Balanchine called Diana Adams and me in about two weeks before the company started to rehearse. During our second week working on it, he said, "This is the longest it's ever taken me to do a pas de deux. But this has got to be absolutely right." At the same time Stravinsky was writing the music in California and mailing it in. We could only go as fast as the music was coming in. I learned an awful lot about partnering, working with Mr. B. on *Agon.* There was a definite use of the skin tones in terms of Diana being so pale and me being so dark, so that even the placing of the hands or the arms provided a color structure integrated into the choreographic one.

For *Figure in the Carpet,* Balanchine wanted a black woman, and I asked Mary Hinkson to come in. He looked at her, liked her very much, and then choreographed a pas de deux for Mary and me. And then he did *Modern Jazz: Variants* with the Modern Jazz Quartet. Again, he asked me to bring somebody in to make the dance quartet: "I'd like you to bring in another man." I asked John Jones to come and work with us.

Midsummer Night's Dream was interesting because logically people would have thought, since I was black and taller, that I would do Oberon and Eddie Villella would be Puck. But Balanchine reversed the roles. He wanted quickness and speed and a lot of acting in that part. In designing the costumes, he tried all kinds of things. He said, "I want a costume where you become invisible with the tree trunk." It got pared down and pared down until I wore only this net. Then he added the little chiffon cloak to give it a sense of fleetness. Finally I took the ointment that you remove makeup with—and outlined all the muscles of my body. Then I took gold, red, and green glitter and patted that on top, so it looked like the dew had coagulated on my body as I flew through the forest. When I came out, he said, "Oh, that's right. Now you look expensive."

In *Metastaseis & Pithoprakta,* Suzanne Farrell and I danced a pas de deux that was one of those eerie things that didn't use steps per se. He'd say, "I want something like this," and he would start moving. You would just have to be free enough to let your body go and do it. I think one of the things that helped me so much with him was that, being a tap dancer, I was used to rhythm and speed. Many times when he was choreographing he would work rhythmically and then put the step in. If you were looking for a step, it wouldn't be there. But if you got *dah,* da-*dah-dah-dah,* it would come out. The rhythm was always the most important. The choreography was set in time and then space.

I had a lot of offers to go to Broadway and Hollywood and do television, and I fulfilled them during the company's layoff periods. When you're young, you think, "Oh, I want to do this, I want to do that," but Balanchine kept saying, "Arthur, that's not the right path for you. Always remember you're classic." He came to see me when I was in Noel Coward's *Sweet Potato,* where I sang too. He said, "That's all well and good, Arthur, but it's not for you." He told me, "You know, I have an idea. You tap-dance?" "Well, sort of," I told him. I'd studied it at the High School of Performing Arts, but I didn't do it much anymore. He said, "I'd like you to do *Slaughter on Tenth Avenue.* " He asked Ray Bolger to come in and work with me. Balanchine said Bolger was a genius and that it was fantastic working with him. But working with Ray Bolger was very hard for me because the way he moved was something that was natural to him and hard to teach. It wasn't just his steps; it was how he did them. "Well, I will learn as much as I can from him," I told myself, but in the long run I just got together with Mr. B. and we worked something out.

Balanchine sometimes referred to Katherine Dunham. He sent some of the ballerinas to study at her school. When he did *L'Enfant* he said, "Arthur, would you come back and dance?" Or when we were doing something he would say, "Arthur, could you come in and show these kids, because they don't know old-fashioned jazz." I knew what he meant. Today kids take jazz, but they don't know the foundations, where these steps came from, like the boogie, the camel walk, the Shorty George.

After being promoted to principal dancer in the New York City Ballet, I did a small part in *Don Quixote,* a pas de deux with Gloria Govrin. She asked Balanchine, "Why are you making Arthur go back to a small role?" He said, "Because one day he may have his own company and I want him to remember everything." And this was his way of thinking about me before I had even thought about anything like that.

After Dr. Martin Luther King passed away in April 1968, Balanchine made *Requiem Canticles,* which was given one performance. After that I went to Brazil in the summer, when Dorothy Maynor asked me to teach up at her Harlem School of the Arts. I came back and said, "Okay, I'll do it." I started in July. In February 1969 I spoke to Mr. Balanchine at the end of the *Nutcracker* season. "I'm very committed to this and I really want to continue," I told him. "The school's getting so big now that we can't be housed anymore at the Harlem School of the Arts." He said, "Well, Arthur, why don't you form your own school?" I said, "Okay, as long as I can use you and Lincoln and Betty Cage as role models and sources to go to." I didn't know anything about the administration of a school or ballet company or even formulating a not-for-profit organization. But McNeil Lowry and Marcia Thompson at the Ford Foundation came to help me.

Today I find myself saying something in class or rehearsal, and I think, "God, I've heard that before, from—Balanchine."

STANLEY

WILLIAMS

Stanley Williams was born in 1925 in Chappel, England, and raised in Denmark. In 1934 he began training at the school of the Royal Danish Ballet, where he rose to the rank of soloist. After an injury curtailed his performing career, he began teaching at the school of the Royal Danish Ballet in 1950. In 1964, he joined the permanent staff of the School of American Ballet, where he is now chairman of the faculty.

I Remember Balanchine

I HAD HEARD ABOUT BALANCHINE, BUT THE FIRST TIME WE ACTUALLY MET WAS IN 1956, when the Royal Danish Ballet performed in New York and he came backstage. Several months later, back in Copenhagen, I saw Tanaquil LeClercq give her final performance, during the closing night of the New York City Ballet's season at the Royal Opera House. Mr. B. stayed with her in Copenhagen for months. While she was in the hospital, he gave us *Serenade* and *Symphony in C* and rehearsed the ballets with the company. He frequently came and watched me teach children's class in the morning, but he never said a word until the day before he left. He asked if I would leave my private address at his hotel; I didn't ask why. Four years went by, and then out of the blue the Danish press called me and said, "We hear rumors that Balanchine is asking you to guest with the New York City Ballet." "That sounds wonderful," I said, "but I haven't been told anything." Then Erik Bruhn came back after having a season with the New York City Ballet. "You know what? The day I was leaving Balanchine said, 'You have a teacher there I would like to invite over, but I can't remember his name.'" And Erik said, "You must mean Stanley." A week later I received an invitation.

I went to the New York City Center, opened the door to the studio, and there was the whole company assembled for class, plus Mr. Balanchine and John Taras. I thought to myself, "What are you doing? You've never taught in English." They couldn't have been nicer as they introduced me to the dancers. There was no pianist, however. Mr. Balanchine said, "No, dear, because if you have music I don't know what you're doing. It will ruin your class. You just do," he said, clapping his hands, snapping his fingers. I started the class and after ten minutes he got up, smiled to me, and left. And that was that. It went well, and I taught company class as a guest for three winters. In 1964 he offered me a permanent position at the School of American Ballet.

Balanchine said, "A lot of people dance till they're forty-five and then they want to be teachers, but it doesn't work because they've started too late. You have to begin to learn the whole craft young." I had started teaching when I was twenty-four. By the time Vera Volkova came to Copenhagen from London, I was just beginning to teach. She took the girls and I taught the boys. I have no idea how I taught then, but I had Peter Martins when he was twelve until he was sixteen, and today he says that's what made him. Yet Balanchine's influence completely changed my way of teaching. It didn't always dawn on me right away what he was talking about. I used to watch his classes and hear him say something, and have no idea what he meant. I'd be teaching maybe half a year later, and suddenly I understood. Subconsciously what he had said suddenly started to make sense to me and then I knew how to use it my way.

I understood his timing in steps. I have a good sense of timing, too, so that appealed to me: how his choreography goes from one thing to the next with no stop. It just continues and, no matter how simple the step, it's always going somewhere. It's always the timing that I'm going for in class, whatever the step is.

One year the program for the School workshop was too short and Balanchine called the School to say, "Could you ask Stanley Williams? Maybe he can do something." That was a week before the performance, and I staged the *Flower Festival* pas de deux for Gelsey Kirkland and Robert Weiss. I then began arranging something of Bournonville's for the workshop every spring. Balanchine said, "Maybe we could put Bournonville onstage, in the company." I knew all the boys' parts, but I went back to Denmark to learn a lot of the patterns. I got it all and came back and I wrote it down.

I remember Balanchine watching a rehearsal of the *Ballabile.* In the coda they all come from the back together, and when they got to the *sissonnes,* they kept ending one beat behind. So I said to Mr. B., "I have a problem." "You know why?" he pointed out. "Because they don't start on one. They go up before the one." It was a very tricky place: there was a beat before, and I hadn't remembered it. He knew exactly what was the matter, but he waited for me to say, "Please." Originally, we ended *Bournonville Divertissement* with the pas de sept from *A Folk Tale.* It was nice, but Balanchine decided, "Not for ending, dear. Do something else." So we added the Tarantella from *Napoli.*

Before one Sunday matinee performance, a girl scheduled to dance a variation in the pas de sept was out sick. One variation overlaps into the next, so we couldn't cut her part out. I arrived at the theater and Balanchine was up in the studio with another girl. I waited onstage and he came down. "Well, dear," he told me, "I just did variation for girl, Bournonville variation. Ten minutes we had. You'll be surprised, dear." And it was kind of incredible, because you could not tell that this new variation was out of place. He did his own choreography, but he did it à la Bournonville.

One day after his class I was sitting next to Balanchine and he started chitchatting a little bit. I could tell from the way he was talking that something was coming, because he didn't waste time; there was always a purpose. Suddenly he said, "Don't you agree with me? You know a teacher's sad when you see him come into the studio and you see the stomach come in first." I'd started living a bit after I stopped dancing and I'd become a little overweight. So I went on a diet, and then I went to Denmark and I hadn't seen him for a long time. He came in and watched class when I came back and was so surprised. "Look at you. Wow! Fantastic! Look at *me* now: potbelly."

CAROL

SUMNER

Carol Sumner was born in New York City in 1940. After graduating from the School of American Ballet in 1958, she danced with the New York City Ballet until 1976, creating solo roles in many Balanchine ballets, including Harlequinade, Don Quixote, Divertimento from "Le Baiser de la Fée," *and* Brahms-Schoenberg Quartet. *In 1976 she founded the American Ballet Academy and Company in Stamford, Connecticut, and directed them until 1989.*

I Remember Balanchine

IT WAS DIFFICULT TO ACCOMPLISH WHAT BALANCHINE WANTED. HE WOULD HAVE YOU do a step—"Let's see, dear." It wouldn't be right and he would just say, "No." And then you would try again and again. If you still didn't get it right he would finally walk away. You would think about it all night long and try the next day until he told you you had it. He really wanted you to learn and there was no in-between. Not with me, anyway.

Balanchine said I looked like Danny Kaye. He was right; I looked like my father, who did resemble Kaye. Later Balanchine started thinking of me as a bird, a canary, during *Harlequinade.* But to tell you the truth, I wouldn't have cared what Mr. B. thought I looked like. The fact that he took me in the company and noticed me was the important thing.

When I first joined the company he was not teaching much. But then he started with his new generation—Patty McBride, myself, Gloria Govrin, Jacques d'Amboise, and others. He began leading three-hour classes every day on the fifth floor of City Center. He took everything apart and I believe may have developed something new on us. He stopped the class once and said, "Dear, do you remember Jimmy Durante saying, 'Did you ever have the feeling that you wanted to stay, did you ever have the feeling that you wanted to go?' That, dear, is how you look when you want to start. But you can't be undecided." It sounds like a simple thing, but it wasn't that easy to just start and not worry about whether you were going to make it or not.

In class he described a little fruit fly that was running around in the egg, thinking, "I'm going to be born. I can't wait, I can't wait!" Finally the day came and the egg cracked. She was born and she was out and she screamed, "Oh, I am born!" And, bang, she dropped dead. That was how he wanted me to jump in second position, as if it didn't matter if I dropped dead later. And after that I jumped with all my might. I tell the same story to my students.

The first ballet I was in was *Gounod Symphony.* He made me be more vivid in my movement. "Dear," he said, "now you come in front and you make *sous-sous* and you go bang! Show yourself. You are transparent. You have to show yourself more."

One day he was talking to a girl standing in front of me, trying to make her do a certain step, until suddenly she screamed, "I can't!" And all of a sudden it hit me that we were not there because we could; we were there to make ourselves dancers. Of course we couldn't do what he wanted; he wanted us to be the best we could. You have to learn to be that good. And maybe we could someday.

VICTORIA
SIMON

Victoria Simon danced at New York City Ballet from 1958 to 1965.

She has staged twenty-one of Balanchine's ballets for over sixty ballet

companies around the world.

I Remember Balanchine

THE FIRST BALLET I STAGED FOR MR. B. WAS *The Nutcracker*, IN COLOGNE, IN 1965. Todd Bolender was running the company there, and Mr. B. needed somebody to go over and put it on. Most of *The Nutcracker* was in my head—it was so much a part of my life. I was still dancing in the company, and I had done almost every part. I had been a child in it and grown up with it. I had helped rehearse the children that year.

I guess I have a photographic memory. I know people who are in ballets for a long time and really only know what they themselves do. I always knew what everybody else was doing too. I was fascinated by how it all fit, how all Mr. B.'s ballets were put together and the way the patterns happened. So I grew up loving them. I learned ballets quickly. If they needed somebody to step into a role, I could do that. It was just there, hanging around. I'm musical, I studied piano when I was a child and can read music. Balanchine knew that, somehow. He was aware of what you knew. I think musical people tend to be able to learn ballets quickly.

For the Cologne *Nutcracker*, Balanchine came over for the last week of dress rehearsals and was pleased with what I had done. That's when I started staging ballets for him. I gave up performing with New York City Ballet and had children. It just sort of happened. I left dancing and started staging, and that's been my life ever since.

Some years I think things are going to quiet down: everybody has all the Balanchine they want. But then there are other requests to revive a ballet that hasn't been done for a long time, or a new director comes in who wants to do more Balanchine in his company. There is always something happening. People want Balanchine ballets for building up repertoire and they are wonderful for the dancers to do. Dancers get so much out of doing his ballets. I believe you build better dancers that way. Some directors have told me that doing their first Balanchine changed the whole way their companies started to dance. His ballets are about dancing, about life.

Balanchine's classes were wonderful learning experiences. They were not the kind of class you would take to get warmed up, certainly not massage-type classes. But they were wonderful learning experiences. I think the technique that you get in class should be related to how you dance onstage. When I go to teach a ballet, most of the time I try to teach some classes too, so the dancers will know what I'm talking about when I'm teaching the ballets.

I saw the Kirov Ballet do Balanchine's *Scotch Symphony* and *Theme and Variations*. I was up in Canada when I first saw them, in Calgary, and I was a little disappointed with canned music. And then I saw them again in New York. I thought *Scotch Symphony*, especially, they did very nicely. With *Theme and Variations*, too, I thought they came up to the challenge quite well, especially hearing what both Suzanne Farrell and Francia Russell had to overcome. I think the Russian dancers learned a lot just by doing those two ballets—about how we work, what things you're not allowed to do. The way they danced those two Balanchine ballets makes you really wonder about how authentic the so-called authentic classics are that the Russians do. They've obviously changed them to suit themselves.

For a ballet company to grow, there must be somebody with a real vision as to where dancing is going and what it is doing. Dance was Balanchine's life, and the New York City Ballet was his family. He spoke of us as his family. That's all he lived for—the dance and the family. That was his purpose, what he was there for. He was lucky to find people like Lincoln Kirstein, who helped him tremendously. Without Lincoln we wouldn't have had Mr. B. as we know him.

RICHARD

RAPP

Richard Rapp was born in Milwaukee, Wisconsin. He studied with Ada Artinian, Ann Barzel, and at the School of American Ballet. He joined the New York City Ballet in 1958 and danced in most of the company's repertory, including Balanchine's Agon, Divertimento No. 15, Ivesiana, Serenade, Western Symphony, and The Four Temperaments. *Rapp played Don Quixote in Balanchine's full-length ballet of that name for many years. Since his retirement as a dancer, Rapp has taught at the School of American Ballet.*

YOU COULD PROBABLY DO A BOOK ON WHAT BALANCHINE EMPHASIZED IN CLASS, IN doing the steps, but over all his emphasis was on beauty, speed, clarity, and musicality. To get those results, he insisted on certain things being done at the barre. He wanted legs and feet and the rest of your body—head, hands, and arms—working in a certain way because he wanted a certain special effect. Rather than a codified technique, what he wanted was similar to what music teachers mean when they speak of bel canto: like beautiful singing, this was beautiful dancing. Great music teachers have the same kind of idiosyncrasy; they want to make beautiful sounds just as he wanted to make beautiful bodies move through space with the music.

Musicality is something that's in your body. Muriel Stuart, one of the wonderful teachers at the School of American Ballet for many years, used to say that about the ability to move; you cannot teach it. A person either has the ability to move well or he does not. It's not just being responsive rhythmically. Let's say you have a variation like the boy's variation in *Stars and Stripes.* He has *cabrioles,* big *jetés battus,* and pirouettes to do. They're all done within the framework of the music. But in a solo, where no one else is involved, you can play with that musical framework. Dancing off the music is something different. Mr. B. used to say that if you're off the music and you're dancing oblivious to the fact that you're off the music, you're in big trouble. While you can teach the mechanics of a step or a movement, the quality of the movement is not going to be improved if somebody just does not have talent or ability. About musicality, I feel the same thing. It's there in a dancer, or it is not.

Balanchine in class one day was attempting to get something out of us, and it wasn't working the way he wanted it to. He said: "You know, dears, I can buy your food for you, I can cut and chop and cook for you. I can even chew for you, but you must swallow." That works well with students when you're trying to get them to accept what you're offering. They go home and they think about it. They think, "Oh, aha, you mean *I've* got to do that? I thought *you* were going to do that for me!"

In ballets like *The Four Temperaments,* you don't really have to act and emote if you do the choreography as it is. It does it for you. Not that you are simply a body going out there doing steps, but you don't have to be John Barrymore to do those roles correctly and do them well. I had the opportunity to do Melancholic in *Four Temperaments* for many years and also, the last couple of years I was with the company, Phlegmatic. I have fond memories of what I hope were a couple of good performances. The roles were challenging, but when you did a good performance, they were emotionally rewarding. It's one of those occasions where musically and technically everything seems to meld together and you come out smelling like a rose. You feel satisfied. You feel good.

Obviously, part of Balanchine's genius was in doing these roles for certain persons. He could see individuals in certain roles. Years ago he took a young girl from the School into the company. I said, "Really, I thought she would be one of the last students you would pick for the company." But he said, "Dear, she will make wonderful Siren in *Prodigal Son.*" So here was this girl I thought was kind of klutzy. But he was thinking years ahead to how he could train her and use her in that particular role. That's how far ahead his mind was.

This genius for shaping a role to fit the gifts of a particular dancer was brought home to me in 1956 when Tanaquil LeClercq was doing a lot of *Swan Lake*s. I've been told she was apprehensive about the role and perhaps that's why Mr. B. was constantly fiddling with the variation. But she did a *Swan Lake* in Brussels with Nicky Magallanes that was the finest *Swan Lake* I've ever seen. Or things that Tanny did in *La Valse.* Although people do the role now and have done the role over the years in beautiful ways and are effective, she is unique in my memory in how she looked and how she danced it. Even though the steps are the same, it's what she did with them. You almost cannot describe what the difference is between someone doing a step and another dancer doing the same step, what makes it different. I guess it's the personality. It's the look of the dancer.

One of the things Balanchine liked to demonstrate was how a dancer should hold her hands with separate curved fingers. He talked about that in different ways: one was like a flower opening. In my classes I elaborate a little more and talk about the time-lapse photography we now see so often, where you can see flowers opening from a bud. Or Balanchine would use the illustration of moving your arms from one position to another, like a parachute opening and softly moving your arm down with a curved elbow and a curved wrist.

For the men, the arms and hands were the same as for the women. I remember a very beautiful picture of Jacques and I believe it was Melissa Hayden on the cover of one of the Sunday supplements years ago. It was *Raymonda Variations.* The hands for both were the same. They were in a pose with one arm raised. There were matching arms and hands and curved necks. It showed what is important for classical ballet, that your head is not straight forward but that you bend your neck, you curve your neck. It carries over into the positions of the body as you do steps and exercises.

Balanchine taught us in pirouettes to look through your fingers to a corner. When you do your first pirouette you bring your spot front flat to the audience, *en face,* as we say. It's something he liked because it was a surprise for the audience. You didn't spot the corner. The audience didn't see profile, they saw *face* when you were turning. Not that it's always done that way, but it's something a little bit different. It's very hard to do when you're first learning.

Students and even teachers tend to look for absolutes. They want to say you must do it this way, it's the only way to do it, and anybody who says something else is wrong. Well, it's not wrong. It's simply a style. It's what your boss wants you to look like. It's up to you to accept it or find another job where you'll be happier.

Even students at the School, when they came into the company, were told: "Now you must learn to dance." Which meant that it was time to learn how to present yourself in the style and the manner Balanchine wanted and not what was being done at the School. Not because the School was incorrect; it was simply that in a performing company the emphasis is on other things. When you took a class from Mr. Balanchine, you sometimes would do sixty-four *battements tendus* in one direction. If any teacher at the School did that, I think they would be run out of the practice room; the students would gang up on him and throw him out the window. I don't think anybody could get away with that. But Balanchine was the boss. He was looking for beauty the way he saw it, what his idea of beauty was. And, genius that he was, he knew how to get it.

LESLIE

COPELAND

Leslie Copeland was born in Featherstone, Yorkshire, in 1927. He left school at fourteen and worked in a print shop, running a Heidelberg printing press. He entered the British Navy at the age of seventeen during World War II and was stationed on the heavy cruisers HMS Ceylon *and* HMS Moriches *in Portsmouth. In 1948 he worked as a dresser for the musical* Oklahoma! *at the Theatre Royal, Drury Lane, in London. On the staff of the Festival Ballet and the International Ballet, as well as the BBC in London, he was hired by Balanchine in 1958 to become men's wardrobe supervisor for the New York City Ballet.*

LUCIA CHASE BROUGHT ME TO AMERICA IN 1958. I WAS WORKING AT THE BBC, and previously, in 1951, I had worked for the Festival Ballet in London, where I had a friendship with Grace Rowsell, the wardrobe lady. Grace Rowsell left London to make a new life in the New World. Finally she got a job as the wardrobe lady for American Ballet Theatre. She wrote to me in London in 1958 and asked if I would take a leave of absence from BBC television and join her in Casablanca for three months of A.B.T.'s world tour. I did. I joined Grace in Casablanca, walked into the dressing room, and there were Nora Kaye, Scott Douglas, and Johnny Kriza. I was very young then. They asked me who I was, and I said, "Leslie Copeland," and they said, "Let's call you Ducky," and I've been Ducky ever since. If people ask at the stage door for Leslie Copeland, very few people know who that is.

I was with Ballet Theatre three months. In that time there was a dreadful fire and all the costumes were destroyed. Two trucks burned up, and they flew me from Nice to London, where I arranged to buy, borrow, and replace all the costumes and flew back to the World's Fair in Brussels, where the company's tour was to close with a final week of performances. I remember it was Whitsuntide, a bank holiday, and it was a dreadful time to try to get shoes from Freed's. Lucia Chase asked me if she should cancel. I said no.

As a reward, Violette Verdy's mother told my fortune with Tarot cards the third night in Brussels. We went to Violette's room, and since her mother did not speak English, Violette had to interpret. Her mother said that very soon a tall dark gentleman would come to me with a letter. She said there would be news from England, and part of my possessions would be gone. "You will never recover them. They are completely gone." But she said the dark gentleman would make me an offer which I would take and that a fair woman would be part of my destiny. She said, "You will cross the water, cross the expansive water twice. You will never live in England again." The next morning, Jeannot Cerone, who was the stage manager of A.B.T. and who was tall and dark, gave me a letter from England. It was from my roommate, saying that we had been robbed, wiped out. Everything was gone, all the valuables. He had been away and when he came back the apartment was a complete mess. Then Jeannot said that Lucia Chase wanted to see me. Lucia had helped sew the costumes for the Brussels performances. She was absolutely terrific. So I went to her and asked what she wanted, and she said, "Yes, dear, you have been wonderful this tour, washing the *Rodeo* costumes in Casablanca by hand. Would you like to come to the States with us as a reward? We will pay you three weeks' wages at the Met." I said, "Certainly." We came to the Met and the three weeks passed by. Jeannot Cerone invited me for lunch at the Carnegie Tavern. He knew George Bardyguine, who was stage manager at New York City Ballet, and introduced me to him.

I said hello, and who should come into the Tavern but Mr. Balanchine. George had just asked me if I had a job, and I said no. I didn't have a green card. So Balanchine mumbled, "Maybe you should come and work for us." And that was that. It was fate really. Lincoln Kirstein was the big instigator for me. He became my guardian. He stood for me with Eddie Bigelow to become a U.S. citizen in 1964. They gave me a lovely party at Lincoln's house downtown.

At New York City Ballet I worked first as a dresser part time and then became the wardrobe master for the company. I've been at City Ballet ever since.

The first big production I was involved with was *The Figure in the Carpet.* The costumes were by Karinska. The first act went on, and the costumes for the final act still hadn't arrived. It was one of those situations, nip and tuck and lots of pins. But I loved coincidences. Karinska and I had a great rapport. All the costumes Karinska made emphasized the feminine figure. And Balanchine loved women. Karinska loved femininity, too. She emphasized it in her costumes. She made them all, and she used the best materials.

Balanchine cared about the smallest details in his productions: lighting, scenery, everything, down to the last touch. Balanchine knew everything. He used all the best people, the best artists—for example, Kermit Love's decor for *L'Enfant et les Sortilèges.* He would only take the best. It was never quantity with him, it was always quality. I think he had those standards all of his life. He always knew what he wanted, and he always got what he wanted. And he always did it in such a gentlemanly way that you would do anything for him. If he had called a dress rehearsal at three-thirty in the morning, I would have been there, and so would everyone else. He would ask in a lovely way, and he wouldn't ask you to do it if it wasn't necessary. You couldn't fool him either. Anyone who tried was quickly sent packing. He wouldn't tolerate fools. He would never hurt people, but he would let them down gently. Like most geniuses, he had a cruel streak. It's in all of us, really—a naughty part. I think that, if he didn't like you, you really became aware of it very quickly. He had no time.

Balanchine and Lucia Chase never got on. He didn't like Lucia, personally or professionally, perhaps because she turned him down for work at Ballet Theatre. On one occasion Lucia was at our apartment for New Year's Eve. We had people over, and Lucia was one of the guests. Balanchine phoned to wish me a happy New Year. Lucia was in the room. I said, "It's Balanchine. Would you like to wish him a happy New Year?" Lucia said, "Oh, no, dear, I daren't." She was horrified.

Lucia was marvelous. The last time I saw her I went to her home for dinner a few months before she died. There were twelve of us. Lucia was always very nice, the best boss for her staff. Not so good with the dancers, but she paid the staff top dollar and people died for Lucia. She respected them, and they certainly respected her; they really gave double for Lucia. We sat around the table, and in a lull in the conversation I asked her suddenly, "Lucia, would you mind if I asked you a personal question?" She said, "No, dear, not at all." So I said, "Well, how much of your personal fortune have you actually spent in Ballet Theatre?" There was a moment of silence. Everybody stopped eating. It was a question that everyone had really wanted to ask for years and was too intimidated to ask. She thought one moment and turned to me and said, "I would estimate $21 million, between $21 million and $22 million, Ducky." There was a gasp around the table. This was when she had just been ousted from the Ballet Theatre board. They had kicked her out. What subsequently happened at A.B.T. I would call poetic justice. My father always said that the wheel always turns. When you go up the ladder, be careful who you step on because you eventually will have to come down that ladder. What you put into your life you get out of it. If you're nice to people, the majority of them will be nice to you. Occasionally, you'll meet the odd bastard, but don't let them throw you. Just be as you are. I've been very, very lucky.

Balanchine used to throw his male dancers on in roles unexpectedly, which they hated. He would make them do it. It was very interesting, because now I find that Peter Martins is doing exactly the same. It's excellent because out of the clear blue sky along comes Peter, and he'll say, "You're going to do this. What about tomorrow?" It's very good training. It didn't work for Balanchine when Erik Bruhn was briefly in the company, however. Erik was a perfectionist. He would never go on ill prepared. Erik could never fake. You never got a secondhand performance. But then he would come off the stage and be very unhappy with the way it had gone. He was a very dismal Dane, but a great artist.

When Baryshnikov joined City Ballet, I think there was a mutual understanding between him and Balanchine. They were both Russian and they were both defectors, but I always got the impression that Misha wasn't ever really too happy with us. He found his niche in Ballet Theatre, for better or worse, for years.

Balanchine had a quirky, clever sense of humor. He tried to keep up an image of himself in public, everything held in, but he laughed a lot with me. It was like a family, a big family. You were part of it. You contributed toward that part of the picture. You really didn't mind coming in at eight o'clock in the morning and working until eleven at night if need be because it was for the family. We felt it. We felt that if he was going to be over at the theater, may as well go in and see what there was to do. And Balanchine was always fun to be around. He would sound people out. I always felt completely free and easy in his presence. Once in a while I would come in and I would have left my money somewhere. I'd say, "I've left my money." "How much do you want, dear?" "Well, only twenty dollars?" "Is that enough?" And then a day later I'd bring in the twenty dollars and say, "That's what I borrowed." "You did?" It would be a surprise. He was very generous to many people.

Balanchine enjoyed being recognized on the street. We were doing *Who Cares?*, and the production had been put together very hurriedly. There wasn't that much money to spend on costumes. He said, "I've ordered these gray pants from the costume shop, and we have shirts. We need five nice ties. Come on, let's go to Bloomingdale's." The ties were for the pants. Balanchine knew that Fred Astaire used to wear a tie instead of a belt around his waist to keep his pants up. So we walked across the park and went to Bloomingdale's. The woman behind the tie counter was one of the students from S.A.B. who had quit dancing, and she almost fainted when we came up. She was now in her late thirties and naturally recognized him. It was fun to see the recognition on her face and Balanchine playing king. She must have put every tie that Bloomingdale's ever had on that counter. Eventually he chose five ties and then chatted for ages with her. A wonderful time was had by all. He came away and said, "Well, you see, somebody knows me." We had a lovely afternoon, shopping at Bloomingdale's.

Clothes did not matter that much for Balanchine himself. He loved neckties and cowboy shirts. He had one navy-blue suit and little sports jackets. He always looked natty, but he didn't cultivate it with his clothes. It wasn't the clothes, it was the man, Balanchine. He didn't need clothes. We would go to sales sometimes. A firm used to come from Hong Kong for suits. We both went down to the Hilton. You could get so many suits and choose your own patterns, so we both went and were fitted by Chinese tailors. We would each order three suits. I went twice with him. They weren't the best suits in the world. But he always got great joy in going down and meeting the Chinese tailors. They'd do his measurements, and we'd choose the fabrics. They were made in Hong Kong and then expressed over. That was a fun afternoon. We'd go from there to the Carnegie Tavern and have a few drinks.

He always had the dancers' interest at heart, always. They are treated very well at City Ballet. That's why they are no good after they leave, because they're all looked after so well here. They're lost when they leave here. It's handed to you hand and foot. Not that they don't work hard, they do—jolly hard.

Balanchine had a great protective shield around him all the time. No one would let him be taken advantage of. If he went to a party, the dancers were always with him. They would rescue him if he was cornered by a bore. There was always an escape route. We would all keep one eye on him, and if he got bored we would prise him away. He was always surrounded by love. And he gave love as well.

Balanchine and I had a rapport from the beginning. He would come to my apartment and cook, and we'd have dinners. He loved to cook. You'd need two people to wash up after him because he used every pot and pan in the place. He brought all the food with him and the wine. I'd say, "How lovely." And he'd say, "Oh, I'll bring wine—and cheese." This could be any time, but usually on a free day, on a Monday. He would go and have a whole filet of beef minced for *koleckti* and dill pickle. He used lots of fresh dill. And he loved boiled potatoes. He relaxed, and it was marvelous.

We had Margaret Hamilton—the Wicked Witch in *The Wizard of Oz*—over on one occasion. I had met her through Phil King, who was staying at our apartment and had worked with her for years. He was part of the Rodgers and Hammerstein office, a stage manager. Balanchine and Margaret Hamilton talked for ages. They hit it off like a house afire. They giggled and laughed like schoolchildren, talking about old techniques, film techniques. Balanchine wanted to know if she was really a schoolmistress, which she was, before she became famous.

Balanchine liked to iron his own shirts. He did his own washing, too, in a little portable washing machine. He planned his choreography while he ironed his shirts and things at about six-thirty or seven in the morning. He was always an early riser, and he always used to do his laundry there at his apartment. He told me, "When I'm ironing, that's when I do most of my work."

He always tried to save money for the company at the State Theater. He would go around after the performances and switch off the lights in the studios. He knew how expensive Con Ed could be, one of our largest expenses.

He hated untidiness. If he saw people grind out cigarettes on the floor in the theater, he would say, "No, dear, this is home and we don't treat home like that." Once I was following him across the Lincoln Center Plaza. In front of him was a lady, and she pulled out cigarettes, took a cigarette out of the pack, and threw the empty packet on the ground. Then she walked on quite nonchalantly. Mr. Balanchine picked it up, caught up with the lady, tapped her on the shoulder, and said, "I think you dropped this, dear." The woman was so embarrassed. She said, "Oh, oh, oh . . ." and put it back in her pocket. I'd seen all of this.

Balanchine and I would reminisce about the past. He had worked in London with Jessie Matthews in the Charles B. Cochran revue, *Wake Up and Dream!* in 1929. That was before my time, but I had worked with her on BBC Television, so I knew her. Jessie couldn't really dance. She could do one thing and that was kick very high from the left. We would talk about Jessie. We used to laugh a lot about it.

Balanchine affected a lot of people. He used to go to my barber, Paul, on Seventy-second Street, between West End and Riverside, on the uptown side, a few steps down from the Royal Bakery. Balanchine asked me once where I got my hair cut. I said, "Oh, Paul's, on Seventy-second Street." So I took him and introduced him to Paul. And Balanchine enjoyed it. It was a ten-dollar haircut. I'm sure he used to give twice as much. On one occasion he went to have his hair cut and was recognized by one of the other elderly guys who was Russian. The man sat in the other chair and said, "Hey, you're George Balanchine, aren't you?" They had a conversation and the whole shop came alive. Paul said the whole shop was turned on. They laughed and talked and reminisced about old times in both Russian and English. Robert Irving discovered Balanchine went to Paul's, and he decided he would go too. During Balanchine's illness, Paul used to go to the hospital and cut his hair, and he and Paul became good friends.

Ballet companies tend to become cliquish. They splinter off into little groups. Then one person will be disgruntled. It's like a sore that festers. Before you know it you are in a hotbed of trouble. A company is like a family. There's nothing that happens in a ballet company that isn't common knowledge within minutes of its happening. There's no such thing as a secret.

New York City Ballet is lucky because there is a vast repertory. It changes all the time, and I think that's the magic of it. The company is getting back to being a family again. At official parties now the kids dress up and look terrific. Also, Peter Martins has done a marvelous job. Balanchine's was a dreadful crown to inherit. Martins is like Balanchine in that he is a gentleman and also has the common touch. It's as though he were becoming more like Balanchine. In meeting people at the stage door, Balanchine used to say, "Yes, how are you," clasping his hands with a little bow, and he would always look in their eyes, talk to them, and listen to what they had to say. Now I see Martins do the same thing. It's a little eerie. I told him about it.

Once Peter Martins was going to do the Don in Balanchine's *Don Quixote* for the first time. Balanchine said, "Try my pants on and see if they fit." Martins tried on the pants, and I looked at Balanchine and said, "How about your shoes?" Balanchine said, "Oh, he will certainly be wearing those one day." That was my first inkling. The way Balanchine said it, I could have predicted that Peter was the chosen one.

Balanchine always wanted to do the Audubon ballet, *The Birds of America*. I never wanted that. I don't think he ever really wanted to do *The Sleeping Beauty* until the last two or three years of his life. In the early years he never really wanted to do the classics as such. He said that if he ever did *The Sleeping Beauty* he would do it from tip to toe, all new.

When Stravinsky would come to visit, Balanchine was marvelous. He treated Stravinsky like royalty. He was humble in Stravinsky's presence. Stravinsky was friendly to Balanchine in return. When Stravinsky died, Balanchine was terribly upset. Stravinsky was his mentor, a father figure. When Stravinsky was there, it was like the dancers were with Balanchine. He was in awe of the composer, with enormous respect. In Balanchine's eyes, if Balanchine was the king, then Stravinsky was the emperor.

I met Balanchine's brother Andrei during a company tour to Russia. He was quite ordinary, really. There again, he looked up to Balanchine. Balanchine was the senior, and he refused to listen to his brother's music. He could be very stubborn. Once in Moscow at the hotel, I think he really wanted to shock the Russians. The band was playing after dinner, and the Russians said, "Somebody should dance." So Balanchine said to me, "Ducky, are you ready?" and we led the dancing. Balanchine danced with me. It was kind of fun. And about halfway around I said, "I think it's about time you switched to a girl now." So one of the girls came forward, and they finished. I think he did it for egg on their face. He hated being lionized by the Russians, since they were doing it for political reasons: local boy makes good.

When there was a new production coming up, Balanchine would mention what sort of thing he had in mind and what I must try and do. He was always caught up with other things. He had so much to do and was always on the go. He never stopped. Before his final illness, I used to tell the kids, "These are the golden years, take full advantage of it. They will never ever return."

I knew that there was something physically wrong with him two years before his hospitalization. He had difficulty with his direction, and he would stumble a little. I would guide him around, pretend to go through his clothes, see if he needed any cleaning done. It was very difficult toward the end. I don't think he was seeing. The vision and the hearing were going a little. But there was nothing anyone could do to help. We were all stymied by it. We didn't know what to do. Chrissie Redpath and I would visit him in the hospital. But I saw him so rarely alone because there was always someone there. I felt like an intruder.

Leslie Copeland

I'm a fatalist, and I think that Balanchine, too, thought it was all mapped out. You couldn't call Balanchine a devout man, but it was there. The religion was all part of his makeup.

He used to come to the theater on Sunday morning. I would always be here at 10:30 A.M., and he would come up and we would sit and chat, and sort of say, "What's gossip?" And we would do a little business—for example, "We must have new costumes" for a certain ballet. But mainly Sunday mornings we would sit and have a cup of tea.

A strange thing happened just after he died. He died on a Saturday morning, and this was the next day, Sunday. I could always tell that it was him when he would come up on the elevator to the dressing room. I was sitting there, and it was 10:30 A.M. Sunday morning. The elevator came up and the door opened. I looked up and almost expected to see him, but there was no one.

VIOLETTE

VERDY

Trained with Carlotta Zambelli and Victor Gsovsky in Paris; danced with Roland Petit's Ballets des Champs-Elysées and appeared in the motion picture Ballerina. *She danced with the London Festival Ballet, Ballet Rambert, and American Ballet Theatre. Joined New York City Ballet in 1958. Balanchine created thirteen roles for her in* Episodes, Tchaikovsky Pas de Deux, The Figure in the Carpet, Liebeslieder Walzer, A Midsummer Night's Dream, Emeralds *in* Jewels, La Source, Sonatine, *and other ballets. Director of the Paris Opéra Ballet (1976–79). A choreographer, Verdy is teaching associate at the New York City Ballet.*

I Remember Balanchine

WHEN I JOINED NEW YORK CITY BALLET, I WAS THE FIRST TO THINK THAT I MIGHT NOT be right for Balanchine's style. I didn't think I would be. But I never felt I would be losing anything. On the contrary, I realized I was graduating to something much more important and much more demanding. I was afraid that I might be a little bit out of tune by an excess of interpretation or personality or individuality. But I was willing to give it a try. One thing I remember is that I was used to rather temperamental, capricious, unreliable European choreographers who depended on their moods for their work and had a tendency to take out on the dancers what they couldn't come up with, while working with Balanchine was Olympian in the sense that he was so quietly sure of what he had to do. He wasn't sure of *himself*, he was sure of what he had to *do* about what he was going to do, and so you were taken care of. We felt completely taken in and included in what he was doing. Then, quickly, you realized that if you were asked to do a thing it was because he could see what you were going to do in it. He never asked you to be put in a false situation, where he had to correct you or scold you or transform you. He was always quietly proceeding with what he knew would be the right choice.

When Balanchine had dancers with personalities, he had no desire to change them. After all, different generations of dancers gave Balanchine different qualities. With me, Balanchine never told me what to do about the repertory pieces because he knew I would get the identity. What he had to do was to tone me down a little bit. I had a little too much garlic. He had to keep me quiet and busy, so I wouldn't make a commentary but dance the text.

Balanchine may have wanted to work with me because of a certain clarity in the articulation of the feet and legs. Some sort of eloquence, a pronunciation of the dancing. Something to be joyous with. It's there in the solo of *Tchaikovsky Pas de Deux* and in *La Source*.

I began doing repertory right away. I remember the first night. I was so nervous. I had to do First Movement Bizet and one of the girls in *Divertimento No. 15*. I was also doing *Western Symphony* that first week and getting ready to go into *Stars and Stripes* in the second girls' movement. Also we were premiering *Medea* by Cullberg, whom I had worked with in *Miss Julie* at Ballet Theatre, and now I was doing Creusa in the new ballet. So I was into everything.

I learned roles from the people who were rehearsing the ballets then, but Balanchine always was there. It was amazing to see how many new dancers he was rehearsing in what were for him already older ballets. He rehearsed everybody sooner or later. As long as he had the energy to do that, he did it.

Balanchine always said that he was not a man of words. But we have a large encyclopedia he left us as his legacy. We find him in his works. All the different aspects of Balanchine he has expressed in what he has done. He would talk about it sometimes. If you brought up an alternative idea about an image or a moment in one of his ballets, he would want to stay with his original conception. He always told me he had learned rather quickly that you never change people. You take them as they are, and you deal with it. You present them at their best. Naturally, you can ameliorate some things, but basically you can never really change individuals.

I discovered things about myself I didn't know but *he* knew. Sometimes it was in a general progression and a general development. But also technically he surprised me by asking me to dare to do certain things with speed. I was surprised at what I was able to deliver. I didn't think I could do it. But I would gain a lot of confidence from Balanchine, partly because I would have to agree with what he had done. It would be so much the best solution that I would gain an extra measure of confidence and faith, and then I didn't have to worry so much and it worked for me. I was carried. He carried you.

One of the first ballets where he made a role for me was *Figure in the Carpet* (1960). I did the first section to the Royal Fireworks Music of Handel. It was extremely formal but very inventive, very beautiful. My partner was Conrad Ludlow, and the costumes were reminiscent of the ones in *Serenade,* except ours were in beige tones, like the sands of the desert. The second scene of the ballet was to Handel's Water Music, and it was set in a palace with ambassadors from all the countries. Balanchine was always very disciplined. Because of union requirements, he would dismiss the corps for their five-minute break, and then take one of the soloists or principals—which the union allowed—and create a little jewel of choreography in that pause. That's how he did it, very often, nonstop.

Figure in the Carpet is no longer performed, but not because it was not a good ballet. None of us who were in the original production remembers enough of the steps. By the time we realized we had forgotten it, it was too late. It's like *Gounod Symphony* (1958), which almost got lost. *Gounod* was one of his most important ballets. Vida Brown really knew the ballet and has staged it recently in revival. This was the first ballet I wanted to stage when I went to the Paris Opéra. When I saw Nureyev after he was hijacked into the directorship of the Paris Opéra, too, the first thing he wanted to stage was *Gounod Symphony.* But the French don't understand or appreciate or wish to retain such *hommages.* All of us keep thinking the French should have the best French things, but they are totally allergic to them! Lincoln Kirstein has defined it forever: the French like cuisine and haute couture—maybe. Balanchine loved France, much admired the Paris Opéra, and whenever it wanted to be a profane kind of place, he kept thinking of it as a Greek temple. He almost went to the Opéra at one point, and forever kept a strong hope that the Paris Opéra would fulfill its high position in international dance. When I left to direct the ballet at the Opéra, Balanchine was very touched and talked about it with a great deal of tenderness, in terms I wish they knew or understood.

I'm glad that Balanchine did not take the position at the Paris Opéra when it was offered because I think he was reserved for a greater achievement—to come to the United States, which is open, ready for anything, with no prejudices. Here he was able to develop himself and give everything he had to offer. I feel that in France, like in many countries in Europe, you have a lot of prejudice against you before you even begin. He was saved.

In works like *La Source* and *Emeralds,* Balanchine gave the French ballet its true identity. We live with clichés all the time, but when you really take an interest in anything you want to go back to the true character, a deeper identity. Balanchine has done so in these works by showing us the different, several, serious aspects of being French. He has shown us the seriousness of the French, which perhaps the French don't practice that much. *Emeralds* in *Jewels* is a very dignified and slightly nostalgic and certainly resigned type of noble French behavior. *La Source* is enchanting because of its invention and the sensuousness of its choreography. The choreography is serious and difficult and intricate. And *Gounod* is a monument, a great big wonderful French palace. And the Bizet *Symphony in C* is another palace, made for the Opéra but brought to distillation by American dancers in this country. I did not see the ballet first in Paris, but I've seen the remnants, the wonderful public ruins. It reminded me of those ruins that you visit.

Usually I danced in nineteenth-century-and-a-half ballets. There were so many pieces. Mr. Balanchine was doing so many ballets at that time! Once I walked into the theater on Easter day when there were no rehearsals, and he was there at the piano. He said, "Oh, I composed a little waltz." He let me listen. It was a sweet, tiny little waltz, nostalgic, sentimental. Mr. B. used to close up the pianos in the theater or the studios before leaving. He would always clean up the pianos, take away the cigarettes or the chewing gum, whatever. He treated pianos like somebody would treat a cat or dog or the plants at home. In class the poor piano usually receives more blows and more accidents than it's supposed to. He treated the piano almost like a person.

When Balanchine made *Liebeslieder Walzer* it was an inspired, important time. It seemed to just flow out of him, irrepressibly. All dancers are concerned with the projection that a person makes from the stage. It must be seen and be important to the audience. In *Liebeslieder* we were exploring an intimacy we had never had before because we were dealing with piano and voice. When you tread on a full orchestra, you know that your steps will be on strong ground. But walking on piano and voice, your feet are much more sensitive. Balanchine had been devising many so-called "abstract" ballets, but in *Liebeslieder* he was giving complete freedom to emotions, feelings, relationships, personal values. People together—it's all there.

It's hard to say which one of the ballets Balanchine made for me is my favorite. Every time was like the first time, falling in love again and thinking, "This is it, this is the best one yet." It's terribly hard to choose. Perhaps *Liebeslieder* because there was so much of the past, of Europe in it. It was so rich. But I took pleasure dancing things that were made for other dancers. Every time I thought it was just so right, what he had done with that music and choreography.

Balanchine's classes were a workshop to prepare his dancers with an absolutely clear sense of the values he wanted them to have, so that when he would prepare a ballet you had received already in the class the elements of some of the choreography. He worked like a sculptor, preparing little preliminary studies, and then you got the sculpture. In his classes, you knew what you were preparing all the time. Also, if he had his mind set on certain dancers for a certain work, you could see him in the class already beginning with those dancers, and everyone else learned from it. Everybody profited from that operation in one way or another. The more specific aim at the time for what he was going to choreograph was made clear in the class. It was a choreographer-director's class, not just a teacher's class.

I'm not the best product of the Balanchine classroom because by then I had had a number of Achilles tendon injuries. Balanchine did not give a long barre or a long warm-up, and all of us knew it. Dancers like me who needed to prepare because of injuries would come early and warm up and try to guess what kind of class he would give so that we would be ready ahead of time. I was not one of the ones who took the most classes from him, but I managed to take enough to understand what he was doing.

Balanchine is no longer with us, and yet we have a solid text to refer to. The company is taught what dancers need to know to dance in the ballets, and the ballets tell you what you need to work on so that dancers go back to practice. The School of American Ballet teaches a normal classical technique, except there's an emphasis on speed that no other school has developed. Balanchine taught something like postgraduate studies in his company classes. The minute they left the School and went to the company class, it was almost frightening for the young apprentices to see how far they still had to go when they thought they were the best students of the School. They discovered that what they thought they had quite solidly, comfortably established was in fact just enough to get in. It's like when you get your driver's license: you go out on the highway and, my God, the cars are coming!

Balanchine's technique was not really different from what I got from Carlotta Zambelli and Rousáne, who were students of Clustine and Trefilova and Gsovsky, who was a student of different teachers in Leningrad. Everything was there. The only difference with Balanchine was the emphasis—from both the music and the scale of the movement. Balanchine made the emphasis for certain steps clearer and more strongly contrasted than what you get at the Paris Opéra, the Royal Ballet, and the Russians now. For example, in Balanchine you don't make a slow *glissade* because it's a small, quick step; but a big arabesque *plié* will always be a big arabesque step. Balanchine would use such families of gesture for particular occasions in his ballets, as the material of choreography. All of Balanchine's disciples are different—Peter Martins, Helgi Tomasson—and yet you can see what they learned from him in spite of their different personalities and approaches.

Balanchine never wrote down his teachings because he was working on certain things in his choreography, reaffirming them, and—depending on the dancers he was working with—working on different material. He came up endlessly with different nuances and accents and timings. He was equally willing to adjust ballets for particular dancers. I never turned well and was always scared of pirouettes. When I did *Raymonda*, I got to that second solo with all those pirouettes and suddenly couldn't do anything, so I did two or three of them, and then I just went on one knee and waited for the conductor to finish the music. It was a terrible experience, an awful moment to live through, one of those things you would rather never remember but which, of course, you remember burningly well. The next day Balanchine said, "Oh, this isn't right for you." Very kind. He said, "Oh, you have a nice little *pas de chat*, let's do a little something nice." He gave me a wonderful step which I notice is now done again. (Patricia Wilde, of course, turned so well. She could do all those pirouettes!)

I never felt that I got really close to Balanchine as a person, ever. There were many reasons. First of all, he was really my director, the great choreographer, and I am not ashamed to say that for me he was a father figure. I never thought of him as a possible lover or husband. Even though he sometimes confided a little bit or told a few jokes, he was not what you call a warm person. That's the way he was. But you got other things from him. You discovered other wonders in the work you did with him. It was almost like too much to expect to think that Balanchine would also be a fantastic, wonderful, socially usable person besides everything else he was and everything he produced. When you run a ballet company, I've learned, it's best when there is no hesitation and everybody knows what's what; you proceed on particular rules. It clarifies everything for everybody. If you try to accommodate everyone's wishes, it is difficult.

I never thought of Balanchine as God, but he made you think of God, which is another story. He himself always said that it was all work, that you had to set yourself to work to create. You couldn't wait for the inspiration, you really had to work, so that you did one ballet, another ballet, a third ballet. And finally something original and unique might happen. If you could get even one or two unique combinations in a ballet, this was already enough to justify the whole thing. He was modest about how good the work could be and how much work had to be done before you would see something that might be called creative. He used to joke that, just as we don't refer to Mr. Poet—it's not a title—so you're not Mr. Choreographer.

He always said that he would have preferred a more ordinary life. He loved to cook, and he loved women, and he wanted to be a very regular person. He said that he had all this knowledge, and yet he always had to work. Sometimes he said, "I'm tired. I wish—there are lots of young, new dancers. They are waiting. I have to give." We always say people don't give, but he would say, "It's very sad because it's not true. People don't take. You give, you give, and they don't take. That's the most heartbreaking thing of all. Lots to give, you want to give; they don't take."

The position that Balanchine eventually reached with the public was unique—he became a star choreographer. It's perhaps the only time that has happened. Not that his performers were slighted. The stars came out no matter what. With that kind of choreography, you have stars. You have to have stars. It's inevitable. That's a solid type of star. I was there when the so-called "no star" policy was presumably in force at New York City Ballet, and I really never knew the rule existed. None of us inside ever thought there was one. I think it was spoken about externally. You did the goddamn best you could just to be good enough. Balanchine never calculated who thought you had attained what—the writers, the historians, the critics, or whatever. We were kept outside those other considerations. We were busy doing it. And whatever was reported, in a way we were rather "not guilty." When good stuff goes into the soup, it's delicious.

Balanchine would compare dancers with flowers and little animals. One very cold year in Saratoga he gave us blankets, just like for horses, when we were cold. He invented little nicknames for some of us. I was called Mistinguette—Hautecole Mistinguette Nelly, because Nelly is my real name. Pat McBride was Mandago Pie. Allegra Kent was Kentucky Cookie. All the good solid things he used as comparisons.

Balanchine treated ballet as a composer's operation. He was less concerned with the visual, the final visual effect, than other choreographers: John

Neumeier, Roland Petit, even Frederick Ashton are much more visually effective, as theatrical choreographers. But Balanchine was much more concerned with music. He forced us to consider the means and method—the place of music and pure dance in ballet.

W. McNEIL

LOWRY

Until 1975, W. McNeil Lowry was a vice-president of the Ford

Foundation, with responsibility for the Division of Humanities and

the Arts. In addition, he was also vice-president in charge of the Office

of Policy and Planning from 1964 to 1966. Prior to the launching of

the Program in the Humanities and the Arts in 1957, he had been

director of the Foundation's Education Program. He joined the staff of

the Ford Foundation in October 1953. Prior to that time, he was a

member of the faculty of the Department of English at the University

of Illinois from 1936 to 1942. In 1940 he helped to establish Ac-

cent: A Quarterly of New Literature. *The Ford Foundation*

Program in the Humanities and the Arts, was the first national

program of support for the arts in the United States and preceded by

eight years the establishment of the National Endowment for the Arts.

During his career in the Foundation, expenditures in the creative

425

and performing arts reached $320 million. In 1978, Prentice-Hall,

Inc., published **The Performing Arts and American Society,**

a volume edited by Mr. Lowry who has continued to work with arts

organizations and artists nationwide and has written widely in the

field. In 1983 and 1986, **The New Yorker** *published his "Con-*

versations with Balanchine" and "Conversations with Kirstein." He

is president of the San Francisco Ballet.

W. McNeil Lowry

MY EARLIEST ENCOUNTER WITH BALANCHINE WAS BACKSTAGE AFTER A PERFORMANCE of New York City Ballet at the City Center. My knowledge of him before that had two sources. One was from the 1950s when I got permission to go ahead with an arts program for the Ford Foundation. The other was from going to the ballet with my wife Elsa, usually watching from the balcony.

Balanchine became interested in the fact that I was in the Ford Foundation and knew people in circles that overlapped his. Lincoln Kirstein had begun to hear that there was a new administration in the Ford Foundation, although everybody who could read the Ford program knew the arts were not in it. But Kirstein and I began to talk. By the time I got approval in March 1957 for an exploratory program in the humanities and the arts, we had had a number of sessions. He may have discussed some of this with Balanchine, though our talks did not often concern ballet.

One evening at City Center, my wife and I went backstage to meet Balanchine. He was courteous and interested. He never knew how to fathom what things meant as they related to the Ford Foundation. Balanchine trusted Lincoln on that. He had seen what it meant with Mrs. John Rockefeller II and the Rockefeller Foundation.

Things changed radically after March 1957, when I asked for a mandate to learn as much as I could about the arts and professional training. I began to spend time inquiring about opportunities for professional training. How, I wondered, are young professional dancers discovered and, once discovered, what are their opportunities? There were ballet schools in those days in Atlanta, Dallas, Dayton, San Francisco, Seattle, Portland, Tulsa, Boston, Wilkes-Barre, et al. When the leaders of civic ballet companies began to understand that I was concerned with training, it didn't take long for them to seek to contribute to my education. In that process, I began to talk with some of the Balanchine dancers: Diana Adams, Melissa Hayden, and others. Gradually I began to ask for time with Mr. Balanchine. He didn't doubt the importance of the subject, but he wondered what could one do about it? Why should he care? At the same time he would talk to me about the difficulty of finding dancers beyond the eight ballerinas he had in the 1950s in his New York City Ballet, the hard core of his company.

I got to know who they were and why they were important. Through that process I began to concentrate on where people had been trained and whom *they* were training. In the biggest continuing program for fieldwork the arts ever had, we traveled to a hundred and seventy-five communities in the United States, talking to everybody we could find in each field of the arts— performers, directors, actors, curators, choreographers, dancers, painters, sculptors, musicians—everybody we could get to form a grapevine. When I saw the School of American Ballet and the San Francisco Ballet School, I began to realize that I needed to concentrate my interest on scholarships.

And then I began the pilot program that has had significance ever since— offering to the San Francisco Ballet School and the School of American Ballet a series of scholarships over a three-year period that they could allocate on their own. Balanchine and his dancers went out to look at candidates east of the Mississippi, and Lew and Harold Christensen took the west. Any students they thought had potential as professionals could be moved to the San Francisco Ballet School or to S.A.B. and paid for by the Foundation, which would have nothing to do with the selection. Over the three years there were an average of thirteen scholarships a year. In the first S.A.B. scholarship class were Roberta Sue Ficker (Suzanne Farrell) and Mimi Paul; in San Francisco, Cynthia Gregory.

I continued visiting ballet studios until I left the Ford Foundation. The whole process was the culmination of my personal fieldwork, though George Balanchine and the Christensens never realized that. I had seen many of the scholarship students in their own classes, where they were later found by the Christensens and by Balanchine's scouts. I didn't pick them, but I was familiar with where they came from. Fourteen months after they arrived in California and New York City, I brought them all together for a day at the Foundation to talk off the record about their careers—how they started, why they started, who encouraged them, what this meant to them, how their present training differed from what they had had before, and what they thought about the future as professional ballet dancers. Five of the S.A.B. scholarship students were late for the meeting, and I remember postponing the start and asking Roberta Sue Ficker, "Where are these kids?" She said, "Oh, they are in the corps de ballet now, and they're getting a schedule for rehearsal." I said, "Don't you worry. I'll bet it won't be long before you are in the corps." She said, "Oh, I don't know. I don't know whether I'll make it. I hope I can make it within the three years of the scholarship." This was only a few months before she was indeed in the corps de ballet, and she immediately began dancing many solo roles.

Balanchine had been invited to the lunch. At one point one of the San Francisco students said to Mr. Balanchine, "I guess Mr. Lowry is what you call a balletomane." And George said, "No. He's not a balletomane. A balletomane is a man who sits in the front row in the theater and tries to look under the skirts of the ballet dancers and wants to take them out to supper. Mr. Lowry cares about dance. He wants to know about ballet."

I knew the civic and regional ballet movement across the country would take no comfort from the 1963 Ford grants because there was no money for them in an $8 million program. So in advance I gathered together the leaders of the regional ballet movement, and I said, "One of these days you are going to be reading about a big action at the Ford Foundation. We are making opportunities for your professional students." A year earlier Balanchine had attended one of the regional ballet festivals, and all the ballet teachers packed into a room asked Balanchine to talk to them. They were all standing on top of one another. I was sitting in a chair in the middle with Diana Adams. One of the teachers asked, "Mr. Balanchine, I would like to know what you consider to be the best book about how to be a choreographer?" George said, "Book? Book? There is no book. You can't learn from a book. It has to be learned from the body and set to music." He got up and took Diana Adams's legs and arms and began to position them. At the beginning, he said, "there may be music, but sometimes not. With me, usually yes. But this is what it's like. How are you going to put that in a book?"

Then, in 1962, Ballet Society, with the participation of others like Lucia Chase, Walter Terry, Freddie Franklin, and others, began an inventory of teachers nationwide. Morton Baum of the New York City Center always saw a chance to ride piggyback on my projects, and he pushed the idea of having a national convention of ballet teachers. It was convened, and Baum, Nancy Lassalle, and George Balanchine all spoke. The fear surfaced that some sort of licensing of ballet teachers was being planned. The teachers knew that, as part of the scholarship program, I had asked Balanchine to undertake a series of seminars for teachers which Ford would pay for through the School of American Ballet. They knew that Balanchine had agreed. Teachers were afraid that certificates might be issued to those who attended the seminars, certificates signed by Balanchine and paid for as a program by the Ford Foundation. None of this was true, of course.

So many teachers attended the seminars, they could fill all the City Center at performances of the company. One of the works they saw the New York City Ballet dance was *Agon,* with Arthur Mitchell and Diana Adams crawling up one another's torsos. Lincoln Kirstein came out into the foyer at the interval and said: "The Virginia delegation has seceded—to the last woman."

Even before this time, Balanchine had begun to foresee the positive results of the Ford Foundation program. In the 1930s, Balanchine and Kirstein had in effect launched the Americanization of classical dance. Now the Ford Foundation completed it, not through Balanchine but through people like Barbara Weisberger in Pennsylvania, Virginia Williams in Boston, and many others. Kirstein couldn't stand the idea of improving American ballet throughout the country. But the Ford Foundation program changed the face of dance in the United States. The program made sense at that time (between 1957 and 1973), and in the hundreds of scholarship students still dancing it continues to be felt.

In 1962, Balanchine agreed to spend two or three weeks going around the country to regional ballet conferences. He said there was a brushfire of young people's excitement about ballet and ballet training. He said that there would be a ballet company in every state. I said, "No, it won't happen." He said, "Why not?" I said that there were two reasons. First of all, you would need talented and compulsively motivated teachers or artistic directors, and you just can't locate them in every state. The second reason was, of course, money. The $7.8 million that I was allocating in our first program was a drop in the bucket compared to what Balanchine was talking about. I said, "I don't think it's going to happen that way. I think what you will see is more and more interconnections in training outlets, companies where S.A.B. graduates can go, and more and more places that send people to S.A.B., San Francisco, and Pennsylvania, and to the New York City Ballet. Otherwise I don't think there are any real prospects." This was before I helped Governor Terry Sanford found the North Carolina School for the Arts. I put up a million and a half to encourage the private money, and he got the legislature to budget the rest. Balanchine's idea of a ballet company in every state was excessive even as a metaphor. It was interesting that he became enthusiastic in 1962 because I did not complete the first grants in ballet until 1963. I didn't like to discourage Balanchine's enthusiasm because it had been awhile coming.

Balanchine had had experience with patrons and patronesses before. But after a time he began to find that what I was getting ready to do gave me a legitimate entrance into the personal province of dance. He had never had to think about such a possibility. Every now and then in our talks I would say, "Mr. Balanchine, I am going to have to ask you a personal question that you may not wish to answer." He would sniff. I would say, for example, "Look, I don't believe you can afford to be both ballet master and chairman of the faculty at the School of American Ballet." From his point of view, how could I ask that? He wasn't getting paid. He had only royalties on his ballets. The royalties were probably something that would give him a living wage, but then he would give his money back to the School or the company. If he had some money, he would give it to the company to buy costumes.

The Ford Foundation gave New York City Ballet $200,000 a year for ten years. Other companies got more. I told Balanchine he had to have a salary, and I tried to fix it at $14,000 per year. That would have been better than what he had, which was nothing. We started on a kind of professional recompense basis, but it took a long time. When he did go on salary finally, he sent around a telegram saying that any ballet company could do any of his ballets. He even had the State Department send out a message offering his ballets to ballet companies around the world. But he really didn't go on salary. He continued only to take royalties and to give them back to the company. In fact, except for his Hollywood and Broadway earnings, I never knew what George lived on, really. I even raised the question whether Lincoln Kirstein should take a salary. I had to ask such questions if I was going to go to the Ford Foundation and say, "I want you to support N.Y.C.B. and S.A.B. for ten years." It took a long time for Balanchine to understand that partnership was possible with close, personal Foundation support. Lincoln Kirstein had understood this earlier. So did Morton Baum and Julius Rudel, the latter in terms of the New York City Opera.

Balanchine came to understand despite the fact that he saw things in black and white. He understood that Lowry had elected to be a partner of the company and of the School, not for himself or his own glorification but because he cared. That's the way Balanchine understood things. So did the dancers around the country. They wanted to look at it rather simply, like that.

In 1963, Balanchine took little specific interest in the grant terms and the conditions for either the School or the company following the grant. He was not affected by the way the grants were reported in the press, as a conspiracy against modern dance. None of that meant anything to George. Other people were agitated, but Balanchine showed little resentment. The fact that the Foundation said nothing in response meant to Balanchine that Lowry was the Foundation, that the Foundation let him talk for it. So, on with the dance.

The following year presented Balanchine with another series of problems with the anticipated move to State Theater. Morton Baum and Betty Cage went to the mat with the board of Lincoln Center, with my assistance. I had made grants to every one of the constituents of Lincoln Center when they were moving in. I could not make a grant to City Center itself at that time (it was not a constituent of Lincoln Center as yet), but I reserved $3 million for that purpose and let it out that it was on my appropriations budget and there was more where that came from. That was on condition that the City Center Ballet and Opera companies would go into Lincoln Center under the City Center title. We all know that Balanchine himself had to threaten to withdraw his company from State Theater when it became apparent that it might be made a musical comedy house for Richard Rodgers. Balanchine had to dynamite an extra two rows of seats to enlarge the pit for his ballet orchestra. That was a scary time.

But Balanchine never regarded State Theater as the theater he and Kirstein had dreamed about. Balanchine thought of it as a wonderful small toy and nothing like a national ballet company's home. Even three or four years before he died, Balanchine explained that Lincoln and he had yet to accomplish their final dream. Balanchine kept saying to me that at critical times—when they were at the Metropolitan Opera in the 1930s or when Kirstein was with Ballet Caravan—he would wait for Lincoln to tell him what they were going to do next. Lincoln knew about strategy, and the two of them would say, "Is this going to be it?" Lincoln thought that Lincoln Center would be the final thing. But George Balanchine never did. Lincoln knew that the State Theater was not the house that George Balanchine would have called the great imperial theater. But Lincoln was a realist compared to George. He knew that if it hadn't been for Morton Baum they never would have had even the State Theater. Even as Balanchine was dying, various parties would cite his views on trying to improve the theater by changing the size of the proscenium or altering the acoustics. I always reminded them that Balanchine felt the State Theater wasn't made for ballet, it was made for musical comedy except for the orchestra pit, which he had enlarged.

When Suzanne Farrell left the New York City Ballet following her marriage to Paul Mejia, there was no diminution in Balanchine's work as a choreographer and artistic director. There were only the shifts in the development of dancers like Kay Mazzo and others in the repertoire that had belonged to Suzanne and then in the new works in which Suzanne had never appeared. As far as I could observe, Balanchine was reticent and less ebullient in company, at least around State Theater. It would be false and simplistic to believe that Balanchine's creative juices were greatly affected by the departure of Galatea. But it is easier even for someone at my distance from the company to believe that the return of Suzanne after five years sparked a tremendous creative burst shared by both the choreographer and the dancer which lasted right up to George Balanchine's final illness.

Some works of that period were often built around particular women like Karin von Aroldingen, but they continued to evolve from the almost wordless collaboration of Balanchine and his prima ballerina. The final creations made expressly for Suzanne seemed indeed an indirect profit, an enhancement. In the last two or three years before his hospitalization, the creative accent of Balanchine showed as much through Farrell's initiative as through his own.

That, of course, cannot be a literally true statement, but Balanchine regularly challenged Farrell by the opportunities he gave her. He regularly challenged her to use her special gifts of movement, speed, accent, pause, and changing a phrase to do what she could with one of his works; after all, Balanchine believed more than most choreographers that each work lived only in performance. The individual work never lost its form, but there were

432

performances when one of his classical works with Farrell reached almost utter perfection. I have no way of knowing how complete the film archives are of these performances—or how palatable such filming would be to Balanchine's concepts of history and change—but at least for a while there could hardly be superior artifacts to those of the Balanchine-Farrell collaboration of the late 1970s and very early '80s.

What would Balanchine have done without Farrell in his history? A great body of creativity and classical style that forever would be associated with a unique ballet master and choreographer. What Farrell would have done without Balanchine is something none of her greatest admirers would like to try to contemplate. But what the collaboration ended up doing was to make Suzanne Farrell perhaps the prima ballerina assoluta of her generation throughout the world, while Balanchine—like any true Pygmalion—wielded the hammer and chisel. Balanchine did not need Farrell's return to put a new cap on his career or his corpus of work. The cap was already there. The ranks of dancers present in 1969 and thereafter were rich and memorable. The real meaning of the relationship between Suzanne Farrell and George Balanchine is not in whatever ties they formed or did not form as human beings but in the release of art and imagination that each bestowed on the other.

But there was an even more unique relationship. Balanchine and Kirstein were not friends in the way we usually think of friends. Nor were they collaborators in the way we usually think of collaborators. The only aesthetic area in which George needed Lincoln was scenic design. Some people would say to George that Lincoln could go astray in that field. But as far as George was concerned, Lincoln had a much better education and background in painting and sculpture and design than he had. In fact, in this area Lincoln once told me that he despaired of what George knew or could see. Balanchine had that gap, as he volunteered to me in the 1983 conversations about the Diaghilev period. For a time he had Pavel Tchelitchew, but after Tchelitchew, there was no one else but Kirstein for Balanchine to lean on in visual matters. Lincoln did some remarkable things with Balanchine. The Franklin Watkins design for *Transcendence* is a tremendous example.

Balanchine would advise Kirstein on occasion, though sometimes destructively. One of the worst examples was the time he had Kirstein destroy two journals which he was working on. This was in 1962–63. Lincoln had been getting up every morning at 4 A.M. to work on them and made the mistake of talking to George about them. He had been upset in that period, and he had also been creative. Sometimes when you are upset, you can be at your most creative. George got the idea that the work on the journals was harming Lincoln, making him neurotic, and that he had to get this monkey off his back. So George told Lincoln to burn the journals, and he did. Balanchine thought the journals would be witnesses against Lincoln in the future, and he didn't want Lincoln to harm himself in that way. But he probably lost for the twentieth century a priceless artistic record.

When Lincoln Kirstein first decided that George Balanchine was *the* choreographer, he was able to control things. Later, for Lincoln it was George's company, George ran it, George made the decisions. Balanchine assumed that role by virtue of being George Balanchine. But all the authority that George was allowed to hold proceeded from Lincoln Kirstein's attitude about George Balanchine. Kirstein made that decision very early, and he never took it back. He gave the example.

What happened for Kirstein and Balanchine after the war was crucial. Lincoln knew what to do. There was a period when Ballet Society was talking to the Paris Opéra about George becoming director, but everyone also acknowledges that the Paris Opéra was then completely hopeless. Balanchine could never have done new things at the Opéra, and he was only interested in doing new things. For Balanchine, if it was ballet, it was always new.

Maria Tallchief is fond of saying that Balanchine was always propping up Kirstein. But she heard the phone conversations only at George's end of the line. George did help Lincoln, but what about the conversation from Lincoln at his end of the line? George's helping Lincoln was the smallest gesture he could make in response to the fifty years of support he had received from his friend. Some of us say that Lincoln's support of Balanchine was the greatest single selfless act in the history of American philanthropy. For that and other reasons, Kirstein is certainly the most important cultural influence of the twentieth century in the United States.

The twenty-six years in which I knew Balanchine began and ended with such reverence and respect mutually paid that it is hard to think of another artist at the same peak of achievement or capacity. This fact regularly displeased or irritated some of the most talented artists with whom I worked in my rather special position in creating the first national program in the arts. I can still hear the voices say, "Mac, you don't think I'm the genius George Balanchine is." I never, of course, relayed any of these remonstrances to Mr. Balanchine. He might not have been embarrassed by them, but he would have sniffed, and that would have meant the same thing.

PATRICIA

McBRIDE

*Trained with Ruth Vernon and at the School of American Ballet;
danced with the Eglevsky Ballet Company before joining the New
York City Ballet in 1959; she was made a principal dancer in 1961.
Balanchine made twenty-one roles for her* (The Figure in the Car-
pet, A Midsummer Night's Dream, Brahms-Schoenberg
Quartet, Who Cares?, Divertimento from "Le Baiser de la
Fée" *et al.) and staged (with Alexandra Danilova) a revival of*
Coppélia *for her in 1974. She became famous for her partnership
with Edward Villella through many appearances on stage and televi-
sion. McBride retired from the stage in 1989 and teaches at Indiana
University.*

MY FIRST TEACHER WAS RUTH VERNON IN TEANECK, NEW JERSEY. I WAS SEVEN. MY mom just sent me to ballet. She thought it would be marvelous. All little girls seemed to be taking ballet lessons, so I went and I cried. I hated it. I just couldn't do it. It was the most difficult thing. I always did the wrong thing. If you were supposed to turn out, I would be turning in. My teacher was sure I would give it up. I just stuck to it, and I got to be pretty good. There were no boys in the classes. There was a tap class that I took that had one boy in it. In those days it was just unheard of to have any boys. But Ruth Vernon was a wonderful teacher. At the Metropolitan Opera she danced in the corps de ballet; she retired at age seventeen. When she was about fourteen, she played all the men's roles because she was quite tall. I'm sure that if Mr. Balanchine had seen her he would have thought she was just beautiful. When I was twelve, she said, "I really can't teach you anymore. I don't want to waste your mother's money. If you really want to dance professionally, you should really go to New York."

So I came there and saw an advertisement for a school, and went there for about eight months. One of the people said, "She looks like she's a Balanchine dancer." At thirteen I was really skinny, the size I am now. They said, "You must go to the School of American Ballet" where I would get "the best training in America." I didn't want to leave. I was happy with Sonja Dobovinskaya, who was a fine teacher; hers was a different kind of training than I had had with Ruth Vernon. Also, Sonja was a very flamboyant character from Russia, with a lot of soul. I once went to see the New York City Ballet with Sonja, and I was just overwhelmed. I saw *Serenade.* I could barely breathe. I didn't know dancing could be that beautiful.

When I went to the School of American Ballet, I had to audition with Madame Tumkovsky. They placed me in B class at fourteen. I had never seen so many beautiful dancers in my life.

I was there for two years, and then I was taken into the company. What was incredible was that I went from Teaneck, where I had one teacher, to another school where I had one teacher, to having suddenly Stuart, Vladimiroff, Oboukhoff, Doubrovska, and Tumkovsky. To have a different teacher every day was a wonderful way to be schooled; you had to work. You knew each teacher, and you knew what they wanted, and you would try to do what they wanted. I found it to be competitive. You go from your little local school to New York, from best in class to suddenly realizing you can't do *entrechat six,* and you've never ever had to do an attitude turn.

Doubrovska was a wonderful teacher. She used to say, "This comes from *Apollo,*" when we'd do it, especially in her pointe classes. Or "This comes from *Sleeping Beauty.*" She adored Mr. Balanchine; he would come and watch her class. I think he was in awe of her. He knew that she would pass things on. Young kids are influenced by what they see visually. If you see something that's beautiful, you pick up on it. That's how you learn. And if you have a terrible teacher and you're doing all kinds of mannerisms like the teacher, you're just an echo of them. Balanchine thought Doubrovska was a marvelous teacher, and she had such elegance. Just to watch her make her entrance in the room was something. It was a theatrical event. She would come in with the most beautiful dress. And always she had a beautiful French scarf tied around her waist, and she had beautiful legs. She would demonstrate with a noble bearing. She wanted to show what Mr. B. wanted. He asked her to give a special class at the School for ten dancers.

Balanchine chose the teachers for his School because he respected them as dancers. Mr. Vladimiroff was a really great dancer in his day. In the old Maryinsky he danced with Pavlova. He had a fantastic technique. Balanchine wanted to show the students what that technique was. He believed in the people he had teaching at the School. I thought that if you studied with Vladimiroff, if you could do his class, you could just do anything. Oboukhoff was a wonderful teacher as well. He was such a character, a dynamic person. I was scared stiff of him when I was fourteen. He would stand in front of you and say, "Dahnce, miss." You would just cringe. He'd stand and look you in the eye, and you had to do everything. He made you extend yourself beyond what you could do because he made really difficult combinations, endurance-wise. When you are young, you have to build endurance.

Muriel Stuart was also a marvelous teacher. She was one of Pavlova's girls and had a beautiful upper body. All the personalities at the School were wonderful. To go from one class to the next was so exciting. Mr. Balanchine always came in. He'd walk in the door and scare everyone. We always felt the teachers were a little nervous too when he was there. In those days he really came often, and he chose each dancer himself. He knew each student. It was such a relief when he'd finally leave. You couldn't wait for him to go. It was too nerve-racking.

Balanchine used to teach the students. I took some classes with him. I feel that I was in a generation in whom he really established the Balanchine technique. Then, in 1959–60, he would give two-hour classes every day. How to do a *plié*. We would start the *plié* and he'd stop us immediately. It was just so difficult. You felt that you could never satisfy him or do it well enough. He would say, "You can go home and you can do *tendus* while you're cooking." Do *tendus* in the kitchen and never stop.

He would say that his classes—which were so difficult—were like a smorgasbord. You could take what you wanted. He made you dance the way he wanted you to use your legs and feet in his ballets. He hated lazy dancers, lazy people. He said, "Oh, you can have time to rest when you're in the grave. But you give a hundred percent, and you do it." He loved to see a lot of energy. If he was choreographing a ballet, he would do it in the style of his classes at the time, the way he would be teaching his class.

We learned how he wanted the hand positions—how to hold your hands. I remember that I was an apprentice and he would make me hold a rubber ball. He said the arm has to be round so that it has life, and the pinky should be out so it doesn't look stiff and rigid. We'd take our rubber balls into the other teachers' classes, and they were very understanding about it. He would say, "You've got to change your hand. It looks like a dead chicken." You shouldn't be "English," with the shoulders down, so correct. He wanted your arms to breathe and to have life to the end of your fingertips so that when you danced it was not just one part of you dancing, you could feel from the tip of your toes to the end of your fingers, from the nose to the end of your fingertips. He didn't want us to have a stiff neck. He wanted to show the girl's neck. He'd come and kiss us. He'd say, "Offer your cheek." Everyone always says, "Oh, Balanchine was so cold!" or he liked "mechanical" dancing. But if you ever saw him in class, how beautifully he would show what he wanted, you'd see how untrue that was.

Demanding uniformity of corps work in Balanchine is very difficult. Dancing Balanchine is harder—the patterns, the way they change in Balanchine ballets. The ballets are so fast, and they travel much more than a lot of the more classical companies. One of the first ballets I danced when I entered the company was *Symphony in C.* I ruined the uniformity. I made a mistake. There's a moment where you use the arms and *tendu* in the finale. My foot went astray. I was sure they would fire me. At sixteen years old I thought I'd had it. But they didn't. No one said anything. I was quite amazed. But they do trust you. They know you know.

The first ballet Balanchine choreographed for me was *Figure in the Carpet,* when I was seventeen. It was a terrible loss that they didn't film that; now it is a lost work. The whole first scene was Violette Verdy, about the building up of the sands of the desert. The corps was in long, flowing *Serenade*-like costumes. The second section was the divertissements, and that's the section I was in, a little court dance with Nicky Magallanes. We were Chinese and I was a Duchess. There were fountains at the back of the stage that kept leaking.

I had danced a few things with Eddie Villella, like *Symphony in C,* Third Movement. I always adored dancing with him because he always gave a hundred percent. He was such an exciting dancer. It was like gangbusters. He never got nervous. It used to kill me. He'd be so relaxed. He'd be checking out his muscles, how he'd feel, but he never got nervous. It was so wonderful to dance with him. We had a great time onstage together. We were both young. I was seventeen and he was twenty-one, an old man of twenty-one! I looked up to him. He was a star, and I was just a little corps de ballet dancer who was lucky enough to get to dance with him. I had a wonderful time. *Tarantella* was a killer. It was an endurance race and great fun.

I don't know how all those incredible ballets Balanchine made at City Center ever fit on that stage. He made the role of Hermia for me in *A Midsummer Night's Dream.* That ballet was the beginning of Mr. B.'s having the dancers move in a different way. I think he always envisioned the bigger stage, from the beginning. He had a great vision of what the company would be.

Harlequinade was a totally different thing. It was *demi-caractère* for Eddie. I think that Mr. Balanchine remembered *Harlequinade* fondly from Russia. Nemtchinova had found the music from Russia for him. He didn't explain the story, it bored him to be so literal, he liked spontaneity, he assumed that you could do things for yourself. He loved challenging dancers. You'd have a week to do a part. He just loved to see what you'd do on your own. Then he was proud, because it was you.

I remember going through the rehearsals for *Harlequinade* beet-red from having to act. I was so shy, and Balanchine put all those kisses into the ballet. I was just dying; I thought, "Oh, I'll never be able to do this the way he wants." He started the first pas de deux in a little practice room and finished it in an hour. The next day I was called for an hour for my first variation, and he whipped that off. The second variation he did in forty-five minutes. He was just the easiest choreographer who has ever existed, he knew what a woman can do. He knew what you could do before you knew it yourself. He knew what it is for a woman to be on pointe. I remember thinking he must have practiced on pointe. It was just innate, there was no experimentation, he would just set it, and it would be right. He also trusted you. When he choreographed, he knew you and trusted you to do what you wanted with what he gave you. He didn't intimidate you by saying, "Now lift this little pinky here, and the head must be like this." That was all done in class.

Balanchine regarded himself as a teacher. He taught us how to dance. But when he would walk into the studio to choreograph, the teaching was over. He would be making something beautiful for us to dance. It would not be a lesson. He would show everything so beautifully. I felt that I could never do it as beautifully as he could. He would never really explain, but he would show. It was extraordinary to see how he would do everything. It would all fall into place. He had such a flair for comedy. He'd be all over the place. He had so much energy. He would go from studio to studio. He'd be there every night. He'd be there for class the next morning. In 1969 he did the variation in *Who Cares?* for me. He was sixty-five and he did that whole variation, the rhythms, the body, much better than I could.

He was a great partner, too. He would lift me, throw me around. He spent a lot of time showing the boys how to partner. What worked with him perfectly well I would have a little trouble trying to do with someone else. It would take a little time. Usually he didn't have to change things. He wouldn't experiment and try things five or ten times to get the result. He used to say he was never prepared until he was in front of you. I felt that was true, but I could never believe it because when he choreographed he would just do it. As Mr. Balanchine worked, the dancer might add a few touches here and there to the choreography, but basically it was all there.

Mr. Balanchine and Jerome Robbins were opposite in their approaches to choreography. Working with Jerry is like working with a real director. The emotional side of the material is important to Jerry, including describing what he wants before you start. He will experiment when he's choreographing. He is so talented, he can do four different variations to the same music and they are all fantastic. He likes to try different versions until he gets the one he feels is right.

Mr. Balanchine always trusted his dancers. It's so wonderful to be trusted. I always felt that he knew me so well that he didn't have to change things; he knew that what he was giving me I would work on. Probably, if it did not work, he would change it for the dancer. He was very open to that because he wanted you to look good. I felt that I was always too slow to catch up with him because his mind worked so quickly and I was always afraid that I wouldn't grasp everything he had to give. It was just so natural for him.

I once asked him to choreograph something for me to be performed outside the company. He said, "Well, bring the score." I took the score, and he set it on the piano. It was Aurora's solo in the vision scene of *The Sleeping Beauty.* I had to dance to a tape that was much too fast. It couldn't be danced to. So he just whipped up the dance, played the music on the piano, and choreographed it in street shoes in ten minutes.

Brahms-Schoenberg Quartet was a really special ballet because I wasn't teamed with Eddie Villella. I felt that Mr. Balanchine had made it as a special partnering experience. It was a much more lyrical role. We were on tour in Tel Aviv, and he had the score. I had heard that he was going to do a new ballet and that there would be four different sections. He never asked me who I wanted to dance with. It was one of those rare exceptions when he said, "Who do you want to dance with?" I said, "It's not for me to decide, Mr. Balanchine. I just can't." So he said, "Um, maybe Conrad Ludlow. It will be different." He made something for me that involved being lifted. The partnering was extremely difficult. Conrad was a superb partner, the greatest partner the company had at that time, and Balanchine made beautiful phrasings and lifts for us.

He asked me to make a *grand jeté*, and I just fell back. He said, "Ah! Keep it. That's good." It was originally going to be a *grand jeté* forward, but he always went for the natural way. This would happen a lot when he choreographed. He would not make you fight your natural instincts. If you fell a natural way, he would incorporate that into the choreography. It wasn't like someone saying, "I am going to choreograph this great work." He hadn't really gone that far in thinking what he was going to do.

I wasn't in the original, first cast of *Liebeslieder Walzer*, but Balanchine used to come before performances of that ballet and sit on one of the little chairs and talk to us. He always felt that the men never knew how to waltz. He would spend rehearsals trying to teach the men how to hold the hand elegantly and how to present the women. He would waltz us around for hours; we really got pretty good. We learned how to waltz with Mr. Balanchine. When the ballet was revived after his death, it had been ten years or so since it had last been done. That revival had a very special feeling. All of us felt he was looking down. We remembered the things that he wanted. Karin von Aroldingen did a very good job of setting the revival. It's a difficult ballet to set. We didn't feel the fact that Balanchine was not there because we felt he was with us. I was lucky because I had worked with him and been in the ballet for many years.

I remember once Balanchine said that he was very happy with my *La Sonnambula*. It was one of the few times he ever came back and said anything. Sometimes he would say "good"—"good" was wonderful. But he said, "Your eyes, it was mysterious, it was just what I wanted to see in it." I was remembering this recently and said to myself, "How special! I wish I knew what I did in that performance! I wish I had a film." It was just a hint of what he wanted for that specific ballet.

Critics have liked my rapport with my partners, including the way I look at them. It's another part of dancing—it's being with the person. I'm actually not sure that Mr. B. liked that too much. He liked the use of the whole body. But there is nothing that would make him angrier than if he felt things were automatic. I think he liked the use of the eyes. He'd have us do *port de bras* and would say, "Look with your eyes to the end of your hand."

Balanchine never told me in words what he wanted. I think he told my husband, Jean-Pierre Bonnefous, what he wanted of me more than he would tell me directly. I know that in *Union Jack's* costermongers pas de deux (1976) he wanted me to be slightly vulgar. He told Jean-Pierre to whisper terrible things in my ear. He must have told him, "She's not doing enough. You've got to get in there and do something." He put in a few bumps and showed me really vulgarly how to do them. He was very expressive.

He had me do *Episodes* once, the second section. It's a pas de deux, and the ballerina's entrance is like on a tightrope. Balanchine had me imagining that I was walking it, balancing, really doing it. I did that millions of times until I got it right. There was another step that was like smoking a cigarette. There were always these little things that you would think about as you did them. I remember in *La Valse* there was an entrance where it was as though the wind was blowing you back. That was so difficult, and I still don't think I ever got it right. He would demonstrate it for me so many times. "No, dear, it's not like that. No, dear." I kept at it, and he said, "Well, you go home and you work on it." He wanted you to be completely relaxed, and you'd like to be in a beautiful position. But in order to do what he wanted you really would have to sort of collapse. In the "Central Park in the Dark" section of *Ivesiana,* he had me really closing my eyes and being like a blind woman to really feel everything. He allowed you to feel that you really were trying to find things in the dark.

When Balanchine made an unsuccessful ballet—like *PAMTGG*—he knew it all right. He knew when he was good and when he was bad. He knew it was just one of those things. You can't do a masterpiece every time. And we knew that he knew. I think everyone was very supportive of him. When he would subsequently say, "Wear what you want," about a particular piece, you knew that it was on the way out. Balanchine's ballets always had a lot to do with the music. He once told me that *Stravinsky Violin Concerto* was his greatest ballet. He loved it. He would watch every performance, until the end.

For the Ravel Festival in 1975 he made *Pavane* for me. It was a very different kind of Balanchine. He left it up to you to make of it who you were. There is a part where it is very evident the woman has a baby from the way she holds the scarf. But I think he trusted what you would do. He had great faith.

Balanchine didn't talk about his ballets, but he taught everybody about cooking and wine. And he would always buy perfumes for us. He loved women so much. The one he chose for me was Guerlain.

FRANCIA

RUSSELL

Trained with the Christensens in San Francisco, with Kschessinska and Besobrasova in Paris, and with Vera Volkova in London. Joined the New York City Ballet in 1956; danced with Jerome Robbins's Ballets: USA (1963). In 1964 she was appointed ballet mistress of the New York City Ballet. She and her husband, Kent Stowell, named ballet masters of Frankfurt Ballet (1975). Since 1977, artistic director with Stowell of Pacific Northwest Ballet in Seattle. One of the first ballet masters chosen by Balanchine to stage his work. Russell has mounted more than a hundred productions of his ballets in Europe, the United States, the People's Republic of China, and the U.S.S.R.

I Remember Balanchine

BALANCHINE SAW ME AND TOOK ME INTO HIS COMPANY IN 1956 AFTER TOO MANY YEARS of too many teachers everywhere and wanting to be in Ballet Theatre. Lucia Chase said I was too tall, so I went to the School of American Ballet. After two weeks Mr. B. came to watch class and offered me a job. That's when I started learning how to dance, really. I was so lucky because he taught company class all the time I was dancing. Except during the time Tanaquil LeClercq was sick, he was around choreographing and teaching. He taught incredible two-and-a-half-hour torture sessions. They stretched your body to the ultimate. You felt like you had never used your body like that before and never did use it again the same way. He demanded so much more. There was nothing—no compromise in anything, so we all produced more, we did everything for him. He was all that mattered. Even onstage it wasn't the audience, it wasn't anything else but Balanchine. As much as we loved to perform, it was like night and day if we knew he was out there or onstage watching.

I was one of the four girls in *Agon* (1957) when he created it, so I watched that whole thing, and it's so incredible to me now. To think that I was eighteen or nineteen, and it seemed so normal to be in the same room with Stravinsky and Balanchine creating together. It was just ordinary. And now I think about it, it might as well have been Mozart. Looking back on it, I feel like I should have had a camera and been writing down my impressions, but of course I didn't think of that. And then *Liebeslieder* (1960) was another wonderful one—I was second cast of that. Right from the first rehearsal, there were two casts learning it, but again we didn't realize how wonderful it was until it was onstage. We didn't know that it was one of the great works of the twentieth century. Nobody ever does know that kind of thing. He always used me a lot to demonstrate. He'd work things out on me, whether it was corps or solos or whatever, but of course mostly in corps things. I understood what he wanted quickly, so I was usually the guinea pig.

You couldn't ever read Balanchine's mind, but I could sometimes be almost a step ahead of what he was going to do next, so that there was a lot that didn't need to be explained. He was always full of surprises, little things, like connecting steps, and I gave what he wanted. And the most memorable experience was the one time that he created a dance in a room with me all alone. This was for the pas de trois in *Agon,* which Jillana and Eddie Villella and I were to do. It fitted my mind and my body. He decided that he didn't like a dance he had done earlier, and he wanted to do a completely new one. But Jillana didn't show up that day, so he did the whole thing on me. She later absolutely hated it, because of course it didn't fit her at all. It was one of the most satisfying things to dance for me. It was like my skin. Mr. B. did it very fast but, on the other hand, I felt I had input because he'd say, "How does that feel?" And I'd say, "Well, I want to go this way." So then he'd make it go that way. It was so exciting. That happens in rehearsal sometimes, where it catches fire and you zoom right through something. It was like that, that day. We never changed a fraction of it.

Balanchine was tough on us all. He did not believe in the Method way of acting. Once when I went to ask him something, he said I was trying to express too much onstage. "Nobody, dear, is interested in your tears." He wanted the show to be in the dance. He knew what all his roles were about, what he intended; he could have explained but I think he was right that it wouldn't have made the performances any better. On the other hand, now I try to talk a little bit about how dancers should approach roles in our own company. But I understand what he meant—you want to see what a dancer does with the role herself, without any preconceived notions. Then you get a kind of freshness.

Figure in the Carpet (1960) was a ballet I'd like to see restored one day. Except for Nicholas Magallanes, most of the dancers who were in it are very much around. Patricia McBride was discovered in that ballet. We all stood in the wings and said, "My God, who would ever have thought little Patty could look like that onstage?" Diana Adams, Violette Verdy, Mary Hinkson and Arthur Mitchell, Melissa Hayden and Jacques d'Amboise, all were in it. I just did one little piece in it. People really liked "The Sands of the Desert," the first part. It was like a beige *Serenade*. *Figure* was a really large-scale ballet. Mr. B. was Russian, and Russians love size. Everything in Russia seems huge to me. Going to Leningrad in 1988 to stage Mr. B.'s *Theme and Variations* made me realize that. The Kirov Theater is not so large, but it has a big stage. They just think big. Out front it's kind of baroque and pretty, but the stage is for big effects. They think in terms of size and numbers of people. Mr. B. grew up on that stage. He loved making things like *Vienna Waltzes* and *Union Jack* because there were so many hordes of people. He was always talking about big sets and was fascinated by the size of the tree in *Nutcracker* and always spoke about having more dancers. In Russia when he was a boy there were hundreds of people in the ballets, and he always wanted that.

The thing Kent Stowell and I always remember, apart from his teaching and his ballets, was Mr. B.'s courage when he almost lost the New York State Theater. There was a move to make it into a musical comedy theater for Richard Rodgers. Mr. B. and Lincoln came back from a meeting one day, and it looked really bad. It looked like the New York State Theater was going to be the Richard Rodgers Musical Theater. Lincoln was monumentally depressed. We asked Mr. B., "Well, what do we do now?" Mr. B. said calmly, "We start over. We just start again. If we have to go back to the beginning it doesn't matter, we'll do it again." The fact that he could face that was unthinkable. *We* couldn't face it. I was a ballet mistress then and Kent was a dancer, and we couldn't face it, but Mr. B. would have gone right back to the beginning again. "Someone will build us another theater," he calmly said. "We'll just start over."

After I stopped dancing in 1962, I taught at the School of American Ballet for a year. Balanchine came and watched my classes. Then he gave me hours of corrections on every detail. He would tell me everything I had done wrong. He gave me so much, and I never really repaid it. He would work on every little detail of everything I was saying and the combinations I gave and also how I was demonstrating. "You must demonstrate everything perfectly because children learn by imitation." If I made the teeny-weeniest mistake or if my little finger wasn't held correctly, he would explain to me exactly how it should be. After that, when I couldn't make enough money at the School because there weren't enough classes for me to teach, I got a job at *Publishers Weekly.* Then Balanchine asked me to stage *Allegro Brillante* (1956) in Montreal for Les Grands Ballets Canadiens. I'd danced it a lot. I did talk to Pat Wilde and Diana about the principals, because I'd done the corps. And then Barbara Horgan called me one day and said, "If you've ever had any thoughts of being a ballet mistress I think you should talk to Mr. B." Obviously he had said something. They needed an extra dancer for *Stars and Stripes* in a benefit for Lyndon Johnson in Washington. So I went, just for fun. I was taking classes but not really wanting to dance. And Mr. B. was sitting out in the audience. I went and said that I was interested in being a ballet mistress. And he hired me. He was waiting for me to come and say something. He wouldn't ask me, but he put the word out that I should come and say something. So then I started working with the company and he kept trying to get me to dance. And I had to be in shape and I had to be able to replace whoever was out and that was fine, I did a lot of that. But then he would say, "You sure you don't want to dance *Apollo,* dear? Next week you could do *Apollo.*" I said, "No, I'm sure. I don't want to be a dancer. I don't." And he kept taunting me with the possibility of *Apollo,* teasing me with things, like the Coquette in *Sonnambula.* And I really didn't want to be a dancer anymore. I liked being a ballet mistress, and so he started sending me off to stage ballets. I went to Germany to do *Symphony in C* for Hamburg, *La Valse* and *Serenade* for Munich, and *Allegro Brillante* for Stuttgart. Four ballets on my first trip out, a real baptism of fire. And there were no videotapes in those days. It was a lot harder to stage ballets because, in order to learn the ballet, you not only had first to write everything down, which I still do, but also to pester each and every dancer to know what their counts were. If the ballet wasn't in the rep that season you didn't get a chance to see it. You just had to capture dancers and corner them, and of course they would run when they saw me coming because they didn't want to spend half an hour showing me their parts. They were tired, and it was boring. I don't use notation. I've never had the time to learn. I just use my own notes and diagrams.

For the Kirov staging, I took a tape of *Theme,* but I never got a chance to use it because there's no tape equipment, no video equipment, at the Kirov. I did look at it once just before I left, the first time, just to make sure I had everything right.

Working with the Kirov was exciting. Of all the nationalities I've worked with, the Russians are the ones I got closest to. Oleg Vinogradov's invitation to stage the Balanchine ballets in Leningrad was a real pioneering gesture that can produce so much for us and for them. He and Mr. B. seemed to get along together very well, from all accounts, when they met years ago. Vinogradov has accepted our invitation to come to Seattle in 1990 to stage *Paquita* on an all-Russian program we will do, with the Prokofiev-Balanchine *Prodigal Son* and *Firebird,* which Kent Stowell has just staged in a new setting by Ming Cho Li. It would be wonderful if this were the beginning of a continual exchange between the United States and the U.S.S.R. in the ballet world. And all because of Vinogradov's enthusiasm for Balanchine, who started out there but built here the new classic dance.

When the Kirov came to New York in the summer of 1989 and performed the Balanchine ballets there for the first time, I was able to work with them again the day before. What thrilled me about that, in addition to working with the dancers again, was the pleasure Lincoln Kirstein took in watching the rehearsal. It was like Mr. B. at a distance was watching too.

Arlington HYATT

703-525-1234

_____

SUKI

SCHORER

Daughter of the distinguished American man of letters, Mark Schorer; trained at the school of the San Francisco Ballet with Harold Christensen; joined New York City Ballet in 1959. Balanchine made roles for her in nine ballets, including **The Figure in the Carpet, Raymonda Variations, Don Quixote,** *and* **Emeralds** *in* **Jewels.** *She danced an extensive repertory at the New York City Ballet. Long a valued teacher at the School of American Ballet, where she directed the lecture-demonstration program for New York public schools, she is writing a book on Balanchine pedagogy.*

449

I Remember Balanchine

MY FIRST KNOWLEDGE OF BALANCHINE CAME THROUGH HIS BALLETS. VIDA BROWN came to the San Francisco Ballet and staged *Serenade* and *Barocco*, and I was in them both. Then in the summer of 1959 I came to New York for the first time and took classes all over the city in addition to those at the School of American Ballet. I lived at the Gorham Hotel across from City Center on Fifty-fifth Street, and after the first ballet of the evening I would go inside with my friends. We would see every ballet except the opening ballet. I fell in love with the company—the way they danced, they way they moved, and the ballets. The City Ballet dancers moved in a very big way, which I had never seen before. It was exciting. The performances were alive. I saw *Agon* —it was just unreal. And in *Stars and Stripes* I saw the boys doing their double *tours*. I don't remember how many boys we had in the San Francisco Ballet but certainly not sixteen. I was very impressed.

I had been trained in San Francisco by Lew and Harold Christensen, and they talked about Balanchine all the time. I would hear people say about Lew, "Well, he's imitating Balanchine, he's 'after' Balanchine," in terms of what he wanted in class or onstage. But when I got to New York, I didn't think about joining City Ballet. I only thought that I might audition, and if Balanchine would take me, then I could go back and ask for more to dance from Lew. Through Vida Brown I got in touch with Janet Reed, who was the ballet mistress then, and she saw me dance. She said, "Balanchine might be interested." A date was made for me to go to City Center on the free day, Monday, at twelve noon, and meet Mr. B. and do a class for him. I came at the appointed hour. He was onstage rehearsing Pat Wilde and Jonathan Watts. I appeared and he said, "Oh, you're the girl who's going to audition." I said, "Yes." He said, "Well, your contract's upstairs." And I said, "Well, I don't want a contract." He said, "But I'm very busy rehearsing. Can you please talk with the company manager? Didn't I see you in class the other day? You had the black leotard on and the pink tights." Well, so did every other dancer. I said, "Oh, yes, I was wearing the black leotard." And he said, "Well, yes, your contract's ready." I went up to Betty Cage and said, "I don't know how this happened. I didn't mean to have a contract. I can't join this company unless I talk with Lew Christensen." She said, "Well, he's coming to town tomorrow. You talk to him at ten and come and sign your contract at eleven." And that's what I did.

Then something happened that brought me close to Balanchine. I was diagnosed as having some form of polio in my arm and neck. Perhaps it was. I had had all the innoculations because my aunt had died of polio. On the summer tour after I joined City Ballet, my arm had been bad. In the Bizet I couldn't lift it up in second, I couldn't do *port de bras* to fifth in time. But I did it anyway. At the end of *Fanfare* I would have to catch my hand and hold it because it would only extend. I looked distorted. A doctor in California said, "Well, if it's not better by August, I want you to see a neurologist in New York." It wasn't better in August. So when we came back from the summer tour—the Greek Theater in L.A., Ravinia in Chicago—I went to a neurologist at New York Hospital, and he said, "What I think you had is polio." He gave me exercises to build up other muscles on my back, and of course when I found out that I had polio I was very upset. I remember telling Mr. B. and crying: "Look at my arm. When I do a back bend my neck just falls over." So Balanchine used to come to me periodically and say, "Well, how is it? Now, show me how is your arm doing today." We would talk about it. He would say, "Well, you know, the nerves are like a carrot. One day there is no carrot, and the next day there is a carrot. It's going to come back. It's under the ground. We don't see it happening, but all of a sudden you'll have your full use of the arm." I wouldn't say that Balanchine and I became friends, but there was communication.

Allegra Kent was going to have a baby, and they needed someone for the third movement of *Bourrée Fantasque,* the "Fête Polonaise." Balanchine said, "Well, let's try Suki." Then he didn't come to the theater for four days. Either he was sick—and he was never sick—or it was Greek Easter. I learned Janet Reed's part. She taught me, and I rehearsed. Balanchine never saw one rehearsal, the performance came, and there I was in costume dancing it. He came to the performance. Afterward I said to Janet Reed, "What did he think?" She said, "He thought it was awful, and you will never do it again." I said, "What should I work on?" And she said, "Everything." I said, "Oh." Actually, I was crying, and she said, "Well, I'll take you out for a beer." So she took me out for a beer, and we talked. That was the beginning—that was when I had to work very hard. I just said, "Well, I'll just continue working." I always worked hard, and when I joined the company I looked very young, younger than I was. People could lift their legs up in the air, and I couldn't lift my leg up. People could do *entrechat six,* and I couldn't. So I took three or four classes a day and, when I discovered the polio, I started going to exercise class—to Carola Trier, who used a Pilates system of exercising to build strength. Balanchine himself believed in the Pilates system. It certainly helped me.

I couldn't work any harder. I thought, "Well, just continue working hard if you want to improve, get stronger," because obviously there was something about me that he liked because he put me out there. After all, if he had seen a rehearsal of *Bourrée Fantasque* something else would have happened. He probably had an image of what he thought I was going to look like, and if he'd been in the rehearsal he would have known what to expect, or he could have made me do something else.

The next thing I did was *Donizetti Variations* (1960). I didn't have a solo but he gave me something a little bit different in the ballet. He seemed to enjoy working with me, showing me the steps, and I remember that I got a write-up. The writer misidentified me, and the management realized that they had to put my name separate from the alphabetical listing in the program so the critics could see who was who.

Years later, perhaps the year after I stopped dancing, Mr. B. said to me, "I can't believe how much you changed." I was able to do it by working hard, listening, changing the way I worked, and learning how to move. Most of this happened in his classes. Right after I joined, I think he was beginning to get involved in teaching the company again. I think he lost a little bit of interest when Tanaquil LeClercq was sick. He was preoccupied at home, so he would just come and make ballets. But then he started teaching a lot. In the layoffs he'd teach two-hour, two-and-a-half-hour classes. I was fascinated by what he had to say. It all made sense. If you listened to his stories, how they related to the movements or the steps, to me it just seemed the right thing. People either believed in what he had to say, in what he taught, or they didn't. If they didn't believe, then they didn't really like him, and they didn't stay around. You couldn't just feel that, "Well, he's okay." You either adored this man and believed strongly in what he believed in or you didn't like him and you couldn't be around him. You were either in love with him or you hated him, and there was very little middle of the road.

I was able to observe him choreographing *Donizetti*. With Balanchine the creative process didn't look that much different from his work in class. He was always making things during class and seeing how they would look. He would make a step in class and say, "This is what I want to see. Do this, do that. . . . No, I don't like that, so let's try it this way . . . or that way." He was very relaxed. He seemed to know what he wanted. He would say, "Now, make *épaulement*. Present yourself. Present your feet. Do this. Now we'll kick here. Now you go on one, she goes on two." He would simply throw things around, and it became a ballet. It was not heavy meditation to produce a step. He had so many wonderful steps and combinations, some of them so simple, just a change of direction, the same step on the other side or in another direction or to the back, something nobody else would have thought of but it was right there at his fingertips. Sometimes we would make up a step in class and he would say, "Let's put all different kinds of *ronds de jambe* in this one step," and we'd do it, and he'd say, "It's never been done before."

I think *Ivesiana* was the first solo thing I did—"The Unanswered Question." I had never seen Allegra Kent, but Balanchine was there, and he said, "Well, you stand up on the shoulders and now you're going to sit down.

And now you're going to do a back bend. And now grab her. And now come up. Now fall back, just straight back." I had no fear—then. Now, I can't cross the street, a cab's coming, ohmygod, only in a crosswalk, in a jaywalk, I say, "I have a daughter. I have to live now." Actually, *Ivesiana* was coolly received in the beginning by the audience. I'm not sure how popular *Concerto Barocco* was with the San Francisco audience when I first danced it there. It was certainly popular with the dancers. I didn't listen to applause, I just danced the ballet.

For *Apollo,* Balanchine wanted a cast of small dancers with Eddie Villella as Apollo. So he found some small dancers: Patty McBride, Sally Leland, Carol Sumner, and myself. It was so beautiful to dance. He rehearsed us and talked to us about the ballet. For example, in Calliope's solo he explained that shot, the arrow hits you and you react, talking and opening. He said not to worry how you look, not to try to be pretty, just do the movement. In the finale I remember he said, "You know, it's like Greek frieze. You should go to the museum." So, of course, I went to the museum and I studied all the vases. He wanted it to look flat. When the Muses come in and drink, it's no perspective. Mr. B. said, "Oh, good, what did you do?" I said, "I went to the museum." "Good."

John Taras taught *Concerto Barocco* to me when I did the lead, the second girl. Mr. B. took the last couple of rehearsals. It was a little different then. They changed the last movement. There was a *grand jeté* entrance where you went around in a circle with the girl. Now they repeat that so that it is one section again. The ballet has a very jazzy feeling. He used to say, "This step is like the Charleston." It's in the finale, an *entrechat* where you *dégagé* to the side. It has the flavor of the Charleston. The ballet has a lot of syncopation, and he actually worked on it the most. The timing had to be exactly so. One girl steps over and moves her leg and dances, then the second girl dances, and he cared a lot about crispness in that. He wanted articulation, musicality.

In *The Nutcracker,* I did "Snowflakes," "Spanish," "Chinese," "Dolls" at City Center, and then "Marzipan" at State Theater in 1964. And then Dewdrop and the Sugar Plum Fairy. With Sugar Plum, Mr. B. said, "Don't get sweet." I think I tried to be sweet with the children. He said, "No, no. Don't get soft. Do the steps in the variation, use more attack, don't be motherly." And in Dewdrop, just basically dance, fly, move. That was such fun to do. I was doing Sugar Plum with Tony Blum, and there's a shoulder-sit. At one performance I didn't get up there. I landed on his chest. And then another time I didn't get up there. So we were to dance it again, and I was scared to death that night. So Balanchine came into the room, and he said, "You know, we're going to change it and don't tell anybody. We'll put a fish in. You'll ride it like the fish-dive in 'Bluebird.' And nobody will know that it's going to be different. So they'll all be aghast that you're going to run and jump at the shoulder, with your hips on his shoulder, rather than your butt." That was funny. So with Tony I did this other lift for a year or two. When I had a different partner, I switched back to sitting up.

I did Third Movement *Symphony in C.* At one point, I did *Tarantella* first, and the next ballet was *Symphony in C* without an intermission. Sometimes if we were very tired they would cut the repeat of Third Movement. So you would only do the circle once. So I went up to Mr. B. and I said, "Oh, can't we cut the repeat? I have *Tarantella,* no intermission, and Third Movement Bizet. I have to change my headpiece and my shoes will be all worn out. I won't have time to change the shoes." He said, "Don't worry. It'll be okay. Take it easy. Nobody watches the girl." I thought, "Oh, you rat! So I can just stay in the wings, all right?" I should have said, "I won't bother coming out." He wanted that repeat, obviously. It wasn't that nobody watched the girl. It was just a way of looking at it: no matter how high I jumped, it wouldn't look as high as the boy, who was going to soar over me.

I did the Blackamoors' Dance in *Night Shadow (La Sonnambula),* and Mr. B. was very much into that little jazzy step in the dance when the dancers come forward. Every time we'd do it, he used to get up and do the little jazzy step.

My first *Stars and Stripes* was with Eddie Villella, and again Balanchine had to leave town. He said, "Well, dear, just smile. Lots of rouge and smiles." That was his advice. It was the same weekend I also had my first *Tarantella.* He just said, "Put on the rouge and lots of flowers in your hair, dear." And then he said, "And when you're not facing the audience you know you have to dance with your back"—I liked that line. He meant that you have to be aware that when you're not facing front you're still modeling and dancing. You can't just take a vacation when you turn around. *Tarantella* was fun for me because I was the original understudy to Patty. When he was choreographing it, I was there the whole time, learning the steps. Other times, you could watch him choreograph, but you couldn't get up and learn. At one point in *Tarantella* there was too much music. He had to cut a little of the music because the dance was a killer.

I can't remember my dance with Eddie and Susan Borree in *The Figure in the Carpet* (1960). I was a Princess of Lorraine. I remember a wonderful wave of the hand and arm that we never got right. Balanchine could do it but we couldn't. "Like the French," he would say, and he would move his hand in a certain way. We would look and we would try. It was a bow with the plume of the hat. But we couldn't do it. I remember our dance had lots of hopping on pointe, and arabesques leading past Villella. Susie would hop, and then I would come and hop and Eddie would be holding the two of us by our hands. I remember the finale: it was step and fly. It was hard to count. There were some charming little divertissements in *Figure.* The one that he did for Diana Adams, the Scottish dance, was lovely.

The music in *Don Quixote* (1965) was hard to hear for a week of repertory performances, over and over again. The dancing in it was beautiful, including the dance for John Prinz and me. The man leaves the girl. She has a handkerchief, like the Greek handkerchiefs in their folk dancing. I always had a feeling that I was holding something, a little scarf or something. I don't think Mr. B. ever said so, but that's what I felt like. You're making designs with the handkerchief.

Even when there is a calmness in Balanchine's ballets, there is an energy within that calmness. Calmness doesn't mean lack of energy or life. He was after something interesting to look at. When he taught a class, he would know what he wanted, but on the other hand he would look at you and see what you had and take from you. And when he was choreographing, he would do the same thing. He could pick up your unique quality or bring it out and use it. If you moved in a certain way, he would use that in his choreography instead of making you move a way that he had preconceived. So often, when he thought of a ballet, he would think of somebody for that part because of the way that person moved. And if that one dancer couldn't perform the resulting ballet one night, then that ballet wouldn't go. I remember that for a long time with *Don Quixote* he felt that if Suzanne Farrell couldn't dance the lead, well then, "It won't go. We won't do it." He only wanted to see her do it, so it was more than a matter of steps.

Mr. B.'s whole approach to dance was about life and individuality. His whole technique could be adjusted to the individual. The approach would be the same, but the result might be achieved in a slightly different way, depending on the dancer he was working with. If you had more suppleness or if you had more flexibility, you could do it one way; if you were stiffer you had to adjust and somehow make the end result. Take the presentation of the foot, for example. You would slightly adjust how you did it depending on who you were. Mr. B. liked individuals, and his dancers were not the same. In past years, no one was the same. There was tall Diana Adams, and there was Melissa Hayden, and there was Violette Verdy, and there was Pat Wilde. They were all different shapes and sizes and they all moved differently and had their own strengths. Something that would look fine on one person would not look so good on another, and so when he made a ballet he would adjust it for a certain look. He would have you do something else.

Let's say you are really turned out, then you're going to sacrifice slightly on the standing foot to achieve a better look with the working leg because the working leg is the leg that the audience is going to see. It's moving. How the moving leg moves is more important than the leg that you are standing on. I'm dealing with such questions in the book that I am now writing, and a writer has to be careful because these questions can be misconceived by the reader and then taught in a distorted way.

My father was going to write a book on Balanchine. Much earlier, Balanchine had come up to me and said, "You know, your father's a writer. I've just looked at his William Blake book, and he's a very scholarly man. . . . And the Sinclair Lewis book . . ." I don't think he read the books, but he probably read more than I've read. My father didn't start the book until I had left the company. (I asked him not to. He had to wait for me to get out. I said, "There are too many father images around here. If you start coming in here, and he's there already . . .") My father certainly liked Balanchine a lot, admired him, and they got along fine. I think Balanchine liked and admired my father. It was a mutual kind of respect. When my father died, the book was only in his head and on some tapes. Balanchine said, "Well, probably shouldn't have been. This book probably should not have been."

Today the Russian companies are beginning to confront Balanchine by dancing his ballets. If they bring more of his ballets into their repertory, if they bring in more teachers, if they don't resist the style, and if they like it—they may have a chance of catching up. There has to be someone in authority there who wants to see it happen. If the administration doesn't want it to happen, it won't. There may be more continuous exchange between us in the future. That would certainly help to widen both of us. We could perhaps work a little more on our chests and arms. And they could certainly clean up their footwork, their articulation and musicality. They don't know phrasing, counting, the timing within a step. They've never seen anything. They only know what they know. But they have to want it. That's what Balanchine always said. "I can tell, but you have to do. I can suggest."

If they had some more Balanchine in their repertories, that might inspire a young choreographer of their own. I believe the Russians were thinking of having a teacher come here and teach some variations classes. And perhaps one of us could go to Russia and teach something there. I don't know if they're interested.

Balanchine moved the teaching of ballet forward. He took what he had, and he made more of it, and he reshaped and redefined basic things. He made it what it was once, and he cleaned it up. Musically, he made every step have a reason, even at the barre. He made a timing to do it. It wasn't just one more *tendu*. Each *tendu* mattered—how you got the foot out, how it came in. He redefined even the timing within that step. Balanchine always said that he never changed anything. He said he just looked through a keyhole when he was a child and he saw ballerinas on the floor. He saw them do *tendu,* and he said, "That's what I'm teaching, what I saw." But I think that he transformed what he saw through that keyhole. Maybe he saw somebody do an incredible *tendu.* We'll never know.

KENT

STOWELL

Trained with Willam Christensen at the University of Utah; became

principal dancer with Lew Christensen's San Francisco Ballet. Joined

New York City Ballet in 1962, where he became a soloist and choreo-

graphed ballets for the School of American Ballet Workshop. Was

leading dancer and choreographer for Munich Opera Ballet (1970–

73). Appointed ballet master and choreographer for the Frankfurt

Ballet (1973) and became co-artistic director with Francia Russell

(1975). Artistic director of Pacific Northwest Ballet since 1977, he

has choreographed many ballets for its repertory.

I Remember Balanchine

BOTH FRANCIA RUSSELL AND I THINK OF BALANCHINE OFTEN AS WE DIRECT PACIFIC Northwest Ballet. It's usually at our worst moments. We think, "Look what Balanchine suffered through, how much he put up with and how hard it was for him." Other times I think not necessarily "What would Balanchine do?" but about matters of substance. Ninety percent of all of the people who talk about what Balanchine said or didn't say about technique and how to do things his way miss the point, I think. Dance is a personal point of view. He had his, but that doesn't necessarily mean that everybody has to have the same view. It isn't a question of absolute fifth position. He gave us enough substance to have our own individual points of view. Each one of us brings to our profession and our life our own characteristics; they shouldn't be subtitled "Balanchine Said." When he was here, he had absolute authority, it was a one-man show to a large extent, but he would not question that after he was gone it had to be another man's show. And the same everywhere else. That's probably why he never consented to do a book on technique that would freeze things. Since his teaching and his ideas often changed, I think he felt, "Why freeze it?"

The never ending refrain "Balanchine said" is usually invoked by persons who don't have anything else to say. Part of the reason is that they never exposed themselves to the risky business of standing on their own. The way that I view my career is similar to the way he coped with his. He came out of Russia and was forced to do every kind of dance and ballet. After Diaghilev, he went to Denmark and Monte Carlo and London to earn a living and choreograph an opera or a ballet here and there. He learned his trade by having to do. He did that on Broadway. My career and my relationship with Francia is pretty much the same. We lived in Europe, and I choreographed operas and a few ballets here and there. Fortunately then Balanchine's contribution to our profession in America made it possible for us to come back and get in Seattle what he didn't get when he and Lincoln Kirstein started out: an extended season and a community of support. What he set up made possible a pattern that we could then duplicate elsewhere. There's talk about a dearth of ballet choreographers, but because of Balanchine there are a lot more ballet companies than there were thirty years ago bringing a lot of dance to America.

As Balanchine ballets are revived, people worry that the letter is going to get across but the spirit is going to be gone. But we must remember that every generation of dancers in the New York City Ballet's history feels that its version was the only version. They see a performance by another ballet company, staged by a person from a different generation, and they yell, "Look, it's all wrong, they made so many mistakes, it was never that way!" Everyone ought to have enough wisdom to recognize that part of the legacy of Balanchine's ballets is that they were ever changing. He made those changes for a good reason: when a dancer, for example, couldn't do a step, he found one that she could do. It's interesting to see these different versions because they all represent different times in the life of a Balanchine ballet. The integrity of particular stagings depends on the people who do them. The version that Francia Russell knows—and she learned a lot of the ballets because she needed to—is the version that was danced when she was in the company. What she knows for that time doesn't mean somebody else is wrong. Nobody has a stranglehold on the truth of a Balanchine ballet. But having a firsthand knowledge of his ballets because we both danced them makes us doubly responsible. We feel that same obligation for any choreographer. I remember when we first arrived in Seattle they'd had Lew Christensen's *Nutcracker*. Some said, "Go ahead and change it. It's all right, nobody cares." I said, "But it's *his* ballet. We have an obligation to protect the integrity of his work. Would you rewrite *Madame Butterfly* just because somebody thought it would be interesting to change a few passages?"

I danced for Balanchine from 1962 to 1969. We were trying to get into Lincoln Center at the time—there was an enormous amount of pressure to get us in there and an enormous amount of opposition to us. And once the company was there, there was an enormous amount of pressure to make sure that it lived up to expectations. There was a lot of anxiety about working in a theater that was so much more costly that first season. At the New York State Theater, lots of people who had never been to the New York City Ballet were coming to see us because we were dancing in a new theater. Out in the audience one night after the Stravinsky ballet *Movements for Piano and Orchestra* (1963) I heard a man say, "This looks like a hippie ballet company to me." Because it was in leotards and tights! The general public which didn't know us had different expectations. To many people the old City Center was a K-Mart version of ballet: good but not expensive, leotards and tights. At the State Theater Balanchine prepared for a bigger scale by doing *Midsummer Night's Dream* (1962) and, once he got in there, *Don Quixote* (1965), *Harlequinade* (1965), and the revival of *Ballet Imperial* (1964).

I feel that at that time Balanchine was preoccupied with moving to the State Theater and with his relationship with Suzanne Farrell. He forgot himself as an artist somewhat. I personally don't think that there were any great new works during those years. It wasn't his heyday as a choreographer. *Don Q* was a big theater piece but not a Balanchine masterpiece. Nor was *Clarinade* (1964). Reviving things like *Slaughter on Tenth Avenue* (1968) was fun but not much more. In a way he sacrificed himself to the needs of the company and his devotion to Suzanne. As an artist he took a back seat for a while. But I don't think it's necessary for an artist to be productive all the time. Not only was Balanchine an artist; he represented an enormous institution with lots of obligations. If they continued with business as usual and didn't produce some fairly large-scale ballets, they might not attract the audience they needed. The fallout from that was Clive Barnes in the New York *Times* saying maybe it was time for a change at New York City Ballet. Balanchine struck back with the full force of the 1972 Stravinsky Festival, which certainly ended that. Maybe artists need a period of change of focus and ferment. I think in any case Balanchine was very aware of the need of the institution over and above his need to choreograph ballets.

My feeling also is that he didn't do any great pieces for Suzanne. In *Jewels* (1967) it was his relation to Stravinsky that made the difference in *Rubies,* the big hit of the ballet, and not *Diamonds. Movements for Piano and Orchestra* he had choreographed for Diana Adams. Suzanne inherited a lot of parts, but the ones he did for her were a little bit off. Sometimes the muse so captivates that we can't see that we're in thrall. The odd part about having a muse is not knowing whether you have it or it has you.

In the ballet profession, the data that are really important you can't talk about; they're there on the stage. When they ask me how I choreograph a ballet, I say, "Painfully." There is nothing else to say. How do you describe it? I'm not a writer, that's a different art. So I sort of make up things. The more specific you are, the more limited you are in your options. The staff calls me D.V.—"Deliberately Vague." That's the best way to preserve all the options because, as soon as you say what it is, they've translated that into their own visual image, and it doesn't come out anywhere near what they expect. I think that Balanchine understood that and utilized all of those funny phrases like, "I am a cobbler, a craftsman," so that he didn't have to corner himself. Whether he was being humorous or simple or clever is beside the point. It was his way of functioning.

PATRICIA
NEARY

Born in Miami in 1942, trained with Georges Milenoff and at the School of American Ballet, Patricia Neary joined the National Ballet of Canada when she was fourteen and the New York City Ballet in 1960. She danced with them for eight years. Balanchine created five roles for her and she danced a wide repertory of his work. Ballet mistress, German Opera Ballet in Berlin (1971–73), she was director of the Geneva Ballet (1973–78) and director of the Zurich Ballet from 1978–85. From 1986 to 1988, she directed the ballet at La Scala in Milan. She is now staging ballets for the George Balanchine Trust and recently mounted Apollo *and* Tchaikovsky Pas de Deux *for the Kirov Ballet in St. Petersburg, Russia.*

BALANCHINE WAS MY GUIDING LIGHT. FROM THE TIME I FIRST JOINED THE COMPANY HE
saw that I would make a teacher. He felt that at eighteen I should already
begin to teach company class. I was nervous about that: I would say, "I can't
do it." After a week I actually refused, because in the company class I had all
these famous ballerinas—Diana Adams, Melissa Hayden, Jillana, Maria
Tallchief, Violette Verdy. I just couldn't cope with that; I kept saying to
Balanchine, "I don't want to teach. I want to dance." But still I was one of
the first teachers he sent out on the Ford Foundation grant to find new
dancers and to look at schools. I often taught the company when he would
leave.

Balanchine was suspicious during our first trip to Russia in 1962. He
thought everyone was being bugged. I'm sure they were. He spent half the
time whispering. When we arrived at the airport, we found all these photog-
raphers and TV people assembled. The lights and cameras went on, and the
first thing Balanchine did was take out his American passport. They said,
"Welcome to your homeland," and he replied, "I'm American."

He was upset throughout the rest of the tour. He couldn't sleep at night;
he told me the phone would ring at four o'clock in the morning, and the
radio would go on suddenly. He got thinner and thinner; he was not well.
Actually he went home, back to New York, in the middle of the trip, and his
nerves had a lot to do with it.

Some of us were a little rankled during the Farrell period; not everyone
survived that time. I think Mimi Paul and I were affected most, of the
younger group. Mimi, Gloria Govrin, Suki Schorer, and I were in heavy
competition. Looking back on it now, I don't think I was usually seeing
things through the right eyes. I was too involved with my own Pat Neary
and wanting to be this and that. I thought Balanchine was just overboard
about Farrell, and none of us were actually able to completely understand
why. Later I could see it. When I really didn't want to dance anymore and
had completely become a director, I watched films of Farrell and I could see
so much. Our difficulty originally was that he had a lot of other dancers in
the company. He used to say to me, "I have a right to love." The day I left, I
said, "There are other dancers, and you've got them too."

I made the mistake once in my career of asking Balanchine what he
thought. I'd hardly even spoken to the man except casually backstage, and a
lot of people had warned me that he was going through a very difficult time.
I was afraid of him, but being as stubborn as I am, with my Irish-German
blood, I pushed him up against the wall, which he hated. "Why am I not
doing this role?" I asked. "Why am I not doing that?" "Well, actually," he
said, "because I don't like you in tutus." "Well then, why am I in all these
tutu ballets?" "But I don't like you in them," he said. "Oh, maybe in *Firebird,*

because you have enough strength to go through brick walls." It got worse. As we got deeper into the conversation, I wished I had never started it. We talked about it afterward sometimes. "Remember that day?" I'd ask. "Oh, that wasn't a good day, no. And I said things to you, but I was right." He would never say he was wrong. It was a very good lesson for me. I survived that and I can still healthily say it actually made me stronger. I am never one to give up. There were certain things that came out of it that were interesting to me: how he saw me onstage, certain qualities he adored and others that he didn't.

Since I've been directing ballet companies I understand Balanchine a lot better. There are days when you just should not try to push yourself onto a person. Usually if a dancer comes toward me and goes, "Pat, I'd like to talk to you now," that means, "I'm unhappy about something. Why can't I do this ballet?" I sometimes say, "I'm sorry, I don't have time right now," or if I'm in the mood, I'll say, "Yes, let's talk." I've got to be ready to either give them some honest views or be a little sympathetic.

I started teaching Balanchine's ballets in 1968, when I staged *Agon* for the Stuttgart Ballet. Then he sent me to be guest ballerina in Geneva, one of his satellite companies at the time. Alfonso Catá was the director. At a particular time there Balanchine said to me, "Why don't you go to Berlin and stage *Four Temperaments?*" As a result I was appointed assistant director and dancer at Berlin in 1969. In 1973 I became director at Geneva, then went on to Zurich in '78.

During the preparations for the New York City Ballet's Tchaikovsky Festival, a videotape of Nureyev's *Manfred* was submitted to Balanchine. Nureyev didn't actually like this particular video because he had an 8mm film that he thought was better. Balanchine did not like the video, however, so he refused to do the ballet. A little while later I said to him, "Guess what, I might as well tell you because you're going to hear about it. We're coming to the States with *Manfred* and Nureyev." And he said, "No. You can't do that. This is *my* company." "Well, I decided to do it," I told him. "We cannot tour the States in any other way. It's good publicity for us." "Oh, plastic stuff." He dismissed it.

Some time later he arrived in Zurich to see the company and work with the dancers. And what do you think we were performing? Nureyev's *Manfred*. I asked him, "Do you know what we're dancing tomorrow night?" "Oh," he said, "I'm not going to come to the performance." "Oh, yes, you are," I insisted. "They are dancers you love and you're coming to see them." He did. Actually, he was not overly critical about it, which surprised me. I would say he was curious and interested, but he would never admit, after deciding not to do it, that maybe it wasn't so bad.

I always thought that Balanchine—in his later years—had a secret dream of returning to Monte Carlo, of spending six months a year in New York and six in Europe. He started in Europe, and he loved Switzerland, Germany, Austria, all of Europe. He would talk about the food and he'd bring back all these mushrooms and condiments he adored. He had a tremendous love of European life, but he couldn't really relieve himself of the New York City Ballet. Occasionally, when they were not dancing, he could take a week or two of vacation, or actually work a little bit, too.

I was sitting in Zurich one day in late 1982, rehearsing the company. I had a sudden intuition that I had to go immediately for a long weekend to New York to see Balanchine. I arrived just before he entered the hospital for the last time. The meal I had with him was the last supper he actually took at home. I had a premonition that I wouldn't see him again.

I knew the one thing he didn't want to be was a vegetable. When Karinska was dying he would tell me, "Oh, it's just so awful. I went to visit her and she doesn't know anyone, and she can't talk. It's awful to see people that way."

We always feel that Balanchine is alive, because his spirit, after all, is in the ballets. He still lives in me very strongly, because I believe that every time I'm teaching one of his dances I'm conveying something of him. I've made people think I'm very funny when I teach his ballets, because often I look up and say, "Is that okay, Mr. Balanchine?" "Mr. B.?" I believe that my greatest gift, besides being able to direct, is that I know about thirty-eight of his ballets. I have taught them to dancers all over the world. It's something that transforms me and I love doing it; it's too full of joy to talk about.

PAUL

MEJIA

Born in Peru and raised in New York City, Mejia trained at the
School of American Ballet as a scholarship student. Joined New York
City Ballet at age seventeen and danced many repertory roles. Joined
Maurice Béjart's Ballet of the 20th Century. Choreographed works
for the Béjart Ballet and the Ballet de Guatemala. In the United
States he assisted Melissa Hayden at Skidmore College. Mejia joined
Chicago City Ballet as assistant artistic director (1981) and was
named co-artistic director, with Maria Tallchief (1983). Became ar-
tistic director of the Fort Worth Ballet (1987) and has choreographed
many ballets, including Romeo and Juliet, Hamlet, Cinderella, Brahms Waltzes, Eight by Adler, Jeux, Joie de Vivre,
Serenade in A, and Sonata.

467

I Remember Balanchine

I CAME TO THE UNITED STATES WHEN I WAS TEN OR ELEVEN, AND I ENDED UP AT THE School of American Ballet because my mother, Romana Kruzinovska, an American from Detroit, had studied there as a child.

When I was a child I was in the New York City Ballet's *Nutcracker*, and little by little I learned who Balanchine was; I did not know what he was until much later. The first year I was in *Nutcracker* I was Fritz and the Prince as well for a couple of performances. And then the next two years I did the Prince. At the time the ballet was rehearsed by Janet Reed; she was wonderful. She made everything so clear and so much fun at the same time. And Mr. Balanchine would come. He was there at the last rehearsals, and we all obviously knew that he was the boss. I always listened. I was an attentive, serious person, though I was having fun. It was a disciplined group of kids, but we had a lot of fun running around the halls of City Center. There were no girls playing boys' parts; we were all a bunch of roughnecks.

It wasn't until I was about fourteen that Balanchine started to take an interest in me. He sent me to Kyriena Siloti, the daughter of the pianist Alexander Siloti, to study piano. I had studied piano when I was in Peru, and I guess he saw something in me. I was at least coordinated, and I suppose he thought I should learn a little bit about music. Mr. Balanchine knew my mother from the past, and he went to her. He never dealt with me. He dealt through Ouroussow with my mother and made sure that I was studying music and that I was surrounded by the right people. He was concerned by the fact that I didn't have a father. He wanted to know, "Who does he talk to?" I did have a grandfather at the time, but Balanchine was interested to know what I was doing. No doubt I was not the only student he was interested in this way. Balanchine was not nosy, he was protective. He felt that I had some talent, and he wanted to see it go in the right direction.

When I was fourteen or fifteen my mother was teaching ballet in New Jersey, where she wanted me to put on a little program. I said sure, why not? I asked at the School if I could use some of the students and if I could have a little workshop. Of course they asked Mr. Balanchine, and he said, "Naturally, have studio and take any dancers you want, and if you want a pianist we will give you a pianist. . . ." I already had my pianist, so I said, "No, thanks." He also let me borrow any costumes that I wanted but he wasn't curious as to what we were doing. So I had a workshop. We had twenty-four kids dancing, and I choreographed three ballets just like that. Eventually he came to a rehearsal with Una Kai. This was my first real contact with Mr. Balanchine. I did a ballet to Schumann's *Symphonic Études* that was pure dance. And a very close friend of the family, George Wehner, a composer, wanted me to use his music. He was like an uncle to us, and naturally I used his music. One of his compositions had to do with a cockfight. It was strange music and probably terrible, but it was new.

Mr. Balanchine came to watch the rehearsal: the *Symphonic Études* was fine. It was a big workshop, but I never thought of doing anything small. But Mr. Balanchine liked that. He said, "That's great to be able to do something like that." Kyriena Siloti was there at that rehearsal. I could see Balanchine with a sort of grin on his face. He was probably laughing his head off at the ridiculous stuff that was going on, but at the same time I think he appreciated the fact that a young kid would take on something so elaborate. After the rehearsal, I was talking to my music teacher, Siloti, and Balanchine came up to us. He said to Kyriena, "You know, you have to teach him what good music is, not teach him how to play. Teach him what good music is." He probably meant the George Wehner compositions. Then he said to me, "You know, you have to learn, you must never work with family or friends. You see, it is not a good idea." I didn't know what he meant at the time, but I always remember what people say to me. Especially since it was then that I started to realize who he was. I also knew that he had sent me to study piano and that he was very aware of who was befriending me and who wasn't. This annoyed me greatly because, like any young kid, I thought I knew what I was doing, but at the same time I felt enormous respect for him. I realized years later what he meant about working with friends and family—how you can not only lose and alienate friends that way but you can accept garbage. But the workshop was a wonderful experience.

That led the following year to Balanchine starting the choreography workshops at the School. He asked me to be part of it. Also, there he began a special C class that Doubrovska taught. Suzanne Farrell, Mimi Paul, Kay Mazzo, and a number of girls that he wanted her to teach were in the special class; he wanted me to take it as well. I was the only boy in that class. I felt a little bit strange, naturally, but Ouroussow always came to the rescue. She said, "I don't know why, but he wants you to take this class. He wants you to know the woman's technique." This had never occurred to me. At that time, choreography was not that serious to me. I enjoyed doing it. So I was stuck in that class, which I didn't mind at all, being the only boy. There must have been at least twelve beautiful dancers. Doubrovska was such a remarkable, feminine, beautiful person to look at; how she taught and how she demonstrated—in the end was what it was all about. That was important to Balanchine—how people showed things, the perfume in the air, the grandness and the scarf, the femininity, the strength. Doubrovska was a powerful lady, with legs that went up, even in those days.

Balanchine never talked to me. Then at a choreography seminar for visiting teachers he put me on the spot for the first time in my life. One day he brought in a little piece of music, some little waltz. He picked five people—Jacques d'Amboise, Kent Stowell, Virginia Williams, Barbara Weisberger, and someone else. Then all of a sudden he pointed to me. In front of all those people, I almost died. He said, "You six go, you take the same piece of music, take two dancers apiece, drop into a little studio and put something together. When you're ready, come in and show us what you did and then we'll decide what to do." I didn't know what on earth to do. I remember sitting there watching Jacques and Kent make dances. They were going to town, they were all finished. Mr. B. said, "Are you ready?" and I hadn't even started. I didn't know what to do. Then, all of a sudden, I just threw something together. The best part of my dance was the ending: three steps—walk, walk, walk. It was absolutely pure accident, out of pure necessity and fear. I had to finish this thing in three counts, and I said "Walk, walk, walk." But at least I had an ending, and it was probably the only good thing in the dance. But I didn't know these things at the time. I could put things together musically. Balanchine said to me, "You dance it." He didn't want to see Bobby Blankshine. Perhaps he thought I would make the choreography clearer. Because I was about fifteen years old and all the others were older, they decided to use my piece. So I had to stand up there with this girl who was about a foot taller than I was and perform the dance. Balanchine said, "Do you like it? Are you happy with it? Is that enough?" Of course I said, "No, well, I don't know." I was brought up never to speak out of turn. I went to a tough English school in Peru, and you never spoke out of turn to an older person. At the same time, I could tell that he was smiling inside, that he was really proud, that he liked it.

But what was great was that Balanchine proceeded to take what I had done and destroy it and put it back together in front of my eyes. I will never forget it. He took the same steps and used them properly with the music and made it a lot more interesting. First, when I said, "It's not enough," he said, "Then fix it." Of course I just stood there. Five minutes went by, and he loved that. He was making it hard on me. Then he said, "Well, you know, we do this, and we do a little here, and now why don't the two of you do it separately? She should go this way. You should go that way. She should do it on this count. You should do it on that count." If the two of us were dancing at the same time opposite each other, he said, "Well, you know what? Why doesn't she do it now and you follow doing the same and change this?" The whole thing started to unfold. Partly because it was in front of everybody, all of a sudden I saw that there is so much to making dances—endless possibilities of listening to one little bar of music, one little phrase, endless possibilities with two dancers, either saturated or as simple as you want.

The only thing he left intact from my original dance was the end—walk, walk, walk—because it was a novelty, a surprise, nobody expected it. He kept it. That also taught me a lesson, that you can't always think in dance steps and that many times you get the best results working with your dancers out of necessity, by accident. Also, having to do it on the spot is a big lesson because you don't choreograph at home. You do it in the studio. You can have ideas at home, but they never come out in the studio. You take from your dancers, and hopefully they give you something, and you use some of it with the music. This was the most that Balanchine and I had talked up to that time; it always stayed with me. From then on I was interested in choreography or in working toward making dances.

I was a good pianist, and I enjoyed it. I could have become a pianist and not a dancer, but it was a question of how many hours do you want to practice and how many do you want to dance? I took music seriously, but I also had school, so the piano suffered, and I wanted to dance. So you have to have your focus. But I remember so many of the things Balanchine said during the seminars for teachers about music. He took beautiful chords—for instance, a major chord, diminished, augmented, or triads—and he would take three girls and visualize the chords for us. Here is a major chord. Now, how are you going to go from a major to a minor, let's say? Can you do it visually? We know that the one note goes down half a step, but that doesn't mean the dancers are going to do that. How can you visualize it? He did it, and it made me think theoretically and musically.

As an apprentice in the company I was involved in dancing the ballets before I really knew them from the audience point of view, and I think that is a good thing. Today, students go to all the performances and get used to criticizing the works and the dancers; then they dance them when they are still students and they think they've done it already. I think it is wonderful to have an open innocence before you do these things. Then you really appreciate them more, you take more care. They can mean more. In my time we thought it was great to do the *Firebird* Monsters. I was doing *Firebird* Monsters on the same program that I was doing *Agon.* Balanchine walked by me one day and saw me in the lion costume and said, "Do you still do that?" I said, "Yes, sure, here I am." I never thought of getting out of things. I love being onstage under any circumstance. John Taras taught me *Agon,* in preparation for the Edinburgh Festival. Casting me in it had created unrest because I was a corps member; the person who was doing the role at the time was left behind so I could go. I had not been to Europe, and Balanchine thought it was wonderful for us to travel. Balanchine was really bent on exposing me to everything.

After John Taras rehearsed, Balanchine would come and make one or two comments. Unless you were really wrong, he would let you develop, which is wonderful. There were a couple of things that he would try to tell me about the role. In the pas de trois, that one *rond de jambe* step with the hand was very important to Balanchine. Somehow, it's got lost along the way. He showed it so well, and I couldn't do it. It was very hard, but I tried. Balanchine showed so beautifully. He had on shoes, but it's the musicality and the idea behind the steps that he would demonstrate. Some people say about *Agon,* "It's Stravinsky, it's steps, and that's all it is!" It's not that at all. People don't realize. The Stravinsky is full of wonderful wit and humor. If you can't hear that, how can you dance it? It's in the music. Listen to the music. It's all there. If it means nothing to you, how can you apply it? So if you don't hear it, then Balanchine would say, "Well, you know, it's like putting out a cigarette on the step." In other words, for this one step in *Agon,* if you hear it, why do you have to put out a cigarette? He had to use such images to make you understand. That particular piece of musicality right there came from somewhere else that led you to the spot. It starts somewhere, and it leads you there. The lead is the harmonic line, which causes rhythms to change, causes everything to change.

There are dancers who are just innately musical. Maybe they don't realize they are hearing the harmonic changes or that they are being led by them. You don't have to know music to be a musical dancer. Sometimes it's better not to know. I am musical, but knowing music helps me to do what I have to do now. Now I am not a dancer. When I was a dancer, I heard music normally. Later on, I realized what I was hearing, from learning about it. But some people are not musical at all, and how do you get an idea across to them? That's when Balanchine must have suffered a lot. He would change things eventually.

For each ballet Balanchine had a concept. When I am choreographing a ballet I know that the construction will move from point A to point B and then to point C. I can hardly wait go get to those points because I know what I'm going to do there. I know what I want, and sometimes it's a struggle getting to those points. If you lose your way, you either have to get a better concept or redo it, but you have to get to those structural points. You don't just start and follow the melody and see where it leads you, like throwing paint on a canvas. Balanchine made me understand this from his workshops.

It's nonsense when people say Balanchine didn't care about male dancers. I think I know what he means when he said that "ballet is woman." It doesn't mean that man doesn't have a part in ballet. If man didn't have an important role, then woman wouldn't be woman. I think one of the things he meant was that a woman's technique is really infinite. Men's technique is more limited. What do you see a man do usually? Jump through the air and spin. Every male dancer has his two spins and one jump, which is put into every ballet, except in Balanchine's ballets, where the dancer becomes like Apollo or the Prodigal Son or Oberon. Think of the variations in *The Four Temperaments, Jewels, Chaconne,* or *Mozartiana.* Where else can you dance like that? Nowhere else.

I made my first dances when I was fourteen, and choreographing was in the back of my mind, but I was just a dancer. I was twenty-one, a good dancer, and I did my job. I adored Balanchine, even though we never talked. I was arrogant and proud and had a big ego, like all young men who are secure in the world. And I was also very naive. I didn't steal Suzanne away from him. I had no idea Balanchine was even in love with Suzanne. I thought he was with Tanny. I didn't really know until obviously it was too late. By then my heart was committed, too, and I felt bad about it. My grandmother had warned me. I was furious with her because perhaps deep down I knew it was true. I said, "It can't possibly be true: this is the great George Balanchine and he's married to Tanny." Suzanne and I had become friends, she had come to our Christmas party, and Mr. Balanchine came too. It was a big family affair, and afterward my grandmother said to me, "Paul, you'd better be careful. He has his eyes on Suzanne." I was offended by her saying such a thing about him. Of course, what bothered me was the fact that she knew I was in love with Suzanne. I was a kid, Suzy and I had become good friends and very close. It just didn't occur to me that I was doing anything wrong. How would I know how he felt? I hardly knew the man. I never talked to him in the elevator when we ended up there together. It was just, "Hello." He never said any more than that. He never asked me, "How's your music?" We never talked, ever. How do you talk to Balanchine, anyway, unless you have something to say, and I had nothing to say. It would be silly for me to say, "Oh, I love doing your ballets."

Little by little, I wasn't dancing. I was no longer cast. I had been the boy doing the Third Movement in *Bizet,* not anybody else. I was the boy doing the pas de trois in *Agon,* no one else. All of a sudden those roles started to disappear. They were going to people who hadn't done them in ten years, not to somebody new. Of course, it hurt me. I became indignant. Even before Suzanne and I were married, the situation was bad. That's why we decided, "Well, why wait, it's already bad, we might as well get married." We waited until we knew that Balanchine would be out of town. We were patient about the whole thing, and then we realized it wasn't going to change.

After we were married in February 1969, I continued to collect my salary, but I wasn't dancing. Then Betty Cage called me one day and she said, "Mr.

Balanchine really doesn't want you around the theater." She said he had offered to pay me a year's salary, and then she said, "Please don't talk to the press about it." Then, sometime later, I got another call. Lincoln Kirstein said that Balanchine couldn't do such a thing. So I was taken back, but I just didn't dance. I sat there in the wings and got paid. It's not as though I had ever demanded roles. What parts would I demand? I had the parts, they had been taken away. I had been sitting around for a year, dancing only a few little things. The final straw was the big benefit night in May. The casting for Third Movement *Bizet* had my name up, and then my name was scratched out, and somebody else's name was put in. That's when I went to Suzanne and said, "Suzanne, I'm really sorry, but I can't do this anymore. I shouldn't stay." She made her own decision to leave on her own grounds. You could not talk to Balanchine, all you could do was send word through someone. I said, "Well, if I don't dance, then I might as well leave, and I will leave." Suzanne said basically the same thing, even though she was there, prepared to go on. The whole thing just blew up, and we were devastated by it.

Looking back now, when people ask me about it, I say, "My God, he had every right to do what he did." I understand his feelings completely, and I am not bitter at all at what he did. At the time I was young. He must have suffered greatly, doubly, because it was me, whom he adored. I know that he loved me, even in the later years when we talked a little bit again, even though he did not want me around. When Suzanne returned to the company, Balanchine wanted me to go to Chicago, but I wasn't ready to go to Chicago as yet.

I've never been bitter, but then I was also fortunate. I did all the dancing I wanted to do at City Ballet. Suzanne and I danced in Europe, but it wasn't the same anymore for me. We were with Béjart for almost five years. Living in Europe alone was extraordinary. Even Balanchine said that everybody should leave for a while and then come back. I learned a lot from Béjart. But after dancing with Balanchine, you miss the work. I had taken his class every day. I never missed. That's how Suzanne and I became so close: we stood together at the barre. We were there every day. When everybody else changed, we were always there. It became part of your life. You don't learn Balanchine, you live it. And so, after we left, one year went by, two years went by, and after a while you realize how much you miss. We worked alone. We did our Balanchine classes. We forced ourselves, and everybody thought we were crazy. But little by little everybody started to work with us. Béjart let me do a couple of ballets. He let me be responsible for part of the company on tour at one point, and so my appetite became whetted for what I'm doing now. I thank him for that. But it was time to come back. I missed the United States enormously. And I knew Suzanne was ready to return. It meant a lot to her to come back. Balanchine took her back, and I was very happy.

When Suzanne came back, we did meet with Mr. Balanchine, and I said to him, "You know, this is the only place I want to dance because you are the only person that I can learn from." And he said to me, "Oh, you know, you don't want to be here. This is too big a place. Go to Chicago. Maria is starting company. I send you there." And I said, "Well, thank you, I'll think about it." I ended up in Chicago two years later. Obviously, he was right. When Suzanne returned, he didn't want me around. I understood.

It didn't bother me that Balanchine did not take me back. I wanted him to know that I wanted to work with him, but if he didn't, that was fine. I did my own thing. For me, ballet dancing was finished. I'm not a frustrated dancer. I'm doing now what I really love and what I feel I've been trained to do and what he trained me to do.

As artistic director of the Fort Worth Ballet, I think of him all the time. I was so fortunate to take so many of his classes. He was so interested in Suzanne that he taught every day, and I was there too. The company had seventy-five to eighty dancers, and thirty people came to class every day. He always wondered where the other fifty were. And out of those thirty, there were maybe eight constant people. The rest sort of came in and out. But I think the most important part of Balanchine to remember is his teaching. If you don't remember his teachings, you can't do his ballets. A lot of people are doing his works, but they're no longer his ballets. His teaching really is our foundation. What he taught was not just steps. He taught everything, just like my old Russian music teacher. She taught me more than music, she taught me life. These were wonderful Russian people with enormous tradition and enormous richness of life. They brought it with them, and they had a lot to give. We are very spoiled in this country. We were born with everything. Not that you have to suffer to accomplish something, but at least you can listen to people who did suffer, who learned through life how to accomplish things. We must remember Balanchine's teachings. That's where I think a lot of people have failed. As Maria Tallchief says, "I don't know what he did in the end, but I do know what he did when I was there." Somebody else has to teach the next step.

I learned a lot from Maria Tallchief. I re-remembered, thanks to her. That which came before what he taught us is a very important step, because what he taught us doesn't always make sense if you don't remember what came before. I am extremely fortunate to have worked with Maria for seven years.

She is a tireless lady, and she teaches the same thing day in and day out. She beats it into you with infinite patience and will not accept anything else.

Between Maria Tallchief's time and our time with Balanchine, there were changes in Balanchine's teaching. For example, Maria's *épaulement* and intensity were intrinsic in her. Not all dancers can be like that. If you look at what's happened since, there's been a lot more freedom, not all of which works. Suzanne is very special. But Balanchine was there nurturing it, watching it, making sure it did not get out of hand. If he liked it, he let it roll because he really liked it. These people took his class every day. They got something, guidelines through the classes, so they could be free. Now we have everybody very free because they think that that's what he wanted. But where is the foundation? Who is teaching the classes? Here at the Fort Worth Ballet, I insist on teaching, and I've developed my way of doing things.

When Balanchine would choreograph, he knew the construction of the music, and he knew how to get from point A to point D. The in-between didn't matter—how he would get there. It was as though he were saying, "Let's just make something interesting." He was very good at making things interesting between point A and point B. That's why you can change the steps in his ballets and still have the same wonderful works. Sometimes the public will not allow you to change things: How dare you change your ballets? And the critics: How dare you? But from his point of view, It's my ballet! I can change it if I want! As a matter of fact, there is a step in *Apollo* that he changed for Suzanne. In Terpsichore's variation the original choreography called for *grands jetés*. Suzanne does *développés*. She couldn't jump at the time because of her knee. We decided that we liked it better than the *grands jetés*. She danced it, so our dancer in Fort Worth does that step as well. Some people might say, "Well, they changed the choreography. They are accommodating." But it's not true. Suzanne danced it, and Balanchine liked it. It's within the style. Frankly, in many instances, the change works better because dancers have changed.

Balanchine was constantly keeping his ballets alive with new dancers. Sometimes the changes were good, and sometimes they were not so good. There's a section of *Agon* that Suzanne noticed had been changed when she returned to the company from Europe. It's a group moment, where each girl had her own count to do a turn. She discussed it with Balanchine: "Why did you change this?" He said, "They can't do it." He finally got fed up because the dancers couldn't do it the way he wanted it. It irritated him to see it done wrong. So he gave up and simplified it. Suzanne staged the ballet here in Fort Worth in 1987 and restored the original choreography.

It is understandable that Balanchine would change things. Like him, I don't remember ballets at all. I rely on dancers who were in the works before. And we have videos now. But to learn from a video is terrible. I have to be here to keep the ballet alive. It's nice to have a video to learn the steps, but that's just the steps, it's not the ballet.

We decided in 1989 to mount the original version of Balanchine's *Apollo*, rather than the later, cut version. Why on earth did he change the ballet, he who was always so meticulous about not cutting a score? Balanchine could be perverse at times. If you said you liked something, he would make sure you wouldn't get what you wanted. And if you didn't like something, you would see it for the rest of your life.

Balanchine told Maria Tallchief, "I will be remembered for my teaching." My theory is that he meant that he hoped that the people whom he had taught would continue with his teaching and keep it going. But it is hard to teach. It's the hardest thing. It's much easier to choreograph. Teaching is hard because it's difficult to make people understand process. Mr. B. never beat it into us. It was our choice. He was there, and we chose to pick it up.

I still play the piano. My first purchase when I got into New York City Ballet was a piano. When I came to Fort Worth, Suzanne let me bring it down. When I do a ballet, I get the score just like Balanchine, and I sit and work with it, and I find the points I want to make.

IRINA

KOSMOVSKA

Born in Moscow, the daughter of an opera singer, and smuggled out of
Russia as a child; trained by Victor Gsovsky, Olga Preobrajenska,
and Lubov Egorova. Danced with de Basil's Ballets Russes de Monte
Carlo. Opened school and concert group at Palacio de la Música in
Barcelona. Coming to America in 1951, she began teaching in Los
Angeles and founded the Los Angeles Junior Ballet (1959), the oldest
ballet company in the city. At the invitation of Balanchine, she
taught twelve consecutive summers at the School of American Ballet in
New York. She teaches at the school of John Clifford's Ballet of Los
Angeles.

BALANCHINE TURNED ME INTO A TEACHER. I HAD HAD MANY RENOWNED TEACHERS in my background, but then I was invited to seminars Balanchine was conducting for teachers around the country at the School of American Ballet. Dancers usually begin teaching because they get on in years or have a severe injury. We never went to college and have no other resources. As for my own training, I only remember that my mother took me to ballet class and I forget what exercises we did or how it all started. But I do remember how Balanchine began his seminar. He began with first position, dancers from the New York City Ballet demonstrated, and he emphasized why we have to do what, what produces turnout, speed, elevation, and extension. He went over the whole thing A to Z, and he crystallized the technique. He always called himself a dentist cleaning teeth: he always wanted everything clean and never distorted. I started to apply this method to my students, beginners, intermediate, and advanced, and I got fantastic results.

Balanchine invited me to teach at the School, and I did that for twelve summers. It was a great honor, and I learned a lot from the wonderful teachers at the School of American Ballet. In addition to what was in the curriculum I also taught what I called dance forms—where I introduced the students to the classical tarantella, czardas, mazurka, gavotte, the waltz, which Balanchine loved so much, sort of neo-character. He felt that every good dancer should be able to waltz beautifully. He really demanded that. When he staged *Vienna Waltzes,* we all knew why. But he wasn't stuck on just the waltz. He wanted all-round dancers. He wanted them to have knowledge of character dancing as well as classical dancing.

Speaking of what Balanchine wanted for his dancers, I read parts of Gelsey Kirkland's book. It made me sick. It's terrible when you think how good he was to her; he made her. And he's not here to reply to her. His principal dancers like Melissa Hayden and Violette Verdy were not emaciated. They looked womanly onstage. Balanchine liked artists. Of course, for his corps de ballet he liked slender bodies. Who doesn't? They won't accept children at the Bolshoi or Kirov if there's any evidence of obesity in their families. They don't allow one ounce of fat! Why should Balanchine? Any great person will have many petty enemies, bugs crawling about.

In Saratoga we only taught straight classical ballet with Madame Doubrovska and Mr. Vladimiroff. Mr. Vladimiroff I knew from my days in the Ballets Russes. He came to London and gave classes. They were both great teachers. Madame Doubrovska was also beautiful. Her specialty was her great carriage; she carried herself like a queen, like royalty. It was marvelous to observe her. This is so important for the ballet students because they have to be dignified and feel ennobled. Otherwise, they are just a bunch of little kids trying awkwardly to dance. That was her legacy.

Vladimiroff was the all-around teacher, the good old-fashioned wholesome Russian technique which is also so vitally important. And of course he was a great partner.

When I was attending the Balanchine seminars in those summer months, I commuted to Saratoga every weekend so that I could attend Balanchine's company classes and watch his ballets. I knew him first as a teacher. I realize for most people it's the other way around: they know his ballets first. But for me the experience was overwhelming. I saw the cleanness of the company, his theory in real practice. And of course he updated everything; the Russians are in mothballs, still with the fairy tales, while he went ahead. His genius carried him on top of a crest and created a completely new thing. This was so vitally important for the American dancer. Here Balanchine caught the essence of what American dancers with their beautiful bodies could produce.

While Balanchine in his classes concentrated sometimes on one particular thing, in his ballets he was like a fountain, it just *went*. He was so generous as a person, as an artist it just flowed out of him.

I have had thirteen students who went on to Balanchine, the School of American Ballet and his company. With Darci Kistler, the first thing I knew she had been picked to do big things in the School of American Ballet workshop. In my training company, the Los Angeles Junior Ballet, she took the audience by storm when she was a child, really, especially when I saw her onstage. She danced a waltz by Offenbach with a country bumpkin; she was so musical. It was cute. She made of a little thing something worth observing.

One day at Saratoga before he gave class, Mr. Balanchine was sitting on a bench in the sunshine. I said to him, "Mr. Balanchine, your method of teaching works like a charm. I can apply it to beginners, to intermediate, and to advanced students." He got up from the bench and pointed a finger at me and said, "Take from me whatever you need, but use your own judgment." I always carry that with me.

Mr. B. remained like a rock in a turbulent ocean. He radiated such calmness that it was awesome. Although he was completely down to earth and had a wonderful sense of humor, one always felt a little afraid to approach him, thereby forgetting that he was very easy to talk to. I am eternally grateful to Mr. B. and only grieve that he is no longer among us. To me, his most outstanding characteristic as a human being and as an artist was always his giving, giving, giving.

RUDOLF
NUREYEV

Born near Irkutsk, U.S.S.R., March 17, 1938, Rudolf Nureyev auditioned at the Bolshoi and Kirov schools before choosing the latter. He studied with Alexander Pushkin and joined the Kirov Ballet as a soloist in 1958. He quickly rose to international stardom through the Kirov's foreign tours. On June 17, 1961, at Le Bourget in Paris, he requested political asylum, the first Russian ballet star to defy Soviet authorities publicly. Not since Nijinsky had the world taken such close interest in a male ballet dancer. Nureyev has appeared as guest star with ballet companies around the world. In 1962 he began a legendary partnership with Margot Fonteyn at the Royal Ballet. Noted as a choreographer for his versions of the classics and for original works, he made a film of his production of Don Quixote *with the Australian Ballet in 1973. He was director of the Paris Opéra Ballet from 1983 to 1989.*

I Remember Balanchine

THE NAME BALANCHINE (OR BALANCHIVADZE AS WE CALLED HIM IN RUSSIA) WAS always in the air in the ballet world of my youth. This was particularly true, I remember, when American Ballet Theatre came to Russia in 1960, with Maria Tallchief, Erik Bruhn, Royes Fernandez, and Lupe Serrano. We knew they were to dance Balanchine's *Theme and Variations.* That was to be my first experience of a Balanchine ballet, thirty-six years after he left us for the West. I wanted to see it badly. Perhaps I made that all too clear because the authorities sent me away to Germany to dance. They didn't want me to get influenced by Western styles or something like that. I heard all about *Theme and Variations* from my friends when I returned to Russia. They filmed it on a very primitive 8mm camera, without music, and showed it to me. I said, "Well, a most beautiful ballet," and I vowed that I would learn it. Sure enough, I did. Erik Bruhn taught me the role. I danced it with Ballet Theatre in November 1962.

The first ballet of Balanchine's I heard about was *Palais de Cristal (Symphony in C)* when the ballet of the Paris Opéra came to Moscow in the late 1950s. That again I did not see because I was in Leningrad, but again there were bits of film of the third movement that I saw. My third encounter with Balanchine, and this one I saw onstage, was the Alicia Alonso company. She brought *Apollo* to Russia. I was agog. I remember that after I saw a performance of *Apollo* I went to a rehearsal with Grigorovich, who at that time was choreographing *Legend of Love* on me. There I repeated all the movements of *Apollo.* I thought, "How strange, how weird, how wonderful!"

When I came to New York in 1962, I met with Balanchine. I went to see his company's performances, and he took me quite a few times to the Russian Tea Room. I can't think why. He wanted to see what kind of man I was, I think. He was extremely friendly. We spoke about Pushkin, Russian literature, and Tchaikovsky. Of the two operas by Tchaikovsky based on Pushkin, I love *Pique Dame,* he preferred *Eugen Onegin.* So we had small differences of opinion.

I recall talking to him after I had danced *Theme and Variations* with American Ballet Theatre in Chicago. I was dying of shyness—I had thought of writing him a letter. I guess Russian laziness took over, and I didn't, but I wanted to thank him, to say how great I thought his ballets were. And speaking of *Theme and Variations,* he said, "Oh, it's the worst ballet I've done. It was Alicia Alonso and Youskevitch—couldn't dance." It was like a cold shower to me.

I danced for the first time in America at the Brooklyn Academy of Music in New York, and I wanted to join Balanchine's company. But he somehow thought I was not right for his ballets. He said, "My ballets are dry," and thought I would not be interested. I said, "But I like them dry. *That* would attract me!" After a while he said, "No, no, go and dance your princes, get tired of them, and then when you're tired, you come back to me." I didn't tire of the princes, and the princes didn't tire of me, but I did come to him. He choreographed for me *Le Bourgeois Gentilhomme* in 1979 in New York.

That was wonderful, except there were complications. Jerome Robbins was supposed to fill in the empty places Balanchine left when he had heart trouble. Jerry said to me, "You are free to cancel the whole thing, you know. If anything happens to George, it will be on your conscience." And I said, "No, with me, things like this are fated. I'm here." I tried to make Balanchine sit and take it easy. But he wouldn't; he insisted on controlling everything. There was no way to force him to sit down or take short cuts. Sometimes I would say, "Mr. Balanchine, I have to stand and figure out the counts." But he would not rest. After rehearsal we went to have a costume fitting which lasted two or three hours. I asked him, "Are you going to go home and lie down or something, have lunch?" And he said, "No, no, no. Home? I don't go home. I just go and snatch a little bit of vodka and that's it." So he went back from those fittings for the costumes for *Bourgeois Gentilhomme,* back to the theater for the performance that evening. I saw him standing in the wings as always, not sitting, standing, watching the performance.

What I loved about him was the way he went about his work. When he did the pas de deux for *Bourgeois,* he said to the pianist, "Play the music." We listened. He then described what tempo it should be and then he asked, "What's the end? What's the climax?" The pianist played it. Balanchine said, "Ah, so what do we do about that? Let me think." Then he would figure out some pose or other combination for how the pas de deux should finish, but that was just tentative because next he asked, "Play now the climax *before* that." He was working backward, analytically, finding where the dance with the music had to climb. After hearing that earlier climax, from which the music would ascend, he said, "Now let's choreograph."

I learned the big Balanchine roles from the best authorities. John Taras taught me both *Prodigal Son* and *Apollo. Prodigal Son* I danced first at Covent Garden with the Royal Ballet. The Royal Ballet would not let me dance *Apollo* so I went to Vienna and had them produce it for me. John Taras came there to work with me on the role. Earlier, Erik Bruhn had taught me many things about dancing *Apollo.* He was supposed to dance *Apollo* once with the New York City Ballet, but somehow he refused. He had rehearsed the ballet with Balanchine. He told me what Balanchine said to him about the ballet, about the meaning of every movement. After I danced *Apollo* in Vienna, I did it at La Scala in Milan and in Amsterdam. I came to London with the Dutch National Ballet and danced it at Sadler's Wells and finally the Royal Ballet was forced to give me the role.

Theme and Variations I danced with Lupe Serrano. I thought she was wonderful. I don't think Gelsey Kirkland or anybody else came near to what Lupe did. *Agon,* too, I loved. I was amazed and thrilled when I first saw it. Edward Villella danced the first pas de trois. I learned it with great pleasure. I remember when I first danced it, Jerry Robbins was extremely complimentary about my dancing, how clear and succinct I was. *Orpheus* I learned from Rosemary Dunleavy and John Taras.

There was some kind of black cat that ran between me and Balanchine for many years. The rift, I think, began between us when an article about me appeared in a magazine. The writer who interviewed me put words into my mouth about why Balanchine didn't do ballets for men. I think Balanchine heard about that.

But we all know Balanchine's male roles are extraordinary. Maybe his great inspiration came from women, but he choreographed very well for men, and when better men came he choreographed better.

Ballet in Russia must try to catch up on Balanchine. They have missed really the major development of their own classicism in this century, and there is a big gap. Choreography is suffering in Russia because they don't know how to deal with music. Think of the Stravinsky they missed! Balanchine had such a wide vocabulary, married so well to contemporary music.

Balanchine had to come to America. I don't think he would have developed anywhere the way he developed in America. I believe Broadway contributed a great deal to his choreography, plus Fred Astaire. Instead of waiting, like Russian-Soviet choreography, for signals from the music, Balanchine imposed his own rhythms.

The Kirov Ballet's doing *Theme and Variations* and *Scotch Symphony* in 1989 is a beginning, but I wish they had started with *Serenade, The Four Temperaments,* and *Agon.*

For the Paris Opéra Ballet, I brought over Balanchine's *Stravinsky Violin Concerto* and *Symphony in Three Movements.* When I came to direct the ballet of the Paris Opéra, I insisted with the head of the school, Claude Bessy, that there should be some Balanchine. I made the children dance his ballet *Le Tombeau de Couperin.* This was not a popular idea then, but I wanted the young dancers at the school to come on to the Opéra fully informed, disciplined, and capable of counting rhythms and to be precise.

The last time I saw Balanchine was in the hospital during his last illness. Rouben Ter-Arutunian suggested that I should go. When I asked Rouben what should I bring, he said, "Caviar and Château d'Yquem, share it with him." Balanchine was very ill when I visited that day at Roosevelt Hospital, but he was so delighted by the taste of the caviar and the wine that his eyes lit up and he reached out to embrace me and Rouben. We talked Russian and

French. It was very sad; I remembered earlier, happier times. I wanted to see if he would give a number of his ballets to the Kirov Ballet in Leningrad but he was totally uninterested. He said, "When I die, everything should vanish. A new person should come and impose his own new things."

KARIN

VON AROLDINGEN

Karin von Aroldingen was born in Greiz, Germany, in 1941. She
was trained in Berlin and joined the Frankfurt Opera Ballet in 1959.
She joined New York City Ballet in 1962 and danced many roles in
the Balanchine repertory. He created twenty roles for her. She now
stages his ballets around the world.

My whole mission in life is to keep Balanchine's work alive. He's alive in his work. He said, "You are the one onstage. I can tell you certain things, but in the end it's you who has to do it. I can chew for you, but you have to swallow it." Sometimes I didn't even know what I was capable of. He brought it out of you. It was a natural thing, the way he gave you material to work with, and I'd say to myself, "Oh, I don't know if I can do it." He knew before that you could. If he saw any sign of struggle technically, he would immediately say, "Stop, we do something else." He was never imposing, and he was so fast in making ballets. I'm not a fast learner, but once I got the gist of it and understood it, it came like second nature to me.

I was eighteen when I did Kurt Weill's *Seven Deadly Sins* with Lotte Lenya in Frankfurt, where I was first dancer. She had appeared in Balanchine's original production of the ballet in 1933. The Frankfurt ballet production was choreographed by Tatjana Gsovsky. Lenya arrived to work with Tatjana, and everything went very smoothly. Lenya had done the revival of the Balanchine production the year before in New York, with Allegra Kent. Tatjana's production opened with the same idea Balanchine had used, the two Annas seen in one big black cape.

Balanchine told me that Tilly Losch had been wonderful in the original Les Ballets 1933 production. It's too bad that the projected Balanchine revival of *Seven Deadly Sins* never happened because of an orchestra strike. In rehearsal we got to the sixth sin. Bette Midler was fantastic. She came to the house on Mr. B.'s seventieth birthday, but the strike had just happened and she had other engagements, so Balanchine could not pursue the production.

In 1961 Lenya said to me, "Why don't you come to the States?" I said, "But how?" She said, "I will speak to Balanchine. Give me some pictures." So I gave some to her, and we had a correspondence. Balanchine was doing a lot of stagings of operas and ballets in Hamburg. Rolf Liebermann was director there, before he went to the Paris Opéra. About six months later Lenya arranged for me to meet Balanchine. He was to stage *Eugen Onegin,* and she spoke to Balanchine and told me, "He expects to meet you." I flew to Hamburg, and I had a private audition with him. I didn't speak English, and there was one Russian ballet mistress. She translated. I never thought he would take me into his company. I was just interested in studying in his school for a year and then returning to Germany. He saw how flexible I was—my legs, my feet. It was the first and last time in my life that I had an audition, and I know it was awful. I fell off pointe because I had new shoes. I was very frustrated. Later on in class, he said, "Oh, I have X-ray eyes. I can see through somebody." He could see my nervousness. "And I count that too." He did not ask me to do a barre, but I did a little warm-up, and I did *sissonnes* and turns. Balanchine said, "Give me your name and address." A couple of weeks later I got a letter from Betty Cage, asking me to join New York City Ballet. Balanchine said to Doubrovska, "Oh, I've got new girl, German girl. Wonderful. New blood." Doubrovska said, "Oh, German—bad feet, everything bad." It really took me years of work, and I worked hard on my own, too.

I had seen New York City Ballet on tour when I was still in school in Berlin. I was fifteen when I saw Tanaquil LeClercq dance *Bourrée Fantasque* and *Pied Piper.* She had a very special quality. I was able to use my memory of her for *La Valse,* even though I never saw her perform the role. I remember how thin she was. The next thing I heard was that she had polio. When I read this, I was very upset. Later I did roles created for Tanny, like Choleric in *The Four Temperaments.* She had an eccentric quality and, in a way, I had that too.

When I entered New York City Ballet, I thought, "How strange, how could this be possible?" When I got the letter to join, I was thrilled. I thought, "Yes, what have I got to lose?" I had never been to the School of American Ballet, but now I took classes there. At the time Balanchine didn't teach as much as he did in later years. I took classes from Diana Adams and André Eglevsky. Basically, I was struggling alone, with dance and English, but the first year I was given solo parts. I did Spanish in *The Nutcracker.* I was in the corps in the Waltz of the Flowers. I did *Con Amore* when Jillana left. And in *Don Quixote* I was the Duchess. I was not made a soloist until I had been in the corps for five years, but I danced all those parts. There were some dancers who were made soloist and never danced as much as I did. But I didn't care about the title, I was happy to dance the roles.

It took me years to unwind myself, to be good. Now I have more understanding of everything. Balanchine invented a new, extended technique, pure classical. Today, even our own people don't believe in it. Only a handful believe in his teaching. I worked very hard on my own, and much later I said to Balanchine, "You never cared about me." He said, "No, dear, I know you can do it on your own." I think he meant that some people are weaker and need more attention. But he left me alone. He knew I was observant and didn't need to be pushed.

I met my husband, Morton Gewirtz, in 1964. I didn't know that Balanchine cared about me, although he did make nasty remarks when I got married. I got married one day at 4 P.M., and at seven I was at the theater dancing. A year later I had a child, and Balanchine told me to give up my career but I danced *Monumentum/Movements* in a white leotard in my sixth month of pregnancy. I finished the season, and Balanchine didn't know I was pregnant. But I finally had to tell him because I could not dance in Saratoga that summer. But I took class up to my sixth month. I was back in class a week after the delivery. A month after I had the baby, I flew up to

Canada, where the company was touring. I didn't miss a season. Balanchine finally thanked me, although he didn't thank people very often or compliment his dancers. I had an interview while I was in Saratoga in which I said, "It sounds terribly harsh, but I am first a dancer, before I am a wife and mother. And I care a lot about my family." My husband knew when I married him that I was a dancer and he accepted it. It's not easy, but it can work. After I had my baby, the next season opened and I was onstage. That's when Balanchine realized that I was not "married" and simply Mrs. So-and-so. I was married to dance.

I was devoted and dedicated and had gotten stronger over the years. When my daughter Margot was two years old and I was a soloist, the company went to Monte Carlo. I had a family problem at home, and I went to Balanchine for advice. I had had a fight with Morty, my husband, and I didn't know how to handle it. I never had a father. He died when I was three years old, and my family was all women. We were three women at home— me, my mother, and my aunt. Balanchine was always a father to me, in addition to many other things. I thought that maybe he could help. A good friend of mine—Lucia Davidova—said, "You should talk to him." In Monte Carlo we got together, Eddie Bigelow, Kay Mazzo, and Balanchine and I— and I realized, "My goodness, of course he is human, you can talk to him." After all, I did not have a language for talking, and I didn't understand him at first with his accent and mine on top of it. But it was very simple. He told me how to "behave as my daughter," and everything worked out all right.

Balanchine was also like a mother to me. One day he said, "Let's go out to the Nabokovs'." That was Nicolas Nabokov and his wife Dominique. I told Morty, "Look, it's all Russians and Europeans. Do you mind?" Balanchine had said, "Bring your other half." It took him four years to say Morty's name. Until then he would say "your other half" or "your better half." When Balanchine met Margot, he adored her, and we became like a family. It was special. Although people were probably talking about our relationship outside, I didn't care because it was so special. It had nothing to do with the dancing. Balanchine never favored me because I was close to him.

Balanchine was so at ease with me. I never threatened him. We cooked together for Russian Easter. We had many Russian Easters when Madame Stravinsky was still alive. We had all the Russians there, and it was great. Balanchine told me a lot about the German food and smells he remembered from his childhood. He taught me things to do in the kitchen that were typically German, and I didn't know they existed. We had fun with cooking. He said I made the best *kogletski,* and he told me a Russian way to make it— sauerkraut and lamb. Russian Easter was a feast. We cooked for a whole week together. I colored Easter eggs. We made pasta together. We would sacrifice a whole week, and then we ate in five minutes. As a child, he had a German nursemaid named Barbara. And he was also very close to his sister Tamara. I think he was very hurt when she died. When Balanchine left Russia, the first country he and his dancers stayed in was Germany. He said that going down the Rhine was the greatest thing because they had been starving in Russia. Food was everything, and food to a dancer means a lot. I think he admired the civilized disciplines of the German people. Tamara Geva's mother was part German. I remember doing the mother at the end of *Serenade* at City Center. Also I did the mother, Leto, in the old version of *Apollo.* I'm a "mother" to everyone, even my husband. I have that in me, Mother Nature. Balanchine had that quality too, always trying to help.

Thank God for Lincoln Kirstein. After Diaghilev died, Balanchine was offered a job at the Paris Opéra, but Serge Lifar took it over. Balanchine was also interested in working in England, but he was also rejected there. He couldn't get the necessary papers. If Lincoln Kirstein had not brought him to America, our history here would be different today. We wouldn't have American dance. One day Balanchine's works will be widely recognized in America. He is like Jackson Pollock, who struggled long in his lifetime but was finally recognized as a genius.

Balanchine said, "God creates. I don't create." He hated when people would say, "You create a new work. Who inspired you—what woman inspired you?" He would say, "It wasn't a woman. It was the music." He adored women, of course. We were his muses. But the ballets came from something music said to him. And sometimes that called out for a particular dancer. We were tools to him. He used everyone—Patricia McBride, Merrill Ashley—and it had nothing to do with what they meant to him outside the work. He always resented it when people made a big fuss over his preferred ballerinas. It's gossip, really.

I knew I was a tool. I was happy to be giving this. He would start *Union Jack* or *Who Cares?* He would make the movement for a new work, and he was comfortable with me. He would call me up, and he would start *Robert Schumann's "Davidsbündlertänze"* with me. In *Who Cares?* we did that pas de deux on me first, Jacques and I, before Balanchine did any other steps for the ballet. And the same for *Stravinsky Violin Concerto.* We would work privately before the rest of the ballet was begun. After that, he would work quickly on the rest.

Balanchine would sometimes speak of ballets as advertisements, or he would compare dancers to certain animals or to desserts. At his parents' country place in Finland as a boy, Balanchine had a baby piglet. It was like his little toy, a pet. He was so jealous because it ate leftovers. One day the piglet was gone. It appeared on the family's plates. He said, "I'll never eat dinner." He was starving. He promised he would never eat pork again. Later on, when he grew up, he made the greatest dishes, including pork. But at the time it must have been devastating for the child.

Balanchine never explained his dances to his dancers. He would give you the movement with the music, and he knew that you would make something with it. That's why he'd choose certain bodies. He knew who was right for a particular sound. He always said, "Feelings. If you talk about them, there are no more feelings." That's why he would never explain. His ballets would make a total impression, very theatrical, although some people never gave him much credit for the theatricality. He taught everyone: the costume designers, the designers of sets, lighting. He did everything. He would sketch, indicate. He gave artists who worked for him ideas for sets and costumes—even Karinska.

The 1972 Stravinsky Festival was Balanchine's prime, when he was so creative. I am ecstatic that I was part of it. One after another, the ballets came out: the *Duo Concertant,* the *Symphony in Three Movements,* the *Stravinsky Violin Concerto.* He went on and on, and so quickly!

I learned to find my own way, and it was so wonderful how he would use your personality. He never imposed on you. Certainly you had to be on time, in space. After years of dancing *Violin Concerto* I heard Morty say to him, "Oh, *Violin* looked wonderful tonight." Balanchine said, "Gets better. It's getting better." For fun, I once said to him, "Everyone interviews you. Can I ask you a question, Mr. Balanchine? Tell me, of all your ballets, is there one which you think you don't want to change or you think is crafted right?" He said, *"Violin Concerto."*

Before dancing *Davidsbündlertänze,* I did not know the story of Robert and Clara Schumann. Balanchine told me a little bit, that Clara was a wonderful pianist, and then Robert went insane. He said, "Oh, we make beautiful ballet someday." He listened to recordings at my home. He brought several different ones, and he didn't like the tempi at all, except for Walter Gieseking.

Balanchine never said, "You're Clara Schumann." He never told Adam Lüders that he was Robert. He just built the ballet, and then we came together. Each partner is so isolated. We never saw each other, all four couples, until much later on in the piece. He choreographed each so fast. It was funny. When we danced, I had the feeling, even when I was offstage, that there was such a wholeness, a togetherness, even when you weren't there: that you were part of the whole thing. The whole ballet was a poem of gestures and so inventive. Balanchine said one sad thing. Mr. B. asked Rouben Ter-Arutunian to design the ballet after Caspar David Friedrich, who was contemporaneous with Schumann. Rouben did just that, and Balanchine said to him, "This is going to be my last ballet." Of course, Balanchine did several ballets later. The only other big ballet after 1980 was *Mozartiana,* but I think he meant what he said. I think it took a lot out of Balanchine. It was a very special work and very emotional.

For the 1981 Tchaikovsky Festival, he also choreographed the *Adagio Lamentoso* from the *Pathétique* symphony. I was injured, but Balanchine said, "Look, would you like to do this? It's a special work." I said, "What do you mean? Of course I would want to do it." I could hardly walk when I was barefoot, but I wanted to be part of it. He said to me, "You are the one person who knows how to mourn." I didn't understand at first. Why did he say that? I have the ability, I am born this way. I never have to act, but I have a dramatic quality that's born in me, that's natural. I first came to see this when he said, "All Europeans act." At that time I had said to myself, "I'll show you, Mr. B., one day, that I can dance as well, too. I don't have to act." Balanchine always put me in all the acting roles, and he said in an interview: "Because Karin knows how to act." He had to tell the American dancers how to act, but no one ever had to tell me. I was there. I knew how to wear the costume, how to react to having my hand kissed. Look at Nureyev. He comes onstage and he's a prince. He's present. He doesn't have to do a step. He's there. You have to tell American dancers all kinds of stories before you get the right feeling from them.

Balanchine believed the *Pathétique* was written by Tchaikovsky about his own death. He drank the water from the Neva even though it was poisoned. The *Adagio Lamentoso* was Balanchine's tribute to Tchaikovsky. The child in the ballet could be the composer. It could also be Balanchine. With the symbolic candle and blowing the light out, it could be whatever one wanted. The cross was incredible—the cross breathing before the child who ran. It was very touching, being on that stage. We were crying.

What was extraordinary about Balanchine's choreography was its relation to the music, even music that wasn't written the way we dancers counted. It was his conception that was so musical. He made the music "look" better. His famous saying was that you could "see the music and hear the dance." The relationship of the music and the dance in one of his ballets was almost sexual. He doesn't merely follow every note. That becomes boring. In *Violin Concerto* I do a back bend in a count of four. The music is counted in nine, and it creates a syncopation.

Balanchine had patience. He had to train an audience to learn to see. In the past, dancers always wore costumes; he eliminated them and stripped everything down. He was sometimes accused of being unemotional and cold, but *Liebeslieder Walzer* and *Davidsbündlertänze* are so poetic and so emotional. And there are *Vienna Waltzes* and *La Valse* and *Ballo della Regina*—every ballet has emotion. Balanchine could not be emotional *about* his ballets being so. He was always very clear so that you, as the observer, would be moved. That's what counts.

Balanchine hated talking about the past. He said, "Now is what matters. I don't care about the future. When I'm gone, there'll be something else." In the last years he spoke about how he would like to do *The Sleeping Beauty.* He remembered what it was like at the Maryinsky. He said, "Our theater is too small."

Balanchine was very religious, but he did not go to church regularly. But he would have his own icons in his home, and I even gave him an icon of St. George. His saint's day meant more than his birthday: St. George. It had an inner meaning to him, a private one. The last dinner we had in his house— Morty and I with Balanchine—he was already suffering from falling. He had more candles in his bedroom with the icons. It was like a little altar. When we were about to leave, Morty said, "I smell something." The doors were open to Balanchine's bedroom, and Morty went in there and flames were going up. A lighted candle had fallen. Morty called, "Karin, get some water." I ran into the kitchen and got some water, and as I passed Mr. B. I heard him falling behind me. He had slipped on the rug. I put the fire out.

A weekend was coming up, and Morty and I went to Long Island. Balanchine didn't want any nurses around him. He was fighting. He said to me, "You come here." I said, "I can't, I'm married." It was really hard. He fired all the people he had. He broke five ribs that weekend. Finally he said, "I want to go to the hospital." He was fighting to the end. He did not want to go.

I don't want to work for anyone else. I just want to live up to his trust, because Balanchine would want me to. I brought *Variations pour une Porte et un Soupir* back, and I want to do *Gypsy Airs.* We have to protect ourselves. That's why we formed the Balanchine Trust, for protection against someone who comes along who doesn't like Balanchine. We will try to keep his ballets alive.

I'm sure Balanchine would have loved the idea of scholastic exchange with the Russians, for example the Kirov learning *Scotch Symphony* and *Theme and Variations.* I saw both performances in New York. The Russians have a long way to go, but it's a beginning. They tried. You can't expect to move a mountain in one day. Look how long it took Balanchine to make dancers out of American body movement!

Years after Balanchine's death, I don't know how other people feel, but I am sometimes so lost. In his last years when I was still dancing, he said to me, "You are a disciple now. You go on your own." He gave me all that trust. It doesn't get any easier. He was ballet for life. He gave me so much. It's almost as if it was your life. It's so hard to live up to that. Balanchine did not take a salary from City Ballet until 1964. He had to borrow money from the School of American Ballet to buy a $50,000 apartment. He was poor. He lived like a millionaire, and he thought he was rich, but he had nothing. Nothing. He was a generous person. When he had no money, he would buy a fancy car. All the Russians who defect are now driving Mercedeses. Balanchine had to wait fifty years to buy himself a little diesel Mercedes. And a little apartment. He would go out to dinner and have champagne and invite people: "We have Russian souls." But he never had a family and children. He said that would be a drawback. You had to worry about how to make money for them. He had enough to live, and that's all he cared for. When poor, starving friends arrived from Paris, he would say, "I'll take them out."

ROUBEN

TER-ARUTUNIAN

Born in Tiflis, Russia, in 1920; educated in Berlin, Vienna, and Paris; studied philosophy at Berlin's Friedrich Wilhelm University and at the University of Vienna and the École des Beaux Arts in Paris from 1947 to 1950; moved to the United States in 1951. He has designed many opera productions internationally and won Emmy and Tony awards for his work on television and on Broadway. His designs for international ballet companies are legion. A collaborator of Balanchine's for a quarter of a century, he made designs for twenty-five ballets. Ter-Arutunian's original designs for these and other productions are in the collection of the New York Public Library at Lincoln Center.

MOST OF THE TIME BALANCHINE HAD A CERTAIN NOTION AS TO WHAT HE WANTED a ballet to look like in its final form, while he was asking for it to be designed. But there were always some areas where he would be grateful for a contribution from the designer, because frankly he would not be very clear about one thing or another he had in mind.

Vienna Waltzes (1977), for instance, started very "clear"—very definitely as waltzes around five tree trunks in the middle of the woods, the Vienna Woods, to the music of Johann Strauss. They were to transform into something as yet not defined for Franz Lehár's *The Merry Widow,* using the "Gold and Silver Waltz"—and this was then to lead into the finale: Richard Strauss's *Der Rosenkavalier* waltzes, which would be danced in a grand ballroom, with the trees of the woods metamorphosed into crystal chandeliers. As long as there was a forest at the beginning of the ballet and a ballroom for the end, there must be something in between. A combination of nature and architecture or of nature *as* architecture. A decorative fusion might perhaps succeed to suggest the extravagance of an Art Nouveau foyer of a Grand Hotel or the elegance of a fashionable *salon de thé dansant,* created entirely through the swirl and undulation of golden roots. Balanchine liked this idea instantly. He later introduced the golden ballroom chairs and tables, which we had made, and ubiquitous toasts of champagne. If *The Merry Widow* attempted to evoke a hint of decadence, and the atmosphere of the Hapsburg Empire at the turn of the century, the *fin de siècle,* the succeeding one of the *Rosenkavalier* would be totally different in character.

To accomplish this second transformation technically—of course, again in full view of the audience—it seemed logical to continue the growing of the forest further (there were now only golden roots left) and to continue to unreel them upward to reveal the always present background: a wall of mirrors of a festive grand ballroom, the stage finally wide open and empty except for a series of chandeliers. Details are cool, geometric—the white checkerboards on top of the mirrors forming the outline of an arch; at their bottom, the abstract renderings of a silver rose connects with the adjacent mirror frame. It is the spirit of the *Wiener Sezession* and the *Wiener Werkstätten*— it is the twentieth century and the new harmonies of the score of Richard Strauss. At a certain moment during the exuberance of the waltz rhythms, the lights of the chandeliers—their root motif provides the only link to the Vienna Woods—suddenly are illuminated, dazzling in the crescendo and building to the final curtain.

The design of *Vienna Waltzes* required trust in the music and a sensibility to relate to it and to respond with visual means. Evidently this appears to be also the approach for the choreography. In retrospect, it seems that Balanchine might not have been at the start totally aware of the importance and influence his idea of the five trees in the forest would eventually have in the context of the development of the decor for the ballet, but it determined and inspired a very specific approach. As in every collaboration with him, he never restricted a proposed decorative solution, though he would have done so without any question had it not been what he had in mind, instinctively. It was not only that he would not confine the thinking of his collaborator, but that so often did he manage to find a suggestion to make which would inadvertently become an inspiring revelation, though frequently in a totally unrelated way. But it would lead to a final, decisive idea.

It was almost always possible to anticipate his response to a new design. There was never any indecision about him. He would react immediately to an idea, and it was either acceptance or rejection, nothing in between—though he would not hesitate to change his mind later, if a better idea had occurred to him. But there was never any insecurity, no self-doubt, and never mistrust. He was always a model of professionalism, of clarity, an inspiration—not only professionally—in all of the twenty-five years that I had the great privilege to work for him.

Style and elegance—that is really what he did have. But it's difficult to define either one of the two. What is elegance? What is style? Whatever it is, he had it. I think those are the words that describe part of his personality. Style and elegance and always asking for the best. If he couldn't have the best, he would rather not have anything. He would never settle for mediocrity. He was a man who made his choices and had his own style and then followed the choice he had made. His choice was the choice of the music, and once the music seemed to him worthwhile and interesting and inspiring, then he would do everything to extract from that music what his sensibility would permit him to do. He didn't really have a surface of style, so to speak. He would submit himself to the inspiration of the composer. It was the ground that he walked on—the music. And so was his choreography. Always really the same approach, through music. Because the music was it.

PETER

MARTINS

*Trained at the school of the Royal Danish Ballet, danced with that
company 1965–69, where he first appeared in Balanchine's* Apollo.
*Principal dancer, New York City Ballet, 1969–83, he made his first
choreography in 1976. Ballet master-in-chief of the New York City
Ballet since 1983, he is the author of* Far from Denmark *(1982).*

I Remember Balanchine

THE FIRST I HEARD OF BALANCHINE WAS WHEN MY AUNT AND UNCLE TOLD ME ABOUT this semi-weird friend from Russia. Balanchine had been ballet master at the Royal Theater in Denmark in 1930–31. He was asked to stage Massine and Fokine ballets. He was furious because the Danes didn't want his ballets. He made a deal. He choreographed Fokine's *Schéhérazade* and Massine's *La Boutique Fantasque* and *Le Tricorne,* staged Fokine's *Prince Igor,* put on his own *Apollo,* and made a new ballet to *The Legend of Joseph.* He had a great time. I remember him telling me that on New Year's Eve, 1930, my uncle and he got drunk. My uncle had to dance *Les Sylphides.* The director of the theater called Balanchine and said, "You must do it." Balanchine said, "I'm drunk too." The director said, "Just pretend." They threatened not to renew his contract. So Balanchine put on white tights, which he hadn't had on for a while, and pretended. It was a huge disaster. The review said, "We only wish Mr. Balanchine would stick to choreography." Balanchine used to speak of my uncle, Leif Ornberg, who danced *Apollo.* He'd say to me, "You look just like your uncle, except he was short and couldn't dance. But he was better-looking."

When he first met me, Balanchine told me stories about Denmark. "They're very stubborn, they won't let you do anything there, I had to fight for everything, and finally I couldn't stand it any longer." The same thing happened to me. He said to me, "I told you." He said, "They have the most beautiful women in the world. They grow like grass. Nobody ever makes anything of them."

I think the school in St. Petersburg was much stricter and much tougher than Copenhagen. Of course we had the Bournonville tradition. The emphasis was on speed and musicality. When I first danced *Apollo* in 1967, substituting for Jacques d'Amboise, who was ill, I thought the performance went well. Then Balanchine told me it was not right, that he had not wanted to bother me the opening night because he needed me to be calm. Then he tore me apart. He told me, "I don't know who the hell taught you this, but . . ." Then he danced the role for me, completely. *Apollo* is not a ballet you analyze in front of a mirror. You dance it the way you were coached by Balanchine and the way you sense it. You can't talk about it. I think he was intrigued by *Apollo* because of the mythical impact, the music, the steps. But he was upset that people didn't stop talking about it.

I always quote to dancers what Balanchine would say to us: "Just dance and don't add anything to it." It should be explained what he meant. In other words, don't act, don't pretend you're anybody, don't think of yourself as anything, don't think of yourself in *Apollo* as a god. Then it becomes phony. It wasn't that Balanchine didn't want his dancers to be themselves. It was exactly the opposite: he *wanted* them to be themselves. He wanted the bare essence. Now I, as ballet master, am in the same position. I look at my own work, and only when the dancers are themselves does a performance mean something to me. That's what Balanchine wanted. It's difficult to get people to just be themselves.

I remember Balanchine coaching Baryshnikov in *Prodigal Son.* You would think he would have told Misha to emote all the way. He didn't. It was all *physical,* not in the facial expression, but in the neck.

Balanchine always experimented. Choreography was a tool. He knew everything about it, and yet it was as if he said to himself, "There's got to be a different way to do the same thing, essentially." He kept experimenting. He would challenge dancers because he was fascinated by what the human body could stretch itself to do. He kept talking about the Olympics. He said, "Four years from now, they're going to jump so much longer and so much higher." The classes he taught were similar. They were cruel sometimes, really tough, difficult because he was not choreographing for you and one other person—instead, he was doing it for fifty people. Sometimes you were praying that he wouldn't single you out and just finish you. Yet it was not fear. You were there because, when he decided to show you and teach you something, you knew he had a purpose.

I do not think Balanchine neglected his best male dancers. I just think he was not as interested in us as he was in the women. That's all. He thought of us, and he put us onstage, and he cast us, but he cast us according to the women.

I am now a choreographer; something happens when you choreograph that you don't experience when you dance. You become totally unaware, you don't know what you're doing, you just do. When you dance, for the most part you're aware every moment of who you are, what you are doing, what you have to do, what the conductor is doing. You have to be aware, otherwise you can't dance. But when I choreograph, at a certain moment I have no idea where I am or what time it is. I don't remember when I ate lunch. I just choreograph. It's therapeutic and weird. You make judgments, but you don't know whether it's a good judgment or not. With the dancer you play around and experiment, but you end up with one particular version that you find is right. And then you go on. When I say "right," it's not that there's some secret answer somewhere. It's instinct. At times you can't choreograph. I remember there was a rehearsal of *Robert Schumann's "Davidsbündlertänze."* Balanchine choreographed it rather fast, and then he came in one day twenty minutes late. We all stood and waited, the entire cast. He walked into the studio and came straight across the room to me. "I just can't do this now," he whispered to me, so nobody would hear. All these principal dancers were waiting for him. Finally, now, here he is. And he said to me, "I can't do this." Of course I was totally shocked. I didn't know what he was talking about. And he said, "You see, you do." And I said, "I do what?" He said, "This is a dance. Four couples. I planned, four couples, you see. And you'll do, you'll make nice little dance. I don't know what to do," he said. "I have no ideas. I can't think about it now. You make a little dance. You have an hour." And he said, "Gordon will help you." I said, "Mr. B., I just can't. I don't know—what kind of a dance?" "You will see." And he walked out of the room. Of course I wasn't going to stand there and choreograph on Suzanne Farrell and Jacques d'Amboise and the others. So I followed him, but I couldn't find him. I walked downstairs. I looked in all of the offices. He was nowhere. I really didn't know what to do. I went back ten minutes later to the studio and two of the dancers had left and one was very upset. Finally Balanchine walked in. He clapped his hands and said, "Come on. Let's go." And he choreographed the dance in two hours—the sequence where three men toast each other with goblets. That whole dance. It was a two-and-a-half- or three-minute dance. He made himself do it. He had to struggle sometimes too.

He was very surprised to hear that I had choreographed my first ballet, *Calcium Light Night.* He didn't realize that I was interested in choreography at all. I told him I had done something, he came to look at it, and he liked it. He said, "Let's do it next week in New York." Just like that.

Balanchine's lesson was "Apply yourself." If you don't apply yourself—talent, musicality, gifts, whatever you have—it doesn't much matter. He always taught his young dancers that. He always told them, "What's wrong with right now?" A little girl would stand there, and she would be a little lazy, and he would say, "Why not now?" And he would say, "Perhaps tomorrow you feel more comfortable about it, doing it tomorrow?" And she would say, "Yes." And he'd say, "Why? Now! Maybe you leave now and a bus—wham! Do it now. Don't wait!" Now, there's something interesting about that lesson. We all laugh about it, and we joked about it. But I tell my dancers today, "Now, now," all of them. I'm going to tell them every day. That's all I can do. It's going to have as little or as much effect as it did when he told us. But now it has an impact because he's gone. I miss Balanchine the man more than Balanchine the artist. After all, we have the artist still, in his ballets. He was very funny, and wonderful company.

ROBERT

WEISS

Born in New York City in 1949, Robert Weiss studied at the American Ballet Theatre School and at the School of American Ballet; performed as a child in Balanchine's The Nutcracker; *joined New York City Ballet in 1966. Created roles in the Stravinsky* Symphony in Three Movements, Coppélia, Gaspard de la Nuit, *and* Ballo della Regina. *From 1982 to 1989 he was artistic director of the Pennsylvania Ballet, for which he choreographed many ballets.*

I STARTED MY BALLET TRAINING AT THE AMERICAN BALLET THEATRE SCHOOL, WITH Schollar, who was a really wonderful first teacher. I was eight years old. My mother had studied there. Even though she never became a professional dancer, she loved ballet. Then I went to the School of American Ballet because I wanted to be in *The Nutcracker.* I stayed at S.A.B. and went through the whole course of study, but I didn't take it very seriously. I took *The Nutcracker* seriously. I was Fritz and the Prince, and then I was too big.

Balanchine rehearsed me in those roles. At that time he was much more involved with the School and with its students. He personally took the time to coach the first act of *Nutcracker* himself. He taught me the pantomime of the Prince. It was a smaller company, the seasons were shorter, and everything counted, every detail, even the children. He was wonderful with the children. He treated them like adults and had great rapport with them. He would say, "This is what you have to do. . . . This is the motivation behind it. . . . This is what you're saying. . . . There are words for each gesture . . . no, not exactly like that . . . you sleep . . . no, it's too rough, you sleep gently . . . now you're surprised." He was terrific.

As a youngster I didn't take the training at S.A.B. seriously. I like to dance, and it was fun. When I felt like doing it, I did it. And when I didn't feel like doing it, I didn't. The School was a serious, Russian-style institution, and you had to take so many classes a week in each division that you were in. Robert Maiorano, Paul Mejia, and I were the male contingent. I had a certain talent, and they were pushing me. But I was always getting together with my friends. I was in a science club and I had taken piano lessons from the age of five. I had all sorts of interests; ballet was only one. I was supposed to be in class three times a week, and I went only once. Then, at age sixteen, I met Stanley Williams. He was so interesting that I started to attend classes five or six times a week. When I was a child, I viewed ballet as an extension of sports. You could do a double *tour* and you could jump high, and it was exhilarating to do it to the music, but I didn't really understand the emotional and intellectual part of dance until I met Stanley. Then I knew I wanted to be a dancer.

Danilova was teaching at S.A.B. She was a great artist. I never saw her dance, but I knew she was a great artist from watching her teach. Danilova's gift was to bring to the students that sense of the past, the tradition, the manners. She's the last one. The next generation of students is never going to know what we learned about that first hand. It will already be one step removed.

I was in the first S.A.B. workshop in 1964 and the transition into the company was shocking because nothing can prepare you for being a professional. It's a whole different ball game. You're coddled at the School in certain respects. The company is like real life. You're thrown in at an age when most people haven't started college. Suddenly, you have to deal with the work place, and competition, and the politics and working from 10 A.M. to 11 P.M., and the responsibility and the discipline.

I learned *Diamonds* (1967) in the corps when Balanchine first choreographed it. He gave us a step, and he was very concerned that you would turn a certain way with a straight leg in the back and your hands extended as fully forward as possible. He didn't like the old-fashioned way of turning with a bent back leg. He got to the point in *Diamonds* where the men do a little step to the side and then do a turn. I bent my back leg, and he said, "I know where you learned that—at the School. Forget the School. Don't go back there." Stanley still taught in this way in 1967. But when he understood why Balanchine didn't want it, he stopped teaching it.

Balanchine was always changing things. Toward the end of his life he cut the opening scene in his *Apollo.* It's a scene that dates the ballet: you know what period it came from. It looks like 1928. The rest of the ballet is so sweetly neoclassical. Balanchine used to talk about "white" ballets, and *Apollo* is a "white" ballet. As Balanchine got older and times changed, he revised a lot of his work. He added parts, left parts out, or changed and divided them three or four times. I think he was trying to distill his art to the point where time literally wouldn't impinge. And I think he succeeded. Without the first scene, in a hundred years *Apollo* is going to look just as fresh. You will not be able to say, "This was choreographed in 1928 or revised in 1979." It is just what it is. It's timeless. I think he had a very acute sense of wanting that to happen in his work.

Balanchine could be complex; I think he definitely had a problem with male dancers. He was in competition psychologically with every man he came in contact with. When a great male dancer appeared, Balanchine felt in competition with him on some level. And yet he wanted and used great male dancers. Everybody who knows his work knows that he did some of the greatest roles for men ever. But with Edward Villella, who was truly one of the great dancers of his generation, Balanchine never had a real rapport.

Balanchine's classes contained elements of his genius, but he really couldn't teach people how to dance, and this was especially true of men. If somebody, particularly a woman, was truly gifted, he knew how to make those gifts shine. The interesting thing is that Balanchine taught Stanley Williams how to be a great teacher. Williams came to the United States from Denmark at Balanchine's invitation. Balanchine had an incredible eye. When he was in Denmark nursing Tanaquil LeClercq, he watched classes at the Royal Danish Ballet, saw Stanley Williams teaching, and became fascinated with his methods. He must have thought, "This is the teacher I'd like to bring to America." Stanley is a great teacher because he has the instinct and talent. That's a completely different instinct and talent from that of a great choreographer. Sometimes one person can have them all. But most of the time one person is a great choreographer, a great director, another person is a great teacher, another person is a great dancer.

Balanchine couldn't really teach the intricacies of technique. He knew how it was supposed to look, but Stanley knew how to make it look like that. The teaching process is a much slower process. Balanchine didn't have a lot of things necessary to be a great teacher. Number one, he didn't have the patience. It takes years and years of unbelievable patience to instruct a dancer over and over again. Balanchine used to get totally frustrated and say, "It's like pulling teeth. Why do I have to pull teeth? I'm not a dentist. I don't want to be a dentist." But teaching *is* like pulling teeth. I know it is because I've been teaching for eight years. It takes patience to say to the same person who did the same thing wrong last week and the week before and the week before, "You know what? That's still wrong. This is what you have to do; and not only is this what you have to do, but *you have to do it.* You must do this, and this, and this. . . ." And the student tries, and you say, "Well, you just did this and this, but you didn't do *that.* You've gotten three of the steps down, but there are nine more to do."

I think Edward Villella wanted desperately to have a real relationship with Balanchine. But Eddie wanted to dance, and he knew Stanley Williams could help him. Eddie didn't have the best body for ballet. But he did have two really important things: one, unbelievable instinct for knowing how to move and how to get his emotions onstage; and, two, an intelligence and drive to know what he needed to do if he wanted to be a *premier danseur.* When he found Stanley, he was like a sponge. Balanchine resented it, but when Eddie became a great dancer, Balanchine used it. I don't know if Eddie would feel this way, but I think Eddie would have ended up a really good soloist if Stanley hadn't arrived. Perhaps he would have found another teacher, but there aren't teachers like Stanley growing on trees. As great a choreographer as Balanchine was, as great an artistic director, Stanley was equally great in preparing a dancer and teaching. He had the instincts of a teacher, he had the knowledge, but he also had an eye. Stanley came here, and he had all the right elements, but what he didn't have was the knowledge. Balanchine had a knowledge that no one else had. Balanchine's knowledge was that ballet in the twentieth century was going to be completely different than it was in the nineteenth century. Through his choreography, Balanchine took ballet and brought it into the twentieth century. For that, there was no one to teach.

As a result, Balanchine took short cuts. When he first came to America, there was nobody who could dance at all. He didn't have time to wait ten years for a generation of dancers to come along. So he took short cuts, and he used his great eye for picking talent. He took talented people, and they danced somewhat the way he wanted them to dance, but they didn't really know how to dance. Balanchine needed classes to prepare his dancers to get out there on the stage and do his ballets.

I took his class for years. Balanchine's was not a class to make your body respond as a performer's must respond, to actually help you do his choreography. What is hard to get at technically is the jumping, the turning, the speed—all the things he wanted. Those qualities are very hard to achieve, and it takes years of training your body slowly. You can't start out dancing in that way. But that's what Balanchine wanted. His short cut was "Just do it." And if it looks right for the moment, then that's enough. If you were Suzanne Farrell, that was fine. She was long and limber and loose, and no matter how he jammed her body, it didn't hurt. But if you were Eddie Villella or if you were me, you couldn't take those classes more than twice in a week and do them full out.

Stanley Williams, who had the instincts of a teacher, the intelligence of a teacher, the eye of a teacher, came to this country and completely changed the way he taught as a result of Balanchine. Stanley had learned in Denmark from the Bournonville background. He had learned through Volkova the old Russian background, too. And then when he came to America and watched Balanchine's ballets and his classes, he figured out what it was that Balanchine wanted. He changed his method of teaching to be able to teach people to dance Balanchine's twentieth-century ballets.

The English dancer and ballet master David Blair came to New York and sat with Stanley during a performance of Balanchine's *Nutcracker*. Balanchine's *pas de deux* is one of the greatest of all time, so elegant, so fluid. Dance on this level is intellect without words. Tchaikovsky's music for the adagio is tragic in some high sense that transcends tragedy. Balanchine expresses it in the choreography, and it's pure genius. There's a point in the choreographic idiom where things are going to happen that can't happen anywhere else, including in any of the other arts. There's a certain moment in that *pas de deux* where, within the pathos of the music, the choreography allows sadness and happiness to intermingle. The border is crossed in some spiritual sense. It transports you to a place no other art can take you to. It's unique. If you look at the old *Nutcracker pas de deux,* or what people remember of parts of it, it's boring. It doesn't capture the music at all. David Blair sat watching with Stanley, and said, "I don't understand this. So dry. This is not the *Nutcracker pas de deux.*" Stanley had been here in America for a while and understood what the choreography was about. He said, "David, you just don't see. You have to come and stay here for a year and watch all the time, and then you'll realize why this is so much better than the other stuff that you think is good."

Balanchine knew that Stanley had changed his method and was successfully teaching it. But he didn't want Stanley to have the credit. He wanted every dancer in the company to be under *his* spell. He needed that security. He could have fired Stanley at any moment. He could have gone to him and said, "Stanley, this isn't working for me, and I would appreciate it if you would leave at the end of the year." Why didn't he? Because he knew Stanley was making dancers for him, dancers at entrance level into the company. Gelsey Kirkland was ready. Darci Kistler was ready. They were prodigies, and they absorbed everything Stanley had to give them, and then Balanchine gave them something else.

Balanchine knew how to make somebody a great dancer. He had an eye for talent, and he was a great coach. A coach is different from a teacher. A teacher instructs you in the intrinsic matters—technique, style, knowledge of movement, knowledge of yourself. A coach is like a director. The great theater director Harold Clurman, when someone asked what it takes to be a great director, said, "Hire great actors." He chose to answer the question flippantly, but that's probably ninety percent of what it does take to be a great director. There's a lot more, but you must know the right person for the right part. If you're going to get it out of them, it has to be there. You can't put it there. As Balanchine and Stanley Williams would say, "God puts it there." That's something nobody can teach. A coach, on the other hand, has a job that is specific to a role. The dancer has to arrive for coaching with a complete preparation in order for the coach to work with him. You can't coach somebody if he doesn't have the technique or the emotional qualities. It's too late. Coaching is refining, fine-tuning, working with the specifics. When Balanchine would joke with newcomers in class—"Dear, where did you learn that?"—he was saying, "Don't go back to your teacher at the School anymore. I want your complete and eternal devotion at this point in your life." That's a hard thing to ask somebody who's independent. Peter Martins had to endure a version of this treatment as well. But Peter learned a vital lesson from it. He had to divorce himself from Stanley for a time just to understand what Balanchine was talking about. It's not as though Balanchine is completely right or completely wrong. Life is complicated. But these perversities could be frustrating if you really had an independence of thought. It was tough. In the end, look at all the great ballets Balanchine made for Eddie. Balanchine could never have made them if Stanley hadn't taught Eddie. Life is never simple.

I was fiercely independent and determined to keep my independence. I also had a strong relationship with Stanley Williams, which I was also determined to keep. Once I understood the potential that ballet held, at about the age of sixteen, I wanted to do more than just dance. I knew that I wanted to choreograph. I even knew I wanted to direct a company. That sounds egotistical, but I think you have to know those things when you're young because then you learn all the way along. The first piece of choreography that I ever did was to Sarasate. Paul Mejia and I took two girls, and I choreographed a pas de deux for him and one girl and a pas de trois with him and two girls. And he did the same with me and the girls. We were embarrassed, and we didn't show the works to anybody. Paul was eighteen, and I was seventeen. We just went into a room and closed the door and locked it in the old S.A.B. building. We had our tape player and the music. Sometimes I would play the piano for Paul, and sometimes he would play for me. Balanchine seldom came to the School because the company had already moved to State Theater. We'd been working for about a week, and one day the door started to rattle. Someone wanted to get in. We knew it was not time for a class. So we just ignored it. Five minutes later someone comes with a key and opens the door. It's Balanchine, the last person in the world we wanted to know about our working. "What's going on in here? Why is the door locked?" "Oh, we were just fiddling around, making a little dance, you know." "Oh, good." He walked out and left.

I learned to choreograph because of Balanchine, and I pretty much work the way he worked. I always look at the score, but I'm not the kind of musician he was, making a piano reduction myself. I could do it, but it would be a painstaking process. I always get four or five interpretations of the piece on recordings, and then I discuss it with my music director. Most of the time I pick a piece of music that I have lived with for two to ten years. Three years ago I choreographed the Bartók Third Piano Concerto, which I'd first thought about choreographing when I was twenty-four. But I wasn't ready to choreograph it then.

Balanchine would sometimes say to the dancers, "Don't think, just do." I don't think "just do" really meant "don't think, just do." What it meant was, *"Get yourself out of the way and become a transparency for the music and the choreography."* Art, when it's great, is selfless. It's not about what you think, but in the end—and this is what is so complicated about it—it *is* about you. In the end, when you get rid of the garbage that you think about yourself, the real you comes through. Then there's something unique, because what we think about ourselves can never be who we truly are. That's what he did when he choreographed. It wasn't about him. It was about an idea, concept, or feeling. It was about something spiritual. It was about a lot of different things. *Who Cares?* is different from *Concerto Barocco.* But what they had in common was that they weren't about Balanchine. In the end they were about something so much greater than Balanchine-the-man. They were about some aspect of truth, of God in some way. He knew that, so he didn't want the ballets mucked up by dancers who thought, "Well, I understand this, I'll put my way of doing this into it." You can't understand just with your brain, and yet your intellect helps you to get to that transcendent understanding. But so many people have ideas. He would say, "Don't think. Don't dance with your soul. There's no such thing as a soul." Of course he didn't believe that.

When it worked, the dancer was just as important as the dance. And not only to the public but to Balanchine. After all, he would substitute for certain ballets if the casts that he had choreographed them for were sick or unavailable. He would put something else on, even if there were understudies. He didn't want to see understudies do it. He had captured the uniqueness of the person in that role, not just the surface of the dancer, the true uniqueness underneath. Eventually, because people are archetypal, when the right person comes along again, it's like a glove is put on or like the slipper in "Cinderella," and that role takes life again. Balanchine choreographed for specific people, and that's a lot of what made those works come alive. A lot of choreographers make dances for themselves or for some ideal that is not real. Balanchine taught me that when you choreograph for individuals it has to be for *them*.

In *Ballo della Regina* (1978) Balanchine used Merrill Ashley's and my quickness, our ability to jump into the air without having any preparation, something that he had taught us. He knew Merrill and me intimately by then. We were both in the company for ten or twelve years. The qualities that work best in that ballet were qualities that he saw in us. When *Ballo* was first done a lot of people said, "Oh, fluff, not very important." And then after a while they said, "Well, fluff, but pretty important fluff." The ballet took awhile to settle down. People don't understand that. Look at a Broadway show— previews and previews. They change it, they fix it. With a ballet, you put it onstage opening night. There it is. You don't have previews. Balanchine fiddled and changed. A lot of times he believed in something more than everybody else, and most of the time he was right.

Remember, it was tough for Balanchine when he arrived in the United States because there really was no ballet in America. He had to create it. Now some people say, "After Balanchine, what is there?" Actually, some of his ballets are danced better now than when he was alive. I think they'll continue to be. He allowed his ballets to be performed all over the world. He didn't just leave them in New York City Ballet. Some people will understand them better than other people and not always in New York. They're that good, they'll survive time and place. After all, it was a hundred years after Bach died before Mendelssohn rediscovered him. Shakespeare survives the worst performances by the worst hams.

Other choreographers today are afraid to have their works performed everywhere. They have to come back and look at them and work with them. They certainly do have to, because if they don't their work falls apart. There isn't any real choreography there. Their ballets are all about them, about the choreographer.

If you take a look at what Balanchine did, it developed slowly over a long period of time. In a sense it's still developing. It's a strong tradition: Petipa, Fokine, the strong tradition of classical dancing that you can see in Balanchine. The Balanchine influence is on all of us who are carrying that tradition forward.

KAY

MAZZO

Kay Mazzo was born in 1946. After studying with Bernardene
Hayes in Chicago, she enrolled at the School of American Ballet.
Mazzo danced with Jerome Robbins's Ballets: USA before joining the
New York City Ballet in 1962. She created many roles in ballets by
Balanchine and danced a wide repertory of ballets until 1982. Since
1983 she has taught at the School of American Ballet.

I Remember Balanchine

I WAS SEVEN OR EIGHT, LIVING IN CHICAGO, WHEN I SAW MY FIRST BALANCHINE BALLET. I sat way up in the balcony of the huge opera house, looking down at *Firebird,* with Tallchief and Moncion: the most beautiful music in the world, and the most exciting, dramatic dancing. "This is how I want to dance," I told my mother.

The next time the New York City Ballet came, Balanchine brought *Nutcracker,* Maria doing the Sugar Plum and Tanny LeClercq dancing Dewdrop. I was nine, and one of three thousand children who auditioned to be in it. I got in, probably because I fit the costume. I had a chance to work with Balanchine, for the party scene and Polichinelles. He came in to check on us at the end, and told us, "Yes, you're fine," or "No, you're not." He was quiet, patient, and nice. He would go out in the evenings after the performance with Maria on one arm and Tanny on the other, and Diana Adams—everyone in their minks and jewels. It looked like such a wonderful fantasy world to me. Here was this god and I was under his influence immediately. I told my parents, "I have to study at his school in New York, the School of American Ballet, because I want to dance for him." I asked my parents to let me audition for the summer course at the School. We told a fib: I was eleven and a half; we said I was twelve. At that point they didn't require birth certificates. I stayed two summers. Melissa Hayden was one of the teachers. I had seen and admired her; she was magnificent. She gave us lots of ideas and pointers and opened up another world and another challenge. You got something of the energy of all the Balanchine training she'd received, so I grew even more enamored of it.

When I was thirteen my parents moved to New York because the School said that I showed some talent. The School gave students a wonderful foundation and it still does, a Russian classical ballet foundation. From there you go to Balanchine and he makes a few changes—not that many. Of course he would turn around sometimes and say to those of us who had just come into the company, "Where did you study? Where in the world?"

Balanchine got all these teachers together at the School and trusted them. He knew each was totally different, and they all had something wonderful to offer. Tumkovsky would give us thirty-two *entrechats six* and I could never do it, but that's where we would get our strength. "Come on, girls, do me, do me—do!" It was important, because in the Balanchine ballets you need the strength. Doubrovska taught pointe class and she had all sorts of little secrets to tell us concerning what she had done and how she did it. Muriel Stuart was the most beautiful creature, with her *port de bras* and the way that she'd walk so elegantly. A lot of people looked at her class and sort of sloughed it off, saying, "Humph, I can do all of this." Muriel gave a fairly easy class, technically, but it was a wonderful place to work on qualities you couldn't concentrate on in Tumkovsky's or Doubrovska's class, where technically you were working so hard on your feet and everything else that sometimes the *port de bras* was forgotten. Muriel was telling you how to land beautifully from a jump, how just to bend, to move, which is the hardest thing you can teach in dance. She also taught that you don't lean against the barre when you're waiting. You stand. All this is still conveyed in our school but not as strictly, perhaps.

I had about two years with Stanley Williams, when he first came to the School. He had great ideas on jumping and wonderful new combinations, sort of Bournonvillesque things, that I had never seen before. His marvelous classes were very different from Balanchine's at the time. Then Stanley started looking at the Balanchine ballets and technique and he meshed all that with his syllabus, and we now have what Stanley teaches. It's a little bit of both, and it works.

Stanley's classes helped me with the Balanchine, because I knew that I could do a different way. I could tell my foot what to do rather than it just going automatically. I could do a *glissade* one way or another, whatever was called for at the time.

I think Balanchine was right not to prepare a textbook. We teach *glissades* at the School a certain way, but in a variation sometimes you do it another way altogether. I remember when Violette Verdy was performing a ballet she would be entirely different than anyone else, because of her phrasing, because of the accents she would use. Then Allegra Kent would do the same role and convey entirely different things. Now we can turn around and say, "Well, Balanchine said you should do a *glissade* this way." But do you think that either Violette or Allegra ever did a *glissade* in exactly the same way?

Doubrovska led a special class for about twelve of us, teaching us all sorts of variations. Mr. B. would come in often and watch us, sometimes giving us steps across the floor. We were all very excited about it, because we felt he was starting to know us at that point.

Years later I was thrown into *Firebird* in a day, because someone was sick. It wasn't a ballet for me, it was so odd for me to do, but Balanchine always liked to give you something that would challenge you. I was a nervous wreck; I wanted to dance it, but I didn't feel I had enough time. He was coaching me, and afterward I said to him, "Please, Mr. B., whatever you do, don't come to the performance." He looked at me and said, "Kay, do you think that there are any surprises that you have to offer me? I've known you since you were nine years old. I've watched you grow up. I know exactly how you dance. Why would it bother you to have me in the wings? I chose you and you can do it." All of a sudden I felt wonderful when he was in the wings, that he was there not to threaten and say, "Oh, you can't do it," but,

"Let's see how you're going to do it differently tonight. I want to watch you, I enjoy watching you."

Balanchine was wonderful in that he didn't get you into a rehearsal and break the whole thing apart from top to bottom. He'd let you go. One day he'd say, "Do this a little differently and maybe try this way or that." You got a feeling that he trusted you and wanted you to do your own thing. You'd be taught a role in repertory by someone and then he'd come in and all of a sudden, musically, there'd be a little something that was missed throughout the other teachings. There was some syncopation in the finale of *Apollo,* say, and nobody I'd ever seen had done it the way he showed me. It wasn't that it was more complicated, it was just that it was more musical. Maybe a little more difficult to do, but it was the way he wanted it. You'd say, "Oh, I've been seeing that step for a long time and this is how you want it. Now I understand." It was like an awakening.

At the beginning of *Duo Concertant,* Peter Martins and I just did this one step, and then we added the hand when the violin comes in. I remember Jerry Robbins coming backstage after the performance and saying to Mr. B., "How did you have the nerve to just do that—I mean, they stand there for eight bars of music doing the same step. That's all they do in the beginning." And Balanchine said, "Well, that's what the music said."

Musically, *Duo* was a little difficult because he had the violin and the piano, but he just rehearsed it with piano. It was lots of counting in the beginning, which I usually didn't do too much. He did it very quickly. I'd go home and listen to the music and practice, because I had to remember what he'd done. He said to us, "Well, I think in the first movement, Peter, you just stand and listen to the music because this dance is about music. I want the audience to listen, to really listen. And then the second movement you come, and, Kay, you are one instrument and Peter is other, and sometimes you switch." The fourth movement, the Gigue, was "a little bit of a variation for both of you." He choreographed it, if I remember correctly, the day before it went on—maybe two days before—very quickly in the studio. It was strange because Balanchine never really did passionate things like that last movement in *Duo.* Peter and I were, I think, both rather embarrassed about it at first, because Peter had to "run back and go to your knees," and the music was sort of schmaltzy. Beautiful, but it just seemed so odd for Balanchine, and we felt uncomfortable doing it.

I had no idea that there was going to be the blackout at the end. He said, "Maybe we'll just see your hand, but I'm not sure." I was trying to figure out how the hand would come down. I had to stand there, but all the fingers had to be shown. I didn't know at that point that you wouldn't be seeing the rest of me, you'd just be seeing this hand. He kept molding my fingers: "No, I want it this way." And then he'd tell Peter, "You have to rise up." Peter felt ridiculous on tippy-toe trying to kiss my hand way up high, and then kneel down. We just felt very uncomfortable with it. The day of the performance we got onstage with Ronald Bates, the lighting designer, and Balanchine said, "Now I want everything black." I was on the stage, so I never got a chance to see it until it was filmed later.

When Jerry Robbins came back to the New York City Ballet, nothing could have seemed more right. Balanchine was choreographing a lot, but there was no one else around, really, who was doing much that was really good. Balanchine gave people chances, they'd come in and go. Then Jerry said he wanted to return and he started working with Patty and Eddie. When I was fifteen, working for Jerry in Ballets: USA, I knew that he adored Mr. B. I think Balanchine has always been his mentor, his god. Jerry never said this to me, but I truly believe that's how he felt. And I think sometimes he has been a little bit hidden behind Balanchine, thinking, "Mr. B. is so great and maybe I'm not."

I didn't think I'd go back to the company after I had my first child. Mr. B. said, "Wait. Let's see after you have the baby." A couple of months after my son was born, I went to him, and I was very sad. I realized that I'd danced for twenty years. I had a bad hip; I wasn't performing that much. I knew that if I went back I would never see my family. I was so ambivalent about it, but I knew the right thing was to retire. He said, "If you're not going to dance, then you have to teach." I'd always wanted to, but I didn't think at that point of going to the School of American Ballet. He said, "Go and see what they need at this point. I want you just to wait. Soon they're going to be needing someone to teach the older girls." I went and I was sort of a substitute teacher for a while. I said to him, "What do you want me to teach?" "I want you to teach them what you know." He came into my class a couple of times. "Fine." It made me feel so good.

I've always been so closed-minded about ballet, unfortunately. Since Balanchine's death I've tried to look at things a little differently. I think we have to see new things and appreciate them. But Balanchine was of the generation that looked at relationships between men and women in a different way than people do now, in the 1990s. As we all heard him say, the woman was always on the pedestal, and the man was at her feet. I look at the ballets that are done now and sometimes the women are dragged and thrown around, and it's very different. Balanchine was a gentleman and made me feel that I was very important to him. I knew he would take wonderful care of me: he would give me something to dance and it wouldn't embarrass me. He was sort of a father figure and a mother figure and a brother. It was a very personal matter, and things aren't done that way anymore.

ROSEMARY

DUNLEAVY

Born in New York City; studied with Bella Malinka, Nina Popova, and Norman Walker at the High School of Performing Arts and at the School of American Ballet; joined the New York City Ballet in 1961. Danced in almost all of the ballets in the company's repertory. In 1968 she began to help with rehearsals, and in 1971 she retired from performing to become Balanchine's full-time assistant ballet mistress. In 1983 she was named ballet mistress of the New York City Ballet.

I Remember Balanchine

WHEN YOU WORKED WITH BALANCHINE, HE APPLIED HIMSELF TO YOU AS AN INDIVID-ual. He would talk about what he knew you were interested in. He met you on your social level, to get to know you, and then he would tell you his stories. If you stood at his funeral and watched the masses go by, you realized the different areas of living, the different types of people, he had touched. I could see this with every single one of them. Every person had a special memory of him, each person knew a different Balanchine.

In terms of his preferences for the stage, Balanchine liked beautiful, long-legged, thin girls. We all have our likes, and we are drawn to them. Balanchine had the luxury in his last decades of being able to have his likes. But even before then, look at what he created on his preferred dancers. They had to have something to inspire him. They couldn't have been fat and ugly. That would never have inspired him. (In fact, he did make a ballet for elephants: I guess he could work with fat and ugly too!)

Today, I'm working for Peter Martins. I've known Peter for years, and I know what he's like. You have to think: "I wonder if Mr. B. was like this when he was young?" I have no idea what he was like in his youth. When I came into the company, everything was organized. The company was running well, and he had his likes and his dislikes and could be demanding when he wanted to be. You wonder what he was like when he was young. Was he impetuous? Was he a tyrant? It's a mystery to me. I only knew him in his later years.

When his early dancers were technically weak, Balanchine must have made it work. He tried so hard to make it work, and he was never antagonizing. I can remember when he would choreograph for us. He would give us a step that was maybe a little bit difficult and perhaps the timing was weird. But he wouldn't become antagonistic. He would find a way to make it work.

I was born in New York City, and I started ballet at a very small school, Sally Lustre's Dance Studio, because my girlfriend went there. I learned tap and ballet and baton twirling, and of course I was the star of the studio. Then I heard about the High School of Performing Arts. It had a good dance department. In modern dance we had David Wood and Norman Walker, people who were just starting out. And in my first year ballet was taught by Robert Joffrey. Later it was Nina Popova and Patty Asmus. That was the beginning of my serious ballet training. I realized that this was serious business, hard work, no game, and I still loved it. It was there that I heard about Balanchine's school. By then I was advanced enough so that I could attend S.A.B. on a scholarship.

When I finally did see New York City Ballet, I knew that was where I belonged. I had stood in line to go to the Bolshoi when they came—and the Royal Ballet. I went to see Martha Graham. In fact I think I may have gotten into the High School of Performing Arts because of modern. I had never had modern dance, but I picked it up very quickly, and it was fun. I remember when we went in, the ballet people said, "Oh, modern. I'm not going to take modern." But those teachers made it so much fun, I really enjoyed it. I think that's why I got my extension, because you stretched and worked so much with it. It was another reason why you learned how to move. It's a good thing for ballet dancers to study modern at some point, to get the technique and the ability to move a bit differently. It does work against the turnout, but Mr. B. used to send his dancers over to take jazz classes. We used to have a jazz teacher across the street from State Theater, and Balanchine used to say, "You know, dear, go take some classes. Learn a little bit how to move." And it would help the dancers. The dancer gets a respect for the different kinds of dancing because he realizes that there is a technique, and it is a little bit harder than you thought and you're not so superior just because you're a classical ballet dancer.

One of the first Balanchine ballets I saw was *The Four Temperaments,* and it just wiped me out. Who isn't wiped out when they first see that ballet? Another ballet that I kept coming back to—I saw every performance—was *The Seven Deadly Sins.* That was a theater piece. It wasn't really a ballet. You saw something like *The Four Temperaments.* Then you saw *Seven Deadly Sins,* and then perhaps you saw *Symphony in C!* I'd come out, and the images of all those ballets would stay with me constantly. Even now, the way I work is through the images, the way it looked, the feeling it gave you when you watched it. So if you're taking a rehearsal, and it doesn't give you that feeling, you know something's wrong. If you're working with a dancer, you can try to explain how you felt when you saw it or how you felt when you saw him choreographing it. You try to make them understand and do it the way he would want it.

I joined New York City Ballet in 1961 and remained as a dancer for ten years, until 1971. During that period the ballet masters in the company went into a turnover. When I first came in, they were John Taras, Francia Russell, and Una Kai. Subsequently, Francia, then Una and John left. So I was left alone. When John Taras left, Francia asked if I could help out, so I did. Then suddenly I was there by myself. In a sense it was the best thing that could have happened, because you really learned the job. Those people were wonderful to work with, but when they left I was forced to learn so much so quickly. Also, I got to work closely with Mr. B. I wasn't the third one in line.

The work requires a good memory, but I didn't know that not everybody has one. People from the School have said that Mr. B. apparently knew it and told them a long time before that I had the ability and that's what I would do one day. But he never gave me any indication of it. I didn't even think he knew me. But they claim that he had planned for me to work in this capacity. Soon after I began to work as assistant ballet mistress in addition to performing, we were casting *Donizetti Variations*. We were bringing it back; I had danced that ballet before, loved dancing it, and wasn't scheduled. I went into his office, and I said, "Mr. B., how come? I just did it the last time we did it." He said, "Dear, you have to remember, you're not going to do that anymore. You have to be here now." He was cutting it off. It was hard, but when somebody like that tells you that's what he wants from you, that's what you do. If you asked Mr. B., he had an answer. Sometimes his answer would be, "Because I want it." And that would be it. Perhaps he realized that I would not have stopped performing as quickly as I did and applied myself so thoroughly to my new task if he didn't say something. If he had let me go on dancing, maybe I wouldn't have been as good. I don't know.

Everything happens for a reason. We may not know it at the time, but you go along with it, and it works itself out. Balanchine had a lot of foresight like that. Over his lifetime he would do things and people would say, "What is he doing!" But sooner or later everyone else was doing what he had done. Also, Balanchine knew how to use people. He would see a lot of things in a person that you couldn't see or that you wouldn't accept in yourself. I feel very lucky, blessed, that I did have twenty years with him, and at a time when I felt that he needed somebody who could get out there and demonstrate the steps that he would want but that sometimes he couldn't do himself.

As a ballet mistress, you realize that a ballet was choreographed on a specific dancer. Take something like *Stravinsky Violin Concerto*. It was choreographed on specific dancers, but it has a flavor and an essence to it. You know you can't make another dancer look completely like Peter Martins or Kay Mazzo looked. But you can get them to have the feeling that those people had. The steps will be the same, and mechanically you can do a step. But it's not necessarily going to have the flavor of the ballet. As you're watching it, you may think, "I don't feel the impulse, I don't feel the beat the way they did it." And that's what you try to get, after you've taught them the steps. That's what you try to remember—his imagery, whether he explained it or did it. In *Violin Concerto* he always talked about the Russian Tea Room. In the finale, there's a certain section, "The Waiters in the Russian Tea Room" number. All that walking around—that was all Russian Tea Room waiters. Not only was that his imagery, but that's what stays with you, so you think it and believe it. It gives you a feeling of the Russian part of that ballet. There's a lot there that you can work on. When you say "Russian Tea Room Waiters" to a dancer, something clicks. The dancer

Rosemary Dunleavy

thinks, "Oh, all right, I'm supposed to be like that." Balanchine had a lot of imagery of that sort. He had ways of explaining things that made them work without saying, "Do *tendu* side, *rond de jambe,*" etc.

Video tapes are wonderful, but the flavor doesn't always get through on them—perhaps it depends on whether you're looking at the dancers who are doing it right. Every section in *The Four Temperaments* has a bit of a key. In the third "Theme" pas de deux the girl goes down in what Balanchine called a little "sukiyaki" slide. He always said that was "sukiyaki," which means oriental. And that's the flavor it has, very gentle. The woman is a little bit subservient, controlled by the man. When I'm in the rehearsals, the key images all flash back. When people come to me and say, "Give me an example," I have to think. But in rehearsal they come to you because that's where it happened, that's what you were doing at the time.

You never stop seeing new things in Balanchine's ballets. You never stop having notions of what they are about. When I teach them and do them a lot now, even *I* am constantly aware of why things happen in the ballets, what his point was. I can logically figure things out when they look wrong. That's because it's so consistent with the music. Balanchine was a very, very logical man. It all works the easiest way possible and the most beautiful, which is generally the easiest and least cluttered. Take *Vienna Waltzes* (1977). At first I was bothered about having to restage it, but then I looked and realized that it's not difficult at all. That last waltz, with all the dancers going crazy and coming downstage, just works out. Anybody who stages Balanchine's ballets has years and years ahead of them doing the same ballet over and over, and every time you find something new. It's not because you don't know the ballet. It's because you've become more aware. Audiences can train themselves in this way too. If they listen to the music and watch the ballet, they'll realize what's happening.

Balanchine kept saying that what he was aiming at was *The Sleeping Beauty.* Now he was going to do the classics. It would have been so wonderful. He said, "I'm going to show them what they can do to that music. We're not going to have people standing around." Just look at the little *Garland Dance* that he mounted for the 1981 Tchaikovsky Festival. That was what it was going to be like. He was talking about his *Sleeping Beauty* all the time. It was his next big project before he died. He wanted to do it for the music and to show people that you could dance in *The Sleeping Beauty* and not just walk around.

In his later years Balanchine hated to be immobile. He didn't like the idea that he couldn't demonstrate. He felt that he looked like an awkward old person, and his back bothered him a lot. When we went into rehearsals sometimes he would say, "I don't think I can do anything today." Of course he would get in there and do a lot, but toward the end everybody was aware that they had to be ready to pick up from a less clear definition than what we had been used to. I myself would concentrate to pick up anything, a little shuffle at times. His back was bad, and his equilibrium was going. It was difficult, and he hated it. But he never showed it. In front of the company he was always alive and energetic to the younger people. To those of us in management he would show it or say something. But the kids never knew it. They realized he was getting older, but they didn't realize how much he was bothered by it.

Robert Schumann's "Davidsbündlertänze" (1980) was choreographed in bits and pieces. It was hard because I think the ballet had a lot of personal attachments in it for Balanchine. He never really spoke to me about them. I do know that he was explaining Schumann's being unable to respond to Clara. Schumann was a very troubled man, and he knew that he hurt Clara and was incapable of giving her the love that she wanted. Balanchine never said these things specifically, but he told me right away that the ballet would deal with Schumann's life. In the section when the critics appear, Balanchine named each one of the critics after one of today's dance writers. He also explained them in terms of the critics in Schumann's life. Everything that he said had two meanings. One was what the public would know. One was something that we would have known backstage.

Balanchine would often come to me before a new ballet and tell me what he had in mind. We were in Washington when he first started to talk about *Vienna Waltzes.* He said, "I have this idea for a ballet, and we're going to do it. *Vienna Waltzes.* Beautiful music." He had the music that he wanted, and he played it for me on a record in the dressing rooms at the Kennedy Center. He said, "This will be the first waltz, and it will have trees, Vienna trees, in the woods, and people dancing around, lots of pretty trees. And then there'll be some more and then some of trees will go away." I looked at him and said, "Fine." "Then there'll be a polka with not so many maybe." And then he said, "Then we're going to have a great big ballroom. All the trees are going to go up, and from the roots we're going to make a ballroom." I thought, "Yuck. Fine. Okay. Ballroom." He explained the whole thing, and sure enough, a year later, there it was. He knew exactly what he wanted. He started the first waltz with Jacques, but Jacques was injured. He redid the section with Patty McBride and Helgi Tomasson. The first version had all the trees down, and then he rechoreographed it because he couldn't see it. He had it all set—how he wanted it to look—before it actually happened.

He wanted the Merry Widow to look like his mother. He had an image of his mother. When she was very young, she used to wear a very dark black dress with a high collar and a big hat. It wasn't like the costume in the ballet now. But his image was that of his mother when she was young. That's the way he had it when Kay Mazzo first did the role. Perhaps the image didn't work for him, because the costume was changed later. He cut the dresses down, and now the women are more exposed. He started the last waltz with the invisible partner on Stephanie Saland. Suzanne Farrell was away, and he wanted to get going on it, so he started it on Stephanie, and then when Suzanne came back he did the rest of the dance.

For *Union Jack* (1976), I even have his sketch. It was his plan for the third part, the Royal Navy. It shows the Wrens, and he tried to spell it out. He explained how the flag was going to come down in separate layers. He drew the first layer, and he drew over it the next one, and then he said it was going to ripple. He tried to add up how many people would be in the Royal Navy section, and he kept making mistakes in his estimate. In the sketch he was explaining the whole thing, how it was going to work, and then he was talking about Suzanne's group, the Wrens, and he was trying to figure out how to spell Wrens.

One of the last things that I can remember Mr. B. saying was, "You know, these are my ballets. In the years to come they will be rehearsed by other people. They will be danced by other people. But no matter what, they are still my ballets." I think what he meant was, first, that dancers in the future are going to be better than the ones he worked with and capable of putting more into them. Second, people who rehearse them may not be as knowledgeable as the people he once had around him. But no matter what you do with the ballets, they're still wonderful works and they were made to be danced. So, obviously, he didn't want them just to be sitting around and not danced because they're not being danced by our company. Personally, I feel that I would like to have kept the ballets with our company for a longer amount of time before letting them go out to a lot of new companies that they're being danced by now. I feel they're being overexposed. When you have too much of something, you don't want to see it anymore.

A lot of people I've worked with and taught Balanchine's ballets to now also hopefully have a knowledge of them. I've passed it on; I feel I have trained the company. Most of the dancers have come into the company since I became ballet mistress, and I feel I have educated them on the ballets. I'm hoping that is how it will continue. I can see that happening when I'm teaching something to a new corps member. If I'm working on a step with her afterward I'll notice her working on it in the back, and one of the older dancers will come over and say, "Well, you know, remember this. . . ." So they are working together and keeping it. After all, a Balanchine ballet is not something you want to keep to yourself.

HELGI

TOMASSON

Born in 1942 in Reykjavik, Iceland; trained at the National School of Reykjavik and in Denmark; performed at the Tivoli (Garden) Pantomime Theater. In the United States studied at the School of American Ballet; joined the Harkness Ballet as a soloist. Joined the New York City Ballet 1970 as a principal dancer. Balanchine made a number of important roles for Tomasson: the Stravinsky Symphony in Three Movements, Divertimento from "Le Baiser de la Fée," Coppélia, Union Jack, *and* Vienna Waltzes. *Tomasson began a choreographic career in 1982. He retired as a performer in 1985 and was immediately appointed artistic director and resident choreographer of the San Francisco Ballet. In 1988 he staged a full-length* Swan Lake *for his company and in 1990 a new production of* The Sleeping Beauty.

I Remember Balanchine

THE FIRST WORK THAT I SAW BY BALANCHINE WAS THEME AND VARIATIONS, DANCED by Ballet Theatre when it came to Copenhagen in the late 1950s. I was very taken with it, it made a strong impression. Royes Fernandez was the *danseur*. This ballet told me that there was a classical ballet in America, classical training. Until then, American dance meant Martha Graham and modern dance, which I knew about from books and magazines. I had heard of Balanchine, but the name meant little to me at that time. In 1959, I auditioned in Iceland for Jerome Robbins, who was there with his Ballets: USA. He suggested I come to America to study and lo and behold he wrote to me that I had a scholarship at Balanchine's School of American Ballet, where I began in 1960. I then danced for the Joffrey Ballet for two years and at the Harkness Ballet for six. I went to Russia in 1969 for the first International Ballet Competition and came away with the Silver Medal. That's when I met Baryshnikov, who won the gold. After the competition, I received a couple of telegrams from other ballet companies saying, "Come and see us." One of the telegrams was from Balanchine. I went straight back to New York to see Mr. B. I met him on the State Theater stage just before a performance. When you talk to the director of a ballet company, you would normally go into an office, close the door, sit down, and be asked, "What do you want?" and "What do you expect?" But Mr. B. said, "Hello, how are you?" I said, "Hello, how are you?" It was the first time that I had really met him. The dancers onstage were getting ready to dance, and they were mingling and we were just standing there. He looked at me, and there was an awkward silence. Don't forget, I had received a telegram saying "Come and see me." Presumably he wanted to say something to me. He finally said, "Well . . . ?" And I said, "Well, I, uh, received a telegram." I felt uncomfortable with the dancers coming and going around us, trying to listen in. He said, "Oh, yes, yes. Well, do you want to see the performance?" And I said, "Yes, very much." So I went out front with him. This was one of the few times that he went out front; we sat up in the first ring in his two seats. As others can testify, it could be hard to carry on a conversation with him. I talked a little about the performance. I said that I liked a particular ballet. But actually there were very few words spoken. We got up and walked backstage, and I thought, "Well, maybe he's going to say something now." He turned to me and said, "Well, if you've nothing much to do, why don't you come and take some classes?" Not knowing Mr. B. at that time, I thought it was a very strange response. I went back to the hotel room, my wife said, "Well, what happened?" I said, "I have no idea what happened. I guess I have to go and take classes."

So I took company class every day. No one said anything. I kept coming back to the class. Mr. B. didn't say anything. He taught the class and he looked at me. I was aware he was looking, and I tried my best. Four or five days later a dancer said to me, "Oh, congratulations." I said, "About what?" She said, "You're in the company." I said, "I don't know I'm in the company. How do you know?" This dancer said, "Well, why don't you go and see Betty Cage?" So I went to Cage's office and she said, "Oh, sure. No one told you you were in?" Later on, I found out that that's how Mr. B. operated.

I found it difficult to talk to Balanchine. For years if we happened to meet in the long hallway on the fourth floor, coming or going from the offices, we would go right by each other. I would start to bow a little bit and say, "Hello, how are you?" And he would say, "Hello, and how are you?" And neither one of us would stop! Because he did not stop, I wouldn't stop! If someone had been watching, they would probably have thought we were Japanese. That was about it. In rehearsal he would say, "You do this" or "Do that." That was fine. But socially, I always had the feeling he was saying, "This is my harem. You can look, but don't touch." I had no problems with that.

When I joined the company, the season was on and I was assigned roles right away. I went through the rigorous introduction to the repertory that Balanchine enjoyed giving dancers. He loved to throw you into everything and see how you would handle it, how you would sink or swim, what was best suited to you or not. I learned lots of ballets, both Mr. B.'s and Jerry's.

As early as my first professional work at fifteen in Denmark, I tried to learn how to handle and partner ladies, who were usually dancers more experienced than I was. I really had to work at it. Over time, I became quite good at partnering, and I took a great deal of pride in it. If the woman is not presented well in a pas de deux, or if she is partnered badly, it's you who are to blame. I think I discovered I had a knack of finding easily the balances of Patty McBride or Gelsey Kirkland. I could switch partners like that. In the beginning, when I joined the company, Balanchine talked to me about handling partners. His approach to partnering was different from the traditional one I had been taught. For example, when you hold the ballerina, you show her off. You watch her and by doing so you make the audience focus on her. There's more distance between you. Before, I had been taught to get in closer and be in the "correct" positions. There was no air, no freedom. Typical pirouettes in Balanchine are in fourth position. When you partner, you step in as she starts to turn and then you stop her and go on. Traditionally, you start closer in, back off when she turns, and then come up close again. Since Balanchine has you start at a distance from her, it creates a wonderful flow in the movement.

Mr. B. would take final rehearsals onstage, where he would take time to stop and correct. He would sometimes come upstairs in the main studio and rehearse with me, knowing that I was doing something new. But not always. I remember one or two years after I had joined, Melissa Hayden came to me one day and said, "Oh, guess what, we are dancing *Tchaikovsky Pas de Deux* in Toronto!" The performance was five days away. Melissa helped me, but I remember asking Mr. Balanchine right away which version I was to learn. At that time there were two for the male solo, one for D'Amboise and one for Villella. He said, "Learn Eddie's. That would be more suited to you." There was no one to teach me the part in the pas de deux except Millie, and Millie grabbed me and said, "Now you hold me here, and now you grab me there." I learned the variation not from Eddie but from Conrad Ludlow. We went to Toronto. Balanchine had still not looked at it. On the opening day in Toronto we rehearsed, as usual, the big ballets first. At five o'clock in the afternoon Mr. B. said, "Okay, let's see it." So there I was, my first rehearsal with Balanchine on the *Tchaikovsky Pas de Deux* at five o'clock the same afternoon that it's going on. He said, "Yes, that's good . . . do a little more this . . . a little more that." He wanted at one point for me to put in a double *assemblé* going backward from downstage right. I tried it going to the left, which is not my strongest side, but I managed. He finally said, "No, do the other step. That is better." I was exhausted at six o'clock, but we danced that evening. I can't remember if it went well or if I was displeased with the performance. It was over, and I didn't drop Millie. That was one time I wished I had had a little more time!

Mr. B. didn't say anything after the performance, and I learned very quickly that if he didn't say anything it meant that he was not displeased. Once he came to the house in Saratoga that we had rented with Patricia McBride and Jean-Pierre Bonnefous. Marlene and I invited him along with Eddie Bigelow for dinner. Everybody was nervous, of course. Marlene cooked Italian food. I had asked him if that was all right. He said, "Oh, sure." Patty McBride made two desserts, in case he didn't like one. We said to Jean-Pierre, "You are in charge of the wine, because you are French." He bought two or three kinds of wine. Balanchine came. Everybody felt everything was wrong. Marlene wasn't happy with her Italian cooking. But he ate. Patty was so nervous. Would he like this dessert? "Oh, that was fine." She asked, "How about another one?" Balanchine said, "No, this is okay." Jean-Pierre came with the wine. Balanchine looked at it, he didn't taste it, he just looked at the bottle and the year and he said, "Well, maybe in a year's time." I remember Bonnefous almost dropped the bottle. So he brought the next one, and Balanchine opened that and tasted it. I guess it was okay.

Balanchine taught me how to dance. He taught me about expanding the movement, about not being satisfied with it. You must push it, stretch, go for the extra. Balanchine opened my eyes to Stravinsky. Stravinsky was

unknown to me when I came to the company. Balanchine opened my eyes—
he made me see music through his choreography. When I was in Russia in
the competition, a woman from Western Europe said to me, "You know, you
are a very good dancer, but basically you are only as good as what you
dance."

I was twenty-seven years old when I made the change. I could have stayed
and had a good salary with Harkness. But Balanchine's ballets challenge
you. You have to live up to them. You have to come up to that level. They
make you a better dancer. They make you grow. To work with Balanchine,
one on one, in *Prodigal Son* was a wonderful experience. He would crawl on
his knees to show you what he wanted, he would be the Prodigal Son and
then the father figure. He broadened my horizons both in how to look at
dance and in my own dancing. That's what I mean when I say that he taught
me how to move. Others had taught me. I had a very good base, good
training. I had danced many things by modern choreographers. But my
dancing blossomed when I came to Balanchine.

He put me in *Symphony in Three Movements;* I opened the ballet. It was a long
diagonal, a shot out of a cannon, and a solo for the man. He changed that
solo five or six times. He never was happy with it. I became very self-
conscious. I thought, "Maybe it's just me, maybe I'm not doing what he
wants." But I somehow got the word back, "No, it's not you." When I saw it
years later, after I left the company, things had been cut.

When *Theme and Variations* was revived, Edward Villella did it for two performances, and then I went into it for years. No one else did it. After one
performance, Balanchine came from his corner of the stage, walked up to
me, and said, "Excellent." In all those years he said that to me only two or
three times. "Good" was wonderful. But after one *Harlequinade,* once after
Coppélia, and perhaps one other time, it was "Excellent." I particularly remember *Harlequinade* because I had learned it on fairly short notice. I had
even started to learn it in Saratoga with Gelsey Kirkland at one point. Eventually the production was brought back into the repertory, and I began
rehearsing with Patty. At the stage rehearsal, he was standing there watching and I expected him to say something but he didn't. So I just kept going.
Finally he looked at me and said, "Good." Later on in the performances, he
said, "Excellent." You knew that you had achieved something on a higher
level. Perhaps on those occasions something special had come together,
something happened to raise you up in your achievement.

Balanchine did not give me one correction in the mime or the dance for
Harlequinade. Of course, I had learned mime in Copenhagen at the Tivoli
Pantomime Theater. The theater had preserved about sixteen of the *commedia
dell'arte* stories, with Harlequin, Columbine, and Pierrot. I started learning to

535

dance those roles when I was fifteen years old. It's a very different, distinct style with fast footwork. For example, Harlequin moves fleetingly, he never really stands still. It's a specific energy. The movement is very calm on top. His arm movement would be telling a story, but the feet are always driven. That was the essence of the role. The stories are always about Harlequin's chase of Columbine, how Pierrot is her escort, how her father wants her to marry some rich old man, and how Harlequin and Columbine finally get together with the help of a fairy. There was not very much partnering or dancing with Columbine, but I learned all that pantomime, and at sixteen I was put into leading roles. Perhaps Balanchine saw the Tivoli *commedia dell'arte* performances when he worked in Denmark. One of the sixteen pantomimes is *Harlequin's Millions.*

I danced *The Steadfast Tin Soldier* after Peter Schaufuss and Ricky Weiss, and I remember working with Mr. B. on the role of the Soldier. He wanted a specific quality when the Soldier goes and retrieves the Ballerina's heart from the fireplace—the simplicity of it. I think he sympathized with the source of the ballet, the fairy tale by Hans Christian Andersen. Here was a one-legged soldier who loves a ballerina. What does a soldier do when his ballerina goes up in smoke? He turns around and sheds a tear or two, but all right, carry on—next!

When I first went to Denmark, I did not have classes in Bournonville ballet technique. But later on, because Denmark is such a small country, I could not help being influenced by dancers from the Royal School. I would take classes with them and pick it up. There is a similarity between Bournonville and Balanchine in the articulation and execution of the steps, the cleanness, the simplicity of the two approaches. Of course, Balanchine's upper body is very different from Bournonville's. And in Bournonville you hardly do any partnering. Balanchine is a master of partnering. Bournonville was himself a wonderful dancer, and he choreographed a lot of those dances on himself.

Stanley Williams, the Bournonville expert at the School of American Ballet, came to the United States at the same time I did, in 1960. I think Balanchine respected the Bournonville training, particularly for the male dancer. As Balanchine would have said, "Things are cooking. Let's put a little Danish dill in here. It's good, let's see what happens. Something good will happen." And I think Stanley has adapted to the Balanchine style and technique: his classes then and now have absolutely nothing in common. After all, Stanley had been trained by Volkova, a wonderful teacher, and his classes were very much in her style. He has become more refined. I am the first to say that Stanley is a wonderful teacher.

I think Balanchine sensed my enormous respect and admiration for him.

And I think that he respected me as a dancer. Mr. B. taught most of the classes at that time. As one of his dancers, I was part of his family. I was around him, I took part in the conversation. The company was a group of people talking. I did not take everything he said literally or put him up on a pedestal. He was a genius, of course, but he was always a human being.

Balanchine choreographed *Divertimento from "Le Baiser de la Fée"* for the 1972 Stravinsky Festival, and I was a little disappointed that I did not have a solo, but who was I to argue with Balanchine? That was it, and I got over it. I was in another ballet, the *Symphony in Three Movements.* And then one day Gordon Boelzner, the pianist, said, "Oh, I think Balanchine is going to add some music in *Baiser.* "Oh." "It might be something for you." "Oh, great, wonderful." And the rehearsal appeared on the schedule. I remember Mr. B. coming into the main studio, and he said that he had "found this music" and "I thought I might do something. Let's just see what happens. This music that I use was when I did *Baiser de la Fée* a long time ago. It was something with a story and a crystal ball and something. Let me see what happens." He started. And one hour and twenty minutes later that solo had been choreographed. It was a fantastic solo. He would say, "Do this and then show me that. No . . . yes . . . good. Go on." He would choreograph another piece of it and then change it perhaps. In the end he said, "Well . . ." and I said, "Let me go back and try to remember everything because it's happened so quickly." I went over it by myself while he talked to Gordon for a while. And then he said, "Okay, let's see it. Do you want to do it?" And I said, "Yes." I went through the whole dance, not forgetting anything. And, typically, he said, "Okay. Work on it. Good-bye." The next time he saw it was the day of the premiere when we had the stage rehearsal. He never came back to the solo, and ten days or so passed. He looked at the solo and he said, "Good." From him, that was a wonderful compliment. To me it meant that he had given me a gift. He had said, "Now it's up to you. You work on it and show me." After all, he could have said, "No." Or corrected. Instead, just that "Good." That was like getting gold bars.

When Baryshnikov joined New York City Ballet, he was given many of the roles I had been dancing with Patricia McBride. It was a difficult time for me because I had had a back problem and was coming out of traction. A number of my old partners—Violette Verdy, Melissa Hayden, Gelsey Kirkland, Allegra Kent—were gone. Patty and I worked very well together, and I enjoyed her dancing.

Balanchine treated Misha exactly as he had all of us—he threw everything at him. That was Mr. B.'s way of finding out what you were suited for. You sink or swim under that pressure. As we all know, Balanchine had the gift of choreographing for an individual and finding the specialty of each dancer.

He would accent that quality. In the process of arriving at that stage, he needed to see you in a lot of different things. I think sometimes it worked by elimination for him. He would say, "Good . . . uh-huh . . . that's not it . . . oh, maybe, yes . . ." So finally he would arrive at the dancer's essence, the bouquet of a dancer. When Balanchine took dancers into the company, he did so because he had agreed he wanted them in the family. He did not expect them to leave. You were there because you wanted to work with him, so there was no hurry. And when he was ready—when he had found the right subject or the music that suited what he needed to do—he would give a role to you. It could be two years after you came to the company or eight years. I think Mr. B. liked Misha for what he could do as a dancer. He was a wonderful dancer. But I think, in all fairness, Misha did not have a very big success in Mr. B.'s repertory. He did not have enough time to adjust to Mr. B.'s way of moving, the speed that was needed, the accents. Certainly Mr. B.'s great dancers were always very individual. But there was a certain approach to dance that he wanted to shape you into, a philosophy about dance. With time, I think Misha could have achieved success. I have no doubt that, given the caliber of dancer Misha was at that time, Balanchine would have done something for him. Balanchine never hesitated to use excellent male dancers when he had them, despite his "Ballet is woman" statement.

Misha strikes me as a person who is very inquisitive. He likes trying things, experiencing them. After he's danced a ballet two or three times, he's ready to move on to the next one. Perhaps it comes from his career in Soviet Russia. (Rudolf Nureyev, of all the Russians who came over, had more than anyone a genuine interest in different approaches to the art of dance. What respect I have for that man!) But, after all, by the time he joined New York City Ballet, Misha had achieved superstar status, and it wasn't easy to come into a company where there was a non-star system. Certainly there were some principals who were more equal than others in the roster. But to come to New York City Ballet meant working with Mr. B. There was undoubtedly pressure on Misha to achieve fame and fortune. These were his peak years, and Mr. B. was in his later years.

Balanchine never articulated his philosophy of dance in words. He expected you to understand it over time and by watching him demonstrate in movement. Much of it was in his classes, how he wanted you to execute certain steps. He would devote one class, two classes, to certain steps, sometimes to one particular step. You might be aching and wanting to get out of there, you couldn't stand it anymore, but it sank in. Once we were in Berlin at the opera house and we had morning class on the stage on the day of the opening. The stage floor is terribly hard, like pure cement. Mr. B. said something to the effect that "Everybody's forgetting *pliés.*" To him the value of a *plié* was equal to standing flat or on pointe. So we started doing *grands pliés* in fifth at the barre. I'm not exaggerating if I say that we did at least thirty-two *pliés* on each side on that hard floor. Our muscles were aching, our thighs were just burning. All Mr. B. had in mind was "Ah, the *pliés* are not what I really want, they're starting to be loose, so I have to get it back, and they have to understand." I don't think that it entered his mind that we had to dance that night. He was not concerned about warming us up. The *plié* was part of his choreography, was part of making it look good, and it was disappearing. So, *pliés, pliés, pliés.* We crawled off that stage. After all, he stressed so much *plié* in his choreography, much of it is on the downbeat. He wanted to get you into the floor. I have looked at New York City Ballet off and on over the years since he died, and that is one thing that I definitely miss.

Sometimes Peter Martins and I would be talking in Danish when we did not want anyone else to understand, and Balanchine would join us. He would throw in the few Danish words that he knew. Sometimes they were a little bit on the dirty side, and we would all giggle and laugh. But, other than that, there was not much contact between us. When I went to Balanchine and asked him to let me choreograph, his assistant Barbara Horgan had set up a time for me to meet with him in his office. Of course I had heard all the stories about Mr. Balanchine giving people music to choreograph. There was no choice: you do what I tell you to do. I thought, "Well, be prepared, at least bring something." I had heard a piece of music which I liked ("Introduction, Theme with Variations, Polonaise" by Mauro Giuliani), and I thought this would be lovely as a first ballet. We sat down in his office on the big sofa there. The atmosphere was very friendly. There was never a cold feeling between us—there just wasn't that much to discuss usually. After all, Balanchine could do all the small talk in the world with the ladies, and he would love them when they did that with him. But he would never stand for a man to talk about insignificant things. Except when we talked about food or ballet or listened to him when he told stories, there was not much conversation. So I was quite nervous in his office. He sat down and looked at me and he said, "Why do you want to choreograph?" I was prepared, but I had not thought that he would ask me that. I just looked at him, and I said, "Because I love music." "Okay."

So I said, "Mr. B., I have brought music. I have no idea if you are interested in listening to it or not, but I have it if you want it." He said, "Oh, yes, I want to hear it." And so I put on the tape. The Giuliani music is about twenty minutes, so I said to him, "I can skip the adagio." He said, "No, leave it." And after four or five minutes I said, "Just tell me what . . ." "No, no, leave it." And he sat and listened to the whole thing. And he said, "Who is this by?" And I said Mauro Giuliani. Balanchine said, "I don't know him." And he said, "It's good. . . . That's fine." He had reservations about the use of a guitar soloist—whether the sound of the guitar would carry in the theater. And so he said, "I wonder if it could be transcribed for a violin? Why don't you see if it can be done? See if Barbara can connect you with Morton Gould." I said, "Can I use company dancers?" He said, "No, no. Go to the School. I did a lot of things for the School, many of my ballets. Go to the School." Of course, I had wanted to use company dancers.

So I contacted Gould on the phone, played the music over the phone to give him an idea of it, and explained what Mr. B. had said. He did not think a transcription could be done, but by that time I was already choreographing to the music. When Mr. B. heard that it could not be transcribed, he thought perhaps we could get a good piano score for it, and in the meantime I kept choreographing. I liked the music with the guitar, and I said, "Can't we just use a microphone?" Finally Mr. B. gave in and said, "Yes, just do it."

I asked him to come and take a look at the ballet, because I had seen him look at other choreographer's ballets-in-progress, Peter Martins's for example. Sometimes he would say, "Take that out," or "Do something like that next time." So he came to the studio and sat down. The ballet was not yet finished but there was a good part of it to see. He sat there for a while. And there was a long awkward silence, as there could be with Mr. B. And he finally said, "You know, uh, why don't you rethink the opening." Silence. I said, "Okay." "Yes, you know? Okay. Rethink the opening." And he got up and he said, "Thank you," shook my hand, and in leaving added, "If you want me to come again . . ." I said yes. So I rechoreographed the opening, and I asked Mr. B. if he had time to come by, and he did, within a few days. I showed it to him and he commented, "Much better. Okay, good-bye."

Then he came to the performance. I did not see him the day after the performance. Mr. B. at that time was not well, he was not always around. Then I was onstage at the State Theater the following morning, and I met Mr. B. coming across the stage. It was dark except for the one light in the middle of the stage. He said, "Oh, hello. How are you?" And I said, "Hello, how are you?" I knew he was going to say something or hoped he would. And he said something to me that astounded me. He said, "You know, now we can talk, because now we have something to talk about. You have choreographed your first ballet. See, now you understand about choreography." To me, that was an enormous compliment. Overwhelming. He had been so right to send me to the School to choreograph my first piece. I had good, well-trained students, but they did not know how to partner. The boys did not know how to lift. I had to use what was available to me. I had to show. I had to take things apart. It was an enormous learning experience for me which I would not have gotten from dancers already seasoned, knowing how to partner, knowing how to lift. So I am grateful for that.

From that day my relationship with Balanchine changed completely. It was as though we were friends now. In Saratoga in the summer of 1982 he wanted to talk to me. At that time he was not coming to the theater that often. I went to see him at the house where he stayed, and we had long conversations, sitting out in the garden. He said that, after seeing my one ballet, I should concentrate on my pas de deux work. He said, "You seem to have the ability to move people in groups or in larger groupings, which is difficult to do. Many choreographers can move two people around, but not many can move groups around." He suggested my using romantic music for work on adagio. Perhaps Glazunov. Or Fauré. We talked about choreography, some of his reminiscences.

I told him I would like to do another ballet. I listened to Fauré and to Glazunov, but I had a very difficult time finding anything. I called him up, and he said to go ahead. Again he said to go to the School, perhaps because there was so much production going on in the company. I thought that I had earned the right to work with the company, but who was I to argue? So, I said okay. I listened to more Fauré and Glazunov. With Glazunov, all I could see in my head was Balanchine's *Raymonda Variations,* all those glorious steps. And I liked some of Fauré, but I just didn't feel that it was right for me. By accident I had heard some music by André Messager which I liked, but I was in a dilemma. So I called him. I mustered the courage to say, "Mr. B., you told me to listen to Glazunov and Fauré, and with all due respect to you, I can't, I see only your choreography, your ballets, to Glazunov. The same thing with Fauré. I feel that my chance of finding anything of my own in them is small. But I do have other music." "What is it?" "It's André Messager." "Ah! You know, he is one of the most underrated ballet music composers. I like him very much. Good. Go with him. You know something? Don't ever let anybody tell you what music you can use. You must like your music, because that's half of it. And if that's what you want to do, go with it."

He never saw the ballet. He died on the morning of the premiere of *Ballet d'Isoline* at the School of American Ballet Workshop performance. His New York City Ballet was dancing at State Theater. Ballet Theatre was opening their revival of his *Symphonie Concertante* (1947) at the Met. It was a very moving weekend. Not only his company and his school but everyone at Lincoln Center was dancing Balanchine.

When Balanchine was in the hospital, he didn't want to see too many people. Of course, everybody wanted to see him. I checked with Barbara. I wanted to see him because I felt that in the last two years, and having been in the company for almost thirteen years, a relationship had started. She said, "Okay, go." I went and he wanted me to come back. "Come back." I went back and brought him some Danish beer, and he loved that. I was there a few times with him alone. Sometimes he would doze off and I would sit with him. They would bring him something to eat and drink, and he had such a hard time feeding himself, drinking out of the straw. I would hold everything for him. To have worked with this genius, who taught me how to dance, about music, about movement from looking at his works—and there he was not even able to feed himself. It was a difficult emotional thing for me, but I kept coming back. Sometimes I would just look in on him. Sometimes Ronald Bates would be there, and we would sit for an hour or so. Sometimes he would ask good straight questions, at other times he would ramble. Sometimes he would ask me what was going on in rehearsals, and at other times he would say, "Oh, I have to get up, they are waiting at the theater. I have to get up. I have to rehearse." He couldn't get out of bed, and he wanted me to help him get up. It was very emotional.

When I worked at New York City Ballet, I did not watch Balanchine with the idea that one day I would be directing a company. That never occurred to me. But it's amazing what I absorbed. Sometimes I get hold of myself and say, "Okay, now use common sense." Often when I do that I am reminded of Mr. B. I am not comparing myself to Balanchine. He was a genius. I am not. Also, when I was with New York City Ballet, Balanchine was very much a father figure. There is no comparison. I just try to be true to my own convictions. I discovered quickly that you can never please everybody; when you are trying to be fair to one person, you are unfair to another. That bothered me for some time, but I've also learned that it's not possible always to be fair. Use your best judgment. Balanchine always said, "Things will change. And they must." The steps stay the same but the style and even the content of the dance change. After all, steps are the only changeable thing you can hold on to. And the farther we get from his leaving us, the less we will remember.

JOHN

CLIFFORD

Born in Los Angeles in 1947; studied with Kathryn Etienne, Irina Kosmovska, David Lichine, Eugene Loring, and Carmelita Maracci; attended the School of American Ballet for two summer sessions and joined New York City Ballet in 1967, where he danced an extensive repertory. Balanchine created seven roles for him including Glinkaiana, Sonata, Danses Concertantes, and Variations pour une Porte et un Soupir. Established the Los Angeles Ballet, which he directed until 1984. As a choreographer, Clifford is known for many ballets, and he has staged Balanchine ballets for companies around the world. He is now artistic director of the Ballet of Los Angeles.

I Remember Balanchine

THE ROLES BALANCHINE MADE FOR MEN DISPROVE THE NOTION THAT HE DID NOT care for male dancers: *Apollo, Prodigal Son* in the early period, the male roles in *The Four Temperaments* are actually more important than the female. And if you look at the Villella repertory, you see that—aside from the early days with Lifar—Villella was the one who inspired Mr. B.: Oberon, *Rubies, Tarantella,* the two-act *Harlequinade.* The only reason people think that Mr. B. did not care for the male dancer is because he kept talking about how much he cared for the female. Mr. B. liked women very much; his statement that "ballet is woman" started the misapprehension. Balanchine came from a nineteenth-century European perspective. No matter how modern Mr. B. got, he was always a courtier. In class he would continually remind the boys that we were there to support the women. There again, that is what he said, but you have to look at what he actually did.

I first met Balanchine when I was eleven. I was studying in Los Angeles, there was an audition for the New York City Ballet *Nutcracker,* a cattle call at the Greek Theater, and I was chosen for the Prince. Balanchine was charming. I remember him distinctly as being not the least bit threatening. He was businesslike. I'd been in the theater before, so I wasn't really stagestruck. My mother and father had been cabaret performers.

I knew who Balanchine was. Everybody knew. We started rehearsing with Janet Reed, the ballet mistress, before we saw Mr. B. He chose us, but he was in and out. Then the first rehearsals with him were onstage, and he demonstrated everything that he wanted us to do even though we had been taught it. He went over everything. Even though we knew that Balanchine was the boss and everyone was whispering, "Oh, Balanchine's going to come . . ." he was not the least bit assuming. He was just there. I remember two incidents. In the opening pantomime of Act Two, the Prince's panto-mime out of Petipa, you *port de bras* to stage right and everybody responds, and you *port de bras* to stage left. I remember I was too far upstage, and I turned too far, so that my back was to the audience for the *port de bras.* Balanchine said, "Well, you know, dear, I know that girl up there is very pretty, but you have to show the audience the *port de bras.* You have to show the audience what you're doing. So don't." I loved the way he worded that. Then, during the fight scene with the King of the Mice, the Nutcracker has to jump on his back. I jumped and grabbed the Mouse King around the neck and went over him, and we both went tumbling. I remember that stopped the rehearsal cold. Everybody got hysterical laughing. Mr. B. said, "You don't have to jump so high, dear."

I went to Eugene Loring's American School of Dance on scholarship, and at the age of fourteen I started a choreographic workshop. One of the conditions of the scholarship I received was an essay on why I wanted to dance and why I wanted to choreograph. I wrote that I didn't know why, that it was just a disease that I had and I had to scratch it. I made mostly jazz dances. At sixteen I choreographed a production of *West Side Story* in which I also sang and danced. That was my first professional work. I had seen the movie twenty-three times. I didn't steal anything. That was the hardest part —to try to make it completely different.

I went to New York when I was eighteen. I had done a lot of television work, so I had money. I had been on the "Dinah Shore Show" when I was fourteen, dancing pas de deux with Suzy Cupito, who is now Morgan Brittany. (She also played Baby June in the movie of *Gypsy.)* Tony Charmoli was the choreographer of the "Dinah Shore Show." When I was eighteen, I went back to TV and Charmoli put me on as a regular dancer on the CBS "Danny Kaye Show" in Hollywood. I was on a weekly salary, so I made quite a lot of money. But I didn't want to stay in TV, so I went to New York and paid for classes at Balanchine's S.A.B. and the Joffrey and A.B.T. schools.

I was paying for classes in all three schools. Robert Joffrey wanted to see me onstage, and it looked like he was going to offer me a job. And Leon Danielian, who was running the A.B.T. school, wanted Lucia Chase to look at me. But I was bowled over by the students at S.A.B. because they were so good. I felt totally inadequate. I felt fine at the A.B.T. and Joffrey schools, but at S.A.B. I realized I didn't know anything. Eglevsky was teaching class then, and was brilliant. It was impressive to have Nureyev and Bruhn come in to take Stanley Williams's class, but I was even more impressed by Paul Mejia and Ricky Weiss because they were more my age and they were much better than I was. They were doing fourteen pirouettes, and I was going, "Jesus Christ!" I really wanted to stay at S.A.B., but after about a month and a half my money ran out.

I asked Diana Adams if there was any way I could audition for a scholarship, and she said, "Oh, you've got one." Diana was dry, very serious. At S.A.B., Balanchine would come in with Suzanne Farrell and look at a class for a few minutes. I was only at the School in New York for about two months. I went back to L.A. because even though I was on scholarship there still wasn't enough money to live on.

I made some ballets for the Western Ballet Association, the company that Balanchine had started in 1964. Balanchine came out to L.A. to see their performance of *Serenade* and saw my two little ballets for them. Barbara Horgan came up to me and said that Balanchine wanted to know why I never told him I choreographed when I was at S.A.B. I said nobody asked me. She said, "Well, he wants you to come back to New York." I said I couldn't live on the money. And she said, "We'll give you whatever you need, and Balanchine wants you to start a workshop at the School and start choreographing." So I said good-bye to L.A. and went to New York.

I returned in 1966, and Balanchine told me to start working with the kids at the School. The first thing I choreographed was Malcolm Arnold's *Scottish Dances* for about twenty-two kids. I finished it in two weeks, and Balanchine came in. Suzanne was with him, and they watched it. Everybody was very nervous and excited, and afterward he said, "That's very good. When did you do it?" I said, "I just did it." And he goes, "No, this is something you did in Los Angeles." And I said, "No, I just did it." He said, "Well, when did you do it?" I said, "The last two weeks." He went, "You did this in two weeks?" I remember he was very surprised by that. I said yes. And he goes, "Oh, well, do something else right away. Do something right away." So I revised something I had started to do in L.A. to Morton Gould's "Spirituals for Orchestra." And then Bizet's "L'Arlésienne Suite." He came in and looked at the Morton Gould, and the funny thing was that the day after I showed him the Malcolm Arnold he took the lead girl in it into the company —Lynn Bryson. He hired her for N.Y.C.B. that day. And the day after I showed him the Morton Gould *Spirituals* he hired the girl who had the lead in it—Renee Estopinal. So I got a reputation at the School that it was very good if you showed up for my rehearsals because Mr. B. might take you.

He sent me to Madame Zaloty's for piano lessons, and I went to performances every night and matinee. Balanchine wanted me to come to the theater. I sprained my ankle doing one of my ballets for André Eglevsky. I asked Mr. B. if he would mind if I watched company class, and he said no. So I watched company class for a couple of weeks, and one day he said, "How's your ankle?" I said, "Fine," and he said, "Well, why don't you take company class?" I said, "Okay, I'll try." That was hell, it was so hard. After my ankle was better, I went back to the School classes, and Diana Adams came up and said, "Why aren't you in company class?" I said, "What do you mean? My ankle's all right." She said, "No, you should take company class. You're in the company." Nobody had told me. She said, "You'd better go to Betty Cage and sign a contract." So I went to Betty Cage and said, "Am I in the company?" She said, "Yes, we wondered when you were going to come in and sign."

Balanchine was teaching company class every day. Then for those who wanted it—about ten of us, Suzanne, Marnee Morris, Pat Neary, Kay Mazzo, Karin von Aroldingen, myself—he would teach on Mondays too. We had seven days a week with him. The Monday classes were fun because he gave a more thorough class. The following June he gave what turned out to be his last teachers' seminar. It was during a week's layoff between the spring season and Saratoga. He invited the company to take the seminar class and, although we didn't get paid, a lot of people took it. The visiting teachers would watch us take his class. There were about one hundred of them. Balanchine would teach the class and explain everything for the teachers. Why he had *pliés* at a certain rhythm. Why he wanted heels off the floor for certain steps. Why he wanted *fondus* done his way. Everything was absolutely analyzed to the nth degree, and it made perfect sense for what he was doing. The most ironic thing for me personally was that in the first row the first day was my old teacher, Eugene Loring, who hated Balanchine. He was livid. Balanchine knew I had come from Loring's school, and so Balanchine made a big deal over me, how I was new to the company, and I had a big jump, and I had to learn how to do certain things differently from the way I was taught. Loring had a tic, and his tic was going nuts.

Balanchine had a specific way of teaching *grand jeté*. He didn't want the jump high. The normal way to teach *grand jeté* is to kick the front leg up, jump up to it, then raise the back leg, as if you're going over a hurdle. Balanchine didn't want that. He wanted you not to kick the front leg up but to ascend. He didn't want you to bring the back leg up into arabesque. You just floated up. There were ways to do it. Sometimes he would have us do *grand jeté* with our legs very close together. Sometimes he'd have us *grand jeté* landing on both legs, just as an exercise to get the feeling of jumping, not kicking and not trying to jump high, because then it always made us look like we were struggling. Also, he didn't want to see the top of the jump. He wanted to see the entire picture of you in the air without changing. He didn't want to see the crest, the up and over.

At the end of the seminar week we got to the big jumps, and he was describing his *grand jeté*, and he said, "We're going to have Clifford demonstrate. First, Clifford, do it the way you were taught." So I just did it the way I was taught. Everybody applauded. Balanchine said, "Well, that's wrong. Now, Clifford, do it the way I've been teaching you and show them the difference." I did *grand jeté* his way. Everybody applauded more, except for Loring, of course. Loring was livid. And Balanchine and I went out to lunch together after the seminar class. He said, "Do you want to get something to eat?"

Balanchine taught the seminars only for one or two days the next year. Then Suki Schorer took over, and after that year he didn't do any more of them. In the seminar of 1967, some of the teachers tried to pin Mr. B. down and trip him up. At one point he got a little exasperated and said, "Look it's like a kitchen. I cook what I like to eat. This is my kitchen. This is what I do. If you don't like to eat this food, you don't have to." He was very autocratic about it, but he was correct. Of course, he had also just got millions from The Ford Foundation.

Balanchine and I were just starting to socialize a bit then. We hit our peak after Suzanne Farrell left the company. Then we were really non-stop together, and that was when I got to know him really well. Up to that point, I was the class pet. The other boys couldn't stand me. Up to that point, Paul Mejia had been Mr. B.'s favorite, but I guess I had more energy than Paul. Or perhaps I was more of a challenge to teach. Mr. B. and I used to have a hell of a lot of fun in class. Jacques d'Amboise also got into this. Mr. B. would give real brain teasers, things that were outrageous. He was training our brains, not just our feet. I loved that part of it because it was a challenge. I don't know where I got the balls, but sometimes Mr. B. would give a step, and I would do it, and Jacques would say, "No, no," and I would say, "No, it's this way." I would disagree with Jacques. But Jacques loved it. He couldn't believe how ballsy I was. He told me later that he couldn't believe that I had the nerve to say no. And I was right. That's the thing that got Mr. B., I think, that I was usually right. Sometimes I was wrong and Jacques was right. Mr. B. was more attracted to somebody who didn't cower around him. I was very there. I probably drove people crazy in the company because I was so damned energetic. Also, he didn't want dancers to save, to hold back, when they danced. I never did.

When Mr. B. and I would eat together, we didn't talk business. We talked about what was going on in the world, we talked about music and about the company.

Balanchine would have breakfast with Suzanne Farrell at the Empire Coffee Shop. I would go in to pick up an English muffin and coffee, and they were there every single morning in those years. In the evening he and I went out a lot. He would visit Ruth Ann King. She was a dancer in the company when she was about fifteen. He liked her very much, but she had a very serious knee problem and had to have knee operations. Or we'd go over to Carol Sumner's or Giselle Roberge's apartments, or later to Ducky's or to Lucia Davidova's. I would be with Renee Estopinal, who was sort of my girlfriend in those days, and Mr. B. was interested in her and in Linda Merrill, the redhead. It would be just the four of us. It was all very silly, but great.

Balanchine was a great romantic. He would get these crushes on the girls who were very "un-" what one would think Mr. B. would like. But in another sense I wonder if he didn't just use all the women as a means of further building his fantasy ideal of what all womanhood was about. But it was a healthy Pygmalion complex because, when the girls became mature and developed their own personas, that released him to find another young one who was developing. And every time he found a young one it released a new spurt of creativity on his part. It was as if he were building these perfect female statues, and the minute they were done he would find another one. It sounds cruel, but in a way don't all artists do that? At the time Mr. B. was in love with each woman. But there was always, I felt, a reserve there that indicated he knew he was going to be on to the next. At the same time, he was devoted, absolutely, heart and soul.

I figured out in the beginning why Balanchine liked me, and that was mainly because I was so determined I was going to choreograph. He encouraged that. Also, I laughed at his jokes. They were so dirty. I couldn't believe it. I was brought up in Hollywood around theater people. Danny Kaye used to have the filthiest mouth I've ever heard; he had a very vulgar and humorous tongue. He didn't hurt anybody, but every other word was "fuck, fuck, fuck." Mr. B. didn't swear, never. But he would say things that were double entendres or innuendos that were just as bad. I remember some that were just X-rated.

He used to say things in class, and I would laugh and everybody else in the company would not—except for Jacques. Violette Verdy would go, "Oh, oh, oh," and do her French thing. Suzanne would just look annoyed, but I loved it. Everybody would look at me like I was nuts. He'd say something before he'd give an exercise at the barre, or he'd make some little aside and nobody else would get it. I would let out this hoot and literally fall on the floor. I would fall on my knees, I thought it was so funny. There he was, George Balanchine, a quiet man. But then he would say something so funny, very dry. He had a dry sense of humor. I would let out these shrieks, and he would look at me. Once he said, "You got that?" I said, "Of course I got it. You forget I'm from Hollywood." He knew I would get his jokes.

In the beginning, I didn't get all of his ballets. I wasn't bowled over by *Apollo.* Works like *Movements* and *Monumentum* left me cold. I loved *Prodigal Son.* And the next one of his ballets that I got was *Brahms-Schoenberg Quartet.* I think part of my reaction to *Brahms* was the performances. I remember Gloria Govrin was unreal in the first movement, which nobody has been able to do since, really. I liked Vicky Hall, who has left the company, she was good in it. She had that lush amplitude. Gloria was just so luscious. I've never seen anything like her movement quality except Plisetskaya, such luscious generosity. Mr. B. kept saying to us in class, "What are you saving it for?" and "Be generous. Why are you all so stingy?" He wanted everything to be so big and grand. Give it, give it. "What are you saving it for? You're going to get hit by a car when you go across the street to O'Neal's." And Gloria gave. I just loved that about Gloria. And Eddie Villella was phenomenal in the third movement. I loved Suzanne and Jacques in the fourth. The ballet just built. Each movement got better. I loved Patty McBride but her section took longer for me to understand because it's the most subtle. The first time I saw that exit at the end of the movement, it was like a special effect. I really couldn't believe it. I went, "What is that?" I couldn't figure out how she got from the lift to the exit position. So I went backstage and asked her, "How did you do that?" It was very simple. That's typical of Mr. B.'s genius: maximum effect with minimum effort. Everything had maximum effect with, considering what was going on, minimum effort. That's why Balanchine ballets are hard. When I teach his ballets in Europe, European dancers put maximum effort to minimum effect. Trying to get them to understand the difference is the hardest part.

Balanchine would continually recommend pieces of music for me to listen to. I would do some things for the School workshop. When I picked some music, it was usually too mushy or too romantic. He would say, "Dear, no, too mushy." He didn't want me to do *Fantasies* for the company with music by Vaughan Williams, but Robert Irving ran interference on it. I said, "Oh, but I did the *Stravinsky Symphony in C,* and you wanted me to do that and I really want to do something mushy." He said, "Well, the music's too big, takes too many strings." I didn't believe him. I went to Robert Irving, and Robert said, "Oh, nonsense." So Robert sat down in the wings one night and started pounding out "Fantasia on a Theme by Thomas Tallis" on the piano, and Mr. B. came over and said, "What is that?" Robert said, "It's the Vaughan Williams 'Fantasia,'" and Mr. B. looked at me. He took Robert over into a corner, and they talked for about ten minutes, and Robert came back and said, "Well, he said you might as well start it. He says you're determined to do it." Robert convinced him that it didn't take too many strings for them to do. And then Balanchine loved the ballet. He gave me a suit to bow in at the premiere because he really loved *Fantasies.* He had a dinner party for me at Lucia Davidova's and told me that he still didn't like the music, but that I did the best that could be done with it, and that he was very pleased. He kept it in the rep until I left the company. It seemed like every Sunday matinee we opened with *Valse Fantaisie.* I had to dance *Valse Fantaisie,* dash, throw on a pair of jeans, and run out into the audience to watch *Fantasies.* That's how I remember 1969.

Balanchine became a father figure to me, but I'm not saying that I became a son figure to him. I was told by other people—Barbara Horgan, Betty Cage, Patty McBride—how much Mr. B. cared for me. I said, "Well, it's mutual, obviously." Only once in a blue moon would he and I have a disagreement.

I remember once when I was working on *Reveries* he didn't like the way the adagio went. He wanted me to do it to the Tchaikovsky Suite No. 1, which he had given me. He had said, "This will be good for you to do." I had said okay. I liked the music very much. I started and after I got one movement—the fugue—mostly done, I invited him to come in and look. He came in, and he didn't like it. I was fed up that day. I was in a bad mood. I said, "Well, Mr. B., I don't understand. It's just classical steps set to the adagio." He said, "Well, dear, it's supposed to be more Russian-feeling and Slavic."

I got mad, and I said, "Well, it's just classical ballet . . ." He said, "No, it's not, it's supposed to be scenes of Russia." I said, "What?" He said, "The music is sweet. Tchaikovsky is being very specific." I said, "Well, I don't know that, I don't hear that in the music." He said, "Well, dear, that's what it is." He had images of the suite that were more specifically Russian folk-lore, which I don't know anything about. I said, "But I don't know that. I can't superimpose that. What about Second Movement *Bizet?*" He said, "What do you mean?" I said, "Well, Second Movement *Bizet* is just classical *grand jeté* and *développé* side, that's not specific." He said, "No, no, it's specific to me." I said, "Oh." He said, "Besides which, it perfectly fits the music." I said, "Well, you can fit music to anything." So I put on the *Reveries* recording, and I got up and proceeded to dance Second Movement *Bizet*. I superimposed his choreography over the Tchaikovsky music. And I'll be damned if it didn't fit, like a glove, even to the change for the *développé*. I wasn't just doing the steps, I was doing it in sequence. He turned red. It was one of the only times I ever saw him really get mad. He said, "That's not fair."

He said, "That's not fair because the Bizet Second Movement is supposed to be dance of the moon." I went, "Dance of the moon?" He'd never tell that to anybody unless cornered. He never gave a clue before in rehearsals or anything. I asked, "What's the moon got to do with it?" He said, "Well, the *grands jetés* where she gets carried back and forth at one point are supposed to be the moon going across the sky." I said, "Oh." I was speechless at that point. Here is the great "abstract" dance master telling me that in *Bizet* the *grands jetés* to him represented the dance of the moon. I mean, how do you argue with that? I said, "Well, fine." He said, "Well, dear, you should think about changing it."

And I stormed out, and he was red. I went to Lincoln Kirstein and I said, "Will you come and look and tell me what you think?" Lincoln loved it. I told him Mr. B. didn't like it, and he said, "Oh, I'll talk to him." So Mr. B. said, "Fine." Gelsey Kirkland got her first solo in that ballet, in the "Marche Militaire." She was sixteen and caused a sensation. She got three curtain calls. Her sister Johnna did very well. Johnna used to get three curtain calls every time at the end of the adagio. In those days *Bizet* was only getting two with Suzanne Farrell. *Reveries* was a pretty popular little work. I don't want to paint a picture of my relationship with Mr. B. that is all kissy-poo. I would argue with him, but it didn't seem to break us up. We would just look sideways at each other for about two or three days.

For the workshop in January or February of 1967, I was doing a pas de deux for Johnna Kirkland and Michael Steele. I had her bend over Michael in a *penchée* arabesque on pointe and be supported just by his lips. It was to the adagio of the Tchaikovsky Piano Concerto No. 1. I invited Mr. B. to look at the pas de deux, and he came in with Suzanne. He looked at the dance, and then he looked very weird. It ended with the *penchée* arabesque with the kiss. I thought it was a little obvious, but so is the Tchaikovsky music. Balanchine asked, "Where did you get that?" I said, "What?" "That. The pose." I said, "I don't know. Why?" He started muttering and just walked off. A couple of days later Pat Neary came up to me and said, "John, where did you get that *penchée* kiss thing?" I said, "Well, I made it up." She goes, "But you couldn't have made it up." And I said, "Well, I did make it up. What's the big deal about it?" Balanchine was very close to Pat and her mother—he would go over to dinner at the house—and he had evidently told her that he didn't know where I got it because it was the same thing that he had done in Russia when he began his Young Ballet. I said, "Oh, it couldn't be." Pat repeated that he said it was the same step, and it had completely unnerved him, that it had freaked him out.

When I left New York City Ballet, Balanchine didn't want me to stop dancing, even though I had started the company in L.A. Barbara Horgan would call me up and say, "Mr. B. wants to know if you're doing something next week? Can you come and do some *Rubies?*" "Of course." So I would run back. When he was dying, Barbara called me and said he was very ill and "If you want to see him, you should come back to New York." I got on a plane in a day. I was told by Barbara and others that he didn't recognize people at that point, and that he would go in and out of recognition. But he was fine to me. I brought one of my dancers from L.A., this really cute blonde, Ellen Bauer. She sat on his bed, he sang *Nutcracker* to us and was fine. Ellen was one of my principal dancers and a very bouncy, aggressive girl. I had in my pocket the scheduling for the next season in L.A.; we were doing about sixteen Balanchine ballets. I was telling him this, and Ellen was sitting on his bed. She was a little afraid. People were saying that in the hospital he could get fresh with the girls. But I said, "Ellen, I want you to go in there, sit on his bed, and kiss him on the cheek and behave yourself." She did. And he perked up. He just looked ecstatic to have a new little girl sitting there. I said, "Mr. B., we're doing every ballet of yours that I can think of doing this season. But you know, I can't figure out which ones to put together musically." I wanted to have something to talk to him about. I knew he felt isolated. He wasn't at the theater, and that was his whole life. And Ellen grabbed the paper out of my hand and asked, "What am I dancing? Am I doing *Serenade?* Oh, I'm not. What am I doing? Oh, I'm doing *Square Dance.* Okay." He looked at her, and his eyes got big, and he looked at me and he said, "Well, you know, dear, she's just like you." I said, "What?" And he said, "Greedy." He used to say that I was greedy because I danced everything. I replied, "Well, you put me in everything. If I'm greedy, you're greedy."

He grabbed the paper, and Ellen said, "Oh, yes, I love dancing your ballets, Mr. Balanchine. Oh, it's the best thing. Ever since I was a little girl, ever since I was twelve years old and John started teaching class, all I ever heard was sex and Balanchine, sex and Balanchine." I turned white. Sex and Balanchine, ohmyGod. Mr. B. looked at her. He couldn't believe what he was hearing. He goes, "What?" She said, "Well, you know, John'll tell dirty jokes in class, we get all these sexy jokes, and then he'll give all these fast *dégagés* and *tendus* and tell us about how you want things done. So all I've heard my whole life is sex and Balanchine." He looked at me, and I went oh-help-me. He said, "Well, you know, dear, next year it will be something else." He was talking about mortality and beginning to get a little morbid, but she just wouldn't let him. You know what she said? "Oh, no, it's always going to be sex and Balanchine." I loved that. He loved that.

Then we began talking about *The Nutcracker* because I did my own version of it. I said to him, "God, the pas de deux was the hardest thing. 'Flowers' and 'Snow' are hard enough to rechoreograph, but the pas de deux! Mr. B., how in God's name could I try to do it? I want to do a pas de deux, but it's nothing but a goddamn descending scale over and over." And he said, "No, dear, it's not." When he had that tone of voice, you knew that you couldn't argue with him. I said, "It's not?" He said, "No, it's not." I said, "Uh, what is it then?" He said, "I'll tell you, dear. You know what it is? It's this." And he proceeded to sing it. There he was, singing away, and he gets to the big climax and he stops singing and says, "And then you know what happens?" We went, "What?" We thought he was going to say a key change. And he starts singing it louder! His point was that it is not the same thing, it gets louder. We had a good time with him. Then when I left the hospital room I found I was shaking. It was obvious that he was not going to be around much longer.

I was making these fantasy plans about kidnapping him from the hospital and taking him to L.A. and putting him in the Beverly Wilshire. Pat Neary was having the same fantasies about taking him to Zurich. I felt terrible about him being in the hospital. I tried to talk him into setting up a private TV hookup so that he could have a TV camera in downstage right wing, where he always used to stand and have it hooked up, like a live broadcast, to his bed, so that he could feel he was standing in the wings. I heard that he used to call up the wings and want to talk to Karin von Aroldingen during the performance.

The next time I saw him was in April. He was very sick, but he recognized me. He couldn't talk. I said, "Hi, Mr. B., it's me." He looked at me and expressed himself with his eyes. I said, "Do you want me to go?" He sort of went "no" with his eyes. So I made small talk for about five minutes. Then I said, "Good-bye. I'll see you. We'll all see each other." I told him I loved him, but I didn't want to be maudlin in case he was really understanding me.

When you teach, it's hard unless you are the director of the company yourself. In Los Angeles my word was law because I was paying the bills. So I taught a very Balanchine class. I can't teach a Balanchine class because only Mr. B. could do that; I taught a very close second. But in Europe and in other places I modify the class, given the fact that they are only doing one or two Balanchine ballets in their repertory. I was in Caracas once and they were doing an all-Balanchine evening that I staged: *Serenade, Concerto Barocco, Allegro Brillante,* and *Apollo.* They wanted me to teach, and so I taught there every day for a month. That was a very Balanchine class. I started off in Monte Carlo with a pseudo-Balanchine class but after a month I was in full swing and the dancers were right with me, once they got over the initial idea that one can work fast and not hurt themselves.

But usually I work gradually because you can't go in and just go shotgun from the hip. That turns people off. The Balanchine style and technique are very important. To my mind, it's the highest development that we have yet of what classical ballet can do. It's the most refined use of classical ballet up to this point. No one else has been able to take the basic classical vocabulary and develop it without distorting it. He really didn't distort anything. He developed it to a fine level of technical prowess, cleanliness, and speed, and with Mr. B.'s ability to entertain the audience as well. Other schools—like the Russian school—can emphasize certain steps, certain tricks for the men, certain *port de bras* for the women. But it's a limited technique because it's only part of the whole vocabulary of dancing. I wish Balanchine had been allowed to work with Valentina Koslova. He would have been able to develop Valentina. He wanted to, he hired her. She's a Balanchine dancer from Russia. And perhaps Sylvie Guillem would have come to him to be trained. So what I try to do in the teaching is to give specific Balanchine exercises. I have a pretty good memory. Every now and then when I give something of Balanchine's that may be difficult I'll turn to the kids and say, "Look, I didn't invent this. This is tradition. This is the tradition of the twentieth century, and this is the tradition developed by George Balanchine, and if you can't dance this, then you can't dance his ballets. So if you can't do these things in class, there's no point in even trying to do *Theme and Variations* and some of the hard ones."

I have staged over twenty of his ballets over the years. I danced some forty-five roles in his ballets. Mr. B. still remains the guiding principle of my life.

Sally Leland called me to let me know he had died. My first thought was, "Thank God." Thank God he's out of that hospital and out of his body. The only person who's made me spiritual in any way has been Balanchine. He believed about the spirituality of everything, really. We'd talk about it. So I believe that he's really around. Even if he's not around, the thought that he is around is a guiding golden rule for me. When he would talk about Mozart being around or Tchaikovsky being around, I don't know if he meant that in the literal sense or if he meant that they are around because of what they were and they have to still be around because of their guidance, the rules of the game. This sounds metaphysical, but every now and then I get a little tap on the shoulder, and "Not bad, dear." I hear it.

RICHARD
TANNER

Born in Phoenix, Arizona, in 1948; studied with Sonya Tyven and Robert Lindgren in Phoenix and with Willam Christensen at the University of Utah. Tanner began choreographing dances at the university and studied at the School of American Ballet. He joined the New York City Ballet in 1971. He was appointed artistic director of the Denver Civic Ballet in 1972. In 1981 he became régisseur générale *at American Ballet Theatre at the invitation of Mikhail Baryshnikov. Beginning in 1984, Tanner began staging Balanchine's ballets across America and throughout Europe. From 1985 to 1989 he was associate artistic director of the Pennsylvania Ballet. He is known for many ballets of his own and in 1990 choreographed Mozart's* **Prague Symphony** *for the New York City Ballet.*

I CAME FROM ARIZONA WHERE I STUDIED WITH BOB LINDGREN AND SONYA TYVEN. Then I went to School of American Ballet. My parents weren't very happy about all of this and were screaming about my keeping up with regular school. We were Mormons, so I went to Utah to go to school and to dance with Ballet West. I was doing choreography there. One of my friends who had been in the New York City Ballet, Diane Bradshaw, said why didn't I bring an evening of my stuff out to Los Angeles where she lived? So I brought my dancers from Ballet West and she invited Mr. B. He said, "Why don't you come to New York?" So I went to New York in 1971 and joined the company as a dancer and as a choreographer. Balanchine was a great teacher. I took his classes, and I thought they were really weird. They were too short; he didn't give you *pliés.* But his classes were lessons in conception, in how to think about ballet. They were lessons in what steps are about. What Balanchine was doing was perfect for somebody like Suzanne Farrell, with those long legs, long tendons, and soft muscles. It was exactly what she needed.

Balanchine called himself a ballet master and saw choreography as only one part of a ballet master's work. He didn't see choreography as a separate matter. It was that old-fashioned way of looking at things. He felt that a ballet master taught classes, took rehearsals, choreographed, made programs, understood lighting, costumes, and scenery, and knew about the orchestra. He thought a ballet master did everything. As a result, he was always after me to do other kinds of work. After I had been in the company for about three years, he had me be Jerome Robbins's ballet master for about a year. He said, "Jerry needs somebody, and I think this would be good for you." I was choreographing, I was dancing, and in addition I worked with Jerry.

When I arrived in the company, Betty Cage, the executive manager, was still doing the subscription programs. She had been doing it for years with Mr. B., and they both thought it would be a good thing for me to learn. The New York City Ballet has a very complicated subscription series. They try not to repeat any ballets from a particular subscription series for two years. It's a matter of figuring out what ballet can go in and when. Making up the subscription programs was a time-consuming process but fascinating. You had to deal with what ballets were available; then the challenge was trying to make programs that Balanchine thought were good. You had to understand what he considered to be a good program. Balanchine had a lot of ideas about what made up an evening of ballet. He paid attention to absolutely everything: which dancers might be on, which dancers might be off, whether the ballets offered variety. He didn't like whole evenings that were just in practice clothes or whole evenings that had too many costumes and sets and not enough dancing. He also liked musical variety. He used to say,

"The whole evening is strings. What are you doing?" Of course, I'd never thought about anything like that. You couldn't begin with *Apollo,* do *Serenade,* and end with *Barocco.* He'd say, "This is dull and nobody else in the orchestra's playing, we're paying all these musicians, and it's dull to hear." The same thing with the size of the ballets. He'd say, *"La Source* and *Barocco* are the same size, essentially. If you're going to put *Barocco* on, then you should put on *Stars and Stripes* or *Who Cares?* or a huge ballet so that the audience can see how many people the company has." He'd say, "Mel doesn't have anything to dance," and "Suzanne has three things on this program, it's silly." It took years of listening to him and arguing in order to learn.

Balanchine had such a vast repertoire that he could mix ballets and worry about his mix. Because he didn't have that many full-length ballets, he considered every night a challenge. Balanchine taught me how to do the subscription programming the same way he taught people about dancing. I'd go into his office with my new set of programs. He would never say, "Why don't you do this?" or "Why don't you do that?" Instead, he'd go through the individual program I'd planned and point out what was wrong. "This one nobody's on in the whole evening. . . . The ballets are too small. . . . *In the Night* and *La Sonnambula* are dark ballets, the evening's too dark." It was the same way he taught ballet. He'd tell you what was wrong and just assume that when it was right you'd know it. I'd go away and revamp the programs. We'd meet again and he'd point out again, "Okay, this one's better. Here's what's wrong with this one." It was fascinating.

Sometimes I'd help out with the casting. He basically did the casting with Rosemary Dunleavy, so I'd help Rosemary prepare what was going to be shown to him, which ballets were on that night, everybody who did them, and sometimes I'd help out if Rosemary was busy. One of the first things I learned from Mr. B. is that casting does itself. So many people mistakenly feel that casting's a big deal. The casting is a political overview of the company that week. He used to say to me all the time, "I never get to pick who I want." And he didn't. That's a big misconception by certain reviewers—the Dance Police, we call them. (When dancers get a bad review from them we say, "Oh, I got a ticket!") The casting does itself in any ballet company. It's who needs what when. Very rarely do you get to say, "This dancer ought to be in this ballet. Let's go for it." The Dance Police think it happens all the time. They thought that Balanchine was sitting there saying, "Ah, let's put Darci Kistler in this. Let's put Darci in that." Of course he wanted to. He thought Darci was great. But it was hard to do sometimes. He had to satisfy Patty McBride. He had to satisfy Suzanne. Merrill Ashley had to have something. He was more aware of that than anybody because he had been doing it all his life. Many recognize what a great choreographer Balanchine was.

I'm not sure how many realize what an unbelievable director he was. He really knew how to run a ballet company. He'd keep most of the dancers happy most of the time. He could keep his public happy most of the time. He checked everything. He oversaw everything that went on in that house: who was there, who wasn't, who was lazy, who was ambitious, who worked and who didn't work, who got paid, how much, who was paid too much, who was underpaid. He'd check programs to see how the information was printed. He'd change it around if he didn't like it. He worked. He was there all the time. New York City Ballet is a really complicated big ballet company. You look at the Kirov and the Bolshoi and their rep is so simple. They do so few things. But City's continues to be huge, with large numbers of dancers dancing many kinds of ballets. He kept his eye on it. It was frightening what he knew of what was going on. He knew every day who was in the house and who wasn't. He knew who hung around. He liked people to hang around. If you don't happen to be on, why go home and watch TV? Hang out! Watch somebody dance. Learn something. He was always encouraging everybody to hang around, and they did to a degree more than I've seen in any other company. Most of those people practically lived in that house. And still do.

The 1972 Stravinsky Festival was an unbelievable accomplishment in putting on that many ballets and organizing their production. Balanchine did everything: he picked every piece of music, decided who would do what, gave the other choreographers first pick among the dancers. He'd take whoever was left and make a better ballet on them. In some cases, of course, he knew whom he wanted. He didn't make *Duo Concertant* (1972) or *Stravinsky Violin Concerto* (1972) on just anybody. But in some cases it was who happened to be available. He was an incredibly flexible man; he could make do. He used to joke that he was making variations in the hallways. And he did!

Symphony in Three Movements was an extremely difficult ballet for him. During the period when I was in the company, it was the hardest thing for him to choreograph. It took months, and they were torturous, traumatic rehearsals, with screaming and yelling. That was extremely unusual. There were sixteen corps girls who might be dancing at the same time as the five couples but have different counts. That took a long time.

He suggested music to me all the time. He would do that with everybody. He was always running around pimping all kinds of music. We all used to say to each other, "Does he like it? If he really likes it, why doesn't he do it himself?" But I felt that he couldn't do everything. There was a lot of music that he felt ought to be played in the theater or that he wanted heard or that he felt somebody should do.

I always felt that Balanchine's view was that, after himself, Jerry Robbins was the best choreographer in the world. He wanted Jerry there for a lot of reasons: his ballets enhanced the repertoire immeasurably, and they were unlike Balanchine's. They drew a different kind of audience and threw a different light on Balanchine's own ballets. I felt personally that at some point Balanchine would become jealous. Jerry always had such an immediate popular success. Jerry would put on a ballet, and the house would come down, people would scream, hanging off the first ring, and all the critics would write, "A masterpiece is born!" Then two seasons later the audience would get up and go have a drink when that one came on. Balanchine respected what Jerry could do. He had a lot of trouble with Jerry's neuroticism. Jerry continues to be extremely confusing, demanding, fussy, and I think that was really tiresome for Mr. B. It made so many in-house problems. Except in a few instances, Balanchine always stood up for Jerry. When somebody was screaming, "He's just impossible to work with, we can't," or dancers were going into the office and saying, "I just don't want to be in his ballets anymore," Balanchine would calm them down, tell them that they didn't understand how good being in Jerry's ballets was for their careers, what they were learning, and the public perception of their dancing.

By and large, Mr. B. was the most gentle, kind person. He didn't like to fight with people. He didn't like to be rude to people. Once in a while he'd have to. All the staff were up there on the fourth floor. His office was in the corner, we all had little offices, and you could hear a lot, too much. Once in a while he'd have horrible screaming and yelling fights with dancers. But I always felt they provoked him. He just wouldn't be rude unless you pushed him over the brink. Like anybody, he'd put his foot down and say, "No, you're not going to get your way." But it was rare. For the most part, New York City Ballet continues to be a calm, polite, easygoing place, for all the pressure that all those people are under.

Balanchine's professional calm was pervasive. It permeated the entire house. He created an atmosphere of professionalism and concentration on what you were doing and a work ethic that was down-home and Western: "Just do it." In other ballet companies there's so much temperament, people throwing scenes. But not at New York City Ballet. When people realize that kind of behavior isn't tolerated, nobody thinks it's glamorous or interesting.

It started from the top. Balanchine didn't act like a big star or a great genius. He acted as a ballet master, a working person who came in and did his job. He didn't act grand or egotistical. From him the attitude seeped down to the principals. In a ballet company that's who all the dancers look up to. They watch the principals.

Some people say that Balanchine only liked "yes" people around him. But I always had enormous respect for the people he had working for him.

Ronnie Bates was very good at what he did and really loyal to Balanchine. Balanchine has been dead for years, but Barbara Horgan still works full time on his behalf. Betty Cage was an unbelievable person in what she accomplished. Balanchine had enormous respect for her. He'd go to Betty and say, "Should we do this? Can we do this? I'd like this. Is it stupid? Is it feasible?" They had adjoining offices. Her door was open all day; she practically lived in the theater.

Betty Cage helped the New York City Ballet become what it is today. I feel that it was because of Betty that the company has become such a stable institution financially. For the dancers, Betty was a mother confessor, Company Mama. If you had a big problem, you went to Betty and somehow she'd get you out of it. And Betty was brilliant with the unions and dealing with corporate people on the board. This woman was a real negotiator. She was so quiet. She'd be doing a crossword puzzle while dramas were going on. She never got ruffled. I never heard Betty scream at anyone ever, although people would go in there and yell at her. She basically did what she did selflessly. She devoted her entire career to building the New York City Ballet, and it is as successful and as stable as it is today because of her.

By the time I arrived in the company, Lincoln Kirstein had a very strange role. He felt exiled to the School, where he had an office. I'd overhear him say things to Balanchine like, "I never see you."

I was in the company when Baryshnikov joined. I didn't think the collaboration worked awfully well, but it wasn't bad. Baryshnikov was fabulous. He's the greatest dancer alive. Misha was surrounded by a lot of people who were not happy he was at N.Y.C.B. Misha had enormous powers of concentration, but I felt he was hampered by all this extraneous advice: "A star like you shouldn't be working for a salary like that" and "How dare they list you with the rest of the dancers?" Misha's a very bright person, and he learned so much from Balanchine. He was like a sponge. He absorbed as much as he could while he was there.

Balanchine adored Misha. He thought he was wonderful, and he loved him. I think he liked him better in his ballets than anyone else did. He loved watching him dance. He loved having him in his ballets. He had Misha to dinner more than any other male dancer in the company. Very rarely did he invite people over to his apartment or out to dinner. I think it was like a father-son thing. Misha's joining the company was Balanchine's idea. Balanchine called him. I was one of the dancers who were friendly with Misha. I'd go out with him and I saw him with Mr. B. a lot. I never saw anything complicated. I saw complicated situations with Edward Villella. I think it was clear that Balanchine was jealous of Eddie's fame. I think with Eddie it was some weird kind of love-hate thing. But I didn't see it with Misha at all, not in any rehearsals, not in any of the things he said to him that I heard or that Misha would say to me that he said.

I think when Misha joined A.B.T. as artistic director in 1981 Mr. B. was disappointed but he also thought it was good for American Ballet Theatre. Baryshnikov invited me to come with him, so I left City Ballet. I was good at my work, I knew I was good, and they all thought I was good. Then I left Ballet Theatre and began to free-lance as a choreographer. One day Barbara Horgan needed to have *Bourrée Fantasque* mounted in Nancy, France. I knew the ballet, went to Nancy, had a great time. It was easy and was fun to do. Barbara then sent me to other places. The dancers there just ate Balanchine's works up. It's like food. They feel so enriched. Wherever you go, the dancers want to be in the Balanchine ballet you're setting. They're all enthusiastic and eager when you're having rehearsals. In addition, every time I do one, I feel like I'm paying the old man back a little. I feel like I'm doing something for him for a change, after he did so much for me. And I've never set a Balanchine ballet for some reason without thinking about Betty, especially the Bizet *Symphony in C.* She owns the Bizet. It's hers. So I don't feel like I'm just paying Balanchine back. I feel like I'm paying Barbara back and Betty back and Eddie Bigelow back and Ronnie Bates back. Those people were unbelievable to me. I was young. It was like a second family.

MERRILL

ASHLEY

Born in St. Paul, Minnesota, in 1950; trained at the School of American Ballet; joined the New York City Ballet in 1966. She danced many roles in the Balanchine repertory, including Square Dance, Divertimento No. 15, *Sanguinic in* The Four Temperaments, Symphony in C, Tchaikovsky Concerto No. 2, *and the* Theme and Variations *from* Tchaikovsky Suite No. 3. *Balanchine created roles for her in* Cortège Hongrois, Coppélia, Ballo della Regina, *and* Ballade. *She published* Dancing for Balanchine *in 1984. Ashley also distinguished herself in Peter Martins's* Barber Violin Concerto *for the American Music Festival at New York City Ballet.*

BALANCHINE IS STILL THE DETERMINING FACTOR IN MY PROFESSIONAL LIFE. I DON'T FEEL he's a figure of history. It's as if it were yesterday as far as I'm concerned. His principles, everything he instilled in me, his patterns of work for the company, the way the company is run—those habits are still present and important. I still talk about him in the present tense. I catch myself, and I can't believe I'm doing it years after his death. I'll see things and I'll think, "Well, he'd be saying this, you know." I think about him in class, no matter who is teaching it.

As time goes on, the dancers at New York City Ballet may understand less and less why things are done the Balanchine way. At the moment there are enough people who worked with Balanchine and who know why we approach things in a certain way—for example, now people just accept that you are not going to have weeks and weeks to learn a role. You are going to have a few days. It's going to be the last minute. Maybe it's not the way you get the best performance at first. But there's another kind of challenge here. It is very spontaneous, it's not going to be an overrehearsed, dull performance. Anyone coming in from outside who hasn't been through that initiation of being thrown on in the corps all the time is going to be shocked by the approach. I don't think that will change. We'll maintain it with the vast repertoire and the limited rehearsal time. We're not going to have casting months ahead so that you can rehearse months ahead. It will never happen.

When Balanchine would throw you on, there was usually a real need. He wasn't just trying to test you. Sometimes I think Balanchine just didn't want to sit down and do the casting. Sometimes the casting would be so late, and Balanchine would think, "Well, it's time to give So-and-so a chance." Then, because the casting announcement had gone up late, there would be that much less time for the dancer to prepare, and that didn't bother Balanchine. He felt, "Well, let's see what they are made of." He kept the limited time in mind if the dancer made a mess of it: "Well, maybe they need more time, let's give them more performances," or "Let's wait." He would judge it individually.

After a performance Balanchine would often not say a word. This wasn't necessarily deadly, but it wasn't necessarily good, either. After all, the individual performance was just a small piece in a big puzzle for the dancer. I think Balanchine sometimes felt that, if he made a statement, too much weight would be given to it. "You did a good job." "Oh, I'm great! Oh, good, I don't have to work anymore." On the other hand, a little bit of praise could often spur somebody on. It's hard to judge. But eventually you began to get a feeling of what his impression of you was, of what kind of job you were doing. But it took a lot of piecing the puzzle together yourself. How did he look at you? How much attention did he pay to you? How often were you cast? Who did he cast you with? How were the other dancers at your level? Sometimes Balanchine himself came to the wrong conclusions.

I never spoke to Balanchine about dancing the classics—*The Sleeping Beauty*, for example—outside the company. I think he was always afraid that his ballerinas were going to go off and do *Giselle* and *Swan Lake*. My impression was that, if you started talking about it, then he felt that you were turning your back on him, and I certainly wasn't going to turn my back on him. I kept hearing toward the end that he was interested in doing *The Sleeping Beauty* himself but that he didn't have the right facilities. As far as Balanchine's own *Swan Lake* was concerned, he really confused me a lot when I first did it. He was very involved in my first performances. He kept saying, "Don't act. No acting at all. Don't look at your partner. Don't do anything. Don't pay any attention to him. You just stand there with him to the end of the ballet. In the old days people never got close. You must just stand there." I had trouble accepting that. I felt that there was an emotion there, and I couldn't just stand there blankly and let the corps run around me. It just didn't make sense to me. My conclusion in retrospect is that he just didn't want it to go overboard. Especially with someone young, he wanted to minimize the acting. He wanted it to come through the movement. Too many dancers go for the facial expressions and elaborate arms, and he wanted it simple. Tchaikovsky's music just seems to pull emotion out of me, anyway. I find myself sometimes in performance thinking, "God, now have I overdone it?" because I'm certainly freer now than when I first did it. I'd like to give the complete *Swan Lake* a try. I'm very blessed with my Balanchine repertoire. There are very few of his ballets I feel I can do without.

When the company revived *Gounod Symphony*, I felt, "If only he were here." There are so many details I just want to see Mr. B. demonstrate. If only he could show me. I just know if he saw me dance the ballet he'd have the comment that would crystallize it in my mind, and then I'd know which way to go. I felt that very much with the pas de deux in *Gounod*. I also felt that very strongly in *The Firebird*. It was interesting that when Ann Bell was putting together her Balanchine film she showed me a clip of Maria Tallchief doing the *Berceuse*. Ann asked me for help because the films were without music and she was trying to set the clips to music. I saw the *Berceuse* footage and I said, "My God. Can I watch this several times, please?" Watching Maria do it just crystallized everything, and I felt that everything was so simple—very powerful, but so simple. It gave me a certain confidence that my approach was valid and right, and I really learned from watching the clip. I feel that it's helpful to see Tallchief over and over again in whatever I can. This is true despite the fact that the *Berceuse* was done in a television studio and she had no room. But I kept feeling that there were certain things that I had been taught that just didn't seem right to me. After all, choreography can change because there's a very clear difference between certain generations. Each is right in its own way, but which should be done and which should be taught? Some companies have old Balanchine versions, and they've had them for ten or fifteen years. A later dancer comes in and looks at the productions and says, "What is this?" There are technical things that can be bettered, but it's just an older version. It's hard to reconcile all of that and decide what approach to take. Often the people who do the choosing don't have the authority or knowledge to make an educated decision.

Ballet has been handed down for so many years from person to person. Now we have video. It's wonderful to have records like that but some people take them as the gospel and just look at a video to learn a ballet and pass it on to the next generation, thereby avoiding using the knowledge of dancers who actually worked with Mr. B. The direct line of information is broken. I don't think that is good. Perhaps sometimes there isn't a dancer available who worked with Mr. B. for a particular ballet, so you do the best you can. But right now there are still a lot of persons around who worked with Mr. B. in all of his ballets. It does perplex me why they are not consultants. You can't call in everybody who did the role. If somebody new is going to dance *Theme and Variations* at New York City Ballet this season, then Kyra Nichols or I should teach the role. It shouldn't just be somebody who's watched a video. After all, there are things that perhaps we don't do in a particular performance. Maybe we were injured. But we know what it should be, and we know what Balanchine asked for. No matter what version it is, they were his words, his wishes, at some point in time. Why just throw that away? There are so many little details that can cause the steps to take on a whole new flavor. That knowledge is still alive with people right now. It doesn't get across and it's not always welcomed. You hold back more and more. When people ask for help, I give it, and sometimes when I can't bear to hold my knowledge anymore I give it and usually individual dancers appreciate it. If you suddenly say it should be some other way or that they are not doing enough of something in a major rehearsal, that can create trouble.

The same is true with foreign productions, like the *Theme and Variations* and *Scotch Symphony* at the Kirov. If you send in a different ballet mistress to check up on a production after it's been mounted, the dancers will hear a different teacher say the same thing in a different way. Suddenly it may make sense or it may strike somebody freshly. We all tend to focus on certain things more than others. One ballet mistress will worry about musicality. Another will worry about technique, another about patterns and energies.

The 1972 Russian tour was really tough, and the audiences for the most part didn't know what they were seeing. They just didn't know how to react. It wasn't at all what they envisioned ballet to be, and they didn't get all the fireworks they are used to. In Tbilisi, where the Balanchines come from, the audience went wild. They loved anything and everything we did. They wanted to celebrate for Balanchine and for his brother, too. But the reaction needn't have been delivered. It really worked, and the reaction wasn't false at all. I don't think Balanchine really liked being in Soviet Russia. He was tolerating it.

Today, dancers approach their career so much more as a job. People love to dance, but there was something about Balanchine's belief in ballet—some spirit that he could instill in you about ballet. Today, dancers find a way to do something new, to be technically strong, to enjoy themselves and be interesting onstage. But there's something missing. Very few people have that kind of spirit. Ballet to me is still something greater than I am. Sometimes I feel like I'm talking about a religion. But ballet is something that must be highly respected, treated with great care and not mistreated. Balanchine gave that feeling to all of us, and I feel it is getting lost.

I don't think that Balanchine wanted to talk to us about such things in words. Perhaps he had some concrete thoughts and feelings about it, but I don't think he wanted to impose that on anyone. He wanted to give that general feeling: it's a noble pursuit, honorable and dignified. You yourself have to be that way. You have to treat the theater and all of the elements that make a ballet the same way. By doing that, you learn the greater meanings of some of these things. It will come through your own personal view.

Balanchine was not imposing but there were certain rules, a certain framework, that he did insist on. With this huge picture frame he gave you, you put what you wanted within it. You put yourself in it. You know that, given certain guidelines, you become yourself. Balanchine wanted individuals. It seems to strike many people when they look at his dancers that they are so unlike one another. It always amazes me that people can think we're all the same and that we fit into this little tiny box and that we are all mechanical dolls who move exactly the same way. Nothing is further from the truth. That was what intrigued him. There was a *battement tendu* that he wanted done in a certain way: the look of the leg, the energy, how the body was attached to it. Somehow, everyone doing a correct *battement tendu* still looks different. He wanted that individuality. Then you add the whole body moving and the personality behind it. There's no way that we can be anything but different from one another. And there was, on the other hand, the greater outline that we had to fit into. That is a paradox.

There were dancers whom Balanchine confused because he would give them all his attention. He would see something there and try to cultivate it, bring it out for weeks, months, or years. And then suddenly he would just give up. He saw that it wasn't going to happen, or they weren't committed to it. Why was he going to spend all that energy on something that wasn't working when there were many others he could work with? Perhaps when you are the one who's getting such attention you don't have the ultimate commitment. Then you may not understand if you're dropped. If your perceptions are a little cockeyed, you become bitter, fall apart, or are crushed with disappointment. If Balanchine saw it was not working after a long effort, he wasn't going to waste his time anymore.

After a performance Balanchine would sometimes keep a dancer onstage for forty-five minutes after everyone else had gone home. If he was in the mood, he would coach you. We waited for those days when he would feel so inspired or inclined to spend that much time with you, even if he was displeased. At least that's the way I felt. I would rather have him displeased and yet interested and feeling I could get it than just giving up and going home.

DANIEL

DUELL

Born in 1952 in Rochester, New York; studied with Hermine and Josephine Schwarz and David McLain in Dayton, Ohio; received a Ford Foundation scholarship to study full time in New York at the School of American Ballet. Joined the New York City Ballet in 1972, where he became a principal dancer in 1979. His repertoire included roles in Balanchine's Coppélia, Harlequinade, Agon, Symphony in C, Donizetti Variations, Stars and Stripes, The Four Temperaments, Danses Concertantes, Brahms-Schoenberg Quartet, *and* Chaconne. *Balanchine added a new finale to* Emeralds *for Duell—a trio for three men. Duell began choreographing in 1980 and his ballets have been performed by the Harkness Dance Theater, Ballet Hispanico of New York, and as part of the choreography projects of the School of American Ballet and Jacob's Pillow Dance Festival. An accomplished classical musician, Duell is artistic director of Ballet Chicago.*

I Remember Balanchine

MY INVOLVEMENT WITH BALLET BEGAN AT AGE ELEVEN IN DAYTON, OHIO, WHERE I spent six years in initial training. My parents had talked me into it. That was around the start of the Ford Foundation scholarship program nationwide, when funds were given to City Ballet and the School of American Ballet to develop talent and bring it to New York. My teachers, Josephine and Hermine Schwarz, had developed their own scholarship program in Dayton and asked a bunch of guys to come and audition. At that time I thought, "Rats, I got hooked into this because my sisters take ballet at the Schwarz school already." But the Schwarzes had engaged a wonderful teacher named David McLain to teach the men as part of the scholarship program. So my dad suggested, "Why don't you go and just try?" In gymnastics class when I could do things like straighten my knees and point my toes, they all asked, "Where have you been taking gymnastics?" I said, "Nowhere, it's ballet." Ballet helped in wrestling too because I was flexible enough to get out of holds. So those things helped me to love it. But what really got me going on my own was the first time I had a serious performance with the local ballet company. It was Violette Verdy who came and collected me, my brother Joseph, and a couple of girls and got us to the School of American Ballet. I took a summer course, and the School said immediately, "Why don't you stay as a scholarship student year round?" I did so, and then three years later I got into the company, having had the good fortune to study intensively with Stanley Williams, along with André Eglevsky, Richard Rapp, Tumkovsky, and Danilova.

In company class, Balanchine was famous for saying to dancers who had just arrived in New York City Ballet, "Where did you learn this, dear?" The dancer would be at a loss because he knew his answer would name teachers whom Balanchine himself had chosen for the School. I think he enjoyed doing this. The point was to make us understand that he would take us beyond what we had been taught in his School.

Lincoln Kirstein mentioned to me once that Balanchine abhorred the idea of a syllabus, and I could see something of that in his company class. He didn't want an organized doctrine that others would misinterpret. He needed to hand it down personally. He would consult with his teachers at the School and get them to offer in their own way what he wanted taught, but he would never entrust this to a written system or codification.

Balanchine's artistic vision is what forms the basis for training in the School. His approach to training was guided more by his choreography than by a way to train the body, although the training of the body became incorporated into the approach. Balanchine was always one for moving expressively and making movements appear musical by their look, and these things were taught in the School. For example, every teacher at the School says you have to lift the elbow, lift the wrist, drop the elbow, drop the wrist, then pick up the arm just so. Training was guided by Balanchine's vision, and he informed all of the teachers of it. Still, each teacher was permitted his own style, his or her individuality.

The same was true of uniformity in the corps de ballet. Balanchine was interested in the individuality of the corps member. Let's suppose that we're watching Patty McBride and Gelsey Kirkland dancing in the back line of the corps. . . . Balanchine would want to see what each could do in that back line rather than see them look like one another. For him, that was true for all dancers.

Balanchine would advise us on how to hold our heads. To the men he once said, "Like *contrapposto* painting. In *contrapposto* painting you never see a face straight on. It's always at an angle." To the girls he would say to tilt their cheeks as if to receive a kiss. The *contrapposto* "angle" is designed to show bone structure and to give some interest to positions facing straight front.

And he had a "thing" about English training. I remember him talking to a dancer who had trained with an English teacher in New York. He said, "But it's so English. Very proper, exactly right, and not very interesting. It's like having tea in England—you have to sit down very proper, and they bring you tea in a tiny little cup, and a tiny little spoon, and a big lump of sugar; you don't know how it's going to get in the cup. You drop it in there, you pick up the tiny little spoon, and you stir. But only once. You aren't allowed to do it more than once. You put the little spoon down, and then you sip, but you can only take a *tiny* sip. That's English. Not me. In Russia we have bread in one hand and a big bowl of soup in the other." He loved to talk in imagery that way, to get us to understand how he thought of things.

Sometimes in class he would concentrate on only one or two values, to the point of exhaustion. We had this terrifying routine in which we'd start with very quick *pliés* and very quick *tendus,* lots and lots of them. My brother described it as being "like a bicycle pump in your thigh." On our own, we would start off warming up nice and easy, doing stretch and *plié.* It feels great. But Balanchine would say, "Class is not therapy." So instead of nice, slow *tendus,* one or two in each direction, we would do sixteen in each direction. Then we would turn around and do it to the left, and then immediately start over, faster and faster. Then we would do *jetés,* finishing with sixty-four in first position. By that time our legs were aching. The whole purpose was to get our blood boiling, no excuses, no indulgence. He would always go around and say, "Um, you don't have to do it if you don't want to. If you're old or sick or tired or you don't like . . ." Everybody did it.

He had a way of gathering loyalty by not demanding it. You can't enforce loyalty. You *can* respond to what people want to do and capitalize on those things. Our individual commitment was exposed; what we didn't want to do showed because he didn't try to *make* us want it. We had to do that ourselves. He did have occasional temperamental explosions, always upon extreme provocation. He was authoritarian, demanding great discipline, but not punitive. He got his results by finding positive ways to get us to go further than we thought we could possibly go. If you could see his intent, most of the time most of us committed to it. If one didn't, then eventually you'd either leave the company or accept a compromised standing.

One of the first major things I did was the Sanguinic section of *The Four Temperaments* (1946). Tony Blum, who was to dance it, was injured. I had been understudying it, and Balanchine came up to me and said, "You know, we have this performance on Sunday, and I think Blum cannot do it. Can you do?" I said, "Yeah, yeah, sure I can do." He said okay. There were only two or three days to work on it, and I think Merrill Ashley and I got one stage rehearsal with him. I remember thinking, "On short notice, how could this guy who was so impossibly demanding in class leave you with such a feeling of being trusted before a performance?" He would be very specific about basic stylistic elements, qualities of movement that were right for his choreographic design, but he never imposed on your personal artistry.

He didn't like to name steps because everybody has an already formed idea of what a step is. He wanted to avoid having such formed ideas imposed on his expressive design. Named steps are like notes on a page of musical composition. A note is only the translating symbol from what a composer hears to what an interpreter is to do; thus, there is much more in that little note than its appearance. An interpreter has to look at notes and turn them into music, just as a dancer has to turn named steps into dance. Balanchine didn't like to nail down anything in so many words. There are always dancers who say, with the best of intent, "I know exactly what it is forever because Mr. B. told me." But, with Balanchine, there was nothing "forever" because his work was ongoing.

In the Sanguinic section of *The Four Temperaments,* there's a section where I'm supposed to leap into the air and do these furious beats and land with my legs in open position, and beat again and land again with them in a closed position. Well, I was trying to do the most beautiful, classical, perfect landing in fifth position that I could muster. And Balanchine said, "That's very good. Very pretty. So pretty, it's going to ruin my ballet! We have to see something else." I think he meant that in this neoclassical ballet the idea was to make it arresting or interesting, not just pretty. He didn't want you to indulge in what you were feeling, which is a private thing, because what we are doing is designed to *evoke* feeling *from* the audience. They are not sup-

574

posed to be involved with what *we* are actually feeling. He would say, "Everything we do, it's manufactured. 'Artistic' comes from 'artifice'; it's man-made." Everything we do with our bodies from the very beginning to the end is man-made. We aren't born ballet dancers; it takes twenty years to become one.

Balanchine thought metaphorically many times. That is, he had his own images that were the basis of what he was choreographing. What came across to me in the gestures beginning Apollo's second variation was his suggestion of his dominion over the heavens and the earth. The winglike *port de bras* connotes Apollo's godly power of flight. The leaps, turns, and control in Apollo's second variation are all expressions of flight and power. It's Balanchine's stylization; he was constantly translating images into movement. Those images were only for him (and for those of us who were fortunate enough to witness his rehearsals) to know. Everybody else sees the effect without having to know what it was that made it.

Balanchine's ability to demonstrate what he wanted was amazing. He would show us variations. He would show us how to partner. He would indicate the steps, show us his way of making movement expressive and understood, particularly in how it fit the music. Rhythm was extremely important for Balanchine, and he himself was so rhythmically accurate it was amazing. He had a gift for elucidating syncopation. He could show enough in rehearsals to make his point without doing the steps "full out." For example, in *Apollo* (1928) he would say that the man jumps as if he's flying and then lands. He would do the jump without doing the beats, but he would indicate clearly and you'd see exactly what he meant. He could get the feeling, the essence of the movement quality, by demonstrating with his arms and his upper body without doing the whole step. You would understand the expressive intent. He'd leave you with the feeling that you could never dance it as beautifully as he did.

WILLIAM G.

HAMILTON, M.D.

Dr. William Hamilton was Balanchine's orthopedic consultant for New York City Ballet, a position he has occupied with the company since 1974. Born in Oklahoma in 1932, he is a graduate of Princeton University and took his premed studies at the University of Wisconsin. His medical training was at Columbia University College of Physicians and Surgeons, and his internship and residency were taken at Roosevelt Hospital and the New York Orthopaedic Hospital in New York. He was a senior fellow in children's orthopedics at the Newington Children's Hospital in Connecticut. Dr. Hamilton has been orthopedic surgeon to the School of American Ballet since 1974 and to American Ballet Theatre since 1982. He serves as orthopedic consultant to many dance companies, including the Joffrey Ballet, the Dance Theater of Harlem, the Pennsylvania Ballet, as well as various Broadway musicals.

BALANCHINE WAS A GENIUS IN HIS OWN FIELD, BUT THERE WERE SO MANY DIFFERENT dimensions to him that everyone found him fascinating in different ways. By 1973 at the New York City Ballet, Dr. Mel Kiddon, who had been their physician, was getting on. Instead of replacing him with another general practitioner, Balanchine wanted someone more interested in sports. After all, most of the dancers' problems are sports-related. I met Balanchine through Michael Arshansky, director of makeup at the N.Y.C.B. for more than thirty years, and I went up to the New York State Theater and talked with him and Edward Bigelow. Balanchine told me what he had in mind, and we decided to begin on a trial basis for six months. It worked so well that six months went by without noticing, and I continued to do it. That was seventeen years ago.

I realized that I knew about sports medicine and athletic injuries but I didn't know very much about ballet. I lived across the street from Balanchine. Almost every weekend I went over to the New York State Theater for his class. I would sit and watch. I had to learn the vocabulary and the technique. With total immersion you can pick it up. That's one of the major shortcomings today with doctors who want to treat dancers. They don't take time to understand exactly what's going on and the fine points of technique. Purely by accident, I was working for Balanchine during his golden years.

I was not Balanchine's medical doctor but, because I came to know him well, in a sense I was his doctor. In late 1982 he fell at home and broke some ribs and a wrist. I had to take him into Roosevelt Hospital just prior to Thanksgiving. We didn't know it at the time but he never left the hospital. I went to see him every day during the whole period when he was wasting away, and I couldn't do anything about it, nor could the other doctors. We were desperately afraid that maybe we had missed something that might have been treatable. As it turned out, we didn't. Even had there been a diagnosis before he died, we couldn't have saved him. The saddest thing of all was to watch him drift away slowly and not to be able to do anything about it. In the beginning, his hospitalization was a cheerful, temporary thing. Everybody was optimistic that he would soon be home. But on his birthday in January they had a big party in his room. Baryshnikov sent a limousine to a Georgian restaurant in Brooklyn and picked up a huge Georgian feast and brought it all back for Mr. B. and his close friends—Karin von Aroldingen, Suzanne Farrell, and Jacques d'Amboise. And it was a disaster.

There had been many wonderful parties at his home. Every Russian Easter, he'd give a big one. I remember twice when Baryshnikov and Jessica Lange were there. It was just a marvelous time. Everybody tried to recreate this on his seventy-ninth birthday in the hospital. For the first fifteen minutes or so, the old excitement was there, but then he just couldn't handle it. That's when everybody realized he really wasn't going to make it.

Balanchine cared a great deal for his dancers as far as their health went. He did want to be in charge, though. He always was the puppeteer who wanted to pull the strings. That was the way it worked. But he was concerned about them. I think that's why he brought me in; he wanted them taken care of.

By the late 1970s the company had gotten fairly large and there really was no in-house medical care provided. I was available for injuries, but otherwise the dancers drifted off to various chiropractors and health practitioners and massage therapists. Everybody was on his own. It occurred to me that all the professional sports, even a professional basketball team with fifteen players, have their own therapists and trainers. I said, "Well, why shouldn't a professional dance company have the same thing?" I approached Mr. B. with that idea. I was interested in setting up an in-house therapy and training system. He thought about it, and he said yes but he had misgivings. He was afraid of a sort of Parkinson's law—that if some sort of therapist was there virtually everybody would start going to him for massage whether they felt good or not. He said, "This should be for people who are injured. If they want a massage, then they can go get a massage. I don't want it to be like A.B.T., where they have a company masseur." I said, "Fine, I agree with that." So he said, "Well, we'll try and see how we like it." The program turned out to be successful not only for treatment but for prevention.

Compared to many sports, ballet is really very safe. Major injuries are rare in ballet compared to football and contact sports. Whether ballet ruins the body from overuse is something we really don't know. For instance, it's our impression that many older ballerinas tend to develop arthritis of the hip. Is that related to the extreme turnout or not? We don't have any hard data about that. We are now accumulating such data. We plan shortly to do a mailing to the alumnae of both the New York City Ballet and A.B.T. and ask them if they developed arthritis of the hip later, have had any injuries specifically while they were dancing, or had arthritis of the hip in the family. The genetic predisposition is something people often ignore. Someone may say that Suzanne Farrell ruined her hips dancing the Balanchine technique, but what is not mentioned is that her father has had two hip replacements. She may have been genetically programmed to get arthritis of the hip whether she had been a dancer or not. We don't really have an answer, and the first step is to do a mailing and try to get an idea of the percentage of dancers who develop arthritis of the hip and then go to the National Institutes of Health and see what the incidence of such a condition is in the American public. Then we could see if the incidence is in fact higher in dancers or not. Studies like this need to be done because otherwise we're simply dealing with impressions which really don't hold up. There's a great expression in medicine, especially in surgery: "Nothing ruins your results like follow-up studies." You may think you've got good results, but until you have your long-term results, you don't really know how good they are.

We don't know, for instance, whether dancing is fundamentally bad for the skeleton or not. There are many older dancers who are in superb shape. And there are many who have arthritis of the hip. But arthritis of the hip is common in the American public. I do not know people who were specifically ruined by dancing under Mr. B. Of course, he was trying to push the art form to the brink. He wanted to see just how far he could go. In that sense what he was trying to find out was just how much the bodies of his dancers could hold up to, what were the limits, the boundaries. That was typical of him to want to know. Certainly it was difficult in many ways on the dancers.

I've always felt that ballet needs a specific type of body. If you have that body, I don't think it's very injurious. If you don't, then it can be hurt. That's why the S.A.B. process of weeding out students is so important—the survival of the fittest that begins at age eight, the children's first division. There's a continuous selection process through the whole career, weeding out the ones who do not have the turnout or the feet or the musicality or the gumption. After the selection process, what you are left with at age twenty is the tip of a very big pyramid. In a sense you've got a thoroughbred racehorse that's highly tuned for this one particular weird art form. Where you get into trouble is if someone manages to elude the selection process and gets in with the wrong body. The excuse might be "I love it so much, I can do it." Or perhaps there's a ballet mother who insists. Those people are at real risk.

My wife, Linda Hamilton, has written on the eating disorders dancers may encounter. In a study she made she found that the people who are at high risk are the ones who are genetically heavy. If you are genetically programmed to be heavy, then the caloric expenditure of the dancing, no matter how vigorous, is not going to be enough to keep you thin, and so you're going to resort to a deviant eating behavior in order to maintain the thinness that's necessary; whereas, if you are genetically thin, then you won't have trouble. You will be able to stay thin without having to resort to bulimia and anorexia nervosa in order to stay thin in your career. This is part of ballet's Darwinism, too, selecting the right person. The right person with the right body can dance Balanchine ballet safely. Gelsey Kirkland's book was sensationalistic, from a disturbed author.

Balanchine had a vision and, like all great artists, he was uncompromising. And he had it right up to the very end. His neurological deterioration resembled going back to the womb. It broke me up completely about a month before he died. There was a certain point when he walked like a toddler, and then he walked like a one-year-old, and then he couldn't walk anymore. When he finally died, he was curled up in bed in the fetal position. It was as if he were going backward out of the world. Many neurological disorders are like that. He watched a lot of television for a while, and then his eyes went bad and he went back to WQXR, the classical music station, which he listened to all the time. In the hospital he would listen to it every morning, and I would go in to see if he was all right. He was in the corner room of the top floor. I'll never forget that room. One morning I went in to see him. Although he knew me very well, he looked through me to the horizon. There was beautiful music on the radio, but it was almost as if I wasn't there. I just waited. Then he saw me and said, "Oh, good morning. You know, I still hear beautiful music and see people doing things, but it's all over." Up until the very end he was seeing a pas de deux in his mind. I'd ask him, "How do you do all this stuff?" And he'd say, "Oh, it's really very easy. I hear music, and I see people doing things, and I just go in the studio and I have them do what I'd seen them do in my mind." He would point up and say, "He tells me." After Balanchine had his open-heart surgery in 1978, everybody was waiting to see if he would still be creative. I used to drop in at that period every morning at his apartment. He got up very early. No matter what time I arrived, he was already up and had his breakfast. He would sit there in the morning in his underwear with WQXR on, ironing his laundry.

He had little icons and candles in his room. Every day I would go in and chew the fat with him. "How are you feeling today?" "Fine." "Do you need anything?" "No, I'm okay." Eddie Bigelow was up there too. One morning I went in there and everything had changed. The radio was on, but the volume was turned way down, the ironing board was out and the ironing was there but there was no ironing going on. There was sheet music all over his apartment. He was running around. Every flat surface in the apartment had music on it. He was moving from one pile to the other and was obviously totally absorbed. He was a bit abrupt with me. He was never really abrupt, but he sort of looked up and said, "Oh, hello." It was obvious that I was intruding. I said, "Are you okay?" He said yes. Before I left, I took a peek at the music: it was *Davidsbündlertänze*. One day he was ironing laundry, and the next day the creative juices were flowing.

I think he knew Schumann's life backward and forward. Later he talked about how Schumann went crazy. It was obvious to me that he knew a great deal about the composer. Of course, the ballet *Davidsbündlertänze* is really about Balanchine, not Schumann. When the hero in the ballet faded off, that was Balanchine, not Schumann. Or maybe it was, but it was as much Balanchine as Schumann. I think that ballet was Balanchine's swan song, his good-bye. When the dancers faded back into the garden, that was Mr. B.

Sometimes he would talk about his youth. I remember one time he talked about how lonely he was when he was left in St. Petersburg so young and how terribly he missed his mother and how he was very homesick. He was eight at the time, and it was difficult for him. He missed his mother's cooking, and he loved to cook. That was his legend. I used to stay with him in the summer at his country house in Saratoga. He and Eddie Bigelow and I would cook meals and make homemade ice cream. One of the best days I ever spent with him was a Monday—a dark night for the company—and it was rainy. We spent the whole day in the kitchen making Ukrainian borscht and talking about food. He talked about how good his mother's cooking was and how that's where he got so interested in cooking. Of all his early experiences, the thing that he mentioned to me most was missing his mother. He also talked about the selection process at the Maryinsky school, and the little uniform that was the same as the cadets' uniform but had a little lyre on the collar.

When he was recovering from his open-heart surgery, they put together the latest souvenir book for the New York City Ballet. In the hospital, Balanchine had a whole stack of the photographs for the book, 4" × 8" photos in color. He said, "Oh, look at these beautiful women, but this is my favorite, this is my next ballerina." And he showed me the picture, and it was Maria Calegari. "Oh, so lovely. Red hair. Oh."

When he and Geva and Danilova left Russia, they knew they weren't going back. That wasn't a decision they made when they got to Germany. He was a White Russian until the day he died. He hated the Reds—"Communist bastards, sons of bitches." He would be so happy today. He's probably up there laughing when he sees what's happening in Eastern Europe. He rejected the Bolsheviks. In that sense, he was very much like Solzhenitsyn. He said, "It's not the Russians, the Russian people are wonderful, it's the Soviet Bolshevik bastards." He loved the Russian people. He loved Pushkin. You'd see him get tears in his eyes when he recited Pushkin. It was like Shakespeare to him.

Balanchine would tell stories all the time. I never knew exactly whether to believe them or not because sometimes he enjoyed telling tales. He used to call me up occasionally and say, "If you're not doing anything, let's have dinner." Even if I was doing something I'd drop it when he said, "Let's go and have a bite together." I'd say, "Yes, I'd love to do that." There used to be a restaurant on Central Park South called Alfredo's. He liked to eat early. We went down about five-thirty. Nobody else was in the restaurant. They said, "Maestro," and sat us in a big corner table, just him and me. And I remember he ordered the best wine on the menu and then spaghetti and a green salad. Obviously the meal was the bottle of wine. He had just a little spaghetti with butter and cheese and some bread and some salad. He loved a good bottle of wine, especially Château Haut Brion, which was his favorite. He called it "O'Brien."

I used to give him a magnum of "O'Brien" on his birthday, and the last one I gave him was when he entered the hospital. I brought it to him so he could have it in the hospital and he said, "No, no, no. This is too good. You keep it and we'll drink it together when I leave the hospital." And of course he never left. At a rehearsal of the *Pathétique* during the Tchaikovsky Festival he said to Karin von Aroldingen, "Come look, I show difference between Russian angels and Roman angels. The wings on the Roman angels go out and down, and the Russian angels go straight up and down. This is Russian angel." That was his funeral mass.

Balanchine knew about pain and illness. He really did care about his dancers. He may have pushed them hard, but not to the point of reckless damage. When they were injured, he cared. Some more than others, because he did tend to play favorites. But I think he played favorites because he perhaps had some vision for that particular person.

DARCI

KISTLER

Born in Riverside, California, June 4, 1964; studied with Irina Kosmovska in Los Angeles and at the School of American Ballet, where
she was given a full scholarship. In the 1980 School of American
Ballet workshop performance, she danced the principal role in Swan
Lake, Act II. Joined New York City Ballet in 1980, made a soloist
in 1981 and principal dancer in 1983.

I REALLY ONLY KNEW ABOUT BALANCHINE WHEN I CAME TO NEW YORK BECAUSE IN California it's a different world. I didn't get to see the New York City Ballet there. My teacher, Irina Kosmovska, who taught in New York for Balanchine in the summer, used to talk about what he liked in a dancer. When I got here, I thought I knew what it was going to be all about. At the School of American Ballet, Balanchine would come and go. There was an atmosphere there that makes you just want to give everything. When Balanchine would come watch, it was like when the house is a mess and your dad walks in the door at five o'clock. Balanchine had a hundred dancers in his ballet company, plus a whole schoolful; I never thought he cared about my work. I loved what he and the School offered. That made me want to work.

He coached me a little bit on *Swan Lake* at the School workshop. He would simply show you. He was soft-spoken, but he put the fear of life into you. He'd show and run, full of energy and a kind of reality. He kind of dared you—you want to do or you don't. What could take somebody else days or weeks even to get you to do, with him it came very rapidly. Somehow he made you want to give back. Just the fact that he expected it of you made you accomplish.

He had me do *Swan Lake* in the company without much time, very few rehearsals. I remember getting to Washington late before the opening night and not having any rehearsal before the performance. Especially at a time like that, you're nervous. You'd like much more, you'd like to think that you could work more on something, but that wasn't the case at all. I was very scared, but it went well. He somehow made you always proud of what you did; it was fulfilling. That was the unspoken trust he transmitted, the respect. He knew the role of Odette in *Swan Lake* asks so much. It's a role identified with all those famous ballerinas. To put someone out there who is very young is risky. I always felt I needed ten years before dancing it because I knew I couldn't get the kind of maturity the woman has in *Swan Lake*. You can't fake it, you can't act it, especially when Mr. Balanchine was telling me, "Don't act! Don't be a Swan Queen. Just dance it." So he took away everything that made me worry about it. So smart! He knew what I was thinking. For me, *Swan Lake* is a role I felt absolutely free to walk in and dance. Even people who are brought up on it and who trained rigorously for it don't feel that way about *Swan Lake,* which is strange. I don't feel I have to *be* something. I felt like I could just dance it. And then other things happen. *Swan Lake* can offer whatever somebody wants out of it if it's just danced. I guess *Giselle* and all the classics would be the same, if you're not afraid of tradition. Anything with a story I think Mr. B. really did fabulously.

Music has always helped me. I took clarinet from second grade up to the time I came to New York. I like playing it, but it wasn't my favorite instrument. I always wished I was an opera singer. I never thought anything was prettier than the voice in song, nothing more perfect. But there's no way I could ever sing. I made the glee club with all the boys when their voices were changing, and it was great. They had a difficult time, and I was the only girl in there with anything approximating a voice. The clarinet is a vocal substitute, it's a singing instrument. The reason I love ballet so much is because of the music. I don't think I'd like to go to the studio every day without the music. That's what's so nice. A *tendu* isn't the same every day there, a *plié* is different every day because the music is different.

We went to Europe soon after I joined the company. During a performance of Jerome Robbins's ballet *The Cage*, Balanchine took me and put me in a dark corner backstage and made me sit and just listen to the Stravinsky music, to find how beautiful that music is. He taught me just to listen.

I remember the first day I got into the company; it was "Wow! You've made it." But, like in a school, you start all over again. You're on the back line, you're in the back row, you're in the corner. I didn't notice a difference in the transition going from the School to the company. It was just more of what I wanted. It was more overwhelming. What was difficult for me were the little things that you have to learn how to do, like putting on your makeup. Who wants to put on makeup? Those kinds of things—the tedious things, the practical things. I feel like I'm just learning them now.

There are a hundred and five dancers now in New York City Ballet. Every single person there has a place. Mr. B. used to say to me, "To want to be like someone else is death." If we want to be in someone else's place, we're never going to be happy. We choose to make ourselves happy or not. And that means not to want anything of anybody else. I have never demanded anything.

Mr. B. used to say, "Dancers need to be told. What's going to happen when no one is told? I'm not going to be around, so you have to remember, you have to drum it into your head, you have to remind yourself, you have to take over the responsibility." It's a pretty scary idea, but I never thought of it in a bad way. I thought, "He's right. This is survival, what he's saying." Sometimes you're not lucky. You lose somebody and they never said, "Look, I'm not going to be here. Remember this." It was nice that he said it.

I think he wanted us to remember that you have to live and perform on edge. I have to admit that I do miss that edge. You always have to find it, you always have to remind yourself of it. You have to bring it into yourself. Mr. B. was like your conscience. You'd walk into the studio, and he used to say, "I know where people have been the night before. I know what they've eaten. I know where they slept. I know . . . everything." And you know, I really believe he did. We don't have that when we walk into the studio now.

It was like having your father keep you always on your toes, trying new things. It's hard to live and grow and keep yourself on that kind of edge. It's double work. It's harder to take on that kind of responsibility. I want to get stronger and keep that edge and always remember that this moment may be your last, so make the best of it.

Mr. B. was great because he liked so many types of dancers. That's why he used to call himself a gardener or a chef. You love everything because you need everything. You need corps dancers, you need soloist dancers, you need principal dancers. Balanchine allowed people to be and to choose what they wanted to be. He wasn't the kind of choreographer who tells his dancer, "I have something that you don't know and won't tell you." Or "You've probably never felt this emotion, so I'm going to show it to you." He respected his dancers by not doing that. He allowed us to be ourselves. If anything, you have more of a person out there onstage because you have less to hide under. He also respected his audience.

Balanchine used to talk to me about the Russian Orthodox Church and how beautiful the services were. He would tell me about his uncle, who was a Russian Orthodox priest. I grew up with the Bible. He said once that at the end of *A Midsummer Night's Dream* he wanted to have a drop curtain based on *The Book of Revelation* where John has a vision of the Woman of the Stars: "Now a great sign appeared in heaven: a woman clothed with the sun, with the moon under her feet, and in her hand a garland of stars." Balanchine said, "You know, they would all think I went too far, they wouldn't get it." He was saying that at times you can say what you believe, and it may be right for you. But you can go too far. Balanchine let you learn for yourself, and he didn't put anything on you, not even his belief.

He taught you how to live life. His dancing isn't just about dance. That's why he's a great teacher of people. He makes you more conscious of what's right and what's wrong.

I knew Balanchine as a master, as a teacher. His teachings and his ballets, all of the things he said to me, echo. I didn't have a deep personal relationship with him, but I got enough to live a whole life on.

ANDREI

KRAMAREVSKY

Born in Krakow in 1928 to a father who was a ballet master and a mother who was prima ballerina at the Minsk Theater; studied at the Bolshoi Theater School. Performed in Frunze during World War II. Returned to Moscow and finished training at Bolshoi school. Joined Bolshoi Ballet in 1949, where he became a soloist and danced fifty roles. Left the company in 1967 and danced with a concert group for four years. In 1976 he emigrated to the United States with his wife and son. Almost immediately he began to teach at the School of American Ballet and the company class of the New York City Ballet. He also dances character and mime roles in N.Y.C.B.'s repertory.

I Remember Balanchine

BALANCHINE IS EVERYTHING TO ME. FOR HIM TO HAVE HAD A HIGH OPINION OF MY work as a teacher is my treasure. He was like my second father. I began teaching at his School of American Ballet one week after I arrived in America in 1976. I showed Molostwoff and Gleboff my credentials—my teachers, colleagues, and background at the Bolshoi Ballet. Natasha Gleboff said, "Oh, today one teacher is ill. Can you teach?" I said, "Of course, immediately." I taught the class without English, showing every movement. The only English words I knew were "please" and "okay." After the class there was applause. Natasha said, "That was a good class, but I am sorry, we have no place. Maybe we'll use you for a summer course." I said, "Thank you for giving me the opportunity." I went home. That night Natasha called me: "Please, come again. Balanchine wants to see your class."

The next day there were some new people from the company taking the class. I started before Balanchine arrived. "Please start," I was told. "Balanchine is busy now and will come later." Balanchine came in after about ten minutes. I stopped the class. I said to him, "Thank you very much for you attention, Georgi Melitonovich. In 1962 I saw the class that you taught at the Bolshoi." Balanchine didn't remember me. He was absolutely without expression. But I remembered that for his class in Russia he had used no pianist. He had clapped his hands in rhythm for the whole class. I asked him then, "Why not pianist?" Balanchine said, "Because there are so many rehearsals, we save pianists for rehearsals." Ten minutes before I finished teaching my class, Balanchine walked out. I thought he didn't like it.

I went into the dressing room and Balanchine was there. He said, "My dear, I really like it. I need man teacher. I waited for you for forty years. From tomorrow, you work and teach class, company and School." I was crying. I had had news from Russia: my father was ill, almost dead. I said, "Thank you, Georgi Melitonovich." "Don't thank me, thank God, because God sends orders," he told me. "I thank you, but from God."

I protested to Balanchine, "Georgi Melitonovich, I can't speak English." He said, "You can be without language. Show, please, one more time for everybody. I still show jumps sometimes. Ten minutes ago I could fly." When I taught the company class, Balanchine would sometimes watch and say to me, "Stop. Show one more time. One more time because I want everybody to do it like you."

In 1978, Balanchine invited me to perform at the New York City Ballet. "Do you want to go onstage?" "That's my life. This is very prophetic." Balanchine offered me the role of Cassandre in his ballet *Harlequinade* when Baryshnikov danced his first performance. It was Baryshnikov and me in our debuts. My name was not even in the program at the debut, it all happened so fast. But over the public address system they announced that Cassandre would be played by Andrei Kramarevsky. Afterward, Balanchine said, "You are an actor. I want to see you in *The Nutcracker* as Drosselmeyer." He gave me one hour of rehearsal before the performance. He himself showed me the *mise en scène*. He said, "Now, go make up, immediately. You are fantastic. I believe in you."

When I first saw the New York City Ballet, on tour in Russia in 1962, I said to my friends there, "It's usual for us, for our government, to say we're the best. I don't think so. Legs work at the New York City Ballet like they never work at our ballet. This is absolutely fantastic." In retrospect I now understand why. Balanchine ballet is especially for the feet. Russian ballet has very good *épaulement* and the arms are better. But the feet are terrible. New York City Ballet was amazing to me in 1962. I saw different work, the tempo was presto, very fast.

I was in Moscow in 1987. I went to the new building of my school at the Bolshoi Ballet. Now it is not called the School of the Bolshoi Ballet but the Academic Moscow School. I asked about watching classes. I got permission and saw an advanced men's class. The tempo was very slow. Afterward the teacher asked me, "Could you show us a typical combination that you use to teach in America?" I asked the pianist to play for me and demonstrated one combination. The Russian dancers could not do it. It was something I give my youngest children here in America—*brisé*, three *jetés battus*, and *pas de bourrée*. "No, it's too fast for us." The Russian school is nice but too slow. I try to mix the best of Stanley Williams and other teachers in America and the best of the Russian school. That is art—it is necessary to take and to mix.

I knew Balanchine offstage, at home, and in the hospital during his last year. That was a terrible time. He was very slow in his decline. At first he forgot English. He asked, "Why do I not understand what people are saying?" Once Makarova and I went to visit him in the hospital. Makarova was rehearsing for the Broadway revival of *On Your Toes.* I would recite Russian poetry to Balanchine in the hospital because, like a dramatic actor, I know many poems. Balanchine would reply to me because he was a very good dramatic actor in his youth in Leningrad. He declaimed poetry in Russian for years. In bed at the hospital, Balanchine would recite brilliantly, with temperament, Chasky's monologue from the play by Liadov. The play is in verse, like Shakespeare. Chasky is a hero who is against everybody in the community. He fights corruption. Of course, he can't win and has to leave Moscow. Balanchine had played Chasky on the stage, he would shout "Corrupt men!" and say Chasky's last phrase, "And everybody looked for me." Balanchine said to me, "I cried onstage." Balanchine read the line "Give me courage to go" with a suppressed cry, without the usual shouting. I praised Balanchine's reading of the line: "Georgi Melitonovich, you are absolutely right." Balanchine also loved Pushkin's *Eugene Onegin* and *Bronze Horse*—and Lermontov. I went to see him every day between classes. When he couldn't walk, I would pick him up and walk around the room. Afterward I would cry.

In art, Balanchine was a very happy man. In life, he was like a zebra, sometimes very happy, sometimes like an ordinary human being. In his art, Balanchine was happy because he could put any idea onstage. Even at the end—*Vienna Waltzes*—the ballets were fresh. Balanchine never grew tired. His occupation was art, only art. Other choreographers begin to repeat their ideas as they grow older. Balanchine wanted a new idea every time.

If he had remained in Russia, he would not have been happy. He was right to leave. Take, for example, Goleizovsky. For thirty years he could do nothing. Before he died, he produced only one ballet that was good. In Russia the one genius choreographer was Goleizovsky, and Balanchine was a greater genius than he. About Lopukhov, Balanchine said, "Very nice. But Lopukhov only start and couldn't do it." An artist can't work under control. The artist must open the way.

Baryshnikov worked with Balanchine, but the result was good, not great. Baryshnikov in our company felt uncomfortable. He had a different style.

Balanchine sometimes talked to me about his mother and brother. He really didn't have a family. He mostly talked about art, about people, and about eating. He was an excellent cook. He would say, "My ballet is like great restaurant. I must prepare new, absolutely excellent food for our guests. Everybody is waiting. I must think about it." In the hospital he said, "Oh, now is a terrible time. I can't go and cook."

EDITH

LANGNER, M.D.

Dr. Langner is a physician in New York City who practices internal medicine. Her specialty is endocrinology and dance medicine. She is a native New Yorker, went to New York University Medical School, and is affiliated with Roosevelt Hospital.

I Remember Balanchine

I CAME TO KNOW BALANCHINE IN 1978. AT THAT TIME HE WAS A BIT UNSTEADY ON HIS feet, probably the beginning of his neurological illness. It was subtle, and did not become a serious problem until 1980, but he was aware of it. There were multiple problems that had to do with his heart, his cardiac surgery, his eye problems and eye surgery. In spite of his many medical problems, his major focus was always his work. He was conscientious about his health, and interested in it. In the course of his illness, he saw many consultants, and was willing to talk to yet another specialist or to have another test in the hope of finding an answer.

Before I met him I was an occasional balletgoer. After I met him, I would go to the theater often, three or four times a week, and sometimes stand backstage with him to watch the performance. I was privileged to spend time observing him at work, teaching class and rehearsing ballets. I will never forget watching one rehearsal of *The Prodigal Son* for television. Frustrated with the entrance of the ballerina, he stepped in to show her how he wanted her to move. Remarkably, this seventy-six-year-old man transformed himself into a graceful young woman. A short time later, he stepped into the role of the father welcoming home the prodigal son. With a few gestures he brought tears to the eyes of all who were watching.

I think one of the reasons George was so appealing to people was that he had such definitive views. *Everything* mattered to him, from the grand to the most prosaic. At Saratoga, where he stayed during the season in a wonderful little cottage on the property of the Richard Leeches, he was known to wash his car, and even other cars that were parked outside the cottage. People would comment on the joyful attention he would give each one. I think they had trouble with the idea that this great man, this famous choreographer and renowned artist of our time, enjoyed washing cars. He used to sit outside his cottage in his white-and-blue-striped bathrobe and read the paper and have coffee. People would deliver the mail and sometimes he'd sit and read the review that was in the local paper. He told me he had been interested in cooking since childhood, and he remembered his mother was a very good cook. He would talk about foods that he had when he was five, describing them as if it were yesterday. He talked about his father winning a lot of money in a lottery, and how he gave it all away. These memories of his childhood must have been very vivid, because he talked about them often.

His love of cooking was famous. He loved to chop things. I sat with him once at a dinner where there was a salesman for Cuisinart, who had tried to give Balanchine one of these efficient machines. George was unimpressed. He explained that he *enjoyed* chopping, and that he wouldn't consider delegating this very pleasurable task to any Cuisinart. He ironed his own shirts.

His joy in all the ordinary tasks in life, caring about the food he ate or the wine he drank or the car he washed, was a part of his charm.

I was lucky enough to get a number of cooking "lessons" from him. One was at the little cottage in Saratoga. The project was borscht. Even here he was a perfectionist, from selecting the beets at the market to the process of baking them (rather than boiling them) to how they were to be peeled and sliced. And no one enjoyed the finished product more.

There is one anecdote George would often tell, which I found really wonderful—it's a story about Stravinsky. Late in Stravinsky's life when he was ill and under a doctor's care, he called together his friends one night to have a great dinner, complete with wine and caviar. Stravinsky organized everything. When his guests were seated at the table, Stravinsky phoned his doctor and said: "Doctor, I have all my friends here and we have a great dinner. Balanchine is here, and so-and-so is here. We have marvelous wine and caviar, too, fabulous caviar; the best. We're all sitting around and we're just about to have it. May I have the caviar?" "Absolutely not." This apparently went on and on. Finally, the doctor said, "What the hell—do what you damn well please." Stravinsky put down the phone, turned to his guests, smiled and said, "He says it's all right." This was a story Balanchine always told me whenever I tried to get him to slow down, eat less caviar or whatever. He had had his heart attack in '79, and then bypass surgery. When I asked him to be prudent in his dietary habits, he would tell me this story.

I remember one visit to Balanchine at the time of his cardiac bypass. I went to see him in the hospital, within the first twenty-four hours post-op. He had come out of anesthesia and was in the intensive care unit and on the usual monitors. It's a point at which most people are at their worst, complaining or dealing with the overwhelming aspects of surgery. But when I went to see George he was talking about monitors. They were taped to his chest, recording his heartbeat. With remarkable precision, he pointed out how poorly the apparatus was designed. An electrode from the monitor goes to a piece of tape that's attached to the body. The connection between the electrode and the piece of tape is fragile. If the patient moves or turns, very often the electrode comes off and the monitors go haywire. At that moment, George was redesigning his monitor. He was going to get the electrician at the New York City Ballet to work with him.

His intelligence was overwhelming. He wanted to know and understand everything that was happening in his body. I would attempt to draw diagrams and schematics for him. There was nothing like "You fix it." Many patients ask, "What are my chances, doctor?" That wouldn't be his approach. He was much more involved in the technical aspects of his illness.

George was interested in so much more of the world than his own professional milieu. He talked about "Sesame Street," about Einstein's theory of relativity, about religion and mysticism. He talked about perfume, politics, cats, and coriander. And when he talked, he was insightful, intelligent, funny, and usually looking at the world from a slightly different angle than everyone else. I feel very privileged to have known him.

ROBERT D.

WICKHAM, M.D.

Born in 1923, Robert D. Wickham is senior attending urologist at St. Luke's/Roosevelt Hospital Center in New York and assistant clinical professor, urology, at the College of Physicians and Surgeons, Columbia University.

I Remember Balanchine

At the time of the Stravinsky Centennial Festival at the New York City Ballet in June 1982, Dr. William Hamilton, an old friend of mine and the resident physician for Balanchine's company, asked me to see Mr. Balanchine, who had suffered a minor accident in his apartment. I saw Mr. Balanchine at the New York State Theater during the dress rehearsal of *The Firebird* and, after examining him, assured him that the black and blue bruises he had suffered were not serious and would gradually subside.

Later, when I saw him for a routine checkup, it was clear that he was beginning to have signs and symptoms of a prostate problem. However, surgery was not indicated at this time, although I thought that sooner or later it might be required. Soon after this the unsteadiness that heralded his final illness became apparent. That took precedence over all other concerns and he entered Roosevelt Hospital in November 1982. I stopped by to see him almost every day thereafter. We all wanted so much to help him.

Mr. Balanchine obviously had some kind of neurological disease but a specific diagnosis could not be reached. Dr. Langner and Dr. Hamilton arranged for all the usual diagnostic tests as well as special neurologic examinations, but it was not until an autopsy was done that the disease was identified. Jakob-Creutzfeldt disease is rare and the diagnosis is ordinarily made only by microscopic postmortem examination of tissues.

I remember a birthday party held in his hospital room in January 1983. Several of his friends were there and he seemed to know everyone. Karin von Aroldingen, a very good cook, had brought in food which she had prepared. We had it with wine and champagne. After about an hour Mr. Balanchine was very tired and, attempting to stand up, he began to fall. Those nearby caught him. All of us were saddened because it was clear that he was losing ground. Two devoted nurses were with him to the end and they made him as comfortable as possible.

Mr. Balanchine was very much concerned about staying as youthful as possible. That preoccupation is common in many men as they age. He once told me that in the past he had obtained "rejuvenation" injections in Switzerland. It is quite possible that he got Jakob-Creutzfeldt disease by way of these injections. Such injections have been available in European health spas and clinics for many years. They oftentimes contain extracts of animal glands such as testicular tissue. Jakob-Creutzfeldt disease is found in sheep and is called "scrapie." As the name implies, sheep so affected scrape their sides against trees to obtain relief. I believe it was first identified in Scotland and is also found in Libya, where many sheep "delicacies" are consumed, as well as in other African countries.

If we were certain of how and where Mr. Balanchine got this rare and fatal disease, it would help prevent others from being inoculated with it.